XL

THE MARKET BOOK

THE

MARKET BOOK

A HISTORY

OF THE

PUBLIC MARKETS

OF THE

CITY OF NEW YORK

BY

THOMAS F. DE VOE

[1862]

REPRINTS OF ECONOMIC CLASSICS

AUGUSTUS M. KELLEY · PUBLISHERS

NEW YORK 1970

First Edition 1862

(New York: *PRINTED for* THE AUTHOR, 1862)

Reprinted 1970 by
AUGUSTUS M. KELLEY · PUBLISHERS
REPRINTS OF ECONOMIC CLASSICS
New York   New York   10001

·   ·   ·   ·   ·   ·   ·   ·   ·   ·   ·

I S B N   0 678 00685 7
L C N   72 121319

·   ·   ·   ·   ·   ·   ·   ·   ·   ·   ·

PRINTED IN THE UNITED STATES OF AMERICA
by SENTRY PRESS, NEW YORK, N. Y. 10019

THE

MARKET BOOK

CONTAINING A

HISTORICAL ACCOUNT

OF THE PUBLIC MARKETS IN THE CITIES OF

New York Boston Philadelphia and Brooklyn

With a brief Description of every Article of Human Food sold therein

THE INTRODUCTION OF CATTLE IN AMERICA

AND NOTICES OF MANY REMARKABLE SPECIMENS

BY

THOMAS F. DE VOE

MEMBER OF THE NEW YORK HISTORICAL SOCIETY ETC.

IN TWO VOLUMES

VOL. I.

NEW YORK
PRINTED FOR THE AUTHOR
1862.

THIS VOLUME CONTAINS

A HISTORY

OF THE

PUBLIC MARKETS

IN THE

CITY OF NEW YORK,

FROM ITS FIRST SETTLEMENT TO THE PRESENT TIME.

———————

WITH NUMEROUS CURIOUS AND REMARKABLE INCIDENTS CONNECTED THEREWITH,
THE INTRODUCTION OF CATTLE, SUPPLIES, TRADING, PRICES, AND LAWS;
SKETCHES OF THE OLD BURGHER BUTCHERS, AND THE LICENSED
BUTCHERS OF MODERN TIMES; TOGETHER WITH A COMPILA-
TION OF FACTS OF EVERY SORT AND CHARACTER
RELATING TO THE SUBJECT.

———————

FACT, NOT FANCY.

TO

GEORGE H. MOORE, Esq.,

LIBRARIAN OF THE NEW YORK HISTORICAL SOCIETY,

THIS VOLUME

IS MOST RESPECTFULLY DEDICATED,
AS A TRIBUTE OF ESTEEM AND RESPECT,
FOR HIS UNWAVERING FRIENDSHIP TO

THE AUTHOR.

PREFACE.

A PREFACE appears to be demanded from all who are guilty of introducing *another* book into life; whether it is done for fame, name, profit, the public good, to be instructive or interesting, or for any other consideration.

In my case, being found here, so much out of *my line*, I do not know under which, or how many, of the above *heads* to place myself; and I must therefore leave the reader to judge, and determine my position from his own estimate of my merit.

For several years, the *unemployed hours* from my business, or rather profession, had hung heavily on my mind, and to fill them up satisfactorily, was a thought I had often indulged in. To be sure, at times, there were no *leisure hours*, not one of the twenty-four, but what were needed for rest; and again, one, two, three, and sometimes four, could be employed in doing something, either useful or wasteful; but what to do, was the question. I knew I had some knowledge, which business and observation had given me; but I also knew that I was very deficient in *learning*, or at least of knowing how to express myself, satisfactorily to *myself*. So I thought to improve, or at least to inform myself, even at this late day; but the reader may say, "An old scholar is not an apt one"—and so I found it. I had the disadvantage of not knowing which end to begin with, but went headforemost into what appeared to me to be the most agreeable to my feelings.

Early in life, (1829,) I had engaged in the *military*, and have continued in it, I may say with but a short intermission, to the present day: this somewhat excited the mind, and sometimes drew heavily on my *leisure hours*, while I sought such information as I could find on this subject. My researches at last extended to the "rooms" of the Historical Society, where I became acquainted with the attentive, obliging, and gentlemanly Librarian, Mr. George H.

Moore, who, after an agreeable acquaintance, unexpectedly caused me to be introduced as a member of this honored association. Here he opened out to me all the rich treasures contained therein, and I eagerly *devoured*, not only the "*military subjects*," but all connected with our city; and at last I began to *feel* that I had either swallowed or been bitten by a *rabid antiquary*. I found there was no remedy for this *dreadful* disease, but by taking, in allopathic doses, sundry *piles* of old musty records, in various forms and at various times. I submitted to the treatment, but, in my case, it only relieved the disease for a short period after the last *time-worn paper* of the *pile* had passed; upon the sight or knowledge of another, it again returned in full force. In fact, I had acquired a fondness for historical information, and more especially for such as related to my native city.

The numerous *Records* and *Files* of the Common Council, with various old books, newspapers, pamphlets, &c., had been glanced over, and the result was, a large mass of historical material, on various subjects, had been collected, as I then thought, more for my own personal gratification and amusement, than for any other use. However, I found my researches had so completed my knowledge of the introduction, time, place, name, and the final exit of the numerous public market-places in the City of New York, that I was enabled to give them, or rather parts of them, to the "press," in answer to some "Reports" and "Communications."

My esteemed friend, Mr. Moore, gently hinted that a *paper* on this subject would be acceptable to the Society; that I had drawn heavily upon the *Treasures* of the Society, and that it was due to them. I admitted the justice of the claim, but pleaded my position and inefficiency, and that I could much better furnish any other than an intellectual *feast*. However, after repeated playful demands, I consented to prepare a *sketch*, with the understanding that he should revise, if he thought proper, and *read* it.

Before it was finished, one other intimate friend, who belonged to the Society, said to me, that I "must prepare and read the *paper* without any assistance." To this I answered, "I would not think of such a thing, as it might not only reflect on the Society, but also upon myself." Says he, "Then you must disappoint the Society, yourself, as well as *one or two others*, who have not displayed very friendly feelings, on learning the proposed arrangement." I had always practiced and preferred a retired position, but I felt stung, and concluded that, if there was anything in me, it must now come out; so, with renewed and my best energies, I finished the *paper*, sought Mr. Moore, explained my position, and asked his presence at my house, to say whether I must fail or succeed. He decided in favor of the latter, and, at my request, gave me an introductory letter to the Rev. Dr. Osgood, one of the Committee on *Papers* to be read, that I might also consult with him.

In the mean time, I found that the "Chamber of Commerce" (the History of which had been so well written by the Hon. Charles King, the present highly esteemed President of Columbia College,) had been a prominent body, with whom the military authorities had consulted on many subjects, including our public markets, during the Revolution. To get at the details on this subject, I was enabled, through a letter of introduction, to consult Mr. King, when he became interested in my *paper*, and I was greatly pleased to be summoned before him, that he might advise with me in relation to it. He listened to the result of my efforts, and in the end he gratified me by saying that he should come to hear it again before the Society. Then, with the approbation of the Rev. Dr. Osgood, who had also heard it read, I felt fully prepared to face this *strong battery* of wisdom, intelligence, and honor, as well as the several regiments of soldiers which I have had the honor to command—without flinching.

On the evening of the 4th of May, 1858, I read my *paper* before the New York Historical Society, and its reception was all, and more, than I expected; and, if confession is proper here, I was elated—it struck in so deep, that—the result is before you. I might also add, that a few days after, a further impetus was given me, by several complimentary resolutions, from some professional and other friends, requesting me to repeat the reading of the above, at an early day, to which, with pleasure, I consented. This took place in the large Hall of the Cooper Institute; and again it was most flatteringly received. On both occasions, the "press" generally and favorably noticed my effort, for which many thanks are due.

The employment of my leisure hours has, at times, been so disconnected, in consequence of my engagements and the usual troubles and trials of business, that it was difficult, sometimes, to get *back on my old trail:* this, with the faults, or rather the neglect, of education, will no doubt cause the style and grammar to be somewhat broken, disconnected, or inelegant. However, my whole aim has been, that it should be *fact, not fancy*—accurate and faithful; to

give precisely what I found and experienced; preserving as much
of the original language and orthography as possible; denoting
extracts, as such, with marks of quotation, and using my own language to connect or carry on the subject in this volume.

I now find myself in that position where my indebtedness is so
much, to so many, that I fear I cannot name all to whom I owe
many thanks. To the courtesy and kindness of David T. Valentine,
Esq., Clerk of the Common Council; George H. Moore, Esq.,
Librarian of the New York Historical Society, and the Librarians
of the several Libraries of our City, as of several others; to
Dr. John W. Francis, (deceased,) Hon. Henry Meigs, Messrs. William J. Davis, Henry B. Dawson, Col. William Appleby, Jacob
Aims, Thomas Jeremiah, Daniel Burtnett, John M. Seaman, John
Scott, (deceased,) and numerous other gentlemen, I specially ac-
knowledge my obligations. I have also derived much assistance
from the works of O'Callaghan, Dunlap, Smith, Watson, Moulton,
Hardie, Horsmanden, Valentine, &c.

Almost every one (more especially the aged citizen) has some
special historical knowledge, connected with family, friends, or
neighborhood, worthy of being known and revealed, for the instruction or gratification of others, or as shedding new light upon the
annals of our city. Permit me, in concluding this *Preface*, to ask
from such as have the power to grant it, that if, while reading these
sketches of the past, their own memories may be stirred by long-
dormant recollections of remarkable incidents or scenes, they will
be good enough to note these recollections, as material for the use
of either myself, or others who, like myself, may adventure upon
the agreeable task of seeking to revive by-gone days.

THOMAS F. DE VOE,
Butcher.

JEFFERSON MARKET,
    CITY OF NEW YORK, 1861.

INTRODUCTION.

In presenting the following historical matter, I do not propose to reveal anything which is new or even interesting to the historian, whose well-worn path is before me ; and although I may not follow in his immediate footsteps, yet I must travel on the same high-road, or I cannot be true to history.

The historian, in seeking his mental fare, looks only for the choicest and most substantial food to satisfy his natural appetite; and his eagle eye merely glances at the stray crumbs which have fallen from his plate, while the hungry gleaner, who follows after, is forced to pick them up, to cover such other rejected food as may be left, but which he gladly seizes and ravenously devours. I therefore hope to find the reader hungry enough to partake of the *gleaner's* fare.

The contents of this volume will chiefly relate to the establishment of the several market-places and public market-houses within the present limits of the City of New York.

No doubt the number will surprise many; there having been more than forty, although several have been found located on or near the same spot where a former one had ceased to exist. They were, however, separate and distinct markets, as will appear from the various sources of evidence presented through the following pages.

In giving each their separate histories, many interesting incidents or local facts will be introduced, to relieve the necessary sameness of so much building up and tearing or tumbling down, which so many *public edifices* would seem to demand. Although not an interesting subject, yet the early age and associations may assist to interest the minds of those who now and then like to look back at the ages past; to see the feeble steps of the first settlers; to follow the more firm tread of their children; and to witness the rapid strides of their fast generations.

The main object of the early settlers of New Netherlands was, no doubt, to better their condition; and when they beheld these beautiful and bountiful lands—as Van der Donk says, "The country fruitful and advantageously situated, possessed good and safe havens, rivers, fisheries, and many other worthy appurtenances;" and, in truth, excelled their Fatherland, (*Netherlands*)—they had good reason to name it New Netherlands. "In short, (says Lambrechtsen,) New Netherlands, to make use of Hudson's own words, was the most beautiful country on which you could tread your feet. The natives were good-natured, peaceable, and obliging; the climate pretty near at par with ours; so that New Netherlands was very properly adapted for our nation, to be settled by it, as there seemed nothing wanting but domestic cattle."

The natives were also found to be agriculturists, cultivating the land, and producing many species of grain and vegetables. Hudson says: "I sailed to the shore in one of their canoes with an old man, who was the chief of a tribe consisting of forty men and seventeen women; these I saw—there in a house well constructed of oak-bark, and circular in shape, so that it had the appearance of being built with an arched roof. It contained a great quantity of maize, or Indian corn, and beans of the last year's growth; and there lay near the house, for the purpose of drying, enough to load three ships, besides what was growing in the fields."

The chase also furnished them, at one and at the same time, with clothing and food from the various species of wild animals, wild fowl, fish, fruits, nuts and roots, and fine oysters, which they, at times, exchanged with or gave to the sometimes almost starving settlers. In an address from the Indians to the ambassadors of Gov. Kieft, they say: "When you first arrived on our shores, you were often in want of food; we gave you our beans and our corn, and let you eat our oysters and fish."*

The West India Company went into active operation in the year 1623, trading principally in peltries, but did not do much to encourage the settlement or population. "Not a particle of the soil was reclaimed, save what scantily supplied a few servants of the Company."† The country, however, was becoming more favorably known to the Directors, who resolved to further improve it, by sending over several families, and introducing domestic cattle. Accordingly, in the spring of 1625, (says Wassenaer,) *Peter Evertsen Hulft* (one of the members of the Board) brought in two ships, of 280 tons burden, "one hundred and three cattle, among which were stallions, mares, bulls and cows, for breeding, as well as swine and sheep. These beasts were all very well provided for on ship-board

O'Callaghan.   † Ibid.

—almost as well as on shore. Each one had his own stall, arranged with a flooring of sand," with plenty of water, hay, and straw.

"The beasts, two of which only died on the passage, were, on their arrival, landed on *Noten Island, (now Governor's Island,)* but there being no grazing-ground for them at that spot, they were, a day or two afterwards, taken by shallops and barges to *Manhattan,* where they eventually throve very well, though some twenty, in all, were lost: many of them by eating some kind of poisonous vegetation, which had also destroyed the first shipment of domestic animals, sent here several years before. These were brought by *Hendrick Christiansen,* but were all of the smaller kinds, consisting of 'bucks and goats, also rabbits.' We may therefore conclude that those brought by *Hulft* in 1625 were the *first* large domestic cattle introduced; and those also of the smaller species brought by him, were the *first* of the breed successfully prolific in *New Netherlands.*"

In 1626,* Director *Minuit* concluded a treaty with the natives, by which they ceded *Manhattan Island* to the Dutch, for the sum of *"sixty guilders."* The land which composes the now great City and County of New York, estimated to contain *twenty-two thousand acres* of land, was purchased for *twenty-four dollars!* So the "West India Company" became the owners, and reserved it for themselves, as stated in their "Charter of Liberties;" but they made very slow progress either in colonizing it, or in producing many of the common necessaries of life.

Dominie *Jonas Michaelius,* in a letter dated August 11th, 1628, says: "We want ten or twelve farmers, with horses, cows, and laborers in proportion, to furnish us with bread and fresh butter, milk and cheese."

The population two years before (1626) numbered but "two hundred and seventy souls, including men, women, and children;"† but in 1629 the Company offered greater inducements, in the forms of "freedoms and exemptions" to families or single persons, and a "patroonship" to those who would, in *four years,* "plant a colonie of fifty souls, upwards of fifteen years old;" the last named, however, were not allowed to settle on the Island of Manhattan, and "all fruit and wares that are produced on the lands situated on the North River, and lying thereabout, shall for the present be brought there, before they may be sent elsewhere."‡

In the "Conditions entered into and made between the Lords the Burgomasters of the City of Amsterdam and the West India Company," favorable articles were also set forth to encourage colo-

---

* Wassenaer. Also, Hol. Doc. Col. His. † Wassenaer.
‡ N. Y. H. C. N. S., vol. i., p. 371.

nization. Article 6 says, "That the said city *(Amsterdam)* shall provide a suitable piece of land on the banks of a river for a proper dwelling-place for the colonists. The place shall be provided with a trench and wall on the outer side, and the inner ground be laid out with streets, a *market*, and in lots, for the advantage of merchants, mechanics, and those who will pursue agriculture—the whole to be done at the cost of said city."

"ART. 9. And to the end that the colonists may be provided with *necessaries* as far as is practicable, the said city shall supply them with clothing and *necessaries* for one year, and also with seedgrain; and for the assurance and certainty of having the necessary supplies on hand, the city shall erect a large magazine or warehouse in said place for the storage of clothing and necessaries for the people, wherein they shall keep their *factor*, who shall supply every colonist with necessary clothing, household necessaries, and husbandry articles, at the same prices of this country, *(Amsterdam)*—the toll of the Company not charged."[*]

The Directors in Holland, in the year 1639, to further encourage emigration, offered free passages to such farmers and their families "as were desirous of proceeding to New Netherlands, where, on their arrival, they were promised to be furnished for six years with a farm, fit for the plough, a dwelling-house, a barn, a suitable number of laborers, four horses, an equal number of cows, sheep and swine in proportion, with the necessary farming implements; for which they were, however, to be bound to pay a yearly rent of one hundred guilders, (equal to $40,) and eighty pounds of butter. On the expiration of his lease, the tenant was to restore the same number of cattle that he had received on entering into possession, retaining for himself whatever increase there might have been, in the mean time, from the original stock. To those who owned farms, but who had not the means of providing stock, the Company loaned cattle for a certain number of years, 'on halves;' that is, on expiration of the contract, the number furnished were restored, with half the increase."

Additions were also made from the settlements in New England and Virginia, where the freedom of conscience had been proscribed. They removed by "whole towns to the Netherlands, to enjoy that religious liberty denied them by their own countrymen;" but in order to secure their allegiance, "they were therefore called on to take and subscribe an oath of fidelity."[†]

[*] N. Y. H. C. N. S., vol. i., p. 239.   [†] O'Callaghan.

WEST INDIA COMPANY'S STORE.

THE Company's large "Magazine, or Warehouse," consisted of five substantial stone buildings, adjoining each other, afterwards known as the "Company's Store-Houses," was erected at an early period. They occupied a position fronting westward, towards "Fort Amsterdam," where an open space, of more than one hundred feet in width, originally laid between them. This open space or street, which extended along the front of the "Store-Houses," was called "Winkle Street," Market Street, or Store Street, and ran nearly on a line of Whitehall Street. On this street, between the present Bridge and Stone Streets, stood the "Company's Store-Houses,"* in which was the *first* regularly appointed depot or *market-place* in New Amsterdam, and from which the settlers were supplied with the daily necessaries of life. This fact, however, will be more satisfactorily shown in a malversation committed by one of the Company's servants a few years after. There is no doubt, however, that previous to the erection of these "Store-Houses," and the introduction of domestic cattle, the inhabitants were chiefly furnished by the Indians with the flesh of wild game, fish, oysters, clams, and such vegetation as they produced.

The town, in 1633, came under the administration of Director Van Twiller, who improved the fortifications, built a church, and several dwelling-houses. But, "scarcely one solitary agricultural settler had been, as yet, sent over by the Company to fell the forest or reclaim the wilderness."†

Governor Van Twiller appears to have devoted the greater part of his time to agriculture. "One of his plantations was at Red Hook; and Governor's Island, which is supposed always, from the first settlement, to have been a perquisite of the Director-General for the time being, was said to have been so near Red Hook, that cattle crossed the channel to and fro at low water."‡ "This Island he purchased, in June, 1634, from the Indian proprietors, who called it 'Pagganck,' or 'Nut Island;' the Dutch lengthened it to 'Noten,' or Nutten Island; and the English further, to Governor's Island. He also purchased two islands at Hell Gate, in July, now known as Randall's and Great Barn Island. These 'plantations' he had taken care to have well stocked, but greatly neglected those of the Company, which were found by his successor, Sir William Kieft, in

* Valentine, Hist. of N. Y. City Records. † O'Callaghan. ‡ Dunlap.

1638, to be without tenants, stock, or cultivation, and thrown into 'commons.' "*

At this period, (1637,) we find the price of provisions and rates of wages for laborers were as follows: "*Rye* was worth two florins and a half *(about one dollar)* per schepel of three pecks. *Maize,* (or Indian corn,) one and a half florin. *Wheat,* three florins. *Peas,* four to five florins. *Broken barley,* four florins. *Pork,* seven stivers per pound. *Meat,* (beef,) six stivers do. A *hog* six months old brought fifteen florins. A keg of *butter,* twenty-five florins. A *laborer* in harvest got about eighty cents a day, on other occasions sixty; while the price of a *negro* was forty florins, or $16."†

At the commencement of Van Twiller's administration, an "Inventory" shows that all the Company's farms had been "liberally stocked with brood-mares, oxen, milch-cows, heifers, yearlings, goats, calves, and the necessary farming implements." While after its close, was found, from their "five or six farms on Manhattan Island—which were now destitute of a creature—16 milch-cows, 10 mares, a number of sheep and other stock, had been sold and otherwise disposed of." So that many of Van Twiller's acts appeared to give cause for suspicion that "he had not hesitated to enrich himself at the Company's expense."‡

His example was followed by another of the Company's servants; as we find, a few years afterwards, the store-keeper, Ullrick Lupold, was complained of for extortion and malversation. "The inhabitants being generally supplied from the Company's store with whatever goods or necessaries they required at fixed prices, being fifty per cent. advance on their prime cost, a list was posted in a conspicuous place for public inspection, which shows that several articles had become lessened in price in a few years, no doubt in consequence of the increasing number of agriculturists. This list is arranged as follows:

Fresh meat,	5	stivers,§ or	10 cts. ℔ ℔.	A hog, (common size,)		$ 8.00
Pork,	5	"	10 " "	Cabbage, (℔ 100,)		12.00
Butter,	8	"	16 " "	Staves, (℔ 1,000 of 1,200,)		32.00
Tobacco.	7	"	14 " "	Sugar,	17 to 24 stivers ℔ ℔.	
Dried fish,	12	"	24 " "	Sour wine,	$31 ℔ hhd.	
Hard bread,	15	"	℔ 100	Spanish wine,	4 stivers ℔ quart.	
Wheaten bread,	7	" or	14 cts. ℔ loaf.	French wine,	10 " "	
Rye bread.	5	"	10 " "	Grogham,	$1.00 ℔ ell.	
Corn bread,	4	"	8 " "	Kersey flannel,	1.20 "	
Indian corn,		60	cts. ℔ schepel.‖	White linen,	18 to 20 stivers "	
Barley,		$2.00	"	Red flannel,	$1.20 "	
Peas,		3.25	"	Children's shoes,	36 stivers ℔ pair.	
Wheaten flour,		1.00	"	Brass kettles,	40 " ℔ piece.	

* Valentine.   † O'Callaghan.   ‡ Ibid.
§ Stiver, valued at about two cents.   ‖ About three pecks.

"The inhabitants complained, it is right to add, that the goods in the Company's store were overvalued: a complaint which was subsequently admitted to have sufficient foundation in fact; for *Ullrick Lupold*, the store-keeper in charge, was found guilty of extortion and malversation, and sentenced by the Director and Council, by and with the advice of the principal inhabitants, to removal from office; to pay, in addition, a fine of eighty dollars, and to be banished to Holland. His sentence was, however, remitted, on Lupold's petition; but he was ordered to satisfy the 'Company' for his malversation."*

The prospects in agricultural pursuits, and more especially in that of cattle and hogs, had become so thriving and favorable, as to cause Governor Kieft and his Council to establish, on the 15th September, 1641, "two Fairs at New Amsterdam: one to be holden annually, on the 15th of October, for cattle generally; the other on the first of November, for hogs."†

We have been favored with interesting descriptions of the cattle, hogs, and other animals, both tame and wild, domestic fowl, birds, fish, with numerous agricultural productions, as they then appeared, by Van der Donk and other early writers, from which the following extracts appear to be suitable:

Van der Donk says, "The *Cattle* in New Netherlands are mostly of the *Holland breed*, and with proper care, they raise as fine cattle as we do in Holland. There are also cattle brought over from the province of Utrecht, which are kept in the highlands at Amersfort, (Flatlands, L. I.,) where they thrive as well as in Holland; the increase is not quite as large, but the stock give milk enough, thrive well in pasture, and yield much tallow.

"They also have English cattle in the country, which are not imported by the Netherlanders, but purchased from the English in New England. Those cattle thrive as well as the Holland cattle, and do not require as much care and provender; and, as in England, this breed will do well unsheltered whole winters. This breed of cattle do not grow near as large as the Dutch cattle; do not give as much milk, and are much cheaper; but they fat and tallow well.

"They who desire to cross the breeds, and raise the best kind of stock, put a Holland bull to their English cows, by which they produce a good mixed breed of cattle without much cost. Oxen do good service there, and are not only used by the English, but by some of the Netherlanders also, to the wagon and plough. The grazing of cattle for slaughtering is also progressing, as well of oxen as of other cattle, which produces profit in beef and tallow."

* O'Callaghan.   † City Records.

" *Hogs* are numerous and plenty—some of the citizens prefer the English breed of hogs, because they are hardy, and subsist better in winter without shelter; but the Holland hogs grow much larger and heavier, and have thicker pork."

" *Sheep* are also kept in the New Netherlands, but not as many as in New England, where the weaving business is driven, and where much attention is paid to sheep, to which our Netherlanders pay little attention. The sheep thrive well, and become fat enough. I have seen mutton so exceedingly fat there, that it was too luscious and offensive. The flocks require to be guarded and tended on account of the wolves, for which purpose men cannot be spared; there is also a more important hinderance to the keeping of sheep, which are principally kept for their wool. New Netherlands throughout is a woody country, being almost everywhere beset with trees, stumps, and brushwood, wherein the sheep pasture, and by which they lose most of their wool, which by appearance does not seem to be out, but when sheared turns out light in the fleeces. These are reasons against the keeping of sheep."

"The inhabitants keep more *goats* than sheep, which succeed best; they also give good milk, which is always necessary, and because they cost little, they are of importance to the new settlers and planters, who possess small means. Such persons keep goats instead of cows. Goats cost little, and are very prolific; and the young castrated tups afford fine, delightful meat, which is always in demand.

" The New Netherlanders also have every kind of domestic *fowls*, as we have in Holland, such as *capons*, turkeys, geese, and ducks. There are also *pigeoners*, who keep several kinds of pigeons. In a word, they have tame animals of every description, including cats and dogs."*

Among the species of wild animals, " were panthers, bears, buffaloes, elk, deer, wolves, wild-cats, foxes, racoons, beavers, otters, fishers, minks, hares, muskrats, rabbits, squirrels, skunks, groundhogs, drummers," &c.

" The bears of this country (says Van der Donk) are not ravenous, and do not subsist on flesh and carrion, as the bears of Muscovy and Greenland do. They subsist on grass, herbs, nuts, acorns, and chestnuts, which, we are told by the Indians, they will gather and eat on the trees. In the fall they always are fat."

" The Indians esteem the fore-quarters and the *plucks* as excellent food. I have never tasted the meat, but several Christians,

* N. Y. H. C. N. S., vol. i., p. 165.

who have eaten bear's flesh, say it is as good as any swine's flesh or pork can be.

"Buffaloes are tolerable plenty. These animals mostly keep towards the southwest, where few people go. Their meat is excellent, and more desirable than the flesh of the deer, although it is much coarser. Their skins, when dressed, are heavy enough for collars and harness. These animals are not very wild, and some persons are of opinion that they may be domesticated and tamed."*

Of *elk*, Van der Donk says, "I have heard from the mouth of a Jesuit, who had been taken prisoner by the Mohawk Indians and released by our people, and came to me, that there were many wild forest oxen in Canada and Nova Francia, which, in Latin, they name *boves silvestres*, (the moose, or elk,) which are as large as horses, having long hair on their necks like the mane of a horse, and cloven hoofs; but that, like the buffalo, the animals were not fierce."

Another writer says, "I have also eaten here several times of elks, which were very fat, and tasted something like venison."

"In the forests is great plenty of deer, which in harvest-time and autumn are as fat as any Holland deer can be. I have had them with fat more than two fingers thick on the ribs, so that they were nothing else than clear fat, and could hardly be eaten."

"We seldom pass through the fields without seeing deer, more or less, and we frequently see them in flocks. The year before I came here, (1641,) there were so many turkeys and deer that they came to the houses and hog-pens to feed, and were taken by the Indians with so little trouble, that a deer was sold to the Dutch for a *loaf of bread*, or a *knife*, or even a *tobacco-pipe;* but now we commonly give for a large deer six or seven guilders."†

"The wild birds were as numerous as the wild animals. Eagles, falcons, sparrow-hawks, sailing-hawks, kites, ravens, castrills, crows, cat-owls, turkeys, partridges, pheasants, woodcocks, snipes, quails, cranes, herons, pigeons, land-runners, woodpeckers, thrushes, blackbirds," &c.‡ Van der Donk says, "The most important fowl of the country is the wild turkey. They resemble the tame turkyes of the Netherlands. Those birds are common in the woods all over the country, and are found in large flocks, from twenty to forty in a flock. They are large, heavy, fat, and fine, weighing from twenty to thirty pounds each, and I have heard of one that weighed thirty-two pounds. They differ little in taste from the tame turkeys; but the epicures prefer the wild kind. They are best in the fall of the year, when the Indians will usually sell a turkey for ten stivers.

* O'Callaghan.   † Ibid.   ‡ Megapolensis.

Sometimes the turkeys are caught with dogs in the snow; but the greatest number are shot at night from the trees. The Indians take many in snares, when the weather changes in winter. Then they lay bulbous roots, which the turkeys are fond of, in the small rills and streams of water, which the birds take up, when they are ensnared and held until the artful Indian takes the turkey as his prize."

"There are also several kinds of quails in the country, some of which are smaller, *(common quail,)* and others larger, (the *partridge* or *pheasant,)* than those of the Netherlands. In the Netherlands it is not believed that they will alight and sit in trees; but it is true that many *(partridges)* are shot from trees in this country. I have done it several times, and have killed a hundred or more from trees. I have also heard from respectable authority that eleven heath-fowls *(prairie hen)* have been killed at a shot—off a palisade fence. There are also woodcocks, birdcocks, heath-fowls, pheasants, wood and water snipes, &c., and many cranes, of which great numbers are shot on the mowed lands in the fall of the year, and they are fine for the table. Quacks and bitterns are also plenty.

"The pigeons, which resemble coal-pigeons, are astonishingly plenty. Those are most numerous in the spring and fall of the year, when they are seen in such numbers, in flocks, that they resemble the clouds in the heavens, and obstruct the rays of the sun." "The Indians, when they find the breeding-places of the pigeons, (at which they assemble in numberless thousands,) frequently remove to those places with their wives and children, to the number of two or three hundred in a company, where they live a month or more on the young pigeons, which they take, after pushing them from their nests with poles and sticks."

Of water-fowls, there "were swans, geese, pelicans, ducks, teal, widgeons, brant, coots, divers and eel-shovelers." "We find these principally in the spring and fall of the year. At other seasons they are not as plenty. But at those seasons, the waters, by their movements, appear to be alive with water-fowls; and the people who reside near the water are frequently disturbed in their rest at night by the noise of the water-fowls, particularly by the swans, which, in their seasons, are so plenty that the bays and shores where they resort appear as if they were dressed in white drapery."

"There are also three kinds of wild geese. The first and best kind are the gray geese, *(Canada geese,)* which are larger than the Netherlands geese, but not so large as the swans." "A great many of those fowls are shot, and they are esteemed before the other kinds for the table. I have known a gunner named Henry de Backer who killed eleven gray geese out of a large flock at one shot from his gun. The other kinds are the black geese, and the white-heads."

Of the fish taken "in the fresh water, were salmon, sturgeon, striped bass, drums, shad, carp, perch, pike, trout, thick-heads, suckers, sunfish, catfish, eels, lampreys, divers, mullets, or frost-fish. Those of the sea, codfish, shellfish, weekfish, halibut, herring, mackerel, thornback, flounders, plaice, bream, blackfish, seal, lobster, oysters, crabs, periwinkle, clams, turtles, and porpoises."

"All the waters of New Netherlands are rich with fishes. Sturgeons are plenty in the rivers at their proper season; but these fish are not esteemed, and when large, are not eaten. No person takes the trouble to salt or souse them for profit; and the roes, from which the costly *caviaer* is prepared, are cast away. Salmon are plenty in some rivers, and the striped bass are plenty in all the rivers and bays of the sea." "The drums are a tolerably good fish. I have heard it said, that the drums were named *thirteens* when the Christians first began fishing in the New Netherlands. Then, every one was desirous to see the fishes which were caught, for the purpose of discovering whether the same were known to them, and if they did not know the fish, then they gave it a name. First in the fishing season, they caught many shad, which they named *Elft*, (eleventh.) Later, they caught the striped bass, which they named *Twalft*, (twelfth.) Later still, they caught the drums, which they named *Dertienen*, (thirteenth.) For those fish succeeded each other in their seasons, and the same are still known by the names which were thus derived."*

In addition to the above list of fish, Van der Donk adds, "snook, forrels, palings, brickens, dunns, roah, scoll, and sheephead. The latter are formed like the sunfish, but much heavier, with cross stripes, being about the weight of the largest carps. They have teeth in the fore-part of the mouth like a sheep, but are not voracious, and are an excellent fish. There is another species of fish, called blackfish, which are held in high estimation by the Christians. It is as brown as a *seek*, formed like the carp, but not so coarse in its scales. When this kind of fish, which are plenty, is served upon the table, it goes before all others, for every person prefers it.

"There are also porpoises, herring-hogs, potheads or sharks, turtles, &c., and whales, of which there are none caught, but if preparations were made for the purpose, then it might be easily effected; but our colonists have not advanced far enough to pursue whaling. A lost *bird*, (whale,) however, is frequently cast and stranded, which is cut up."

* O'Callaghan.

The same writer, in his description *of the North River*, says: "I cannot refrain, although somewhat out of place, to relate a very singular occurrence which happened in the month of March, 1647, at the time of a great freshet, caused by the fresh water flowing down from above, by which the water of the *(North)* river became nearly fresh to the Bay, when at ordinary seasons the salt water flows up from twenty to twenty-four miles* from the ·sea. At this season, two whales, of common size, swam up the river forty miles, from which place one of them returned and stranded about twelve miles from the sea, near which place four others also stranded the same year. The other ran up the river and grounded near the great Chahoos Falls, about forty-three miles from the sea. This fish was tolerably fat, for although the citizens of Rensselaerwyck broiled out a great quantity of train oil, still the whole river (the current being still rapid) was oily for three weeks, and covered with grease. As the fish lay rotting, the air was infected with its stench to such a degree that the smell was offensive and perceptible for two miles to leeward. For what purpose those whales ascended the river so far, it being full forty miles from all salt or brackish water, it is difficult to say, unless their great desire for fish, which were plenty at this season, led them onward."

"Lobsters are plenty in many places. Some of those are very large, being from five to six feet in length; others, again, are from a foot to a foot and a half long, which are the best for the table. There are also crabs, like those of the Netherlands, some of which are altogether soft. Those, the people call weak-crabs, and they make excellent bait for hook-fishing.

"There are also sea-cocks, (horned crabs;) sea-colts, sea-conks, and periwinkles are very plenty, which in some seasons are cast ashore by the sea in great numbers. From these the Indians make wampum.

"Oysters are very plenty in many places. Some of these are like the Colchester oysters, and are fit to be eaten raw; others are very large, wherein pearls are frequently found; but as they are of a brownish colour, they are not valuable. The price for oysters is usually from eight to ten stivers per hundred.

"Muscles of different kinds are plenty; the St. Jacob's and mother-of-pearl shells, with alis or stone crutches."

"There are also shrimps and tortoises in the waters and on the land. Some persons prepare delicious dishes from the water terrapin, which is luscious food."

Of vegetables, Van der Donk says: "The garden products in the New Netherlands are very numerous; some of them have been known

* A Dutch mile is about three English miles.

to the natives from the earliest times, and others introduced from different parts of the world, but chiefly from the Netherlands.

"They consist, then, of various kinds of salads, cabbages, parsnips, carrots, beets, endive, succory, finckel, sorrel, dill, spinage, radishes, parsley, chervil, (or sweet cicely,) cresses, onions, leeks," "together with laurel, artichokes, and asparagus."

"The herb-garden is also tolerably well supplied with rosemary, lavender, hyssop, thyme, sage, marjoram, balm, holy onions, wormwood, belury, chives, and clary; also pimpurnel, dragon's-blood, five-finger, tarragon, (or dragon's-wort,) &c."

"The pumpkin grows with little or no cultivation, and is so sweet and dry that it is used, with the addition of vinegar and water, for stewing, in the same manner as apples; and notwithstanding that it is here (Netherlands) generally despised as a mean, unsubstantial article of food, it is there (here) of so good a quality that our countrymen hold it in high estimation."

"The English, *(in New England,)* who in general think much of what gratifies the palate, use it also in pastry," *(pumpkin pies, no doubt,)* "and understand making a beverage from it." "The Spanish *(or mammoth pumpkin)* is considered the best."

"The natives have another species of this vegetable peculiar to themselves, called by our people *quaasiens, (squashes;)* a name derived from the aborigines, as the plant was not known to us before our intercourse with them. It is a delightful fruit; as well to the eye, on account of its fine variety of colors, as to the mouth, for its agreeable taste." "The natives make great account of this vegetable; some of the Netherlanders, too, consider it quite good, but others do not esteem it very highly."

"Melons, likewise, grow in the New Netherlands very luxuriantly, without requiring the land to be prepared or manured; they will thrive, too, in newly-cleared wood-land, when it is freed from weeds; and in this situation the fruit, which they call *Spanish pork,* grows large, and very abundant. I had the curiosity to weigh one of these melons, and found its weight to be seventeen pounds."

"The citrull, or water-citron, *(water-melon,)* also grows there, (here;) a fruit that we have not in the Netherlands, and is only known from its being occasionally brought from Portugal, except to those who have traveled in warm climates." "They grow ordinarily to the size of a man's head. I have seen them as large as the biggest Leyden cabbages, but in general they are somewhat oblong." "When they are to be eaten, the rind is cut off to about the thickness of the finger; all the rest is good, consisting of a spongy pulp, full of liquor, in which the seeds are imbedded; and if the fruit is sound and fully ripe, it melts as soon as it enters the mouth, and nothing is left but the seeds."

"Cucumbers are abundant. Calabashes, or gourds, also grow there: they are half as long as the pumpkin, but have within very little pulp, and are sought chiefly on account of the shell, which is hard and durable, and is used to hold seeds, spices, &c. It is the common water-pail of the natives, and I have seen one so large that it would contain more than a bushel," *(about three pecks.)*

"Turnips, also, are as good and fine as any sand-rapes that are raised in the Netherlands."

"Of beans there are several kinds; but the large Windsor bean, which the farmers call *tessen,* or hot-house beans, and also the horse-bean, will not fill out their pods." "The Turkish beans which our people have introduced there grow wonderfully; they fill out remarkably well, and are much cultivated."

"Before the arrival of the Netherlanders, the Indians raised beans of various kinds and colors, but generally too coarse to be eaten green, or to be pickled, except the blue sort, which are abundant; they somewhat tend to flatulency, like those we raise in Holland; but in other respects they furnish an excellent food, of which the Indians are especially fond. They have a peculiar mode of planting them, which our people have learned to practice: when the *Turkish wheat, (Indian corn,)* or, as it is called, *maize,* is half a foot above the ground, they plant the beans around it, and let them grow together. The coarse stalk serves as a bean-prop, and the beans run upon it, and thus two crops are gathered at the same time."

Another writer (De Vries) says of Indian corn, or maize, "They sow the maize in April and May," and gather it in September and October; "and when they have shelled the corn, they bury it in holes, which they have previously covered with mats, and so keep as much as they want for the winter and while hunting." "When they travel, they take a flat stone, and press it with another stone placed upon the first; and when it is pressed, they have little baskets, which they call *notassen,* and which are made of a kind of hemp, the same as fig-frails—which they make to serve them as sieves—and thus make their meal. They make flat cakes of the meal mixed with water, as large as a farthing cake in this country, and bake them in the ashes, first wrapping a vine-leaf or maize-leaf around them. When they are sufficiently baked in the ashes, they make good, palatable bread.

"Our Netherlanders raise good wheat, rye, barley, oats, and peas, and can brew as good beer here as in our fatherland, for good hops grow in the woods; they are in want of nothing but men to do the work."

"Barley grows well in the country, but it is not much needed." "Flax and hemp will grow fine, but as the women do not spin much, and the Indians have hemp in abundance in the woods, from which they make strong ropes and nets, for these reasons very little flax is raised."

"Wild fruit was equally abundant," observes another writer; "consisting of acorns, (some of which were very sweet,) chestnuts, beech-nuts, walnuts, butternuts, hazlenuts, mulberries, cherries, currants, plums, gooseberries, medlars, bilberries, blackberries, raspberries, cranberries, and strawberries; the latter in such abundance, that people lay down in the fields and ate them to satiety. Pignuts, artichokes, wild leeks and onions, wild-peas, and other wild fruit, also abounded."

Of imported fruits, Van der Donk says: "The Netherlands settlers, who are lovers of fruit, on observing that the climate was suitable to the production of fruit-trees, have brought over and planted various kinds of apple and pear trees, which thrive well. Those also grow from the seeds, of which I have seen many, which, without grafting, bore delicious fruit in the sixth year." "The English have brought over the *first* quinces, and we have also brought over stocks and seeds, which thrive well. Orchard cherries thrive well, and produce large fruit. Spanish cherries, forerunners, morellaes, of every kind we have, as in the Netherlands; and the trees bear better, because the blossoms are not injured by the frosts."

"The peaches, which are sought after in the Netherlands, grow wonderfully well here." "We have also introduced morecotoons, (a variety of the peach,) apricots, several sorts of the best plums, almonds, persimmons, cornelian cherries, figs, several sorts of currants, gooseberries, calissiens, and thorn-apples."

"Although the land is full of many kinds of grapes, we still want settings of the best kinds from Germany, for the purpose of enabling our wine-planters here to select the best kinds, and to propagate the same." "The entire land, both forest and bottom-land," observes O'Callaghan, "was, moreover, covered with vines, climbing up the loftiest trees, or creeping along the lowly valleys, and bearing loads of grapes: some white, some blue; some large, some small; some very juicy, and others not so good, yet all promising, if properly cultivated, an ample return to the vine-dresser." "In short, every kind of fruit which grows in the Netherlands is plenty already in the New Netherlands, which have been introduced by the lovers of agriculture; and the fruits thrive better here, particularly such kinds as require a warmer climate."

> " Why mourn about Brazil, full of base Portuguese?
> When Van der Donck shows so far much better fare ;
> Where wheat-fills golden ears, and grapes abound in trees ;
> Where fruit and kine are good with little care."
>
> *Evert Nieuwenhof.*

At this early day, it will be seen, the natural advantages of this beautiful country—producing so much, and still capable of growing every luxury wanted by man—were not fully appreciated, so badly was it managed and sadly misgoverned by many of the Company's servants, more especially by Governor Kieft himself, who afterwards confesses that he was instructed to do so ! "For he said he had express orders to exact the contributions from the Indians"—to prosecute the people—"when there was no offence, and to consider a partial offence an entire one, and so forth."* These unpopular acts, and especially his exactions and enmity towards the Indians, the consequences of which had become very grievous to the settlers, and more particularly to those who lived away from the protection of the Fort, as the settlement then extended about thirty English miles to the east, and twenty-one to the north and south from Fort Amsterdam—to assist in reforming some of these grievances, the Commonalty at large chose "twelve men" to co-operate with the Governor and Council.

Among some of the local improvements which were introduced in 1642, these "twelve men" represented that, in consequence of the sale in New Netherlands of cows and other stock by the English, the cattle owned and introduced by the Dutch were held in small esteem, and were not so valuable as they had heretofore been." That "it was near-sighted and destructive to the improvement of their own stock; and that the English should not be permitted hereafter to sell either cows or goats within the Dutch jurisdiction, but that this privilege should be confined to oxen and poultry."†

The Dutchmen, at this early day, began to admit the superior qualities of the *red cattle* of New England; at least in producing better working oxen than their Dutch breed; but they wished to exclude their breeding cattle. Theirs were generally good milkers, producing good fleshy beef, and withal, this solicited exclusion of the English stock would tend to enhance the value of their own breeding stock. The Governor, however, concluded that the "English should not be permitted to sell cows or goats for the future within

* Murphy's translations.   † O'Callaghan.

New Netherlands." In this act, he had acceded to the wishes of the "twelve men," but many of their movements and acts were looked upon by him with a jealous eye, and by a proclamation he disbanded them, and forbade them to meet.

His enmity towards the Indians also was such, that he had made up his mind to attack them unawares, and without notice, and expressed himself to De Vries, who was dining with him one day, that "he had a great desire, he said, to make the savages wipe their chops." Sure enough, the night after, he ordered an attack to be made upon two separate parties of Indians that had moved near the settlers, as a sort of protection from a stronger tribe which was at war with them. So, in the silent hour of midnight, Kieft's brave and valiant soldiers approached the unsuspecting victims, and in cool blood cowardly murdered above one hundred of them. This unwise and cruel act caused all the neighboring Indians, those who were friendly as well as other tribes, to retaliate, by murdering all the men they could find, (leaving the women and children,) burning and desolating the farms, destroying the crops, killing the cattle, hogs, &c., and driving the settlers panic-stricken into the town.

Within two weeks after, peace was proposed, and partly effected with a few Indians; yet many were not satisfied, and they again commenced murdering families and individuals, and some who were quite near the Fort. The inhabitants were now almost confined to the precincts of the fortifications, and in a dreadful situation; so they appealed to the Honorable Lords in Holland, and say: "Our population consists for the most part of women and children; the freemen (not counting the English) are about *two hundred* in numbers, who must protect by force of arms their families, which now lie concealed in straw huts around outside the forts." The cattle are partly burnt and killed; the remainder conveyed to the fort on the Manhattes, where, for want of forage, they must starve through the coming winter, if not immediately slaughtered."*

Still further to add to their miserable condition, internal troubles broke out among themselves. "Complaints were daily made of stealing and killing of hogs, goats, as well as of the irregularities which increased so fast that it 'threatened to end in plunder and robbing,' and it was found that people would at last murder one another in consequence of the impunity of the delinquents."

The situation of the country at that time was certainly a very discouraging one; with a jealous, sordid, and an unpopular Governor, and the people almost rent asunder, distressed by their losses of friends and protectors, of property, and many of them almost in

* O'Callaghan.

despair. However, assistance came; their complaints and appeals had been heard; the Dutch West India Company, in 1647, recalled Governor Kieft, and sent a man much more fitted for the position than either who had preceded him.

Peter Stuyvesant, the last of the Dutch Governors in this city, arrived in the month of May, 1647, when he assumed the reins of government. His character appears somewhat pompous and arbitrary, yet he had the vigilance, firmness, and force which were necessary to raise the country up from the disorder and confusion in which he found it. He made friends of the Indians, and introduced a successful trade with them, as well for the resident traders as the " West India Company."

Numerous proclamations and ordinances of a stringent character soon appeared, which were posted in the " public market-places."* In the following month of July, an ordinance, in relation to the trespassing of cattle, was enacted, declaring that all the inhabitants of the New Netherlands are hereby charged and commanded to set off and put into good fence all their plantations, so that the cattle therein may be kept from committing trespass ; which cattle, whether they be horses, kine, and in a special manner goats and hogs, must be taken care of, or otherwise disposed of, that they cannot commit any trespass; to this end the Fiscal Van Dyck should build a *pound*, in which cattle shall be detained until the damages shall have been made good, and the fees of officers shall have been paid: let every one take warning, and look out for costs."

In the early part of the following year, (1648,) a law was introduced to confirm the privileges of trade in New Amsterdam to permanent residents; for it was ordered that henceforward no person should keep a shop, or carry on any retail business, except such as " have already taken the oath of allegiance," were rated, at least, at from two to three thousand guilders, and had entered into an engagement to remain in the country four successive years, " and to keep fire and light" at their own expense. This regulation was not, however, to extend to "old residents," who were to be allowed the privileges of trade, though not rated as above, provided they bound themselves to remain in the province the required time; not to quit the same without permission from the Director and Council, nor to use any weights or measures except those of "Old Amsterdam, to which we owe our name;" and for the further encouragement of trade, " each Monday in the week was declared to be a *market-day*"—"as well for strangers as residents." The "strangers," no doubt, were the Indians and country people who had, prior to

* City Records.

the establishment of this "market-day," brought with them, in their skiffs and canoes, their productions, from the chase, of the land and of the water; some of which, such as peltries, corn, &c., were taken to the "Company's Store," either for the purpose of trade or sale, and the balance sold to the residents who were in the habit of finding them at the "store," or landing-place; but at no stated time or particular day: therefore it appeared necessary to appoint a particular day—"Monday of each week a market-day," when they would be sure to find each other, near this depot of trade or market, which, no doubt, gave the space between the "Company's Store" and the "Fort" the name of "Market-field."*

About this period an "Annual Fair," or "kermis," was also established, for the sale of home productions, (those appointed previous were for cattle and hogs,) to commence on the first Monday after the "feast of St. Bartholomew," (24th of August,) and continue for ten days; at which all persons were privileged to sell their goods from their tents.†

Many of their productions were sold for cash, or such currency as was then recognized as such; a great deal of which was Indian money, called "wampum," or seawant, (or zeawant,) "half-beavers, and beaver" skins. The common value of "wampum or seawant," when strung on a string, passed "six white," or "three black seawant," for one stiver; the value of "beaver" was "eight guilders," or about three dollars; divided in "half-beavers," the value was much less in proportion. The early English settlers, however, used their £ s. d. currency when an opportunity offered. This Indian currency, seawant, afterwards became much depreciated in value, by the unskillful tinkering at the currency; it being loose, not perforated, and badly finished. The authorities notice it at a meeting held May 30, 1650, and they "have observed, both now and for a long time, 'loose seawant;' many are not perforated, and half finished, and also made out of stone, bone, glass, muscle-shells, horns, and even out of wood, and broken ones, whereby occasion is given for repeated complaints from the inhabitants, that they cannot go with such seawant to the market; nor yet procure any commodity, not even a mean white loaf of bread, or a can of beer at the merchant's, the baker's, or the tapster's, for the loose seawant." The authorities resolve, "from this time forth, no loose, unperforated, or clumsy seawant shall be current, nor be a lawful tender, except that the same shall be strung on one string, as the general custom has been heretofore. They ordained that the common seawant shall be as formerly; that is, six white, or three black seawant, for one stuyver;

* O'Callaghan and City Records.   † O'Callaghan.

and the *base strung seawant* shall pass *eight* white, or four black, for one stuyver."*

Part of these instructions were unheeded: "the *base strung seawant* being still refused and rejected for trifling articles by shopkeepers, brewers, bakers, tapsters, mechanics, and day-laborers, to the great confusion and discommoding of the inhabitants in general; there being at present *no other specie* with which the inhabitants can accommodate one another." The authorities, on the 14th September following, " do ordain and decree, that the *base strung seawant* shall be current—in payment for small and daily necessary commodities in housekeeping"—and " that the sum of twelve guilders and under shall be paid *all* in *base strung seawant;* from twelve to twenty-four guilders, half-and-half; that is to say, half base and half good strung seawant; from twenty-five guilders to fifty guilders, one-third *base strung*, and two-thirds good strung seawant; and in large sums agreeably to the agreement between the buyer and seller."† In case of refusal, certain heavy penalties were ordered to be inflicted. We find, a few years after, one of the Government officers refused to receive this currency from Solomon La Scheen's (La Chair) wife, who appeared in court on the 17th January, 1656, " with a certain box of white stringed '*zeawan*,' to the amount of ff. 84.3, complaining that Warner Wessells, the Farmer of the Excise, refused the same, and will not give any license; and whereas she is obstructed in her business, requests the W. Court to decide if the same be good *zeawan* or not, and to order him accordingly to receive the same, and not impede her. The W. Court decides that the *zeawan* exhibited by the petitioner is good merchantable *zeawan*, and hath heretofore sealed the same in Court."‡

At this period the prices of several of the domestic animals are noticed, and " were to be had at a reasonable price, except *sheep*, which the English (in New England) do not sell, and are rare in New Netherlands."§

"A milch cow, with her 2d or 3d calf, ff. 130.

A year old sow, ... 20 to 24.

A sheep, being a ewe, . . . 20 to 24."

"Maize *(Indian corn)* can be always had in season from the Indians;" " the schepel cost ordinarily 10 to 15 stivers, when bought from them."

Although the above valuation of animals appears to have been made for breeding stock, yet this valuation, in our day, usually, would not vary much if the *same* were fit for consumption. In 1640 the price of "fresh meat" was five stivers (10 *cents*) per pound;

* **City Records.**   † Ibid.   ‡ Ibid.   § Col. His., vol. i., p. 369.

—at this period, (1650,) according to the above, it could be afforded at about the same price. Seven years afterwards (1657) we find it about the same, by the following extract from a letter of Vice-Director Aldrich, dated April 13th, 1657,* who says: "I understand that pork, beef, peas, etc., are to be had cheaper here than they can be sent from Holland, to wit: beef and pork at 4 and 5 stivers the pound; peas, 3 and 3½ guilders the schepel, payable in merchandise, such as duffels, linen, etc., at the aforesaid prices. These, however, were the prices in trading for merchandise, or other than the *Indian currency*, which had become much depreciated; instead of *four black seawant* passing for one *stiver*, as in 1650, it had been lowered, first to six; then, in 1659, the white wampum (or seawant) was reduced from 12 to 16, and the *black* from 6 to 8 for a stiver. The only effect of this was to oblige the holder to give more wampum for any article he might require from the trader, who in return allowed the natives a larger quantity for his beavers, *(skins,)* 'so that little or no benefit accrued.' Prices nominally advanced: beavers, which sold for 12 to 14 guilders, (seawant,) rose to 22 and 24 guilders; bread from 14 to 22 stivers the 8 lbs. loaf; beef, 9 to 10 stivers per lb.; pork, 15 to 20 stivers; butter, 30 stivers; common shoes from 3½ to 12 guilders the pair; coarse stockings from 36 stivers to 4 or 5 guilders the pair; and wrought iron 18 to 20 stivers the lb. Beaver and specie were all this while of equal value, and the difference between these and wampum was 50 per cent. Finally, the price of beavers fell, in 1663, from 8 guilders (specie) to 4½ guilders; white wampum from 16 to 8, black from 8 to 4 for a stiver; and this was the state of the currency when the English came into possession of the province."†

Let us now return to the period of about 1650, when the increasing numbers of inhabitants had caused trade to rapidly advance, and many who were anxious to make a good or quick bargain on the "market-day," were on the lookout, watching and waiting at the *beach* or *strand* at the East River side, for the market-boats and canoes, which were sometimes belated in consequence of the tides, storms, ice, or other causes; and when landed, the inhabitants were as ready to purchase there at the strand as the farmers and Indians were to dispose of their produce, to save them the trouble of carrying it up to the "market-field." This strand, which had been the regular landing-place for small craft many years previous, extended along up the shore from about the present Whitehall Street, along the line of the present Pearl, to the foot of Broad Street, then called the (Grafht) common ditch or creek. This "creek," at that early

---

* Hol. Doc., vol. ii., p. 6.   † O'Callaghan.

period, did not appear to be in a proper condition for the accommodation of the market and other boats; but it is supposed to have been in a state of nature; the shores on each side muddy and full of weeds, and in winter obstructed with ice, so that it appearednot to have been used much until about the year 1660, although they were at work filling it up on the sides, in 1657 and '58, as will appear from the City *Records*, February 21, of the latter year, when " the three laborers of the Graft (*canal*) being summoned to court, appearing, are asked how it happens that they do not come any more to work; answer—the weather is unfavorable; whereupon, they were told that complaints were made that there has *nothing filled up*—and therefore ordered to proceed to do so, and that they should not stop." Then, on the 7th of March, 1659, " Resolvert Waldron is ordered to appear in Court, to receive a commission to superintend the Grafht, according to the placard dated 3d December, 1657, published in front of the City Hall, and renewed on the 4th of March, 1659. He was ordered to take good care, and superintend on the newly-constructed 'Graft,' that no filth be cast into it; also, that the boats, canoes, and skiffs be placed in regular order therein."

We now pass over a period of almost twenty years, when we find it not yet dyked, nor the street (*Broad*) leveled or paved, which is shown from the proceedings, as follows: "Ordered, that all and every p(er)son & p(er)sons being inhabitants and living within the streete called Here Graft, shall forth with & without delay fill up the Graft Ditch or Common shoare, & make the same level, with the streete, and then so pave & pitch the same before their doores with stones, soe far as every inhabitant's house shall be fronting towards the Graft or Ditch, upon pain of every person soe neglecting shall have such fines inflicted upon them as the Courte shall thinke fitt.—Dated this 9th day of May, 1676, then proclaymed."

Although the houses were ordered to be built fronting the "Graft Ditch," at that time, yet the line of the Here Graft (*Broad*) Street was not laid out until about twelve years after; this is shown in the appointment of two carpenters, as surveyors, to lay out some lots along the shore of the East River, from about the present Moore Street, along the east line of Pearl Street, up to Coenties Slip. The proceedings May 4, 1688, show the appointment of "Peter King & Adolph Pieterson, surveyors for ye Citty of New York," were required to "survey ye vacant land within this Citty, near and in ye Dock, beginning ffrom ye Weigh-house to ye Citty Hall, and to lay ye same out in lotts of eighty foot long, into the Dock, and about Four and Twenty ffoot broad, leaving sufficient spaces ffor ye street; as also to lay out ye street, ranging with ye Here Graft, as you shall receive further directions,"—"and that they lay out a convenient inlett in y⁰ middle of y⁰ said street ffor y⁰ Water to fflow in at, and y⁰ channell of y⁰ Here Graft to run into it." Again, on the 14th of June following, it was "Ordered, that the Carpenters, Mr. Adolph Pieterson and Peter King, forthwith sett up the fframes of the inlett into the Here Graft of sixteen ffoot wide, leaving on each side twenty-eight ffoot for the (*Broad*) Street."

In consequence of the war between the *Fatherland* and England, the citizens began to fear that the feeling had extended to the English Colonies; and if a sudden attack should be made on the city, it would be found defenceless.

Orders were therefore given, on the 13th of March, 1653, to repair the "Fort;" that the whole body of citizens should mount guard every night; and to "inclose the greater part of the city with upright palisades and small breastworks, so that, in case of necessity, all the inhabitants may retire within the inclosure." This wall of palisades was made of hard wood, of twelve to thirteen feet in height by eighteen inches in circumference, and sharpened at the tops; they extended from the East to the North River, along the northerly side of the street, which took and yet retains its name from this *wall*, or barrier, of palisades. There were but two entrances on the land side, by which the city could be entered: one on the present Broadway, and the other on Pearl Street.

After the "wall" was finished, the "Night-Watch" became careless, and neglected to *mount guard* every night, as directed: so, on the 24th of November following, Governor Stuyvesant summoned the Captains of the Burgery, *(citizens,)* Arent Van Hatten and Martin Krigier, before him, and told them he "was highly displeased that the Burgers should have intermitted their night-watch without his knowledge; whereupon they answered, that this happened through the want of *fire-wood;*" to which "Stuyvesant" said, "that they *set to* and procure some." Van Hatten pleaded the resolution previously made, "refused to do so, and requested his High Mightiness that they should go, according to request, to the Burgomasters and Schepens."

An attempt was made, in the month of November, next year, to "ordain and establish a '*Rattle Watch,*' of four to six men, to guard this city by night; wherefore all persons, who desire to undertake the same, are warned to repair to the aforesaid place, *(City Hall,)* to hear the conditions, and to act according to circumstances." The Court met at the appointed place and hour, and after stating the "conditions," there was not *one* offered himself to undertake this important trust; so the idea of forming a "Rattle

Watch" at that period was given up, although they succeeded a few years afterwards to organize one. The Burgomasters, on the 4th of March, 1658, say they "have above *eight* persons for 24 stivers every night they watch, it being well understood *four* and *four* shall watch each night; and they are promised one or two beavers for candles, and two to three hundred pieces of fire-wood."

On the 12th inst. following, Lodowyck Pos was appointed Captain of the "Rattle Watch," when Articles or Rules were established.

The trading at the "Strand," already referred to, no doubt increased from year to year, as the agriculturist advanced; and the Town of Manhattan, in February, 1653, formally became a city*— the City of New Amsterdam.

Although there were large crops raised, yet they were not such as furnished food for the increased immigration. The growing of tobacco was found more profitable than the growing of grain, and the agriculturist excessively cultivated it. "For the last two years, a scarcity of food now became imminent." "To prevent this, the export of breadstuffs was prohibited; tobacco-planters were ordered to set as many hills of corn as they did of tobacco, and the consumption of grain by brewers and distillers was strictly forbidden."†

About two years after this scarcity of food, the inhabitants were again visited with another more terrible infliction. "Sixty-four canoes landed at the city, with nearly two thousand Indians, who broke into several of the houses, on pretence of looking for other Indians. The magistrates, however, succeeded in prevailing upon them to quit the place by sundown, and to retire to 'Nut (Governor's) Island.'" In the evening they again appeared, and attacked some of the citizens; but they, in return, had prepared for them, and after killing several, drove them out of the city. The Indians then proceeded to lay the country around in waste. In three days, one hundred of the Dutch were killed, one hundred and fifty taken prisoners, twenty-eight "boweries" and a number of plantations were burned, twelve or fifteen thousand schepels of grain destroyed, from five to six hundred head of cattle killed or driven off, and the farmers driven into the city for refuge.

Governor Stuyvesant being an old soldier, and withal a diplomatist, brought his threatening or persuasive powers into action on the Indians, and, with some presents, soon restored peace. Many of these Indians were ofttimes found treacherous, and were not generally liked by many of the settlers, who would occasionally bring charges against them, which very often were proved false; and this had no doubt a tendency to establish the following regulation in "the month of January, 1656."* "Various complaints were made, 'that under the notion and name of Indians, horned cattle, hogs, and other animals on the plains have been seized, slaughtered, and offered for sale by Christians, or at least by those who go under the name of Christians. To prevent, from this time forth, neither in this city, nor on the plains belonging to this province, shall any cattle, hogs, goats, or sheep be permitted to be slaughtered, not even by the owner himself, unless the owner first, on the same days he intends to slaughter, shall have given in such creature as his own, to the magistrate of the respective place to which he belongs, and from him have obtained a slaughter certificate' "—for which he had to pay a fee, according to the size and value of the animal.

The city and citizens no doubt severely felt these drawbacks, but, under Governor Stuyvesant's vigorous administration, both kept on increasing. "A survey of the city at this period showed there were 'one hundred and twenty houses,' with extensive lots, and 'one thousand souls.' "† The houses were more substantially built, the streets were better regulated, and a more rigid system was introduced into all the local affairs of Government.

"MARKET-PLACE AT THE STRAND."

1656. The increasing number of the inhabitants in the year 1656 no doubt wished better regulations, especially in the one specified as their "market-day." Monday was objectionable, because the butchers had to slaughter their animals, and the farmers to gather their productions on the Sabbath-day; and as no particular public market-place had yet been appointed by the authorities here, although, as has been before noticed, the inhabitants, in the course of trade, had first made the open ground before the "Company's Store" and the fort a "market-field;" then, likely, the scarcity of food in 1653 and '54 had caused the citizens, in their pressing wants, to meet the market-boats and canoes as they ran upon the shore or *strand*, which extended from "Whitehall" along Dock *(now Pearl)* Street, up to the "Graft" *(Canal)* at the foot of Broad Street."

The continuation and increase of business at that place, and the

* City Records.   † Brodhead.

fact of Governor Stuyvesant having been a strictly religious character—not only not countenancing, but positively forbidding labor
on the Sabbath-day—had afforded good reasons, with the assistance
of his counselors, to change the "market-day," and on the 12th day
of September, 1656, formally, to appoint a public locality in the following language: "*Greeting:* Whereas, now and then the people
from without are in the habit of bringing into the city different commodities, such as veal, pork, butter, cheese, turnips, roots, straw, and
other products of the land, for the purpose of selling them; and it
frequently happens, particularly here at the 'Strand,' that they are
obliged to tarry long, and to lodge to their great damage, for the reason, because the community, or at least the greater part, especially of
those who live away from the 'Strand,' are not aware that such
commodities have been brought for sale, not alone to the discommoding of the 'Burgerers,' but also to the notorious injury of the
enterprising man from without, who frequently has to lose more
in his time than the profit on his commodities will warrant;
therefore, for the purpose of making provision in the premises, the 'Director-General and the Councillors' aforesaid, by these
presents, do ordain, that from this time forth, here in this city, *Saturday* shall be the market-day, and market shall be held at the
strand, at or around the house of Mr. Hans Kierstede, where, after
him, every one shall be permitted to enter that has anything to buy
or sell."* This location was between Moore and Whitehall Streets,
on the east side of Pearl Street.

Here, then, the public wants and accommodations of both producer and consumer appear to have been consulted by the public authorities in establishing the *first public market*-place in our city, without
a direct gain to the public coffers, although one part of the public
revenue was received in the form of "excise" on all the slaughtered
cattle, which all had to pay alike, whether for sale at the "Company's Store" or for family purposes. "They who slaughter oxen,
cows, calves, hogs, or goats, for consumption, shall be taxed for each
guilder (40 *cents*) of their value, one stuyver, (2 *cents;*) and those
who do not produce their animals for valuation previous to slaughtering, shall forfeit the same, for the benefit of the officer, the town,
and the informer."†

This "Excise"‡ was first *farmed* or leased, for one year, to Solomon La Chair, Burgher, for the sum of seven hundred and ten ca-
role guilders, (about $284.) He appeared in Court on the 6th of
November, 1656, and requested that "sworn butchers" may be or-

---

* City Records.   † City Records and Doc. Hist. of N. Y., vol. i., p. 646.
                        ‡ City Records.

dered and confirmed. The Burgomasters and Schepens appointed " *William Clasen, Gerit Jansen Roos*, and *Jan Van Haerlan*," "who shall each be bound to serve in butchering and cutting up, and to provide, have, and possess their own ropes, hand-barrows, troughs, and other articles requisite for slaughtering, and receive for butchering and cutting as follows:

"For every ox or cow, - - - - 4 guilders, or $1.60 *cents.*
" every pig under 80 lbs. wt., 20 stivers, " .40 "
" over that (weight,) - - - 30 stivers, " .60 "
" a calf, - - - - - - - - 1 guilder, " .40 "
" a sheep or goat, - - - - 12 stivers, " .24 *cents.*"

Some of the inhabitants, in giving in the valuation of an animal to La Chair, were apt to place their worth at too low a figure, as he petitions to the Court "to be allowed to value them himself, and to bind himself to take the animals at such valuation, if the owner is satisfied." This the Court grants him. About the same time, a complaint is made against William Harck, for slaughtering cattle without paying excise. He states, in answer, "that he killed four cattle for Mr. Thos. Willet, o'er at the Ferry, *(Brooklyn,)* and he is ignorant if he must pay excise for them." The Court decides he must pay "either himself, or by Mr. Willet.'"

The next year, (1657,) this "Excise," as a "*Slaughter Farmer*," was leased to Gerrit Hendricks, who received the same rate of fees on "all steers, cows, calves, sheep, lambs, hogs, bucks, or goats;" and also, "that for all salted meats or pork coming from without into this city, whether in barrels or casks, to be consumed, shall be paid to the *farmer* aforesaid one stuyver in each guilder of the value of the same."

"That all fresh or salted meat coming into this place and not to be consumed here, but for exportation, the person who brings the same in shall be obligated to procure from the *farmer* a certificate of delivery, containing an account of the just quantity or weight of the meat; and moreover, to procure from the said *farmer* a certificate of inspection, and shall also pay therefor three stuyvers." Hendricks, no doubt, was the first "inspector of salted meats" here.

In the month of July, the year following, (1658,) "the Heer President" states, "that the Burgomasters have resolved that the Board should fix certain hours of the day when the working people should go to their work and come from their work, as well also their recess for meals."

Near this "market-place at the strand," in the "market-field," a cattle-market, or the first "Bull's Head," was established on the 13th of December following, and the Secretary was ordered to draw up a "placard," holding a cattle-market for about forty days in the fall of the year, "for the sale of *fat* and lean cattle." This placard says: "The Schout, Burgomasters, and Schepens make known that they establish, for the accommodation of the public, a market for store and *fat cattle*, steers, cows, sheep, goats, hogs, bucks, and such like, and to that end, they mean to erect stalls and other conveniences for those who bring such animals to market. This market will be opened the 20th day of October, and close the last day of November, precisely, in each year; during such time it shall remain a free cattle-market, and no stranger shall, during that time, be liable to arrest or citation, but shall be permitted to attend to his business without molestation or hinderance." It also orders the Burghers not to meet any one for the purpose of buying cattle, except only at the place appointed; that "posts shall be erected by the side of the Church, *(along the west side of the 'market-field,' against the fort,)* where those who bring fat cattle to market for sale shall present them."

At another meeting held March 7, 1659, "it was thought good," *(as all the proceedings at that time were kept in Dutch,)* "that the proclamation concerning the cattle-market be translated into English, and sent to the magistrates of the following places: Stamford, Fairfield, Southampton, Southhold, Stratford, Milford, and East Hampton, and to be accompanied with the following letter:

"Worthy Lords—The object of this is to make known to you our resolution to erect and establish within this city a market for fat and lean cattle, and to request of you to make known the same to your people; and that every one has leave to come to said market with his cattle who may be inclined to extend his voyage hitherward." "We remain, &c."

The English and Dutch traders were sometimes sorely troubled in their trading transactions, on account of their different languages, and there were but few who could translate well enough to allow them to drive a satisfactory bargain. Three years previous to this "proclamation," Jan. Peeck had been occasionally employed, and found very useful, so the Court, on the 25th February, (1656,) appointed him as a translator, or "broker," between the Dutch and English merchants, who paid him a per centage on the amount of their trade or sale.

These Cattle Fairs first introduced the New England *(English)* breed of cattle into our city, which were soon after preferred by many to the Dutch breed. The New Englanders appeared to understand their breeding, rearing, and feeding much better than the Dutch settlers, and their fine animals were more eagerly sought after, which soon caused a regular trade to be opened at all seasons of the year.

In 1667 the trade from New England had become so flourishing as to demand the establishment of a ferry across the Harlaem River, which, as the Records show, on the 9th of July, was in the possession of Johannes Verveshe, of Harlaem, to whom the authorities " have solled the fferry as followeth : Itt is agreed hee shall have the fferry for ffive years, provided hee keepe a convenient house and lodging, for passengers att Harlam, and he shall have a small pecce of land on Bronckside, about an acre, and a place to build a house on, which he must cleare, and not spoyle the meadow, which shall bee layed out by the Town, which must bee a morgan of land, and att the end of ffive years itt is to be farmed out, and dureing the five yeares hee shall pay nothing for itt; and in case itt shall be lett to another, the house shall be vallued as itt stands, and he must be payed for itt, provided hee may have the preffernence of the hyring of itt att the tyme expired.

" Heere followeth what he shall aske ffor every man passenger, or horse or cattle.

" Ffor every passenger, two-pence silver, or sixpence wampum.

" Ffor every ox or cow that shall bee brought into his fferry-boat, eight-pence, or twenty-foure stivers; and cattle under a year ould, sixpence, or eighteen stivers wampum. All cattle that are swome (*swims*) over, pay but half price. Hee is to take for dyett every man for his meale, eight-pence, or twenty-foure stivers wampum. Every man for his lodging, two-pence a man, or six stivers in wampum. Every man for his horse shall pay foure-pence for his night's hay or grass, or twelve stivers wampum, provided the grass be in fence.

" All men going or coming with a packett from our Governor of New Yorke, or coming from the Governor of Connectcott, shall be fferried free.

" Also, in regard the said Verveshe must be att the charge of building a house on each side of the fferry, the Governor hath freed him from paying any excise for what wine or beare hee shall retayle in his house for one yeare after the date hereof."

In the year 1668, Verveshe (*or Verveelen, as he is now known,*) " and the remaining inhabitants of New Harlaem," complains of certain travelers using a place to cross near *Spitenduyvel,* and have broken down fences with their cattle and horses. The Court and Governor order, " that among others, also, one John Barcker has passed with a great number of cattle and horses over the Spytenduyvel." They order, " that said Barcker shall pay the ferry-money of all horses and cattle conveyed by him over the Spytenduyvel, whilst the ferry has been at Harlaem, which ferry-money the petitioner shall employ for the repairs of the fences on Spytenduyvel aforesaid; and the ferryman is in like manner well and expressly ordered and charged to finish the house and korael, *(pen,)* according to his agreement, at the earliest opportunity."

On the shore or "strand" near this market-place, the sale of fish, oysters, &c., it may reasonably be supposed, took place from the boats, skiffs, and canoes, or they had about this time been removed to the "canal," which was reported at a meeting held 7th March, 1660, that, "Good care and superintendence on the newly construct-ed graft, *(canal,)* that no filth be cast into it; also that the boats, canoes, and skiffs be placed in regular order therein." A complaint was made in the month of September, against Wessels Everzen, for "having sold fish on last Sunday forenoon." Everzen's' wife ap-pearing, says, "that it happened before the ringing of the bell." Another fisherman, by the name of Albert Trumpeter, was also com-plained of for the same thing; his wife also said, "it occurred be-fore the ringing of the bell."

The Court, after some consideration, dismissed them, by saying that it "took place before the preaching."

Forestalling also appeared to have been quite extensively prac-ticed, through a trade with the Indians, who visited the city with their various articles for that purpose. The Burgomasters and Schepens had repeatedly warned those who engaged in it, but it ap-pears it had not produced the desired effect; so, at a meeting on the 11th of October, 1661, the authorities say, "they had spoken about the forestalling of what the Indians bring to sell, such as venison, maize, and fish;" whereupon it was declared, "that no Indian shall bring any articles to any place, except such as shall be ordered and appointed therefor."

Then, on the 26th of June, 1663, "Otte Gerrits complains of Joris Dopzen and Roelef Jansen Van Mepplen, for having 'brought in two quarters of veal without a permit.' Gerrits demands the veal, and a double fine." Both of the defendants admit "it to be so," and, it is reasonable to suppose, were fined accordingly.

Another curious case is noticed on the 13th of November, in the same year, when a woman named *Aaght Jaes* sues Cornelius Jansen Van Horn. She states her case before the Court, and says, "Her *boy* shot a bear, which he tried to put into his boat, and that the defendant came by there, who said that he had chased the bear, and that the half belonged to him; forcing him to *toss up* for who should have the skin, which her *boy* lost: maintaining that the de-fendant has no right to the skin, but her *boy*, because he had shot it."

Defendant says, "He chased the bear, and that he was on one end of the Island, and the *boy* shot the bear on the other end: admits he told the *boy* to *toss up* for the skin, and that he had eaten half of the meat." Burgomaster and Schepens having heard the parties, decree that "the bear belongs to the *boy*, as he shot him; but since half of the meat has been consumed by the defendant, and the plaintiff is content with the skin, that defendant shall deliver up to her *(Mrs. Jaes)* the skin of the aforesaid bear."

These *trial scenes* certainly appear very curious and laughable to the present generation; while there is no doubt the *scenes* of the present day will be looked upon by future generations with the same feelings. These "Old Netherlanders," who laid the foundation of our great city, brought many of their "old fatherland" habits, customs, and laws; but the currency, or principal part of it, as noticed before, had been already established by the Indians, and to deal or trade with them, it was necessary for the Burghers to adopt it; although a great deal of trading was done, principally among the settlers themselves, by barter.

One of the earliest cases of trading and worthy of notice appears from the Translations of Van der Kemp, dated 10th of October, 1638: "Cornelius Petersen appeared before the Secretary Van Tienhoven, and declared with true Christian affirmation, in lieu of a solemn oath, that it was true that he had purchased a *hog* from *Ann Jackson*, in payment of which, she took from his store so much of purpled cloath as was sufficient for a petticoat." There appears no evidence given as to the size of the *hog* or the *garment;* we may therefore rationally conclude that, if the *garment* was as expansive or expensive as those worn *two hundred and twenty years after! why,* the hog ought to have been of an enormous size!

The trading price of *pork* and *beef* at this period (1664) is shown in the following extract from the "Register of the Resolutions,"* dated May 31, 1664: "Agreed with Captain Tomas Willet that he will procure for us, on account of the Honorable Company, if he can, a quantity of pork and beef equal to 600 lbs., the beef at 4, and the pork at 5 stivers the pound, payable in negroes, at such price as may be agreed on; in case of not agreeing, in beaver or goods—beaver price."

In the city the prices usually ranged higher, especially at retail, and they also were regulated by the *currency* paid for them: if the pay was in "*good hard money*," it was at a less price than "*pay as money*," or "*trust.*" "*Pay as money*" meant, pay in provisions of

* Hol. Doc., vol. ii., p. 474.

any kind, at one-third less than Government valuation; and *"trust"* was still worse, as one-fourth or one-fifth more was charged than the article could have been bought for with *"good hard money."*

"Government valuation," after the change of government from Dutch to English, appears to have been the standard price for all kinds of stock or produce, which was fixed by the "Governor and Court of Assize;" and all such, at this fixed rate, paid debts, taxes, rates, &c., especially out of the city, where there was but little business done except by trading or paying in this manner.

We find the Assessors were ordered by law, in 1665,* to value stock at the following prices:

"A horse or mare, 4 years old and upwards, - - £12 0 0
An ox or bull,   " " "   -   6 0 0
A cow,   " " "   - -   5 0 0
A steer or heifer, between three and four years old, 4 0 0
A goat, one year old, - - - - -   0 8 0
A sheep,   "   " - - - - - -   0 6 8
A swine,   "   " - - - - -   1 0 0 "

" The prices of many articles of food varied but little from 1665 to 1687, and were also received for taxes, and contracted for in trade, at the following prices:

"Pork, £3, 10s., 0d. per barrel, or 3d. per lb.
Beef,   1, 10s., 0d.   "   2d.   "
Wheat, 0, 4s., 0d. per bushel, to 5s.
Rye,   0, 2s., 6d.   "   3s., 6d.
Indian corn, 2s., 6d. do. Oats, 2s. do. Butter, 6d. per lb.
Tallow and hog's fat, 6d. do. Dry hides, 4d. per lb.
Green hides,   2d. do. Board, 5s. per week.
Victuals,   6d. per meal. Lodging, 2d. per night.
Labor, 2s., 6d. per day. Beer, 2d. per mug."

"The practice of paying in produce continued until about the year 1700, when trade had rendered money plenty, and introduced it into general circulation."

In the year 1670, some interesting particulars of the city, its in-habitants, and of the country around, have been given by Denton, who says, " New York is built most of brick and stone, and cover-ed with red and black tile; and the land being high, it gives at a distance a pleasing aspect to the spectator."

" The inhabitants consist most of English and Dutch, and have a considerable trade with the Indians, for beavers, otter, racoon skins, with other furs; and also for bear, deer, and elk skins; and

* Wood, L. I., p. 16 and 17.

are supplied with venison and fowl in the winter, and fish in the summer, by the Indians, which they buy at an easie rate."

He says of the country around, and more especially of Long Island, that "it is inhabited from one end to the other—is plentifully stored with all sorts of English cattel, horses, hogs, sheep, goats, &c.; no place in the North of America better."

"To give some satisfaction to people that shall be desirous to transport themselves thither—(*this country*.) The best commodities for any to carry with them is clothing. They sowe store of flax, which they make every one cloth of for their own wearing, as also woollen cloth, and linsey-woolsey, and, had they more tradesmen amongst them, they would in a little time live without the help of any other countrey for their clothing."

"Here you need not trouble the shambles for meat, nor bakers and brewers for beer and bread, nor run to a linnen-draper for a supply, every one making their own linnen, and a great part of their woollen cloth, for their ordinary wearing."

"Were it not to avoid prolixity, I would say a great deal more, and yet say too little, how free are those parts of the world from that pride and oppression, with their miserable effects, which many, nay almost all parts of the world, are troubled, with being ignorant of that pomp and knavery which aspiring humours are servants to, and striving after almost everywhere; where a waggon or cart gives as good content as a coach, and a piece of home-made cloth, better than the finest lawns or richest silks; and though their low-roofed houses may seem to shut their doors against pride and luxury, yet how do they stand wide open to let charity in and out, either to assist each other, or relieve a stranger."*

In the year 1671 numerous complaints were made, "that great quantities of unmarked horses and cattle, contrary to the former ordinance, still are found in the common wood-land of the Island of the Manhattan. It is therefore ordered by the mayor, that the persons heretofore appointed (of whom there were four) for branders, as well as at Haerlam, shall give notice that no horses or cattle, after the space of six weeks next ensuing, are permitted to feed in the common lands of this Island, except they are branded with the *cittye's* or *towne's* brand upon. Those found not branded 'shall be brought up to the S. Overseers to be branded, and the owner of the same shall pay as followeth: for bringing up a horse, six guilders, and for branding, two guilders; for bringing up a steare, oxe, or cow, three guilders, and for branding, one guilder. If no owner

---

* Denton's "New York," published by William Gowan.

appears for those which are not known, they shall be kept during the space of six weeks, and then publicly sould.'"*

This "Market-Place at the Strand" continued as such until the year 1675, when the "Custom-House Bridge Market-House" was erected, and its attractive "fitt" shelter drew the market people from what, during a period of almost twenty years, had been known as "at the Strand, at or around the house of Mr. Hans Kierstede."

"BROADWAY SHAMBLES."

EARLY in the year 1658, a meat-market was established, and a shed or shambles were built for that purpose, on the plain in front of the "Fort Amsterdam," the present site of the Bowling Green. This appears to have been the first place erected expressly for the sale of the meat of large animals, as, previous to this, we have before noticed that "fresh beef and pork had been sold, and no doubt *cut up*, at the Company's Store." Smaller animals, such as mutton, veal, goats' flesh, &c., had been sold from the baskets of the producers, at the "Market-Place at the Strand."

The market-place having been established, an elderly Burgher, or rather "Claas Van Elsant, *the elder*," on the 21st of February following, petitions, "that the magistrates may be pleased to allow him to be keeper of the shambles, as it is frequently demanded, both by the English and outside people, that some one may be appointed to fix a block, scales, and weights in the hall, so that they may not be at a loss when they come there with their meats."† His request was laid over until another meeting, when it was denied. The next year he again presents himself at the Court, and "requests to be Clerk of the Market;" soon after, Teunis Kray (who held the public office of a measurer of apples, onions, and turnips,) petitions "that his wife may superintend the market, to keep it clean." The Court answers, "that nothing will be done about the market for the present time."

This market "shambles on the plain" did not appear to answer the purpose of its erecters, as there is no doubt that it was a small, rough shed; open, leaky, and not suitable for stormy or cold weather. As the Records show, on the following 18th of April, "the Burgomasters resolved and concluded to erect the *meat*-market; further, to cover it with tiles; to have a block brought therein, and to

* City Records.   † Ibid.

leave the key with Andries (*de Haas*) the baker, who shall provisionally have charge thereof."

We have previously introduced three sworn butchers, whose chief business was in "butchering and cutting up," for the private citizens and the "Company's Store;" but now having established this *meat*-market, and many complaints being made of frauds which had been committed by cheating the Government out of their lawful excise, called for additional "sworn butchers." These facts brought the Burgomasters and Schepens together on the 24th of September, 1660, when they resolved to appoint more "sworn butchers," who are to be bound under certain instructions. At a meeting held on the 15th October following, therefore, a placard was prepared in the following terms: "In accordance with the laudable custom of our own Fatherland, and for the accommodation of the Burghers and inhabitants of this city, *(we)* have thought it expedient that sworn butchers be accepted and chosen, who shall be empowered to slaughter all cattle consumed within this city's jurisdiction—they have therefore accepted and selected thereunto

Egbert Meinderzen,	Asser Levy, *(a Jew,)*
Roelof Jansen,	Veeter Maacker,
Gerrit Jansen Roos,	Jan Van Harlaem,
Pieter Jansen,	Vande Langstraat,
Hendrick Volkersen,	Daniel Tourneur,
Paulus Van de Beeck,	Gerrit Fullewever,

who are made known to the community, that every one who has any cattle to be slaughtered may speak to them, and pay them the following fees:

One ox or cow,	- - - -	5 guilders, *(about $2;)*
" hog,	- - - - -	1 thaler;
" sheep, calf, or goat,	- - -	1 guilder, *(40 cents;)*

small animals in proportion." In their instructions, "they shall be bound to accommodate every one without delay, and bring with them their tools; and shall not kill any cattle without a permit from the Slaughter Farmer."

They all submitted to the instructions, and were sworn, except Asser Levy, who "requests to be excused from killing hogs, as his religion does not allow him to do it; which was granted him." He then took the oath which the Jews are accustomed to take.

The municipal officers occasionally engaged in a little of the slaughtering business, and no doubt received some extra privileges from the "Slaughter Farmer," when preparing meats for the Company's Store; or it appears so from the proceedings which took place on the 19th October following. "The Heer Schepen, Cornelis Steenwyck, proposes, as the season for slaughtering is at hand, and he is about to kill some cattle, therefore requests that he may pay the Farmer for what he consumes, as well as for the meat which he may deliver to the Burghers, and for what he should send or deliver to the *(Company's) Store*, that he might convey with a permit, merely paying an excise."

Burgomasters and Schepens having considered the request, decide that the Heer Cornelis Steenwyck shall have to pay the farmer for what he consumes and sells to the Burghers of this city; and he shall procure merely a permit for what he sends or delivers to the " Company."

These "sworn butchers" were very partial to litigation in settling their difficulties, which appears usually to have been done through referees, and without the assistance of the legal profession. Some of these trials are quite original in their way, and, in their details, show how much of the business was conducted, as well as the history of the citizens of that early day. The Jew, Asser Levy, is found often engaged, both before and after he was made a "sworn butcher," in suits of various kinds. The first he brings against Egbert Meinderzen, in relation to the division of profits.

This case was before the Court January 18, 1661, when Levy states, "he bought and slaughtered some cattle with defendant, and receiving the balance from defendant after settlement of account, he said he should count it *(money)* after him, and acquainting him thereof, that defendant abused him, as one who supported thieves and such like; for which he demands reparation. Defendant denies it. Plaintiff says he can prove it, which the W. Court ordered him to do by the next court-day."

On the following 3d of May, Levy is engaged in another against Frans. Janzen Van Hooghten, a carpenter, who "hath agreed to build a house for Wessels, (*Evertzen,*) the fisherman, which must be finished by May, and to this time (*3d May*) the agreement is without effect; and whereas he has hired the same house from the above-named Wessels, and cannot occupy it, he claims the damage he shall suffer thereby, as he must remain so long in another man's house.

" Defendant says he undertook the house, but for no time, and must moreover wait for the materials to make the roof tight; he has spoken to Wessels Evertzen about them, who gave him for answer, he could not bring them so soon.

" Plaintiff says he laid the roof on long ago, and that defendant went to other work, leaving that stand." The Court orders the "defendant to go to the work, and remain there until it be finished, without working on another."

Again, a few years after, (November 21, 1665,) this Levy brought a suit against Johanus La Montayne, about some goats, which were at that time extensively used for the dairy and slaughter. In La Montayne's answer, he says, the "eight goats were not refused to be paid, on condition that Levy restored to him the butter, etc., the produce of the seven goats which he sold Mr. Gysbert, before the expiration of the contract on which he had the goats."

The evidence which follows shows that an attempt had been made to have it settled by arbitration. This says: "On date, 27th October, appeared before me, Nicolaes Bayard, the above-mentioned plaintiff, Asser Levy, who declared that he agreed with the defendant, Johan Montayne, that defendant should pay him for his claim 8 goats, 2 wethers, 150 ps. fire-wood, and 2 cocks, provided the plaintiff paid the costs of this suit."

Another of these "sworn butchers," named Daniel Tourneur, must have been also fond of the "law," but otherwise he appears unlike Levy, as he slaughtered and dealt in hogs. He brings a suit against Frans. Jansen Van Hooghten, on the 10th February, 1660, from whom he demands one beaver, balance of a hog, and two guilders for slaughtering. Defendant says that, on buying the hog, he was told by the plaintiff that he had no measled hogs among his; and on slaughtering it, found it measled. Defendant is asked if he killed the hog shortly after buying it? Answers, No; but three or four weeks after. The W. Court order defendant to pay the plaintiff the beaver, and the two guilders for killing. This case having been decided, Tourneur and Jans Schryver, on the same day, were called upon as witnesses in another hog case. They were "asked about the sale of the hog which took place between Captain Jan Jacobzen and the Rector Alexander Carolus Curtius. Daniel Tourneur declares that, after many words of praising and bidding, the hog was sold to Dom Rector for five beavers, saying that Captain Jacob would not sell that hog less than five beavers, which was told to the Rector; to which the Rector answered, saying, in God's name, he had but two beavers, and he must wait for the other three; to which Captain Jacob would hardly agree. Finally, through the mediation of Joannes Van der Mezlen, he let himself be persuaded; offering to confirm the same on oath.

Jan Schryver declares that Dom⁰ Rector bought the hog for *two blankets* and *two beavers;* offering also to confirm the same on oath.

The W. Court give parties eight days' respite to recollect themselves, and if they have any proof, to bring it also in."

This case was decided on the 24th of August following, by the Court, "who condemned the defendant to pay the plaintiff five beavers, which he proved."

Next we notice Daniel Tourneur in the position of a defendant in a suit brought before the Court, on the 13th of September, 1664, by Albert Trumpeter, who complains "that he missed a hog, being a sow, which he had placed on Baren Island with other hogs, which the defendant removed from there. Defendant admits having taken a hog from the Island; saying that some of the N. Haerlem have hogs also running there, and that *one* requested the *other*, when going to the Island, to look after his hogs; and as he was there to cut grass, returning from work, he saw a hog lying on the strand very sick, which he laid loose in his canoe and brought to the village, making the same known, in order to learn whose hog it was; whereof he produces declaration; then, as no one claimed the hog, he will let it lay over the night, to see if some one would not come in the mean while to whom the hog belonged, but he found it dead on the next day. The W. Court having heard parties, decree that the defendant shall replace such hog on Baren Island for the plaintiff from which he removed plaintiff's hog, or that he make good the removed hog to the plaintiff."

Two of these sworn butchers were afterwards engaged against each other on the 18th January, 1661, when Roelef Janzen Van Mepplin complains of Egbert Meinderzen, (who appears to have been rather a troublesome Burgher.) Van Mepplin "says he hath slaughtered some cattle in company with the defendant, and agreed with him for wages, at 26 stivers per head. Demanding a balance of sixty-one guilders, nine stivers, according to account exhibited in Court.

Defendant acknowledged he hath entered into such an agreement with the plaintiff, and that no money has yet been received; that plaintiff is unwilling to pay the expense of the men. He was to have slaughtered three with them, and did slaughter five with them.

Plaintiff is asked if he helped to slaughter the cattle which he brings into account? Answer—they slaughtered them together.

Defendant says he can prove by Pieter Jansen and Willem Jansen Van Borckeloo that plaintiff said he would help to bear the expense. Which being stated to plaintiff, he says, if defendant can prove that, he will bear the expense alone." The Court order "defendant to pay the plaintiff, and decree that the defendant shall bear three-quarters and the plaintiff one-quarter of the expense."

Another novel *suit* was brought against one of the early sworn butchers, at a Court held on the 3d of August, 1673, where "Thomas Walton brings action against Roelef Jansen, butcher, for sheep sold him." He claims "the quantity of three ankers of rum." The Court condemns "Jansen to pay the said debt." Then again, in 1674, Jansen was sued by David de Four, who demands from Jansen "the sum of ff. 200, for an ox sold about two years ago to the defendant, and offers to deliver to defendant a certain cow which he bartered with defendant whenever he is paid." Jansen says, "that De Four did not deliver him the cow according to agreement, notwithstanding he sent his children for her divers times." The Court ordered, "that Jansen shall pay De Four the demanded sum within eight days' time, provided the cow be first delivered to the plaintiff the time the same is paid, and that said cow shall meanwhile run at defendant's risk."

We turn back, and find, three days after these butchers were sworn in, (October 15, 1660,) Egbert Meinderzen, who had a complaint lodged against him "by persons bringing meat to market, that he obliges them to purchase a *Burgher-right* first before they can sell it." The Court warns him not to do so any more, or he will be attended to.

This Burgher-right, or freedom of the city, appears to have been of two kinds, which vested certain rights and privileges in the holder when obtained, and were known as the "Great Burgher-right" and "Small Burgher-right."

The "Great Burgher-right" was established in this city on the 30th of January, 1657, as will appear from the "Records," in the following language: "The Court allow and concede to the Burgomasters and Schepens the establishment of a Great Burgher-right, for which those who may request to be therein, shall pay fifty guilders, ($20;) and all such, and such only, shall hereafter be qualified to fill all city offices and dignities within this city—be exempt for one year and six weeks from watches and expeditions—be free in their proper persons from arrest by any subaltern Court or judicial benches of this province." The "Small Burgher-right" it was necessary to obtain before they could do any business, and some bought it only for short periods; however, the following proceedings will more fully explain this privilege.

On the 25th of March following, "The Heer President states that there are several of the inhabitants of this city who have purchased their 'Burgher-right' for a year and a day, and do not pay; and whenever the city messenger goes for payment, they answer, they have no money, proceeding to scoff at and censure the Burgomasters;

and though it be a matter which concerns the Burgomasters alone, nevertheless, that it be known to the Heer Schepens, it is therefore communicated to the Court to remember it."

Two days after, " the Schouts and Burgomasters, pursuant to the privilege granted on date 30th January, 1657, that some of the newly-arriving passengers may, through ignorance, presume to sell here in this city by the ell, measure, or weight, or pursue some other business, have thought proper, in order to save every one damage, again to inform them by this publication, that no one can sell in the city by the ell, measure, or weight, or do any other business, unless he have received the Burgher-right of this city, and have his ell, measure, or weight stamped; and whoever is inclined so do to shall have to apply to receive their Burgher-right to the Hon. Presiding Burgomaster, Allard Anthony; and for the stamping their ell, measure, and weights, shall apply at the City Hall, on the afternoon of Saturday, from two to four o'clock; every one is warned to take heed of damage." The same day "Marcus Vogelsangh appears in Court, requesting to be admitted a Burgher; claiming, as he lived here before three years, that it cannot be refused him; and also that he is to be preferred to the new-comers, who were not here in the troubles with the English. But as there was no Burgher-right at that time, Burgomasters decree that he, the petitioner, must purchase it like others, or he cannot be considered a Burgher."

On the 9th of April following, notice was given "that those who claim the Great or Small Burgher-right, by virtue of gift or favor, shall communicate their names within eight days to the Burgomaster of this city, who, for this purpose, beginning to-morrow, the 10th inst., shall sit during the eight days at the City Hall, from two o'clock till five o'clock in the afternoon, to inscribe the names, with warning, that those who do not communicate theirs within the assessed time, shall be deprived of the claims of Burgher-right."

Two days after, "Asser Levy, the Jew butcher, appeared in Court; requests to be admitted a Burgher; claims such ought not to be refused him, as he keeps watch and serves like other Burghers, showing Burgher's certificate from the City of Amsterdam, that the Jew is Burgher there; which being debated on, 'tis decreed as before, that it cannot be allowed, and he shall apply to the Director-General and Council."

"Lourens Cornelius Van der Wel" also appears in Court the same day, "representing that he hath already performed divers extraordinary services in time of need, &c., both as a gunner of the city, as also in the South (Delaware) River, and that, if necessary, he is ready to serve; requesting, therefore, the benefit of a Great

Burgher-right. Burgomasters, considering the manifold services of the petitioner, and his good disposition to continue, if necessary, grant his petition, and he is therefore inscribed, and has taken the Burgher oath."

The next year, on the 28th February, (1658,) "Tomas Swartwout appears in Court, requesting the Small Burgher-right, and took the oath in Court, signing an obligation for 20 gl. beavers, payable for it." On the 22d of the following month, "It was ordered, that from now, henceforward, that all who will purchase the Great and Small Burgher-right, shall promptly pay into the Treasury; and those who have already bought it, to pay within the space of twenty-four hours, on pain of execution."

Two years after, on the arrival of the ship *Gilded Beaver*, the Court permanently fixed the price of these *Rights*, which took place on the 18th of June, 1660, when they say, "To those who come in the ship *Gilded Beaver*, and those who may yet come," must pay "for the Small Burgher-right twenty guilders, ($8,) and for the 'Great Burgher-right' fifty guilders, ($20;) or in beavers, the beaver to be the value of six guilders."

Referring again to the sworn butchers, we find a man by the name of Symon Joosten is noticed in Court, October 16th of this year, (1660,) "and was told if he be desirous to be a sworn butcher, he must first purchase his Burgher-right. He declares he is not desirous to be a sworn butcher, but requesting that he may sell his meat that he may bring for sale on payment of the excise, which is allowed him."

Meinderzen (before noticed) was again complained of on the next Court-day, held 29th October, 1660, but this time impleaded with one William Jansen Van Borckeloo, (*an unsworn butcher*,) and from the evidence on trial, both are *found guilty*. Meinderzen is fined twenty-five guilders, with costs, and forbidden to slaughter for the space of six weeks. Van Borckeloo was also fined, although pleading ignorance of the *placard*, in the sum of twenty-five guilders and costs. The next day Meinderzen petitions to the Court, "after paying his fine, and requests their Hon" will be pleased to permit and allow him to slaughter along with the other 'sworn butchers.' The Burgomasters, through special considerations, release the petitioner from his condemned six weeks, with this reservation—that he demeans himself for the future as an honorable Burgher." Van Borckeloo also petitions that "he has settled his fine, and requests, in all humility, that your Hon" may be pleased to accept him as a sworn butcher." His request was also granted.

Cases of theft were most severely punished, and sometimes *torture* with the *rack* and *chains* were applied to force confession from the culprit. The following extracts from the trials of two individuals show these facts: The first is noticed in the month of May, 1661, in the trial of one Marten Van Weert, when under examination by the magistrates. "The prisoner, under threats of being placed on the *rack*, was asked where he got the silver-handled knife. Answers, persisting in his (*former*) confession, that he was half drunk when he took the spoons, and laid them the next morning under the little shelf." After the conclusion of the trial, the magistrates proceed to show his many unlawful acts, and then the sentence follows: "For his grave and shameful act of theft, committed at various times and divers places, according to his own voluntary confession and acknowledgment, without *torture* or force—first having stolen, seven or more years ago, a quantity of zeawan from the house of Pieter Kock, deceased; having stolen from the Heer Cornelius Steenwyck's house, at divers times, a quantity of otters and beavers, (*skins*,) together with some pieces of manufactured or Harlaem stuffs, and a piece of fine-napped cloth; also a piece of fine linen; having lately stolen from Christyne Capoens' house, at the feast or celebration of the marriage of Lawurens Van der Spygel and Sarah Webbers, to which wedding he was invited, half-a-dozen spoons," the magistrates "condemn the above-named Marten Van Waart, as they hereby do, that he shall be severely scourged with rods in a closed chamber, banished ten years out of this jurisdiction, and further in the costs and mises of justice."

On the 15th of November following, another case is found in "Mesaack Martenzen, brought forward, was, at the request of the Heer Officer, for further interrogation, examined by *torture* as to how many cabbages, fowls, turkies, and how much butter he hath stolen, who his abettors and co-operators have been. Answering, he persists by his reply, as per interrogatories, that he did not steal any butter, fowl, turkies, nor had any abettors; being again set loose, the Heer Officer produces his demand against the delinquent, concluding, that for his committed theft, voluntarily confessed, without *torture or chains*, he shall be brought to the usual place of criminal justice, well fastened to a stake, and severely whipt, and banished from the jurisdiction of this City of Amsterdam, for the term of *ten years*, all with costs."

At the Court this day, January 31, 1662, "Pieter, the negro, entering, requests payment for executing the sentence on one Mesaack Martenzen and Marten Van Weert; is promised that arrangements shall be made that he have that for Mesaack, but that of Marten Van Waart is promised him by the Heer Officer."

Ten years after, John Clarke, in a letter dated "ffrom yᵉ Secretarye's Office in Ffort James, the 28th day of January in the evening, 1672–3," furnishes us with some other interesting facts of the same character. He says: "Lastly, for our own city news, lett this satisfy: that 'tother day wee had like to have lost our hangman, Ben Johnson; for hee being taken in diverse thefts and robberyes, convicted & found guilty, scapᵈ his neck through want of another hangman to truss him up, soe that all the punishment hee receivᵈ for his 3 yeares roguery in thieving & stealing, (which was never found out till now,) was only thirty-nine stripes at the whipping-post, loss of an ear, & banishmᵗ. Capt. Manning had likewise 2 servants that hee employed at his island, (*now Blackwell's,*) taken wᵗʰ him in their villany, but they being not found soe guilty as hee, came off with whipping and banishmenᵗ. All this happened about a ffortnight since, but 'tis 2 months since they were apprehended. Another disaster about 12 dayes since befell a young man in this towne, by name one Mr. Wright, a one-eyed man, & a muff-maker by trade, who drinking hard upon rum one evening, wᵗʰ some ffriends, begann a health of a whole halfe pint at a draught, wᶜʰ hee had noe sooner done but downe hee fell and never rose more, wᶜʰ prodigy may teach us all to have a care how wee drink, in imitation of that good old lesson, *Fœlix quem faciunt,* &c. This young man's untimely (*end*) doth somewhat parallel that person in yoʳ letter, who you write was killed with a sley, the wᶜʰ in like manner could but strike a great amazemᵗ into all that heard it, by wᶜʰ wee may see that though there is but one way of coming into the world, yet there is a thousand wayes of goeing out of it."*

We again look back to the year 1664, on the 3d day of September, when New Amsterdam became New York, (after *James,* Duke of York,) by its seizure, and Governor Stuyvesant was forced to surrender it to Col. Richard Nicolls, who appeared in the harbor with a powerful English fleet, causing an open war between England and Holland; this was settled soon afterwards, and New York was ceded to the English by a treaty. The city, at this period, contained about 1,500 inhabitants.

Colonel Nicoll immediately became the Governor, but the Dutch laws, with the name of Schout, Burgomaster, and Schepens, were not repealed until the following June 12th, (1665,) when Mayor, Aldermen, and Sheriff were introduced; and soon afterwards they were importuned with petitions and complaints of various characters: one of which was, that the city was defrauded by the inattention of Timothy Gabrie, collector of the excise on slaughtered

---

* Historical Magazine, vol. iv., p. 51.

cattle, who is informed by the Court that "the city is seriously defrauded in the entering of cattle for slaughter; that before he grants a license, he must inspect the cattle, to see if they be entered according to the just value."*

The butchers, also, on the 31st of October following, petition for increased "fees and wages;" which, after some deliberation, the authorities only raised "one guilder on each beast, whether ox or cow; and from all other small cattle, not more than was granted and allowed heretofore."

Additional "sworn butchers" were considered necessary, and the following were appointed: Jan Hendrickson Van Gunst, Richard Nicholls, and Richard Dodomit, who were *sworn* with the following oath: "We doe swere, in the presence of the Almighty God, that we, as *sworne Butchers* of this Citty, shal kill noe Cattle, Hoggs, etz, without a Ticket of consent from the Collectors of the Mayor and Aldermen, except it be for the Right Hon[ble] Governor, Richard Nicolls. So help us God Almighty."

At some seasons of the year these butchers were busily employed in slaughtering, especially in the fall season and part of the winter, but the spring and summer months found them seeking other employment, which sometimes appeared to interfere with the rights of others, or was so thought in these *early days;* and no doubt called forth from the authorities, on the 25th of August, 1676, the following order: "That noe Butchers bee permitted to be Curriers, Shoemakers, or Tanners; nor shall any Tanner be either Curriers, Shoemakers, or Butchers; itt being consonant to the Laws of England, & practised in the neighbour Collony's of y[e] Massachusetts and Conecticott."

Prior to the 1st of November, 1676, cattle were slaughtered in the citty (then below Wall Street) at the private establishments of the butchers; and no doubt they were not as careful or as cleanly as they should have been, or at least the following proceedings, which appear on the previous 7th of June, lead us to think so: "Whereas, there is found sev'all inconveniencys by the Butchers keeping theire Slaughter-Howses in this City, as well as the annoyance thereof to y[e] inhabitants of the same. Itt is ordered, y[t] *(that)* for y[e] future there shall not bee any Slaughter-House w[th]in this City, nor any Oxen, Cows, Hogs, Sheepe, or Lambs killed w[n]in y[e] same after the first day of November next ensuing, upon paine not only to forfeit all and every such meate soe killed contrary to this order, but forfeit to y[e] use of the Citty the sum of £10 sterlinge."

* City Records.

This *order* caused them to be so scattered about the suburbs, that it gave the "Farmer of the Excise" a great deal of trouble to examine the different animals which were to be slaughtered on the same day; and no doubt this called for the establishment of a large public slaughter-house, to be conducted by the Government, on the 16th of February the next year, in the following language: "It is ordered that, for the necessary and publique use, a Generall or Publique Slaughter-Howse shall be built for the use of the Cytie over the Water, without the Gate at the *Smith's Fly*, neare the *Half Moone*"—Battery.

"Without the Gate" meant just outside of the Gate of the *Wall* of the City, and on the east end of *Wall Street*, on the river-shore, stood the "*Half Moone*" Battery; between this and the present *Pine* on Pearl Street this "Publique Slaughter-Howse" was built, one year afterwards. The proceedings show on the 8th of January, 1678, that "Ashur Levy, (*Jew Butcher*,) then makeing his addresse to their Court, that hee might be admitted to build the Slaughter-House," (*mentioned in the above*,) "and to take in Garrett Jansen Rose to be partner therein, and that all persons should have libberty to kill & hang therein meat, there paying for the same as formerly in other places." The Court granted his proposal, and on the 10th of February following, he "affirmed that hee had built" it; when the Court confirmed the same upon him and his partner.

This building was used for public slaughtering until the 12th of March, 1696, when a committee was ordered, (after the representations made by the inhabitants of Pearl Street, setting forth the great apprehensions they have of being injured by the "*Gunpowder* lodged in the warehouse near Whitehall,") "doe view whether the Slaughter-Howse *formerly imployed* for that use be sufficient for yᵉ lodging the same—which if itt be, that they order the powder be removed thither accordingly," and the Slaughter-House became a powder-house.

Asser Levy, the Jew butcher, while keeping this "Publique Slaughter-Howse," also kept an old-established tavern near by or just within the "Water Gate," which many previous years was kept by the widow of Daniel Litschoe, from whom he purchased it. Levy died in the year 1682, when his family removed to Long Island.

Gerrit Jansen Roos was a carpenter by trade, but he became a sworn butcher, and in 1665 lived and owned property on the present Broadway, above Wall Street; then, thirteen years after, he is found engaged with Levy in the public Slaughter-House.

Glancing back to the change of government from the Dutch to English rule, with the second Governor, Colonel Francis Lovelace, who succeeded Nicholls in 1668, did not altogether change the language of the "Records," as they were yet kept in both English and Dutch. This change, however, did not last long; for on the 29th day of July, 1673, a Dutch fleet sailed into our harbor, and, with some manœuvring, again took possession of the country, changed the name of New York to that of "New Orange," (in compliment to the Prince of Orange,) and with it the form of government to its former character of Schout, Burgomaster and Schepens, and Captain Anthony Colve as the Governor. This continued only for a short period, as, by a treaty of peace made on the 9th of February, 1674, between England and Holland, the Dutch restored this country to the rule of the English, when Sir Edmund Andross became Governor, William Dervall Mayor, and our city was once more called New York.

Many propositions were soon after offered, followed with *orders* and *proclamations* to improve the local affairs of the government, some to undo and others to add to those already in existence. "Itt being taken into consideracon wether itt bee not proper to have English weights and measures too bee used according too the Law. It is ordered, thatt in three months after the publicacon thereof, the same shall bee put in practize in the City, Long Island, and parts adjacent.

"And in six months in all other parts throughout the government. And thatt whosoever shall after that time presume too use any other weights and measures, shall forefeite all they shall soe sell, and bee lyable too such further punishment ffor contempt as the case shall require. The time off Proclamacons prohibiting the exportacons off corne, ande also that off fflouer, &c., being expired, the same being taken intoo consideracon, and the present scarcity. Itt is ordered that the prohibicon ffor exporting off corne or ffloure doo still continue inn force ffor the terme off six months after the dayte hereoff."* ("*A Dutch pound contains eighteen ounces.*")†

Several other changes were made at the General Court of Assize, held in the city, beginning on the 6th and ending on the 13th of October, 1675, among which, "A Fair or Market is ordered to be held three dayes at Breucklin," and three more in this city, which is fully noticed in the following proclamation made by Governor Andross on the 29th of January, 1676: "And the ord^ce of the Court of Assize for a Ffayre to bee also observed, to witt: at Breucklin for cattell, &c., graine, &c., produce of the country, the first Monday, Tuesday, and Wednesday in November, and in the Citty at the *market-house* and plaine afore the forte, the Thursday, Fryday, and Saturday followinge, and

---

* Wooley's Journal, by Gowan, p. 35.   † City Records.

that every person or persons cominge to the same are and bee free from any arrest or arrests, for debt or debts in their persons or goods, cominge to or returninge from the said Markett of Fayre day or dayes, of wch all persons are to take notice, and conform themselves thereunto accordingly.

"This ord^r to be and remain in force for the space of three yeares from the twenty-fourth of March next."*

Governor Andross, in 1678, in some answers about New York, shows us some facts in relation to the buildings, productions, trade, wealth, slaves, &c. He says, "Our buildings, most wood, some lately *(built of)* stone and brick, good country houses & strong of their severall kindes. Our produce is land provisions of all sorts, as of wheate exported yearly about 60,000 bushells, pease, beefe, pork, & some refuse fish, tobacco, beavers, peltry or furrs from the Indians, deale & oake timber, plankes, pipe-staves, lumber, horses, & pitch & tarr lately began to be made. Comodityes imported are all sorts of English manufacture for Christians, & blankets, duffells, &c., for Indians about 50,000 lbs. (£) yearly.

"Our merch^{ts} are not many, but with inhabitants & planters about 2,000 able to beare arms; old inhabitants of the place or of England, except in & neere New Yorke, of Dutch extraction, & some few of all nations; but few serv^{ts}, much wanted, and but very few slaves. Some few slaves are sometimes brought from Barbadoes, most for provisions, and sould att ab^t 30 lb. or 35 lb. country pay.

"A merch^t worthe 1,000 lb. or 500 lb. is accompted a good substantiall merchant; and a planter worthe halfe that in moveables, accompted (rich?) with all the *Estates*, may be valued att about £150,000." "Noe beggars, but all poore cared for."

About this period Mr. Wooley, in his "Journal," also gives some interesting facts, in the following words: he says, "The price of Indian commodities as sold by the Christians is as followeth:

	£. s. d.		£. s. d.
Beavers, -	00 10 3 a pound.	Grey Foxes, -	00 03 0 a pound.
The Lapps,	00 07 6 "	Otters, - -	00 08 0 "
Minks, - -	00 05 0 "	Rackoons, -	00 01 5 "

"Beaver is fifteen pence a skin custom at New York, four-pence at London; three-pence a skin freight, which is after the rate of fifteen pounds a tun.

"The value of other skins: a deer skin, 00 00 6 a p.; a good bear skin will give 00 07 0; a black beaver skin is worth a beaver and a half of another colour; a black otter's skin, if very good, is worth twenty shillings; a fisher's skin, three shillings; a cat's skin,

* City Records.

half a crown; a wolf's skin, three shillings; a musquash, or a musk-rat's skin, six shillings and ten-pence.

"An oxe-hide, three-pence a pound wet, and sixpence dry. Mo-lossus, three-pence a pound, and fifty shillings a barrel in winter, that being the dearest season. Sugar in Barbadoes, twelve shillings the hundred, which contains a hundred and twelve pounds, which at New York yields thirty shillings the bare hundred. In Barbadoes, (new negroes, *i. e.*, such as cannot speak English,) are bought for twelve or fourteen pound a head; but if they can speak English, sixteen or seventeen pound; and at New York, if they are grown there, they give thirty-five and thirty or forty pound a head, where, by-the-by, let me observe, that the Indians look upon these negroes or blacks as an anomalous issue, meer Edomites, hewers of wood and drawers of water.

"The price of provisions: Long Island wheat, three shillings a (*schepel*) skipple, (being three parts of a bushel;) sopus wheat, half a crown a skipple; Indian corn flower, fifteen shillings a hundred; bread, 18 a hundred; pork, £3 the barrel, which contains two hundred and forty pounds, *i. e.*, 3d. the pound; beef, 30s. the barrel; butter, 6d. a pound; amongst provisions I may reckon tobacco, of which they are obstinate and incessant smokers, both Indians and Dutch, especially the latter, whose diet, especially of the boorish sort, being sallets and bacon, and very often picked buttermilk, require the use of that herb to keep their phlegm from coagulating and curdling. I once saw a pretty instance relating to the power of tobacco, in two Dutchmen riding a race with short campaigne pipes in their mouths, one of which being hurl'd from his steed, as soon as he gathered himself up again, whip'd to his pipe, and fell a sucking and drawing, regarding neither his horse nor fall, as if the prize consisting in getting that heat which came from his beloved smoke."

In 1680, another extraordinary market-day is ordered to be kept every week, on Wednesday. This, however, is to be held at the market-place, near the bridge and weigh-house.

These particular days were no doubt designated in the laws and ordinances for the purpose of enabling the country people to meet on certain days, to establish them as market-days, "Wednesdays and Saturdays," at the market-place "near the bridge and weigh-house," *(see Custom-House Bridge Market;)* and the only place for the sale of fresh meat was at the Broadway Shambles, where the regular market-days were "upon Tuesday, Thursday, and Saturday," which fact is shown from the laws "ordained and enacted on the 15th day of March, 1683." They read, "that Tuesday, Thursday, and Saturday in each week be and are hereby appointed *market-days* in this city, for the exposing to sale at the market-house all butchers' meat and flesh whatsoever; that is to say, on Tuesday and Thursday, from 8 to 12 of the clock in the forenoon; and on Saturday, the same time of the forenoon, and from two to four of the clock in the afternoon, for the market shall be opened and shut by the ringing of the bell. No butchers'-meat victuals is to be exposed for sale in the said market, under the penalty of forfeiture."*

Before the close of the year, it appears that "butchers' meat is to be sold every day, except Sunday," from the proceeding held on the 6th of December same year, which first notices the fact that "the Lycenses always belong to yᵉ Governoᵉ, the benefitt of yᵉ Markett and Markett-Houses is granted, provided there be nothing sold but upon Wednesday and Saturday, beginning betwixt nine & ten of yᵉ clock in yᵉ fforenoon, and all brought in yᵉ markett-place, nothing being sold in any vessell, boate, or canoe w'soever; only *Butchers' meat is to be sold every day* in yᵉ weeke, Sunday excepted, but to be sold in yᵉ markett, & no where else. That it is convenient a Clerke of yᵉ Markett be appointed, and that by yᵉ Governor, who shall see after yᵉ weights & measures, & due regulations of markett."

The "Dongan Charter," which was proclaimed three years after, also says, that "Tuesday, Thursday, and Saturday" were the regular market-days; this is dated April 22d, 1686, and also says: "Whereas, the citizens and inhabitants of the said city have erected, built, and appropriated, at their own proper costs and charges, several public buildings, accommodations, and convenience for the said city; that is to say, the City Hall or Stadt House, with the ground thereunto belonging, *two market-houses, &c.," (one the "Broadway Shambles," and the other the "Custom-House Bridge Market.")* It further says: "The granting to the Mayor, Aldermen, and Commonalty, that they and their successors shall, and may forever hereafter, hold and keep within the said city, in every week of the year, *three market-days;* the one upon Tuesday, the other upon Thursday, and the other upon Saturday, weekly, forever."

In 1691, the "Broadway Shambles" still continued to be the only meat-market, and were so represented on the first day of April of that year, in the proceedings, which say: "That there be but one butchers' shambles within this citty; that it be still daily kept at the (*Green*, or) Groon, before the ffort, until further; and all butchers' meat to be brought to the said shambles for sayle, and no other place."

* City Records.

This was followed on the 18th of the same month with market regulations, as follows: "*Resolved*, That the market for *flesh* be kept three dayes in the week—Tuesday, Thursday, and Saturday—and that the market bee opened by seven of the clock in the morning, and notice to bee given for the opening of the same by the Ringing of the Bell; and in case by Tydes, weather, or any other accident, that Flesh, Fish, Poultry, Eggs, Butter, Cheese, hearbes, ffruit, and Rootes, or other provisions vendible, should come to the Citty on other days wh^{ch} are not markete days—yett they may nevertheless be sould in the said markett-place under the same Circumstances and Regulations as on the Dayes on wh^{ch} the marketts are appointed."

"No Hucksters or persons to sell againe shall b(u)y any flesh, fish, fowles, Egges, butter, Cheese, or any other sort of provision sayable, till it hath bin two houres in the markett, upon forfeiture of six shillings, and also what shall bee so brought or sold."

"Any person that buyes or cheapons any Flesh, Fish, &c., and coming to the markett, to forefeit six shilling."

"That all the above said provisions—as Flesh, Fish, &c., that shall be exposed to sayle in any other place then afore appointed, to be forefeited to the Clarke of the Marketts."

"Ordered, that the Clerke of the Marketts receive for all Cattle killed for the markett, for each head one shilling; for every hogg or shoate brought or cut out for sayle in the Markett-House, threepence; and for every sheep, calfe, and lamb, two-pence. And for sealeing of weights and measures one penny a p., both great and small."

One individual, named Henry Coleman, soon after became insubordinate, when a "complaint was made (on the following 9th of May) by Captain Lockard against *Coleman*, Butcher, who denys any obedience to the Rules and Orders of this Citty." This appears to have been of so much importance, that a committee was appointed to "wait upon His Excellency to acquaint him of the said complaint."

An addition was made to these laws on the 16th of October following, when it was "Ordered, that no Butcher, on any of the markett dayes appointed within this Citty, shall sell any meate under the quantity of a whole quarter of Beefe att a time in any place but the Markett-House appointed, shall forfeit six shillings; one-half to the Clarke of the Markett, the other half for the use of the Citty." Ten days after, it was further "Ordered, that all fforfeitures by any Law or order relating to the Markett-House, half the ffines to goe to the Clarke of the Markett, the other halfe to the Citty."

An additional *flesh* or meat market being required, on the 15th of the same month and year it was also "Ordered, that there be *two* markets for *flesh-meat* kept; the one in the Broadway over against the ffort, ('*Broadway Shambles*,') the other under the Trees by the Slipp; and that the Butchers shall be obliged to keep flesh in both places; and the Country people shall bring *flesh* to either of the two places, suiting their conveniency"—"to pay nothing for anything they bring in killed"—"and that no butchers' meat be killed within the City Gates."

The establishment of this new *meat* market-place, "under the Trees by the Slipp," had no doubt the effect of reducing the trade at the "Broadway Shambles;" and in addition, its locality appeared much against it. The city on the East River side, with its ferry, dock, slips, Weigh and Custom Houses, and City Hall, all tended to increase the growth and prosperity on that side, and also in that of the sale of property. Several lots, in 1692, were sold at "publick vandeu" along the shore in the "Smith's Vlie," for about sixty-five dollars per lot; each buyer was bound to "dock out," within a specified time.

These lots had been surveyed a few years before by Peter King and Adolph Pietersen, surveyors for the City of New York, when a warrant had been given to them by the Mayor, which is noticed the 4th day of May, 1688, as follows: "You are required and commanded to survey yᵘ vacant Lande within this Citty near and in yᵉ Dock, beginning from yᵘ Weigh-House to yᵉ Citty Hall, and to lay yˢ same out in Lottes of Eighty foot long into the Dock and about Four and Twenty ffoot broad, leaving sufficient space for yˢ street, as also to lay out yᵉ street Ranging with yᵉ Here Graft, (*canal in Broad Street*,) as you shall receive further instructions from me uppon yᵉ surveying & laying out yᵉ sid Lottes; & for so doing this shall be your warrant. Given under my hand in New York, this 15th day of September, Aᵈ 1686."—N. BAYARD, *Mayor*.

The grounds around the "Broadway Shambles," however, had the advantage of being occupied several times through the course of the year with fairs and cattle markets. An act was passed by the General Assembly, in 1692, "for settling the Fairs and Markets," of which the following is a part: "That there be kept yearly, for the City and County of *New York*, two Fairs at the City of New York. The first Fair annually, to commence the last Tuesday of April in every year, and to end upon the Fryday then next following, being in all four days inclusive, and no longer. And the second Fair to commence the first Tuesday of November in every year, and to end on the Fryday then next following, being in all four dayes inclusive, and no longer."

To these "Fairs" and open markets were brought "cattle, horses, mares, colts, grain, victuals, provisions, and all other necessaries, together with all sorts of merchandise, of what nature soever, and them to expose to sale or barter, in gross or by retail, between the hours of eight of the clock in the morning and sunset of the same day, without payment of any toll, or any other let, hinderance, or molestation whatsoever."

The various domestic animals that were brought to the city from the northward had to cross in the ferry-boats or swim, as no bridge had yet been built across the "Spikendevil" or Harlaem River. We, however, find, in the month of January, 1693, the "Council" met to consider the offer of Frederick Phillippse to build a bridge where Kingsbridge is now located. "They doe find that itt cannot be well accomplished without a great charge unto this Citty, which at present they are not soe capable to defray; and understanding that Frederick Philips, Esq., will undertake to build a Bridge at the said place (Spikendevil) for y conveniency of all travellers & Drovers of Cattell att a moderate and reasonable Toll, they doe therefore humbly pray your Excellency, (the Governor,) that if the said Mr. Philips will undertake in one year's time to build a good and convenient *Drawbridge*, for the passage of all Travellers, Droves of Cattel, & passage of Carts & Waggons, for the Toll of one penny ffor each neat Cattel and two-pence for each Man and Horse, and twelve-pence for each score of Hogs & Sheep, & six-pence for each cart & waggon that shall pass thereon, that he may have the preference of their Majesties' Grant."

The bridge appears to have been built soon after, and it became established as a toll-bridge, and the only bridge connecting the Island of New York with the main-land for a period of more than sixty years.

Madame *Knight*, in her Journal of 1704, says: "Thursday, December 21, set out for New Haven with my kinsman, Trowbridge, and the man that waited on me about one afternoon, and about three *(o'clock, P. M.,)* came to *half-way house, (which once stood at the bottom of the hill on the old middle road, about* 107th *Street, between the line of the* 5th *and* 6th *Avenues,)* about ten miles out of town, where we baited and went forward, and about 5 came to *Spiting Devil*, else Kingsbridge, where they pay three-pence for passing over with a horse, which the man that keeps the gate set up at the end of the bridge receives. We hoped to reach Frenchtown *(New Rochelle)* and lodge there that night, but unhappily lost our way about four miles short, and being overtaken by a great storm of wind and snow which set full in our faces, about dark we were very uneasy. But meeting one Gardner, who lived in a cottage thereabout, offered us his fire to set by, having but one poor *bedd*, and his wife not well." She was taken further on, where she obtained quarters.

At this period, across this *Bridge* was the only road to Boston, and that but seldom traveled. The Albany Turnpike had not yet been opened, and only a few very rough by-roads, which answered the purpose of a few farmers to reach the North or East River, as they usually came by water to the city with their produce. However, some few farmers in the interior, and drovers from Connecticut, with cattle and horses, occasionally passed over it. But at a later period, when the turnpikes were opened, and traveling on them became general, occasionally the farmers and drovers would complain of the many detentions, and "at times the toll was so variously charged as to become grevious," which no doubt led Jacob Dyckman, (the grandfather of ex-Alderman Isaac Dyckman,) a blacksmith, a farmer, and also a tavern-keeper, with several other public-spirited farmers, in the year 1758, to erect another bridge across the river near this old one. This new bridge, as appears from the following communication, was called "Free Bridge Dyckman's;"* and then follows on, "Whereas the crossing at Harlaem River, on the high-road to Boston by Kingsbridge, according to an established toll, became very changeable and burthensome to travellers in general, and to the inhabitants of Westchester and Dutchess Counties in particular: the toll received passing the bridge being for each carriage, 9d.; each horse and head of cattle, 3d.; and a man 1d. Notice is therefore hereby given that certain public-spirited persons have lately contributed a large sum of money, and therewith built a fine new bridge across the said river, a little to the southward of the said bridge, which shortens the public road about half a mile; and the said new bridge is free and exempted for all toll whatsoever. (Signed) Jacob Dyckman, Jun'r; (dated) Harlaem, 11th November, (1758.)"

The following letter from Benjamin Palmer to Colonel Aaron Burr, Member of Assembly of the City and County of New York, in the year 1798, will further explain how this bridge was built, and its cost: "Sir—I called at your house the day you went to Albany, but you was gone on your journey. I had a desire to inform you personally concerning the *Free Bridge*, which I built over Harlaem River.

"Sir, I undertook to raise the money by subscription, and expected to build it near the old bridge, called King's Bridge; but when I

* N. Y. Mercury, December 18, 1758.

found that Col. Philips had got that right from the Government of this State, it could not be built in any other place than from Thomas Vermillia's land, across to Jacob Dyckman's land; therefore, I took them into partnership with me to build said bridge. We chose Walter Briggs (since deceased) to be our treasurer, to receive the subscription money, and to pay the workmen and other costs arising from the building said bridge, but there was not money enough by a considerable sum to finish it, because it took twice as much to build it in that place as it would where I first proposed; therefore, there was not money enough to build said bridge raised by subscription. I then paid into the hands of Mr. Briggs, our treasurer, £120 in cash to finish it, and he allowed me £20 14s. for my time, trouble, and expenses in getting the subscription signed, collecting the money and attending the building of said bridge, which sum makes £140 14s., according to my petition; which sum I have never been paid, nor ever received any satisfaction for it.

"Besides this loss, I was twice pressed in one year, as a soldier, to go to Canada, there then being a war between England and France; therefore I was obliged to hire two men to go in my place —the one cost me £5, the other £20, supposed by the people in general, as well as myself, to have been the orders of Col. Philips; because he knew it would stop his bridge from taking toll. Notwithstanding this, I continued building the *free bridge* until finished.

"Sir—the reason of my writing particularly to you, was because Mr. John Bartow was acquainted with you—he told me that he had talked to several gentlemen about the building this *bridge*—they said it was just that I should be paid; for it had saved many thousand pounds to the people of this State. He told me if I would draw up a petition, and send it to the Assembly, he would sign it, and speak to you, sir, concerning it, and desire you to lay it before the Honorable the House of Representatives, and speak in favor of it, as it was a just debt, and ought to be paid.

"Mr. Bartow further said, he knew it was Col. Philips' interest in the House to stop the petition from being granted.

"I shall be much obliged to you, sir, if you will lay this petition before the House, and speak in favor of it, as in your wisdom you may think fit.   BENJAMIN PALMER."*

The following remarks in relation to it are also interesting: "When Col. Burr returned from the Legislature, he told Mr. Palmer that there were no hopes of ever getting any assistance from the Legislature for building the above *bridge;* and told that if Mr. Palmer would draw up a subscription paper, he would subscribe to

* N. Y. Gazette, September 6, 1800.

it himself; for, that it was not worth his while to petition any more concerning it; and that, as it was begun by subscription, there was no other way than to finish it by subscription.

"And whereas said *bridge* was then considered as a grievous and heavy tax on the public. The profits went into no public funds, but only to enhance the private fortune of a particular subject; and also it was a neat imposition on the public, for said bridge separated the City and County of New York, and the people from the country from coming into and going from the city—they could neither pass nor repass, by land, without going over said bridge, paying an extravagant tax or toll. The gates were locked and barred at night, so that if people's business was ever so urgent, they were obliged to stand and knock, let the weather be ever so cold or stormy, until a servant pleased to come and unlock the gate, the house being 12 or 15 rods from it; therefore, Mr. Palmer, on the frequent complaints of the people, undertook to build a *free bridge* over Harlaem River by subscription; and there not being money enough raised to finish said *bridge*, Mr. Palmer advanced £120 in cash to finish it, besides his time and trouble, and other expenses. This *bridge* was finished in the year 1759.

" Walter Briggs, who was treasurer, allowed Mr. Palmer £20 14s. for the purpose above mentioned, which may be seen by Mr. Briggs' book of accounts—the two sums, with the interests, make upwards of 1,500 dollars—a sum too great to lay on one man, when we all had the honor and profit of a *free bridge*, as well as himself; therefore let us consider Mr. Palmer's situation, and do unto him as we would desire others to do unto us.

"Such gentlemen as can spare a few dollars to make up his loss, do it freely; and not say, this *bridge* was built before we was born. If nothing for the public good had been built before we were born, we should be in a deplorable situation.

"Suppose young people should say, the Independence of these States was declared before they were born, and that they would not pay the old debts contracted to obtain their independence; but there is a law to oblige them to pay. Mr. Palmer has no law to oblige the people to pay him for freeing them from a grievous and heavy tax laid on them for passing a toll-bridge, by building a *free* one. And whereas, it was the first step towards freedom in this State, and it is hoped the *Sons of Freedom* will step forward and cast in their mite; for it was almost as difficult for Mr. Palmer to get a *free bridge* in those days, as it was for America to get her freedom and independence from Great Britain.

" When this *free bridge* was finished, there was a fine fat ox roasted on the Green, and thousands from the city and country partook of the ox, and rejoiced greatly.

"When this *free bridge* was finished, Col. Philips was obliged to make his a *free bridge* also; and it would have continued a toll-bridge to this day, had it not been for the spirited exertions of Mr. Palmer."

This *free bridge* was noticed as having been finished in the year 1759, and the public opening of it was thus announced: "These aie to acquaint the public, that to-morrow (2d of *January*, 1759,) the *free bridge* erected and built across Harlaem River will be finished and completed; and on the same day there will be a stately ox roasted whole on the Green, for and as a small entertainment to the *loyal* people who come."*

In the month of April following we find, "To be let, and entered upon immediately, the house, farm, and *bridge* at King's Bridge, in the manor of Philipsburgh, in the County of Westchester. For particulars inquire of Frederick Phillipse."†

From a petition and report made in the year 1824, a few more interesting facts are brought forth. The first introduces "the bridge formerly called the 'free bridge' across Harlaem River, leading from New York Island to Westchester, has become much decayed, and in a condition to be dangerous to persons and carriages passing and repassing over the same.

"The bridge is much used by persons from Westchester, coming to the New York market, and others, and is highly necessary to be kept in good order." This was dated October 7, 1824, and signed by Jacobus Dykman, James De Voe, Aaron Post, Henry Post, Denis Post, Henry Thison, and Benjamin Lynt. In the month of December following, the "Road Committee" reported: "The bridge to be repaired connects the island of New York with that part of Westchester County lying on Harlaem River, called the 'Manor of Fordham,' and is a short distance from the mouth of 'Spyt den Duyvel' Creek, through which the waters of said river flow into the Hudson.

"This bridge was erected about sixty years ago by individual subscription, to avoid the unjust exactions of the proprieters of Kingsbridge. But during our struggle for independence it was destroyed by the enemy to prevent the passage of the American Army across the river; the passage of the other bridge being defended by a redoubt. Ten or twelve years since, however, the inhabitants in its vicinity raised another subscription and rebuilt it, at an expense, as your Committee are informed, of about *one thousand dollars*, and have kept it in repair at their own cost, excepting the appropria-

* N. Y. Mercury.   † Gazette, April 9.

tions made by this Board three or four years ago of two hundred dollars, twenty of which remain unexpended. It is now in such a state of decay that it cannot be passed without great danger, and humanity at least requires that it should be immediately and substantially repaired, or that it should be entirely removed, that the safety of travelers who do not know its situation may not be endangered. It is virtually the property of the corporation, as the sovereignty of that body over Harlaem River to low-water mark on the northern or Westchester side of it has never been disputed."

"Your Committee are informed that there is considerable traveling over this bridge; that the inhabitants of a large district of Westchester County pass it with produce for our market; if so, may it not in time be productive of the most beneficial effects, by reducing the price of such vegetables as come daily to our city? For it cannot be denied that a toll-bridge is a tax on all the produce which passes over it, which the consumer has to pay; if, therefore, the produce which crosses Harlaem River, and reaches our market by land, can toll free, it could be afforded and would be sold at a less price than it now is." "The Committee recommend the appropriation of two hundred and eighty dollars to assist to rebuild in a safe and substantial manner the aforesaid bridge, and to keep the same in repair for the space of seven years."

Returning to the latter part of the sixteenth century, we find the inhabitants rather a mixed people; some doing illy and some well, but the Dutch Burghers had the credit of being the most industrious and prosperous. Charles Lodowicke, in a letter to his uncle, Mr. Francis Lodowicke, dated May 20, 1692, says, "Our chiefest unhappyness here is too great a mixture of nations, and ye English y^n least part; ye French protestants have in ye late King's Reign resorted hither in great nu(m)bers proportionately to ye other nations' inhabitants. Y^r Dutch generally ye most frugall and laborious, and consequently ye richest; whereas most of ye English are y contrary, especially ye trading part."

"Most sorts of European animalls thrive here very well, tho' ye country before y^r discovery was not known to have produced any of those usual sorts of Beasts, as Horses, Cows, Sheep, Hoggs, or Goats; Sheep would increase here and do very much. English or clover grass agreeing very well with ye land, yet y^r stature of ye cattle seem rather to decrease here, wch might doubtless in a great measure be helpt by care and good husbandry. An Ox shall ordinarily weigh here six hundred weight, rarely one thousand." "All sorts of Cattle are now in abundance and increase dayly: a Horse is sold from 2 to 6 pound, an Ox or Cow from 2 to 5 pound, this country money, wch is 25 per cent. worse than sterling."

The General Assembly, however, in the following year, regulated the price of slaves, domestic animals, and other property, in the following terms: " *Resolved,* 1. That all negro and Indian slaves, from twelve years old to sixty, be valued at twelve pounds per head.

" 2. That all horses and neat cattle, from three years old and upwards, be valued at thirty shillings per head.

" 3. That all sheep and goats, from one year old and upwards, be valued at three shillings per head.

" 4. That all hogs, from half a year old and upwards, be valued at three shillings per head.

" 5. That all lands, meadows, and houses, throughout this province, shall be valued according to the yearly income of the same."*

On the 25th of September, 1694, the Broadway Shambles, in the Broadway, were ordered " to be lett to Farme unto Henry Crosby, of this City, *Butcher,* for the term of seven years, att one pound per annum, upon condition that he put the house in good repair, and soe to maintain and give up the house att the expiration of the term aforesaid."† The next year Crosby sought and procured a better bargain from the Common Council, as appears on the 19th of June, 1695. " Upon the humble request of Henry Crosby, yᵉ Butcher in the Broadway, that the Citty would be pleased to grant him liberty to fence in a small piece of ground, the breadth of his shop, and about fourteen or fifteen feet long, for the keeping of sheep and for slaughter, which was granted."

Crosby's lease expired, when a committee was ordered, on the 3d September, 1702, " to lett to Farme the old market-house in Broadway, not exceeding the term of five years." This term it changed hands, for I find it in the possession of "Jeremiah Calcutt, of this city, butcher," at the expiration of the term, who afterwards, on the 29th September, 1703, had influence enough in the Common Council to be appointed " High Constable." Whether he was appointed for *efficiency,* or from political favor, or whether it was necessary to *fee-ed* the whole of the Common Council, (which at that period included the Mayor,) before the important office could be obtained, is not now known; although, if the latter, the expenses for a " *grand feed,*" or *feast,* would not now be considered a large sum; but at that period, however, when a grand dinner was given, or ordered for the Common Council, every item was afterwards made out in the bill, of which the following is a specimen:

"An account of Richard Harris, against the Mayor, Aldermen, &c., Dr.   Dated December 19, 1704.

"To a piece of beef and cabbage,   -   -   -   - £0   7 6

* Journal of Assembly, vol. i., p. 37.   † City Records.

To a dish of tripe and cow heel, - - -	0	6	0
To a leg of pork and turnips, - - - -	0	8	3
To 2 puddings, - - - - - -	0	14	6
To a surloyn of beef, - - - - - -	0	13	6
To a turkey and onions, - - - - -	0	9	0
To a leg of mutton and pickles, - - - -	0	6	0
To a dish of chickens, - - - - -	0	10	6
To minced pyes, - - - - - - -	1	4	0
To fine cheese, bread, &c., - - - -	0	7	6
To butter for sauce, - - - - - -	0	7	9
To hire of two negroes, to assist, - - -	0	6	0
To dressing dinner, &c., - - - - -	1	4	0
To 31 bottles of wine, - - - - -	3	2	0
To beer and syder, - - - - - -	0	12	0

£10 18 6"

The above was considered an enormous *bill*, but after considering the large number of *items*, "it was allowed." The *wine item* appears very heavy, but in those days it was a custom to prepare largely of liquid stimulants, in the event of a victory, birth-days, or even the "making of vendues." When the "great victory over the Spanish and French fleets at Vigo" was celebrated, a few years before, it was "Ordered that a public bonfire be made, and ten gallons of wine and a barrel of beer provided, and all the houses to be illuminated."

At this period, Madame Knight, a Boston lady, made a journey to this city on horseback, and in her "Journal" she notices many interesting customs, fashions, &c., of the citizens on certain occasions. She says: "They are not strict in keeping the Sabbath as in Boston and other places where I had been, but seem to deal with great exactness, as far as I see or deal with.

"They are sociable to one another, and courteous and civil to strangers, and fare well in their houses.

"The English go very fashionable in their dress; but the Dutch, especially the middling sort, differ from our women, in their habit go loose, wear French *muches*, which are like a cap, and a head-band in one, leaving their ears bare, which are set out with jewels of a large size, and many in number. And their fingers hoop't with rings, some with large stones in them of many colors; as were their pendants in their ears, which you should see very old women wear as well as young.

"They have vendues very frequently, and make their earnings very well by them, for they treat with good liquor liberally, and the customers drink as liberally, and generally pay for 't as well, by paying for that which they bid up briskly for, after the *sack* has gone plentifully about, tho' sometimes good penny worth are got there.

"Their diversion in the winter is riding sleys about three miles out of town, where they have houses of entertainment at a place called the *Bowery;* and some go to friends' houses, who handsomely treat them. Mr. Borroughs carry'd his *spouse* and daughter and myself out to one Madame Dowes', a gentlewoman that lived at a farm-house, who gave us entertainment of five or six dishes, and choice beer and metheglin, cyder, &c., all which she said was the produce of her farm.

"I believe we met 50 or 60 slays that day; they fly with great swiftness, and some are so furious that they'le turn out of the path for none except a loaden cart. Nor do they spare for any diversion the place affords, and sociable to a degree, theyr tables being as free to their neighbours as to themselves." We must, however, take leave of these happy people, and at a later period again refer to them or their generations.

On the 28th of October, 1707, a "resolution passed, that the butcher's shop in the Broadway now in the occupation of Jeremiah Calcutt be demolished and pulled down, and that the said Jeremiah Calcutt have liberty to convert the materials thereof to his own use, by the Mayor's lysense, he producing his lease thereof to the Mayor."* It was soon after taken down, but no doubt the *place* was held as a market-place for fairs and the like for many years after, as I find, in 1720, "the old market-place in the Broadway be and are hereby held as a public market-place, until further orders."

CUSTOM-HOUSE BRIDGE MARKET.

1675. IN the year 1675, a General Court of Assize was held in this city, "beginning on the 6th and ending on the 13th day of October," when, among other proceedings, "a weekly markett" was ordered to be held, and "a fitt house to be built by the water-side," near where the "Market-Place at the Strand" had been formerly held. This was soon followed by a proclamation from Governor Andross, which came before the Common Council on the 29th of January of the following year, and read as follows: "Whereas, as a weekly markett in this citty hath beene thought necessary for the

* City Records.

convenience, good, and welfare of the inhabitants and neighbour-
hood, for wh^{ch} a fitt house being now built by the water-side, neare
the Bridge and Weigh-House, I have, by the advice of my Councell
and Cort of Mayor and Aldermen, resolved and ordered, and doe
hereby publish the said markett to begine on Saturday, the 24th of
March next ensuinge, in the afores^d house, and soe every Saturday
followinge, for the space of *three yeares.*"*

The location of this *"fitt house* by the water-side, neare the
Bridge and Weigh-House," stood about where the corner of Pearl
and Moore Streets now meet; and no doubt, when it was erected,
the business which came to the "Market-Place at the Strand" was
removed into it.   It appeared to accommodate the country people
and Indians, who came by water with poultry, fish, butter, cheese,
&c.; while those who brought "flesh-meat" went up the canal in
Broad Street, to the Marketfield Street, and so across into the
"Broadway Shambles."

About this period, the Rev. Mr. Wooley, in his Journal, notices
the Indians, with their swift canoes: "In which they bring oysters
and other fish for the market; they are so light and portable, that
a man and his squaw will take them upon their sholders and carry
them by land from one river to another, with a wonderful expedition; they will venture with them in a dangerous current, even
through Hell-gate itself, which lies in an arm of the sea, about ten
miles from New York eastward to New England, as dangerous and
as accountable as the Norway whirlpool or maelstrom: in this
Hell-gate, which is a narrow passage, runneth a rapid, violent
stream, both upon flood and ebb; and in the middle lieth some islands of rocks, upon which the current sets so violently, that it
threatens present shipwrack; and upon the flood is a large whirlpool, which sends forth a continual hedious roaring; it is a place
of great defence against an enemy coming that way, which a small
fortification would absolutely prevent, by forcing them to come in at
the west end of Long Island by Sandy Hook, where *Nutten Island*†
would force them within the command of the fort of New York."

Mr. Wooley, in another part of his Journal, says: "The City of
New York in my time (1678–9) was as large as some market towns
with us, all built the London way; the Garrison side of a high situation and a pleasant prospect; the Island it stands on all a level
and champain; the diversion especially in the winter season used

* City Records.

(† This evidence would lead us to suppose that there could not have been much of a
channel, even at that period, between Red Hook and Nutten or Governor's Island, and
very likely some fifty years before, as noticed on page 15, had been in the state as there
represented.)

by the Dutch is aurigation, *i. e.*, riding about in wagons, which is
allowed by physicians to be a very healthful exercise by Land. And
upon the Ice it's admirable to see Men and Women as it were flying
upon their Skates from place to place, with markets upon their
Heads and Backs."

He further says: "All Commodities and Trades are dearer or
cheaper according to the plenty of importation;" and "for what I
had occasion, some things were reasonable, some dear. I paid for
two loads of Oats in the straw 18 shillings to one Henry Dyer; to
the same, for a Load of Pease-straw, six shillings; paid to Thomas
Davis, for shooing my Horse, three shillings, for in that place
Horses are seldom, some not shod at all, their Hoofs, by running
in the woods so long before they are backed, are like flints: Paid
to Derick, *i. e.*, Richard Secah's Son, for a Load of Hay, twelve
shillings; Paid to Denys Fisher's Son, a Carpenter, for two days'
work in the Stable, eight shillings; for a Curry-Comb and Horse-
brush, four shillings; to Jonathan, the Barber, £1 4s. the year; to
the Shoo-maker, for a pair of Boots and Shooes, £1 5s.; to the
Washerwoman or Laundress, £1 5s. 6d. the year."

Of the inhabitants he says, "Both English and Dutch (are) very
civil and courteous, as I may speak by experience, amongst whom I
have often wished myself and family, to whose tables I was frequently invited, and always concluded with a generous bottle of
Madera. I cannot say I observed any swearing or quarrelling, but
what was easily reconciled and recanted by a mild rebuke, except
once betwixt two Dutch Boors, (whose usual oath is sacrament,)
which, abateing the abusive language, was no unpleasant scene.
As soon as they met, (which was after they had alarm'd the neigh-
bourhood,) they seized each other's hair with their forefeet, and
down they went to the sod, their vrows and families crying out because they could not part them; which fray happening against my
chamber window, I called up one of my acquaintance, and ordered
him to fetch a kit full of water and discharge it at them, which immediately cool'd their courage, and loosed their grapples; so we
used to part our mastiffs in England. In the same City of New
York, when I was Minister to the English, there were two other
Ministers, or Domines, as they were called there, the one a Lutheran,
a German or High Dutch; the other, a Calvinist, was Hollander or
Low Dutchman, who behav'd themselves one towards another so
shily and uncharitably as if Luther and Calvin had bequeathed
and entailed their virulent and bigotted spirits upon them and their
heirs forever. They had not visited or spoken to each other with
any respect for six years together before my being there, with whom

I being much acquainted, I invited them both, with their vrows, to a supper one night unknown to each other, with an obligation that they should not speak one word in Dutch, under the penalty of a bottle of Medara, alledging I was so imperfect in that language that we could not manage a sociable discourse; so accordingly they came, and at the first interview they stood so appaled as if the ghosts of Luther and Calvin had suffered a transmigration, but the amaze soon went off with a *salve tu quoque*, and a bottle of wine, of which the Calvinist Domine was a true carouser, and so we continued our *Mensalia* the whole meeting in Latine, which they both spoke so fluently and promptly, that I blush'd at myself with a passionate regret that I could not keep pace with them."

The growth of the city had at the end of three years so much increased, that it seemed to demand more than one market-day; and as this (*Saturday*) was about to expire, according to the order of the 24th of March, 1675, it was necessary to renew it, and also to appoint another day; which, however, did not take place until the 9th of March, 1679–'80, when "for ye better supply of ye Cytie"—with provisions and other necessaries—"from this day forward another market extraordinary shall be kept every week, weekly, on Wednesday, att ye usual market-place, neere ye Bridge and Weigh-House."* The population two years after is shown to have been about 2,000 whites, besides negroes and slaves; number of houses 207, besides barns and sheds.

The market regulations in existence (prior to 1683) did not answer altogether, or were not rigid enough to meet forestallers and sellers of unsound meats, to provide in what manner certain articles should be sold, &c., which this increased and mixed population would seem to have demanded. The city, however, was soon afterwards supplied with such laws, which were ordained and enacted on the 15th of March, 1683; part of them read as follows: "That fish, butter, cheese, eggs, poultry, fruit, roots, and herbs may be sold every day in the week at any time, in the market or other convenient places."

"That no person shall forstal any provision or victuals coming to the markett, as to buy in any private or other place than the markett, under pain of forfeiture of the same, whether it be found in the hands of buyer or seller.

"No person shall engross any provision or victuals which is in the market, or by the market, to retail there again, especially such as be known for Hucksters, Butchers, or other people occupying their living by such provisions or victuals as they shall so engross, under pain of such provisions and victuals so engrossed.

* City Records.

" No butter, cheese, or other provisions sold by weight, shall be sold but according to the weight established.

" No Huckster shall engross any poultry, eggs, or fresh butter coming to the market, under pain of forty shillings.

" No unwholesome or stale victuals shall be sold in the market, under the pain of forty shillings.

" No blown meat or leprous swine shall be sold, under the pain of forfeiture the same and forty shillings.

" That there be a person appointed by the Mayor and Aldermen to be Clerk of the Market, who is to take care that the above orders are duly observed and prevent defaults, and set out and appoint convenient boarths, stales and standings for all persons that come to the market, shall not be put in execution until the week after Easter, when the same is to be duly observed and kept."

In the repairs of this market-house, in 1683, I find from a report that " 1,500 *(feet)* of inch oak plank, 16 feet *(in length,)* cost £5 5."

This "fitt market-house" had not been used quite ten years when Governor Dongon ordered the removal of this market-place; which subject came before the Council held on the 24th of May, 1684: " Mr. John Tudor, bringing a message from the Governor, desiring that the market may be removed from the place where itt is now kept, to the vacant ground before the Fort, and that the authorities would order the same to be done accordingly." " That from henceforward the market for butchers' meat be held in the same place *(Broadway Shambles)* according, they erecting their scales and other conveniences at their own charge."

The removal of this market-place from the " Bridge and Weigh-House" no doubt was caused by the accumulation of business at this place. The laws had granted them the privilege to hold market-days every day of the week; this, and the shipping and the receiving of goods, all took place on and around the Dock, Bridge, and through the 'Weigh-House,' and '12d. per ton bridge money' was exacted on all merchandise exported or imported."*

Although the market-place was removed, yet the " fitt market-house" was not; but in 1687 it was "Ordered that the market-house of the city be employed as a warehouse for goods; each ton or cask paying 9 pence for 24 hours, and the Mayor appoint a fit person to keep the same, who shall have half of the profit for his services." Accordingly, on the 26th February following, (1688,) Anthony Demilt was ordered to "keepe ye key of ye market-house until the 25th day of March," and the allowed fees, which in addition "for every half bar¹" be collected "two stivers wampum for ye use of ye city."

* Picture of N. Y.

At the expiration of the term, he was again appointed to this important office " until further order."

On the 16th of March, in the year 1689, the Common Council
agreed with Captain John Tudor "for a place to build a shop in the
market-house for the term of three years, for the sum of forty shillings
per annum." Then, on the 30th inst., "George Brown hath hired a
lott for a shop in the *market-house* for the same time at £2 10, and
another lott was lett to Peter Panburnge at £3, to be paid quarterly."

The Mayor made a report on the 24th April, 1691, "that he hath
lett out the shop in the *market-house* to one John Ellison for three
pounds ten shillings per annum, to be payed quarterly, and he to receive the same att his owne charge, a pair of hinges for the door,
onley accepted." On the 18th of February, in the year 1692, a committee was appointed to "lett *it* out, what is to be lett thereoff."

Next we find it with an additional name, from the proceedings on
the 15th March, 1694: " The *market-house* or *store-house (no doubt the
whole)* at the Bridge was let to John Ellison, citty joyner, *(carpenter,)*
for the space of five years, from the first of May next, for the sum
of sixteen pounds per annum; he having permission to build an addition of ten feet in breadth, with chimney—part of the *market-house*
to be used as a *store-house* for merchants."

Ellison's lease expired in the year 1699; he, however, on the
20th of September, agreed with the Authorities to "put up a house
of brick and stone, two stories high, in the room and on the ground;
the old market-house stands to have a lease of twenty-one years;"
but I find the inhabitants enter a protest against giving "the possession of a lease to John Ellison for the market-house at the 'Custom-House Bridge,' until such time they are heard;" and there appeared two parties who wished that privilege; one to build a market-
house, and the other a place for the meeting of merchants.

The first was before the Board on the 16th October of that year,
"praying that they have liberty to make and erect a publick market-
house for the ornament and benefit of ye Citty, on ye ground whereon
ye old market-house stands on which John Ellison lives; he, the said
John Ellison, having relinquished his agreement with ye Citty."
The other, signed by some eighty-three inhabitants of the South
Ward, states, "That whereas Sir Edmund Andross, Knt., late Governor of this province, did order a certain building to be erected
near the *Bridge* in this city, which has since been called the *market-
house;* and whereas your petitioners have been informed that the
same was by this Board to be let out for some term of years to one
Mr. Ellison, on condition to erect a new building on the same ground,
and pay as a rent *twelve* pounds a year to the City:

"Your petitioners therefore humbly pray that the said agreement may be quashed, and that the same ground may be allowed to your petitioners for the use of this City, they offering to erect there a convenient place for the meeting of *merchants*, on their own cost and charges; it being a very convenient place for the same, being nigh the Custom-House, and will be of ornament to the City, and also pay *twelve pounds* a year to the City, they having the benefit of the store-money of merchants' goods allowed them," &c.   A committee was ordered " to consult with the inhabitants of the South Ward what building they propose to make on the premises, and what yearly rent they will pay for the same, and make report thereof to the next Common Council."

This report was not made until the 19th of February, 1700, when it was "Ordered, that yᵉ said market-house be granted to yᵉ *(South)* Ward for the terme of fifty years, they, the said Inhabitants, in ten years' time, erecting a publick building according to the moddell exhibited to this Courte; they yielding the yearly rent of twelve pounds, and keeping and delivering the same in good repair att the expiration of the said term of fifty years."

It appears, by this order, the inhabitants were not immediately bound to erect this public building, but were allowed ten years to do so; and our old friend, John Ellison, a few years after, turned his attention to " catching porpoises," as his petition sets forth, " that he has been at great charge in inventing a method to catch porpoises," and wishes encouragement for the same, which was not given him by the Board.

The old market-house had been, many of its former years, used as a " store-house and shops," and lost its reputation as a public mar-ket-place; others, also, had been in the mean time established; the inhabitants around it felt anxious to restôre its trade back again, and applied to the authorities to assist them, who, on the 30th June, 1701, "*Resolved*, That the old market-house near the Custom-House Bridge be forever hereafter appropriated for a publick market-house, for the benefit and conveniency of all persons that should resort thereunto, in as full and ample manner as any other market-house or market-place within this city now is, or lawfully ought to be."

In 1703, it appeared to have needed some repairs, as, on the 29th of November, " ten pounds is appropriated for the covering of the market-house by the Custom-House Bridge."   So it stood until the 2d November, 1708, when the sheds or "shops" on the sides had become useless, and it was "ordered that the inhabitants have lib-erty to pull down the boards about the market-house by the Cus-tom-House Bridge, and that Alderman Thong dispose of the same."

He reported, on the 1st February following, "that he had sold the boards for one pound, three shillings and sixpence; whereof he expended for thirty-four loads of sand, and for a laborer for mending the street near the Custom-House, eighteen shillings and one penny half-penny."

It then rested quietly until the 16th of November, 1720, when it was presented as a public nuisance, and the Common Council gave permission to the inhabitants, or rather to "have liberty to remove the old market-house near the Custom-House to a more convenient place near the water-side, at their own cost, provided they do the same within ten days; if not, the said market-house will be pulled down, according to an order of the Supreme Court." Thus was disposed of the old market-house, which I have designated "*the Custom-House Bridge Market.*"

BROAD STREET MARKET.

1691. I HAVE designated the *first* market-house built in Broad Street with the above title, there having been several market-houses and market-places established at various intervals in that street.

The first notice we have of this market-place is found in the proceedings of the Common Council, July 9, 1691, in which "Captain William Merritt, Mr. Johannes Kipp, Captain Brandt Schuyler, and Mr. Teunis de Kay are appointed a Committee to build a market-house att the end of Heere-graft *(Broad)* Street, for all *but* Butchers' meat." This market-house was finished, as is shown from the following instructions, given to a committee, on the 18th of February, 1692, "for the letting the new Market-House over against Anthony Farmer's, which said new market-house is allowed to be made shambles, *(stalls for butchers' meat,)* or any otherwise."

"Anthony Farmer's" appears to have been located *over* or on the east side of the Heere-Graft, *(canal in Broad Street,)* near the present Water Street, near what was then known as the "Little Bridge."

The Laws and Ordinances in 1702 say, "That there be three market-days, *one whereof* be at the 'Little Bridge' by the dock."

In the month of March, 1704, "Two pairs of stairs be made in the Dock on each side of the 'Little Bridge;'" "and that two posts be put up in the 'market-house' by the Great Bridge, *('Cus-*

tom-House Bridge Market,') in order to keep out the cows." Then, in the month of June, 1705, it was ordered that "the street fronting the Dock, between the 'Great and Little Bridges,' the south end of Broad Street to the Little Bridge, on both sides of the *(canal)* way," should be paved.

At this early period, just about this market-house appeared rather a favorite place for the merchants and traders; it being so nearly located to the "Great Bridge," Dock, and Custom-House on the one side, where all goods of every character were exported and imported for the city; and on the other side, the "Coenties Slip *(Fish)* Market" and the old City Hall, which had now been given up by the authorities, and sold, a few years previous, (1699,) to one John Rodman, a merchant, for the sum of £920; and another at the head of this *(Broad)* street, in Wall Street, had been erected in the year 1700.

These attractions gave an idea to a prominent individual, named Cornelius Sebring, who lived opposite, on the Long Island shore, to petition to the Governor, on the 23d January, 1708, for an additional ferry. He stated, he "stands possessed of a certain farm on the Island of Nassau, directly over against the centre of the City of New York, being a most fit and convenient place for being a ferry to and from the said city;" "and can be of no hurt or dammage to the *old ferry*, it being not so convenient for that ferry to send their boats to the south end and centre of the city, where he proposes to send his." "To be limited on the Island of Nassau on the one side of the *old ferry*, and on the other side by the Red Hook; and on the side of New York between the (Old) Slip, at Captain Theobald's, unto the 'Great Bridge,' for the loading and landing of all persons, goods, wares, and merchandise, except cattle, to be landed at or near the *slaughter-howses;* (nevertheless, not excluding the old ferry-boat from the places aforesaid.")

The Corporation remonstrate against the granting of this petition, and state that this ferry "hath been commonly esteemed & reputed for *seaventy years* past to extend from a heap of Rock Stones gathered together on a small wharfe or landing Bridge near the Ferry-House on the said Island." "That some private persons, for their own Lucre and gain, have solicited your Excellency for another Ferry on the said Island fronting to this City, which, if Granted, would be of great damage to this Corporation, and all the Inhabitants thereof." "And also, that your Excellency would be further pleased to order unto the petitioners & their successors her Majesty's Grant of Confirmation for the said Ferry on both sides of the said River, with power to Establish one or more Ferrys, if there shall be occasion, &c."* Their remonstrance was granted, which denied the petition of Mr. Sebring.

This "old ferry," (says Mr. Valentine,) "from the earliest settlement, and for many years afterwards, was from the present landing on the Brooklyn side, at Fulton Ferry, to the nearest point on this island, which was at the present Peck Slip."

The Records inform us that on the 28th of February, 1683, "Mr. William Merritt beeing sent ffor, and discoursed about the fferry too Long Island; offered, iff he might have the same ffor twenty years, too give twenty pound p^r annum, and to mayke houses on each syde, and have two Boats ffor cattle and horses, and two Boats ffor passengers; and too carry cattle and horses att 6 sciple p^r head, men at 1 sciple, and corne att 1 sciple p^r bagg; wheat 3 sciples."

A committee was appointed "too drawe upp suitable orders ffor the future management and accomodacon thereof, and the rates and prises, and too lett the sayme ffor terms off years, by advise and consente off the Mayor, reservinge a Rente too be annually payde bye quarterly payments ffor the publique use off the Citty."

It appears, however, that no regular ferry-house and other necessary accommodations had been prepared until the year 1698, when the conditions were made known in again farming or leasing it for a period of five years, beginning from the 25th of March of the above year, (1698.)

These conditions read in the third section: "That ye said farmer shall provide and maintain two great Boats or Scows for ye carrying and transporting of cattle, corne, &c.; and two small Boats sufficient for ye carrying of passengers, and that the great Boats shall be kept one on each side of the river, &c.; the small Boats ye likewise constantly going to and fro, but not both to remaine on the same side of ye River att any time, and also to keep good and able men to Row in the said Boats, who shall give their constant attendance, and be ready att all times according to form and custom."

They shall "keep and maintain one sufficient pound for security of cattle to be transported to and from the Citty of New York, and when delivered at ye Ferry to take charge thereof, and to find all Roapes & other necessaries." Section 5th says: "That the Mayor, &c., within the first year of ye said lease, shall cause to be erected and built at ye Ferry, on Nassau Island, a good sufficient house of stone and brick, of two stories high, fourty foot in length, and twenty-four foot in breadth, for ye accommodation & conveniency of ye persons that farmeth ye said Ferry. And the farmer to keep it a Public House of entertainment."

---

* Doc. Hist. of N. Y., vol. iii., p. 422.

The ferriage rates were fixed as follows: "Every single person to pay for going over eight stivers in wampum, or a silver two-pence. Each person in company fower (4) stivers in wampum, or a silver penny—if after sunsett, double ferriage. Each horse or beast single, *one shilling;* in company, nine-pence. Each colt or calfe, three-pence. Each hog, eight stivers in wampum, or a silver two-pence. Each sheep, four stivers wampum, or a silver penny," &c.

This ferry was ordered to be sold or "demised to yᵉ fairest bidder."

From the above we perceive the cattle that crossed the ferry were landed at or near the "Slaughter-Houses," (previously noticed,) then located above Wall Street on the East River shore; as shown in a survey made of the north side of Wall Street in 1686, they "Have laid out yᵉ northeast side of Wall Street, beginning at yᵉ wester-most corner of yᵉ Butchers'Pen," the yard belonging to the Slaughter-Houses; and they are also so put down on the Rev. John Miller's plan of New York, printed in 1695.

This "public institution," or the slaughtering part, was ordered, on the 23d June, 1696, to be removed, and "no butcher or other person whatsoever doe slaughter any cattle of any kind, after yᵉ seventh day of July next." Captain Ebenezer Willson having previously (*May* 11) petitioned "for a grant for some land from the street to low-water mark on yᵉ west side of yᵉ house of Thomas Hooks for yᵉ building of a Slaughter-House," which was granted to him for "thirty years, and that yᵉ surveyors lay out yᵉ same." This location appears to have been "fronting to the East River at the east end of Queen (*Pearl*) Street," near the present Peck Slip. This fact, however, is more fully shown from the report on the petition of John Kelly, before the Common Council, October 11, 1720, in which he states:

"That the petitioner hath lately purchased from Richard Sarkett three water lotts contiguous, seventy-four foot wide, convenient for the present for the situacon of a Slaughter-House for Cattle. That the places where the two slaughter-houses of this City are now situated, by the increase of buildings & the number of inhabitants, are not only become offensive to the inhabitants, but dangerous to them and their children, being exposed often to the danger of mad oxen and doggs.

"That the three lotts of this petitioner are likewise convenient for the landing of *Black Cattle* by the Ferryman from the Island of Nassau, and that the petitioner is willing, at his own private charge, to erect and build upon his said lotts such convenient Sloughter-House as may serve all the Butchers of this Corporation, provided he may have a grant for the same for a reasonable term of years without increasing of the ffees." This was referred to a Committee consisting of Aldermen Andrew Marschalk, Jacobus Kip, John Roosevelt, John Cruger, and Philip Cortlandt, who reported on the following 3d December, "That wee find the said allegations to be true, and are humbly of opinion that the present Sloughter-Houses fronting the East River at the east end of Queen (Pearl) Street in the East Ward of this City, now or late belonging to the Widdow Cortlandt and Johannes Beekman, are becom a publick nuisance, and ought in a short time to be removed, in order more convenient and ornamental buildings may be erected there, and in that neighborhood, which now are retarded by occasion of the said Sloughter-Houses.

"We are also humbly of opinion that the place proposed by the petitioner, John Kelly, for the erecting Public Sloughter-Houses and Penn upon the East River of this City, a little to the westward of the now dwelling-house of Mr. John Deane in the said East Ward, is a convenient place for that use and service, being the freehold of the said John Kelly, and that the petitioner ought to have a grant to him, his heirs, executors, and administrators, for the erecting of *three* or more substantial and convenient Publick Sloughter-Houses at the place aforesaid, at his own proper cost, charge and expense, at which all persons whatsoever shall and may sloughter their neat cattle, paying to the said John Kelly or his assigns *one shilling* or the *tongue* of each neat cattle so sloughtered for the use of the said Sloughter-Houses and Penn & convenience for sloughtering the same in full of all fees, dues, and demands for so doing."

They further say, that the said grant " ought to be for the term of twenty-one years;" also " to be restrained from farming" the same "to any butcher whatsoever during this term;" also "to inclose a sufficient quantity of ground for a publick Penn or Pinfold, sufficient to hold and secure all neat cattle that shall or may be brought thereunto in order to be sloughtered at the said Sloughter-Houses, and shall and will supply, furnish & provide all necessary ropes, trees, and tackle suitable and convenient for the well and easy sloughtering and hanging up all cattle;" also to keep all " in good and sufficient repair, plight, and condition—well and sufficiently scoured & clansed."

To have them all built and regulated " on or before the first day of October next;" " the same shall be deemed & esteemed the Publick Sloughter-House of the said City of New York, & that no other Sloughter-Houses from thence forward shall be built & erected on the East River during the said term."

Perhaps these few facts in relation to the " Sloughter-Houses" of the olden time will not be so acceptable to the reader as some more interesting subjects. My answer is, they were public institutions—built and conducted for more than a century and a half by some of the first men of that day, several of whom have given their names to certain public streets, as Cortlandt, Beekman, Bayard, &c.; and withal, they are noticed or marked down on many of the early maps of the City in the most prominent form; and if they are an eye-sore or an evil, they are a necessary one, where people will be carnivorous.

A complaint was made against the ferry-master five years after, (1725,) through a petition, by a butcher named William Weblin, in which he states, "That he has received many abuses of late from James Harding, the ferryman, not only by abusive words, but several times by his carelessness has had his creatures destroyed and killed in bringing from the ferry to New York; the particulars of which would be too tedious to trouble this Honorable Court with all, and therefore your petitioner will confine himself to what has been transacted by said Mr. Harding, since the 26th of this instant month of July, on which day, about noon, your petitioner had *two* cattle brought to the ferry, and put into the common pen or yard where cattle always use to be put, in order to be brought over to the Slaughter-House in New York; on which day, in the afternoon, your petitioner went over to said Harding, and *treated him* handsomely, and pray^d him to bring said two cattle over by the first opportunity, which he said should be done; but said cattle not being brought over according to expectation, on Fryday, the 28th instant, your petitioner went over again, to know what was the reason the said cattle were not brought over in *four high waters*, at a time of calm good weather; and when your petitioner came, the said Harding told him he could not carry them now, nor could he tell when they could be carried over, so that your petitioner was forced to turn said cattle into a pasture after they had stood starving in a pen for the space of *four high tydes*, during which time your petitioner had no beef for the market but what he borrowed; and when your petitioner expostulated with this ferryman about his neglect herein, his answer was, that Jeremiah Calcutt was dead, and he would make all the butchers in New York *truckle* to him before Christmas; nor would he bring said cattle over, unless your petitioner would come over and help to load them.

"As your petitioner has lived in this city and followed the trade of a butcher for the term of about nine years, during which time the ferrymen have always thought it their duty to load and bring over the cattle that have come to the ferry for the butchers. And why the butchers shall be forced to goe and load the cattle themselves, now Jeremiah Calcutt is dead, more than they did before, your petitioner cannot perceive, nor will the circumstances of the trade allow your petitioner to hire hands and goe over to load the cattle when they come to the ferry. He wishes the Hon. Court to order the said ferryman to do his duty—as has always been the practice of the said ferry."

Two years after the butchers and other keepers of dogs were complained of for allowing their dogs to run loose about the city, and the authorities on the 17th of March notice it in the following manner: " Whereas the butchers and other inhabitants of this city superabound in a very great number of mischievous mastiffs, bull-dogs, and other useless dogs, who not only run at coaches, horses, chaises, and cattle in the daytime, whereby much mischief has ensued, but in the night-time are left in the streets of this city, and frequently bite, tear, and kill several cows and render the passage of the inhabitants of this city upon their lawful occasions very dangerous in the night-time through the streets thereof, by attacking and flying at them, and are become a publick nuisance and grievance," &c.

The butchers in general, from my first recollections, were notorious for keeping bull-dogs, and no doubt at this very early period they were used to assist in catching runaways or dangerous animals, which had become so from fright or other causes. Cattle raised on large ranges, where they almost run wild, are apt to be dangerous, and if penned into a small yard singly or almost alone, they will not allow any person to approach them, but turn and charge you at a full run. Such animals, when about to be haltered in *olden time*, were worried with bull-dogs, who seized them by the nose with a vice-like grip of their strong jaws, and by a muscular twist of the body, threw the animals or held them until they could be haltered.

Some stubborn animals would not step after being haltered, but lay down; then the bull-dog would soon arouse them, so that they can be pulled in. It is, however, many years since butchers have used bull-dogs for this purpose, although they were kept by some of the *bull-lies*, when it was the fashion for bull-baiting. The few which are now kept here are by sporting characters of the dog-fighting and rat-killing fanciers.

In the month of September, 1710, a committee was appointed to "cause the wall under the market-house at the south end of Broad Street, near the Dock, to be repaired." We then pass on to the 1st of June, 1714, when it was "Ordered, that the market-house by the Dock, at the south end of the Broad Street, be repaired;" which I find, from records in the Comptroller's office, cost £7 10s. Again, in December, 1719, a committee was ordered to " view the wall fronting the Dock which supports the Market-House at the south end of Broad Street, and take care that the same be put into some tolerable repairs, to preserve itt from falling this winter, in order it be better repaired in the spring;" which no doubt was done.

The next year the laws ordained "what places to be public markets;" among which were "the market-places at the *Great* and *Little Bridges;*" that is, the one at the *Great* Bridge was the "Custom-House Bridge Market," and the one at the *Little Bridge* the "Broad Street Market." Then also, in the boundaries of the South Ward, from the Charter, dated 1723, it includes "the market-house at the south end of the said (*Broad*) street."

Now let us look at the plan of New York, surveyed by James Lyne, in 1729. He places a building at the foot of Broad Street, which he calls *Exchange;* the laws, however, the next year call it "Market by the Long Bridge."

This Long Bridge was formerly the Little Bridge, which at this period had been widened and extended.

We here turn aside to notice a great rejoicing, which ended with great sorrow and death to several prominent citizens. It was a great fashion in "olden times," on great occasions—such as victories, birth-days of distinguished men, or the finishing of some important edifice or great work—to have an ox roasted whole, with barrels of liquor furnished to the inhabitants. From "Zenger's" *Weekly Journal*, of the 21st July, 1735, we learn that "on Wednesday last His Excellency, William Cosby, Esq., our Governor, caused an ox to be roasted whole on the new Battery, where he was attended by several gentlemen of distinction; the day was spent with firing and drinking of the loyal healths by a great many people, as is usual on such occasions. But the day ended with more real and sudden sorrow than we have known in this city within twenty-four years last past. For the last piece *(cannon)* unfortunately burst, and wounded three persons mortally, viz., John Hendrick Lymes, Esq., Sheriff of the City of New York; a fragment of the piece struck on the groin and thighs, and bruised him that he died within a few hours." One of the others was "Catharine Courtlandt, the only daughter of Philip Courtlandt, Esq., one of His Majesty's Council for this province; she had her skull fractured, so that she died within a few minutes after she received the hurt. She was about nine years of age."

This market-house, for many of its latter years, was used principally as a country market, and when vacant, the merchants took possession of it, where they transacted their selling, trading, or exchanging. Near by was the "Long Bridge," which had been

used by them as a place of meeting for about seventy years, and
was first established by Governor Lovelace, in 1669, in *order* that
merchants should meet "near the Bridge" (Long Bridge) on every
Friday, between the hours of eleven and twelve o'clock; and the
Mayor was ordered "to have the bell rung to congregate, and again
to disperse;" and also "to take care that they be not disturbed"
while in session.

This market-house was not noticed in the laws of 1737 as a public market-place; but the "*Gazette*" of July 24, 1738, refers to it in
an advertisement for the sale of property at Harlaem, as follows:
"On Saturday, the 2d of September next, at ten o'clock in the
morning, in the *Exchange Market-House*, near the 'Long Bridge,'
will be exposed to sale, by publick vendue, the plantation of the
late Captain Thomas Coddrington, containing about thirty acres of
land, besides two out-lots of about eight acres;" "all in the bounds
of Harlaem, in the outward of the City of New York."

Four years after, David Grim, on his map, marks it down with
the name I have adopted for it, viz., "Broad Street Market." Two
years later, an excellent old side-view map, or the "South Prospect
View of yᵉ flourishing City of New York," printed in London,
1746, now in the possession of the "Society Library," shows this
market-house, directly at the foot of Broad Street, but no reference
is given to it. A mistake, however, is made, by noticing the "Meal
or Wall Street Market-House" as the *Exchange*, (No. 15.) The
"Old Exchange" in Broad Street was not built, or commenced,
until the year 1752; and the intention, no doubt, was to represent
this old "Broad Street Market" as Lyne did, when he called it
"the *Exchange*," in 1729.

I find no further reference to it; and as it had stood more than
fifty years, I am inclined to think that about the period of 1746 it
was taken down.

"OLD SLIP MARKET."

1691. AMONG the proceedings which took place before the "Court,"
on the 15th of October, 1691, was that of designating where "Flesh-
Meat" shall be sold. The "Court" ordered "that there be two
market-places for Flesh-Meat: the one in the Broadway over against
the Ffort; the other under the Trees by the Slipp."

The first I have noticed as the "Broadway Shambles," and the other I will proceed first to locate. This "Slipp" is marked down on an old map as being near the present lower end of Hanover Square and *Old Slip*, where no doubt at that time stood several large shady trees, under which the country people coming from the ferry from Brooklyn, with their productions, were wont to stop and rest, sheltered from the sun. They were here met by the purchasing Burghers, and it soon became a market-place recognized by the authorities in the above "order."

The "Burger's" or "Slip Battery of Ten Guns," and also the Burger's Path, was near this spot, where the first *Slip* was made, or noticed as such, gave it the name of *Old Slip*—it being the oldest Slip.

This additional "Flesh-Market" was ordered no doubt in consequence of the rapid growth of this part of the city for several years previous, as this would appear to have been a reasonable supposition from the many improvements suggested by the authorities. One of which was the "ordering all the lotts from *Burger's Path* to the foot of the Hill, by Alderman Beekmans, *(Beekman Street,)* be exposed to sale;" and on the following 5th of December it was "ordered that the lotts lying between *Burger's Path* and the Block-House *(Wall Street)* be laid out into thirteen lotts, the first lott next to the *Slipp* to yᵉ *(be)* fifty foot in breadth, and the other twelve to yᵉ *(be)* each forty-two foot." These were all sold, and many of them were soon built upon, as well as many others which formerly belonged to the Government.

The rapid progress of the city was, however, checked for a period by what was then called the "Bread Famine." This took place in the year 1696, when the citizens, in the month of October, appealed to the authorities to assist them, in the following language: "Upon complaint of the inhabitants & poor of this city, that there is no bread to be bought to supply their wants, soe that they cannot subsist unless some speedy method be taken to furnish the same; and the bakers being summoned before this Board, doe complain that they have no *corne*, neither can gett any to purchase att a reasonable rate, whereby to occupy their trade in order to supply the inhabitants of this citty with bread as aforesaid. It is therefore ordered that yᵉ Aldermen and Assistants of each respective Ward within this Citty doe goe through their several Wards & make dilligent search and enquiry of what quantities of *flower*, wheat, and bread are in the same Ward, and make return thereof on Munday next att two of yᵉ clock in the afternoon, in order that effectual care be taken for to supply the inhabitants with bread."

At their next meeting (October 23d) it was ordered that a com-

mittee "joyn the Recorder to consult of such proper methods as may
be most effectual for the causing *corne* to be brought to this citty for
the releif of the inhabitants."

On the 17th of November following, the Mayor reported to the
Board, "that the inhabitants have made daily complaints for the
want of bread. That the Aldermen had made strict enquiry at
every house of what store of *corne* they had at that time; there did
not exceed the quantity of *seven hundred bushels;* upon which it was
taken into consideration what number of inhabitants was within this
citty, and what might be needful for their daily subsistense with
bread. Whereupon itt was computed that there was about *six thousand souls* within this citty, and that stock of *corne* would not be
sufficient for a week's maintenance."

"Thereupon this Board fell into consideration of what should be
the cause of soe great a scarcity, when lately there had been soe
plentiful a harvest, and did finde that the true and only cause did
proceed from yᶜ liberty & latitude that every planter had lately taken
of making his house or farme a markett for wheat, or converting the
same into flower by *bolting of itt,* and that under pretense of a priviledge they conceive they had obtained by virtue of a law made in
Genˡ Assembly." A committee was appointed to take measures to
have this law repealed, and they were successful with what was then
called the "Bolting Act."

This market-place soon became a successful one, visited by many
country people, and butchers who cut up and sold "flesh-meat,"
which no doubt afterwards gave it the name of the "Great Flesh
Market." Prior to the erection of a market-house, they protected
themselves from the stormy weather under their several temporary
sheds and tents until the prosperity and wants of the "inhabitants
of the neighborhood of *Burger's Path* asked leave to erect a market-
house at their own charge." This took place on the 8th of July,
1701, when the Board ordered that they have liberty to erect such a
house "on the vacant lotts of ground fronting the houses of Leonard
Huygen, and that late of Jacob Teller, for the conveniency and
accommodation of the public."

A statement was made showing the increase of cattle, and those
that were killed for the use of the city, in several of the previous
years. The proceedings of the 16th of July, 1698, show "A considerable increase of stock of cattle, and sould att double yᵉ price of
what they were formerly; and for instance, about fourteen years
ago, (1684,) there was not above *four hundred neat cattle* killed for
the service of the inhabitants of this citty, and now near *three thousand* head, besides sheep and other small cattle, which fully demon-
strates the increase of the trade."

The introduction of a landing-place for the ferry-boats was also established here; it was, however, chiefly for the landing of flour at certain tides. The lessee of the regular ferry, Dirck Benson, had got behind with his payments to the Corporation, who sued him, but they afterwards proposed terms of settlement, (in the Court held January 27, 1703,) by abating "£30 per annum, for the remaining term of the lease," if he would "land all flower brought over to the city in the ferry-boats att the *Slip* att *Burger's Path*, and also to land passengers and other commodities brought over *one tide* att the said *Slipp* at *Burger's Path*, and the other tide at ' Countess Key,' (*Fly Market;*) and if these terms were not agreed to, then the action now depending against him for the said rent be prosecuted to the utmost."

This arrangement of the ferry was, on the 1st of October, 1707, somewhat altered in the terms of the lease to James Harding; "that is to say, every Monday and Thursday, at Countess Key, every Tuesday and Fryday, at *Burger's Path*, and every Wednesday and Saturday, at the Dock Slip, near Col. Cortlandt's house, and at no other place whatsoever." Then, in the early part of the year 1722, the same was "demised and lett to ffarm to William Weblin, butcher, for the term of five years, at seventy-one pounds," but this arrangement was not completed.

The war with the French at this period (1705) found, as Smith says, "Our harbor being wholly unfortified; a French privateer actually entered it in 1705, and put the inhabitants in great consternation." They, however, soon began to prepare with fortifications, ship of war, and privateers; one of the latter, a brigantine, called the *Dragon*, commanded by Captain Guicks, carrying about 130 men, lay in the harbor preparing for sea; several of her crew being allowed on shore, "went on a spree," which ended in a riot and the death of several persons. The particulars we find noticed in "The Boston *News Letter*," October 1, 1705, (*dated New York, September* 24:) "On the 19th instant, about 10 at night, some privateers began a riot before the Sheriff's house of this city, assembled the sheriff at his door without any provocation, & beat and wounded several persons that came to his assistance, & in a few minutes the privateers tumultously met together in great numbers; upon which forces were sent out of the Fort to suppress them, and the Sheriff, Officers, and some men belonging to Her Majestie's ships made a body to do the same; but before these forces could meet with them, the privateers unhappily met *Lieut.* Wharton Featherstone-Hough and *Ensign* Alcock, (two gentlemen of the Hon. Col. Livesay's Regiment, that came in the Jamaica Fleet, who were peaceably going home to their lodgings,) and barbarously murdered the first, and greviously wounded the latter in several places in the head, and brusied his body; & after they had knock'd him down several times and got his sword, some of them run Lieut. Featherstone-Hough in at the left side thro' his heart, (as is supposed with Ensign Alcock's sword,) of which wound he immediately dyed. Just as the fact was done, the privateers were attacked by the Sheriff, Officers, and Seamen of Her Majestie's Ship, and some of the town, & in a short time were obliged to fly; several of both sides were wounded; some of the privateers were then taken prisoners, and several since, who were committed, & do believe will suffer according to law; the soldiers killed one of the privateers that was flying from them. One *Erasmus Wilkins* was apprehended on Saturday last & committed, and by the evidence 'tis believed he is the man that murdered Lieut. Featherstone-Hough; it would be too tedious to relate the particulars, but their insolence is beyond expression: this riot was chiefly acted by the privateers belonging to the Briganteen *Dragon*, Capt. Guicks, Commander."

The next year (1706) greater exertions are made for the defence of the city; the Mayor and Council petition Governor Cornbury on the 8th of May, stating " the iminent danger wee conceive the city to be in by an invasion of the common enemy," and " the vigorous defence by reason our fortifications are wholly out of repair." They wish them repaired, and "the making of others in convenient places; the mounting of artillery and the compleat arming of our inhabitants." The next meeting of the " Council," (14 May,) it was "ordered that what beams the carpenters shall use of the Widdow Helena Cooper's for the making of carriages for the mounting of the guns," " to be paid for by the city, as shall be appraised."

On the 11th of July following, an ordinance was passed compelling all the inhabitants, or their providing sufficient laborers, " to work att or upon the fortifications by equal terms & wards soe often as they shall have notice; to appear with a good spade, shovell, ax or pick, or other necessary tool or instrument."

The " Council" again petitioned (on the 22d July) to the Governor, saying, "We haveing received advice from Antigua that *four French privateers* are sayled out of Martineque for this coast, and also that Monsieur Deberville, with a strong squadron of ships of war, designs speedily to attacque this city and province. We therefore must humbly pray your Excell^cy that your Lordship would most favorably be pleased to lay an *embargo* in this port for such term as your Lordship shall judge requisite."

From the " Boston News Letter," August 5, (1706,) following, we again extract the news from New York, dated 29th July, which tells us that " Last week an embargo was laid here for 60 days, and all persons forbid all manner of labor, and all shops shut up until the fortifications of the city be finished, so that we have near 1,000 men at work every day." The next week after, the same paper says, " Our fortifications we hope will be compleat this week, and we shall have 100 cannon mounted in this city, besides the Fort, (*George,*) which is also put into very good repair & order."

The people, however, had no confidence in Governor Cornbury; he had deceived them before, when money, &c., were granted for the defence of the city, he appropriated to his own private use. Smith says, " We never had a governor so universally detested, nor any who so richly deserved the public abhorrence. In spite of his noble descent, his behavior was trifling, mean, and extravagant.

" It was not uncommon for him to dress himself in a woman's habit, and then to patrole the Fort in which he resided. Such freaks of low humor exposed him to the universal contempt of the people; but their indignation was kindled by his despotick rule, savage bigotry, insatiable avarice, and injustice, not only to the publick, but even his private creditors; for he left some of the lowest tradesmen in his employment unsatisfied in their just demands." However, the numerous complaints presented to the Queen obliged her to revoke his commission, and his creditors threw him into one of the jails of the City Hall, in Wall Street, until released by the inheritance obtained by the death of his father.* His successor, John Lord Lovelace, Baron of Harley, arrived here in the month of December, 1708, and before a period of six months had passed, he was laid into his grave, " from a disorder contracted in crossing the ferry on his arrival here."† The Lieut. Governor, Richard Ingolsby, was then placed in command, until his character and actions became known; who, like Cornbury, was dismissed from the office; and in 1710, we find Robert Hunter, " a man of wit and personal beauty," at the head as the Governor.‡

About this period, the Mayor, Jacobus V. Cortlandt, held several other public offices besides, which were attached to this high position, and among these was that of *Clerk of the Market*. In the latter office, he had been engaged in prosecuting several delinquent butchers, from whom his counsel or collector had recovered certain fines or penalties. This subject was brought before the Justices and Vestrymen on the 17th of June, 1712, when " Mr. (Thomas) George having acquainted this Board, that he has in his hands thirty pounds —— shillings, which he recovered of several butchers at the suit of Coll. Jacobus V. Cortlandt, which moneys he, the said Coll. Cortlandt, hath given to the use of the poor of this citty, and de-

* Dunlap's Hist. N. Y., p. 263, vol. i. † Smith's Hist. N. Y., p. 191. ‡ Ibid., p. 199.

sires this Board will order how he shall dispose thereof. Ordered, he pay the same to the Church Wardens of this city, for the use of the poor of this city, whose receipt shall be a sufficient discharge for so doing.

"Ordered, the Church Wardens lend Phillip Batten, butcher, *thirty shillings*, in order to go on with his trade, (he being reduced to great poverty by reason of his wife being delirious,) being an object of charity."*

In the year 1711, the war with the French had made it necessary for the authorities to take possession of and use all the public market-houses in the city to build battoes in, except this one at Burger's Path,† which then appeared to be the principal market-place, as it was more central and in the more thickly settled portion of the city. "Twenty ship and house carpenters (says Smith) were impressed into the service for their building, while commissions were appointed to purchase provisions and other necessaries, and empowered to break open houses for that purpose, and to impress men, vessels, horses, and waggons for transporting the stores." The following will give some idea of the prices that were paid for some kinds of these provisions:

		£.	s.	d.
"Good prime pork, per barrel,		3	10	0
Indian corn, per bushel,		0	2	6
Pease, do.		0	5	0
Buttock of beef, per pound, (smoaked,)		0	0	7
Cheese, do.		0	0	6."

After peace was concluded, which took place in the month of March, 1713, the prices of provisions became much reduced, and so remained until the hard winter of 1717, when a large portion of the country was covered with a deep snow, and supplies were stopped from many places, and again the price advanced.

The farmers in the Eastern States suffered severely, which is particularly described in "Lewis' History of Lynn." He says, "Two great storms on the twentieth and twenty-fourth of February covered the ground so deep with snow, that people for some days could not pass from one house to another. Old Indians of an hundred years said that their fathers had never told them of such a snow. It was from ten to twenty feet deep, and generally covered the lower story of the houses. Cottages of one story were entirely buried, so that the people dig paths from one house to another under the snow. Soon after, a slight rain fell, and the frost crusted the snow; and

* Records in the possession of G. H. Moore, Esq.
† See "Flatter's Barrack Market-Places."

the people went out of their chamber windows and walked over it. Many of the farmers lost their sheep; and most of the sheep and swine which were saved lived from one to two weeks without food. One man had some hens buried near his barn, which were dug out alive eleven days after.

"This snow formed a remarkable era in New England; and old people, in relating an event, would say that it happened so many years before or after the great snow."

Three years after, in the month of January, it is said, "on the 9th, 10th, 11th, and 12th instant, great numbers went over Hudson's River upon the ice from New York to New Jersey, since which the weather has been very warm, like the spring, and all the ice gone."*

In the spring of 1726, prices of provisions were noticed in *The New York Gazette*, on the 9th of May, as follows: "Pork, 55s.; Beef, 34 to 35s. per barrel; Flour, 11s. to 11s. 6d. per hundred; Fresh Beef in the market, 3d. ½ penny per pound, by the quarter, and 4d. per pound smaller pieces; and Pease, 4s. 6d. per bushel."

In the Laws of 1720, this market-place is noticed "as the market-house at Burger's Path," and we find eight years after it was still known by that name, when the Board gave the inhabitants "liberty to repair the *market-house at Burger's Path*." Again, in May, 1721, "John Brown, at Mrs. Beurk's, over against the 'market-house by Burger's Path,' sells European goods at very reasonable prices, and takes for pay Flour, Biskets, Beef, Pork, Gammons," &c.† Two months after, however, the name assumed the proper one, as we find in the same paper, "Thursday next, at nine in the morning, at the 'Old Slip Market,' will be exposed for sale, by publick vendue, goods of various kinds;" and Lyne's Map of this year, marks No. 9, "Old Slip Market," standing on a line of the present Pearl Street, with the rear next to the "Slip." It continues in the "papers" with its right name, although at times slip will be spelled with two p's in describing the residence (in 1734) of a "Book-binder, lives in Duke Street, *(formerly called Bayard Street,)* near the 'Old Slipp Market.'" "Looking-glasses, new silvered, and the frames plaine japan-éd; also, all sorts of Picktures made and sold, and all manner of painting work done. Also, Looking-glasses and all sorts of painters' coulers and oyl, sold at reasonable rates, by Gerardus Duykinck, at the sign of the two Cupids, near the 'Old Slip Market,' where you may have ready money for old looking-glasses;" and in 1736, "Stephen Bayard has Muscovada sugar to be sold between the *Old Slipp* and Koenties Markets."‡

From about the years 1725 to 1733 this market appeared at the

* Boston News Letter, February 1, 1720.   † N. Y. Gazette, 1729.   ‡ N. Y. Journal.

height of its prosperity, and it was then considered the best in the city; but in 1735 the "*Fly Market*" became its rival, as an equal number of stands were leased, as will appear under the head of "Fly Market," at that date.

This leasing of all the stands took place on the 10th of December, when the Market Committee reported that they had met and agreed with the following butchers for stands in the "*Market-House at Burger's Path:*"

" To Israel and Timothy Horsefield, 2 stalls, Nos. 1–2, at £22 0 0.

To Samuel Brown,	-	-	1	"	3	"	1 0 0.
To Samuel Hopson, -	-	- 1	"	4	"	3 0 0.
To Eliza Carpenter,	-	-	1	"	5	"	16 0 0.
To Widow Davis, -	-	- 1	"	6	"	1 0 0.
To Mich¹ Christopher Row,	1	"	7	"	3 0 0."

Israel Horsefield lived at Brooklyn near the ferry, where he had built several buildings, and in doing so, had no doubt by accident overstepped his bounds, and got upon the property of the Corporation; but was fortunate in securing a lease on the 26th February, 1735, " of that part of the wharfe and slaughter-house he has lately built and put upon the land of this Corporation, near the ferry at Brookland, at the annual rent of *five shilling.*" This part of the corporation's no doubt he purchased afterwards, and it became possessed by Israel, Junr., who advertised it for sale in the *New York Gazette and Weekly Mercury*, February, 1769, " consisting of a house and lot of ground, slaughter-house and barn, situate at Brooklyn Ferry, on Long Island."

The market-house, even with an increased number of stands, soon appeared too small, as the country people were crowded out, and caused many to stop at the "Fly," which was close by the ferry. This was a spur to the "inhabitants of the East Ward, near and adjoining the market-house, contiguous to the Old Slip, called Burger's Path, who applied to the Board on the 21st ——, 1736, through Alderman Walter, to enlarge the market-house at their own charge and expense," so that a part thereof be for the use of the country people. This enlarging did not tend to give much encouragement to business, as I find but five stands leased for one year in March, 1737, to the same persons, and Nos. 6 and 7 are not noticed.

Some of these butchers, with others of "*Fly*" and "Coenties Markets," were so unfortunate as to have negro slaves engaged in the "Great Negro Plot," which occurred a few years afterwards. This information is derived principally from Horsmanden's account, whose conclusion was, that these conspirators, both white and black, had designed to destroy the city by fire, and massacre the inhabitants; but fortunately, in consequence of a robbery having been committed some weeks before the appointed time, which was fixed on St. Patrick's night, (*March* 17,) 1741, and while the police and magistrates were engaged in tracing out the thieves, several fires occurred, of which the governor's house, the chapel, and other buildings in the Fort (*George*) were burnt to the ground. A few days after, the roof of Capt. Warner's house was found in flames, but was soon put out by the fire-engines: then followed the partial burning of the store-house of Mr. Van Zandt; then the cow stables, near Guick's, in the "Fly;" then at the house of one Ben. Thomas, next door to Capt. Sarly's; then the haystack standing near the Court-House and stables of Joseph Murray, Esq., in the Broadway; then at the house of Sergeant Burns, opposite Fort Garden; then at Mrs. Hilton's house, at the corner of the building next to the "Fly Market;" then at Col. Philips' store-house; and then the alarm which proceeded from the cellar of a baker near *Coenties Market*, which was all of a smother, and chips in a blaze, but was soon suppressed; added to all this, the evidence from the criminals, which had begun to be developed of this infernal plot, and the thoughts of the former conspiracy,* (1712,) all tended to create the most intense excitement among all classes of the citizens.

"At this time the City of New York contained a population of about twelve thousand souls, and of whom one-sixth were slaves."† So numerous were they, that it was thought they were more fully organized than was afterwards proven, and so strong was the feeling against them at first, that they were without defence; "all the counsel in the city were arrayed against them, and volunteered their services in behalf of the crown."

Some who had always born good characters, were deserted by their masters, who believed they were all guilty alike; many were persuaded to plead guilty, and throw themselves upon the mercy of the Court; and others, again, were convicted on the testimony of other negroes, who gave false evidence to save their own lives.

The two butchers, Timothy and Israel Horsefield, noticed as occupying stands Nos. 1 and 2, in this *market*, lived at Brooklyn, L. I., and, as it appears from the evidence, they had three slaves on trial, two of whom were found guilty, and their sentence was transportation. Mrs. Eliza Carpenter, who occupied stand No. 5, had two, one of which was burnt, and the other transported. Edward Kelly, of "Fly Market," had one transported; and Isaac Varian one also transported.

* See "Coenties Slip Market."   † Smith's Hist. N. Y., p. 438, 439.

It appears they had the city divided into two districts, and organized in two parties: one of which called themselves "Long Bridge Boys," who met at John Romme's in Broad Street; and the other, "Smith Fly Boys," who met at John Hughson's, living at the North River, where he kept a low place of resort, near the foot of (*now*) Liberty Street, in John Thurman's house. Hughson and Romme were white men, and were both engaged in this conspiracy: the former appeared to be the "ringleader;" and at a great meeting, where some forty or fifty negroes met at his house, he swore them all, "to burn and kill," every one to (set on) fire his master's house, "kill master and mistress, and then fire the Fort." "That when the city was on fire, the negroes were to meet at the end of Broadway, next to the *Fields*," (*Park*.) The following evidence from confession made, shows the fact of the slaves of the above butchers being interested: from *Pedro*, (Depeyster's slave,) "says, he went out one Sunday morning with *Mrs. Carpenter's* negro *Albany;* that as they went along the Broadway, they met with Mr. Sleydall's *Jack*, who was going to Comfort's for tea-water; that at the (*Fly*) market, near Mr. Delancy's house, they met two other negroes; that *Albany* asked them to go down to Hughson's, and drink with them; that they first drank cyder, then raw drams." Braveboy (*Mrs. Kierstede's*) says, "that some time last summer, *Carpenter's Albany* came to his mistress's house to bring meat, and called him into the yard, saying he wanted to speak with him, and then asked him whether he would join with them?" "Then *Albany* told him, he would help him to a gun to kill his master." "*Varian's Worcester* said, that in Christmas holidays, Lefferts' Pompey carried him to Hughson's, where were many negroes at supper; that they had punch, &c., and after supper, Hughson, his wife and daughter, swore to a plot against the white people, and that he (*Hughson*) swore most or all of the negroes then present, among whom the prisoner was sworn; that some swore by one thing, and some by another; there were present the following negroes, viz.: Lefferts' Pompey, *Kelly's London, Carpenter's Tickle,* and *Albany* and *Bastian.* Codweis's Cambridge asked *Horsfield's Cæser* and *Guy* about it, who both confessed they had been sworn at Hughson's, and told him, when the *work* was going forward at York, (meaning the city, as the Horsfields, or masters of these two negroes, were butchers, who lived over the water, Brooklyn, Long Island, opposite to this city,) they would give the prisoner notice, and take him over with them in a canoe to assist them. William Nail, servant to *Thomas Cox*, of the City of New York, butcher, (*in Coenties Market*,) being duly sworn upon the Holy Evangelists of Almighty God, deposeth and saith, that he, the deponent, having discourse with one *London*, a negro man slave, belonging to *Edward Kelly*, butcher, concerning negroes that were taken up on account of the plot, heard the said *London* swear, by G—d, that if he, the said *London*, should be taken up on account of the plot, he would hang or burn all the negroes in York."

One hundred and fifty-four negroes were committed to prison, of whom fourteen were burnt at the stake, (about half way in Augustus Street, between Duane and Pearl Streets;) eighteen hanged. *Cæser*, Varick's negro, was hung in chains on the Island, near the powder-house, not far from the corner of Centre and Pearl Streets. Seventeen were transported, and the rest were pardoned or discharged for want of proof.

Twenty white persons were committed, of which the following were executed: John Hughson, his wife Sarah, Margaret Kerry, and John Ury. Hughson was hung in chains, on the grounds now occupied by the "Catharine Market." In the month of October, the Common Council petition the General Assembly, praying that the negroes executed for the late conspiracy be paid for out of the revenue.

In the evidence shown in this "Great Negro Plot," the name of William Nail, *servant* to Thomas Cox, is noticed. The name *servant* was usually given to those of any age or sex who were unable to pay passage-money across the ocean, but instead of it, bound themselves for a period of time agreed upon to the shipping merchants, which time the merchant or captain had liberty to dispose of to the best advantage, on their arrival. At a later period, many such persons were known as "Redemptionists;" that is, they had power to redeem their persons by paying certain sums of money instead of labor or service.

The arrangements to obtain a home in the "New World" in this manner commenced at a very early period, and some cases are indeed quite novel. Among the earliest noticed, appears in the following law-suit which took place on the 27th of March, 1656. Gristie Rutzersen brings action against Dirk Van Schelluyne before the Court, when she states, "that she brought last year a girl, named Mayke Cornelissen, with her from Holland, and disbursed ff. 50 (florins) in Holland for her passage, on condition that if she did not remain here with her, she should pay her in place of the ff. 50 Hollands, ff. 100 here; and whereas, the maid hath been engaged by others, and deft. (Schelluyne) hath order to satisfy her; the pltff. requests that he be condemned to pay her the ff. 100. Deft. says, that Mayke Cornelissen hath left an act. with him, which he exhibits in Court, in which she acknowledges that ff. 50 were paid in Holland by the pltff. for her passage, for which she should serve here one year; but

in case she came to marry in the meantime, she should give her here
ff. 100 for the ff. 50 paid in Holland; and whereas, pltff. could not retain her in her service, she hired herself with another; maintains,
consequently, that she owes only ff. 50." The Court adjudges the
defendant to pay ff. 100.*

In the following month of July, "Loaurens And^r Van Boskerk, a
turner, here complained that Frederick Adryasen, Senr., his man, ran
away from last Sunday morning, without either words or reasons,
and he hired him in Amsterdam for 3 years, & he is not bound yet
more than 1 year; requests that he be constrained by order of the
Court to serve out his time."

We leave the "Records," and pass to a period when "Newspapers" were first printed on this continent, to which Boston must
claim the honor. In the *advertisements* which then appear, "few
and far between," we find these "servants" noticed. In the Boston
News Letter of September 3, 1705, we read: "Ran away at Boston,
about 3 weeks ago, from his master, Capt. Samuel Rymes, commander of the *Barbadoes* merchant, a *man-servant*, named Joseph
Ingerson, aged about 22 years, a well-set young man. Whoever
shall apprehend said *servant*, and him safely convey to his said master, shall have forty shillings reward and reasonable charges."

The same paper, dated 3d of June, next year, in an "editorial,"
thus shows the advantage of encouraging the importing of these
white *servants*, instead of black slaves: "By last year's bill of mortality for the Town of Boston, in No. 100, 'News Letter,' we are
furnished with a list of 44 negroes' death last year, which being computed one with another at £30 per head, amounts to the sum of one
thousand three hundred and twenty pounds, of which we would make
this remark: that the importing of negroes into this or the neigh-
bouring provinces is not so beneficial either to the crown or country
as white servants would be.

"For negroes do not carry arms to defend the country as whites do.

"Negroes are generally eye-servants, great thieves, much addicted
to stealing, lying, and purloining.

"They do not people our country as whites would do, whereby
we should be strengthened against an enemy.

"By encouraging the importing of *white men-servants*, allowing
somewhat to the importer, most husbandmen in the country might
be furnished with servants for 8, 9 or £10 a head, who are not able
to launch out 40 or £50 for a negro, the now common price.

"A man then might buy a white man-servant, we suppose, for £10,
to serve 4 *years*, and boys for the same price, to serve 6, 8 or 10

* Records.

years. If a white servant die, the loss exceeds not £10, but if a
negro dies 'tis a very great loss to the husbandman; three years' interest of the price of the negro will near upon, if not altogether, purchase a white man-servant.

"If necessity call for it, that the husbandman must fit out a man
against the enemy, if he has a negro, he cannot send him; but if he
has a white servant, 'twill answer the end, and perhaps save his son
at home.

"Were merchants and masters encouraged, as already said, to
bring in men-servants, there needed not be such complaint against
superiors impressing our children to the war; there would then be
men enough to be had without impressing.

"The bringing in of such servants would much enrich this province, because husbandmen would not only be able far better to manure what lands are already under improvement, but would also improve a great deal more that now lyes waste under woods, and enable this province to set about raising of harvest stores, which would
be greatly advantageous to the crown of England and this province.

"For the raising of hemp here, so as to make sail-cloth and cordage to furnish but our own shipping, would hinder the importing it,
or save considerable sums in a year to make returns for which we
now do, and in time might be capacitated to furnish England not
only with sail-cloth and cordage, but likewise with pitch, tar, hemp,
and other stores which they are now obliged to purchase in foreign
nations.

"Suppose the government here would allow forty shillings per
head, for five years, to such as should import every of these years
100 white men-servants, and each to serve 4 years, the cost would
be but £200 a year, and a 1,000 for the five years; the first 100
servants being free the 4th year, they serve the 5th for wages, and
the 6th there is 100 that goes out into the woods, and settles a 100
families to strengthen and barricade us from the Indians, and also
a 100 families more every year successively.

"And here you see that in one year the town of Boston has lost
£1,320 by 44 negroes, which is also a loss to the country in general,
and for a less loss, (if it may not improperly be so called,) for a
£1,000, the country may have 500 men in five years' time for the 44
negroes dead in one year.

"A certain person within these 6 years had two negroes dead,
computing both at £60 per head, to have served 24 years, at 4 years
apiece, without running such a great risque, and the whites would
have strengthened the country, that negroes do not. 'Twould do
well that none of those servants be liable to be impressed during

their service of agreement at their first landing. That such servants being sold or transported out of this province during the time of their service, the persons that buy them be liable to pay £3 into the treasury."

Some twenty years after Boston, New York began by publishing the N. Y. Gazette, in which we find, dated May 9, 1726, "The ship *Happy Return* is lately arrived at the City of New York from Dublin, with men and women *servants;* many of the men are tradesmen, as blacksmiths, carpenters, weavers, taylors, cordwainers, and other trades. Which *servants* are to be seen on board of said vessel laying over against Mr. Read's Wharf, and to be disposed of by John & Joseph Read, on reasonable terms."

Professor Kalm, on his arrival at Philadelphia, in 1748, in the ship "Mary Gally," Captain Lawson, says he went on shore with the captain, "but before he went, he (*the captain*) strictly charged the second mate to let no one of the German refugees out of the ship, unless he paid for his passage, or somebody else paid for him, or bought him." Of the various kinds of servants then employed, he further describes as follows: "The servants which are made use of in the English-American Colonies are either free persons, or slaves, and the former are again of two different sorts.

" 1. Those who are quite free, serve by the year; they are not only allowed to leave their service at the expiration of their year, but may leave it at any time when they do not agree with their masters. However, in that case they are in danger of losing their wages, which are very considerable. A man-servant who has some abilities, gets between sixteen and twenty pounds in *Pennsylvania* currency, but those in the country do not get so much. A servant-maid gets eight or ten pounds a year; these servants have their food besides their wages, but must buy their own clothes, and what they get of these they must thank their master's goodness for.

" 2. The second kind of free servants consists of such persons as annually come from Germany, England, and other countries, in order to settle here; most of them are poor, and have not money enough to pay their passage, which is between six and eight pounds sterling for each person; therefore, they agree with the captain that they will suffer themselves to be sold for a few years on their arrival. In that case, the person who buys them pays the freight for them; but frequently very old people come over, who cannot pay their passage; they therefore sell their children, so that they serve both for themselves and for their parents.

" They commonly pay fourteen pounds *Pennsylvania currency* for a person who is to serve four years, and so on in proportion.

"When a person has bought such a person for a certain number of years, and has an intention to sell him again, he is at liberty to do so; but he is obliged, at the expiration of the term of the servitude, to provide the *usual suit of clothes* for the servants, unless he has made that part of the bargain with the purchaser.

"The English and Irish commonly sell themselves for four years, but the Germans frequently agree with the captain before they set out to pay him a certain sum of money for a certain number of persons; as soon as they arrive in America, they go about and try to get a man who will pay the passage for them; in return they give, according to their circumstances, one or several of their children, to serve a certain number of years; at last they make their bargain with the highest bidder.

"3. The negroes or blacks make the third kind. They are in a manner slaves; for when a negro is once bought, he is the purchaser's servant as long as he lives, unless he gives him to another, or makes him free. Formerly the negroes were brought over from Africa, and bought by almost every one who could afford it. The Quakers alone scrupled to have slaves; but they are no longer so nice, and they have as many negroes as other people. The price of negroes differs according to their age, health, and abilities. A full-grown negro costs from forty pounds and upwards to a hundred of *Pennsylvania currency*."

We again turn to the N. Y. Gazette, to notice these "servants," who, it appears, occasionally *ran away* from their masters. We read that "William Fletcher, a bought servant, is run away from his master the 19th of last March, (1726,) and carried with him some paper-money belonging to his master. Whoever can apprehend said *servant*, or discover by letter where he is, so that he may be apprehended, shall have five pounds paid by the collector of His Majesty's Customs in New York. Or if he will return and give security for his good behaviour, he shall be forgiven. He had on when he went away a dark-colored kersey coat, with brass buttons and braid, with duroy; has leather breeches, short dark hair; by trade a brush-maker; pretends to be a turner; he makes mops, makes, and mends bellows."

Four years after, 11th of May, 1730, in the same paper, is the notice of a runaway "servant-man," which, from description, would appear to have been a useful mechanic. "Ran away from Nicholas Mathiessen, of the City of New York, brewer, one servant-man, named Henry Fisher, about 26 years of age. He is by trade a house-carpenter, a mason, and a pump-maker; some time past he lived with Mr. Hold in this city, brewer. Whoever can take up said *servant-man* and bring him to his master, or secure him and give notice, so that his master can have him again, shall have five pounds reward, and all reasonable charges paid."

Another, at a later period, is also worthy of notice, and reads, " Ran away from Doctor William Rand, of Boston, on the third day of July last, an indented German servant-man, named George Ducart, about 22 years old; is well set, of a brown complexion, and has brown hair. He took with him a suit of blue clothes, with metal buttons, a pair of cotton breeches, ozenbrigs frock and trowsers, and yarn stockings. He also took from his master a silver-hilted sword, a cross-cut saw, and a fine French gun. He is supposed to be gone towards Philadelphia, but 'tis said has been lately seen in New York, in the employ of a butcher. Whoever takes up said servant, and secures him in goal, shall have three pounds reward, paid by the printer of this paper; or returned to Boston to his master, three pistoles reward, and all reasonable charges."*

The manner of disposing of the unexpired time of these servants, in case of death or otherwise, is shown by the following: " On Thursday, the fifth day of August next, will be exposed to sale, by way of public vendue, the times of two men and one woman servant, and several other things belonging to the estate of His late Excellency Governor Montgomerie." On the following 11th of October, "a very good, handy servant *girl's time of six years*, to be disposed of; enquire of the printer hereof."† Advancing forty years, the " N. Y. Journal," June 27, 1771, says, " *Twenty-three months* of the time of an indented *servant-woman*, named Hannah Scott, is ' to be sold for *eight pounds;*' inquire of Samuel Bayard, opposite the Old English Church." " Rivington's *N. Y. Gazetteer*," July 22, 1773, " *Servants* and *Redemptioners*.—A few boys and girls, men and women, on board the ship *Needham*, William Chevers, commander, just arrived from *Newry*, whose freights are payable to the captain, or to William Neilson." In the same paper, on the 29th of July following: " To be sold, upwards of four years' time of an English indented *servant*, a *young man* about twenty years of age; he has been used to accompts, and writes a very good hand." After the Revolution, we find in " The Daily Advertiser," May 25, 1786, noticed, " To be disposed of, the time of *two German Redemptioners*, man and woman; they are likely, healthy, and strong, and have four years and a half to serve; enquire of the printer."

We turn back to this now ".Old Market-House," and find two *items* noticed in relation to it in an *editorial* of the N. Y. Gazette, June 17, 1754, which says, " The 'Old Slip Market,' at the foot of Smith Street, which for a long time has remained in a very ruinous

* N. Y. Gazette, Sept. 25, 1752.　　　　　† Ib., July 26, 1731.

condition, is, by order of the Mayor and Corporation, now repairing, having a good stone foundation already placed and a strong
boarded floor preparing for the same; and will in a very little time,
from the close application of the workmen, be in an extraordinary
good condition to receive both city and country produce. We are
told that the front part (if not the whole) of the market is to be re-
shingled." Then follows, "At the aforesaid market, on Friday last,
was exposed to sale the largest veal of its age that has been known
for many years to be brought into our market. It was but six weeks
and four days old, and bred at Woodbridge, Rahway, in the Jerseys,
and was sold for 9 shillings the quarter, one of which weigh'd upwards of 30 pounds."

On the first of November following, the market-house appears to
have been finished, when a committee was appointed " for the letting
of the sellars under the ' Slip Market,' for the use and benefit of this
Corporation."

As late as 1762, the Laws designate it as " the Market-House at
Old Slip, commonly called Burger's Path ;" but whenever noticed
in the press, it is usually found with its proper name, used as a
" guide-post," in advertising somebody's wares, and very seldom in
an editorial. One of an unfortunate occurrence which happened to
one of the butchers is thus noticed in the Gazette of July 3d, 1766:
" Mr. Giles Cooper, a butcher of the ' Old Slip Market,' *partner of
John Foster, another butcher*, fell from his horse, between Hamstead
and Jamaica, Long Island, last Thursday (27th ult.) afternoon, and
broke so many of his bones that he died next morning."

Occasionally meat and other thieves visited the markets for the
purpose of procuring a good dinner, without paying the current coin,
and occasionally they were caught; when, if they did not willingly
pay, they received a *coin* " well laid on," which would do some of the
light-fingered gentry now-a-days some good; but in those days, there
were no " shysters," either judges or lawyers, who would like to divide their plunder or run the risk of receiving some of the same sort.
Not only were men publicly whipped, but women too. In the month
of September, 1756, the N. Y. Mercury says, " This day, between the
hours of nine and eleven, Mrs. Johanna Christian Young, and another
lady, her associate from Philadelphia, being found guilty of grand
larceny, at the Mayor's Court, last week, are to be set on two chairs
exalted on a cart, with their heads and faces uncovered, and to be
carted from the City Hall, to that part of the Broadway near the
new English Church, from thence down Maiden Lane, then down
the Fly to the Whitehall, thence to the Church aforesaid, and then
to the Whipping Post, where each of them are to receive 39 *lashes,*
to remain in goal for one week, and then to depart the city."

The pay of the "Publick Whipper," some twenty years before this took place, is noticed in the following entry, dated 15th January, 1736: "To Edward Breuwen, the public whipper of this city, £2 10, in full for 1 q^{rs} sallarry, & also the sum of 15s. for setting in the pillory & whipping through't the Town, at a cart's tail, one Patrick Bulter for issueing contrefetted dollors," &c.*

The pay of this "publick" officer was very much increased in 1751, as no doubt the duties of the office had become more onerous and arduous to the professed office-seeker, which caused an advertisement as follows: "The Public Whipper of the City of New York, being lately dead, if any person inclines to accept that office, with *twenty pounds* a year, he may apply to the Mayor, and be entered."†

A few years after, another mode of punishing criminals is noticed in the same paper, January 25, 1768, as follows: "One John Clayton Morris was committed to goal of this city for *sheep stealing;* it seems he had successively stole four or five, which he killed, and retailed in the markets. On a search, the skins were found in his possession. He was tried last week at our Supreme Court, and found guilty, but had the *benefit of the clergy* granted him; was burnt in the hand, and discharged."

The next year, (1769,) on the 14th of September, the "Chronicle" says, "On Tuesday last William Smith and Daniel Martin, the former for stealing a quarter of lamb, and the latter for stealing fiddle-strings, received 15 lashes each at the usual place of flagellation."

A few days after, Richard Ely, for attempting to defraud and cheat, "was exalted on a wooden horse in a triumphal car, with labels on his breast; after which he was conducted to the public whipping-post, where he received a proper chastisement."

We find the counterfeiter was more severely dealt with, as the following will show. The same paper on the 15th of May, same year, says, "On Thursday last, one John Jubeart was committed to goal, for passing false dollars. Upon examination before Alderman Gautier, he said that he was born upon Staten Island, and followed the business of a tinker. There was a millinix found upon him, and an instrument which he said he used to straiten gun-barrels. He had passed some of the bad dollars in this city, which were brought in and delivered to the Alderman. Upon his being detected and threatened to be carried before a magistrate, he endeavored to make his escape, and went into the 'Old Slip Market,' where he buried some dollars among a parcel of rubbish, which was taken up by some people who had observed him, and produced at his examination.

"The public are desired to observe, that the mounts upon the side

* Records.   † N. Y. Gazette, March 4, 1751.

of these false dollars, instead of being raised, are indented, and the millinix upon the edges open, and distinguishable from a genuine Spanish dollar."

On the 3d of August he was found guilty, and received sentence of death, to be hanged on the 23d; but was respited until the 6th of September, " when he was executed at ' stone fence,' near the city."

The gold and silver money, although scarce, gave considerable trouble among the traders, who sometimes differed about its valuation; some of it was either much worn, or had been lessened of its weight by the dishonest.

The question of its valuation came up before the Chamber of Commerce on the 3d of October, same year, (1769,) when " it was unanimously agreed, that all the members will receive and pay the undermentioned gold and silver coins at the following rates, and their lesser denominations in the same proportions, viz.:

	£.	s.	d.
" A *Johannes*, weighing eighteen penny-weights, for -	6	8	0
A *Moidore*, weighing six penny-weights and eight grains, for - - - - - - - - - -	2	8	0
A *Caroline*, weighing six penny-weights and eight grains, for - - - - - - - - - -	1	18	0
A *Spanish Doubloon*, or 4 pistole pieces, weighing seventeen penny-weights and eight grains, for - - -	5	16	0
A *French Pistole*, weighing four penny-weights and five grains, for - - - - - - -	1	8	0
An *English Guinea*, weighing five penny-weights and six grains, for - - - - - - - - -	1	17	0
A *French Guinea*, weighing five penny-weights and five grains, for - - - - - - - - -	1	16	0
A *Chequin*, weighing two penny-weights and five grains, for - - - - - - - - - -	0	14	6
An *English Crown*, and also a French Crown, cast -	0	8	9

An *English Shilling*, 1s. 9d.; a Pistareen, 1s. 7d.

" That for every grain any of the above specified gold coins shall weigh less than the above respective weights, four-pence must be deducted therefrom. (Signed,)   ANTHONY VAN DAM, Sec'y."

The paper currency was also a source of trouble to the citizens; the principal part in circulation was Jersey money, which appeared to rank higher than New York bills, as will be shown from the proceedings of the Chamber of Commerce, March 3d, 1772. At this meeting William McAdam stated, " Soon after the establishment of this society, I proposed to your consideration, whether it was for the interest of the community that Jersey paper-money should pass in this province higher than it is taken for in the Treasury of the province of New Jersey. The loss and inconvenience arising to the traders in this city, from the present practice of passing Jersey money for more than its acknowledged value by their own Legislature, will, I hope, plead my excuse for receiving my proposal. That this Corporation may enter into an agreement to fix a time when they will no longer depreciate their own currency by accepting that of another above par.

"I therefore propose that a time be fixed that this Corporation do agree to pay and receive Jersey money at the same rate it is received and paid in their own treasury."

This proposition was referred to further meetings; however, on the 5th of November following, a resolution was passed, "that it be received on the same terms that it passes for in New Jersey; that is to say:

"A bill of £6 proclamation money for $16, or £6 8 N. Y. currency,
A bill of £3   "   "   8, or 3 4   "
A bill of £1 10   "   "   4, or 1 12   "
A bill of 15s.   "   "   2, or 0 16   "

and in like proportion for bills of a less denomination," which was to take place "from and after 3d of September following, (1773.")

This resolution was, however, rescinded, in consequence of its unpopularity, at a meeting held on the following 7th of December.

"Rivington" came out with an editorial on the 20th January, 1774, saying, "Jersey Bills are now, in the general course of trade, restored to the old standard at which they were ever current in this province, viz.: Bills of *one shilling*, at *thirteen pence;* those of *one pound ten shillings*, at *thirty-two shillings* and *sixpence*, &c. At these rates they are freely taken, either for goods, or to purchase the best Bills of Exchange in our city."*

From the following advertisements, we glean some further facts relative to the currency of that period: "Jacob Remsen has for sale besides, beef, pork, flour, and bread," "and a parcel of 'wampum,'† (or *Indian currency*.)" "Lost or mislaid, on the first of this inst., in the 'Oswego (*Broadway*) Market,' 3 thirty shilling Jersey Bills; one 6 and 6 penny do., 2 18 penny do., in a blue paper. Two dollars reward, and no questions asked; it being lost by a poor man, and the money not belonging to him."‡ The next refers to counterfeit money. "The public are hereby notified that there are now passing among us a number of counterfeit Jersey twelve shilling bills, dated December 31, 1763, signed *Johnson, Smith,* and *Skinner.* They are

* Gazetteer.   † "Gazette and Weekly Post Boy," March 13, 1766.
‡ N. Y. Mercury, September 14, 1767.

printed with common types, but so badly executed as to be easily discovered on close inspection. Twelve shilling bills made out of three shilling bills have also appeared in this city lately."* "Lost or stolen, last Monday, between the North River and 'Coenties Market,' a worked pocket-book lined with read; had in it cash, 1 bill New York currency, old emmission; 2 of forty shillings ditto," &c.†

The next will show the ridicule, as also the value of a Congress bill, by the royal editor "Rivington," in his "Royal Gazette," December 22d, 1779: "Monday se'night was offered for public sale, at the Coffee-House, a Congress bill of 70 dollars; the first bidder offered three shillings New York currency for it, the next 6d. more, and it went on at 6d. more till 6s. 6d. The bidders began then with coppers, and came up to 7s. and 3 coppers; at last they offered farthings, and the 70 dollar bill was knocked off for eight shillings and three-pence half-penny."

After the "Revolution," we find "Indian money" yet for sale: the N. Y. Packet, May 11, 1786, gives notice to "any person desirous of purchasing a quantity of Indian Corn, may be supplied by applying to Nicholas Hoffman & Son, No. 12 Little Dock Street, where also may be had a quantity of *black and white wampum*, pipes and shells."

In the preparations for the *Revolution*, the city was laid out into districts or company beats: No. 20 is noticed as "beginning at **Mr.** John Siemons', fronting the corner of the *Old Slip Market*, running down to the East River; then from said Siemons' along Queen Street to the corner of Smith Richards, and then down King Street to the East River, taking in Dock and Water Streets below." This beat was commanded by Oliver Templeton and Garret Kettletas."‡

The next year, this *market* is noticed in connection with a horrid murder, which took place near by it, which appears in the "Penn**a** Evening Post," and reads, "On Sunday last, July 7, 1776, a number of felons, confined in the New Goal, attempted to escape. The ringleader, it seems, is one Armstrong, a murderer, of whom we have the following account, viz.: That he was a deserter from the Regulars at Boston, and entered himself in one of our Rifle Companies before that place; that he was a remarkable wicked, disorderly, desperate fellow ; that some months ago, soon after the arrival of the army from Boston, he broke into the house of Mr. Jacob Pozer, at Whitehall, and took from thence all his wearing apparel; same night he went into the house of Mr. James Meldrum, at the (*Old*) 'Slip Market,' when most of the family were in bed; that a young woman of the house asked his business, and desired him to walk out,

<hr>

* N. Y. Journal, April 19, 1770.   † Gazette, March 23, 1776.
‡ Prov. Congress, August 22, 1775.

which he refused, and attempted to take hold of her, when she threatened to scald him with hot water from a tea-kettle, and endeavored to leave the room; that he followed her and struck the edge of a tomahawk into her skull, of which she instantly died; that he then rushed out of the house, was pursued by the men of the house and others, who, by the assistance of the watch, secured him. That at the last Supreme Court, he was brought on his trial for the murder, but there not being a jury to be had, he was remanded till the next session; that having, with a number of confederates, formed a conspiracy to escape, on Sunday afternoon he fired a pistol at the sentry, which luckily missed him; that he seized the sentry's gun and knocked him down with it, and then wrenched a sword from the hands of Mr. Sheriff Roberts, who was endeavoring to quell the mutiny, just going to plunge it in his body, when the sergeant of the guard saved him, by shooting the villain through the head."

The days of prosperity of this lingering old market-house appear at that time to have been drawing to a close, as I find it but seldom noticed; although as late as the year 1778, it appears to have been in existence, as we learn from Holt's N. Y. Journal, August 24th, where it was noticed in connection with a very large fire as follows: "The fire began on Monday morning about 1 o'clock, the 3d inst., at the house of Mr. Stewart, on Cruger's Dock, (*now Front Street;*) that it consumed all the houses between 'Coenties' and the 'Old Slip Market,' from the water-side to Dock (*Pearl*) Street." Another account says, the "fire broke out in the store of Mr. Jones, ship chandler, on Cruger's Wharff, and, notwithstanding the utmost efforts of the Navy, Army, and inhabitants, soon consumed all the buildings on the east, south and west end of said wharff, and every house on the south side of Little Dock (*Water*) Street. The street being narrow, the flames soon communicated to the north side of Little Dock Street, and consumed the whole (five houses excepted) at the west end. The fire soon caught the back buildings in Dock Street, and burnt every house to the east of Mr. Isaac Low's, as far as the Old Slip, and three opposite the Slip."* The next issue states those who suffered from loss, as follows: "Col. William Bayard, 6 houses and store that rented for £520, (this worthy gentleman suffered greatly in the fire of September, 1776.) Messrs. John and Henry Cruger, 6 houses; Mr. Gerardus Duyckinck, 7 houses; Mr. Peter Mesier, 2 dwelling-houses, (this family and their relations have lost in the course of 23 months no less than 15 houses and stores, some of them large and elegant buildings,) and Mr. David Provoost, 4 houses, and 2 pulled down; Capt. Thomas Brown, 4 houses; Mr. Varack, 1 house;

* N. Y. Gazette, August 3, 1778.

estate of Mr. Andrew Myer, 1 house; Mr. Henry Van Vleck, 1 house;
Mr. Samuel Schuyler, 2 houses; Mr. Thomas Doughty, 1 house; Mr.
Isaac Low's house, and that of Mr. Lawrence Kortwright, adjoining,
greatly damaged; Capt. Deale, 2 houses; Mr. Edmund Seaman, 2
houses; Mr. Andrew Breasted, 3 houses; Mr. Humphrey Jones, 1
house; Dr. Van Solingen, 1 house; Mr. Richard Ten Eyck, baker,
1 house; Mr. Wandelham, 1 house; Mr. James Wells, a house and
2 stores; Mr. Benjamin Moore, 1 house; Mr. Benjamin Davis, 1
house; Mrs. P. De Lanceys, 1 house; Mrs. Ten Eyck, 2 dwelling-
houses and several stores."

Another account of this fire is taken from a letter, dated at " Camp
at the White Plains, August 8, 1778," which says, " Yesterday came
out from thence (*New York*) two Hessian officers, (who deserted,) left
the city about 8 o'clock in the evening, the 6th inst., and passed
King's Bridge about one in the morning.   One of them, a handsome
young fellow, whose brother is aid-de-camp to Gen. Clinton, tells me
he saw the fire.   That it began in a house filled with king's stores;
68 houses and a vast quantity of stores, amongst which 30,000 blankets
or pairs of blankets, I think the latter; 10,000 suits of cloaths, and
a great deal of provisions, computed at four weeks' supply."*

David Grim says, in addition, " The cause of so many houses
(about 300) burned at this time, was the military officers taking the
ordering and directions of this fire from the firemen; the citizens
complained to the Commander-in-Chief, who immediately gave in
general orders, that in future, no military man should interfere
with any fire that may happen in the city."

The Major-General commanding, in a proclamation, says, " Many
of the inhabitants suspected that this fire was not the effect of accident, but design;" which induced him to offer a reward of *one hundred guineas* on conviction of the offenders.   This amount was increased by a somewhat notorious member of the law, *(John Coggil
Knapp,)* who occasionally showed some outward liberality, but
whose reputation was not of the best.   He promises an additional
reward of *twenty guineas*, upon the same terms as set forth by the
major-general commanding.

This large fire was followed the next day with another calamity,
thus noticed: " Last Tuesday afternoon, about one o'clock, during
a heavy rain accompanied with thunder, the lightning struck the
Ordnance Sloop Morning Star, lying off the Coffee-House, *(Wall
Street,)* in the East River, with 248 barrels of gunpowder on board;
it produced a most tremendous explosion.   A number of houses were
unroofed, many windows broke, and some furniture demolished by

* Penna. Packet, August 15, 1778.

the blast; the effects of which were similar to an earthquake. Happily there was only one man in the vessel when the accident happened,"[*] who perished; the other part of the crew being on shore, fortunately escaped.

At this period an extract of a letter says, "The inhabitants are most distressed at their present situation, and a vast many want to take their chance in the country, but cannot obtain permission."[†] Their situation continued to grow worse, and in the long, severely cold winter of 1779–80, caused an inefficient supply of both provisions and fire-wood. "Fuel was so scarce *(says a writer)* that garden fences, old sheds, &c., were taken down to supply the want of cord-wood. Provisions were as scarce as fuel. Everybody, except the rich and the dissolute, was put upon short allowance. Potatoes were sold for a guinea per bushel! while biscuits, made of oatmeal, as coarse and containing as little nourishment as ground straw, were served out to the (British) troops. Early in the spring the Cork Fleet arrived, and brought provisions in abundance. Fine rose butter was sold immediately at 2s. 2d. per lb., and almost everybody was soon relieved and made comfortable."[‡]

No doubt among the "old sheds," &c., this then old and unused market-house was torn down and taken for fire-wood, as I find no further notice of it.

"COENTIES SLIP MARKET."

1691. THE establishment of this market-place took place, no doubt, from the fact, that after the "Great Dock" had been made, it excluded many of the fishing craft from landing at that old place, and, of course, changed their location above the dock. There the large vessels could lay in a well-protected cove, and the smaller ones were drawn upon the beach or strand near the attractive public-house, kept many years before by Mary Polet, commonly known as *Long Mary.*

The first notice in the "Records" of the establishment of this noted market-place was on the 15th of July, 1691, when the authorities designate where *Flesh Meat* shall be sold, and adds, "Fish to be brought into the dock, over against the City Hall, or the house that *Long Mary* formerly lived."

* N. Y. Gazette. August 10, 1778.　　† Penna. Packet, August 15, 1778.
‡ Pamphlets, No. 238, p. 57, H. Society.

Long Mary must have been quite a character in her day, as I find her name often noticed, as early as the year 1671. In that year a committee was appointed " to take a view of the corner waal wch the Towne is to make before the house of *Long Mary's;*" and a few months after, " the Court do allow to the karmen, for the work done for the Towne in filling up the Wharfe before *Long Marie's*, eight stivers per load" for gravel. No doubt her person and well-kept house attracted the attendants at the City Hall, the fishermen and others, who resorted there, and being very tall, she acquired the name of *Long Mary* with her numerous visitors.

The old Stadt House, or City Hall, stood near by on the line of Pearl Street, opposite the Coenties Slip, which fact is well authenticated. It was originally built for a large City Tavern, of which parts were used by the officers of the W. I. Company; soon after it became known as the State House or City Hall, where the Schout Burgomasters and Schepens held their sessions; then, at a later period, the Mayor, Recorder, and Aldermen, with the Courts of Justice and Prisons; and near this *market-place*, on the shore, were many of the necessary implements of punishment. We find on the 20th of October, 1691, that it was "Ordered, that the Sheriff immediately cause a ducking stoole to be built upon the Wharf before the City Hall, and goe to the Treasurer for his pay."

This market-place having been established for the exclusive sale of fish, the fishermen usually sold from their boats and canoes on the few market-days then allowed, except in their fishing seasons, when they provided sheds or other covering, while salting and laying up *stores* for the inhabitants; and the business increased so fast that it became soon after known as the "Great Fish Market."

We find at this early period the various kinds of fish were usually very plentiful and cheap, particularly shell-fish, which were caught in abundance along the shores in every direction. So quiet was the harbor, that whales came up to the city and visited both the East and North Rivers. Several were taken near the city at different intervals, as will be shown, with several other interesting facts connected with the subject of fish. In another part of this work is noticed the description given by Van der Donk of the stranding of two whales up the North River. From the " Boston News Letter," dated February 24, 1707, we find, " Last week a whale, about 40 feet long, was struck a few miles to the eastward of this city, and afterwards passed thro' the harbour, and was killed in the Hudson River and brought down hither, where she is exposed to view." Then, in an address made by Lord Cornbury to the Board of Trade, in July, 1708, he says, " The quantity of train oyl made in Long Island is uncertain; some years they have much more fish than others; for example, last year they made four thousand barrils of oyl, and this season they have not made above six hundred: about the middle of October they begin to look out for fish; the season lasts all November, December, January, February, and part of March: a yearling (*whale*) will make about forty barrils of oyl, a stunt or whale two years old will make sometimes fifty, sometimes sixty barrils of oyl, and the largest whale I ever knew of in these parts, yielded one hundred and ten barrils of oyl, and twelve hundred weight of bone. There might be good improvement made in the fishery of codfish & mackeril; but fish of several sorts is so plenty in the river and bay before the city, that our people will not take the pains to go to sea."*

Samuel Mufford also gives interesting information in his testimony on the whale fishery in 1716, when he says, "It hath been a custom for above 60 years (several years before New York was subjected to the crown of England) for their Majesties' subjects on the east end of Long Island, then belonging to Connecticut Colony, to go out upon the seas adjacent to their land, six men in a small boat, to take and kill whales and other fish, and the captors to have all they killed brought on shore with wind and sea."† There also appears at an early period, an "Agreement made the 4th of January, 1669, between yᵉ Whale Companies of East and South Hampton. If any Companie shall find a dead whale upon the shore, killed by yᵉ other, a person bringing the news to bee well rewarded. And if one Companie shall find any whale so killed at sea, they shall endeavor to secure them and have one-half for their pains, and any irons (*harpoons*) found in them to bee returned to yᵉ owner."‡

In the year 1721, a proposition was made by Josiah Quincy to supply the New York markets with fresh fish. He presents a petition to the Corporation on the 8th July, 1721, " praying for land at or near Kingbridge to erect a fishery, with liberty to fish in the river at that place; and proposes to supply the markets at New York with fish very fresh and at very easy rates, and in payment, rendering therefore yearly, on every fourteenth day of October, to this Corporation *a good dish of fresh fish.*"§

The "Journal of the General Assembly" shows *an Act* was passed, in the month of April, 1726, "to entitle *Lewis Hector Piot De Langloiserie* to the sole fishery of porpoises in the Province of New York, during the term of ten years." The length of this gentleman's name no doubt was taken in consideration, when the length of time was given to him for this value(less)able right, that he might retire on

---

* Doc. Hist., vol. v.   † Doc. Hist. N. Y., vol. i., p. 372.
‡ Thompson's L. I.   § City Records.

the proceeds, and be no longer doomed to sign his *name* to the many documents called for in that business.

An intelligent writer gives a good article on fish and oysters, which is found in the "Independent Reflector, November 22, 1753;" he says, "Tho' we abound in no one kind of fish sufficient for a staple, yet such is our happiness in this article, that not one of the colonies affords a fish-market of such a plentiful variety as ours. *Boston* has none but sea-fish, and of these *Philadelphia* is entirely destitute, being only furnished with the fish of a fresh-water river. *New York* is sufficiently supplied with both sorts. Nor ought our vast plenty of oysters to pass without particular observation; in their quality they are exceeded by those of no country whatever. People of all ranks amongst us, in general, prefer them to any other kind of food. Nor is anything wanting. save a little of the filings of copper, to render them equally relishing, even to an English palate, with the best from *Colchester*. They continue good eight months in the year, and are, for two months longer, the daily food of our poor. Their beds are within view of the town, and I am informed that an oyster-man, industriously employed, may clear *eight* or *ten* shillings a day. Some gentlemen, a few years ago, were at the pains of computing the value of this shell-fish to our province in general. The estimate was made with judgment and accuracy, and their computation amounted to ten thousand pounds per annum. Their increase and consumption are since very much enhanced, and thus also their additional value in proportion. I confess it has often given me great pleasure to reflect, how many of my poor countrymen are comfortably supplied by this article, who, without it, could scarcely subsist, and for that reason beg to be excused for the length of this reflection on so humble a subject, tho' it might justly be urged to the honour of oysters, that, considered in another view, they are serviceable both to our king and country."

Following up the taking of whales, we find in the N. Y. Gazette, December 11, 1752, says, "Last Saturday a whale, forty-five feet long, ran ashore at Van Buskirk's point at the entrance of the *Kills* from our bay, when being discovered by the people from Staten Island, a number of men went off and killed him, and may now be seen at Mr. John Waters', at the Ferry-house on Staten Island."

Then the same "paper" at a later period, (April 13, 1756,) says, "On last Tuesday, 5,751 shad were caught at one draught on the west side of Long Island." Enormous!

"We hear," says the Gazette and Weekly Post Boy, September 4, 1766, "that on Monday, (*September* 1,) Mr. Holman, of Elizabeth-town, N. J., with five other men and two boys, being out a-fishing, discovered a whale swimming about, near Coney Island, on which soon after it ran ashore, and before it could get off, they came up and killed it with a *rusty sword*, that happened to be on board the vessel. We are told Mr. (*Saml.*) Waldron at the Ferry, opposite this city, on Long Island, has bought it, (for about £20,) and that it is now brought up to that place: it is said to be forty-nine feet in length, and that if cut up, would produce about seventy barrels of oyl."

Occasionally a short supply of oil (or *oyl*, or *oyle*, as it was spelled in the "olden time,") was found for the city's use; an instance of this character occurred a few years after, when there was none to light the public lamps for a period of about three months. A *citizen* asks the question, through the N. Y. Journal, (October 8, 1772,) " Why the publick lamps in this city have not been lighted for these three months past, when a tax is levied for that purpose?" It is answered in the next paper, (October 15,) through the editor, as if coming from the Corporation, as follows: " You are desired by the Corporation to answer the question of the *citizen*, by informing him that no oil was to be had."

Among the news dated New York, October 25, in the New Hampshire Gazette, November 5, 1773, which says, "Several days last week a large whale was seen in the North as well as the East River, near the city." Since this period several have been taken near our harbor, and towed up to the city for exhibition; the last noticed was on the 25th of April, 1857, when the "Herald" says, "Captain Cobb, of the fishing schooner *Wm. Riley*, and Captain Harris, of schooner *B. F. Brown*, while cruising off Sandy Hook on Saturday last, came in contact with a stranger, which proved to be a *right whale*. Preparation was immediately made for his capture, and in about three hours the prize was taken. He was immediately towed to Staten Island, where he was cut up, and yesterday the blubber and bone were brought to the city. The *whale* measured 48 feet in length, 10 feet across the breast, and will yield about 40 barrels of oil and five hundred pounds of bone."

Reverting again to this market-place, as no market-house had yet been built here, until we find from the orders given on the 16th of November, 1720, to have the " Custom-House Bridge Market" taken down, and the inhabitants have liberty to remove the old market-house to a more convenient place near the water-side.

The Laws published this year do not yet give it a name, but describe it as "at the slip at the east end of the dock." Ten years after, the Laws say of the "five several places" to hold markets, "One market at Coenties Dock." Then on Lyne's Map of the City, published in 1729, it is noticed as the "Fish Market," and is so known on all the early maps.

Two years after, in the N. Y. Gazette, dated August 28, 1732, it appears with its common name, although differently spelled, in an advertisement of William Thurston, school-master, dwelling at the corner house by Koenties Market, over against the "Scotch Arms;" and the reasonable supposition is, that if the school-master was abroad then, he would have showed his *learning*, in having the name spelled as it was then known.

It no doubt took the name of *Coenties* from a wealthy tanner and shoemaker, named *Coentract Ten Eycke*, who owned and resided on the corner of now Pearl Street by the side of this market-place. The Christian names of the inhabitants were then mostly used, and for shortness, or a nickname, no doubt this was given him: this has been pronounced *coon-re, coon-tre*, coon-je, or *coenties*.

Its proper name after this period it began to enjoy, although variously spelled, as will be shown in the press " of the olden time," of which nearly every one and the greater part of the advertisements and other notices also show, that the market-places, and other public places, were the *guide-posts* to trace out individuality, prior to the Revolution; after that period the houses were properly numbered. The first is taken from the N. Y. Weekly Journal, April 24, 1734, which speaks of a " House to be sold in Duke (*Stone*) Street, fronting the alley that leads to *Coentjies Market*." The same paper, March 29, 1736, says, that "Stephen Bayard has Muscovada Sugar to be sold, between the 'Old Slip and Koentjies Markets.'" The *Mercury*, May 13, 1754, has " to be sold, by James Jarvis, next door to Doctor William Farquar's, between Coenties Market and the Long Bridge, (*Broad Street*,) a variety of chints and callicoes." The same, August 11, 1755, " By Robert Doyle, pewterer, at the sign of the Gilt Dish, in Dock (*Pearl*) Street, between the Old Slip and Coenties Markets." " Colden and Kelly," says the same paper of January, 1756, have for sale, " at their store near Coentjies Market," &c. In the Gazetteer, July 16, 1759, Thomas Doughty advertises " to be sold, cheap, at his store in Dock Street, between the (*Old*) Slip and Coenties Market." The " Mercury," November 21, 1763, notices a sale at public vendue, " at Coentjies Market, of sugars & Lisbon wines." The "Gazette and Weekly Post Boy," April 23, 1766, has " to be sold at public vendue, on Friday, the 4th inst., at 12 o'clock, at the Coenties Market, twenty-five hogsheads of Muscovada Sugars." Then, in the Revolution, we find in the N. Y. Gazette, January 12, 1778: " Stolen out of the house of Henry Minugh, in Little Dock (*Front*) Street, near Coenties Market, a silver watch;" and on the 25th of May, "A negro woman to be sold in Dock Street, between Coenties and *(Old)* Slip Markets."

At this period the Coenties Market did not stand very high, except as a "Fish Market;" we find, however, one butcher named Thomas Cox, in March, 1737, renting one stand, for one year, at £2; and the next year but two are leased: one to Samuel Brown at £1, and the other to Cox at £2 10. Then, in the month of May, 1740, Roelef Van Meppel is found occupying one stand.

This Cox was unfortunately killed a few years after, the account of which I find in the Weekly *Post Boy*, October 28, 1745. It appears that a young man had been aboard of the *Clinton* privateer, and brought off two pistols, one of which was loaded; "he set down in order to mend the flint; in doing of which the pistol unhappily went off, and shot Mr. Thomas Cox, butcher, through the head—when he fell dead without speaking."

The English being at war with the French, privateers were in active operation, collecting recruits and fitting out for the service, while the Government vessels of war that lay in the harbor were in the habit of impressing boatmen and seamen from off their vessels when they arrived in port, which soon had the effect of deterring the market and other vessels from coming to the city, and occasioned a short supply of the necessaries of life. This brought forth a proclamation from Sir Peter Warren, which appeared in the *Post Boy*, September 10, 1744: "Whereas, I am informed that several boatmen and others, intending to come to the market of New York with wood and other necessaries, have been under apprehension that they should be *impressed* for his Majestie's service; I do hereby give notice, that none shall be impressed but such as belong to inward-bound vessels from sea. Given under my hand, on board his Majestie's ship *Launceston*, at New York, the 24th September, 1744.

"PETER WARREN."*

However, this *impressment* did take place, although many years after, to some four fishermen, who were supplying the market with fish. They were, in the month of July, 1764, "seized by a press-gang in the harbor and carried aboard a tender *(from Halifax)* which lay off in the bay. It came to the knowledge of some of the citizens, who, when the captain came on shore in his barge, suddenly assembled and seized the boat, but offered no injury to the captain." He publicly declared, "he gave no such orders; offered to release the fishermen; and, going into the Coffee-House, wrote and delivered

---

* "Sir Peter Warren," whose wife, "Lady Warren," after his death, long resided in the "old *Van Ness* house," yet standing between Fourth and Bleecker, Charles and Perry Streets.

an order for that purpose." In the mean time some of the people carried the boat up to the Fields, *(Park,)* where they burnt it; and others of the company went on board the *tender* with the captain's order, and brought the fishermen on shore.

This market-place being the principal fish market at that early period, it has been thought not improper to introduce into its history all that pertained to fish among the sketches noticed in its history. About the year 1748, Professor Kalm says, "Among the numerous shells which are found on the sea-shore, there are some which by the English here are called clams, and which bear some resemblance to the human ear. They have a considerable thickness, and are chiefly white except the pointed end, which, both without and within, has a blue color, between purple and violet. They are met with in vast numbers on the sea-shore of New York, Long Island, and other places. The shell contains a large animal, which is eaten both by the Indians and Europeans settled here.

"A considerable commerce is carried on in this article, the Dutch and English who live in Long Island and other maritime provinces. As soon as the shells are caught, the fish is taken out of them, drawn upon a wire, and hung up in the open air, in order to dry by the heat of the sun. When this is done, the flesh is put into proper vessels, and carried to Albany upon the river Hudson; there the Indians buy them, and reckon them one of their best dishes. Besides the Europeans, many of the native Indians come annually down to the sea-shore, in order to catch clams, proceeding with them afterwards in the same manner I have just described. The shells of these clams are used by the Indians as money, and make what they call their wampum; they likewise serve their women for an ornament, when they intend to appear in full dress. These wampums are properly made of the purple parts of the shells, which the Indians value more than the white parts."

Between the years 1768 and the breaking out of the Revolution, this market-place appeared to be at the height of prosperity. A large amount of mercantile business was transacted both at public and private sale; and the more particular evidence of this fact is shown by the citizens of this *(Dock)* Ward asking leave, on the 22d of August, 1771, "to enlarge Coenties Market at their own expense;" and they also wish it to be recognized as one of the meal markets; which was granted so far as related to the enlargement; but for meal, the producers were provided with two other places, the "Meal or Wall Street," and the "Broadway Market;" the latter afterwards known as the Oswego Market.

A short period after, we find another petition from the inhabitants, who state "that they have furnished at great expense the addition to Coentjies Market for the use of the country people, only five feet to the westward of the old market, agreeable to the directions of the committee; yet notwithstanding said expense, much beyond their expectation—considering the irreparable condition of the old market-house, which is daily in danger of falling—have by subscription raised the sum of fifty pounds towards rebuilding the said market upon a range with the new end lately finished." They wish the Board to assist them; and while the subject was under consideration, the market-house and other buildings had a narrow escape of being destroyed by fire and gunpowder, of which the "N. Y. Journal," January 22, 1772, gives the following account: "At the late fire (16th inst.) on the Dock, (*house of Mr. John Burns,*) near Coenties Market, the city was in imminent danger of a most dreadful calamity, there being then lodged in a store-house, joining or very near the fire, a large quantity of gunpowder, the explosion of which would probably not only have destroyed most of the buildings near the place, but hundreds or thousands of people by whom the docks and streets were crowded."

On the 16th of April following, a committee was appointed " to examine and view in what condition the Coenties Market is in, and whether any necessarys ought to be made, and how much, and make report with all convenient speed;" and the result was, that they "order a cover to be made over the fish market at Coenties Slip."

For many years the fishermen had met with very poor success and encouragement in bringing fish to market, which had caused the business to be neglected, and necessarily a short supply was the result. It was thought some public assistance ought to be given to encourage the fishery.

The General Assembly took up the matter, and on the 8th of March, 1773, passed an ACT, as appears from the proceedings of the Chamber of Commerce, Tuesday, April 6, of that year. " Mr. Henry White, the President, stated at this meeting, that the House of Assembly, in the last session, did grant the sum of £200 per annum, for five years, to be paid to the Treasurer of this Corporation, for the encouragement of a fishery on this Coast, for the better supplying the markets of this City with Fish."

A committee reported the following, which was: " Resolved and agreed, that the following premiums be paid by the Treasurer of the Chamber of Commerce:"*

To the Owners and Crew of any Boat or Vessel, who shall supply this market with the greatest quantity of Fish, taken on the

* Rivington's N. Y. Gazetteer, April 29, 1773.

Coast with Trawl Nets, (Ray and Skate excepted,) from the first of
May, 1773, to the first of May, 1774, the sum of -   -   -   £40.
  To the same, "for the next greatest quantity," -   -   £30.
  To the same, greatest quantity of Codfish, from 1st November,
1773, to the 1st May, 1774, -   -   -   -   -   -   -   £30.
  To the same, next greatest quantity, -   -   -   -   £20.
  To the same, for the greatest quantity of Live Sheephead, from
the 1st May, 1773, to the 1st May, 1774, -   -   -   -   £15.
  To the same, for the greatest quantity of Fresh Mackerel, from
the 1st of May, 1773, to the 1st of May, 1774, -   -   -   £10.
  On the 4th of May following, the "Chamber" "Ordered, that all
persons who mean to apply for the aforesaid premiums, that they
do, every *Fare* they make, carry an account thereof to the Sec'y
of the Board for the time being, who is to keep a regular account
thereof; and that the persons make oath before a magistrate of the
quantity brought to market each time, if required."
  The next year, on the 5th of July, a committee from the "Chamber," after examining the various parties and their proofs, offering
for the premiums, reported, "That Peter Parks exhibits ample proof
that he hath brought to this City, and exposed to sale in the publick markets, upwards of eight hundred Live Cod-Fish" within the
limited time, and was accordingly paid £30. "That Robert
Heartshorne exhibits proof that he hath at divers times between
(the same dates) brought four hundred and fifty-six sheephead," and
was paid £20.
  These are all that were noticed as having been awarded premiums at this period. They, however, on the 14th inst., renew the
premium list, and make several alterations, by demanding *above*
certain numbers or pounds weight, with the same conditions as represented in their first list.
  The sum of £50 is offered to those who shall supply this market
with the greatest quantity of fish, not less than seven hundred and
fifty pounds weight; and £20 for the next greatest quantity.
  The sum of £30 for the greatest quantity of live codfish, not less
than one thousand fish; and £20 for the next greatest quantity.
  The sum of £20 for the greatest quantity of live sheepshead,
not less than one thousand fish; and £15 for the next greatest
quantity, not less than seven hundred and fifty; and £10 for the
next greatest quantity, not less than five hundred fine sheepshead.
  The sum of £10 for the greatest quantity of fresh mackerel, not
less than seven thousand; and £5 for the next greatest quantity,
not less than five thousand mackerel.
  The sum of £20 for the greatest quantity of dried herrings, from
the first day of May, 1774, to the 1st day of July, 1775.

On the 22d of June, 1775, " Peter Ketteltas, Joseph Bull, Gabriel H. Ludlow, and Edward Laight, being appointed by the
Chamber of Commerce to examine fishermen claims, that have
furnished the market with fish, as the Corporation thought fit to
grant a bounty upon: Give this public notice, that they will attend
at the house of Mrs. Brock, on Friday, Monday, and Tuesday next,
at 11 o'clock, when all persons claiming are desired to attend with
their proof."*

The breaking out of the Revolution soon afterwards, put an end
to this annual awarding of premiums through the Chamber, although they were occasionally called upon to advise and assist the
authorities.

The great preparations for the war caused the more general use
of the city on the East River side, which tended to drive many of
the fishing and other vessels on the North River side; and it also
assisted to destroy much of the trade of the city.

The military occupation of it by both parties, at different periods, brought forth proclamation and orders, which were issued by
those in power.   General Putnam issued an order, dated "Head-Quarters, New York, April 8, 1776.   The General informs the inhabitants,
that it is become absolutely necessary that all communication between the *ministerial fleet* and shore should be immediately stopped; for that purpose, has given positive orders, the ships should
no longer be provided with provisions.   Any inhabitants or others
who shall be taken that have been on board, will be considered as
enemies, and treated accordingly.   All boats are to sail from Beekman's Slip: Capt. James Alner is appointed Inspector, and will
give permits for oystermen.   It is expected, and ordered, that none
attempt going without a pass." †

On the 17th inst. another order from General Putnam follows in
the "Gazette" of that date.   He says: "In order that it may be
more convenient for the people at the North River, His Excellency,
General Putnam, has been pleased to order that a person should be
appointed there to give permits to oyster-boats, &c., going down;
and Mr. Simon Schermerhorn is appointed for that purpose."

The next day, we find another order in the Penn[a] Evening
Post, signed by Horatio Gates, Adjutant-General: "Whereas, the
Asia (British man-of-war) having quitted her station, and left the
harbor, the navigation between this city and New Jersey, by the
Kills, is become quite safe.   The troops upon Staten Island and
Bergen Neck are to let all boats coming to New York or returning
to Jersey, to pass and repass without molestation."

* Rivington's Gazette, July 14, 1774.   † N. Y. Packet, April 18, 1776.

The same "paper," on the 6th of August following, says, "The public are desired to take notice that no person whatever, either male or female, above the age of fourteen years, will be permitted to pass any of the ferries in the State of New Jersey without a proper *pass* from the place they leave."

Three years after, the city being in possession of British officers, fresh provisions, and also fresh fish, had become scarce, and the markets very poorly supplied; and, by way of encouragement, the military commandant (through the Royal Gazette, April 12, 1779,) gave "Notice that permissions will be granted by the police to any persons properly recommended, who may incline to employ themselves in fishing, with seines or otherwise, any where within the protection of his Majesty's ships, for the purpose of supplying the markets of this city."

Soon after the military commandant, "Major-General Pattison," desires the "Chamber of Commerce" to give their opinion "respecting the expediency of regulating the markets with regard to the prices to be paid for butchers' meat," &c. This subject was laid before this *body*, July 12, 1779, when a committee was appointed, and on the following meeting (19th July) they reported as follows: "With regard to regulating the prices of butchers' meat, experience justifies our apprehension that the remedy may prove worse than the disease; but we are of opinion, that limiting the time of butchers, greenwomen, or hucksters, being in the market, may be attended with very good effects. We therefore beg leave to recommend, that no butchers, greenwomen, poulterers, sellers of vegetables, or any huckster, to be in the market (Saturday afternoons excepted) after 10 o'clock in the morning, from the month of April to October; and not after 11 o'clock the remaining part of the year; and that no fresh provisions, (fish excepted,) vegetables, or poultry should be suffered to be put into stores or cellars, on penalty of being forfeited for the use of the Alms-House."

Two days after the following proclamation was issued by General Pattison: "Whereas it is highly expedient that further regulations should be established respecting the boats and small craft passing to and from this city: I have therefore thought fit to order and direct, that from and after the first day of August next, all boats and small craft bringing provisions, fuel, forage, or *fish* to this city, and other market supplies, must have passes from the office of police, specifying the names of the persons and the places to and from which they are to pass and repass. That every such boat or small craft as shall be detected without such pass, or in going to or coming from any place or places, but such as are particularly mentioned in their passes, will be seized, and the persons found therein detained, and are to be reported to the police, in order that the same may be laid before the commandant.

"That any person or persons intending to bring supplies to this city, and who shall obtain a pass from any of His Majesty's officers commanding at out-posts, or the commanding officer on Long Island, or from the Colonel of the Militia of the County in which they reside, shall be permitted to bring supplies to this city, either by land or in any craft, having a pass aforesaid.

"That every person or persons discovered on board any boat or small craft coming to or going from the city, without such pass as aforesaid, or a pass from the office of police, shall, together with said boat or small craft, and the hands thereunto belonging, be detained and reported as abovesaid.

"That from and after the publication hereof, all boats or small craft attempting to pass from this city after dark, and before gun-fire in the morning, (except such as are in His Majesty's service,) will be seized by the gun-boats and forfeited, and the persons found therein imprisoned.

"That all boats or small craft that shall be discovered passing to this city after dark or before gun-fire in the morning, (except such as are in His Majesty's service, or that are coming with provisions, fuel, forage, fish, or supplies for the market, having passes for that purpose,) will be seized and forfeited, and the persons found therein imprisoned as abovesaid.

"That all forfeitures incurred by virtue of this proclamation shall be divided: one moiety thereof to the person or persons making the seizure, and the other to be paid into the hands of John Smyth, Esquire, Treasurer of the City Fund, for the use of the poor.

"Any person or persons offending against this proclamation, may depend on being punished with the utmost rigor. Given under my hand, in the City of New York, the twenty-second day of July, 1779, and in the nineteenth year of His Majesty's reign. JAMES PATTISON.

"By order of the General, John L. C. Roome, Secretary."

"During the whole period of the occupation of the city by the British, viz., from 1776 to 1783," (says Mr. King,) " the *Chamber* seems to have co-operated very zealously with the British authorities, naval and military; and they on their part seem to have relied very much upon the influence and exertions of the Chamber to render their rule of the city easy and acceptable."*

In 1781, Mr. Isaac Low, then the President of the " Chamber of Commerce," presented, (on the 8th of May,) at a meeting of the

* History of the "Chamber of Commerce," by Charles King, Esq.

Board, several suggestions in relation to the fishery. He says, " I am directed also to represent the fishery upon the Banks of Shrewsbury as an object of great importance to this garrison; and that unless a proper armed vessel can be appointed daily to protect the fishermen from the gun and whale boats that are preparing upon the adjacent shores to attack them, they will find it totally impracticable to pursue that business." This subject was addressed to His Excellency Mariot Arbuthnot, Esq., Admiral, &c.; whose answer is as follows: "With respect to the protection of the fishermen employed on the Banks of Shrewsbury, for supplying your market, I cannot help mentioning to you, that early after I took the command on this station, I purchased a vessel mounting twelve carriage guns; she was fitted out at a considerable expense; I requested that the city would *man* her; that I would pay the men, and that her service should never be directed to any other purpose than giving such protection; my offer was received with a strong degree of coolness, and till now I have never had any further solicitation on the subject." The "Chamber" thought this answer from the Admiral was from the effect, that their suggestions had been misunderstood by him, and they again wrote: "They meant no offence;" "that they knew of no application about the vessel, &c., but if he would furnish this vessel, they doubt not they will be able in a short time not only to procure as many men as your Excellency may think sufficient for that purpose, but also to raise funds for paying them; provided protection from *impress* can be granted by your Excellency to the men, and that they shall be discharged as soon as the fishing season is over."

No doubt the "Old Market-House" was yet standing, although it had not been used as a market-place since the commencement of the "War," when it was taken possession of by the military as a barracks, store-house, &c. The Royal Gazette, July 1, 1780, notices it as a *Regimental Store*, in an advertisement for a "deserter, named Richard Hutchinson, private soldier from the 64*th Regimental Store*, at Coenties Market. Whoever will give information of the said Hutchinson to Sergeant McDonald, at the said store, so that he may be apprehended, shall receive one guinea reward. M. WOOD, Ensign 64th Regiment."

The same "paper," on the 19th of August following, notices " a ship's boat taken up on the Bergen shore: whoever can prove their property and pay charges may have her again by applying to Ebenezer Wan, in the 'Coenties Market.'"

Then again four days after, notices " Rum, dry goods, &c., for sale at John Williams and Co's Store, No. —, 'Coenties Market.'"

Soon after this period the market-house must have been destroyed, and the place where it stood was again proclaimed a *public market-place*, as will appear in the following "Market Regulations, dated May 28, 1781, by Samuel Birch, Esqr., Brigadier-General Commandant of New York," &c.

"Whereas divers persons, influenced by a desire of inordinate gain, have been guilty of engrossing and forestalling all kinds of victuals and provisions in this town, whereby the prices thereof are excessively enhanced, and other great and criminal abuses have been committed by persons as well acting as butchers as by others who frequent the markets in this city, to the manifest injury of the inhabitants, particularly those in indigent circumstances. For prevention whereof in future, I do hereby order:

"I. That all fresh meats, victuals, and provisions of all kinds, (fish excepted,) shall be openly sold in one or other of the public market-places, and no where else in this city, (*the place where Coenties Market stood* to be considered as one,) on penalty of forfeiture; one moiety to the informer, and the other for the benefit of the poor of the city.

"II. That no person shall presume to sell any fresh meats, victuals, or provisions, (fish excepted,) in either of the said markets before sunrise; and the said markets shall continue open until twelve o'clock in the forenoon, and no longer, (except on Saturday,) on pain of forfeiture as aforesaid.

"III. That no negro, or other slave living in town, shall be permitted to buy or sell victuals or provisions of any kind for the use of his or her master or employer without a ticket in writing for that purpose from his or her said master or employer; nor shall persons residing in the country suffer their negroes or other slaves to sell the produce of their plantations in the said markets without such a licence or authority specifying the nature and quantity of the articles sent under their care and directions and observing the foregoing regulations, on pain of forfeiture to be applied as above.

"IV. That no butcher or other persons shall presume to *blow*, or cause to be blown, any meat brought to the said markets; nor shall they add to or stuff the said meats or the kidney thereof with any *fat*, or other thing whatsoever; but the same shall be brought to the said markets in the natural state as killed, on pain of forfeiture to be applied as above.

"V. That no person or persons bringing fish to the said markets for sale, shall, on any pretence whatsoever, store the same or lodge them in any cellar, warehouse, or other places whatsoever; but shall expose the same either in the public markets or in the boats they are brought in, on forfeiture to be applied as above.

" VI. That no person acting as a butcher and residing on this island, do presume to kill any kind of cattle, but at a public slaughter-house, on pain of forfeiture the same, to be applied as above.

" VII. That Ephraim Smith, the Clerk of the Market, shall once in every month at least, examine the weights and measures made use of in the said markets, and seize to his own benefit all such as he shall find deficient by the standard.

" VIII. That all and every person and persons exercising the trade and occupation of a butcher in this city shall be obliged, within twenty days from the date hereof, to take out licenses for that purpose from the office of police, and enter into bond in the penalty of two hundred pounds, with one sufficient security, unto the office of police, conditioned for the due and faithful observance of these regulations on their parts; and all fresh meats, victuals, or provisions sold or exposed for sale by any person or persons without entering into bond, and obtaining such license as above, shall be forfeited and applied as above.

" IX. That the Clerk of the Markets be as active as possible in promoting the due and faithful observance of these regulations and detecting offenders; and prevent any contentions between the inhabitants and military. Two orderly sergeants, one British and one German, will daily attend the Clerk of the Market superintending thereof, until these regulations and good order are effectually established therein; which sergeants are to be paid for such service two shillings currency a day each, out of the money arising from the receipts of the stalls and standings in the said market.

" X. And whereas the penalties and forfeitures hereinbefore inflicted may not be sufficient to restrain the lawless and avaricious pursuit of those who had a practice of committing the criminal abuses alluded to in the said markets: In order, therefore, effectually to enforce the due observance of these regulations, it is determined that if any person belonging to the military be guilty of transgressing the same, such person shall be tried and punished by the sentence of a court-martial, as for a breach of order; and if any inhabitant or other person shall violate the said regulations, or enter into any combination or conspiracy to defeat or invalidate the same, or to enhance the price of any of the victuals, provisions, or commodities usually offered for sale in the said markets, such inhabitant or other person shall be immediately put in confinement and expelled the line, as soon as an opportunity offers for that purpose; and it is ordered, that no market be held on Sundays, except for selling fresh fish.   S. BIRCH.

" May 28th, 1781.   By order of the Commandant.

" JOHN ST. CLAIR, Secretary."

After this " proclamation " it is noticed sometimes as the Coenties Market, and again as Coenties Market-Place. In the Royal Gazette, nearly a month after, (June 20,) it is said, "One, two, or more rooms, either on the first or second floor of an exceeding good house, to be let, situated in Dock Street, near the Coenties Market." The same paper two years after, (May 14, 1783,) refers to the removal of James Griffiths "to the house No. 15 in Little Dock Street, between the Old Slip and Coenties Market-Place." Five days afterwards, the *N. Y. Gazette and Weekly Mercury* fixes this market-place as the starting-point for Newark. "Peter Stuyvesant, who for many years drove a stage waggon from Powles Hook to Brown's Ferry, proposes to begin again next Wednesday for the like purpose, and will sett off from Comonapa, at nine o'clock in the morning and four in the afternoon, on every Monday, Wednesday, and Saturday, and drive to Brown's Ferry, where Joseph Crane will be ready with another waggon to receive all passengers, and proceed to Newark. The price for each person is 2s. 6d. in the whole. A boat will attend at Coenties Market to receive all passengers on the days above mentioned, at seven o'clock in the morning."

This "Market-place" was not used as such after peace was proclaimed, but the Slip was a *grand depot*, principally for all the market-boats, which brought farming produce and live stock that came down the East River, and this continued until about the year 1835.

" F L Y   M A R K E T ."

1699. THE adoption of the singular name of *Fly*, which was given to this once famous old market-place, no doubt proceeded from the name of a long, low, salt-water marsh or meadow, which at an early period extended from about Wall Street, along the East River shore, on the crooked line of Pearl Street—then the high-water mark—up to the rising ground about Beekman Street. The *Records* show, as early as 1655, that this marsh was called by the old Dutchmen *Smee's Vlie, Smidt's Vley,* which the English portion of the citizens called *Smith's Fly, (Smith's Valley,* or *Smith's Meadow,")* adopting the sound of the name, without the sense; and the name of *Fly, Smith's Fly,* or *in the Fly,* was known for this portion of the city ; (and it also became occasionally used, when denoting the present Pearl Street,) until near 1800.

The name of *Vlie*, or *Vley*, and *Fly*, no doubt meant to designate meadow-land, as we find occasionally *Smith's Meadow*, or *Middow*, noticed.   From an inventory of goods belonging to the estate of Elizabeth Thyson, deceased, made January 2, 1686, she possessed, "first, one small house and lott of ground, standing and being in yᵉ Smith's Middow, *(Meadow,)* where yᵉ said Elizabeth Thyson is deceased, and lett out to John Carrelson."*   In the disposal of several tracts of land near Roundout Creek,† Robert G. Livingston offers "all the *Fly* or *Meadow*, and upland, &c.;" and again, the "Flushing *Fly* or *Meadows* on Long Island"‡ are noticed.

To further prove the above statements, the Records, in December, 1691, show "all the lands in front of the *Vley*, from the Block-house *(Wall Street)* to Mr. Beekman's, ordered to be sold."   On the 6th of May following, it was "Voted, that from the Block-house to the Green Lane *(Maiden Lane)* be vallued at five-and-twenty shillings pʳ foot, and from the Green Lane to Mrs. Van Clyff's, *(now the present John, between Pearl and Cliff Streets, the latter of which took its name from this family,)* be vallued at eighteen shillings pʳ foot; and from Mrs. Van Clyff's to Mr. Beekman's, *(near Beekman Street,)* be vallued at fifteen shillings pʳ foot."

In the month of August following, the purchasers of these lots in the *Smith's Fflye* obtain liberty to "Digg the Hill by Mr. Beekman's, so much as belongs to the City as the common or highway, *(present Pearl Street,)* as the Surveyors shall direct."

We find in the "press" further evidence.   "On Saturday last, in the afternoon, one Thomas Smith was driving a cart, which was laden with iron, along the street in *Smith's Fly:* the horse (which was naturally skittish) took fright and ran; and he, in endeavoring to hold him, was so violently hurrled against a stoop or porch before a Door, that his scull was fractured."§   "John Browne, lately married to the Widow Breese, continues to carry on the leather-dresser's trade, at the dwelling-house of the late John Breese, in the *Smith's Fly*, near Beekman's Swamp, or Creple-Bush; at the south end of the house a staff is erected, with a Vane on the top of it, &c."‖   The "Weekly Gazette" of 1749 also says, "The removal of Charles Arding from the Meal Market to the Dock near Beekman's Slip, *in the Fly*, where he continues to sell several sorts of European Goods."

Then, to be sold by Evert Pels, "a very good lot of ground, opposite the Hon. William Walton, Esq., on the north side of a certain

* Files.   † Gazette, 1769.   ‡ Royal Gazette, Feb. 23, 1782.
§ Boston Weekly News Letter, Dec. 20, 1737.   ‖ Weekly Post Boy, Dec. 16, 1744.

street called or known by the name of Queen Street, or *Smith's Fly:* adjoining on the west side the Ground of William Elsworth, Jun'r; east side, the house and ground of the Widow Darcey— containing in breadth and front to said Queen Street, or *Smith's Fly*, 24 foot; and in length on each side from said Queen Street, or *Smith's Fly*, to the said Creple-Bush or Swamp, 244 foot, be the same more or less."*

" The origin of this name *(says Valentine)* is ascribed to the circumstance that Cornelius Clopper, a blacksmith, established himself on the present corner of Maiden Lane and Pearl Street. Here he intercepted the country people from Long Island, and pursued a profitable business, making his shop a point of sufficient attraction to give distinctive appellation to the road on which it lay." This stopping-place no doubt originated the idea of establishing a market-place here.

In the year 1692 a Slip (or *Key*, as it was called in those early days,) was made at the east end of this " Green Lane," (*now Maiden Lane*,) about on the line of Pearl Street, at the mouth of a creek, which put up that Lane to near Gold Street. This appears with the name of *Maiden Slip* in the Records of the 9th of August of that year, which say, " As also two other wharfes twelve ffoot wide, one on each side *Maiden Slip*, running to high-water marke, and the *Slipp* are to be twenty-four ffoot wide."

After the arrival of the newly appointed Governor, *Richard Coote*, Earl of Bellamont, in 1698, this *Maiden Slip* was named after and in compliment to the Countess or wife of the Lord Bellamont, when it was afterwards known as the *Countess Key*.

On the 6th of September, (1699,) the inhabitants of Queen (*Pearl*) Street laid before the Court a petition, " praying that a market be appointed at '*Countess Key*,' and that they will build a convenient market-house at their own charge, for the publick benefit." The petition was granted, and it was ordered, " that the inhabitants of the said street, at their own cost and charge, have liberty to erect any publick building at ' *Countess Key* ' aforesaid, for the convenience and ornament of the city." Although their petition was granted at this time, yet it appears by the following, that it was not built until nearly seven years after. In the proceedings held 20th June, 1706, we read, "Pursuant to an order of the Court, bearing date the 6th day of September, 1699, authorizing the inhabitants of Queen Street to build a convenient markett-house at their own charge, for the public benefitt, at ' *Countess Key*;' it is hereby ordered, that such

* Gazette, April 9, 1759. The old " Walton House" is yet standing, (in Franklin Square,) in Pearl Street, above Peck Slip.

markett-house as the said inhabitants shall erect and build, at their own charge, betwixt the houses of Captain John Depeyster and Barnardus Smith, att the north end of the Slip in '*Countess Key*' aforesaid, be appointed and continue a publick markett and markett-house of this city forever."

One week previous, (14*th June*,) the "Council" had given "the inhabitants of Queen Street liberty, att their own charge, to build a Bridge over the Slip att '*Countess Key*,' att the south end thereof, leaving a Draw-Bridge for boats to pass" (up the "creek," noticed before.)

"The inhabitants of the City of New York," says Smith, "consisted, at this time, of Dutch Calvinists, upon the plan of the Church of Holland; French refugees, on the Geneva model; a few English Episcopalians, and a still smaller number of English and Irish Presbyterians, who have neither a minister nor a church, used to assemble themselves every Sunday at a private house, for the worship of God. Such were the circumstances, when Francis M'Kemie and John Hampton, two Presbyterian ministers, arrived here in January, 1707. As soon as Lord (or Governor) Cornbury, who hated the whole persuasion, heard that the Dutch had consented to M'Kemie's preaching in their church, he arbitrarily forbid it." M'Kemie, however, did preach with open doors at a private house, as also did Mr. Hampton at Newtown. They were arrested and imprisoned for six weeks.

Part of the duties of the Church Wardens appear to have been the care or charge of the poor of the city, as they were, on 29th of September this year, "Ordered, the Church Wardens of this city put a badge upon the clothes of such poor as are clothed by this city with this mark, N. Y., in blew or red cloth, att their discretion."

Great preparation for the war with the French had been made, as noticed before, and still greater preparations were making in the early part of the year 1709 for a grand expedition in the reduction of Canada. "Commissioners were appointed to purchase provisions and other necessaries, and empowered to break open houses for that purpose; and to impress men, vessels, horses, and waggons for transporting the stores." Twenty ship and house carpenters were impressed into the service for building battoes, of which we find "one hundred were built, and as many canoes;" and after expending above twenty thousand pounds, it proved a failure.[*]

In 1711 another grand expedition for the same purpose was made; the market-houses were all taken except *one*,[†] to build the battoes in. The Market-House at Countess Key was set apart for the build-

---

　　　[*] Smith.　　　　　　　　　　　　[†] See "*Old Slip Market.*"

ing, "and for no other use or service whatever, until the same be compleat and finished." This expedition in the end, after losing a great many lives by shipwreck and other disasters, proved most unfortunate for the country for several years.

The market-houses were closed but a few months to those persons who supplied them, among which were several countrymen, who were in the habit of defrauding the city out of the fees, by making a quick sale, and leaving the markets before the clerk could collect them. This called for an ordinance on the 16th of October, same year, when "it was ordained that from henceforth the country people who frequent the markets of this corporation, have liberty to expose their meat for sale in the publick market by the joynt or otherwise, as they shall see convenient, *first* paying the fees of the clerk of the market for the same; and that if any flesh be exposed to sale by the joynt by any country people before the fees of the clerk of the market are paid, the same shall be forfeited to the use of the poor of this city."

This market, in the Laws of 1720, is thus noticed: "The Market-House at Countess Key;" after this period, in all the printed laws, it reads, "At the Market-House at or near the Countess Key, commonly called Countesse's Slip;" and the first notice found of it being called "*Fly Market*" is from Lyne's Map, 1729, then continued by F. Maerschalcks, 1755; T. Maerschalcken, 1763, and so further continued by all other surveyors on their maps of the city, as long as it stood.

In 1735 many country butchers and others presented themselves in the garb of countrymen, and claiming their rights, who were allowed, in the different markets, the best standings, without paying the regular fees; this gave cause of great complaint to the regular butchers, who in the month of August, (1735,) presented a petition, "praying relief from the many impositions practised, and wishing to take charge of the public markets, and paying a certain amount of fees for the same," &c. "A committee was appointed to examine into the allegations thereof, and make their report." Before their report was ready, "a law for the better regulating and ordering the publick markets" was passed, and appeared on the 4th of November following, which no doubt gave some relief, as will appear from a portion of it: "And be it further ordained, that (in regard the marketts are principally intended for the benefitt of housekeepers, who buy for their own use,) the hucksters and retailers within this city, who buy to sell again, shall not enter into any of the aforesaid markets to make their provisions, and buy to sell again any sort of market provisions of any of the market people there, to sell again, or carry tne same to their several houses and shops, until the afternoon of every day, to the end, that the housekeepers may provide themselves in the forenoon of every day at the first hand." And "in order for making the several marketts of this city more commodious and convenient for the future, as well for the butchers being FREE-MEN of this city, as of all other persons who resort thereto for the supply thereof, a standing committee shall be appointed by the Common Council, who shall be empowered and authorized to enlarge, alter, repair, and support from time to time all the market-houses at the expense of the city." "That no more than two stalls or standings in any one of the said marketts shall be let or leased to any one butcher." "And whereas, by virtue of divers Laws of this Corporation for many years past, the clerk of the markett had took and received certain fees for all neat cattle, hogs, shoats, sheep, calves, and lambs that were killed for the markett : Be it therefore further ordained, by the authority aforesaid, that it shall not be lawful for the clerks of the marketts of this city to intermeddle with the receipts of dutys, fees, or profits, or take any money of any butchers or other persons resorting to, or standing in any of the common marketts aforesaid, upon any pretence whatsoever, other than for examining and sealing of weights and measures by virtue of his office."

On the 16th of same month a report was made on the petition of the butchers previously presented, in the month of August, as follows: "That it was the opinion of the committee that it would be for the benefit of the Corporation to take the several market-houses under their own care, and should at their own charge support and maintain the same from time to time for the future with all necessary repairs, and that they cause the several stalls in the several markets to be numbered and marked, and let out by lease to the petitioners or such other person or persons as shall agree to take the same at a reasonable and annual reserved rent for the use of the Corporation."

On the 10th of December following, the committee who were empowered to "cause the stalls in the severall markets to be numbered and marked, and let" for one year, reported to have "mett and agreed with the following butchers for stalls in the Fly Market:"

"To Richard Green, - - - 1 stall, No. 1, £6 0 0
To Widow Laurier, - - - 1 " 2, 1 0 0
To Isaac Varian, - - - - 1 " 3, 2 0 0
To George Young, - - - 1 " 4, 4 0 0
To Charles Dawson, - - - 1 " 5, 5 0 0
To John Stockford, - - - 1 " 6, 3 0 0
To Edward Kelly, - - - - 1 " 7, 5 0 0."

The several lessees of these stands "were ordered to give bonds to the Chamberlain, to pay the said rents quarterly for the use of this Corporation."

Although the Common Council had taken "the several market-houses under their own care, and should at their own charge support and maintain" them, yet I find the very next year the people, anxious to preserve and add to their market accommodations, petitioned to be allowed to enlarge this market; and the Authorities on the 21st, 1736, granted their prayer, giving to "the inhabitants of the East Ward liberty, at their own charge, to enlarge the Market-House at Countess Key Slip, in such manner as the Aldermen and Assistants of the said Ward shall direct, and that the butchers' stalls, or some of them, be removed into the new enlargement at the south end thereof."

On the 22d of May, 1737, the same six butchers again lease stands for another year, but the *butcheress*, the Widow Laurier's, name is missing.

This system of leasing these stands continued until the year 1740, when several of the butchers refused to agree with the "Committee," in consequence of their not having been protected in their rights. This Committee, finding they could not make the former arrangements with several of the butchers, made the following report to the Board on the 4th of May, (same year:) "That we have, after many and frequent meetings, great trouble and difficulty, agreed with the several butchers who have subscribed their names to the paper hereunto annexed, for the stalls and standings in the several market-houses." "We also further report, that George Young and Thomas Cox, two butchers of this city, did not appear before the Committee, though sundry times summoned for that purpose. That Israel Horsefield and James Ruffhead (though they frequently appeared and attended the Committee) yet refused to agree, notwithstanding a considerable abatement was offered the former. The Committee do beg leave also humbly to inform this Court, that one Evardus Brower, and many others, living on Nassau (Long) Island, who make it their chief business to buy, kill, and sell cattle, do daily come and take up the stalls or standings in the said market-houses, without paying anything for the same. Lastly, the Committee are humbly of opinion that some other method can and ought to be taken less burthensome, and more profitable to the Corporation, in letting the stalls and standings in the market-houses, than have been heretofore. All of which is humbly, &c."

(Signed,) WILL. ROOME,   S. JOHNSON,   PETER JAY,
     PETER VAN RANST,   H. DEPEYSTER,   SAM'L LAWRENCE.

" Which report is approved of by this Board, and ordered that the Common Clerk commence an action in the Supream Court against Israel and Timothy Horsefield for the rent due from them for their stalls and standings in the *(Old Slip)* Market-House."

At this period an occurrence took place near this market, which introduced its proper name, and no doubt it had then become the common one. It read as follows: "Sunday last, about five o'clock in the afternoon, a fire broke out in the stable of Mr. John Rosevelt, over against the Fly Market, in this city. It burned the said stable, his bolting-house, chocolate engine-house, and part of his linseed oil mill-house, &c."*

The slip near this market, which had been so long known as the "Countess Key Slip," appears to have been changed to "Smith's Fly Slip" about the year 1740, when no doubt the Countess of Bellamont had been publicly forgotten. A petition from Peter Schuyler and others, in 1744, states, " that they are the proprietors and owners of the wharfs and soil between the *'Smith's Fly Slip'* and Burling Slip, in the East Ward."

The business around the Fly Market began now to show an improved state; in fact, the city on the "east end" or side far outstripped the "west end," and just around the public markets appeared to be the common centre for the transactions of trade and sale of almost every character. Slaves were then kept, principally by all who could afford such help, and they were bought and sold both at this and the meal markets. The "old papers" about this (1744) and various periods would often show a notice of this kind: "To be sold at public vendue, on Saturday morning next, at 10 o'clock, at the Fly Market, a negro man, who can cook and do all sorts of household work." Here, then, at this age, our public markets answered a double purpose: for in them were not only sold the *dead flesh*, which tended to keep the soul and body together, but the *living flesh*, with the soul and body too.

The improvements also appeared to keep pace with the business. In 1748 a very important one was finished by the Corporation, who "have, at a very great expense, made a drain or common sewer from the East River, under the Fly Market, up Maiden Lane to the high grounds." It was not, however, satisfactory to the neighborhood, as it was not sufficient for the purposes intended; so they propose to consult, and, if necessary, to assist, the Corporation in enlarging and extending it farther out into the East River. A committee was appointed from the Corporation, on the 11th of July, 1749, " to view and examine the Fly Market, and advise and

* Boston Weekly News Letter, December 20, 1737.

consult what the expense and laying out a good and sufficient drain." This Committee reported, on the 17th inst., "that the present drain be run out and extended so far into the '*Fly Slip*' as to range with the rear of Captain Robert Livingston's store-house, and to be filled in on both sides level with the peers." "That the cost or expense thereof (exclusive of the subscriptions of that neighborhood) the Committee cannot ascertain;" and "advise the work done with the utmost expedition." Another committee, of *six*, was appointed to have the work done, but they found the expense would be so great, "as neither the neighborhood or the Corporation would consent to allow for that purpose." "That in order to prevent the same from being a nuisance, there be dug out of the said slip so much of the mud, dirt, and ground as to leave twelve inches water at low water, which will keep the same sweet, and prevent its being a nuisance; and which is also conceived by the neighborhood to be the most easy and effectual method; and forasmuch as the doing thereof will be an annual charge, and as all other common sewers and wharfs of this city are maintained and repaired and cleansed at the publick charge of this city, they, the neighborhood, have proposed to the Committee to pay into the hands of the Chamberlain or Treasurer of this city the sum of *sixty pounds*, current money of this colony, to be expended for that purpose, as far as the same will extend: provided the Corporation will, at their own expense, advance such farther sum as will be necessary to keep the same clean; and shall and will, at their own expense, keep the same in repair, and from becoming a nuisance for the future."

The next year (1750) a proposition was made to build a large cistern near the Widow Rutger's brew-house, near Gold Street, "to serve in case of fire." It was expected this cistern would fill with clean water at every high tide, by the proposer; who failed to convince the public of the great benefit, and the project fell through.

In the spring of the next year, (1751,) among the parliamentary proceedings of the *mother-country*, a most remarkable act was passed for regulating the commencement of the year, and correcting the calendar according to the Gregorian computation. The proceedings of the General Assembly on the 11th of April, in the year 1696, had "Ordered, that the said year begins the first day of May, *anno* 1696, and terminates the first day of May, 1697." But by this new law, it was decreed that the new year should begin on the first of January, and that eleven intermediate nominal days, between the second and fourteenth days of September, 1752, should for that time be omitted, so that the third should be denominated the fourteenth.

This change was thus announced: "Thursday next the new style begins to take place in all the English dominions, when this day, which would have been the 3d, must be reckoned the 14th of September; and from thenceforward, our reckonings of time will be agreeable to that of most foreign nations."* "Our calendar is of Roman origin, and was originally divided by Romulus into ten months, comprising 304 days. Numa Pompillus added two months to the year; and Julius Cæsar subsequently arranged the solar year at 365 days, 6 hours. As the solar year really consists of 365 days, 5 hours, and 49 minutes, the error amounted in 1582 to ten days, when Pope Gregory XIII. ordained that 1582 should contain 365 days only, and made other alterations, which brought the vernal equinox to the 21st of March, where it should be."† This change has since been known as the *New Style;* the *Old Style* is seldom noticed, except occasionally letters received from Russia will be marked with both, the *new* and the *old* dates, or in the connection with some event prior to this period.

In March, 1754, the Corporation advertise, "These are to give notice to all persons, that on Thursday, the 21st day of March, instant, at two o'clock in the afternoon, at the Common Council Room, in the City Hall of this City, will be let to farm, by publick outcry, to the highest bidder, the stalls and standings of the several markets of this City." On the 14th of June following, the same body appointed a committee to receive " proposals from the inhabitants near the Fly Market towards enlarging the said market in length, to be att their own expense."‡ Their proposals were accepted, and soon after the market appears enlarged, which was very acceptable, as the business had been increasing and much increased for the ten years previous; at which period (1744) provisions were represented to have been very cheap, "*by those who knew,*" who says, "The rich never have wanted luxuries, and the poor have been able to subsist upon the earnings of a few hours' labour; 3 pence in fish, bread, and drink afforded a comfortable meal; 6 pence would procure meat, bread, and drink. Such have been the opportunities of earning money by different kinds of labour, that none willing to work were in want; hence there were few beggars, except the lazy, drunken wretches not fit subjects for the Alms-house."§

These prosperous and plentiful times no doubt continued for several years; and to further assist the cheapness of at least one kind of provisions, the " papers" in the month of April, 1754, state, " We had such great quantities of (*wild*) pidgeons in our markets last

---

* N. Y. Gazetteer. August 31, 1752.　　† Sunday Times, January, 1861.
‡ N. Y. Mercury, March 11, 1754.　　§ " Olden Time in New York," &c.

week, that no less than six were sold for one *old penny*." In the face of all this plentifulness, we find several of the products which ought to have overrun the generous soil of our country imported from another at this period. The N. Y. Mercury, December 23, 1754, gives an instance, as follows: "There is to be sold on board of the snow *Lord Russel*, James Hathorn, master, Irish potatoes, butter in crocks and firkins, and Irish beef." Then, nearly two years after, the high prices of meats are particularly noticed in an editorial of the N. Y. Weekly Post Boy, April 19, 1756, as follows: "The end of last week, on the departure of most of the officers of His Majesty's forces, fresh beef was sold in our markets at 6d. per pound by the whole quarter. This seemed to be a gloomy prospect for many of our poor, who buy from hand to mouth; but that *Being who careth for them* happily sent, in a few days, large supplies of fish; and on Thursday last, Mr. Bernard Johnson, of Gravesend, on Long Island, caught *five thousand seven hundred shad* at one hawl of a sein, beside large numbers of several other hawls; and the next day sold the greater part of them in our markets."

These high prices and scarcity continued for many years after, and caused many to intercept the country people on the ferry-boats, and purchase their marketing, thereby taking the advantage of the many who expected to purchase in the markets when they arrived. A communication from an *officer* to the editor of the N. Y. Mercury, (February 27, 1758,) addressed to Mr. Gaine, says, "As it is a daily practice among servants and others to purchase many kinds of provisions out of the ferry-boats and other boats, in contempt of the law, therefore be pleased to publish the following Abstract from the Laws of the Corporation, in order that no ignorance may be plead, as the same will be put in execution without distinction.

"No person or persons shall buy, sell, or cause to be bought or sold, any victuals or other provisions or things whatsoever, within the City of New York, or the liberties thereof, coming to any of the common markets of the said city, or making any contract, promise, or bargain, for the selling, having, or buying of the same, or any part thereof, so coming to any of the common markets aforesaid, before the same shall be brought into one of the said markets, ready to be sold, (fish of all kinds only excepted,) upon pain, that as well every person selling or contracting, as every person so buying or contracting, either by themselves or their white servant or servants, shall respectively forfeit, for any offence, the sum of six shillings.

"And if negro or other slave shall offend, he shall receive 15 lashes on the bare back at the public whipping-post or house of correction, unless the master will pay six shillings to execute the same."

The next year followed with a great scarcity of fire-wood, when hundreds of families suffered from the long season of cold weather. A somewhat singular appeal for assistance is found in the N. Y. Mercury, December 31, 1759, headed, "Help! Help! Help! Wood at *three pounds ten shillings a cord*, a price never before heard! The countryman says, 'We have wood enough.' The boatman says, '*I could fetch two loads while I am bringing and unloading one!*' The merchants employ the carmen in carrying their sugars, &c. The widow hears a noise in her yard, rises from her bed at midnight, from her window sees a thief, and asks him what he is doing; he answers, *I must have wood!* In the morning views her small pile, and laments the loss of half a cord. The rich engross, when perhaps two hundred families have not a stick to burn, and (it is said) thus it is! in one house where two persons now lie dead of the small-pox."

"Should not the *Fathers of the City* do something in this extremity? Cannot our magistrates appoint an officer or officers to inspect every boat, to agree on the price of the whole, distribute their wood in small quantities at the price agreed on, command the carmen from every other service to attend the boat till unloaded? If this or something to the same purpose be not done, what may be the condition of this city before the beginning of February next?"

"At this period," says Rev. Mr. Burnaby, "the City of New York contains between 2 and 3,000 houses, and 16 or 17,000 inhabitants, is tolerably well built, and has several good houses. The streets are paved, and very clean, but in general they are narrow; there are two or three, indeed, which are spacious and airy, particularly the Broadway. The houses in this street have most of them a row of trees before them, which forms an agreeable shade, and produce a pretty effect. The whole length of the town is something more than a mile, the breadth of it about half a one."

Among the public buildings, " the College, when *finished*, will be exceedingly handsome; it is built on three sides of a quadrangle, fronting Hudson's or North River, and will be the most beautifully situated of any College, I believe, in the world."

Of the inhabitants, "more than half of them are Dutch, and almost all traders; they are, therefore, habitually frugal, industrious, and parsimonious." Their amusements are " balls and sleighing expeditions in the winter; and, in the summer, going in parties upon the waters, and fishing, or making excursions in the country.

"There are several houses pleasantly situated upon the East River, near New York, where it is common to have turtle feasts; these happen once or twice a week. Thirty or forty gentlemen and ladies meet to dine together, drink tea in the afternoon, fish, and amuse themselves till evening, and then return home in Italian chaises—a gentleman and lady in each chaise. In the way there is a bridge, about three miles distant from New York, which you always pass over as you return, called the *Kissing Bridge, (over De Voor's Mill Stream, just below 'Old Cato's,' about* 54*th Street, between* 2*d and* 3*d Avenues,)* where it is a part of the etiquette to salute the lady who has put herself under your protection."

"The province in its cultivated state affords grain of all sorts, cattle, hogs, and great variety of English fruits, particularly the Newtown pippin."

The manner of bringing the market productions to the *Fly* and other markets at this period was usually by water. Those living in the interior on Long Island brought them in wagons and ox-carts to the ferry, then unloaded on the ferry-boats, which came direct to the markets. The boats were propelled either by a fair wind or rowed across, usually three or four trips a day, and seldom a loaded team crossed with them. The farmers living in New Jersey and the neighboring counties, both on the North and East Rivers, brought theirs also down in the same manner to the nearest water-side—unloaded into their skiffs; then, with the *tide of ebb,* easily rowed to the city direct to the various markets on the shores, where they usually disposed of their products in time to return with the *flood tide.*

Such were some of the inducements offered in the following notice of the sale of "Little Bern Island, at public auction, belonging to the estate of Mr. St. George Talbot, deceased, situate opposite New Harlaem Church, in the out-ward of this city, containing upwards of one hundred acres of land and meadows. It abounds with wild fowl, as ducks, geese, pidgeons, quails, &c., and has the advantage of a fine *seine-fishery,* and black-fish, oysters, lobsters, &c. Being in the vicinity of New York, the produce may be brought to the 'Fly Market' with the *tide of ebb,* and the *flood* will waft the craft home."*

We find, however, in their haste to and fro, they would seek a *tow* from some of the larger sailing vessels, which sometimes proved a dangerous assistance, as we read: "Last Saturday afternoon, as a market skiff was returning home with four men and one woman in, they very imprudently took hold of a *tow* rope from a sloop at Cor-laer's Hook under full sail, by which the skiff was instantly filled with water, and overturned; the man that had the rope held fast till he was taken on board of the sloop, the other four were thrown out of the skiff; when, fortunately, the three men, one of whom could

* N. Y. Journal, July 23, 1772.

only swim, got fast of the boat, and in attempting to get hold of her bottom, she turned up again with the woman in her, who had come up under the boat, and taken hold of one of the benches; they then all got hold of the skiff, and just kept their heads above water till Mr. Morgan, ship-carpenter, and another man, in a small boat, at the risque of their lives, took them off, or they must have perished with cold or been drowned."*

The principal part of the farmers and gardeners near the city, during the Revolution, were engaged in the war, either on the one side or the other, which obliged the women and boys to labor in the fields raising such products as they were able; and then,

> "The country maids with sauce to market come,
> And carry loads of tatter'd money home."

They came rowing down past the numerous guards and sentinels to the city, being protected usually with a "pass."

From "Poems of the Olden Time," we have a suitable description of

"THE MARKET GIRL."

> " At dawn of day, from short repose,
> At hours that might all towns-men shame,
> To catch our money, round or square,
> She from the Groves of *Flatbush* came,
> With *Kail* and Cabbage—fresh and fair.
>
> At *Brooklyn* wharff, in travelling trim,
> Arriv'd an hour before the Sun,
> Young Charon's boat receives her stores,
> Across the wavy waste they skim ;
> And thus they, laughing, come to town,
> She at the helm, and he, the oar.
>
> Full early taught the arts of gain,
> No sharping knave that walks the street,
> (Tho' versed in all the tricks of trade,)
> No city nymph, or powdered swain,
> With all their art, can hope to cheat
> A bargain from this country *maid.*
>
> The *market* done, her cash secur'd,
> She homeward takes her wonted way ;
> The painted chest, behind the door,
> (With many a *golden guinea* stor'd,)
> Receives the gainings of the day ;
> Laid up—to see the sun no more !
>
> Sweet nymph ! why all this causeless pain,
> Such early toil, and evening care,
> This hoarding for the age to come !
> If he that courts you, courts in vain,
> And you, regardless of an heir,
> Refuse, alas ! to take him home."†

* N. Y. Packet, January 9, 1787.   † Freneau.

"The ferries between Brooklyn and New York," says Mr. Jeromus Johnson, about the year 1777, "were under the surveillance of a military guard. All the inhabitants were compelled to obtain passports for themselves and their families, *by name*, to cross the ferries; and every market-boat, with her hands, were licensed to come to the city. Nor was this all. Every farmer or person who wished to take any goods from New York, was compelled to take a bill of the goods to the police office, in the city, for a permit to take the same from the city. Every permit cost two shillings. The passports to cross the ferries, and the licenses of the market-boats, were renewed and paid for every year. In this manner, favorites were provided for. During the war, a continual trade was carried on between favored individuals of the British and treacherous Americans."*

The ferry which landed at the foot of this market, and the increased trade in the year 1761, with the numerous market and other vessels that crowded into this Fly Market Slip—the larger ones having the powerful advantage, generally used it—caused a law to be passed in that year, "That no sloop, boat, or vessel, except small craft, such as ferry-boats, market-boats, pettiaugers, and canoes, shall come within the slip"—"at the end of the common sewer (that leads under the market-house, commonly called and known by the name of the Fly Market,) that empties itself into the East River, under the penalty of forty shillings."

An excellent article from "CENSORA," in showing the scarcity and the eagerness of procuring provisions, appeared two years after, in the N. Y. Gazette, January 10, 1763, where the *Lady* says, "I have frequently observed, and sometimes felt, great rudeness and ill manners in our public markets; especially when any kind of provision appeared of which there was a scarcity. I have seen people press and shove with such rudeness and violence, as sufficiently shew'd an intention truly hostile, and that force alone could determine the purchasers; and sometimes the prey has been seized, and in danger of being torn to pieces, by two furious combatants, equally voracious, who seemed, by their actions, to be upon the point of starving, and to contend for their lives. I, who am a woman, unused to war, and of a peaceable disposition, have been obliged to give up my pretensions to the goods, half purchased, and give place to one of more strength and resolution, being not quite reduced to the necessity of fighting or starving.

"All that are weak and peaceable like myself, have been excluded from purchasing in the market, by rudeness and force. It is to be hoped that persons guilty of such misbehavior need only to be told

* Naval Magazine, vol. i., p. 568.

of it, to avoid it, and as they value their own liberty, not encroach upon that of their neighbors. Such conduct has also a direct tendency to raise the price of provisions in the market, to the extravagant price that we all have had reason to complain of."

The prices of provisions had become so exorbitant, that the "principal freemen and freeholders asked for a law to regulate the prices of all kinds of provisions;" which subject was before the authorities on the 15th of August same year, (1763.) They set forth, "That in all populous citys the regulation of the publick marketts, respecting the prices of provisions, hath always been esteemed a matter of great importance to the inhabitants, and worthy the attention of the publick; that the petitioners had for some time past observed many of the common necessaries of life sold in the marketts in this city at exorbitant prices, considerably higher than in any of the neighboring colonies; and wish the Board to regulate and assize butchers' meat, and such other provisions as might be thought to require the like regulations."

This was referred to a committee, to inquire what power the Board had, and whether they can legally do so. They reported, on the 24th inst., "That they are of the opinion the Board are fully authorized to regulate and assize the prices of all kinds of provisions set to sale in this city. And to expedite the work, the Committee presented the following ordinance," which became the law, and is an interesting document:

A Law for Assizing all Kinds of Victuals to be set for Sale in the Public Markets.

PUBLISHED IN COMMON COUNCIL, AUGUST 24, 1763.

Forasmuch as, through the avarice of those who usually supply this City with provisions, the prices of all manner of victuals daily brought to market for the sustentation of its Inhabitants are grown excessively great, and not only ruinous to Families of the poorer sort, but intolerable even to people of better estate: In order, therefore, to remedy this great and growing evil, and to fix and establish between the Buyer and Seller reasonable prices for all sorts of Victuals hereafter to be brought to market, and to regulate the sale thereof, except the articles hereinafter excepted:

I. *Be it ordained* by the Mayor, Aldermen, and Commonalty of the City of New York, in Common Council convened, and it is hereby ordained by the authority of the same, That no kinds of Provision or Victuals whatsoever, hereafter to be brought to this City, or offered, or set for sale or sold within the same, (except live Fish, Bread, Flour, and salted Beef in Barrels and half-Barrels, and salted Pork in Barrels and half-Barrels, and Butter and Milk, and Hog's Lard in Firkins, and Oysters, Clams, and Muscles,) shall be set, offered, or exposed to sale, or sold, at any other place or places whatsoever, other than the Public and Common Market-Houses of this City, under the penalty of *forty shillings* for every offense; to be paid by him or them so setting, offering, or exposing the same for sale, or selling the same; and that the like penalty of *forty shillings* for every offense be paid by the Buyer.

II. *And be it further ordained* by the authority aforesaid, That no regrator, huckster, or other person, usually practising the buying of provision or victuals, such as are hereby directed to be sold, or are usually sold in the common markets, with design to sell them again, shall either by himself, or any other or others, purchase or buy any sort of provision or victual, before or earlier than the hour of *eleven of the clock in the forenoon*, in any day throughout the year, under the penalty of *three pounds*, to be paid by the offender for every such offence.

III. *And be it further ordained* by the authority aforesaid, That no person or persons whatsoever shall hereafter presume to house, or put under cover, except in the public markets, or conceal any sort of provision or victual whatsoever brought, or to be brought to this city for sale, (except as before excepted;) but that every person and persons that shall hereafter set, or expose for sale, or sell, or shall bring to this city with design to set or expose to sale, or sell, any sort of provision or victual whatsoever, (except as before excepted,) shall bring or carry the same, or cause the same to be brought or carried straitways, if the same shall arrive at this city after *sunrise*, and one hour before *sunset*, to some one or other of the public market-houses of this city; and if the same shall so arrive after an hour before the setting of the sun, and before sunrise, then to be carried immediately after sunrise to some one or other of the public market-houses of this city; and her or they shall there openly and publicly expose the same to sale, under the penalty of *three pounds*, to be paid by the offender herein for every offence; and that the person or persons who shall permit or suffer any provision or victual whatsoever (except as before excepted) to be housed or put under cover within his, her, or their houses, out-houses, buildings, or yards, during the time hereby provided for bringing the same into the public markets, shall forfeit the like penalty for every offence.

IV. *And be it further ordained* by the authority aforesaid, That the prices for all sorts of provisions and victuals shall hereafter be as follows; that is to say, the prices of beef and pork shall be as follows, viz.:

For beef, from and including the *first day of March* to and including the *last day of August,* a price not exceeding *four-pence* by the pound weight; and from and including the *first day of September* to and including the *last day of February,* a price not exceeding *three-pence* by the pound weight; the tallow included at the same rates, when the beef is sold by the *quarter.*

For a bullock's head, not exceeding *one shilling.*

For a neat's tongue, not exceeding *one shilling.*

For *pork*, from and including the first day of March to and including the last day of October, a price not exceeding *four-pence half-penny* by the pound weight; and from and including the first day of November to and including the last day of February, a price not exceeding *three-pence half-penny* by the pound weight; and,

For roasting pigs, by the pound weight, *five-pence.*

For Veal, from and including the first day of March to and including the last day of August, a price not exceeding *four-pence* by the pound weight; and from and including the first day of September to and including the last day of February, a price not exceeding *five-pence* by the pound weight.

For a calve's head and pluck, and the four feet, *eighteen pence.*

For mutton, from and including the first day of July to and including the last day of November, a price not exceeding *three-pence half-penny* by the pound weight; and from and including the first day of December to and including the last day of June, a price not exceeding *four-pence half-penny* by the pound weight.

For lamb, from and including the first day of March to and including the last day of April, a price not exceeding *nine-pence* by the pound weight; and from and including the first day of May to and including the last day of August, a price not exceeding *five-pence* by the pound weight; and from and after that day to and including the last day of February, at no greater price by the pound weight than mutton is hereby directed to be sold at during that period.

For Venison, not exceeding *five-pence* by the pound weight.

And the prices of poultry, as well wild fowl as tame, shall not exceed the respective rates herein annexed to the names of the several species or sorts, to wit:

For a full-grown dunghill fowl, whether *cock* or *hen*, one shilling.

For a *pullet*, after midsummer, *nine-pence.*

For a *chicken* of the larger sort, *seven-pence.*

For a *chicken* of the smaller sort, *five-pence.*

For a large fat *goose, eighteen pence.*

For a *green goose, fifteen pence.*

For a large *cock turkey, four shilling.*

For a large *hen turkey, two shilling* and *sixpence.*

For a *cock chicken turkey, two shillings.*

For a *hen chicken turkey, eighteen pence.*

For a large full-grown tame *duck, one shilling.*

For a *duck* not full grown, *nine-pence.*

For a dozen *wild pidgeons, eighteen pence;* and in the like proportion for a greater or less number.

For a *quail, one penny half-penny.*

For a *heath hen, fifteen pence.*

For a *partridge, one shilling.*

For a *black duck,* or other *wild duck* of the larger sort, *one shilling.*

For a *teal,* or other wild fowl of the smaller sort, *sixpence.*

For a large *wild cock turkey, five shillings.*

For a large *wild hen turkey, three shillings and sixpence.*

For a *wild cock chicken turkey, two shilling and three-pence.*

For a *wild hen chicken turkey, one shilling and nine-pence.*

For a large *wild goose, two shillings.*

For a *wild goose* not full grown, *eighteen pence.*

For a *brandt, fifteen pence.*

For *snipes* of the larger sort, by the dozen, *fifteen pence;* and in that proportion for a greater or smaller number.

For *snipes* of the middling sort, by the dozen, *twelve-pence;* and in that proportion for a greater or smaller number.

For *snipes* of the smaller sort, and other small birds, by the dozen, *sixpence;* and after that rate for a greater or smaller number.

And for twenty eggs, from and including the first day of March unto and including the last day of October, not exceeding *one shilling;* and so in that proportion for a greater or smaller number; and from and including the first day of November to and including the last day of February, not exceeding *one penny* for each *egg.*

And for *fresh butter,* from the first day of May, inclusive, to and including the last day of October, not exceeding *nine-pence,* by the pound weight; and from the first day of November, inclusive, unto and including the last day of April, not exceeding *twelve-pence,* by the pound weight. (In the month of April, 1762, "Fresh butter sold in our market at 2/6 a pound.")

And that the prices for *fish* shall not exceed the sums herein annexed to the several sorts or species, viz.:

For a *large bass,* by the pound weight, *two-pence.*

For a *small bass,* by the pound weight, *two-pence half-penny.*

For a *black-fish, sea-bass,* and *sheep-head,* by the pound weight, *three coppers.*

For a *fresh cod*, by the pound weight, *four-pence*.

For *fresh-water perch*, by the pound weight, *four-pence*.

For *salt-water perch*, by the pound weight, *three coppers*.

For *trout fish*, or *tom cod, one shilling* by the dozen; and in proportion for a greater or lesser number.

For *lobsters*, by the pound weight, *sixpence*.

For *oysters* in the shell, clear of weeds, beards, and empty shells, *two shillings* by the bushel, heaped up, and after that rate for a greater or lesser quantity.

For opened *oysters*, by the gallon, *three shillings;* and after that rate for a greater or lesser quantity.

For *clams*, by the hundred, *nine-pence*.

For *milk*, from and including the first day of May to and including the last day of October, not exceeding *four coppers* by the quart; and from and including the first day of November to and including the last day of April, not exceeding *five coppers* by the quart.

For *American cheese, four-pence half-penny* by the pound weight.

V. *And be it further ordained* by the authority aforesaid, That if any person or persons whatsoever shall, at any time or times, from and after the fifteenth day of September next, presume to set, offer, or expose to sale, or sell any species of provision or victuals whatsoever hereby directed to be sold in the public or common markets, or whereof the price or prices are hereby fixed, at any greater or higher rate or rates, price or prices, than is hereby fixed, he, she, or they so offending, shall forfeit and pay for every such offence the respective sums following: that is to say, for every such offence in or relating to the sale of *beef*, the sum of *three pounds;* and for every such offence in or relating to the sale of smaller *meats*, the sum of *thirty shilling;* and for every offence in or relating to the sale of *poultry*, whether *wild fowl* or *tame*, or in or relating to the sale of *fish*, or any other article or articles of provision not here enumerated, the prices whereof are above fixed, the sum of *ten shillings;* and that every purchaser, in such case or cases, shall forfeit and pay the like respective sums for every respective offence; and if the offending purchaser be a *slave*, he or she shall receive such punishment at the *public whipping-post*, as the Mayor, Recorder, or any Alderman of this city, shall in his discretion think fit, unless the *master* or *mistress* of such *slave* will and do immediately pay the fine or forfeiture hereby imposed for such offence.

VI. *And be it further enacted* by the authority aforesaid, That the fines and forfeitures that shall or may accrue or arise upon or by the breach of this ordinance, or any article, matter, clause, or thing whatsoever in the same contained, shall and may be recovered before the Mayor, Recorder, or any one of the Aldermen of this city, by any person or persons who will sue for the same; the one *moiety* thereof, when recovered, to be his, her, or their use; and the other *moiety* thereof to be paid by him, her, or them to the Church-Wardens of this city, for the use of the poor thereof.

Published August the 24th, 1763. By order of the Common Council. AUG. V. CORTLANDT, *C'lk.*

This law created a great sensation among the market people, and more especially the butchers and farmers, who were very indignant, and somewhat contemptuous. The newspapers took hold of them, and handled them "without gloves," as appears by the following effusions:

"There was perhaps never a more just or necessary law passed in this province, than the late By-Law for regulating the prices of provisions sold in our markets. For the impositions of the butchers, and the extravagant demands of some of our country people, have loudly called for redress, and must soon have proved to the poorer sort absolutely ruinous.

"As to the affront offered to the dignity of the butchers, and the *airs* they assume on the occasion, I doubt not they will soon be made sensible that the law is not, like a sirloin, to be rescinded with broad-ax and cleaver; and should they refuse to continue their business on the law's taking place, I hope the gentlemen of the city will not hesitate a moment to raise an adequate sum, by subscription, to supply the markets at a lower rate than that prescribed by the ordinance; upon which the Corporation, 'tis hoped, will instantly turn every butcher's stall out of the market, nor ever suffer them to be replaced, till after suitable proofs of contrition and remorse.

"For we have really been imposed upon by one of the most impudent combinations that was ever suffered among a free and thinking people. Was it not astonishing, and beyond all human tolerance, that beef should be sold from 7d. to 8d. per lb., when it might be offered for 3d. and 4d., and yield a sufficient profit! Cattle were perhaps never plentier or cheaper in the country than the greater part of the time during which this exorbitant price has been enacted. Nay, what is more notorious, than that beef is sold at 4d. per lb. in the neighboring provinces, and in some parts of this very province? Why, then, should this city be under the peculiar curse of being fleec'd, or rather flea'd, by the butcher? In a word, was not 2½d. and 3d. per lb. reckon'd a good profit, when he gave from £5 to £6 for a beast; and is not, therefore, 8d. per lb., when a beast of equal weight and goodness can be now purchased at the same rate, intolerable and extortious? Besides, what title has a butcher, who ought to be considered in the light of a common laborer, (and special little doth he labor,) to accumulate riches? Wou'd not three or four hundred pounds per annum be sufficient for the rank and station of a slaughterer of sheep and oxen? And more than that wou'd arise from the profit of a penny per lb.; whereas I am confident they make above three-pence.   PLEBEANUS."

"Plebeanus" had not so high an opinion of the butchers on this side of the "water," as the same Government had for them, a few years before, on the other side. The "London Review" of November, 1749, says: "A grant has passed the Great Seal, wherein His Majesty is pleased to reincorporate singular, all the freemen of the art of butchers of the City of London, and all others who now use and exercise the art within the said city, the liberties and suburbs thereof, or in any place within two miles from the said city, by the name of the '*Master Wardens and Commonalty of the Art or Mystery of Butchering of the City of London.*' "

We now turn again to another article which followed "Plebeanus," found in the "N. Y. Gazette," dated September 12, 1763. "It is, I think, impossible to offer a stronger argument for the necessity and excellence of the law for regulating the price of provisions, &c., than that it gives so great disgust to our butchers, and the neighboring farmers, who used to supply our markets." "It is evident, from the clamor of the country people, that they did not intend to lower their prices without such legal compulsion. They, indeed, pretend that they would have done it voluntarily: but when? Why, at the swift-approaching period when the city should be so impoverished as to be incapable of purchasing." "If they dislike the law, it is on account of the appraisement; and if they are dissatisfied with the appraisement, it is because they would have demanded more; and if they would have demanded more, it was necessary to prevent them." "Compulsion must" "be called in to remedy the defect of voluntary justice; and the force of law to supply the want of *bowels*. With such a power every community must, in the nature of things, be invested, as to those particulars which are brought among them for their own consumption; and with such a power the Corporation of this City is invested by its Charter, which is confirmed by act of Assembly. And whether it was not high time to exert this power, when beef was raised to 8d., butter to 2s. 3d. per lb., and veal to 14s. a quarter, and most other esculents in proportion."

The farmers or country people took a bold stand, and sent through the Gazette (*Sept.*, 19th *inst.*,) a spicy letter of invitation to the citizens, to step up into *Westchester County*, on Tuesdays and Fridays, and purchase for cash such articles as they have to sell; and from the tenor of it, we suppose they were not guided by the *established* city prices.

This letter is dated from Philipsburgh, *(Westchester County,)* Sept. 12, 1763: "Whereas the gentlemen of the City of New York have been pleased to make a law, and prefix a certain price upon country produce, such as eatables or provisions, brought to the City of New York; and lay a certain fine upon all persons that give a *greater* or *larger* price for what they buy. But they forgot to insert in their laws, that no *lesser* prices should be offered, or given, under the same fine. We thought we were born free Englishmen, and had the liberty, as such, to sell our own effects at our own liberty. But finding the case not to be so, we, the inhabitants, and country back, have fixed upon a store-house on a dock at Martling's Cove, (Tarrytown;) when, on every Tuesday and Friday in the week, the county inhabitants do bring all sorts of country produce to sell there; and where all gentlemen and ladies of the Corporation of the City of New York may be supplied for their cash: for no boat or craft will, after the fifteenth day of September instant, carry off any victual kind, upon a fine of twenty shillings.

"We are your humble servants, and friends to the liberty of *Englishmen.*"

But few country people brought their butter to market, and consequently a short supply was the result, although they were threatened through the "press," by the merchants, with importations of that article. They also appeared anxious to impress on the minds of certain producers rights which the laws granted them, of which the following will more fully explain, as taken from the N. Y. Gazette, October 3d following: "The better to undeceive the people of this province," (the printer of the Gazette was particularly requested to insert in his paper,) "those of New Jersey, Connecticut, & in their being prevented from bringing their cattle to town by a report industriously propagated amongst them, in direct contradiction to the liberty intended and given by the law"—"that every day in the week (Sundays excepted) be, and are hereby appointed public market days, within the said city, from the sun-rising to sun-setting; and that the country people, and others, resorting to the said markets, may stand or sit in such part or parts thereof as are not from time to time particularly appropriated and allotted to other person or persons, and there vend their flesh, fish, poultry, herbs, fruit, eggs, butter, cheese, bacon, and other provisions and commodities, in the public markets." A gentle hint also accompanies the above, in the following language: "We are credibly informed that the merchants of this city expect in a few weeks, from Ireland, about 6,000 firkins of best Irish butter; on the arrival of which, 'tis not impossible the country people who used to supply our markets may be obliged to purchase large quantities of *salt.*" Sure enough, "on Tuesday last (25*th December*) arrived here the ship *Pitt*, Captain Montgomery, in five weeks from Belfast. It is said she has brought upwards of 2,000 firkins of *choice butter*, which sells cheap; and as great quantities are daily expected from the same quarter, the *country stomachs* will soon be brought to." Then we find the prices had induced frauds in the making of it, of which "a quantity of *bad butter* was seized in our market belonging to one Mr. Rosea, of Staten Island; the rolls were very artfully cased over with excellent *fresh butter*, and the inside so bad that it was fit for no other use than the soap-tub."

The reputation of the city and province was anything but good in the packing of this article, and this reputation it appeared to have enjoyed many years previous. This fact is strongly shown in the "Independent Reflector," May 10, 1753, where the writer says, "I cannot learn that the packing of butter for exportation was ever regulated by any act of this province, tho' it constitutes a branch of our trade so considerable, that ten thousand firkins have in one year been brought to market in this city. Nor is there any reason for supposing it would, under proper regulations, be inferior to the *butter* of Ireland. Yet by the frequent frauds committed, and the little care generally taken in its packing, it hath so greatly suffered in its character, at almost every market whither we transmit it, that while there is any *Irish butter* to be purchased, it will not sell, save at a price too low for a reasonable profit. In proof of those reiterated frauds and complaints, I believe I might appeal to every merchant trading to the West Indies. I have myself seen twenty odd pounds of salt taken out of one firkin; and not only hogs' lard and tallow, but even stones and brick have been sold for merchantable butter."

This *Assize Law* also created a great commotion among the butchers, who were very indignant; and some even defied the authorities. Complaints were made on the 23d December (same year) of two of the most prominent of them, which appears in the following language: "Whereas it hath this day been represented to this Board, that John Carpenter, butcher, hath openly and contemptuously declared that he would sell his beef for 4½d. per ℔. in spite of all the *wise heads* that made the law could do, or words to that effect." "He is ordered to appear before this Board, at the house of Walter Brock, Inn-keeper, near the City Hall, to-morrow morning, to show cause why he should not be disfranchised."

Jacob Arden, another butcher, was also " complained of for speaking in contemptuous manner and publicly violating the law for assizing all kinds of provisions. The Board request the Mayor to remove him out of the markets until he shall have obtained the Freedom of the City."

The next day, John Carpenter, of Kings County, (L. I.,) butcher, who claims the *Freedom* of the City, attended, and William Bayard, Esq., proved on oath the charge against him. The Board " ordered his license taken from him, turned out of market, and also disfranchised."

This " Freedom of the City" is noticed by a " freeholder of the Second Ward," who says, " The Charter permits the Corporation to exact the sum of five pounds (besides eight shillings to the Mayor, seven and sixpence to the Clerk, and one shilling to the Cryer, prescribed by law,) of every merchant or trader, as the price of his admission to the privileges of a *freeman;* and twenty shillings for a mechanic or laborer, with the above perquisites."*

A committee of citizens of the First Ward, in the month of August, 1797, petitioned the Common Council to grant a *freemanship* to a certain person whom they wished to elect as a Constable for that Ward. They state, they "have long been unfortunate in the choice of their constables, and wish to avoid this, if possible, in future. In their endeavors to suppress vice and disorder, they readily discover the necessity of having peace officers, in whom confidence can be placed, and who are willing to discharge their duty. They have found a difficulty in discovering a person of this description willing to accept of the office, but are informed, with an opinion that Mr. (Philip) Fulkerson will answer their wishes and expectations. To render him eligible to the contemplated office, it is necessary that he should be a '*Freeman of the City*.' " They "beg leave to recommend him to your notice, as a person worthy of receiving his *freedom*."

We now leave this subject, and turn to Carpenter and Arden, who were among the most prominent butchers of their day; and although they were found guilty and punished, yet they proved, to the satisfaction of the Board, that meats, &c., could not be honestly and profitably sold at the prices assized by this law. The Board having had the subject of changing the *assize* previously under consideration, at the same meeting, after awarding the punishment to these butchers, changed the prices, as will be shown by the *Order:* " That for the future, all kinds of meat be sold by weight, and that the price of beef be at the rate of *four-pence, half-penny,*

* Minerva, Dec. 21, 1796.

by the pound weight; pork, five-pence, half-penny; veal, (hind quarter,) sixpence; fore quarter, four-pence, half-penny; mutton, four-pence, half-penny; fresh butter, one shilling and three-pence; milk, five coppers by the quart," &c.

We find the price of "milk" is noticed in this Assize Law, but it does not appear that it was then allowed to be sold in the markets, if we may judge from the tenor of a communication addressed to *Mr. Weyman.* "SIR—I am surprised, and all my offspring astonished, what can or may be the reasons that I am not admitted or ordered into the public markets? Tho' that I am the support and only nourishment of almost every creature, the poorer sort of mankind are deprived of me, as they cannot bribe my bearers. The richer sort do enjoy me, by the means of bribes, but not in my purity; for I am obliged to run *barefoot* every evening and morning, through so much water, that I am near being wasted to nothing. All which might be prevented by your ordering me to be carried into the market-houses, where every person, rich and poor, might enjoy me in my purity, and should be obliged to runn the risque of being entirely drowned. I beg some people will take this into mature consideration, and they'l oblige many a person and their humble servant,　　　　　　　　　　　　　　　'NEW MILK.'"*

It does not appear that milk was sold in the markets until after the "Revolution:" then "Bear Market" took the lead; but the citizens were usually served by the country milkmen and women, who, after *rowing down* or up to the city, carried it from house to house with a *yoke*, in two kettles, which is peculiarly described in a "Traveler's Letters" as follows: "There are the venders of milk: instead of awkwardly traveling along with a heavy bucket of milk in one hand only, they are thus accoutred: A piece of wood, (which I call a yoke,) about two feet long, is made to fit around the back of the neck, and rest upon the shoulders. To each end is affixed a chain, with a hook at the end. This chain is of such length as to enable them, by stooping a little, to hook the handles of two large milk-vessels, made of tin, resembling a grocer's *tea-canisters.* One of these is carried on each side, to the houses of their customers. A loud cry of 'Milk come!' awakened me from a late sleep, this morning; and when I arose and went to the window, saw a Dutchman thus yoked."† This *fashion* of carrying a *yoke* continued, with a few milkmen, up to as late as 1835.

We find the price of lamb is not noticed in this "Assize Law:" no doubt the cause was, that it was then but little used, on account of its scarcity; or rather it would seem so to appear, from the fact

* October 8, 1763.　　　　　　† Literary Magazine, Philadelphia, vol. vii., p. 120

that a great number of the principal inhabitants subscribed to the following agreement, made on the 3d of February, 1766: "We, the inhabitants of the City of New York, do hereby engage and promise that we will not buy, or suffer to be bought for our use, any lamb before the first day of August next; and that we will not buy any *meat* from any butcher that shall expose any lamb to sale before the day aforesaid, and will give all manner of discountenance to such butchers for the future. Given under our hands at New York, this 3d February, 1766." An editorial says:

"The resolutions against eating lamb before the first day of August, or employing butchers that kill it, having been so generally received in this town, must give great satisfaction to all well-wishers to this country, as it will both save our money and employ our poor, many of whom have been in a starving condition for want of materials to keep them at work. To show the great consequences of these resolves, let us only consider that in this town there are at least 2,000 families that eat lamb, suppose two quarters each week, from the first of April to the first of August, being seventeen weeks, 17,000 lambs saved; the increased value of their wool and skins in that time, at the medium of 2s. each, is £1,700, which, if manufactured, will be six times the value of the materials, and produces £10,200. Another consideration in the eye of the public is, that a quarter of lamb, at an average, before the above period, weighs 3 lbs. per quarter, and afterwards about 8 lbs., though sold nearly for the same money. But the greatest advantage to the public still remains; for it cannot be doubted that, if all the lambs were preserved as above, (which would cost the farmer scarce anything,) a very considerable number would be kept over winter, to increase our stock in this most profitable and useful animal."

In the month of February, the year after, (1767,) it was again recommended, "as the season now approaches for killing lambs, it is hoped that all humane persons will abstain from buying a few months, to increase the breed of sheep, and provide wool for the employment and cloathing for the industrious poor."

Then appears the next year, that "It is expected that all the members of the society will strictly adhere to their engagements against eating lamb before the first of May."

The disposition made of the unfit or unwholesome meat, when offered for sale in the markets at that period, was its immediate seizure, and then burnt, which now would be considered a disagreeable and unprofitable mode of disposing of it; however, but few cases are on record, and no doubt the reason was the prompt action of efficient officers against offenders, who not only lost their *meat*, but had to pay a heavy fine—part of which was used to buy the wood to consume it by fire. I find but two cases in a period of about thirteen years: one is noticed (*March* 17, 1755,) as follows: "Saturday a carrion veal and a lamb were seized in the Fly Market, and burnt at the ferry stairs, by order of Alderman Philip Livingston, of this city, it being diseased and unfit for use." The other, November 14, 1768: "Some few days ago, nine pigs were seized in the Fly Market as perfect carrion, which on the Mayor's view were sentenced to be burnt publicly on the Common, (*Park*,) and the owner of them fined forty shillings; the sentence was immediately put in execution, and part of the fine taken to purchase wood to burn them with."

The death of an old man, described in the N. Y. Gazette, Nov. 28, 1763, brings forth an "old land-mark" near this market: "We hear from Jamaica, L. I., that last week died there one John Cockfer, who was born so long ago, that for many years he had forgot his age. He often said he was a soldier in the Fort (*William*) in Governor Leysner's time, (who was here during a civil war,) and had been a man grown several years before he enlisted, and that, when a young man, he had often shot squirrels, quails, &c., on or near Pot-Baker's Hill* in this city, which was then a wilderness."

"Pot-Baker Hill" at that time was not the Pot-Baker Hill before Chambers Street, known as Crolius'; but its location is described in the following advertisement from the same paper and year, dated February 4: "Jarvis Roebuck, cork-cutter, from London, living at the foot of *Pot-Baker's Hill*, between the *Fly Market* and the New Dutch Church."

In the year 1770, alongside of this market-house, a "skirmish" took place between two of the "Liberty Boys" and some six or seven of the King's soldiers. One of the "Sons of Liberty," Captain Isaac Sears, appears to have picked up a *ram's-horn*, the only weapon belonging to a male sheep, and used it with such effect as to have taken two prisoners, and put the rest to flight.

Some extracts from the N. Y. Journal, March 1st, give some interesting particulars of some of these troubles. In the month of January several attempts had been made by the soldiers to cut down or blow up with powder the *Liberty Pole*, which had been erected by the friends to liberty on the Common, (*Park*.)

"The soldiers, determined to execute their project, availed themselves of the dead hour of the night, and at one o'clock they cut down the *Pole*, sawed and split it in pieces, and carried them to Mr. Montayne's door, where they threw them down and said—let us go to our barracks."

* Liberty, between William and Nassau Streets.

"This act so exasperated the citizens, that they concluded, with the assent of the authorities, to pull down an *old house* which was sometimes used as a barrack by the soldiers, and also a fortification or shelter, to cover their retreat when engaged in pulling down this *pole*. The soldiers drew their cutlasses and bayonets, and dared the inhabitants to come and pull it down. The magistrates and officers, however, interposed, but the soldiers were bent on further insult to the citizens; so they published a handbill, reflecting on their place of meeting, (*which they called*) the Gallows Green, a vulgar phrase for a common place of execution, for murderers, robbers, traitors and rioters; to the latter they compare the Liberty Boys, who have nothing to boast of but the flippancy of tongue," &c. The Journal further says, that " Mr. Isaac Sears and Mr. Walter Quackenbos, seeing six or seven soldiers going towards the *Fly Market*, concluded they were going to it to put up some of the above (handbills) papers; upon the former coming to the *market*, they made up to the soldiers, and found them, as they had conjectured, pasting up one of the papers. Mr. Sears seized the soldier that was fixing the paper by the collar, and asked him what business he had to put up libels against the inhabitants? and that he would carry him before the Mayor. Mr. Quackenbos took hold of one that had the papers on his arms. A soldier standing to the right of Mr. Sears drew his bayonet; upon which the latter took a *ram's*-horn, and threw it at the former, which struck him on the head; and then the soldiers, except the two that were seized, made off, and alarmed others in the barracks. They immediately carried the two to the Mayor, and assigned him the reason of their bringing them before him. The Mayor sent for Alderman Desbrosses, to consult on what would be proper to be done in the matter. In the mean time, a considerable number of people collected opposite to the Mayor's. Shortly after about twenty soldiers, with cutlasses and bayonets, from the lower barracks, made their appearance, coming to the Mayor's thro' the main street. When they came opposite to Mr. Peter Remsen's, he endeavored to dissuade them from going any further, (supposing they were going to the Mayor's,) represented to them that they would get into a scrape; but his advice was not taken, owing, as he supposes, to one or two of their leaders, who seemed to be intoxicated. The people collected at the Mayor's determined to let them pass by peaceably and unmolested, and opened for them to go thro'. Captain Richardson and some of the citizens, judging they intended to take the two soldiers from the Mayor's by force, went to his door to prevent it. When the soldiers came opposite to his house, they halted; many of them drew their swords and bayonets; some say they all drew; but all that were present agree that many did, and faced about to the door, and demanded the soldiers in custody; some of them attempted to get into the house to rescue them; Captain Richardson and others at the door prevented them, and desired them to put up their arms, and go to their barracks; that the soldiers were before the Mayor, who would do them justice; the soldiers within likewise desired them to go away to their barracks, and leave them to the determination of the Mayor. Upon the soldiers' drawing their arms, many of the inhabitants conceiving themselves in danger, ran to some sleighs that was near, and pulled out some of the rungs. The Mayor and Alderman Desbrosses came out, and ordered the soldiers to their barracks. After some time, they moved up the Fly. The people were apprehensive that as the soldiers had drawn their swords at the Mayor's house, and thereby contemned the civil authorities and declared war against the inhabitants, it was not safe to let them go thro' the streets alone, lest they might offer violence to some of the citizens. To prevent which, they followed them and the two magistrates aforesaid to the corner of Golden Hill, (John Street and Pearl,) and in their going, several of the citizens reasoned with them on the folly of their drawing their swords, and endeavored to persuade them to sheath them, assuring them no mischief was intended them, but without success. They turned up Golden Hill, and about the time they had gained the summit, a considerable number of soldiers joined them, which inspired them to re-insult the magistrates, and exasperate the inhabitants; which was soon manifested by their facing about, and one in silk stockings and neat buckskin breeches, (who is suspected to have been an officer in disguise,) giving the word of command, ' Soldiers, draw your bayonets and cut your way through them,' the former was immediately obeyed, and they called out, Where are your Sons of Liberty now? and fell on the citizens with great violence, cutting and slashing." " One of them made a stroke with a cutlass at Mr. Francis Field, one of the people called Quakers, standing in an inoffensive posture in Mr. Field's door, at the corner, and cut him on the right cheek; and if the corner had not broke the stroke, it would have probably killed him. This party that came down to the main street cut a tea-water man drawing his cart, and a fisherman's finger; in short, they attacked every person that they could reach, and their companions on Golden Hill were more inhuman; for, besides cutting a sailor's head and finger, they stabbed another with a bayonet; two of them followed a boy going for sugar into Mr. Elsworth's house; one of them cut him on the head with a cutlass, and the other made a lunge with a bayonet at a woman. During the action on the hill, a small party of soldiers

came along the Fly by the market, and halted near Mr. Norwood's,"
where they drew their bayonets and attempted to strike Mr. Jon.
White. After which many of the magistrates and officers collected
together and dispersed the soldiers.

The accommodations for the country people at this market had
now become insufficient, and the benches allotted for their use were
usually taken up by hucksters; so, in order to accommodate them,
the Board, in the month of February, 1771, ordered "Four tables
and a platform to be erected, to lay quarters of meat upon, and that
no butcher or huckster shall use any part of the above under forfeiture of the provisions exposed." Before the close of the year a
further enlargement was asked for by a "considerable number of
freeholders living and residing near the Fly Market," "at their own
expense." They wish to build "an additional *market-house* in the
middle of the street, to begin opposite the house formerly posses'd
by Thomas Randel, and to extend toward the river as far as the
Smith's Shop now posses'd by John Roome." On the 28th October
this privilege was granted to them.

At this period some idea of the prices of meats may be formed
from a letter by Joseph Outen Bogert,* a butcher of this market,
who writes to the "Council," on the 2d September, 1771, and says,
"I have served the Alms-House for some years past, and not doubt-
ing in the least but that your worthy gentlemen was fully satisfied
therewith, I have served the house with beef, tallow, mutton, lamb,
and veal, at 3d., at $3\frac{1}{4}$d., at $3\frac{1}{2}$d., and at 4d., according to the season
of the year, and the different prices of cattle, at such seasons which
upon a leavel I compute it about $3\frac{1}{2}$d. per pound, and we have had
a fine season for grass and hay. I'll undertake to serve the said
house at $3\frac{1}{4}$d. per year ensuing."

In the month of August, the next year, the Justices and Vestrymen invited "*contracts*" again to serve the "Poor-House" for the
same articles, and notify "that no allowance or abatement whatever
will be made therein, at the end of the year, should provisions unexpectedly rise from the badness of the season, scarcity of cattle, or
otherwise. Signed, &c., AUGUSTUS COURTLANDT, C'k."

The exact number of the inhabitants at that time (1772) we find in
the N. Hampshire Gazette, August 6th, dated New York, July 22,
which says, "An exact account has lately been taken at New York
of the inhabitants of that city and county, as follows, viz.:

Whites, 3,720 males under 16 years of age, ⎫
"   5,083 males above 16 and under 60, ⎬   **9,083**
"   280 males of 60 and upwards,   ⎭

---

* The death of Joseph Outenbogart, butcher, is noticed in February, 1783. His son
Abraham, and also John Woods, were appointed his executors.

Whites,	3,779 females under 16,	9,643
"	5,864 females above 16,	
Blacks,	568 males under 16,	
"	890 males above 16 and under 60,	1,500
"	42 males above 60,	
"	559 females under 16,	1,644
"	1,085 females above 16,	
	Whole number, - - - - -	21,870."

Crime at this period, such as robbery or burglary, was punished with death, on both woman and man. The N. Y. Gazette, November 4, 1773, noticing an instance, says, "On Saturday last ended the proceedings of the Supream Court of Judicature for this City and County, when *Elizabeth Donohough*, for picking the pocket of Mr. Abraham Van Gelder,* in the Fly Market, and *Neptune*, a negro man, for burglary, were sentenced to be hanged on Friday, the 10th of December next."

After the new market-house was finished, it began to attract into it many persons not intended to occupy it, to the exclusion of certain country people, some of whom were fishermen, who now began to visit this market. This caused a law to be published, August 10th, 1774, as follows: "Whereas the Mayor, Aldermen, and Commonalty of the City of New York have lately caused to be erected a market-house at Countesse's Slip, in the East Ward of this City, on the southeasterly side of Dock (Water) Street, for the better accommodating of the country people who come to this city with provision for sale, and those who bring fish to market only, notwithstanding which sundry butchers have of late occupied the *benches* in the said market, contrary to the intention of the said Mayor, Aldermen, and Commonalty, and to the exclusion of the country people; to prevent which for the future,

"*Be it ordained* by the Mayor, &c., of the City of New York, in Common Council convened, and it is hereby ordained by the authority of the same, That if any person who now does, or hereafter shall, follow or practice the business or occupation of a butcher in this city, shall, after the fifteenth day of August (1774) instant, either by him or herself, or his or her apprentice or servant, or by any other person on his or her behalf, presume to sell, or offer or expose to sale, any butchers' meat whatsoever in the aforesaid market at Countesse's Slip, or shall lay any butchers' meat on any of the *benches* within the same, every person so offensing shall forfeit for every such offence the sum of twenty shillings. And whereas,

* This Mr. Van Gelder, on the 3d of April, 1775, "leased at auction all the public markets for one year, at £275."

some butchers have made a practice of slaughtering and dressing *sheep*, *lamb*, and *calves* in the publick markets in this city, which occasions filth, and is offensive to the people in the neighborhood:

"*Be it therefore further ordained* by the authority aforesaid, That if any butcher or other person shall, after the said fifteenth day of August instant, *slaughter* or *dress* any *sheep*, *lamb*, or *calf*, in any of the markets of the said city, he or they so offensing shall forfeit for every offence the sum of *ten shilling:* which fines and forfeitures shall be recovered before the Mayor or Recorder, or any one of the Aldermen of the said city, with costs, by any person or persons who shall prosecute for the same."

The continued exciting circumstances which followed caused the "spirit of freedom and patriotism to show themselves, and soon they marched boldly forward into the 'War of the Revolution.'" The inducements held out by the British officers led many of the slaves to desert their masters: among whom were several belonging to the butchers of this market, one of whom was our "contemptuous John Carpenter;" and they advertised them as "Run a Way's,"* in the month of March, 1776. Carpenter says, "Ran away last Tuesday, the 5th inst., from the subscriber, living at Brooklyn Ferry, a negro man named *Tom*, about 23 years of age, 5 feet, 8 inches high; had on, when he went away, a blue jacket, buckskin breeches, blue-and-white spotted stockings, a tow shirt, and old beaver hat, cut small, a half-worn pair of shoes, with odd buckles. He is a likely, well-set fellow; understands butchering very well; was late the property of John Beck, of this the City of New York, butcher; speaks Dutch and English tolerably well." "20 shillings reward if he is taken in the city, and 40 shillings if taken out," "and all reasonable charges paid, by JOHN CARPENTER." Goodheart Seigler, butcher, also notices his "negro boy *Prince* as having run away, he being a butcher by trade." Another, by the name of Daniel Enslee, (Ensley, Insley, Inslow, &c.,) advertises his, and agrees to give "twenty shillings reward for the taking of *Tom*, a negro man, if this side of Kingsbridge; if on the other side, forty shillings paid by me, DANIEL ENSLEE, Butcher in Fly Market."

An incident soon after occurred, which rather reflected on this Mr. Enslee. Before the "Patriots" left the city, provisions had become scarce, and it was quite difficult for several of the butchers (among whom were John Carpenter, Mathew Gleaves, John Pessenger, and others,) to supply the Continental troops, hospitals, &c., with fresh beef. Neat cattle were very scarce, and what few were obtained,

* "Constitutional Gazette."

it was hazardous to bring them to the city by the drovers, although they were usually engaged before their arrival.

This incident, however, is better explained in the following petition, which was presented to the " Provisional Congress," then the acting magistrates: " The humble petition of John Carpenter, Sen'r, and Mathew Gleves, victuallers, *(supply butchers,)* and Willbur Wood, drover, sheweth: That the said Willbur Wood has been employed by the said John Carpenter and Mathew Gleves, as a drover, to purchase cattle for them. On the 16th of June instant, set out with them from his place of abode in Dutchess County, in this province; that yesterday evening, about four o'clock, after said Willbur Wood had delivered the cattle at Richard Verian's, (Varian's,) the Bull's Head, in the Bowery Lane, for said Carpenter and Gleves, he went over to acquaint them of having brought such cattle, and where he had left them; that on his return to New York, near the *Fly Market* he met with one Mr. Daniel Inslow, and two other persons, who invited said Willbur Wood to go with them and drink some beer, which he did, as having been before acquainted with said Inslow, when, in discourse, said Wood was asked if he did not bring down cattle for said Carpenter and Gleves, which he answered in the affirmative. They then replied, that Carpenter should have none of them, for if he had, said Wood would meet with trouble, and directed him to come to said Bergen's, this day, at two o'clock in the afternoon, and he should be paid for them by the said Inslow. That said Carpenter and Gleves have frequently supplied the Continental troops with provisions, and said Carpenter at this time supplied two of the hospitals; and if these cattle are wanted for the troops, they are willing they should part with the cattle for that purpose; but if that is not so, your petitioners most humbly pray that this Honorable Board will be pleased to take the premises into consideration, and make such order as shall appear necessary for the said cattle to be restored to your petitioners, John Carpenter, Sen., and Mathew Gleves, who wait on this Honorable Board with this their humble petition, to give such further account and satisfaction in the premises as this Honorable Board may require.   JOHN CARPENTER,

" WILLBUR WOOD,   MATHEW GLEAVES.

" NEW YORK. Friday Morning, June 21. 1776."

Daniel Inslow was called before the " Congress," and also the petitioners, who were respectively heard; after which, the " Congress" " Thereupon *Resolved* and *Ordered*, That Daniel Inslow do immediately redeliver to Willbur Wood the cattle which he took from him, and that he see them safely driven to the yard from which they were driven." "He was also reprimanded from the 'Chair' for his improvident conduct, and discharged."*

John Pessenger also supplied one portion of the Continental troops at that period, while occupying stand No. 1 in this market. He being a somewhat remarkable, as well as a patriotic character, perhaps a few incidents connected with his varied life may be found interesting.

About the year 1740 his parents resided in a German settlement called Stone-Arabia, some fifty miles from Albany, in the State of New York. At that early period many of the Indians were very troublesome, especially those living among the French in Canada, who occasionally made war excursions among the settlers in the northern part of the State, when they murdered the people, burnt their dwellings, and destroyed their crops. In one of these excursions, the residence of the parents of Pessenger was attacked and burnt, when they fled for their lives towards Albany, but on their way were obliged to stop among some friendly Indians, and then, in a wigwam, John Pessenger was born, in the year 1742.

Some protection was afterwards afforded them by the Government, when they and many others returned; only, however, for a few years, as the continued difficulties with the French and their Indian allies led to a declaration of war. Then again commenced the destruction of human life, of property, and the carrying off captives by the savages, both French and Indians. The thriving village of Saratoga and some thirty families were sacrificed by them; and at this time the brother of Pessenger, named SEFFRENES, was carried into captivity, and kept among the Indians *ten years*, before he was able to return to his parents, who had long given him up as one of the murdered victims.

Pessenger afterwards came to the City of New York, and served an apprenticeship with Andreas Regler, when he commenced business in this market, where we find him before the Revolution. Previous to that, he had married a young widow, with an only daughter, named *Dorothy*, who, after the Revolution, became the wife of Henry Astor; and she proved a valuable assistant to him, being not only a fine-looking woman, but very active, hard-working, and withal quite frugal. Mrs. Astor was childless, which no doubt left her but few household duties to perform; and as it was then quite fashionable, as well as it was considered a respectable duty of the "working ladies" of that day to assist their husbands in the prosecution of their business, she, at an early period of her married life, occasionally took part with her husband in the slaughter-house, in assisting

* Proceedings of the Provisional Congress.

to prepare the *small meats* for the market. Their combined industry and frugality soon placed it in their power to enjoy a residence in the Bowery, and the owners of considerable property. The great and continued attachment which Astor had for his helpmate was ofttimes displayed in his bringing her home the gayest dresses, or other fancy articles, which he thought would please her. As there was nothing too good for his wife, in fact, he often (in his crooked English) expressed himself to his associates, that his "Dolly was de pink of de Powery." But I am straying from her step-father, John Pessenger, who, among other children, had two sons by this wife, named Andrew and John, and both became butchers.

Andrew, in 1797, obtained a stand in this market, formerly occupied by George Arnold, and in 1810 changed it to No. 5; but on the breaking out of the war of 1812, he entered into the naval service, on board of the U. S. sloop-of-war *Wasp;* and he was in the engagement between that vessel and H. B. M. sloop-of-war *Reindeer*, on the 28th of June, 1814. In the list of "severely wounded" in that action was the name of Andrew Passinger, who soon after died of these wounds.

The other son, John, Jr., in the year 1796 purchased, at public auction, stand No. 62 in this market, where he continued business until the year 1812, when he exchanged with Adam Hartell for No. 35 Bear Market; and when the new Washington Market building was finished, he was transferred into that. Previous to the war of 1812, he had served his military term out in an artillery company, under Captain John Menus; but the war demanded from him further duties, and he became drafted in a militia company, when he performed three months' duty, for which his widow received 160 acres of land, he having deceased in the year 1818.

The patriotism of the father of John Pessenger, Sr., early led him into the ranks of the "Liberty Boys," and no doubt, when the Continental troops were assembled in the city, he was sought after to supply a portion of them with provisions; and being well known to most of the farmers and graziers in Westchester County and Long Island, he was enabled to keep them well supplied; which fact brought him to the notice of General Washington, who found in him a trustworthy and confidential man. On the retreat of the Continental Army to Harlaem Heights, Pessenger went with them; and he became installed with additional duties, in the purchasing of cattle and other live stock, for which he was liberally supplied by the Commissary with the Continental paper money, which at that period was at par.

The morning on which the "Battle of Harlaem Plains" took place, Pessenger being at work, slaughtering in a barn near by, the battle had commenced, when Washington sent word to him to order all hands out, to assist with the wounded, and to his personal care he assigned Major Leitch, of Virginia, whom he said was a particular friend; and on leaving him he impressively said, "Pessenger, I commit him to your charge, and do not leave him until I see you again, unless I am killed." Pessenger had the wounded Major conveyed to a farm-house, where he remained with him, doing all, and more than all, that was ordered by the surgeon. The next day Washington visited his sinking friend, and found, from the nature of his wounds, that he could not live; although, no doubt, from the careful nursing and attention, he lived some fourteen days afterwards, when he expired. Pessenger said that Washington was very much affected, after every visit, and more especially when he died.

Pessenger continued with the army to White Plains, where he occasionally had in possession sometimes 50 to 75 head of cattle at one time, which were usually inclosed in a barn-yard. One night the cattle broke out and strayed off towards the British lines, when all hands were ordered out to hunt them up, and it was near daylight before they all reached home. Pessenger had also strayed quite near the British lines; "hoping," as he afterwards said, "of bringing in a tory or two," and while wending his way back, in passing a piece of woods, he heard the sound of a voice or voices. It being yet quite dark in the woods, he crept along behind the trees and bushes, when he got near enough to hear, as he thought, somebody in distress; the indistinctness, however, led him nearer, when he discovered it to be Washington, who had early gone out to visit the lines and reconnoitre the enemy's position, as he expected an attack that morning, and on returning he had stopped in this quiet place, where, on bended knees, Pessenger found him praying for his country and the success of his patriotic countrymen. Pessenger quietly withdrew and returned to his quarters, to find all the missing cattle closely yarded. Sure enough that morning the "Battle of White Plains" began, and again his services were demanded, and again he assisted with the wounded.

The acquaintance in this county was no doubt the cause of Pessenger's remaining here during the war. In the mean time Gen. Howe, in New York, had been very anxious to procure several persons, who were acquainted with the country round about the City of New York, to procure him the necessary supplies, and having heard through *Manold*, a tailor in New York, (who happened to be Pessenger's brother-in-law,) his relationship with Pessenger, when he induced him to go and visit Pessenger, and with large rewards to engage him if possible. Manold found Pessenger, and offered him 500 guineas as a bonus, and a large salary besides, to engage in the service of Howe. Pessenger's patriotic blood was up in a moment, and he quickly told his brother-in-law, that "General Howe could not buy him with all his golden guineas, and he might take them back and tell Howe to—" do something else with them.

Previous to the war he had purchased at private sale of Colonel De Lancey the corner lot and an old farm-house which stood upon it, then known as the corner of Bowery Lane and Fisher Street, (the present corner of Bowery and Bayard Street,) where he had taken up his residence, but which of course he had to vacate when the British took possession of the city.

When peace was proclaimed, he returned and took possession of his old habitation, as well as his stand No. 1, from which he had been deprived of for seven long years, and again he commenced his old business.

It was not long before he found the property of De Lancey was confiscated, and his own along with it; when he applied to Gen. Washington for his opinion and advice in relation to it; the General informed him that he thought the receipt given by De Lancey when he purchased this property was sufficient to entitle him to hold it; but it appears not to have been satisfactory to the Commissioners of Forfeiture, and it was sold at public auction, and again purchased by Pessenger, who then thought, that as the country was so much embarrassed in her financial affairs, that he would say no more about it to Washington. Another loss, or rather an affliction, soon after took place, in the death of his beloved wife.

Washington became President of the United States in 1789, and shortly after removed his residence to Franklin Square, then known as No. 1 Cherry Street, in this city, and where he sought Pessenger to furnish his table with meats, which in the course of time led Pessenger to occasionally visit Mr. Tobias Lear, the secretary of Washington, at the latter's residence, where, after a time, he became acquainted with one of Mrs. Washington's waiting-maids, Miss Maria M. Henigar, the daughter of Christof Henigar, a fine rosy-cheeked girl, and somewhat remarkable for beauty and healthfulness. The visits became quite agreeable to both parties, and finally it was so interesting, that when Mrs. Washington moved to Philadelphia, Miss Henigar could not be induced to remove with her, as she had made up her mind to join Pessenger in the holy bonds of matrimony; and she is yet (1861) living, being more than 94 years of age.

John Pessenger continued his business on his old stand in this market until he died, which event took place on the FOURTH OF JULY, 1811.

After the British troops had taken possession of the city, officers for the various departments were soon after appointed by the chief officer in command, from whom emanated various proclamations and orders to establish the necessary rules and regulations governing the markets, police, prices to various articles, to prevent extortion in seasons of scarcity, to order supplies; all of which were usually promulgated through the press. Other sources will also show how the city was supplied with provisions, their prices at various dates, with other matters connected with the workings of the government under Martial Law.

The first is an order from the Commissary-General,* addressed to "John Hewlet, Esq., Long Island:" Commissary-General's orders for cattle and sheep, dated Jamaica, October 2d, 1776: "You are to use your utmost endeavors to procure and bring to me cattle and sheep for the use of the army. When they are delivered to me, a receipt will be given for them, to be paid for at a certain time and place. If you find any butchers or other persons interfering with you in this business, or buying from the country people, under pretence of bringing it in to me, without a written order signed by me, you will seize their cattle from them for His Majesty's use, put a fair value on them, and drive them in to me; and on delivery, such butchers will be paid for them, or have a receipt. You will also secure and seize for His Majesty's use all cattle and sheep belonging to *Rebels*, who have left their habitations, and bring them in to me. And you will employ proper persons to assist you. For doing whereof, this shall be your warrant. I expect your utmost care and dispatch in this business; and be sure to report to me what you do in it.   JAMES CHRISTIE, Commissary for Cattle and Sheep."

Mr. George Cherry was appointed agent for supplying or victualing His Majesty's fleet in North America, and he was found on board of the ship "Grand Duke," at Brownjohn's Wharf, near this market.†
Andrew Elliott was appointed the next year, on the 4th of May, "Superintendent-General of the Police, with powers to issue such orders and regulations, from time to time, to suppress vice and support the poor—direction of the night watch—the regulations of markets and ferries, and all other matters, &c.; he will be assisted by David Matthews, Esq., Mayor, with the police."‡

The prices of provisions, soon after the occupation of the city by the British troops, became much enhanced. Eddis, in his letters

---

* N. Y. Packet, February 20, 1786.   † Gazette, May 12, 1777.
‡ Ibid., May 11, 1778.

written in 1777, gives a few remarks in relation to the supplies, as follows: "Notwithstanding the war, New York is plentifully supplied from Long Island with provisions of all kinds. It must, however, be confessed that almost every article bears an exorbitant price when compared with that of former happy times." From another source, in the same year: " Every article of provision is scarce and dear—the beef which formerly sold for 8 coppers sells for 24. No fresh butter to be had; only Irish butter, *very strong*, at three shillings per pound."* On the following 20th of April, the same paper says: "Beef at 14d. sterling per pound by the quarter; mutton and veal at 18d.; butter at 4s. 1d. a scant two-pound roll; milk 7d. per quart; bread very dear, and all sorts of poultry, which is now very scarce; cabbages, small, from 7d. to 20d. apiece; spinage at 10d. and 12d. for a half a peck; three, four, and five eggs for 7d., and everything in proportion." Then, following on the 3d of November: "As fresh beef and pork now bear a very generous price in this city, it would be advisable in the country people to bring down as much as they can of that species of provisions, and not all at once, but at different periods, and in return they can supply themselves with the best beef and pork in the world, (ready salted to their hands,) for one-third less than they sell their *fresh meat for*."† The same paper on the 22d of December following says: "On Wednesday next, being Christmas Eve, forty poor widows, housekeepers, having families in this city, will receive 40 lbs. of fresh beef, and a half-a-peck loaf each, on a certificate of their necessity, signed by two neighbors of repute, which is to be determined at the Rev. Dr. Inglis's house in the Broadway, between 10 and 12 o'clock that day, who will give a ticket for the above donation." This was the gift of an advertising member of the law, named John Coggil Knapp.

The same paper also notices the seizure from a set of monopolizing hucksters, who " for some time past, undiscovered, made a practice to purchase up great quantities of potatoes, turnips, &c., brought to this market for the use of the inhabitants of this city, stow them in cellars near the dock, and afterwards introduce them into the market, and dispose them at a very exorbitant price. This being made known to our Mayor, he ordered a large quantity of different vegetables that had been stored in order to be sold as mentioned above, to be seized last Friday, and the same were sent to the public Alms-House for the use of the poor."

The N. Y. Journal, August 10, 1778, speaks of "a gentleman who left Flushing, on Long Island, last Lord's Day, represents that there are about 12,000 of the enemy's troops stationed at New York, Long

---

* American Remembrancer, Feb. 3d.   † N. Y. Gazette and Weekly Mercury.

Island, Staten Island, and King's Bridge, and about 5,000 at Rhode Island. That bread is very scarce with them; pease and oat-meal being served out instead thereof; the Commissary's rations are entirely stopped, and the soldiers' wives, who were entitled to half a ration, are reduced to a quarter. That the Long Island people are selling off their small cattle, poultry, &c., as they are daily robbed of them by the soldiery."

From the (N. Y.) "Gazette," November 14, 1778, which had previously become both *royal* and loyal, we learn the condition of the workingmen, and its editor's somewhat generous treatment towards his workmen, as will appear from their appeal, headed "The journeymen printers to the master printers: Gentlemen—As the necessaries of life are raised to such an enormous price, it cannot be expected that we should continue to work at the wages now given, and therefore request an addition of three dollars per week to our present small pittance. It may be objected that this requisition is founded upon the result of a combination to distress the master printers, at this time, on account of the scarcity of hands; but this is far from being the case, it being really the high price of every article of life, added to the approaching dreary season. There is not one among us, we trust, that would take an ungenerous advantage of the times. We only wish hardly to exist, which it is impossible to do with our present stipend. There is scarcely a common laborer but gets a dollar per day and provisions, and the lowest mechanicks from 12 to 18s. per day." The editor of this paper says, " I do consent to the above requisition. JAMES RIVINGTON."

In the year 1777, the farmers on Long Island were found possessed of great quantities of wheat, rye, and Indian corn, as it was unreasonable that those who stood in need should be left at their mercy, so the price of wheat was fixed at 12s. per bushel of 58 lbs.; rye and corn at 7s.; wheat flour, 35s. per cwt.; rye, 20s., and Indian corn at 17s. They were ordered to thrash out one-third of their crop immediately, one-third by February next, and the balance by the 1st of May, 1778. The price put on upland hay was 8s.; salt hay, 4s.; straw, 3s. per cwt., and 2s. 6d. per ton for carting or water carriage.

The prices of wood were also regulated in the same manner. In 1778, "it was ordered, that from and after Saturday, the 5th day of December next, no more than *five pounds* currency shall be demanded or paid for a cord of walnut wood, and four pounds for any other sort of wood. The above *rates* being deemed from the best information amply sufficient, the owners of *vessels* and the boatmen that have usually supplied this city with *wood*, are hereby warned not to attempt to distress the inhabitants by desisting from bringing the same, as their vessels and boats shall, upon proof thereof, be seized and assigned to others that will undertake to supply the city, and all protections and passes shall be withdrawn from such delinquents. Those persons that have cut *wood* for the use of this city in consequence of the permits granted, are to send it to New York as soon as possible; upon proof of unnecessary delay, the *wood* shall be forfeited for the benefit of the poor, and their permits withdrawn."*

Then follows "A proclamation of His Excellency Sir Henry Clinton, dated New York, December 20, 1778: the farmers of Long Island and Staten Island were ordered to thrash and bring to *market*, by stated periods, such proportions of wheat, rye, and Indian corn in their possession as they did not stand in need of for the support of their families and the sowing their lands. They were required also to give an account to the Colonels of Militia of their respective districts what quantity of grain they possessed, and what it might be necessary to reserve for the above uses. The Commander-in-Chief has been pleased to order that proclamation to remain in force, and be strictly observed, the rates excepted, which, as an encouragement for an ample supply of the markets, are to be as follows:

"Wheat,   -   -   26 shillings currency per bushel.
Wheat flour, -   - 80   "   "   per cwt.
Rye,   -   -   -   10   "   "   per bushel.
Rye meal,   -   - 30   "   "   per cwt.
Indian corn,   -   10   "   "   per bushel.
Indian meal, -   - 28   "   "   per cwt.
Buckwheat,   -   7   "   "   per bushel.
Buckwheat meal, - 26   "   "   per cwt.

"It is therefore ordered, that from and after the first day of February next, no greater price for any of the above articles shall be demanded, offered, or received, on the penalty of the person so offending forfeiting (on being convicted on oath before the police of New York, or the Colonels of the Militia of the district on Long Island or Staten Island, where the offence is committed,) the grain, flour, corn, or meal so offered to be sold or purchased, or the value thereof, and to suffer imprisonment till the said forfeiture is paid; the one-half of the forfeiture to be paid to the informer, and the other half for the use of the poor of this city, or the township where the offence is committed.

"The police of New York and the Colonels of Militia on Long Island and Staten Island are hereby required to take an account of what quantities of wheat, rye, Indian corn, grain, flour, or meal are

* Royal Gazette, January 22, 1779.

in their respective districts, and in whose possession, and report the same as soon as possible to the Commandant of New York.

"D. JONES, *Major-General.*"

" In the month of March, 1779," says Johnson, " flour and bread-stuff were nearly exhausted in the British store-houses at New York. There was no good flour; and the Hessians, who were in Brooklyn, drew damaged oatmeal instead of bread. This meal, baked into cakes, was unfit for use; and the writer has seen them cast to the swine, which would not eat them. The soldiers were mutinous. All the grain possessed by the farmers was estimated, and placed under requisition. The timely arrival of a few victualing ships relieved the scarcity, and saved the British from a surrender to the Americans to escape starvation."* The price of flour, on the 15th of December, 1780, is shown from a petition of the bakers of the city, who state, " That the price of flour—being advanced beyond the assize of bread—that they cannot afford to carry on their business." The Board of the Chamber no doubt assisted the bakers, as they " are of opinion that good flour cannot now be purchased under *three pounds* per hundred weight."† However, the timely arrival of vessels from the mother-country greatly assisted the citizens with supplies, and at this period is found noticed in the press the arrival of beef from the " Leaden Hall Market." " Uriah Hendricks has for sale ' the best London beef, fresh put up in Leaden Hall Market,' preserved by a new method, with saltpetre, spice, &c., and is in excellent order for family use, being in casks, of 112 lbs. each; *its cost at London* was more than double price of Irish beef."‡ The Royal Gazette following, October 13, notices " ' *London Beef.'*—A few barrels of the prime London beef, put up at the *Leaden Hall Market*, for private family use, and imported in the ship *Bowman*, yet remains on hand, and may be had by applying immediately to Captain Taylor, on board of said vessel, now lying at Marston's Wharf."

Vegetables and fruit also appeared very scarce, at times; there was but little raised, and that little almost clandestinely grew in some place beyond the reach of the numerous marauding troops, or immediately under the protection of the commanding officers. The consequence was, but a small supply ever came to the markets, for as soon as it was landed, it was immediately taken up at almost any price by the wealthy, or the most favored tavern-keepers.

"An officer lately returned from New York reports that vegetables and fruit are so excessively scarce there, that an ordinary din-

---

* Naval Magazine, vol. i., p. 568.   † Proceedings of the Chamber of Commerce.
‡ N. Y. Gazette, &c , June 21, 1779.

ner at any of the taverns in the city, the garden stuff and dessert generally exceed the charge of every article of the entertainment besides, wine and firing (*fire-wood*) only excepted."*

A few months before, the inventor and patentee of the preserved meats was brought to light, in the following notice: "Portable soup—veal, mutton, and beef—fresh imported from Mr. Piper, the patentee, successor to Debois, the first inventor of these excellent *cakes* for invalids and persons traveling by land and water, proving the most excellent succedaneum in the world. Enquire of the printer."†

The same paper notices the loss of ten fat cattle, which, by description, would be considered now-a-days *a hard lot:* "Stolen or strayed, the 6th inst., from the farm of John Houls, living at Gowanus, four miles from Brooklyn Ferry, *ten fat cattle:* two oxen, one large black cow, one black two year old bull, two one year old stears, one three year old steer, three two year old heifers. Twenty dollars reward will be given to any person that secures them, so that the owner may have them again; either acquaint John Houls or William Mooney, butchers in the *Fly Market.*"‡

The winter of 1779 and '80 was a most remarkable cold winter, for the long continuance of cold weather not only closed both the North and East Rivers, but also closed the Bay of New York with solid ice. Near every article of provisions and wood was brought across in sleighs, and "a troop of horse and artillery crossed to Staten Island on this immense bridge, which connected all our islands one with the other, and with the main-land."§ "Fuel and provisions were scarcely to be purchased by the citizens, even those who had means of paying exorbitant prices. In many instances household furniture was broken up to supply the fire necessary to support life."

Perhaps the following will more fully demonstrate the above facts, which we find in the "Penn^a Packet," as follows: "Poughkeepsie, January 10. The very remarkable and long-continued severity of the weather (*the like not having been known*, as we are informed, *by the oldest man living*,) has stopped all the avenues of intelligence, and almost cut off all social intercourse between people of the same neighborhood.

"The incessant intenseness of the cold, the great depth and quantity of the snow, followed in quick succession one on the back of another, attended with violent tempests of wind, which for several days made the roads utterly impassable, has put a stop to business

---

* Upcott's Collections, vol. vi., p. 143. † N. Y. Gazette, August 19, 1780.
‡ Ibid., November 20, 1779. § Dunlap's Hist. N. Y., p. 166.

of all kinds except such as each family could do within itself. And
as many were slender provided with necessaries for subsistence, we
have reason to apprehend that we shall shortly hear many melancholy accounts of private distress in the country; and that from the
sea-coasts and vessels at sea, the accounts will be dreadful."* "The
sound between Long Island and Connecticut is almost froze over
in the *widest part*, and some persons have passed over from Long
Island to Norwalk and other parts of Connecticut *on the ice*. Wood
is brought from Long Island to New York on sleighs. It is also
passable from Paulus Hook to New York."† A party of mounted
refugees who had been making *surprisals*, among which, an account says: "The further trophies of this successful excursion are
three handsome sleighs, with ten good horses, all of which were
yesterday (Feb. 1) driven to New York *over the ice* from Staten
Island, an enterprise never yet attempted *since the first settlement of
this country*."‡ " Yesterday, (Feb. 6,) 86 loaded sleighs went from
this city to Staten Island *on the ice*."§

"A few nights since a number of prisoners escaped from one of
the prison ships in New York *on the ice*, one of whom froze to death
before he reached the shore."‖ (No doubt he was almost dead from
starvation and disease before he started.) At a later date another
escape from this prison ship is thus noticed: " Last Sunday, (20*th
August*, 1780,) came to town (Phila.) Captain Richard Grinnell,
who made his escape from the Scorpion prison ship in New York,
on Tuesday, the 15th inst. He informs us that on the day he left
New York, there was the hottest *press* ever known there; they
pressed about 700 men that day, and the press still continued; that
they not only took seamen, but all the refugees, laborers, and merchants' clerks they came across. Captain Grinnell further says,
that there was on board the two prison ships, Scorpion and Strom-
billo, about 300 prisoners."¶

In the year 1782, the cold weather must have been more severe
than that two years before, but not so long continued. The news from
New York, dated January 31, states: "We have had a more intense
frost since Monday last, than any inhabitant of this city remembers
to have happened for twenty years past. It has rendered the arrival of vessels, and, conseque..tly, the means of obtaining intelligence, impracticable."** Then appears on the 4th of February, "In
the late severe weather on Tuesday and Wednesday last, some people were found frozen to death in their crafts in the East and Hud-

---

* 1780, January 27.   † Ibid., Feb. 8.   ‡ Ibid., Feb. 12.
§ Gaine's Mercury, &c., Feb. 7.   ‖ New Hampshire Gazette, February 5.
¶ Penna. Packet, August 22.   ** Penna. Packet, Feb. 12, 1782.

son's Rivers; and, indeed, the bay was so full of ice all the last week that our navigation to Staten Island has been greatly impeded."

The manner in which the authorities at this period disposed of the stands in the several markets is thus noticed: "By permission of the Commandant, the stalls and standings of the several markets in this city will be exposed to sale at public auction on Monday, the 13th of March next, at 12 o'clock, at the house of Mr. John Roome, inn-keeper, the corner of Water Street and the Fly Market. Conditions will be made known at the time of sale. In *Vestry*, 21st February, 1780.*

The formation and peculiar duties of this *Vestry* are more fully shown in Butler's letter, who says, "At this time, December, 1777, the poor were greatly distressed, and General Robertson, then Commandant of New York, was pleased to appoint nineteen gentlemen from the different wards of the city, to solicit contributions for their relief. These gentlemen, with the magistrates of police, were then formed into a *Vestry*, and the Alms-House and poor of the city were committed to their care; and latterly, the pumps, lamps, &c.—proper funds for the execution of the trust reposed in them were necessary—therefore the rents of such houses and stores as were not wanted for the service of government, and the five (*six, viz., Coenties Slip, Old Slip, Fly, Peck Slip, Bear, and Oswego*) markets were appropriated to the funds for the *Vestry*."†

The street which ran alongside of this (*Fly*) market was not known at this period as Maiden Lane, but as "Fly Market," and occasionally as "Fly Market Street," from the corner of Queen (*Pearl*) Street, where the numbers began; in fact, we find but few streets properly numbered, until after the British troops had taken possession of the city. The "Gazette" furnishes us with several evidences of the above facts. In 1778: "Joseph Collins, Taylor, takes this method to acquaint the gentlemen of the navy and army that he has lately removed to No. 22 'Fly Market.'" Then there appears in 1779: "Wanted, empty soap and candle boxes. Any person who has them to dispose of may hear of a purchaser by applying to Gregg and Laffan, Tallow Chandlers in the *Fly Market*." 1780: "To be sold, the lease of a house in the 'Fly Market,' late the property of Mr. Timothy Slandert, deceased." 1781: "William Torrence & Co. have removed to No. 2 *Fly Market*, next door to William Campbell's, where they are opening for sale broadcloths and Rattinetts, &c." In 1799, the numbers were continued through; that is, Maiden Lane from Broadway, where the numbers began, to No. 112 corner of Pearl Street, was then known by this name, and

* Royal Gazette. † The Tomlinson Papers, Mercantile Library Association.

from 112 to the East River was called the "*Fly Market*," although the numbers continued on to the end of the market.

Fly Market Street continued in existence until the 26th of April, 1824, when Assistant Alderman Samuel St. John called up his "resolution" for giving the name of Maiden Lane to the whole street running from the North to the East River, "now known as Cortlandt Street, Maiden Lane, and Fly Market Street," which was adopted; but Cortlandt Street still survives.

We turn to the 26th of April, 1780, and find the following: "Notice is hereby given that no persons whatsoever are to be admitted into the British lines without having previously obtained passports for the purpose, from the Commandant of New York, except those who come to and go from the markets. They will report themselves to the police, whose permissions for taking out horses, &c., will be sufficient. OLIVER DELANCEY, Adjt. General."*

Some three years after, on the 1st of January, (1783,) "Notice is hereby given to any person or persons inclined to enter into a contract for supplying *fresh beef* to His Majesty's ships at this port, to send in their proposals to me, in writing, sealed, on or before the 18th of January next, on board the 'Centurion' Victualler, at Hallet's Wharf, or at No. 217 Water Street.

"JOHN DELAFONS, Agent Victualler."

Followed soon after this: "By order of the Commandant, permission is hereby granted to all persons coming from any part of the country with live stock for the use of the markets, to kill and dispose of the same, provided the stock is slaughtered at such places as are set apart for that purpose. Hucksters, or any other persons who may be detected in forestalling any provisions or vegetables brought to this city for the supply of the markets, may depend on being treated with the utmost rigour. JOHN ST. CLAIR, Sec'y.

"New York, 7th June, 1783."

The last "proclamation," made before the "evacuation," in relation to markets, is noticed in the N. Y. Weekly Mercury, July 7th, same year, as follows: "Whereas, the butchers who have stalls and standings in the public markets, make common practice of throwing the feet and other offals of their meat, either under their stalls, or in the streets adjoining the same, whereby the inhabitants living near the said markets are greatly incommoded and distressed by the nuisance occasioned by such practices. The said butchers are therefore hereby strictly forbidden from committing such practices in future, and are hereby directed to keep their several stalls and standings clean and clear of all such filths; and in case any of the said

* Royal Gazette.

butchers shall be convicted before the police of transgressing this order, their license shall be forfeited, and the offenders be delivered from having any stall or standing in the said markets. By order of the Commandant. JOHN ST. CLAIR, Secretary."

We turn back, and find from an examination of David Hunt, of Westchester, (New York,) noticed in the New Hampshire Gazette, December 24, 1776, in which he states, "That provisions in general were scarce and dear, flour in particular, and all kinds of vegetables." " That they (*Rangers*) had collected (*in Westchester County, New York,*) 1,200 sheep, 900 hogs, and several hundred cattle, and drove them on Willet's Neck, and since gone off to New York."

These " Rangers" were organized in New York, principally from the refugees, as a foraging party, under the command of the city's former Governor, (Tryon,) who made himself quite extensively known as a " Cattle Thief," and was one of the most efficient in supplying the city with fresh provisions. The following will give the reader some idea of his accomplishment in that line. The "same paper," 1778, September 8, gives the news from " New Haven, August 26," which states that "Governor Tryon, with his foraging party, it is said, are returning, having collected on Long Island upwards of 9,000 cattle, sheep, &c." The same, March 9th, (1779,) next year, says, "The troops which lately went to the east end of Long Island, we are informed, were foraging parties; they have since returned towards New York, taking with them a considerable booty in cattle of various kinds." *March* 16*th:* " 3,000 men landed at Elizabeth Town, under General Clinton. A large body of them, under General Jones, immediately marched a few miles in the country, and had collected about 40 head of cattle, when a detachment of Continental troops attacked them, retook the cattle, and drove the enemy to their boats." The same paper notices a "large body of the enemy, commanded by Governor Tryon, advanced by the way of King's Bridge as far as Horseneck. About two hundred head of cattle and a number of sheep fell into their hands." *May* 18*th:* " Last Saturday a party of the enemy landed at Point Judith, and stole from there about 900 sheep, and between 60 and 70 cattle." *June* 8*th:* " Last week about 1,500 of the enemy made an excursion to Scrallenberg, a small village in the neighborhood of Hackinsack, where they burnt some houses, abused the inhabitants, and plundered their effects; but by the timely exertions of the army, who collected speedily, they were obliged to embark with precipitation, carrying but few cattle and little of their plunder with them. We learn that this party consisted chiefly of the *Associated Refugees,* as they term themselves, but more properly *Associated Thieves* and Murderers. They stabbed an old gentleman of about 90 years of age, named Talman, in order to oblige him to confess where his money was. He died shortly after of his wounds. They also killed Mr. Zabriskie, by frequently stabbing him with their bayonets, and a negro girl, as she was driving off some cattle." *July 13th:* "A party of Tories from New York landed at Monmouth, and marched with upwards of 50 men to Trenton Falls, undiscovered, where they surprised several persons, and drove off a few sheep and horned cattle." Also, "Thirty-two Refugees, commanded by Captain Bonnel, landed at Greenwich, in Connecticut; they plundered the houses of nothing but arms and ammunition, the principal object being horned cattle, of which they brought off thirty-eight, also four horses. The Refugees proceeded about six miles into the country, collecting cattle; and on their return, were attacked by a body of *Rebels*, supposed to consist of about 150, with two field-pieces, but got safe on board, and arrived at Oyster Bay about noon with the cattle and prisoners."

The American soldiers were not behind, and would occasionally return the compliment, even going so far within the opponents' lines as to reseize this kind of stolen property. Says the Penn^a Packet, July 31, 1781, "Last Saturday Colonel Sheldon's Dragoons went to Frog's Neck and Morrisania, and brought off upwards of 200 horned cattle, a considerable number of horses, hogs, sheep, &c., said to be Colonel De Lancy's property, which he had plundered from the inhabitants, in order to fatten and sell to the New York butchers; a profitable trade he has practiced a long time."

Again, we return to the "Royal Gazette," dated January 2, 1779, where we find the loyal editor indulging his readers with a species of burlesque on General Washington's proclamation in relation to cattle. The editor states, "Mr. Washington last winter issued a proclamation, requiring the inhabitants of certain districts to fatten their cattle, in order to subsist his army the ensuing campaign. The British light infantry, having at least an equal interest in that measure, one of them, in the name of the whole, composed the following exhortation to accompany and strengthen the Rebel General's requisition:

"Great Washington, thou mighty son of Mars,
Thou thund'ring hero of the *Rebel* wars!
Accept our thanks for all thy favors past;
Our special thanks await thee for the last.
    Thy proclamation, timely to command
The *Cattle* to be fatten'd round the land,
Bespeaks thy generosity, and shows
A charity that reaches to thy foes!
And was this Order issued for our sakes,
To treat us with *Roast Beef* and savory steaks?

Or was it for thy *Rebel* train intended?
Give 'em the Hides—and let their shoes be mended;
Tho' shoes are what they seldom wear of late;
'T would load their *nimble* feet with too much weight!
And for the Beef—there needs no puffs about it;
In short, they must content themselves without it;
Not that we mean to have them starv'd—why marry!
The *live stock* in abundance, which they carry
Upon *their backs*, prevents all fear of that.
Then, *honest Whigs*, make all your cattle fat;
We, to reward you for your care and pains,
Will visit soon your crowded stalls and plains;
And for your pamper'd *Cattle* write, at large,
With bloody bayonets, a full discharge.
You know that we light bobs are tough and hardy,
And at a push you'll never finds us tardy;
We have a stomach both for *Beef* and battle;
So, honest Whigs, once more, feed well your *Cattle;*
Obey your *Chief's* command; and then, 'tis plain,
We cannot want for *Beef* the next campaign!
And if we want for fighting, be it known,
The fault, good neighbors, shall be all your own!   McL——N."

It also says, on the following 5th of June, "On Monday last a party of about forty Refugees embarked on board two sloops and proceeded to Sandy Hook. On Tuesday evening they landed at Shoal Harbor, and went to the houses of some notoriously violent *Rebels*, whom they took and brought off with their cattle, &c., without the loss of a man." "The party returned safe here on Wednesday, bringing with them 27 milch cows, 7 horses, 2 waggons loaded with goods, &c."

The manner of disposing of their cattle and other plunder was by auction, which usually took place at the "Bull's Head in the Bowery," then the grand depot for *stolen goods*. The same paper which notices the above, also notices the sale of their plunder, as follows: "To be sold this day, at public auction, at the Bull's Head Tavern, in the Bowery Lane, between XI and XII o'clock, several good milch cows, one very fine ox, several horses, waggons, &c." Then, on the 17th inst., were "to be sold, at the Bull's Head Tavern, twenty-one elegant horses, which have been in the *Rebel Dragoon service;* also, near *thirty head of horned cattle*, saddles and bridles, some *sheep*, three waggons, &c." One more sale we shall notice, July 10th following, at the same place: "For ready cash only, a number of horses and cows, &c. By Feegan and Deane."

"N. B. As a bell is not allowed, the Hibernia Flag will be hoisted and a *cryer* at the door."

The "same paper," on the following 29th of November, notices the "police regulations" of bread. "That on and after Thursday, the 23d instant, all bread made of sweet flour of the first quality must be baked into *long loaves* of two pounds weight each, and stamped with the initials of the baker's name, and sold for sixteen coppers each loaf; and all bread made of merchantable flour of an inferior quality must be baked into *round loaves*, weighing two pounds and one-half each, stamped and sold same as the preceding."

The prices of every article continued high, and the " dry summer of 1782 they were very high. Beef then ranged from 1s. 6d. to 3s. 6d. per lb.; turkeys, half a guinea apiece; potatoes sometimes sold at 18s. and a half a guinea per bushel; butter, 8 and 10s. per lb., and the price of oysters was at the enormous rate of 16s. the 100." The poor suffered much, especially the " Refugee poor," but were occasionally assisted from the proceeds of a theatre, gotten up by the British officers, many of whom were amateur performers; and also from a lottery, called in the royal paper of May 4th, 1782, the " New York Poor Lottery, which positively commences drawing on Wednesday next, the 8th instant, at Kirk's Tavern, near the new Bridewell, under the inspection of Captain *Linus King, Frederick Rhinelander* and *Robert Dale*, who are appointed by authority for that purpose."

But *where* were some of these " Old New Yorkers," when the poor starving *Rebels* (as they were called) lay locked up in the many loathsome prisons and prison-ships, where so many *thousands* were suffering the martyrdom of freedom for *seven long years?* I ask, where were the *many* who afterwards grasped at the only chance to stay among those brave and successful patriots, that they might, with their ill-gotten wealth, take advantage of the poverty of those suffering patriots, and accumulate not only riches, but give to their generations a title, or at least the appearance of *nobility*, and that *royal blood* which will never leave their veins until they shall wipe that eternal stain from their records? Read in the N. H. Gazette, April 26, 1777, where " The enemy at New York continues to treat the American prisoners with great *barbarity*. Their allowance to each man for 3 days is 1 lb. of beef, 3 worm-eaten, musty biscuits, and a quart of *salt water*. The meat they are obliged to eat raw, as they have not the smallest allowance of fuel. Owing to this more than savage cruelty, the prisoners die fast, and in the small space of three weeks (during the winter) no less than 1,700 brave men perished." In the History of Litchfield we find, from Lt. Catlin's account, that they were " confined with no sustenance for 48 hours; for 11 days had only 2 days' allowance, pork offensive to the smell, bread hard, mouldy and wormy, made of canail and dregs of flax-seed. He, with 225 men, were put on board the Glasgow at New York about Dec. 25, to be carried to Connecticut for exchange. They were on board 11 days, crowded between decks, and 28 *died* through ill-usage." Then we find from the "grievances that the prisoners are under," "close confined in jail, without distinction of rank or character, amongst felons, without their friends being suffered to speak to them, even through the grates. On the scanty allowance of 2 lbs. hard biscuit, and 2 lbs. raw pork per man per week, without fuel to dress it. Frequently supplied with water from a pump where all kinds of filth is thrown that can render it obnoxious and unwholesome, when good water is as easily obtained. Denied the benefit of a hospital, not allowed to send for medicine, nor even a doctor permitted to visit them when in the greatest distress; married men and others, who lay at the point of death, refused to have their wives or relations admitted to see them, and for attempting it often beat from the prison."* From the Life of Silas Talbot, there were "Two young men, brothers, belonging to a rifle corps, were made prisoners, and sent on board the '*Jersey*.' The elder took the fever, and in a few days became delirious. One night (his end was fast approaching) he became calm and sensible, and lamenting his hard fate, and the absence of his mother, begged for a little water. His brother with tears entreated the guard to give him some, but in vain. The sick youth was soon in his last struggles, when his brother offered the guard a guinea for an inch of candle, only that he might see him die. Even this was refused. 'Now,' said he, drying up his tears, 'if it please God that I ever regain my liberty, I'll be a most bitter enemy!' He regained his liberty, rejoined the army, and when the war ended, he had 8 large and 127 small notches on his rifle-stock."

> " But such a train of endless woes abound,
> So many mischiefs in these Hulks are found,
> That on them all a poem to prolong
> Would swell too high the horrors of our song—
> Hunger and thirst, to work our woe, combine,
> And mouldy bread, and flesh of rotten swine;
> The mangled carcase, and the batter'd brain,
> The Doctor's poison, and the Captain's† cane,
> The Soldier's musquet, and the Steward's debt,
> The evening shackle, and the noon-day threat."
>
> "See, Captain, see! what rotten bones we pick—
> "What kills the healthy cannot cure the sick;
> "Not dogs on such by *Christian* men are fed,
> "And see, good master, see what lousy bread!"
> " Your meat or bread (this man of death replied)
> " 'Tis not my care to manage or provide—
> " But this, base *Rebel dogs*, I'd have you know,
> " That better than you merit we bestow."
> "Here, *generous* Britain, generous, as you say,
> " To my parch'd tongue one cooling drop convey;
> " Hell has no mischief like a thirsty throat,
> " Nor one tormentor like your *David Sproat*."‡

* Onderdonk, L. I., p. 226.   † Cunningham.   ‡ Freneau's Poems, p. 169.

The term *Rebel*, which had been so many years applied to the Friends of Liberty by the royal editors, Rivington and Gaine, had at last become not only disagreeable, but uncalled for, and appears to have been the cause of the following threat: "Provoked at the insolence of the insignificant Tory Printers in New York, who have the impudence to use the term REBEL in their papers, in contradiction to the declaration of their King, in his late speech to the contrary, a number of determined WHIGS have agreed, that should that term, or any other reproachful word, be further used after the first of March next, in any of their papers, that printer, or printers, *shall have their ears cropt* if found in any of the thirteen United States of America after the war.   This public intimation is given them to prevent their further abuse of words, and to *save their ears*, should any of them presume to tarry in that country, and amongst those people who have been the objects of their repeated scurrility and abuse."*

The evacuation of the City of New York by the British troops appears to have been ordered by the authorities in England to take place some five months previous to the 25th of November, 1783, if the following extract of a letter is true.   This letter is dated New York, July 21, 1783, and reads: "This instant the *Mercury* packet is arrived, and Admiral Digby has sent me an assurance that the definite treaty is in his possession, and shall be sent to me presently. The day appointed in England for the evacuation of New York was this very 21st of July."†   This no doubt was true, as Sir Guy Carleton in the following month "informed Congress that he has received orders from England for the immediate evacuation of New York; but observes in his letter, that this movement will be considerably retarded by the number of persons who *must* go with him in consequence of the resolutions of the people throughout the United States, forbidding the return of the Refugees."‡   In the month of April previous, large numbers of Refugees began to leave; the press says, " The number of inhabitants going to Nova Scotia in the present fleet consists of upwards of nine thousand souls."§   In the month of June following, the Adjutant-General, Oliver De Lancey, informs "All persons who have returned their names to the Adjutant-General for passage from this place are desired to apply to the gentleman appointed by His Excellency, the Commander-in-Chief, to examine their several claims, who will attend for that purpose at the City Hall, from 11 o'clock until two every day, Sundays excepted."   On the 16th of August following: " Notice is hereby given to all loyal-

* Penna. Packet, March 4, 1783.   † Ibid., July 24, 1783.
‡ Ibid., August 23, 1783.   § N. Y. Gazette, &c., April 28, 1783.

ists within the *lines*, desirous to emigrate from this place before the *final evacuation*, that they must give in their names, at the Adjutant-General's office, on or before the 21st instant, and be ready to embark by the end of this month." September the 12th following, the Commissioners "give notice to all loyalists who have been recommended for passages to Nova Scotia, that ships are prepared to receive them on board, and it is expected they will embark on or before the twentieth instant; that if they neglect to embrace the opportunity now offered, they must not expect to be conveyed afterwards at the public expense." The two latter were signed "Abijah Williard."

" The most authentic accounts agree (*says a correspondent*) that there are yet between 12 and 15,000 Refugees, men, women, and children, to be embarked at New York, Long Island, and Staten Island for Nova Scotia, St. Johns, and Abasco; among these are many passengers of fortune and landed estates, who leave nothing but *terra firma* behind them."* In the following month of October, Rivington says: " Such persons discharged from the several departments of the army, and have already agreed to form a joint settlement at *Port Mattoon* in Nova Scotia, and are desirous of proceeding thither immediately, are requested to give in, without loss of time, a return of themselves and families to the heads of their respective departments, in order that a proper vessel may be obtained for the purpose of conveying them and their baggage. They will hold themselves in readiness to embark in eight days from the date hereof. Refugees and discharged soldiers, who have been admitted to join this settlement, are required to give in their names, if desirous of going at present, to Mr. Hugh, next door to the Bull's Head in the Bowery. By order of the Managers."

The time was drawing near when the last of the Refugees and other British subjects and soldiers were about departing our shores. One *Tory* "officer-holder," however, in his eagerness to steal and destroy public property, has left his name behind, to be again brought to light in the following transaction: " Last Friday evening, (*four days before the evacuation,*) Mr. Ephraim Smith, heretofore *Inspector of Markets*, assisted by a party of soldiers, determined that the DAMNED REBELS, as that *worthy character* is pleased to term them, should not enjoy so small a convenience when the insolence of his office should be no more, cut down and carried to his house the BELL OF THE FLY MARKET, with threats of prostrating the whole of the *erections* there. But it is with great pleasure we inform the public that the Commandant, having been made acquainted with the trans-

* Penna. Packet, September 4, 1783.

action by a gentleman who happened accidentally to be present, he not only severely reprimanded Mr. Smith for his conduct, but Mr. Smith, by his order, will have the mortification of replacing the *bell* in its old situation. (*Le malleurss, Ephraim.*"*)

All the market-houses which were left standing were found in a ruinous condition, having had no additions or repairs during the occupancy of the city by the British troops. "Above £100 were spent on these market-houses alone."†

The prices of provisions, just previous to the evacuation, are thus noticed in Rivington's paper, (October 22d:) "As sold yesterday in the public markets in this city. Beef from 6d. to 15d. per lb.; mutton, from 7d. to 1s. 1d. per lb.; lamb, 10d.; veal from 1s. to 1s. 6d. per lb.; fowls from 4s. to 4s. 6d. per pair; turkeys from 6s., weighing 8 lbs.; potatoes, 3s. 6d. per bushel; Indian meal, 16s. per cwt.; and butter, 2s. 6d. per lb." Four days after the evacuation of the city, the prices showed another decreasing change, in the same royal editor's paper; but that paper had undergone a change in its name, and appeared with the title of "*Rivington's New York Gazette and Universal Advertiser.*" Its *royalty*, as also its *editors*, had ceased with the departure of the British troops, who also had taken with them the *loyalty* of a great many persons, and left their *royal* bodies behind to propagate and spread discord and *disunion*, if it had *then* been possible. Many thousands, however, who were strictly conscientious and honestly *loyal*, left immediately after finding the *royal* power here had to succumb.

A very few of the *royal* butchers remained after the evacuation; but those who belonged to the markets previous to the war, and remained in the city through and after the war, by continuing under various pleas, were often subjected to insult and mortification in being pointed out as a *tory butcher*, with other more unpleasant names.

For the first few months after the *patriots* had regained the city, very little business was done, as there was but little to do with. The city and the country round about were almost stripped of all kinds of provisions to supply the departing troops and former citizens. In fact, the whole market fees of the city, as appears from an account of Alderman Van Gelder, the *collector*, for nine days, ("from December 9th to the 18th, 1783,") were but £14 4s. 5d.

The poor returning troops and citizens were almost naked and moneyless, but the pleasure of once more beholding their homes and firesides instilled into them a new life; while there were among the poor farmers some who were unable to rise again, being obliged to mortgage their farms to obtain the necessary stock and farming im-

* Penna. Packet, November 25, 1783. † City Records.

plements to cultivate the recovered barren acres, with the hope that a few years would enable them to live as before. The long war had so exhausted the country, that it was many years in recovering sufficiently to relieve its liberators, and, of course, many were impoverished. In the year 1786 we find noticed, "As an instance of the deplorable situation of New Jersey for want of cash, a correspondent assures us that he, last week, counted posted up over the mantle in a tavern no less than sixteen real estates taken by execution, and advertised by the Sheriff of Morris County for sale."*

How much do *we all* owe these suffering liberators for our freedom and independence! And if we cannot repay them in any other way, we can and *must* watch, guard, and *battle* if necessary, and also instruct our children to do the same, that the Union may be preserved as they have left it to us.

This subject has led me astray, although I feel that the sufferings in obtaining our liberties should be engrafted in our every-day thoughts, conversations, books, schools; in fact, in our very dreams, so that we shall be prepared to combat the enemy in any form he may assume. Beware, however, of the demagogue or the smooth-tongued politician, as *this subject* is their forte, which reaches quickest the soul of the patriot, and warily leads him on, to be at last entrapped into their fatal clutches, and robbed of their manhood. Other pens than mine have, and will spread again, pages of this history, which will have more influence than can be found on these, and I can safely resume the history of this market again.

On the 22d of April, 1784, "The neighborhood and butchers at the *Fly Market* were desirous of covering the slip at the lower end of the said market, and extending the said market over the slip to the bridge across the same, to make room for the country people," which then again began to crowd this market. The Board gave their consent on the 12th of May following to extend to the bridge near the ferry stairs, and "That the market thus extended be covered in the same manner as the one it joins on."

A countryman, about two years after, in this market, displayed a remarkable feat or feast, which is noticed in the N. Y. Gazette, 29th May, 1786: "Yesterday, a countryman in the Fly Market, for a trifling wager, eat *fifty boiled eggs*, shells and all! He performed the task in about fifteen minutes, being elevated on a butcher's block during the operation."

A feast at the best hotels (or rather taverns and inns) was not so expensive at that period as the present, as the following charges will show: "Breakfast, two shillings; dinner, two shillings and nine-pence; supper, two shillings; cut of beef, one shilling; cut of ham,

* Independent Journal, March 4.

one shilling and two-pence; do. of beef-steaks, one shilling and six-pence; chicken, one shilling and nine-pence; oysters from 6d. to 2s., as called for. Single bed, one shilling; horse, one night at hay, two shillings; double do., one shilling and sixpence; oats per quart, three-pence; bating at hay, sixpence. Madeira, 8s.; Champagne, 10s., claret, 8s.; Sherry, 6s.; port, 6s.; porter, 3s.; beer, 1s.; cyder, 8d. per bottle; sangaree, (per bowl,) 4s.; punch, 2s.; toddy, 1s. 2d.; grog, 1s.; spirits, (per gill,) 6d.; brandy, 8d.; gin, 8d.," &c.*

" *Eboracus*," a very *great traveler*, also gives us a bill of fare of the several States the next year; he says: "As I have travelled thro' all the States, I will furnish the *Bill of Fare:* for *New Hampshire*, beef and Indian dumplings. *Massachusetts*, cod and haydock, (*had-dock*.) *Rhode Island*, tontog (*black-fish*) with plain butter, not with soy or ketchup—they are quintessences and extracts. *Connecticut*, pork and molasses. *New York*, oysters and lobsters. (New) *Jersey*, a Burlington ham and Newark cyder. *Philadelphia*, soft sheeps-head. *Delaware* does not deserve a dish; they must subsist as Lazarus did—upon the crumbs. *Maryland*, a canvass-back duck, roasted by a stop-watch. *Virginia*, fried chickens and hominy, with New England rum. *North Carolina*, corn-fed pork and peach brandy. *South Carolina*, a pye of rice-birds and a roast turkey-buzzard. These vain people will have two dishes if their creditors have none. *Georgia*, a poor-man's pudding with a glass of water."†

There is no doubt some truth in the general character of the *living* in the several States as noticed above; but the reader will conclude that the following description of the *living* in the States is a more reasonable one: "Notwithstanding the general charge of its being hard to live in America, there is not at this time a civilized country on the face of the earth in which a poor man may live with so much ease as in the United States. Every traveler knows with what diligence farmers and mechanics, in foreign countries, are obliged to labor through the year. In the winter the work begins before day, and in summer it continues thro' the day. They have little respite or time for spending money. If one of them is accost-ed, he seldom stops to answer—his work must go on. This is not the case with us, nor have we any example of what Europeans call industry. The citizens of America may live with half of the labor which would support them in France, England, or Germany. Is he candid or honest who complains of such a country, or says that his troubles are occasioned by the necessary difficulty of living, by the difficulty of paying taxes, or of providing food and raiment, or by any other course than his vices, his idleness and dissipation?"‡

* N. Y. Packet, March 12, 1786.   † Daily Advertiser, May 16, 1787.
‡ N. Y. Packet, June 26, 1787.

There were, however, complaints about some of the currency at this period, and more particularly the copper coin.

The ferrymen who own the boats which ply between this *Market* Slip and Brooklyn apply to the Board for relief, and state they "have for this some time past taken a quantity of *coppers* for ferriage, &c., at the rate of twenty to a shilling, which is now lying on their hands, and must of course be a very great loss in their present depreciation, and involve your petitioners into many embarrassments. We therefore beg your Hon. Body to consider our situation, and to receive them on the same conditions from the 1st to the 20th of July, (1787,) and your petitioners will be in part released of the loss in the 'copper coin.' They also beg leave that your Hon. Body will assist them with advice in respect to those coppers which are now in circulation, as the public in general, which uses the ferry, very seldom presents any other money to pay their passage, and which we have received since your Hon. Body was pleased to recommend their passing at *forty-eight to a shilling;* but as there still arises great inconvenience in taking them even at that rate, and still likely to be attended with some additional loss, unless received for rent by your Hon. Body, we pray your counsel in the premises, &c." HENRY DAWSON, GILBERT V. MATER, and JACOB WILKINS, JUN'R.

The bakers also follow with another on the same subject, on the 8th of June, who state, "That the greatest part of the bread which the petitioners have sold for some time past has been paid for in 'coppers' and Jersey money; that they cannot purchase flour with the moneys they have so received, and are daily obliged to receive; neither will the merchants receive these moneys in payment from them for flour they have already purchased. That in this embarrassed situation, they cannot carry on their business without involving themselves in debt."

In the month of June of the next year, a petition, signed by above forty inhabitants, praying "that the south part of the market now called *the Fish Market* may be covered, and appropriated solely to the use of the country farmers; that the slip may be filled up half of the width of Burnet Street, and a new fish market erected over the water in the middle of the slip." A committee reported, on the 26th of the same month, in favor of the above, and the "additional market-house across the slip, and that proper blocks or wings be laid in the slip, to extend sixty-four feet beyond the south side of Front Street, for the purpose of supporting a market, which may be erected at the expense of the neighborhood."

It may not be uninteresting to know how the stands were arranged in the first and second markets, after the third or fish market was finished. This regulation was adopted by the Board on the 31st December following. In the first or upper market-house, beginning at Queen *(Pearl)* Street: "One stall at the head of the market, and eighteen on the sides," (37 *stands*.) "That every butcher's stall be no more than eight feet long, and three feet, six inches broad, and that no part thereof extend any further into the market; that the back of each stall be placed to range with the inner side of the market-posts, and eleven feet passage-way through the centre." The whole length is represented as being 224 feet, and about 20 feet wide. The same arrangement was made with the six butcher stalls in the next or middle market-house.

The rapid growth around, and the increased business in this market, appeared to outstrip all the others; and notwithstanding the "late enlargement, it is still insufficient for the accommodation of the citizens." The neighboring inhabitants and owners of property were always quite willing to subscribe certain amounts to further increase its success; but we find some—just such, or whom knowledge has made worse, now-a-days—exceedingly willing to subscribe, but exceedingly *un*willing to pay over. But I must go back to this less corrupt age, and speak of a reported list of persons on the 17th July, 1789, "who had subscribed (£54!) to the late addition to the Fly Market, and either neglected or refused to pay;" when suits were ordered to be commenced against them.

The law for collecting the public market fees was altered on the 4th of March, 1790; weekly sums were to be collected from all the butchers who occupied stands. In this market, the sum of £16 9s. was the stated weekly sum, and the lowest sum for any stall "be four shillings." This law was, however, repealed before it was a month old, as we find, on the 26th of the same month, it changed to the old system of paying: "For the four quarters of beef, 2s.; of mutton, lamb, and veal, 4d.; and of fresh pork, 6d., in lieu of all other market fees."

Towards the close of the year, quite a compliment was paid to the Collectors, by the "Board," (on the 24th December,) who state, "That from the diligence of James Culbertson and Rinier Skaats, Collectors of the market fees, considerable more moneys have been collected than usual. Therefore ordered, that Mr. Culbertson be allowed £20, and Mr. Skaats £7, in addition to their usual allowance to the first of January next; and that from that day they be allowed a commission of *ten per cent.* on the moneys by them respectively collected." What a pity we had not *a few* Culbertsons and Skaatses now-a-days to handle the public moneys, as well as to fill many of the public offices! And what a satisfaction to the public, if the whole city were better governed, on *one-half* (or even less) the expense! Such kind of men would build or rebuild our City Halls, our (Tompkins) market-houses, clean our streets, and, in season, attend to all other necessary matters which might lay suffering, and wanted by the people. Their consciences, as well as their *oaths*, would not allow them to leave their desks or duties, during business hours, (which number should count as many as of those of the mechanics and other workmen,) to while away the people's time in Tom's, or Dick's, or Harry's place, or traveling the road with a *turn-out* of electric speed, or to attend a political convention. We all know that there are those of that class who live among us, but of course they are not the flexible tools that this *minority* of well-organized political workmen want; their metal is not tempered in the modern political furnace to suit their purposes: in fact, *they are* only suitable for the *mass*, who appear to have no choice, or, at least, *who do not use it*.

One of these collectors, (James Culbertson,) in making his regular returns in the month of April, 1792, also makes a return of fines collected from nearly fifty delinquents, to the amount of £16 15 0. Seventeen of these were for *light butter;* nine for *forestalling;* eight for *blowing meat;* two for *blowing turkeys;* the others for *exposing meat by an agent*, and *goods* contrary to law. Their fines were generally *five shillings*, and a few £1, which was immediately paid after the decision was made, or the Bridewell key was turned upon them.

In the month of May, 1790, the "inhabitants around this market-place praying aid to erect an arched walk across the kennel (*sewer*) at the end of the market in Queen Street," and also, "that the stall of Henry Astor, butcher, be removed to the lower market," which was granted. This stall of Astor's stood across the head of the upper market, and no doubt tended to block up the entrance gangway, which caused its removal.

An anecdote was told to me by an old drover, several years ago, of this thrifty and hard-working man. When he commenced business here, he began in a small way; his purchases were made at the Bull's Head, (which at that time took up the grounds where now stands the old Bowery Theatre;) here he selected his *small stock*, of which he bought but few at a time, placed them in his wheelbarrow, and wheeled them home; then, with the assistance of his wife, he dressed and prepared them for market. Hours before daylight, the next morning, his stock in trade was placed in the same carriage, when he conveyed it to the Fly Market; and he became one of the most wealthy of our butchers.

He came to this country during the Revolution with the British troops; but, after a short period, he managed to escape their service, and entered into that of the "Art and mystery of Butchering;" when he became known and continued with the name of *Ashdoor*. In 1783, 11th of April, he advertises his horse as—"Stolen from the subscriber, on the night of the 10th instant, from the door of Israel Seaman's, Rosevelt Street, a dark-brown horse, about fifteen hands high, a small star in his forehead, the hair worn off his breast by a collar; trots and carries well; saddle and double curb bridle on the horse when stolen." Three guineas reward for the horse, saddle, and bridle. "For the thief, horse, saddle, and bridle, ten guineas will be paid by Henry Ashdoor."

After *peace* was declared he sought citizenship, and was naturalized under the act passed May 4th, 1784; soon after which he began to thrive, and when his brother John Jacob, the millionaire, arrived here, the frugal butcher Henry assisted him with his first stock in trade: a *basket of trinkets*, which he sold and traded with those who brought furs and skins on board of sloops and other vessels which lay around the docks; and *these* were the rough foundation-stones that were built upon, and now, no doubt, this structure of wealth stands among the highest.

But their lives are only an edition of many of the "Old Families," whose posterity are now enjoying the fruits of the labor of their self-denying and hard-working forefathers and *foremothers;* who, if they could rise up from their graves—Rip Van Winkle like—they would gaze *horror stricken* on the idleness, extravagance, and dissipation of their *fast* generations. And these *fast* generations should be forced to look back into the ages past and see their ancient sires, (or *Governors*, as they are now usually termed,) with their old greasy leather breeches—the only pair ever owned by the wearer—the thick, coarse woolen stockings, with the heels run and well darned; the cowhide boots, with two patches in front and one behind; the coarse flaxen shirt, which thread had been spun on a spinning-wheel for a *resting spell* on a winter's evening; and a hat, or part of one, which twenty years before was said to have been sold for a " cocked hat," and the second one ever owned by the wearer; and then again, their old-fashioned *great-grand dames*, with linsey woolsey short gowns and petticoats, the wool of which had been prepared by their own useful hands; their hair without a comb, but plainly arranged under a close-fitting cap; and their feet incased in a pair of shoes, so heavy and substantial, that their noise and healthfulness would frighten a modern doctor out of his senses, as well as deprive him of his annual income. In the *de*-generations that have followed those "*good old times*" which I have endeavored to illustrate, many no doubt will exclaim against this picture of their ancestors as being a shocking satire upon themselves, with their thin shoes and thinner constitutions; and if they did not faint away outright, they would say that history was a tell-tale, and ought not to be countenanced in this enlightened and fast age.

We follow on with a petition dated 20th of July following, from several farmers and gardeners, whose names will be recognized among many of the worthy families of the present generation. They complain that they were not allowed to place themselves among the farmers of Long Island and other parts of the country in the markets, and wish that proper places may be set apart for the petitioners, where they may be free from the inconveniences they have hitherto experienced. Signed by

Henry Brevoort,	Henry Spingler,	Henry Low,
Isaac Varian,	Samuel Van Orden,	Lawrence Ulshofer,
Thomas Rose,	Richard Amos,	Yellis Mandeville,
Nicholas Romaine,	George Campbell,	Gilbert Coutant,
William Graham,	John Samler,	Samuel Hallett,
	David Williamson,	John Amos, &c.

Then complaints were made of the great interruption and noise of carts, carriages, &c., in market hours. The Board, on the following 20th of August, "Ordered the Deputy Clerk, Mr. Culbertson, to place chains across Front Street, thirty feet west of the side or range of the street leading along to the river; and in December, 1799, chains were ordered on both sides across Water Street."

In the month of January, 1792, "A terrible fire broke out in a frame house in Front Street, near the Fly Market, which in two hours entirely consumed 7 houses, and damaged a number of others before it was extinguished. The Fly Market was on fire several times, and the shipping at Taylor's and Brownjohn's Wharves were obliged to haul into the stream. The heat was so great that several panes of the windows on the opposite side of the street were melted."

There was a scarcity of neat cattle several years after peace had been declared, but since 1788 they increased very fast. Long Island and the lower counties of the State of New York almost wholly supplied the city's wants. Connecticut exported a large number in '89 and in '90: " there were exported (in 1790) 7,072 horses, cattle, and mules, it being 394 more than was shipped the preceding year from the district of New London."* The " Complaint of a Queen's County Farmer" gives us some ideas of the difficulties of the time in getting market price for his cattle. He says: " It takes about six or seven

* N. Y. Journal, &c., January 24, 1791.

years for a farmer to raise a pair of excellent well-grown oxen and make them fat enough for beef of the first quality; he hopes, when he has got them fit for the knife, some butcher will come along and purchase his cattle at their value; instead of this, he finds the country is infested by a set of underling drovers, or rather butcher agents, who fabricate a thousand lies about the glut of the markets, and the cheapness of meat; and who, after haggling and teasing him a long time about the price, worry the poor farmer at last into a bargain, and buy his beef for twenty per cent. less than the current rate of the market. The agent thus adds to the prime cost as much as he thinks proper, and forwards them to the butcher at the new price. In addition to this, he gets his purchase fee, and laughs in his sleeve at the thought of having cheated both the farmer and the butcher."*

The animals, being purchased, were driven to the ferry, then they were put on board of a low flat scow with sprit-sail; and if in crossing they were caught in a stiff breeze, over they went, often drowning several persons and animals too. "On Friday last (17th Dec., 1795,) one of the Brooklyn ferry-boats was overset in passing the East River; one man and seven fat oxen were drowned."†

These occurrences were quite common, and frequently attended with great loss of life and property, on both the North and East Rivers. The sail ferry-boats were considered very unsafe, especially on a windy day, or from floating ice, when but few persons would trust their horses, carriages, cattle, or other property on them; preferring to wait a day or two for calm weather. The oar-barges, for foot-passengers, were thought more safe, and were more regular in crossing. They, however, were a great annoyance to travelers and business men, and continued so until *team* or *horse* and steam boats were introduced. But no doubt a few incidents, since the Revolution, will be more acceptable to the general reader.

In the year 1784, on a "Tuesday afternoon, *(January 15th,)* as a ferry-boat was coming from Powles Hook with passengers for this city, it unfortunately got between two cakes of ice, which so damaged it, that when they separated, it soon after sunk, leaving the people in the water, to struggle for life. A cake of ice close at hand afforded them a temporary relief. The North River eddy, setting in around the Battery, carried them into the East River, where, getting into the ebb-tide, they were carried out into the Bay. All the slips being full of ice, it was with difficulty that two or three small boats were got out to attempt their relief; but the large fields of ice at that moment in motion rendered every effort of the boatmen fruitless, and cut off every prospect of deliverance from

* N. Y. Journal and P. R., March 10, 1792.   † Ibid., December 22, 1795.

their miserable, anxious situation, but by death—till the river, being somewhat free from ice, a boat, manned with hardy soldiers, went in pursuit of them, braving every danger, and persevering through every difficulty. To the inexpressible joy, though contrary to the expectation of the town, they returned just at dark, (having been almost to the Narrows,) and rescued from the jaws of death seven of the unfortunate people. The other, a negro man, perished with cold. Among the number saved are Mr. Buchanan, of Morristown; Mr. Laboyteaux and Mr. Thomson, of this city; and we are happy to inform the public that they are doing very well. To the spectators the sight was truly distressing, to behold our fellow-creatures upon the verge of death, invoking our assistance in vain, and experiencing the most torturing anxiety of mind, between the hopes of being saved and the dread of entering the inscrutable state of eternity."* Then—" On Saturday afternoon last, when a ferry-boat passing over from Brooklyn to this city was suddenly overset. This accident is said to have been occasioned by the shifting of one of the horses, of which there were five on board; which so startled the rest, that they all removed to one side, when the boat immediately filled. The passengers, viz., Mr. Thorne, Mr. Stackhouse, and a servant-man, together with two ferrymen, saved themselves by swimming till they were picked up, when almost exhausted, by several boats from the shore and the different vessels in the harbor."† Following this, we find—" On Wednesday last, about one o'clock, as a ferry-boat was attempting to cross over the North River to Powles Hook, she was overset by a sudden gust of wind at no great distance from the shore, and notwithstanding the utmost exertions of several who immediately set out to their assistance, to the evident danger of their own lives, three passengers, namely, a Mr. Elias Cowenhouse, of Allantown, a Mr. Young, driver of one of the Philadelphia stages, and a negro boy, servant to Mr. Van Voorst, near Powles Hook, were unfortunately drowned. An old gentleman and the two ferrymen continued to hold fast by the ropes till they were picked up."‡ Another more "melancholy accident happened," (*April* 3, 1798.) "Yesterday, about 12 o'clock, one of the large ferry-boats which plies between (the old ferry stairs, Fly Market,) this city and Brooklyn, across the East River, was unhappily sunk in a gust of wind. There were eight men in the boat; five of them were boatmen, and three passengers; all of whom were drowned, except one of the boatmen."§

The business of carrying neat cattle on the ferry-boats was at

* Penna. Packet, January 22.   † Independent Journal.
‡ Ibid., November 8.   § N. Y. Journal, &c.

times objectionable to the passengers; sometimes having to wait after the regular periods for starting, when taking them off or on, and also when discharging them at the ferry landings, at this and the Catharine Markets, among the crowds, was also a cause of complaint. So, on the 30th of September, 1793, "it was ordered that no cattle be landed at any place in this city to the westward of Col. Rutgers," that being much nearer the public slaughter-house, than at Corlaers Hook.

Other complaints were also made to the ferry-master, which sometimes came from a belated passenger, of the want of promptness; another, of the boatmen, whom they dreaded to sail across with, considering their knowledge of navigation, when either in *sailing trim*, or *half-seas over*, was of the smallest possible description. The imagination would lead one to think of the many wrangles that occasionally took place at the ferry landings and on board of the boats; one of which grew into a matter of much importance, and worthy of notice, took place in the year 1795.

It appears that Alderman Furman "came to the ferry stairs on the Brooklyn side and wanted to cross" before the usual time. Unpleasant words passed between him and two of the ferrymen, named Timothy Crady and Thomas Burk, and when Mr. Hicks, the Conductor of the Ferry, came down to order the boat off, the Alderman complained to him that these two men had abused him; on which Mr. Hicks said to the Alderman, that it was the rule to have civil treatment given to all the passengers, or words to that effect. On the passage across, the Alderman being not yet satisfied, gave the men a reprimand, which again brought forth hard words, and finally a threat from the Alderman that he would commit them to prison. Timothy Crady said "he would put his boat-hook through any man that would touch him;" so says the Alderman, in his testimony before what was then known as the "Bridewell Court."*
When they reached the ferry stairs at the Fly Market, the Alderman ordered the Clerk of the Market *(Mr. Culbertson, an officer,)* to arrest them and take them to jail. The manner of their being taken to the jail is described by John Bennet, a Long Island farmer, attending this market, in a deposition, that "he saw Timothy Crady and Thomas Burk in the custody of Mr. Culbertson, on their way to the Bridewell; and that Alderman Furman did punch them in the back with his cane, saying 'Move on, you rascals—I'll fix you;' and that he punched the said Burk and Crady with so much violence, that they frequently would yield to the force of his cane."
They were, after a time, brought up before this Bridewell Court,

* N. Y. Journal, &c., December 26, 1795.

composed of Mayor Varick, Aldermen Beekman, Van Tuyl, and Lenox, usually held at the Common Jail in the Park, when the testimony of Alderman Furman was taken; no other was offered against the prisoners. On their behalf, Jacob Hicks stated, "That he had known Thomas Burk as a ferryman these eighteen months, during which time he sustained the character of a good citizen and a civil man." However, in the end the Court sentenced, "That you, Timothy Crady, receive, to-morrow morning, twenty lashes on your bare back, to impress on your mind that you are not to insult men in office; suffer two months' imprisonment in Bridewell, at hard labor. And that you, Thomas Burk, be imprisoned two months in Bridewell, at hard labor, excused from whipping, being interceded for by Alderman Furman."

Other testimony taken before the Grand Jury shows "they were imprisoned on the 10th of November, and were confined twelve days before being brought to trial." The judgment and sentence which followed is reviewed by some of the "Press" in communications, cards, and editorials; the conclusions of which are not at all flattering to this "Court," particularly to Mayor Varick and Alderman Lenox, the latter being severely handled.

The affair created no little excitement; and several citizens, (among whom were Mr. William Kettletas, the Messrs. Hicks, and others, who witnessed the transaction and thought these ferrymen had been improperly and unjustly punished,) finding they could not obtain their liberation or justice, appealed through petitions to the Legislature to impeach this "Bridewell Court." The case was brought before the House, who appointed a committee to investigate it; they after a time reported, and, after a severe struggle, the House "*Resolved*, That the testimony produced in support of the charges against Richard Varick, &c., does not furnish sufficient ground for impeachment; acquits them, or either of them." This conclusion was quite unsatisfactory, and more especially to Mr. Kettletas, who wrote several communications, showing the case more fully, and somewhat reflecting on the committee.

These were noticed by the "House," who ordered the arrest of Mr. Kettletas; which is shown in the proceedings, March 3, 1796. The Sergeant-of-Arms, being attended with William Kettletas in his custody, "was set to the bar of this House, and was questioned if he was the author of a certain publication? To which he said: '*I am the author, and did direct the same to be printed.*' He was ordered into the custody of the *Sergeant-of-Arms*. A resolution was passed pronouncing him 'guilty of a misdemeanor and contempt of the authority of this House.' That he 'be brought to the bar of this

House, and upon his asking pardon of the House for his offence, and paying the Sergeant's fees, he be discharged from custody.' He was brought before them again, when he answered: ' *I am not conscious of having committed any offence, and therefore I will not ask the pardon of this House.*' He then was delivered to the keeper of the goal of the City and County of New York, and confined in the same prison with the two ferrymen. "

From this prison he addresses a note to the editor of the New York Journal, which is found in that paper, dated April 1, 1796, as follows:

"*Mr. Greenleaf*—It is with the deepest regret I announce to my fellow-citizens a confirmation of the late melancholy report of the death of the unfortunate *Timothy Crady.* Whether his death was in consequence of the 25 unjust stripes he received by order of the ' Bridewell Court,' or not, is reserved for the decision of that tribunal, before whom it will be my duty, as well as every other citizen's, to submit this solemn question. The confirmation of his death was made known to me, on the 28th instant, by *Thomas Burk*, the surviving fellow-sufferer, who has returned to his former place of residence at Brooklyn. Which fact I immediately communicated to William Slo, the Bridewell master, from whose custody, it has been said, the said *Burk* escaped before the sentence of the ' Bridewell Court' was executed. Mr. Slo returned me for answer, that he should not trouble himself about the said *Burk*, except he came in his way. This fact, relative to the conduct of Mr. Slo, I think proper to make public, that the ' Bridewell Court' may take such steps to support the law as the law expressly enjoins."

Mr. Kettletas was confined in prison until the Legislature adjourned; he was then by a *habeas corpus* liberated on the 12th of April. The "*Journal*" says: "On this occasion a number of citizens attended at the prison, and forced him into a phaeton, in which they paraded him in triumph.

"On the phaeton were displayed the American and French flags, the *Cap of Liberty*, supported by Mr. Kettletas, and a painted representation of a man *whipped* at the whipping-post, after the Bridewell mode, with a scroll in these words over the head of the whipper: ' *What! you rascal, insult your superiors!*' The phaeton was drawn by citizens through the principal streets in the city, drums beating, with a numerous body of attendants, to the Tontine; from thence up Wall Street into Broadway, down by the Government House, and back to Hunter's Hotel, where Mr. Kettletas made a short speech to the people in nearly the following words: ' *Fellow-citizens*—I thank you for the respect which you have this day paid

me; in a particular manner for the honor of bearing the *Standard
of Liberty*, which you have placed in my hands. Your decorum,
combined with all your insignias, evidence to me your attachment
to the Constitution and the laws of your country; they are the best
supporters of liberty, and I am sure you revere them.' He was then
set down at his own door, and the company, after giving *three cheers*,
retired in the utmost order, enraptured with the virtues of their fel-
low-citizen, who had endured near *five weeks'* imprisonment, by what
has been called an *arbitrary edict*."

Mr. Kettletas was not yet satisfied that justice had been done to
Burk, so he brings a suit "for cruelty and injustice" against this
" Bridewell Court," for Thomas Burk, and in the end recovered, or
rather it was settled, by paying Burk 500 dollars.*

Another melancholy accident, occurring through the inefficiency
of the ferrymen, is noticed in a "communication," about four years
after, which reads: "Having seen several erroneous accounts in the
papers respecting the upsetting of the ferry-boat at Fly Market,
and being myself on board at the time, will thank you to publish the
following: We started from Fly Market Ferry Stairs with little
wind, but there was a prospect that the wind would blow very fresh,
so that the passengers desired the boatmen to brail up the sail, which
they would not comply with. Some of the passengers wished and
talked of taking charge of the boat themselves. We considered the
boatmen incapable of conducting the boat, owing to *intoxication:*
however, we concluded that no man would be employed in that business unless they were capable of the task; but unfortunately we suffered them to proceed. The first gust that came upset us, and several of the passengers were immediately lost. As near as I can
recollect, there was in the boat about twelve persons—one woman
and five men were immediately drowned—six of us were saved after
having been upset, nearly one hour and an half in the water. One,
after the storm was over, being spent, could no longer hold fast, but
let go and was drowned. There were three horses and a chair (*a
two-wheeled carriage on leather springs*) on board."†

Then we have a communication from an " Enquirer," in the month
of January, 1804, who says: "On Wednesday morning, I had occasion to cross from the Powles Hook Ferry Stairs, New York, to the
Jersey side. On my arrival at the boat, I found the wind to blow
quite fresh; upon which I asked the ferry-master if the boatmen had
not better take a reef in their sails? He answered me, no; and the
mulatto captain also replied, there was no danger; he would carry
us across safely. Though after these answers, I did not feel myself

* N. Y. Journal, &c., February 8, 1797.   † American Citizen, May 27, 1801.

free from apprehension of danger, I agreed with the rest to take my passage, with a promise to myself, that if there should be an increase of wind, I would endeavor to persuade our *captain* to take in sail. I soon found my fears were not unfounded, as at every flaw the pit-tiauger went gunnel under. I then expressed my wish that they would either reef the sails or take in one—this was also answered by a cry on the part of our *captain*, There is no danger. Soon after a flaw took us, and one or two afterwards, so severe that it is a miracle of miracles we were not all sent into eternity. Independent of this, there was a person on board with a horse and chair, who miraculously escaped having his leg broken by the carriage tumbling about, and jamming his leg against the side of the boat. This person lost several articles of his travelling apparatus overboard. He appeared much enraged, and after his arrival on the other side, applied to the ferry-master for his property to be replaced. The only satisfaction he got from the ferryman, that the ferrymen's lives were in as much danger as the passengers'. The person alluded to said he would publish the circumstance the next day; but as I have not seen it, if you think these lines in a fit state for publication, you will please give them a place in your paper."*

Three years after, in the month of February, was noticed: "On Friday, at 5 P. M., a large boat of the old ferry, laden with flour, which was stowed too much on her bows, sunk in the middle of the river, with six persons on board, who were picked up by boats which went off to their assistance." The next year: "On Monday night, (January 14,) the Powles Hook Ferry-boats, *Dolphin* and *Rambler*, owned by Mr. Holdram, were cut by the ice in Whitehall Slip and sunk. They were laden with country produce; the greatest part of which was saved." Then following, on the 21st instant, "One of the Powles Hook Ferry-boats, with a quantity of wood and 25 passengers, had nearly been lost on Saturday (19th) at noon. She was coming before the wind, when a sea struck her, and went over her fore and aft, and filled her nearly half full of water. The passengers waved their hats for assistance, but were fortunately landed in safety."†

We are shown in the following verses some of the troubles of the olden time, in

"CROSSING THE FERRY."

" T' other day, being call'd to New York in a hurry,
And obliged, *nolens volens*, to cross o'er the Ferry,
I had waited impatient some time on the stairs,
When ' Hurry—she's going !' saluted my ears.

* Daily Advertiser.   † Morning Chronicle, January 16, 1805.

So I scrambled on board, took my seat in the stern,
And (as usual) was *waiting for freight*, in the sun!
Till at length, 'mid some oaths, and ' For G— sake push off!'
The men took their oars, and were leaving the wharf.
' Hold on, there—hold on! here's a man coming down
With a cart-load of things to go over to town—
Hold on, there—hold on! here's a woman in sight—
Hold on just a bit—I shall get two-pence by 't!'
With a smart spunky crew, who were not in condition
To bear any longer such great imposition,
We all rose at once—spoke in language of thunder,
And our great noble Captain was forced to knock under."*

"Crossing the Ferry," at New York, with the first steam ferry-
boat, was made on the North River, by Mr. John Stevens, on or
about the 18th of September, 1811. The first announcement of it
appears in the "Press" of that date, as follows: " *Hoboken Steamboat*.—Mr. Godwin respectfully acquaints the citizens of New York
and the public at large, that he has commenced running a steamboat
on the Hoboken Ferry, of large and convenient size, and capable of
affording accommodation in a very extensive degree. The boat
moves with uncommon speed and facility, and starts from the usual
Ferry Stairs, at the Corporation Wharf, foot of Vesey Street, New
York, where passages may be taken at any hour of the day."†

On the 24th of the same month, the following editorial appears:
" Steamboats are rapidly getting into ' the full tide of successful experiment' in this country. Last week one of Colonel Stevens' ferry-
boats, employed by Mr. Godwin, of Hoboken, was started into operation, and yesterday made 16 trips back and forth, between that place
and this city, with a probable average of 100 passengers each trip.
Her machinery, we understand, is somewhat different from that of
the large North River boats, and we presume she sails considerably
faster than any other heretofore constructed in our waters."‡

The North River boats, or rather the first successful steamboat
introduced on the North River, appeared and commenced the first
trip to Albany on Monday, the 17th of September, 1807, at 1 o'clock,
P. M. She was called " *Clermont*," after the country seat of Chancellor Livingston, on the North River, about 110 miles from New
York. The particulars of the " Clermont's" first trip to Albany
with passengers are thus given by a number of witnesses who have
subscribed their names, as noticed in the Press:

" STEAMBOAT.—On Friday morning last, (*September 4th,*) at 18
minutes before 7 o'clock, the North River steamboat left New York,
landed one passenger at Tarrytown, and arrived at Newburgh at 4
o'clock in the afternoon; landed a passenger there and arrived at

* L. I. Star, September 4, 1811.   † " Columbian."   ‡ Ibid.

'Clermont,' where two passengers were landed at 15 minutes before 2 o'clock in the morning, and arrived at Albany at three-quarters of an hour past 10, making the whole time 28 and a half hours—distance 165 miles. The wind favorable but light from Verplank's Point to Wapping's Creek; the remainder of the way it was head wind or a dead calm. This was signed by

"Selah Strong,	Garrit Van Wagennen,	Thomas Wallace,
John L. Wilson,	John P. Anthony,	Wm. S. Hicks,
Dennis Moore,	G. O. Wetmore,	J. Bauman,
J. Crane,	James Braiden,	Stephen N. Power.

"Dated Albany, Sept. 5, 1807."*

This boat was built by Mr. Charles Brown, at his ship-yards on the East River, from which she was launched in the spring of 1807. The engine put into her was made in England, and in the month of August, she was found completed, so as to be moved from her berth around to the Jersey shore by her machinery, much to the surprise and admiration of hundreds who witnessed this first successful steamboat in our waters.

With the ferry-boats there was quite a competition between Fulton, who represented the Powles Hook Ferry Company, and Col. John Stevens, that of the Hoboken Ferry. Colonel Stevens, as it appears, brought forth the first passenger steam ferry-boat; but Fulton produced, although at a later period, a boat (or rather a double boat) which proved successful for the general wants and uses of a ferry-boat.

The remarks of the "Press," made at that period, will give the reader a much better knowledge of their several merits; and having noticed Colonel Stevens', we turn to Fulton's, which is found in the month of July following. "The large and commodious *steamboat* which has been for some time erecting in this city by Mr. Fulton, as a ferry-boat to ply between this city and the City of Jersey, will be in full operation on Thursday next, (*July* 2.) The crossing the North River has been such an obstacle to the communication with this city, that it is a matter of real congratulation to the public that their difficulties are removed. The most timid may cross now without fear. As the fare of a market wagon, loaded, will be but fifty cents, there is no doubt but our markets will be better supplied than ever they have been."†

On the 20th of July following, a description is given of "*Fulton's Steam Ferry-Boat.*" "This excellent machine, consisting of a boat with two hulls, connected by a single platform, with a wheel in the space between them, and rudders at each end, built for the convey-

* Daily Advertiser, September 11, 1807.   † "Columbian," July 1, 1812.

ance of passengers across the Hudson, has got into successful operation, and promises extraordinary facilities for traveling.   Horses
and wagons stand on each side of the machinery, driving in at one
end from a floating bridge fitted to the boat, and out at the other,
without rising or descending six inches in accomplishing the passage from street to street on each side the river.   The boat is
constructed with both ends alike, and never turns in sailing, but
goes back and forth by changing the motion of the wheel."

"On Sunday, the corps of Flying Artillery crossed in the boat
from Paulus Hook to the city, on its way to Albany, at four trips;
on the first of which it brought 4 pieces of artillery, (6-pounders,)
and limbers, ammunition-wagons, 27 horses, and 40 soldiers, besides
other passengers."   Another account says, "The 'steam ferry-boat'
crosses the Hudson twice in each hour during the day.   Yesterday,
(*September* 15,) in crossing from Paulus Hook, the boat contained
about 500 persons, besides a coach and a pair of horses, a phaeton
and pair, a horse and chair, and five saddle-horses."

The great number of soldiers and other persons crossing the ferries at this period was on account of the preparations for war with
England.

The want of a team or steam ferry-boat on the East River was
the occasion of a large amount of property lost by fire on the 23d
of September, 1812, in Brooklyn.   The "Press," the next day, says,
"Last evening, about eight o'clock, a tremendous fire broke out at
Brooklyn in Ben'n Smith's large stable, (in which nine horses were
destroyed,) situated near the old ferry, east side of Main Street,
which consumed the building where it originated, together with
Chas. Hewlet's grocery-store, T. Hicks and Van Mater's stables,
and the large store-house known as the Corporation Buildings."
Three dwelling-houses were also injured.   "We are informed that
if it had not been for the arrival of the floating and other engines
from this city, the fire would in all probability have crossed the
street, and the whole town would have been in danger.   It is supposed the flames would have been sooner arrested, had not the New
York firemen been hindered at the ferries; the large ferry-boat
happened to be on the Brooklyn side at the time of the alarm."

The editor of the "Long Island Star" says, "We are proud to
acknowledge the services of the firemen of New York, who came
over to the assistance of Brooklyn during the late fire.   Besides
the Floating Engine, there were Nos. 5, 7, 11, 13, 21, 22, and 37.
We observe in several daily papers the acknowledgments of the
firemen to individuals of our village for the refreshments provided
for them on that occasion.   In one communication is observed, that

every public, as well as many private houses, were solicitous for the refreshment of the firemen. The engineers of the town, in behalf of the members of the Fire Department, thanked the firemen of New York, and also 'to Captain Robert L. Gardiner, of the *(fishing)* smack, for his willing and friendly exertions in transporting two engines, with their members, across the East River, and to our townsmen for the refreshments they afforded to the firemen generally.' JOHN DOUGHTY and DAVID SEAMAN."

The New York firemen "send the following to be published: The disastrous fire of the 23d which your village suffered, and the sundry late fires, ought to awaken the inhabitants to make all possible preparations to facilitate the extinguishing of fires. Whenever you have been visited by a fire of any magnitude, some of the firemen of New York, with their engines, have gone to your relief. Had there been any ferry-boats or other conveyance at command, you would at all times receive much earlier assistance. Not a boat belonged to your ferry sufficiently large to convey one engine, nor did any cross till after the fire had raged for two hours. I would propose to your inhabitants that they build two scows, one for each ferry, sufficiently large to take in two or three engines; that these boats be deposited in our ferry slip, in which case you may at all times calculate upon assistance from the New York firemen."

It was not long after, when a decided improvement was made on this river, by the introduction of a "horse ferry-boat," first started on the "Catharine Slip Ferry," and particularly noticed in the "Long Island Star," as follows:* *"New Ferry-Boats.*—On Sunday last *(April* 3, 1814,) the public were gratified by the performance of a new-invented ferry-boat on the New *(Catharine Street)* Ferry, between this village and New York. This boat was invented by Moses Rogers, Esq., of New York. It is in some respects similar to the Paulus Hook ferry-boats, and calculated to receive wagons in the same commodious way; but the water-wheel in the centre is moved by *eight horses.* It crossed the river twelve times during the day, in from eight to thirteen minutes each, and averaging two hundred passengers each time. It makes good way against wind and tide, and promises to be an important acquisition. Another boat, to go by horses, is now building for that ferry; and a steamboat, belonging to William Cutting and others, is nearly ready for the ferry between Brooklyn and Beekman Slip. These great improvements on the ferries cannot fail to benefit this village and the adjacent country." It was announced, two days after, "The horseboat will continue to run from the New Ferry to Brooklyn until

* "Columbian," April 7, 1814.

the first of May, as a temporary arrangement. Passengers will be
charged four cents; two of which are for the owner of the ferry,
and two cents for the owner of the boat. All other articles at the
rates heretofore charged in the *row-boats.*"

On the 8th of the next month after, was introduced the first
"*Brooklyn Steam Ferry-Boat.*—The 'Nassau,' the new steamboat
belonging to Messrs. Cutting & Co., which commenced running
from Beekman Slip to the lower ferry at Brooklyn a few days ago,
carried in one of her first trips 549 (another counted 550) passengers, one wagon and a pair of horses, two horses and chairs, and
one single horse. She has made a trip in *four minutes,* and generally takes from four to eight, and has crossed the river forty times
in one day."* "Yesterday, *(Sunday, May 10th,)* between twelve
and one o'clock, Mr. Lewis Rhoda accidentally got hurled into the
machinery of the new steamboat '*Nassau,*' which cut off his left arm
a little below the elbow, and broke his neck. He expired in about
three hours after."†

"The boat impelled by horses from the New (*Catharine*) Slip to the
upper Brooklyn Ferry carried at one time 543 passengers, besides
some carriages and horses. And a horse-boat is to run soon from
Grand Street Dock to Williamsburgh," which boat was noticed on
the following 4th of June: "This morning was launched, at the ship-
yard of Mr. Charles Browne, an elegant double boat, intended to
ply as a ferry-boat from Corlaes Hook to Williamsburgh, Long
Island. This beautiful boat is called the '*Williamsburgh,*' and is to
be propelled by horse-power, with machinery very different from that
already constructed and used in the Hoboken or Brooklyn boats, and
is thought by competent judges to be very complete. It is supposed
that two or three weeks may yet be required to complete the machinery, &c., before she can be placed in her station."

The benefit arising from these *steam* and *team ferry-boats* soon began to be experienced by our city, as well as by Long Island and
New Jersey; from whence loaded wagons were hourly seen through
the day crossing these ferries, laden with the productions of the
farmers of these different places, and more especially from Sag Harbor and the lower parts of Long Island.

From this period, year after year, were introduced new boats of
various styles, and with increased speed and accommodations, upon
the various routes, which have also much increased.

To the year 1795 we again turn, and find the principal part of
these market buildings had been built many years, and being mere
wooden sheds, had now become dilapidated, leaky, and greatly need-

---

* "Columbian," May 18, 1814.   † L. I. Star, May 11, 1814.

ed repairs; besides, the market was on certain days overcrowded, and afforded no shelter from the storms or sun, especially for the many country people. Petitions were presented asking for repairs and greater accommodations, which the Common Council wished to accede to, but they thought the neighborhood, or those who were enjoying a large business or benefit, ought to assist in furnishing the necessary accommodations, as they had always done on former occasions. Many of the "neighborhood," however, thought the market revenue was more than sufficient to maintain it, and they would not subscribe as usual. But several young butchers, who had "*shirk stands*" in the "lower market," and others, came forward with petitions, among whom were Daniel Winship, George Goodheart, John Pell, George Markler (*Merkle*,) Cornelius Schuyler, and John Corbey, present one on the 17th of August, (1795,) in which they state: "They have served regular apprenticeship to the butcher's trade in the city, and some have been working for themselves three or four years. They have been killing 'small creatures,' and selling their meat by the quarter." They "find this mode of doing business will not answer their purpose; they have nothing but their trade to depend upon;" they "conceive they might be accommodated with stands in that part of the Fly Market where they now sell their meat, without taking up more room than they do at present, and in such case the petitioners would each of them willingly pay 'one hundred dollars,' to be expended in repairing or enlarging the market, &c.; and they are all recommended as proper persons by many of the older butchers." Then, on the 19th instant following, George Messerve, Jr., says: "He has served a regular apprenticeship to the butcher's trade, with his father, Mr. George Messerve, and he now wishes to set up for himself, and carry on his business, which he cannot do without having a proper stand (*in the 'lower market'*) for that purpose." He "is willing to pay *one hundred dollars* towards repairing or enlarging the markets, or for any other purpose," &c.

The following certify, that he sustains the character of an honest, industrious man, and recommend him, &c.:

John Lamb,	John Lasher,	M. Willett,
G. Bauman,	Peter T. Curtenius	Walter Bicker,
John Stoutenburgh,	S. Roorbeck,	John J. Montayne,
Geo. Marvin,	Stephen M'Crea,	William Edgar,
Richard Varian,	Ezekiel Robins,	Michael Varian.

Caleb Vandenburgh also petitions in the following November, and says: "He is a native of this city, and has served an apprenticeship; requests a stand in the lower Fly Market." We find the following old butchers certify to his "apprenticeship:"

William Wright,	William Post,	John Lovell,
John Finck (*Fink*,)	John Doughty, Jr.,	John Norman,
Isaac Varian,	William Mooney,	George Robert Beck,
Joseph O. Bogert,	John Fitzgerald,	William Everett, Jr.,
Edward Mooney,	John Pessinger,	Abraham Bogert,
James Sullivan,	Joseph Nott,	Stephen Hilliker, and
James Marsh.		

There were large numbers applying for these and other stands; and others, again, to be licensed as regular butchers; the Board, however, had not yet concluded to enlarge or rebuild, but recommended the Mayor to "License all persons of good character who shall apply for license, provided they shall have served an apprenticeship to the business in this city."

A law had many years before passed, that "No person shall exercise the office of a butcher in this city, unless he is licensed for that purpose by the Mayor, under the penalty of five pounds for every offence; and that every butcher shall hold his office during the pleasure of the Corporation only."

The next year, (1796,) on the 7th of March, a committee, consisting of Aldermen Robert Lenox, Andrew Van Tuyl, and Nicholas Carmer, reported on the condition of these old buildings; part of which appears as follows: "That the upper and middle markets require new floors, and the latter a new roof; but as the repairs, if carried into effect, would only be temporary, and ill comport with the public spirit, they conclude it cheapest in the end to make permanent improvements." This conclusion encourage a petition to have a new building placed along Front towards Wall Street, which was soon followed with a stronger one opposed to it; however, the old site was decided on, and on the 22d of August, the committee were ordered to proceed in the rebuilding the market-house, running from Water to Front Street, by contract, and cause the old building to be sold.

It appeared finished early in the month of November, "supported with brick pillars, and ceiled with lath and plaster."

In consequence of it being next to the country and fish market, there were many applications for the stands; so numerous were they, that the Common Council concluded to sell them at public auction; and on the 14th of the same month, a committee reported, "that the following fourteen unappropriated stands in the *lower market*" were "exposed to public sale in the market on Saturday last, (12th *inst.*,) under the conditions and for the sums mentioned (below,) and that they allowed Mr. (Frederick) Jay, the vendue master, for his commission, eight dollars. Signed, ROBERT LENOX, &c."

They were sold to the following persons, at the prices named:

No. 72. George Manolt,	-	£530	No. 65. Benjamin Cornell,		£165
" 71. David Seaman,	-	290	" 64. Henry Lovell, -	-	280
" 70. John Pell,	- -	285	" 63. Isaac Bayea, -	-	180
" 69. Daniel Winship,	-	205	" 62. John Pessinger,	-	150
" 68. George Messerve,	-	320	" 61. Cornelius Schuyler,		175
" 67. Whitehead Cornell,		170	" 60. Burdet Striker,	-	210
" 66. James Young,	-	310	" 59. Andrew Ross, -	-	200
		£2,110	Whole amount, -	-	£3,470

These conditions were: "None to buy but licensed butchers, subject to such regulations and fees as the Corporation may make from time to time, and no transfer of any stall so purchased to be made without leave of the Corporation.

"Butchers who have stands in the *upper market*, and becoming a purchaser in the *lower market*, are considered to have forfeited their stalls in the *upper market*.

"None of the butchers in the other markets are to have leave to become purchasers in the Fly Market.

"A credit of thirty, sixty, and ninety days is given for the purchase money, upon giving such notes to Mr. (*Daniel*) Phoenix as he shall approve;" when he gave a receipt as follows:

"New York, November 14, 1796, received of (*John Pell*,) his notes, payable at thirty, sixty, and ninety days, for two hundred and eighty-five pounds; which, when paid, will be the consideration money for stand No. 70 in the lower market.

"DANIEL PHOENIX, *City Treasurer.*"

These *fourteen stands* were the cause of a long-contested law-suit in 1822, at which date they will be referred to. The large amount of money which these stands brought induced the Corporation to order all the vacant stands in the *upper* market to be sold at public auction on the following 28th instant; when a committee reported their sale as follows:

No. 3. David Man.	- -	£58	Brought up, -	- -	£303
" 7. Matthew Fox,	- -	85	No. 17. James Reading,	-	75
" 9. Matthew Fogel (*Vogel*,)		62	" 19. John Barr, -	- -	60
" 13. Daniel Ensley, Jr.,	-	43	" 18. John Carby, -	-	40
" 15. Nicholas Smart,	-	55	" 8. John Deavenport,	-	20
Carried up,	- -	£303	Whole amount, -	- -	£498

These *nine stands*, it will be perceived, brought less than one-half as much as those previously sold; the cause, no doubt, was, they were the rejected inside stands of the *upper market*, and the farthest from the country and fish markets. Those which are located the nearest to these markets, and especially those on the *corners*, are always considered the most valuable.

Although these butchers had bought these stands, as it were, in fee, yet they were nevertheless liable any moment for violation of the established laws, ordinances, rules, or regulations; with the infliction of the penalty, either fine, imprisonment, or the removal from their stands were sure to follow. The authorities then were more honest, capable, and strict in the performance of their duties than those of the present day, and carried them out, not as politicians, but as sworn conscientious officers; and the people were more satisfactorily governed.

A few years previous to this sale, the *Proceedings* inform us, on the 14th of November, 1787, that William Everit, in the Fly Market, butcher, " having totally neglected to attend his business at his stall," it was resolved by the Board, " that his license be terminated." He immediately petitions to the Board, and states, that he " has been many years past used the trade of a butcher, and kept his stall in the *Fly Market*, and duly paid for the privileges and immunities, and also paid the sum of *fifteen pounds* for these privileges; that during the time he was in said business supported the character of an honest and upright man, and a good citizen." He gives as a reason for neglect of business, was on account of family matters, or difficulties, and wishes again to be placed in the possession of his stand. But this is denied him; in fact, it placed him out of business for many years after.

In the month of August, 1796, "A complaint was made against N—— S——, butcher, in this market, for affixing false Jewish seals on his meats, and offering it for sale." He was ordered to appear before the Board at their next meetings, (10*th and* 15*th*,) when they ordered, "That his license be suppressed." But after another hearing on the 26th September, " he was restored to his office," which, no doubt, was butchering for the Jews.

Then several butchers were represented as having neglected personally to attend at their stalls, and had put others in their places, without permission of the authorities, " who thereupon, on the 4th day of September, 1797, Ordered, that if any butcher shall neglect personally to attend his business at his standing in the market for the term of *fourteen days*, his standing shall be considered as vacated, and sold to some other licensed butcher, except in cases of sickness or other accidental causes." " The Deputy Clerk of the Fly Market was ordered to notify John Fincke, Henry Spingler, John Doughty, John Lovell, Alexander Peacock, and James Sullivan, butchers, to appear at this Board on Monday afternoon next." On that day John Fincke, John Doughty, John Lovell, and Alexander Peacock attended, and assigned satisfactory reasons for their absence. Henry Spingler also attended, and acknowledged that he had abandoned his stall, "when it was ordered to be sold." John Triglar, the nephew of Spingler, had worked and served for him many years, was at this time occupying his stand, and wished to retain it, so he petitions to the Board on the 18th September, (same year,) and says: "Having served a regular apprenticeship to the butcher's trade in the said city, he about twelve months ago obtained a license to carry on and exercise the trade of a butcher in the said city; and since, he has worked part of his time with his uncle Henry Spingler, and part of the time he has sold meat on his own account at the stall No. 46, occupied by the said Henry Spingler; that the said Henry Spingler being about to decline the butcher's business, the petitioner is desirous of obtaining a license for the said stall, for which he is willing to pay this Corporation the sum of fifty pounds. That the petitioner has it not in his power to pay a larger sum; having but lately begun his business, and being in low circumstances. That the petitioner's *father lost his life at Fort Washington in the service of his country*, and left the petitioner an orphan in his infancy, dependent on his friends for support. He therefore prays that this Honorable Board will be pleased to take his case into consideration; that the sacrifice of his *father's life* in his country's cause may plead in the petitioner's behalf, and that the said stall No. 46 may be granted him." The Board however, demanded £70 from *Triglar*, which he paid, and took possession.

For a few hundred pounds, Spingler several years previous had bought some 22 acres of land, which then lay west of the "Bowery Hill," now located near Union Square, where he turned his attention to raising garden truck and other field products; part of which he conveyed and sold at this and the Bear Market. His property, by its fortunate location, as time has proved, has constantly increased in value; and he has left his heirs very wealthy, (one of whom now resides in the splendid mansion No. 21 West 14th Street,) while his name yet lives, represented by the "Spingler Institute," on Union Square.

Previous to the sale of these butchers' stands, a law had passed which deprived the hucksters from selling fruit from their stands in the markets, caused from the many complaints against their engrossing and storing all that came to the markets for a rise in price. The law was so unexpected and sudden that it found them with a large surplus on hand, and not time to dispose of it; and they appealed to the authorities, on the 26th of November, in the same year, saying that "they now have on hand many of the prohibited articles, which to them will be a great detriment. Should your Honorable Board allow them to sell as usual, they will ever pray."

Catharine Montaynie, Catharine Spicer, Arabella Truce,

Wilhelmina Shaffer,	Catharine Staale,	Elizabeth Totten,
Bridget Nash,	Jane Wood,	Jane Gilmore,
Nancy Lott,	Mary Appleby,	Caty Buyshe,
Eliz. Marks,	Sarah Conklin,	Barbary Varvoser,
Sarah Burton,	C. Shearer,	Mary Baker,
Mary Calp,	Abigal Doil, all of Fly Market.	

A few of them, however, exposed their fruit for sale, and were fined; and in the month of January following some of them appealed again, and state, "that the support of our needy, destitute families depends in a great measure upon the privilege of exposing for sale fruit in the public markets, under any restrictions your honors may think fit to impose in your justice; and at the same time, most humbly pray, after due consideration of our case and the inclemency of the present season, that you will remit the fines at present imposed," &c.

Their appeals appear to have been unnoticed; yet they did not despair, but with the assistance of some forty subscribing citizens, they again made a last trial, and "trust with confidence in your goodness for a repeal of the law above alluded to." This was read on the 6th of February following, and rejected.

In the month of December previous, (1796,) the Fish Market was torn down, for the purpose of stopping what proved to be a very destructive fire, which is noticed in the *Minerva* December 9, 1796. "About one o'clock this morning, a fire broke out in one of the stores on Murray's Wharf, Coffee-House Slip. The number of buildings consumed may be from fifty to seventy—a whole block, between the above Slip, Front Street, and the Fly Market. The progress of the fire was finally arrested by cutting down the *Fish Market.*"

So many fires occurring just about this period, led many of the citizens to believe the slaves were again conspiring to destroy the city, which caused great excitement, and much preparation to guard against such a calamity. The same paper, of the 14th inst. following, notices this. "*Serious Cause of Alarm.*—Citizens of New York, you are once more called upon to attend to your safety. It is no longer a doubt—it is a fact, that there is a combination of incendiaries in this city, aiming to wrap the whole of it in flames! The house of Mr. Lewis Ogden, in Pearl Street, has been twice set on fire—the evidence of malicious intention is indubitable—and he has sent his *black man*, suspected, to prison. Last night an attempt was made to set fire to Mr. Lindsay's house in Greenwich Street—the combustibles left for the purpose are preserved as evidence of the fact. Another attempt, we learn, was made last night in Beekman Street. A bed was set on fire under a child, and his cries alarmed his family. Rouse, fellow-citizens and magistrates! your lives and property are at stake. Double your night-watch, and confine your *servants.*"

The Common Council, on the 15th December, passed resolutions offering *five hundred dollars reward* for the conviction of offenders, and recommend the "good citizens in the several wards to arrange themselves into companies or classes, to consist of such numbers as shall be necessary for the purpose of keeping such watch for the safety of the city."

A citizen says: "The yellow fever produced not such extraordinary commotion. The present alarm, as it is contagious, it may be called the *fire fever.*" The *fever,* however, soon died out; as the precautions taken had the desired effect, even if there had been a sign of conspiracy.

The Fish Market was used without a cover until the 24th of February (1797) following, when the fishermen petitioned "That, in consequence of the Fish Market being destitute of a cover, that it is very injurious to them. Respecting the fish—as in a clear day the fish will not survive but a few minutes, in consequence of their being exposed to the sun, which not only materially affects the sale of them, but we are entirely exposed to the inclemency of the season. They beg a redress of a grievance of this kind, as it will affect the community at large." (Signed,)

Joseph Latham, Nicholas Darow, Elias Lewis,
Jasper Latham, Thos. Wilcocks, Henry Harris,
Joseph Lewis, John Potter, Thomas Geoffery.

On the 27th of March following, a new market-house was ordered to be built. "That in rebuilding the market, the uniformity already established should be continued, and that it should be extended from the south side of Front Street to the door of the house occupied by John C. Frecke;" and to be built in the same manner as the *upper market.*

The next year will always be known as the "*dreadful yellow fever year,*" when we find 2,086 deaths registered in a few short months. It became known to many of the prominent physicians in the year 1791, when several of our first citizens fell victims to its fury; then again in 1795, when 732 were carried off; and the various accounts given of it were quite melancholy.

One, given October 17, states: "This city has been in a truly melancholy situation; but the accounts of the mortality have been greatly exaggerated in the country. Consternation has added greatly to the distress of the city; the poor have suffered much, but their wants have been liberally supplied from the hands of benevolent donors. Very little business has been done—a *solemn calm* has reigned through every street. We are now blessed with salubrious western gales, which is conceived to be sent in mercy, and presages to our hopes that the city will be free from the epidemic in a little time. It certainly puts on a less terrible hue— not more than one in twenty die. Those who have died were the greatest part new residents."*

In the years 1799, 1800, 1803, and 1805, the city was again visited by this dreadful visitor, more or less; but in 1798 it came on so sudden, that it grasped a great many in its fatal clutches before they were hardly aware of its presence; and so fatal was it in the month of August, that it was believed "nearly one-half of those cases reported died; and after that period the proportion diminished to about one-third." What made the matter worse, the country people were so alarmed that they would not bring their provisions to the city, although every encouragement was given them. "No fees were demanded from country people bringing provisions to our markets." The committee appointed to afford relief to the indigent and distressed sick, in a communication to the public, say: "They entreat their fellow-citizens of the surrounding country not to withhold from the markets the usual supplies of poultry and *small meats*, as well as other articles so essentially necessary to both sick and well, in this city, in this distressed season."† These appeals are answered from many of the citizens who had removed; and others, living in New Jersey and elsewhere, sent large sums of money, as well as gifts of beef, pork, mutton, butter, cheese, flour of all kinds, poultry and vegetables, by the wagon and sloop loads.

The markets in the infected district were deserted, but not before this disease had marked its victims among the butchers, of whom no less than eleven, now known—eight from this and three from the other markets—viz.: John Barr, James Place, James Young, William Mooney, Simmons Potter, Adam Van der Bergh, William Everit, Jun'r, and George Messerve, of the *Fly;* and William Blank, Gilbert Knapp, Edward King, from the others.

In briefly noticing the death of John Barr, the occupant of No. 19, it is also a duty, and withal a pleasure, to notice the occupant of No. 13, Matthew Vogel, for his fearless acts of humanity displayed by him in that dreadful season, when many of its first victims were almost deserted or left with those who could not assist them.

Mr. Vogel at that time was a young as well as strictly a Christian man, without a particle of the braggart or of personal fear, as

* N. Y. Journal, &c. † Daily Advertiser, Sept. 28, 1798.

he went wherever he could hear of a case of this fearful disease that needed assistance, whether rich or poor; and I am told he was the means of assisting many, or *smoothing the pillows* of the afflicted and dying sufferers.

Yet living, (1858,) and nearly *ninety years of age*, is the active, intelligent widow of one of the victims of 1798, who told me the following facts. She said her husband, John Barr, was a butcher in the "Old Fly Market," where he took the yellow fever. He came home to his residence, then at the southeast corner of the Bowery Lane and Grand Street, and with the assistance of his wife, dismounted from his horse—no carts being allowed after a certain time around the markets—when his relatives and friends deserted him all, except his affectionate wife—and she for two days and nights was at the bedside, alone with her, at times, deranged husband; and when in his senses, his wishes were, if he died—that he might not be taken by *Parker*, in his *horrid dead-cart*, to "Potter's Field." His faithful wife promised he should not if she lived. The humane Vogel heard of his sickness through the doctor, (*Underhill*, she thought he was a doctor,) and hurried there to find that the husband was speechless and the wife worn out. He stayed and done all that man could do, but the poor distracted wife knew he could not live, and she also knew that no other help could be obtained; she prepared his *winding-sheet*, that he might have the Christian burial she had promised him.

He died, and Vogel, having previously procured a coffin, laid him out; then, before the expected *dead-cart* came along for the body, he harnessed the dead man's favorite horse before his butcher-cart, to be at last used as his hearse, and in this he conveyed the body, followed by *one*, the chief mourner, to the family burial-ground in the Dutch Reformed church-yard, at the corner of Eldridge and Houston Streets, where he wished it to lie. There the noble-hearted Vogel dug the grave, and the faithful wife redeemed the last promise made to her once affectionate and her only husband.*

The action of the "Board of Health," who bestowed on Mr. Vogel a "vote of thanks" for his many fearless acts of humanity, which soon after became generally known, brought him much trade; but his generous nature, which hung to him through life, caused many of the deserving as well as the undeserving to visit him, and they went away not empty handed. Another generation, and *Uncle Mat* (as he was familiarly called) found himself poorer only in purse, and his heroic services almost forgotten, save a few friends who were with him in that deadly season. In the year 1830, he petition-

* A sketch of Mrs. Barr will be found in Union Market.

ed for a small office, but as a *political qualification* had then begun
to show its *demon head*, he could not succeed. His few friends
among the leading men then came forth, and among their acts placed
the following before the Board on the 13th of February: "I certify
that I have been personally acquainted for many years with Mr.
Matthew Vogle, and understanding that he is an applicant to the
Common Council for the appointment of *Ward Street Inspector*, I
recommend him as worthy, and as an applicant having strong claims
to their regard. Mr. Vogle in the gloomy year of 1798 did great
service to our city during the mortality occasioned by the Yellow
Fever—he volunteered his services to aid the sick and distressed
among our citizens, which services he most humanely and perse-
veringly discharged at the hazard of his life—and in a manner so
much to his credit and our satisfaction, that the Board of Health,
of which I then had the honor to be a member, also an Alderman,
deemed it proper to bestow on Mr. Vogle a *vote of thanks*.

"GABRIEL FURMAN, *Chairman of Board of Health.*
"New York, 13th of February, 1830."

We, the subjoined signers, are all acquainted with the facts as
above set forth, and unite in the petition and recommendation of Mr.
Vogle.

Samuel Stilwell,   Edward Sturman,   John Mann,
James Donaldson,   John B. Smith,   George Taylor, Jr.,
                                           Peter Parks.

"Uncle Mat" did not receive this appointment; as the position of
a "Ward Street Inspector" would not suit an honest man—so says
the politician—so says, *not the people;* the politician rules and *ruins*,
and the people bear their burdensome load like heroes. This office
had too many votes, working with the *broom*, and that broom on
election day was wonderfully useful in sweeping in enough illegitimate votes in the ballot-box to keep some other party, who likely
were still more dishonest, out. Mr. Vogel, however, through the assistance of Colonel Appleby, George Pessinger, and many more old
friends, succeeded in obtaining a clerkship in the Essex, Monroe,
and Gouverneur Markets, where he honestly and faithfully discharged the duties until his death, which occurred in 1852.

For another incident of the fever of '98 I am indebted to Dr. Anderson, who was a very great sufferer by the loss of many dear relatives at this period. He told me, that "in the month of September,
he first lost his brother by the fever; a few days after his father,
then living in Wall Street, was attacked, and soon after died; he
then removed his mother to his residence in Liberty Street, when
she was taken down with it, and, notwithstanding the careful nursing of himself and wife, she too died. By this time his wife, who

had been ill of consumption, died also, no doubt hastened from excessive duties and excitement; then her sister, (his sister-in-law,) having performed her duty with his sick mother, and her sister, caught the fatal fever, and also died." While her body was yet lying in the house, Dr. Anderson, who had now become so much overcome by these afflictions that he gave up, supposing that all were gone, his turn would come next. He proceeded up to the garret of his house, when he perceived a piece of rag carpet lay stretched on the floor, threw himself upon it, where exhausted nature caused him to sleep.

In that situation John Ferguson, his friend, found him, who had come to visit and assist him with the sick; but finding the rooms deserted, except the deceased, he proceeded up to the garret, where he remained after finding him. When Anderson awoke, says Ferguson to him: "*Sandy, what is God Almighty going to do with you next?*" These words of pity and sorrow from a "friend in need" encouraged and renewed his before drooping spirits, and again he went forth to the world.

John Ferguson was then a law student, and having been disappointed in love, became reckless of his life, and everywhere, at all times of day and night, he was found assisting the sick or dying of this fatal fever. His freak of recklessness, however, in the end proved to be a humane one; and several years after he became the Mayor of the City of New York.

A Mr. Jacob Underhill, a benevolent gentleman from up the North River, came to the city at this period on purpose to assist the victims of this disease, and faithfully he devoted his time and purse in doing so. His principal medicine, says Dr. Anderson, was plain *Sage Tea*, and, it was said, he cured many with it.

Dr. Alexander Anderson, referred to above, is now about 85 years old, and daily he may be found engaged in an art of which he may properly claim to be the father in the United States; that is, wood engraving. In his youth he studied medicine, and received his degree from Columbia College, but following the bent of his taste for the arts, he relinquished the study of medicine and engaged in that of engraving. Years after, he found some of Bewick's wood engravings on natural history, when he became attracted by their general effect, and without instructions he adopted this branch, and he has followed it to the present day.

We again look back into that dreadful year 1798, and find that the widows of several of these deceased butchers petition to be allowed the use of their stands; others, again, whose stands had been purchased from the Corporation, wished to sell them. The

first is from Catharine, the widow of George Messerve, on the 29th
of October, same year, when she obtains permission " to continue in
the occupation of the standing in the Fly Market of her late husband"—" for one year, or during the pleasure of the Board." The
widow of Adam Van der Bergh, and Sarah, the widow of William
Everitt, Jun'r, were " indulged with the *little (like?)* priviledge as
that granted to Catharine Messerve."

Joseph Outen Bogert petitions for leave to purchase of the widow
of James Young, deceased, stand No. 66, which was granted. She
sold it to Bogert for $1,700; and when she accompanied him to the
Mayor's office, to procure a license, " the Mayor told the widow
that she got more than the husband gave for it"—" and instantly
recommended that it would be proper to take less." To this Mrs.
Young replied, that " the stall was her own, and that, as she was
left with three children, she must make the most of it." No doubt
the trade to it was considered in the sale.

James Campbell also petitions for the stand of Simmons Potter,
No. 19, which formerly belonged to John Barr, which was granted,
on condition that " he pay off the note, with the interest, due from
Potter," to the Corporation. In this manner the Corporation collected all moneys due to them, whether of the principal, interest, or
rent. If one failed to pay either or all of these, it was charged to
the next occupant.

The butchers, after deserting the markets in consequence of the
fever, sold meats at their houses or other places; and as they were
liable to the city for a stated sum *(market fees)* on each head of
stock they sold, after their return to the markets, they were called
on to render an account on oath of such market fees; and they not
doing so immediately, on the 13th of November of the same year,
" the butchers of the Fly and Catharine Slip Markets respectively
do, on or before twelve o'clock on Monday next, of the fees due
from the 30th of July last to the 27th of October last, inclusive;
and also that they do by that day pay the amount of those fees."

In the month of June, 1800, some nine of the butchers in this
market petitioned for the " Manhattan Water" (which was just introduced through several of the streets) in this market, to make
pickle and clean the market, and wish to bring it in at their own
expense; which was granted to them.

At this period there were several petitions and memorials before
the Board, showing the crowded state of this market; and another
against a butcher here, who neglected his business in the market to
forestall cattle. This is dated June 2d, 1801, and says: " That
Henry Astor, and certain others, who are also licensed butchers, leav-

ing the care of their stalls and the selling of their meats to journeymen, and others who are not licensed butchers, are in the constant
practice of forestalling the market, by riding into the country to
meet the droves of cattle coming to the New York markets, and
purchasing cattle for other stalls besides his own; and does not
personally attend to any stall. That it is also become very customary for drovers of cattle from the country, after selling their own
cattle, to purchase other droves, and sell them out singly at an advanced price, thereby forestalling the market. That your memorialists, by their regular and constant attendance at their stalls,
have it not in their power to counteract these pernicious practices,
but are thereby prevented from purchasing cattle upon so good
terms as they otherwise could, and are often obliged to purchase
from the said forestallers at an advanced price. That in consequence thereof, the price of butchers' meat is very considerably enhanced, to the great detriment of the city." They wish the Board
to adopt "such rules, regulations, and active measures as they
shall think fit and expedient, to restrain the said Henry Astor, and
all others, from forestalling the markets in manner aforesaid."
This was signed by several of the principal butchers in several of
the markets, as follows:

Wm. Wright,   William Post,   David Marsh,
Edward Patten,   Alex'r Peacock,   John Norman,
Philip Fink,   Alex'r Fink, and   Joseph O. Bogart.

At this period the market is represented as being much crowded,
by several citizens and some of the butchers, who state: "From
the extreme narrowness of the said market, and from the present
crowded and unequal distribution of the vacancies between the
stalls, they are impeded in the prosecution of their business, and
the citizens frequenting the said market greatly incommoded; insomuch that, in full market-day, it is difficult to pass and repass."

This extract would lead us to suppose that this market, at that
period, was near its height of prosperity; and no doubt it was, as,
two years after, every stand and space appears to have been occupied, and all doing well. Seventy-two butchers' stands were occupied by the following persons:

No. 1. John Pessinger.
   2. John Hilliker.
   3. John Fitzgerald.
   4. John Basley, (*Baisley.*)
   5. Thomas Hall.
   6. William Kline.
   7. James Wilt.
   8. John Deavenport.
   9. George Mason.
  10. Nicholas Stall, (*Stael.*)
  11. George Rierson, (*Ryerson.*)
  12. John Philips.
  13. Mathew Vogal, (*Vogel.*)
  14. Thomas Gibbons.

No. 15. Jacob Nichols.
16. George R. Beck.
17. James Redding.
18. William Dick.
19. William Mooney.
20. John K. Floor.
21. Andrew Ross.
22. John Norman.
23. Abner Curtis.
24. Francis Arden.
25. Scale & Passage.
26. Charles Bird.
27. William Wright.
28. Joseph Graff.
29. Isaac Varian.
30. Eliphalet Wheeler.
31. Sam'l Ackerman.
32. Andrew Van Deusen.
33. John Whitehand.
34. John Roper, or Raper.
35. John B. Smith.
36. John Williams.
37. David Mann.
38. David Marsh.
39. Stephen Hilliker.
40. John Tier.
41. William Post.
42. Isaac Beyea.
43. George Thompson.

44. John Triglar.
45. Daniel Ensley.
46. John Fink.
47. Edward Patten.
48. Alexander Peacock.
49. John Lovell, Jun'r.
50. John Doughty.
51. John Lovell, Sen'r.
52. James Carr.
53. Michael Varian.
54. Richard Varian.
55. John Garrison.
56. Christian Stamler.
57. Henry Astor.
58. William Messerve.
59. John Raynor.
60. James Marsh.
61. Cornelius Schuyler.
62. John Pessinger, Jun'r.
63. William Everitt.
64. Henry Lovell.
65. Benjamin Cornell.
66. Joseph O. Bogart.
67. Whitehead Cornell.
68. George G. Messerve.
69. Daniel Winship.
70. John Pell.
71. David Seaman.
72. George Manolt.

Of all this large number, I know of but two who are yet in the land of the living, (*July*, 1859:) one the occupant, at that period, of No. 30, Eliphalet Wheeler; and the other, of No. 56, Christian Stamler. Both have long and successfully battled with the world, although their long road of life has not been traveled together.

Eliphalet Wheeler is now almost eighty years of age, enjoying good health, both in body and mind. When a boy of nine years old, he began by earning a *few shillings* a week from working in Lorillard's Tobacconist; at the age of sixteen he was apprenticed with John Norman, a butcher in this market, where his perquisites soon placed a few dollars in his pockets. About this period, it was a great habit for the apprentice boys, and of course young men, to meet together certain evenings at Mrs. F's in Elizabeth Street, below Bayard's Lane, (Broome Street,) where she kept quite an attractive shop, dealing out mead, cakes, etc., and where card-playing and other games of chance were performed. Young Wheeler was induced to visit this place one evening, and before he left, he had just *four shillings* less than when he entered. The loss was not so much, but the idea of losing it by gambling was more than his sensitive mind could bear. It preyed on him so much, that on his way home late in the night, he had to cross near the old family vault of Alderman Bayard, which was then looked upon as a sacred spot by many of the rising generation. When he came to it he stopped, and on bended knee made a vow, " that he would never again, in any manner, engage in 'games of chance;' and further, to devote his whole life and energies to serve the Lord." From that hour his earnings were placed in what is called a "money-box," and he continued to thrive: purchased this stand (*No.* 30) in 1802; and in 1822 he purchased No. 2 in Fulton Market, from which he retired more than twenty years ago, with abundance of this world's goods; and he has lived such a life as conformed to the vow made upon the old " Bayard Vault."

Christian Stamler is now about eighty years old, and quite helpless. His life has been devoted to one of money getting, and he has succeeded. He was ever very eccentric, both in looks and conversation. Many anecdotes are told of him; one of which appears quite suitable to his general character. He happened on board of a sloop one day, looking for stock; after finding some to suit and agreeing about the price, the captain not knowing him, and judging from his appearance that he could not raise *five dollars*, asked him for a retainer. " Chris" was somewhat nettled, but very coolly took out a small dirty roll from a corner of his old vest pocket, opened it out, and handed the captain a *one-thousand dollar bill*, at the same time showing many others; told the captain to take out the amount demanded. The captain was nonplused, but some butchers came up—gave the captain his name, which was generally known to him, as well as to all the dealers in stock—but he said, " He did not expect to find a man of his reputed wealth in such shocking bad clothes."

John Fink, noticed as the occupant of No. 46 in this market, had many years previous been a keeper of an old public-house, known as the "Butchers' Arms," on the corner of the Bowery and Bayard Street, where many young butchers and others almost daily congregated; and from this latter fact no doubt was the cause of Mr. Fink becoming a prominent character in the once famous "Miranda Expedition," which originated in this city in the year 1806.

This expedition was started by a native of Caraccas, South America, known as General Francisco De Miranda, who appears to have had some political difficulty with his government, and who had been obliged to leave his country, and to seek safety in France, where he had engaged in her army, and soon after received the rank of General. Some dissatisfaction about promotion had induced him to leave that country also; and the year 1805 found him in the City of New York, where he became acquainted, through letters of introduction, to several prominent citizens. Among these were Colonel William Smith, Samuel G. Ogden, Colonel Armstrong, and Captain Thomas Lewis, the latter belonging to an armed trader, called the "*Leander.*" It appeared soon after Colonel Smith became a frequent visitor at Fink's public-house, which was a sort of head-quarters for the young butchers after the market hours; and after a short period, he induced Mr. Fink to engage in the enrollment of men, as was said, "for the service of the United States," to form a Cavalry Company, by the name of "President's Guards," whose principal duty was to guard the President while traveling, and at other times to guard the mail at New Orleans, at which place they were to immediately proceed. The inducements held out were, that they were to receive one month's pay of $15 in advance as bounty money, besides all the necessary clothing and rations, which were to be supplied gratuitously.

Mr. Fink's influence being very considerable, he soon enrolled above thirty persons, most of them butchers, and several of them married men; and there is no doubt that he was deceived in the real character of the expedition, because he had engaged himself to go, with many of his intimate friends; but when they saw the secret and unusual manner of the ships leaving the harbor, and of embarking the troops, he refused to proceed, and he also induced many of those whom he had induced to join also to refuse; although several of them, on the assurance of several of the officers "that they should not be deceived, with also some additional advance paid," resolved to go.

At this late period but few are left who can recognize many of those who were butchers who went on that expedition; but I have been able to present the following: John Parsells, David Vinton, John Edsall, Alexander Bahanan, Matthew Bahanan, Benjamin Davis, Richard Platt, John Burk, Henry Sperry, and others.

After the ship "Leander" was ladened with a large quantity of war materials, and the Custom-House Officers had been deceived respecting her cargo and destination, she dropped down to Staten Island, where she received General Miranda and the enrolled troops on board; and she put to sea on the 3d day of February, 1806, arriving at Jacmel in due time. Here she remained some six weeks giving those whom "Miranda" intended to attack time enough to learn all his intentions, and the necessary preparations to receive him. Two other vessels were engaged by Miranda at Jacmel, when troops and ammunition were placed on board, and all three proceeded to the Island of Buen-Aire, and after many difficulties arrived off that coast, where soon after they were attacked by two Spanish vessels, and the two vessels of Miranda were taken, although he escaped in the "Leander."

Some 60 prisoners were taken to Porto Cavello, where they were imprisoned, and soon after tried for piracy, when all the officers were ordered to be hung, and afterwards to have their heads cut off; the others were ordered to be imprisoned ten years at labor, part at Omoa and the other part at Porto Rico, where many of them died of wounds and sickness, and those who remained suffered almost death. Some few were pardoned, but many of them remained in prison for years, although many efforts were made to secure the interposition of our Government; to secure which, in their behalf, some twenty of them stated in a memorial: " That we, your memorialists, are natives of the United States of America, and for the most part of the City of New York, and are part of a number of men of the same description who were brought from New York in February last, in the ship Leander, Thomas Lewis, commander, under circumstances of treachery and imposition, which your memorialists will proceed to explain: Samuel G. Ogden has been known for some time as owner of the ship Leander, which vessel had for some time been employed by him in a forced trade, for which purpose she had been heavily armed; consequently, there was less danger of her warlike equipments awakening suspicion on the part of the public, or in the breasts of your memorialists, of any illegal undertaking. Of the whole number of your memorialists, some were attached to the vessel, some were employed for military service, and others for the exercise of their ordinary occupation and trade. Those of the first description were shipped in the usual manner, on a voyage to *Jacmel* and back to New York; the rest were engaged by Colonel William Smith, *Mr. John Fink*, Colonel William Armstrong, and Mr. Daniel R. Durning, to proceed to New Orleans, and other places not mentioned, under the command of Mr. Armstrong and Mr. Durning, who, as was falsely and shamefully mentioned, had been appointed by Government to carry thither a certain number of men as a guard to the mail. Your memorialists predicate their right to claim the interference of Government in their behalf upon the original innocence of their intentions and the veracity of the statement they

have offered. To establish these to your satisfaction, they beg that
the persons hereinafter mentioned, who are informed of the intrigue
that was exercised by Colonel Smith and others, his colleagues, may
be appealed to, viz.: Mr. Daniel Kemper, whose son was executed;
Colonel Marrinus Willet; Mr. Brinkerhoof, tavern-keeper; William
Rutledge, ship-joyner; Samuel Winship and Francis White, butchers, all of New York. And if it shall appear by the testimony of
these persons that the account be worthy of credit, they will be entitled to their country's protection and support." This was dated
"Carthagena, December 30, 1806."

We find also from a petition of John Parcell's, dated July 25,
1812, he says: "About eight years have elapsed since the expiration of his apprenticeship, (with John Pell,) *three years and four
months of which time he was confined in prison in South America in
irons, on account of being on board of a vessel under the command of
Miranda,*" &c. Several others of these butchers, after enduring almost every hardship and suffering, came back broken down in spirit
and constitution, at last to lay their bones with their kindred.

The principal portion of the supplies which at this period (1802)
furnished the markets still came to the city by water, either in small
boats or across the ferries, and but few were brought in wagons or
carts, except by those who lived a few miles from the city on New
York Island. Occasionally the markets were poorly supplied,
caused either from certain tides, storms, &c., which gave opportunities for the now numerous forestallers to take advantage of these
circumstances, by advancing the prices. The prices of certain articles in favorable seasons were usually about the same in certain
months, but the winter and spring months they all ranged higher.
This, however, was expected; but the forestallers had for several
years past exceeded this expectation, and bought up all they could
before its arrival at the markets, by which means they controlled
the markets, and gave much dissatisfaction and cause of complaint.
This brought forth a report in the month of February, 1803, from a
Committee consisting of Aldermen John Oothout and Philip Brasher,
who state: "That it has hitherto been the policy of this Board to
encourage a resort of country people bringing provisions to the markets in this city by land carriages; the Committee are persuaded
that this policy has been attended with the most beneficial effects,
as supplies in this way not only tend to reduce the price of provisions, but frequently defeat the injurious practice of forestallers;
the Committee therefore recommend that *no market fees* whatever
be demanded from persons bringing into this city any provisions in
wagons, carts, or sleds, provided the same are vended out of such

wagons, carts, or sleds in which the same may be brought to this city. The laws against forestallers have been for a great length of time but partially executed, if not totally neglected, whereby the prices of provisions are much enhanced, and the inhabitants generally, but more especially the poor thereof, feel its baneful effects. The Committee are of opinion that the clerks of the different markets ought to be instructed from time to time by the Mayor of this city 'to be vigilant in the execution of their duty in this particular.'" They further state, they "have taken a survey of the Fly Market, with a view to recommend additional shelter from the rain and sun to be provided for women and others who dispose of vegetables; find it impracticable, owing to the space being very narrow between the eves of the market and the opposite houses; any further extension would prove destructive in case of fire. The Committee, however, recommend that the Mayor direct the Clerk of the Market to make a more convenient disposition of the several stands, by obliging many green-women who occupy the lower parts of the Fly Market to remove nearer Pearl Street; by this arrangement, they would have more room, and the country people from Long Island better accommodated."

In the month of April of this year, Mr. Grant Thorburn observed a man, for the first time, selling flower-plants in this market. He says: "As I carelessly passed along, I took a leaf, and rubbing it between my fingers and thumb, asked him what was the name of it? He answered, 'A *rose geranium.*' I looked a few minutes at the plant, thought it had a pleasant smell, and thought it would look well if removed into one of my green flower-pots, to stand on my counter to draw attention. Next day some one fancied, and purchased plant and pot. Next day I went when the market was nearly over, judging the man would sell cheaper, rather than have the trouble of carrying them over the river, as he lived at Brooklyn—and in those days there was neither steam nor horse-boats. Accordingly I purchased two plants, and having sold them, I began to think that something might be done this way, and so I continued to go at the close of the market, and always bargained for the unsold plants. The man finding me a useful customer, would assist me to carry them home, and show me how to shift the plants out of his pots and put them into green pots, if my customers wished it. So I found by his tongue that he was a Scotchman, and being countrymen, we wrought to one another's hands; thus, from having one plant, in a short time I had fifty.

"The thing being a novelty, began to draw attention; people carrying their country friends to see the curiosities of the city, would step in to see my plants. In some of these visits the strangers would express a wish to have some of the plants; but having so far to go, could not carry them. Then they would ask for the seeds, and also those of cabbage, turnip, or radish seeds, &c.; but here lay the difficulty, as no one sold seed in New York, not one of the farmers or gardeners saved more than what they wanted for their own use; there being no market for an overplus. In this dilemma, I told my situation to George Inglis, the man from whom I had always bought the plants in the Fly Market. He said he was now raising seeds, with the intention of selling them next spring, along with his plants, in the market; but if I would take his seeds, he would quit the market, and stay at home and raise plants and seeds for me to sell. A bargain was immediately struck; I purchased his stock of seeds, amounting to *fifteen dollars;* and thus commenced a business on the 17th of September, 1805, that became the most extensive of the sort in the United States."*

We find in the month of March, 1805, the Clerk of this market represented, "That many persons have received severe falls from the steps, which are placed at each end of the market, arising from their being too narrow on the tread," which was so altered as to make them more safe and convenient.

In 1803 the yellow fever appeared here, but it was not so fatal as in 1798, although very bad, and in some instances fatal to whole families. The first case which will be noticed here was a man of the name of John Sebring, who died of this dreadful disease on one of the butchers' stalls in this market, on the 19th of August. He had just arrived from New Orleans, and belonged to Fredericksburgh, Virginia. When taken sick he sought his boarding-house, but was denied admission; so he went into the market, laid down on one of the stalls, and soon after died. Just above the market, at No. 55 Maiden Lane, lived a family named *Westerns,* consisting of a mother and two daughters; all three died at nearly the same hour, and were so reported on the 5th of October following. Mr. Abraham O'Kie, his wife and three children, all died from the same cause within ten days. He was the keeper of the " City Assembly Rooms," but he died at his residence No. 163 Greenwich Street, as noticed October 3d following.

The next year it again appeared in some few cases. However, we find at a meeting of the Humane Society, held August 6th, that the Visiting Committee reported a donation of two hundred pounds of meat received from the butchers here, and two other donations of meat from Mr. Francis Arden, also of this market, for the benefit of the poor and the sick.

* " Life and Writings of *Grant Thorburn,*" p. 62.

The year following (1805) the fever again prevailed with some considerable violence, when the butchers in this market petitioned, on the 6th of September, that "conceiving the health of the city in the vicinity of the Fly Market to be such as to induce them to believe that their stands will be of no public utility during the unhealthfulness of the season," they pray for permission to remove during the sickness, which was granted to them. Some of them removed their business to their residences, from whence they supplied their patrons; while others moved their stalls to Franklin Square, Chatham Square, Broadway, and on both sides of the Park.

Eliphalet Wheeler says his place of business was located on the Park, just below Chambers Street, on Broadway. A few years before he had become acquainted with a most remarkable colored woman, who lived on Golden Hill, corner of Cliff and John Streets, named Mary Simpson, usually known as Mary Washington, as she had once been a most faithful slave of General Washington, whom he had set free, while President of the United States, residing in New York. After she had left Washington's family, she had opened a little store in the basement of this house, where she sold milk, butter, and eggs, with cookies, pies, and sweetmeats of her own manufacture; and she also took in washing for several bachelor gentlemen who resided in the neighborhood. She never forgot her old master's birthday, nor did she want her friends or patrons to forget it, as that day was above all the holidays with her; and she kept it most faithfully, by preparing a very large cake, which she called "Washington Cake," (once a favorite of Washington,) a large quantity of punch, then a fashionable drink, and hot coffee. These were nicely arranged upon a large table; then against the wall hung an old portrait of Washington, which graced the head of the table, and a small leather trunk, on which was marked the initials "G. W.," made of brass-head nails; both of which had been given to her by Washington himself. Every anniversary morning, some of the first men, old and young, paid a ceremonious visit to this much respected colored woman, to eat her "Washington Cake," drink her punch and coffee, praise her old master's portrait, and his many noble and heroic deeds; and thus was passed every Washington's birth-day until her death. She said she "was fearful that if she did not keep up the day by her display, Washington would be soon forgotten."

During the several yellow-fever seasons, about the year 1800, Mr. Wheeler says, "Mary often came to see me and beg offal meat, sheep-heads, &c.; some of which she made soup of for the many destitute and sick and the rest she fed to numerous starved cats, which had been left behind by many families, in their haste to leave the infected district.

Grant Thorburn says, (in a letter to me,) " When the yellow fevers prevailed, people fled, and left their cats to starve; soon the hungry cats came howling round the dwellings of those whose doors were open. *Mary Washington* and her stout colored servant-girl went every morning with two large sacks to the butchers, who always cheerfully gave them as many sheep-heads as they could carry. On arriving home, they found five-score and five starving cats waiting their return; straightway each with her hatchet split the sculls and scattered the brains, when the cats ate and were satisfied. I had full share of starving cats to provide for. The weather being hot, and the windows open, the cats came in. We were obliged to keep a woman with a stick to sit by the table, while the servant was placing the food before us. Every day scores of cats met on the pavement opposite his house; every day I placed dishes on the side-walks, and got many gallons of milk from the kind milkman for the poor cats. Soon the cats found their way up town, and got better quarters."

At an early day Mary became attached to St. George's Church, and after a time she became acquainted with the minister, Reverend Doctor Milnor, who found in her a quiet, respectful woman, with a most excellent heart, full of kindness and attention, especially towards the sick and needy. She was very fond of hearing the Bible read, and became so anxious to know how to read it, that she was placed in the Sunday-school, where, by great exertions and the kind assistance of Doctor Milnor, she soon obtained this knowledge, and this good book became her daily companion. Even when going to market she carried it with her; and if she found Mr. Wheeler not engaged, he was pleased to hold her Bible while she recited, sometimes, whole chapters at a time, without missing a word, so retentive was her memory.

At all the meetings of the Church, no person was a more regular attendant than this colored woman; in fact, she was looked upon, and felt herself, a little above some of the colored persons who came to this Church, and would not sit with them. Her many good qualities were considered by Doctor Milnor, who had a *chair* especially provided for her in the gallery. She could do nothing of importance without consulting her "*Boss*," as she kindly called the Reverend Doctor Milnor; and when she died, she bequeathed about eighteen hundred dollars to the Sunday-school, and to be expended under the direction of Dr. Milnor. One of his sons said to me, "If anybody ever deserved a monument, that colored woman, Mary Simpson, was one of them." So let her name and example live!

In the spring of 1806 several complaints had been made against some uncleanly slaughter-houses, not without just cause. Several volunteers among some of the more respectable portion of the butchers offered their services to the Board of Health; and a Committee of the Board of Health was appointed and conferred with this Committee of Butchers, on the subject of regulating all the slaughter-houses in the city. In their report, dated June 14th, 1806, the Committee state that they had met with the following butchers: "David Marsh, William Wright, Jacob Tier, William Chivers, Daniel Winship, Jacob Varian, and Christian Miller, who will undertake on the part of the butchers to inspect the slaughter-houses, and carry into effect such parts of the law for preventing nuisances as related to butchers; for which purpose the Committee recommended that the aforesaid persons should be appointed inspectors of slaughter-houses by the Common Council, and empowered to prosecute offenders for the transgressions of the law for preventing nuisances, and of such regulations as the butchers may adopt among themselves for the purpose of conducting their business with every possible propriety."

Several of these butchers were also leading spirits in the two great political parties of the day, then known as Federalists and Republicans, and they occasionally brought their power to bear, either on one side or the other. An instance of a great wrong was attempted by the party in power in the month of July, 1806. Twelve Republican butchers petitioned to the Board for as many stands in the lower, or "Fish Market," which caused a resolution to be passed in the Board, granting and directing the Market Committee to assign stands for them; although several of them occupied stands in this and other markets. In a few days after, this Committee reported, "That they have deliberately considered the nature of the duty enjoined on them, and with all due deference to the judgment of this Board, do give it as their opinion, that it would be improper and unjust to give away these stalls to any individual whatever, inasmuch as an offer has been made for one of these middle stalls, at the rate of $120 per annum, and numbers of butchers stand ready to give the same amount yearly for the remainder of them, (and more money, if required.) They are clearly of opinion that a considerable revenue may be derived to the Corporation funds by leasing the said stalls for 1, 3, 5, or 7 years. To give away these stalls in the manner contemplated by the resolution of last *Monday* will certainly cause a great clamor and discontent by the citizens; and there will be evidently a want of room for the country people, as also a deficiency for the use of the fishermen."

This subject did "cause a great clamor and discontent," especially among the "press" of both parties, who indulged in criminations and recriminations; each party showing up the favoritisms or rascalities of the other by turns, and it is now difficult to judge *which was the worst*.

The butchers petitioned, and also held several meetings, in relation to this subject, and at one of them the following proceedings took place:

"At a meeting of the butchers who occupy stands in the different markets in the City of New York, held at Pierson's Tavern, 31st of July, 1806:

"It being well ascertained that the Common Council of this City have lately resolved to convert part of the lower Fly Market, at present used by the fishermen and country people, into a *flesh market*, and to allow fourteen stalls to be erected therein for the use of as many butchers, who have been selected and named for that purpose, and conferred upon them these stands gratuitously, when many of the butchers occupying stands in the Fly Market have paid large sums of money for theirs—in confident expectation that no stalls were to be erected in the lower or fish market, but have granted to fourteen select favorites privileges which would have produced, either at public or private sale, at least *twenty thousand dollars* to the treasury of the city.   JOHN PESSENGER, Chairman.

JOSEPH O. BOGERT, Secretary."

As the prosperity of this market increased, ofttimes the greater part of the country market would be in possession of persons whom the laws excluded. From this fact originated "*Shirk*," or "*Shark Butchers*," who were generally a set of shiftless characters, devoid either of principle or honor; made up of those who had worked a while at the business until discharged; or others from about the country, who could not obtain licenses; and others, again, who had been in business, but not succeeding, either from their extravagance, dissipation, or otherwise, were obliged to adopt any measure whereby they might exist. Many of them often assumed the garb of countrymen, in which they almost daily visited this portion of the market with their quarters of *small meats* nicely laid in the country farmers' baskets; while others represented themselves as agents for countrymen, or made certain arrangements or collusion with the officers in charge; and when driven off from the stands or benches, they would "*shirk*" around for another; and they became known as "*shirkers*" and "*sharks*." There were also a few of the regular butchers who were *permitted*, or specially licensed, "to sell *small meats* by the quarter" in this lower market; they, however, were confined to certain parts and particular stands.

In 1807 these "*shirks*" became so formidable as to almost exclude the country people, who, with several citizens, complain to the authorities, which was followed by the regular butchers, who also asked for relief. They wished none but farmers, "who bring their stock to market, raised on their own farms, to sell meat by the quarter," in this part of the market. The Deputy Clerk was "instructed to use his utmost vigilance to detect such offenders as shall sell contrary to the tenth section of the law," &c., which had the desired effect for a short period.

About this period a Philadelphian visitor, who had been to this market, was comparing it with the principal market in Philadelphia, in a letter to one of the editors of a Philadelphia Magazine, when he says: "This morning I accompanied 'mine host' to the Fly Market, which is the principal one in this city—the whole forming a line perhaps as long as one of the ranges of the Philadelphia 'High Street Market.'" "Fish," he says, "may be had in greater plenty, variety, and freshness. There is not found here that regularity or convenience which distinguish the 'markets' of my native city. The fruits and vegetables, &c., with the owners, are exposed to all the injuries of the weather; they are ranged on the side of the market-house in the street, on the pavement, so that there is no more empty space than is barely sufficient to accommodate the foot-passengers. Everything which is exposed for sale may be bought without walking *half the distance* which it is necessary to do at Philadelphia."*

The prices of provisions are also noticed by Melish, in his Travels, who also refers to this market, as follows: "There are five public markets in this city, of which the principal is the Fly Market, and those are well supplied with wholesome provisions, vegetables, fruit, and fish; and the prices are generally reasonable. A few of these may be quoted: beef, mutton, and veal, 9 to 12 cents per pound; a turkey, 75 cents; a goose, 62 cents; ducks and fowls, 25 cents each; eggs, 14 cents per dozen; butter, 22 cents per pound; fish and fruit plenty and cheap."

The fishermen were now increasing, and were in a thriving condition, although much incommoded in the slip for want of room for their fishing vessels, and they were obliged to pile their empty fish-cars on the dock or wharf, which created trouble between them and the Street Commissioner. The Board, at a meeting May 18, 1806, ordered this officer "to inquire on what terms a water-lot at Brooklyn can be purchased for the accommodation of fisherman cars." Before this arrangement was made, the fishermen petitioned "the necessity of our having our cars out of the water, that they may

* Literary Magazine, vol. vii., p. 188.

dry, and by that means be cleared from the grass, &c., which will otherwise collect and destroy our fish; and it is necessary to have the cars near our place of keeping fish, as it is very frequently the case that our *smacks* or fishing-boats arrive at the dead hours of the night, and in the slack time of tide our fish will die almost instantaneously, unless they are shifted into cars. The number of smacks employed regularly in this business will exceed seventy, and the number of cars now upon the wharf will fall short of two to one smack; and as the fish increase the cars will materially diminish, and the principal part of the summer season there will be but few upon the wharf." This was signed by

George Rogers, Joseph Latham, Joseph Ashbey,
Roger Crandall, Jasper Latham, Jonathan Crocker.

Their petition, with other influences, stopped their removal for a period, but the Corporation eventually (in 1810) removed them to Brooklyn. The fishermen had threatened, that if they were removed or ordered to be removed from Fly Market Slip, they would stop the supplies of fish; and they kept their word. This created considerable feeling with the public on being cut off from one of the principal necessaries of life, and the fishermen were much blamed.

One of them appeared in the " press," in these words: " The present suppression of the regular supply of *sea-fish* at the markets in this city having justly excited the attention of the public, one of the condemned feels himself called upon, by the respect always due to the constituted authorities and the citizens at large, to give some explanations of the case.

" It is well known that for a number of years past the fishermen have been accommodated with room on the wharf adjoining the Slip, as a deposit for their cars. It was necessary that the cars should be kept out of water, and it was not practicable to keep them at Brooklyn, or at any other place at a distance from the market. Let it suffice to say, without going into a detail of the whole business of catching fish, bringing them to market, and keeping them alive, sweet, clean, and wholesome while there, that this arrangement is indispensable, and without it the fish market will lose one-half of its worth and usefulness." " The Harbor-Master, also, on Friday last, gave us express permission and direction to place our cars in the position in which they were found." " And the result is, that we must be allowed our old privileges, or others that will answer the same purpose, or we cannot go on with our business."

This removal of the cars, even if the city had been regularly supplied, would have subjected the fishermen to a great deal of trouble and labor, in conveying these unwieldy *fish-cages* across the

East River, and back again, against the usual strong current of that river. The fact was, however, established, that the City of New York was without a supply of fish, when they could so easily be obtained; and of course, the consequent rise of the small quantity that were otherwise brought there. This soon brought forth appeals from the public press, followed by petitions, and more especially from the poor retail fishermen, who depended upon their daily sales for a living. Those from this market who signed were:

Elisha Lymans,	James Griffing, Jr.,	Russel Beckwith,
Wm. Stebbins,	Nathaniel Harris,	Clark Trumans,
Edward Tinker,	Joshua Parker,	William Baxter,
Jonathan Crocker,	Juorry Tinker,	Bradley S. Wiggins,

and Jeremiah Tinker, who asked for relief; and the Board acceded to their request, "by placing the cars at the end of the Slip."

In the "war of 1812," one of these Fly Market fishing smacks engaged and captured the British sloop or tender named the *Eagle*, which was prowling around the Hook, seizing all the market-boats and other small craft that came in her way. The manner in which this capture was performed is thus described: "The fishing smack, named the *Yankee*, was borrowed of some fishermen at the Fly Market, in the City of New York, and a calf, a sheep, and a goose purchased, and secured on deck. Between thirty and forty men, well armed with muskets, were secreted in the cabin and fore-peak of the smack. Thus prepared, she stood out to sea, as if going on a fishing trip to the *Banks:* three men only being on deck, dressed in fishermen's apparel, with buff caps on. The *Eagle*, on perceiving the smack, immediately gave chase, and after coming up with her, and finding she had live stock on deck, ordered her to go down to the Commodore, then about five miles distant. The helmsman answered, 'Aye, aye, sir!' and apparently put up the helm for that purpose, which brought him alongside of the *Eagle*, not more than three yards distance. The watch-word, '*Lawrence*,' was then given, when the armed men rushed on deck from their hiding-places, and poured into her a volley of musketry, which struck the crew with dismay, and drove them all down so precipitately into the hold of the vessel, that they had not time to strike their colors. The *Eagle*, with the prisoners, was carried to the city, and landed at Whitehall, amidst the shouts and plaudits of thousands of spectators assembled on the Battery, celebrating the 'Fourth of July,' 1813. Those engaged in this successful affair were Sailing-Master Percival and several volunteers from the flotilla."

Provisions at that period had become quite scarce and high, and more especially in the supplies of fish, which many poor families had previously, through the summer season, almost exclusively lived upon. A remarkable circumstance occurred in the fall of 1813, which tended to relieve them for several weeks; and is thus noticed in the press: "Since the interruption of our accustomed supplies of fish from the eastern coast, by the British blockaders, the want is in a great measure provided for by remarkable quantities of chub or small mackerel, with which the New York markets abound. They are taken in nets, in the head of Long Island Sound, in such great numbers, that 72,000, we are told, were caught at one haul a few days since. Such an abundance of this species of fish has never been known in this country since a similar occurrence during the Revolutionary War."* I am told that the rivers, inlets, and creeks in and around the harbor of New York, and more especially along the East River shores, were so well stocked with these fish, that they were taken by thousands, with little trouble; and the common price for them in the markets was "a shilling a dozen."

The few regular butchers which were "permitted" in the country part of this market had from time to time extended or otherwise encroached on the market space, to suit themselves, without consulting the Clerk or Committee. In consequence of this, the Board, on the 17th of April, 1809, passed a resolution, " That persons having permits to sell small meats in the lower or country market, are hereby directed to use, in future, instead of their present stalls, *benches* of such form and dimensions as the Deputy Clerk may direct."

The troubles and duties of the Clerk, John Minuse, are also noted in another form, with some of these occupants. On the 3d of September, 1810, the Clerk complains of an individual, whom we shall call Charles Conlin, to the authorities, and says: "Mr. Charles Conlin, a permitted butcher in the Fly Market, has been guilty of giving in false returns, *(of the number of animals he killed,)* which I have detected several times, and he won't refrain; he says that he don't care about it, for he will cheat whenever he can; and if they turn him out of the market, he can sell meat wherever he pleases." A resolution passed revoking Conlin's permit. About a week after, Conlin presented a petition, in which he says: "That for the last four years past he has sold meat by the quarter in the lower market, and was a few days ago deprived of his license, on account of some person having informed the Clerk that he had not given in a true account of the meat sold; which conduct he is sincerely sorry for," and wishes to be restored.

The Market Committee, after hearing the case, on the 15th of the

* National Intelligencer, October 23, 1813.

same month reported on the facts as were presented: "That the day on which the petitioner was complained of, he killed *eighteen* sheep; ten of which were sold in the market, and the market fees regularly accounted for; of the remaining eight, three were placed in the market in a basket, covered, where they remained not more than half an hour, when they were sent to a Mrs. McK's boarding-house, and sold to her for *one shilling the quarter*. ('*Cheap meat for boarders!*') They were never offered for sale in the market, it being the practice of the petitioner, at different times, to send his meat of such *poor quality* to the above-mentioned boarding-house. The remaining five were never taken out of the market-cart, but were sent to Mr. Winship, for the supply of the Navy-Yard and *frigate* at the Wallabout." The petitioner being a man of family, and of respectable connections, the Committee recommended to the Board " to pardon his offence, and restore to him his license;" which was done.

Another case took place at this market in the early part of next year, for an infringement of the market law. It appears that the Clerk complained of John Miller for forestalling, &c., but he represented that he had a permission from the Alderman to make such sales. He was summoned for trial before Justice Henry Meigs, who reported on his case as follows: " It appeared to me, in the trial of the cause mentioned in the preceding petition, that although the defendant, John Miller, was without a legal authority to sell, as charged against him, yet he must have considered himself justly authorized, by virtue of the permit mentioned; and that he has not, therefore, willfully infringed the ordinance regulating public markets. March 18, 1811. H. MEIGS, Ass't Justice of the First Ward."

This country market was a continual source of trouble not only to the citizens and regular butchers, but to the " Board," which usually took place after a change of officers and their different parties. New committees came into power with new ideas and wants, many of which were not practical, being either too stringent, or tinctured too strongly of free trade, to be suitable for the protection of the citizens.

Laws were passed and rescinded, and licenses and permits were given to favorites by one party, to be taken away by the other. This state of things had originated and grown with those parties; and now (1858) they have so much enlarged and perfected on that dancing-in and dancing-out system of government, that the clever, honest people " pay the piper" any amount demanded, as naturally and faithfully as if they had agreed with them on prices to be named after their election. This is not all: these parties have continually added to their numbers; many an honest, independent-minded man, through his necessities and wants, which actually have been driven into their destructive and detested ranks, taken from them their independence and self-respect, to be at last turned into the *pot-house brawler, drunkard, liar, perjurer, thief, &c., &c., &c.;* or if he has been successful of this world's goods, through rascality, peculation, or collusion, he assumes the model man in conversation *only,* loudly condemning those who attempt to mount the same ladder which carried him above the level, high upon the aristocratic throne of fashion and worldliness.

But I have strayed from the subject I had intended to introduce, which were two resolutions offered to the Board by the Market Committee, December 8th, 1817. The first reads: " *Resolved,* That the Clerk of the Common Council be directed to make a register of the stalls held by the butchers in the several markets of this city; and that for this purpose, the several butchers holding stands be directed to make return to the Deputy Clerks of the respective markets of the number of stalls they hold, and that the butchers renew their licenses in the month of April in each year, for the better regulation of the markets.

" *Resolved,* That all butchers holding *permits* from this Board be required to report on or before the first day of January next, as all *permits* will after that date be considered void, unless renewed by the Corporation."

Many of the old permit and " Shirk Butchers," who had been permitted to stand in this market for many years, considered they were not called upon to renew their privileges, and failed, or would not obey the last resolution. The Clerk complained of them, and they were suspended, along with several others, who almost daily smuggled themselves in against the law. Among the most noted " Shirk Butchers," who petitioned in the month of August, 1818, to be " restored to that privilege," was Jacob Patchen, Jesse Coope, and Israel Reynolds. Their petition was referred to a committee, who, on the 7th of September following, reported that " The small meats brought to the *lower market* are, with very few exceptions, just bought by the persons offering them for sale, or the animals are sent them by some persons residing a few miles in the country to sell on commission, or as pretended agents for the owner, to the great detriment of our own butchers, who are restricted to a public stand. The system now pursued, it is a rare thing to see a farmer in the market with meats, &c., of his own raising; the truth is, that nearly, if not all, these agents are butchers or hucksters in disguise. The Committee cannot perceive the propriety of permitting the market thus to be occupied to the exclusion of our own citizens, who are regular butchers and subject to taxation." This petition was denied, and an ordinance was ordered to be reported on the subject accordingly.

About this period died, at a great age, a very venerable and most eccentric man, known to many of our citizens who visited this market; some of whom even at this day remember "Johnny Day," or rather he was more generally known—some say from ten to twenty years—under the affectionate and familiar name of "Old Johnny." His appearance was that of an old salt or broken-down sailor, always noted for wearing a dirty pair of patched duck trowsers; a once blue, short monkey-jacket; a slouched tarpaulin for head covering, and on his feet a pair of old stout shoes, which had been pretty well worn and patched before they came into his possession.

His history no doubt was one full of events, and of a character somewhat strange as well as romantic. His daily habits and manners, however, appeared somewhat like his wardrobe, and were quite as eccentric. Long before the sun peeped over the Long Island hills, every morning found him at this market waiting the call of his patrons for any light work or odd jobs they might offer him, whether to transport a tray of meat, carry a basket of potatoes, or toddle home after some good housewife with her marketing—not that he was an admirer of the softer sex, or was willing to serve them, as he seldom spoke to or answered their questions, but received their directions and their rewards in dumb show. Previous to his coming to this market, he said, he had not spoken to a woman for about sixty years.

This peculiar habit of "Old Johnny" towards the female sex rendered him not a favorite, and therefore he was rarely employed by them, although there were one or two old hucksters who could occasionally prevail upon him to do some little service; among these was Mrs. Spicer and Mrs. Tallman, who now and then gave him a cup of warm coffee or other refreshment, after finishing their breakfast.

Old Johnny's residence and lodgings were in the cellar of a house in Banker (Madison) Street, where he went regularly every night to sleep; but his boarding-house was in and about this old market.

At the commencement of the war of 1812 he was then acknowledged to be over one hundred years of age, although he still retained the appearance on his visage and gait of the earlier days, when he first became known here. The only complaint he ever made was from occasional "sick turns," no doubt the effect of his extreme age; and in one of these, Mrs. Spicer induced him to go and see Mrs. Brownell, a most benevolent lady, residing on the corner opposite the market, and who was held in high repute for her knowledge as a medical doctress. A few simple remedies applied, with the more important nourishing diet supplied, soon placed "Old Johnny" in a position to pursue his usual routine; in addition to this, it opened a channel to the old man's heart; he began to look upon the sex with a less bilious eye, and with a clearer heart, he began to think there were some kind, true-hearted women, even in this world; as an acknowledgment of this newly-discovered magnet to his heart and soul, he was now more than willing to go to the pump a dozen times a day for water, to carry fire-wood as often into the house, or to do any little or great service within his power for the "Fair Lady," as he now and ever after fondly termed her, who had not only acted as his physician, but now had become his friend. While suffering in one of these "sick turns," Mr. Brownell, (whom he honored with the title of "General,") as well as Mrs. B., frequently questioned him concerning the early history of his life. Johnny was not communicative on this matter in the presence of Mr. B., or would only utter a few exclamatory sentences, and then suddenly stop with a common expression, "Take care, Johnny—you have said enough;" then put his wiry fingers to his mouth, close his lips, and so remain a few moments.

Mrs. B's kindness, however, would occasionally induce him to unfold portions of his life's history. "That he once had the honor to hold the commission of Lieutenant in the British naval service; that he was engaged to be married to a girl of good family—young, beautiful, rich, and accomplished; but, unfortunately, he left his betrothed in the charge of a supposed friend, who cruelly deceived and slandered him; gained her affections, and married her; when he afterwards, in a duel, shot him dead, fled from England, and left all behind." Having gone thus far, he would suddenly exclaim, "Take care, Johnny—you have said enough;" and then remain silent, though often followed by two large tears rolling down his wrinkled face.

This was all that she, by questions put to him, could ever elicit. Years passed rapidly away, still "Old Johnny" was at his post and haunts around this market, till about the year 1818, when one day he was taken suddenly ill in Pearl Street, before the meeting-house of the Society of Friends; here he had lain some time; the people passed by unheedingly; none assisted him; many supposing he was a drunken vagabond lying on the side-walk.

Mr. Brownell learned at his store, from some of the passers-by, of "Old Johnny's" situation. His wife was informed, and immediately this good Samaritan was on her way, and found "Old Johnny"

almost dead. The services of an old honest colored man were secured, and the old man was removed carefully to his home, where,
under faithful nursing and the ancient vigor of his constitution, he
soon recovered his usual health and haunts at the market. He first
visited Mrs. Brownell, and kindly thanked her; at the same time,
he said, in a sort of confidential, mysterious warning, "Fair lady,
you will never regret this act of kindness. Many passed and pit-
ied me; none, however, but the 'Fair Lady' would care for me."
And again he earnestly said, "The 'Fair Lady' shall never regret
it." "No, Johnny," said Mrs. B., "I never regret doing a deed of
humanity." "No, no, 'Fair Lady,'" said Johnny, "I mean—I will
give you all"—and he stopped a moment, to think whether he had
not said enough, but finished with—"What I have never dared to
touch." Mrs. B. thought no more of this, until Johnny was missing
for several days from the market, when she proceeded up to his un-
derground lodgings, and sure enough, Johnny was there lying upon
his death-bed, as it afterwards proved. He quickly recognized her,
with an expression, "Heaven be thanked for this! My prayer is
granted. Again I see the 'Fair Lady,' to tell her that my time is
short in this world. To my knowledge, I have no relatives, and I
want proper assistance to make a will." Mrs. B. said to him,
"Johnny, what have you to leave, that you should wish to make a
will?" Johnny turned on his side, with a groan, saying, "There"—
pointing to a couple of very old seaman's chests, which were almost
hidden from sight by the old sail-cloth, iron, and rough fire-wood—
"There, in those old chests, and a large covered pot, which lies buried
beneath that hearth—all their contents I shall bequeath to you,
'Fair Lady.' I told you you would never regret your kindness to
'Old Johnny Day.'"

Mrs. B. thought these might contain the gatherings of the many
years around the Old Fly Market, and likely not more than enough
to have him decently buried; but, to satisfy "Old Johnny," the will
was made, and properly drawn up, by his dictation—recorded in
the Surrogate's office, and dated the 4th day of December, 1819.

However, before "Johnny" died, he wished to disclose something,
which appeared to greatly disturb his mind; and to his colored
nurse he several times, in detached sentences, commenced to unfold
that he knew where "hoards of silver coin, bars of gold and doub-
loons, and jewels of vast value, lie buried—enough to fill twenty
chests like those; but I cannot, I must not, reveal it now. I will—
I will before I die."

"He had some horror when speaking of it," said his old nurse;
"but I believe he intended, and tried to do so, when he was so far
gone that his speech was inaudible." This was about the substance

of all that "Old Johnny" ever revealed; although there were some people who thought he had been an old pirate, and that before he died he made such a confession; but this was not so, as the old negro nurse was truth itself.

The will was opened, and in it was found, he had bequeathed all his property, of all kinds, which proved to be about $35,000, in solid cash, besides other valuables, to the fair, kind, and Christian lady, Mrs. Brownell, the mother of the well-known and highly-esteemed Judge J. Sherman Brownell, who so honestly inherits those good qualities once possessed by his parents.

On the 26th of April of this year, (1819,) a return of all the butchers who were licensed was made, when a resolution was passed, "That they be licensed agreeably to the returns of the Deputy Clerks of the different markets; and that the price of license be reduced to *one dollar*."

Two years after, the Deputy Clerk reported the following for license:

1. William Pullis.
2. Nicholas Steel.
3. Matthias Smith.
4. George Ryerson.
5. Vacant.
6. John Chappel.
7. Vacant.
8. Do.
9. John Bridle.
10. Vacant.
11. Do.
12. Do.
13. Do.
14. Thomas Gibbons.
15. Vacant.
16. Zavier Broadway.
17. Vacant.
18. Do.
19. Do.
20. John Hyde.
21. Vacant.
22. Do.
23. John Abeel.
24 and 25. Scale and Passage.
26. Christian Truss.
27. James Wright.
28. Vacant.
29. Vacant.
30. William Winter.
31. John Whitehead.
32. George Ewen.
33. Martin Silber.
34. Harvey Lyon.
35. John Rudman.
36. William Warlow.
37. Henry Shop.
38. Eliphalet Wheeler.
39. John Norman.
40. Willet Cornell.
41. Andrew C. Wheeler.
42. Peter Wilt.
43. Daniel Burtnett.
44. John Nash.
45. Henry Marsh.
46. David Marsh.
47. Edward Patton.
48. William Reynolds.
49. Andrew Fisher.
50. John Doughty.
51. William Patton.
52. James Carr.
53. John Stamler.
54. John Perrin.
55. George S. Messerve.

56. Christian Stamler.
57. Effingham Marsh.
58. William Messerve.
59. Michael Crawbuck.
60. William Foster.
61. Cornelius Schuyler.
62. Nat. Underhill.
63. Albert Fisher.
64. Elnathan Underhill.

65. Lanning Ferris.
66. Joseph O. Bogert.
67. Daniel Winship, Jr.
68. George G. Messerve.
69. Daniel Winship.
70. John Pell.
71. David Seaman.
72. George Manolt.

Many of the stands are found vacant at this period; and one year later, more than one-half of the butchers and others had left this famous old market, never more to return.

But we are loth yet to part company with this ancient relic of "by-gone times," which had lived so long in the history of our city; known and fed so many generations of almost all the civilized nations of the world. In childhood it had first appeared with a very small covering to shelter and accommodate its original visitors, who daily passed along at a "slow and sure" pace towards it, wearing huge breeches and pockets capacious enough to contain a week's stores when in danger of short supplies; and while the trade was progressing for the season's supplies of kale and cabbage, their old dingy *meerschaum* was replenished with that then *common weed*, to be whiffed away in assisting their thinking organs in the prosecution of a satisfactory bargain. Although many changes of authority, with rebuildings and additions to the *Vley*, yet these old Dutchmen held fast to their old customs, manners, and language, until time has found them merged into the English, French, German, with a few of other nations, to be at last called and known as *New Yorkers*.

Two years after the war of 1812 had commenced, "the scarcity of specie, and the drains made upon the banks, induced a suspension of specie payments, which continued until the first Monday in July, 1817. The want of specie and small change for a circulating medium induced the Corporation to cause to be issued a substitute, in the shape of paper money, in 6¼, 12½, 25, and 50 cent bills, to the amount of one hundred thousand dollars; signed by John Pintard, Thomas Franklin, and William M'Neal; which bills being endowed with public confidence, passed current in all payments, and facilitated business."*

These Corporation bills, however, were not sufficient for the usual wants, and many tradesmen also issued their own bills; but glad enough were all classes when the time was approaching for the general use of specie again. The butchers and all others who stood in the markets promised, through the "Press," to sell "for one week

* Goodrich's Picture of N. Y., p. 102.

twelve per cent. cheaper than they have done," by way of welcoming the recommencement of the silver age. " Silver is silver—and chaff is chaff," said they.

The city soon after became flooded with the bills of the country banks, which at that period stood upon very slender foundations; some of which were every few weeks or months stopping specie payments or closing for a period; then with their agents buying up their bills for 25 or 50 cents on a dollar, while others stopped entirely, and defrauding thousands of poor mechanics and others. In 1819 it had become so intolerable that a large meeting of the butchers of this city was held on Tuesday, 22d June of that year, at which they passed several resolutions; one of which was, " That after the 30th instant they will receive no country bank-notes that are below par in New York."

In the mean time provisions of all kinds had become scarce and high, and so continued for several years. The prices of cattle varied from 10 to 15 dollars per cwt. from 1814 to 1820. Meat at retail sold as high as 2s. 6d. per pound, and even " rough-fat " sold at 16 to 18 pence per pound. In 1815 the milkmen come out in the press and state, that " in consequence of the high price of fodder, the milkmen, after the 1st of December, have agreed to charge a shilling a quart for milk."*

In the month of January following, " Hickory wood sold at 23 dollars per cord; oak, fifteen—the severe frost having cut off all supplies;" and in the same month of the next year, " Flour sells for $15 per barrel, and a further advance is apprehended."

The February following, "A vessel has lately arrived from Belfast with 562 firkins of butter, 200 of lard, 50 barrels of beef, 54 do. of pork, and a quantity of potatoes;" and in the month of December following, the "Gazette" states: " If there are any *hogs* yet remaining in the country, now is the time to bring them to the New York markets, as the price is from ten to eleven dollars a hundred, which has most of this season been their current prices."†

The number of animals killed and exposed for sale in this market during the months of January, February, March, and April, in the year 1816, was reported as follows:

	Sheep.	Cattle.	Calves.	Hogs.
January, - -	1,544	671	225	220
February, - -	1,066	572	485	158
March, - -	554	569	1,164	157
April, - - -	501	463	1,948	134
Total, -	3,665	2,275	3,822	669

* Gazette, November 30. † December 12, 1817.

In the year 1818 another report shows all the animals sold at the four principal markets, from January 1st to September 30, 1818:

		Cattle.	Calves.	Sheep.	Hogs.
Fly Market,	-	4,402	9,105	19,154	1,725
Washington, -	-	3,168	5,539	14,412	605
Catharine,	-	3,616	5,210	14,384	332
Centre, -	- -	617	1,186	4,357	60
Total,	-	11,913	21,040	52,307	2,722

" The above is a true copy of the returns of the Deputy Clerks of the different markets."

The subject of removing this market-place from Maiden Lane had begun several years before it was accomplished.

Petitions for and against it were presented at intervals; some said: "It was an unfit place, being over a sewer, which in the summer-time is considered very unhealthy; that it blocked up the street, so much so, that mercantile business was partially stopped." And others, again, "Because its trade was decreasing;" and no doubt this latter was the greatest cause, as the new Washington Market was beginning to be the attraction, both for the country people on the North River side, and great numbers of our citizens. In January, 1816, a committee reported on the expediency of removing it, and "that the ground at Beekman's Slip, Front Street, Crane's Wharf, and East River, should be the site fixed upon;" which was adopted, (by a vote of 12 to 5,)* but not carried out at this period; and no doubt the cause was, that more opposition had been made to it than had been expected, especially from the press. The Gazette, August 19, 1819, has rather a sensible " communication " upon the subject, which says: "The public mind has been long occupied with the question—Ought the Fly Market to be removed? The question appears to be at rest by a resolution passed by our Corporation to remove it to Crane's Wharf. This resolve has not been put into execution; nor, unless my judgment is extremely erroneous, is it at all likely it will be. Perhaps the question never was discussed with so much obstinacy as it is at this time in the Common Council.

"The enormous sum required for the completion of the project, the pressure of the times, the difficulties with the owners of property, the advantages to accrue to the Corporation by selling the property prepared for the market, are urged with vehemence on the one side; while the other, with equal warmth, call for its removal by every consideration of their high and responsible stations as guardians of the public health, and solicitous for the public good. The present

* N. Y. Spectator, January 3.

site of the Fly Market is undoubtedly best suited for the convenience of citizens, as the whole community south of it are supplied
there.   The main objection to its present situation is its being so
confined by the adjacent houses as to render it unhealthy, by the
unavoidable collection of filth in a narrow street, and want of a
free circulation of air."

The Grand Jury, in the following month of September, presented
it as a nuisance, and say in their report, that "this market is built
over a common sewer, conducting the water from Maiden Lane and
the adjoining streets to the East River.   The sewer has no covering under the meat market, between Pearl and Front Streets; but
the floor of the market, which is loosely laid, is taken up whenever
it is necessary to cleanse it.   On the sides of the market are a
number of apertures into this sewer, which are receptacles of filth
and garbage from the taverns, fruit-stands, and cook-shops adjoining
thereto, creating offensive and pestilential matter, and infecting the
atmosphere with the most nauseous vapors at this season of the
year.   But although a sense of duty compels the Grand Jury to
present this market as a nuisance, they are pleased to avow that it is
in as cleanly a state as its confined situation will admit, but which
forces on them the conviction that this market ought to be removed
to a site more favorable to cleanliness and comfort."

This presentation of the Grand Jury, however, had no effect with
the Market Committee, who, on the following 24th of January, reported against the removal; and, in answer to the several reasons
urged as causes for the removal of this market, they say: "But
your Committee cannot perceive any unfitness for the public accommodation, or any unhealthiness in the present site of this market, nor any other objection to it, that would not apply with nearly
equal, if not greater, force to any other situation.   They are also
of opinion that, if this market were removed, the inhabitants of the
southwesterly part of the city would immediately require a new
market to be erected for their accommodation somewhere to the
southward and westward of Maiden Lane.   They would then say,
and with great force, that the Oswego Market, the Exchange Market, and the Fly Market had all been taken away from them, and
that another ought to be erected for their convenience."

The business, however, decreased so fast, that the butchers in the
Upper Market petition on the 27th of May following, and wish to
be removed to some part of the Lower or Country Market; stating
that "but little business is done in that part of the market."   They
followed it up the next year, in the month of February, stating that
they "have several times prayed to be removed; but as their pray-

ers have hitherto been in vain, though they have, as they believe, been founded in justice and equity, they have bowed in silent sorrow to your honored will. But as they are now encouraged by many of their much respected and sympathetic brethren in the *Lower Market*, who will make a voluntary sacrifice of personal interest to subserve public good, they appeal with confidence, and humbly pray that your Honorable Body will be pleased to embrace the opportunity offered by the late fire, *(which destroyed all the buildings on the proposed site,)* of erecting a public market, and that the butchers at present in Fly Market may be permitted to remove to and occupy the stands in said market."

The farmers and other inhabitants of Kings County, L. I., who attended this market, also "asked to discontinue it." A remonstrance from several of the property owners and store-keepers was also at that time presented against its removal; but the fate of the Old Fly Market was soon after decided, and the Fulton Market was ordered to be built.

Before this decision was made, however, an interesting display took place in the city, part of which pertained to this market. One of its most prominent butchers, a great friend and co-worker of the New York County Agricultural Society, purchased a number of prize cattle at one of their Fairs held at a place called "Mount Vernon," (but previously known as "Smith's Folly,") at that day a little above "Cato's," on the East River, (now nearly on a line of Sixty-first Street,) on the 13th day of March, 1821.

" '*Premium Cattle.*'—Twenty best cattle that have ever been exhibited in this city, and which obtained the first premium—value $100—on the 13th inst., at Mount Vernon, will be offered for sale on Saturday, the 17th inst., in Fly Market, by the subscriber, assisted by many of his worthy friends, who have, in the most handsome and generous manner, offered him their services; and he hopes that his efforts to promote the agricultural interest of this State will meet the approbation and support of a magnanimous and generous public.   T. GIBBONS."*

After these animals had been dressed, an average of 182½ lbs. of rough-fat was taken from each animal, and in forty butchers' carts, handsomely decorated, "was carried through the principal streets of the city;" while "the 'Star-spangled Banner' was displayed, and the premiums of silver pitchers, &c., exhibited in the first cart." Mr. Gibbons announced through the press, "The price of this beef will be *one shilling* a pound." A card from the Debtors' Prison announced, on the 19th, "With gratitude, the prisoners

* "Gazette," March 15, 1821.

in the Debtors' Jail acknowledge the receipt of a plentiful donation of 'Premium Beef' from Mr. Gibbons, and the joint Society of Butchers of the Fly Market."

The days of the existence of the *Old Vlie* had become numbered, and brought the period when the owners of the fourteen stands, purchased in 1796, wanted to know what compensation the Corporation intended to give them, in lieu of those they intended to take from them. So they presented their claim in the shape of a petition, dated 13th December, 1821, "stating that the Corporation, in the year 1796, caused fourteen new stands in the Fly Market to be sold at auction; and that they were purchased by the petitioners, or those from whom the petitioners have bought them. That they understood the Corporation intend pulling down and removing said market; against which they protest, and request that no measures be taken therein, until a compensation is made to the petitioners for the loss they will incur by the removal of said market;" which was referred, and no action taken upon it. It, however, brought forth a resolution, on the 21st January following, from their friend, Alderman Abraham Valentine, "That the voluntary relinquishment of fourteen butchers to certain stands in Fly Market, which they claim to have purchased from the Corporation, shall not be construed by the Common Council as invalidating their claims to compensation." Which was adopted.

The next morning's (22d) "paper" says: "The Fly Market, or, as our forefathers used to call it, the *Vlie*, is to be deserted this day. The bustle commenced yesterday, and many an epicure, who for years has been habitually fatting upon the good things of the Fly, will hereafter be gratified by visiting the Fulton Market; and, although he cannot dispense with his eating habits, he will soon become reconciled to his new and daily visits to the more extensive one now brought into use."

Several of the butchers continued their business in the markethouse, until the tearing down over their heads drove them out. Mr. John Seaman (now of stand No. 34, Centre Market,) was at that time assisting his father, David Seaman, (the occupant of No. 71,) and engaged in making sale of a piece of meat to a captain of a vessel, and while weighing it, a piece of the roof fell down between the traders; which soon closed the *last sale* made in this once famous *old market*, after having been established *one hundred and twenty-three years* in one place.

This settled the "Old Market-Place," but the claims which the owners of the 14 stands bought of the Corporation in 1796 were yet to be settled. With this purpose, on the following 10th day of

June, a communication was received by the Counsel of the Board, stating that George Manolt, David Seaman, and Albert Fisher had commenced action in the Supreme Court against the Corporation for the damages which they have sustained by being deprived of their stalls in the Old Fly Market, in consequence of its being pulled down. Whereupon the Counsel was directed to enter his appearance for the Corporation, and to defend the suit. It was also referred to the Law Committee, " to employ such additional counsel as they may judge proper."

This suit did not, however, then take place, as there were some hopes and promises of settling it with the Corporation; but after waiting two years, it was agreed that but one should go on, and the suit was entered in the name of David Seaman against the City, before the Honorable Samuel R. Betts; having as Counsel Peter A. Jay and Thomas A. Emmet for plaintiffs; and for the Corporation, M. Ulshoeffer, D. B. Ogden, and William Slosson, Esq., as Counsel. On the 19th of July, 1824, the Counsel to the Board reported: "That on the 15th instant, the cause of 'Seaman' against the Corporation (one of what are commonly called the butcher causes) was tried, and on the 16th a verdict was found for plaintiff of $600."

This was followed with a petition from the other plaintiffs on the 25th of October, of which the following is an extract: " That your petitioners therefore caused certain suits to be commenced against the Corporation, supposing that if *their title* should be once settled in either of these suits, the Corporation would no longer contest their claim to compensation; that one of these suits was tried on the 16th of July last, when a verdict was found against the Corporation. On this verdict judgment has been rendered—no exception was taken to the charge of the judge, which was not favorable to your petitioners—no motion has been made for a new trial—no writ of error has been brought, but the Counsel for the Corporation have acquiesced in this decision. Your petitioners therefore suppose that the question of *titles* may be considered as no longer in controversy, and that the amount of compensation due to your petitioners respectively only remains to be ascertained. It appears to your petitioners, that in this state of affairs, it cannot be necessary or desirable to increase expense by protracted litigation, but that an amicable arrangement may now be made."

This subject came before the Finance Committee, who reported on the following 22d of November, which concludes in these words: "On the trial of one of these suits, a verdict of $600 was found for the plaintiff, and under all the circumstances of that case, your Committee did not deem it advisable to recommend any further defence in those suits; since that trial, the petition now reported on was presented to the Board, and referred to your Committee, and they have had interviews with the petitioners and their Counsel, Peter A. Jay, Esq., and have treated respecting an amicable settlement of the matters in question.

"The result is, that your Committee have concluded to recommend to the Board to allow to the petitioners the amount paid for the stalls which they held at the time the market was pulled down, together with the interest from that time to the present.

"And the petitioners have agreed to accept this compensation, together with their expenses; which also your Committee have agreed should be allowed to them. Your Committee have been induced to recommend this liberal settlement towards the petitioners, not only because of the verdict of the jury before referred to, but principally from the peculiar hardship of the case of some of the petitioners, who paid very large sums of money for these stalls to others from whom they purchased, and not long before the market was pulled down. It is true that this Board have not been parties to these transfers in but few instances; and in none, as your Committee believe, also, they ever countenanced the idea that the purchaser was to hold beyond the life of the original purchaser by auction. But these are questions that your Committee do not mean to enlarge upon; they have met the claimants in a spirit of liberality and amity, and have concluded to recommend a compromise to the Board, as before stated, and with the express understanding on both sides that, in case this proposition should not be accepted by the Board, neither this report, nor such proposition, nor anything that has taken place in regard thereto, shall be considered as prejudging any right on either side. The case of *Seaman* being disposed of as above stated, the claims of *thirteen* of the stalls in question alone remain; and the annexed statement shows the numbers of the stalls sold at auction, which the petitioners either bought then or purchased since; it also shows the names of the petitioners; the amount paid for each stall; the amount of interest on each sum; the total of each claim; and adding the expenses agreed to be allowed as before stated, it makes a total sum of $10,272.46.

"Your Committee therefore offers for the consideration of the Board the following resolution:

"*Resolved*, That in case all the petitioners shall, on or before the next meeting of this Board, make and execute a proper release or releases in the premises, which shall be considered sufficient by the Finance Committee, (who may require security in any instance that they may think proper,) the Comptroller shall report a warrant in favor of Peter A. Jay, Esq., for the total sum above named; and which shall be delivered to Mr. Jay on his delivering to the Comptroller the said release and his receipt for the amounts." Signed, Reuben Munson, William H. Ireland, Henry J. Wycoff, and William Burtsell.

The "Board" approved the report, adopted the resolution, and the whole was acceded to by all the petitioners who represented these various stands at this date, as follows:

No.	Names.	Cost in £.	In $.	Interest.	Total.
59.	William Foster, - - -	£200	$500 00	$100 62	$600 62
60.	Michael Crawbuck, -	210	525 00	105 65	630 65
61.	Cornelius Schuyler, -	175	437 50	88 04	525 54
62.	Nath. Underhill, - -	150	375 00	75 47	450 47
63.	Albert Fisher, - - -	180	450 00	90 57	540 57
64.	Elnathan Underhill, -	280	700 00	140 88	840 88
65.	Lanning Ferris, - - -	165	412 50	83 25	495 52
66.	Joseph O. Bogart, - -	310	775 00	155 85	930 85
67.	Daniel Winship, Jr., -	170	425 00	85 53	510 53
68.	George Messerve, - -	320	800 00	161 00	961 00
69.	Daniel Winship, - - -	205	512 50	103 15	615 65
70.	John Pell, - - - - -	285	712 50	143 40	855 90
71.	David Seaman, - - -	(Test case at law settled.)			
72.	George Manolt, - - -	530	1,325 00	266 65	1,591 65

		$9,549 83
For expenses, taxes, costs, &c., allowed, - - -		722 63
Settlement for the whole amount, - - - - -		$10,272 46

Thus terminated the career of the once famous "Old Fly Market;" but many old citizens and merchants near it had become so partial to the name, that they continued to use it even after the last vestige of the old market-house had disappeared. An old and a well-known highly respected firm, yet in existence, at that period says in an advertisement: "Just published by E. & G. W. Blunt, No. 147 *Fly Market*, a Chart of the Harbor of New York, with the Coasts of Long Island and New Jersey, from Fire Island to Barnegat Inlet, &c.*"

In concluding the history of this market-place, we may say that, while in existence, it could claim the merit of being the best, and most liberally supplied with all the various articles used for human food, in the United States.

* American, December 13, 1823.

"MEAL OR WALL STREET MARKET."

ON the 4th day of October, 1709, "the inhabitants of the East Ward petitioned for liberty to erect a market-house at the south end of Clark's Slip, at the east end of Wall Street;" and permission was granted to them "to erect the same at their own charge, provided it be finished within two years from date."

For more than fifty years previous, a noted tavern had been kept near where this market was to be established, which appears to have been the resort of country people from Long Island, who usually put up here when visiting the city. It was the first house inside of the wall or city gate, which opened on the present line of Pearl Street. This tavern was established by Daniel Litschoe, who died about the year 1660, when his widow continued the business for a number of years; but having become advanced in life, she sold her property to the Jew butcher, Asser Levy, who continued it,* and (with his partner, Gerrit Jansen Roos,) he also kept the neighboring "Public Slaughter-House." After that period, there appears to have been a noted public-house kept near the same place. The old Coffee-House afterwards became famous, which was followed by the celebrated "Tontine," both being in that vicinity.

This market-place, soon after its erection, became rather a favorite place for the merchants to meet to transact their business, and it has not lost its character yet on that point; the only difference is a slight change in the business. In the "olden time," "all negro and Indian slaves that are let out to hire, within this city, do take up their standing in order to be hired at the market-house at the Wall Street Slip, until such time as they are hired, whereby all persons may know where to hire slaves as their occasion shall require, and all masters discover where their slaves are so hired;"† and now a very large business is done there with the products of slave labor.

At that early period the masters, when they had no work for their slaves, (many of whom were Indians,) sent them to this market-place, where they were obliged to wait during business hours until hired, which would sometimes be by the day, week, or month; however, they were occasionally a great deal of trouble to their masters and employers, no doubt in consequence of ill-treatment, neglect, and being improperly cared for; and, of course, the slaves were usually

* Valentine.   † Records, November 30, 1711

lazy, vicious, thievish, and at times revengeful, although many stringent orders and laws were made to keep them in order. As early
as 1690 they were not allowed to cross the ferry either way, as it
was "Ordered that the fferryman shall not bringe or sett over any
negroes or slaves uppon the Sabbath daye without a tickett from
their masters."

In 1706 Governor Cornbury issued the following proclamation:
"Whereas, I am informed that several negroes in Kings County
have assembled themselves in a riotous manner, which, if not prevented, may prove of ill consequence: You, the Justice of the Peace
in the said county, are hereby required and commanded to take all
proper methods for the seizing and apprehending all such negroes as
shall be found to be assembled in such manner as aforesaid, or have
run away or absconded from their masters or owners, whereby there
may be reasons to suspect them of ill practices or designs, and to
secure them in safe custody; and if any of them refuse to submit,
then to *fire* upon them, *kill* or *destroy* them, if they *cannot* otherwise
be taken; and for so doing this shall be your sufficient warrant.
Given under my hand, at *Fort Ann*, the 22d day of July, 1706.

"CORNBURY."

Then we find, in the year 1712, a great excitement was made
among the citizens in consequence of a conspiracy or rising of the
negro slaves in this city. Horsmanden says: "On the 7th of April,
about one or two o'clock in the morning, the house of Peter Van
Tilburgh was set on fire by the negroes, who being armed with guns,
knives, &c., killed and wounded several white people as they were
coming to assist in extinguishing the flames. Notice thereof being
soon carried to the fort, His Excellency, Governor Hunter, ordered
a cannon to be fired from the ramparts to alarm the town, and detached a party of soldiers to the fire, at whose appearance those vil-
lains immediately fled, and made their way out of town as fast as they
could, to hide themselves in the woods and swamps. In their flight
they also killed and wounded several white people; but being closely pursued, some concealed themselves in barns, and others sheltered
in the swamps or woods, which being surrounded and strictly guarded till the morning, many of them were then taken. Some, finding
no way for their escape, shot themselves. The end of it was, that after
these foolish wretches had murdered eight or ten white people, and
some of the confederates had been their own executioners, nineteen
more of them were apprehended, brought upon their trials for a
conspiracy to murder the people, &c., and were convicted and executed; and several more that turned evidence were transported."

Governor Hunter, in a letter dated June 12, (same year,) to the

" Lords of Trade," gives the following particulars concerning it:
" I must now give your lordships an account of a bloody conspiracy
of some of the slaves of this place to destroy as many inhabitants
as they could. It was put in execution in this manner: When
they had resolved to revenge themselves for some hard usage they
apprehended to have received from their masters, (for I can find no
other cause,) they agreed to meet in the orchard of Mr. Crook, the
middle of the town; some provided with fire-arms, some with swords,
and others with knives and hatchets; this was the sixth day of
April; the time of meeting was about twelve or one o'clock in the
night; when about three-and-twenty of them were got togeather, one
Coffee and negro slave of one Van Tilburgh set fire to an out-house
of his master's, and then repairing to the place where the rest were,
they all sallyed out togeather wth their arms, and marched to the
fire; by this time the noise of fire spreeding through the town, the
people began to flock to it; upon the approach of severall, the slaves
fired and killed them; the noise of the guns gave the allarm, and
some escaping their shot, soon published the cause of the fire, which
was the reason that not above nine Christians were killed, and
about five or six wounded; upon the first notice, which was very
soon after the mischief was begun, I ordered a detachment from the
Fort, (*George*,) under a proper officer, to march against them, but the
slaves made their retreat into the woods, by the favour of the night;
having ordered centries the next day in the most proper places on
the Island to prevent their escape, I caused the day following the
militia of this town and of the County of Westchester to drive the
island, and by this means and strict searches in the town, we found
all that put the design in execution; six of these having first laid violent hands upon themselves, the rest were forthwith brought to their
tryal before ye Justices of this place, who are authorized by act of
Assembly to hold a court in such cases. In that court were twenty-
seven condemned, whereof twenty-one were executed, one being a
woman with child, her execution by that meanes suspended; some
were burnt, others hanged, one broke on the wheel, and one hung
a live in chains in the town. One *Mars*, a negro man slave to
one Mr. Regnier, *was twice indicted and twice tryed*, and again acquitted, but not discharged; and being a third time presented, was
transferred to the Supream Court, and there tryed and convicted on
ye same evidence on his two former tryals: this prosecution was car-
ryed on to gratify some private pique of Mr. Bickley's against Mr.
Regnier, a gentleman of his own profession, which appearing so partial, and the evidence being represented to me as very defective,
and being wholly acquitted of ever having known anything of the

conspirracy by the negroe witnesses, I thought fit to reprieve him till Her Majestie's pleasure be known therein."*

The "City Records" also show some of the particulars, and the punishments awarded to a few of the culprits, of which the following are among the most prominent who were tried and convicted: *Clause,* the slave of Allen Jarrott, with *Quacco,* slave of Abraham Provoost, and *Sam,* slave of Peter Fauconieier; also *Robin,* who stabbed his master, Adrian Hoghlandt, in the back, and killed him: all were convicted of murder, but their mode of punishment appears quite different. *Clause* was "broke upon a wheel." *Robin* was hung in chains alive, and "so continue without any sustenance until he be dead." *Quacco* was burnt, and *Sam* was hung. Nicholas Rosevelt also had a slave named *Tom,* who was "burned with a slow fire until he be dead and consumed to ashes," as was also Ruth Shepard's *Tunis.* Ephraim Pierson, a "constable of the watch," was badly wounded by Jacob Regnier's *Mars:* his punishment was to "be stripped from the middle upwards and tyed to the tail of a cart, at the City Hall, and be drawn from thence to the Broadway, and from thence to the Custom-House; thence to Wall Street, and from thence to the City Hall again; and that he be whipped upon the naked back, ten lashes att the corner of every street he shall pass, and that he afterwards be discharged from his imprisonment, paying his fees, &c."

The Sheriff, Francis Harrison, Esq., was ordered to be paid £36 10s. for cost of "iron-work, gibbets, cartage, and laborers, firewood, and other materials and expenses for the execution of several negro slaves, for murders by them committed in April last."

Negro slaves, when they suffered death for committing crime, were not always a total loss to their masters; the authorities were usually appealed to, through petition, for the amount of a valuation made by persons who no doubt dealt or were in the *trayd;* and such valuation was paid by Government.

The following petition on this subject was before the Board September 19, 1719, asking "for payment of a negro belonging to Hermannus Burgher, blacksmith, who is to suffer death for burglary."
"That your petitioner is a poor, aged, and lame man, and hath nothing whereby he may sustain himself but the labor of a negro man slave, named Harry, who is now under sentence of death, and therefore, as your petitioner hath reason to believe, execution will be speedily done. But your petitioner being informed that there is an act of General Assembly in force for allowance of a certain sum of money to the owners of such slave or slaves as shall be le-

* Col. Hist., vol. v., p. 341.

gally put to death—he therefore prays he may have the benefit of the said act; and as in duty bound, &c.   HARMANYS BUGER."

The value of his slave was referred to the following gentlemen, who reported as follows: "We, Alburtus Bosch and Nichlas Maettaysan, being desired of Harmanus Burger to vallow the slave called by the name of Herry, now in prison, are of opinion that he is worth sixty pounds, if hee was to be bought by any of *our trayd:* as witnesses our hands, &c., September 3, 1719."

Eight years after, the punishment for passing false bills of credit is meted out to a couple of individuals in a style which I think would deter or make such kind of *business* very unfashionable at the present day. "At a Supreme Court of Judicature held at the City Hall of the City of New York, the fourth of December, 1727, were presented for sentence David Wallace and David Willson, having at the last Court been convicted of a cheat, in passing some bills of credit of the Province of New Jersey, were now brought to the bar, and received the following sentence, viz.: That the said David Wallace and David Willson do stand in the pillory between the hours of ten and eleven in the forenoon of the same day, (12th inst.,) and after that be placed in a cart, so as to be publickly seen, with halters about their necks, and carted thro' the most publick streets in this city; and then be brought to the public Whipping-Post, and there David Wallis, on his bare back, to receive thirty-nine stripes, and David Willson twenty-eight stripes. And within some convenient time after, the Sheriff shall deliver said prisoners at the Ferry-House in Kings County, and on the third Tuesday in January next they shall be set on the pillory, and then Wallis to receive at Flatbush thirty-nine stripes, and Willson twenty-eight. Then they shall be conveyed to Jamaica, in Queens County, and there, on the fourth Tuesday in February, to stand on the pillory, and afterwards each of them to receive the same number of stripes. Then to be conveyed to Westchester, and there, on the fourth Tuesday in March, to stand on the pillory, and then at the Whipping-Post Wallace to receive twenty stripes on the bare back, and Willson ten. After which, at the end of King's Bridge, they shall be delivered to the High Sheriff of the City of New York, and from that time, Wallace to remain in prison six months, and Willson three months. And then each to be discharged, paying their fees!"

The Laws of 1720 notice this market as the Market-House at Wall Street Slip; and the "Proceedings" on the 16th of November, same year, order, "That the neighborhood of the *Wall Street Market-House* have liberty to remove the said market-house higher up into the said street, or repair it where it now stands, at their own proper cost and charge." Six years after, a law was ordained, that the market-house " commonly called *Wall Street Market-House* is hereby appointed a public market-place for the sale of all sorts of corn, grain, and meal; and that from and after the 25th day of March next, (1726,) no corn, grain, or meal be sold in publick market within this city at any other place" but at this market, under a heavy penalty.

After this period, it became usually known in the " papers' advertisements" as the *Meal Market*, until it ceased to exist. Lyne's Map, 1729, marks it down, No. 10, *Meat Market;* which no doubt was the printer's mistake, as no *cut meat* was allowed to be sold in it until about 1740, when an .ordinance was passed, "allowing country people to cut meat up," and also in the Broadway Market; which fact is more particularly referred to in the history of that market.

Bradford's Gazette, 1734, says: " To be sold by John Briggs, at his *shop*, at the corner of the *Meal Market*, all sorts of Drugs and Medicines by wholesale." I don't suppose there is at present a *shop* in that neighborhood that sells at wholesale, or even one at retail. The " Weekly Post Boy" of 1743 notices their " new printing-office is removed from Hanover Square to Hunter's Key, *(Quay,)* about midway between the Old Slip and *Meal Market*." " The printer hereof" (" Mercury," April 29, 1754, says,) " is now moved next door to Mr. Robert G. Livingston, in Queen *(Pearl)* Street, between the Fly and *Meal Markets*." The same paper, May 6, notices "European and India Goods—to be sold by Richard Van Dyck, at his store in Hanover Square, near the *Meal Market*." The same paper, March 3, 1760, has—" To be sold at public vendue, on Wednesday, the 12th of March inst., a large and convenient dwelling-house, with the lot of ground thereunto belonging, on the corner of Wall Street and Queen Street, opposite to the *Meal Market*, neare the Merchants' Coffee-House, now in the occupation of Mr. Daniel Bright."

We look back into the Records in the year 1737, when we find " William Cornell " had—" Farmed (or *leased*) the ferry between this city and Island of Nassau, *(L. I.,)* and petitioned to amend and enlarge the *market-house* at Clark's Slip, *(then at the foot of Wall Street,)* as it is mightily out of repair, and sundry conveniences wanting for the better landing and preserving the ferry-boats, at their own cost and charges, with the assistance of such as will contribute to the same." Which privilege was granted.

The year previous, Joseph Reade had repaired this *market-house*, at a cost of £28, 16s., 10d., upon which he had received £25, 10s.,

8d., "raised by subscription and money received;" leaving a balance of £3, 6s., 2d., which the Corporation agrees to make up.

William Cornell, on the 15th of May, 1739, petitioned for abatement of rent for the ferry, and pleads, "That he has sustained very considerable loss by the spreading of the *small-pox*, which deters both strangers and travelers from comeing to town, and the country people from coming to market as usual. That your petitioner's family was very soon visited with the said distemper, and by it had the misfortune to loose *two fine negro men*, for which he gave *one hundred and ten pounds*, besides a young negro woman, born in his own family, of great value. That when he first took the ferry, he offered sixty-five pounds per annum rent more than the former tenant had given, and had provided himself with boats, negroes, and all other conveniences, at a very great charge and expense, in order to perform his duty and gain a comfortable subsistence for himself and family, which was all he expected thereby. But as it pleases Almighty God still to suffer the *distemper* to spread, and continue not only in the city, but also in many parts of the country, your petitioner's loss does daily continue; and unless he be relieved by the charity of this Board, in an abatement of the great rent he is to pay, he knows not when or where his losses will end," &c. The Board, "upon mature consideration, ordered that the sum of sixty-five pounds be abated out of this year's rent."

The small-pox was, no doubt, brought into the city the latter part of the year previous, as the authorities were, in the month of June, adopting such sanitary regulations as were then proposed, in consequence of the "fears and apprehensions of the citizens that the small-pox and malignant feavers being brought into the city from South Carolina, Barbadoes, Antigua, and other places where the same diseases of late have been attended with great mortality." It was also stated at a meeting of the Council at "Fort George," 27th June, "That the 'small-pox' was pretty rief at South Carolina, and that a purpled or spotted feaver began to spread there." One of the pilots for this port was ordered "to be constantly in waiting at or near Sandy Hook, and go on board all vessels bound hither, and acquaint all masters that it was the order of the Board, that before they come within this harbour, they first anchor near Bedlow's Island, to be examined by Doctor Roelof Kiersted, who was appointed for that purpose."

This Doctor Kiersted was a descendant of Doctor Hans Kiersted,[*] who emigrated from Holland about 1636, and died in the year 1666, leaving several descendants who have followed his profession. The

* See "Market-Place at the Strand."

well-known and highly-esteemed citizen, General Henry T. Kiersted, is also one of the descendants, and one of the oldest and most popular druggists in the city. For forty years he has kept an excellent store on the corner of Broadway and Spring Street, from whence he lately removed to the corner of Broadway and Forty-sixth Street, where yet he prepares a valuable ointment from a *recipe* left by his ancient forefather, Doctor Hans Kiersted.

About this period (1732) the established ferry rates between Long Island and New York were, " For transporting every person, two-pence in bills of credit current in this colony; and if after sunset, double that rate. For every horse or beast, one shilling; calf or hog, *four-pence;* sheep or lamb, *three-pence;* dead hog, *three-pence;* dead sheep, lamb, or calf, *two-pence;* bushel of grain, *one penny.* For every waggon, *five shillings;* for every gammon of bacon, turkey, or goose, *one half-penny;* and for every hundred of eggs, *three eggs,*" &c.

Interesting scenes are said to have been sometimes enacted at the ferry; often in the payment of the ferriage. "Among the rates fixed was one giving to the ferryman three eggs for every hundred carried to market, which put the women and girls to no small inconvenience, in stopping, when on their way to market, to have their eggs counted; besides, it must have occasioned no trifling merriment to travelers, to see the ferryman overhauling the eggs, and arranging them in rows on the sand, where he and the females occasionally disputed about the numbers and the amount of duty, which often led to a second or third counting before the contested point could be settled."

The accounts given of the winter of 1739 and '40 describe it as a severe one, when the farmers on Long Island were "in so great want of fodder for their cattle in several places, that 4 cows are given to have one returned in May; and that the cold has been so severe that even deer, squirrels, and birds have been found frozen to death. Great quantities of sheep have perished. Wood sold this day for 40 shillings per cord."

The first regular butcher stands in this market were introduced in the month of May, 1740, when Charles Dawson and Isaac Varian leased two of them. The principal business done here, however, was by the country people with their surplus grain, flour, and meal, which they brought altogether in bags, when, if not sold on the first day, the arrangements were so unsatisfactory, they were obliged to store it in the neighboring shops until the next market-day; and then, when sold, if the purchasers were not satisfied with the weight, it must again be carried to these shops and reweighed at an additional cost. This, however, was remedied in the month of September, 1740, by the Council, who "Ordered that Mr. John Marschalk have liberty at his own expense to make such conveniences as he shall think proper in the *meal market*, for storing meal brought to market there, and providing scales and weights for weighing the same, and to receive a reasonable reward for storing and weighing the same."

Another affliction visited the city, both in the summers of 1742 and '43, which was then known as an *epidemical distemper* or *plague*, no doubt the yellow fever. The population of the city was then about 10,000 inhabitants, and so fatal was it in 1743 that an average number of deaths, for three months, was 17 weekly, with large numbers out of the city. "An account of persons in the City of New York, from the 25th of July to the 25th of September, 1743," is given by the Mayor, John Cruger: "Children 51, grown persons 114, in all 165. From the 25th of September to the 22d of October, children 16, grown persons 36, in all 52. And do find by the best information I have of the doctors, &c., of this city, that the late *distemper* is now over."*

The fatality of the "Small-Pox," through the winter of 1742–3, kept the usual supplies from the city, together with the necessary wants of the increased number of shipping which visited New York, caused provisions to advance very much in price. In the month of February, 1743, a committee was appointed " to meet such of the practitioners of the law as they think convenient to desire their opinion, whether this Corporation can by any law, and in what manner, prevent persons buying *quarters of beef* in the markets and shipping of the same, which has greatly raised the price of beef to the inhabitants." A continuation of high prices appears to have ruled for several years. In fact, when prices are raised from scarcity. a mere supply will not reduce them; but it demands a continuous surplus or glut to bring them down again.

These high prices were again greatly assisted from the long cold winter of 1746–7, which caused a great scarcity of fuel as well as provisions. This fact is particularly noticed in the " Press," February 9th, 1747: "The deplorable circumstances this city is under from a long series of cold and freezing weather is matter of concern to all; this now not only hinders our foreign navigation, but occasions our fire-wood to be so scarce and dear as was never equaled here before; the price being from 40s. to 58s. a cord, and almost half of the inhabitants in want. Provisions also are excessive dear. A good turkey, which scarcely ever before exceeded 3s. 6d., has lately been sold for 5s.; a fat fowl for 15d.; a pound of butter for 14d., and many things proportionable."

* American Magazine, October 24, 1743.

For several seasons high prices continued, and this (with the universal practice, as it is at the present day, of selling "small meats" by the quarter, and especially when the quarters are very small and light; and also the meat from the large animals by the piece, when a much smaller-sized piece was given for a *sixpence*, or a shilling, than was formerly given,) gave considerable dissatisfaction, and no doubt caused an addition to the market laws in the month of May, 1749: "That from and after the first day of April next, no beef, pork, veal, mutton, and lamb, shall be sold in any of the public markets of this city by any butcher, country people, or others, in any other manner than by the *pound*, under the penalty of ten shillings for every offence." The enactment of this law was thought expedient and necessary, in order that the butchers and others might not plead ignorance for want of information.

But a few months after this law was passed, when the following was announced through the press: "It must at last give some ideas of comfort to the poor people of this city, as well as to the honest trading part, that provisions must soon fall from the exorbitant price which they have been held at here for upwards of twelve months past."

The legitimate business of this market-place after 1750 began to fail, while another had arisen. Mercantile trading, with sales at vendue almost daily, had begun to encompass it. The "fast" merchants of that day were springing up, with little or no veneration for antiquity in any form, (except the almighty dollar with very plain pillars,) and more especially for this then old market-house, which stood upon the grounds of their future wealth and prosperity. Their peculiar looks when the old market-house crossed their observation, if interpreted into speech, would have been, that its absence would be more agreeable than its presence. However, it stood until 1760, when we find Gilbert Outen Bogert and Robert Croburn were ordered to be paid "forty-three pounds and five-pence in full for work done and materials found and provided to repair the *Meal Market* and the dock and drain."

This repairing, however, did not save it, as a strong petition was before the Board, February 23, 1762, "from several persons living near the *Meal Market* ask for its removal." They state, "that they conceive the building called the *Meal Market*, in the East Ward of this city, is of no real use or advantage, either to the community in general, or with the inhabitants living near thereto; that poultry and other country produce being generally carried to other markets, and no provisions are sold in the *Meal Market*, except by a few butchers, who might be as well accommodated with standings in other markets in this city.   That the said building greatly obstructs the agreeable prospect of the East River, which those that live in Wall Street would otherwise enjoy—occasions a dirty street, offensive to the inhabitants on each side, and disagreeable to those who pass and repass to and from the Coffee-House, a place of great resort," &c. The Board ordered it to be removed and affixed to the "Broadway Market," which at this period was generally known as *Oswego Market;* "and to remove so much of the materials of said market as will suffice to make a platform over the common sewer, which would be uncovered by the removal" of the old building.

FLATTEN BARRACK MARKET-PLACE.

1711. THE establishment of this market-place was caused by the seizure of all the market-houses in the city, except one, (*Old Slip,*) to build battoes in, by the order of Governor Hunter, in 1711, when the English, being then at war with the French, were secretly organizing an expedition to surprise the French in Canada.

This order was placed before the Board on the 28th of June of that year; when they ordered, "That all the market-houses of this city (except that at Burger's Path) be set apart for the conveniency of building the said battoes, and for no other use or service whatsoever, until the same be compleat and finished; any former law, order or ordinance of this Corporation to the contrary hereof in any wise notwithstanding."

This deprived the butchers, country people, and the inhabitants of their usual accommodations for a period; but their wants were soon after supplied by the establishment of this then intended temporary market-place, on the following 7th of September, when it was "Ordained, that the north end of Broad Street, between the City Hall of this city and the cross street which goes from the Broadway to the Dutch Church, be and is hereby appointed, ordered, and established a public market-place of this city, in as full and ample manner as other public market-places of this city," and "the inhabitants in and about the Broad Street have liberty to erect and build such stalls and sheds and other convenyences as shall be directed by the Clerk."

These battoes were flat-bottomed row-boats, and sharp at both ends.   Kalm says, they were "made of boards of white pine; the bottom flat, that they may row the better in shallow water; they are sharp at both ends, and somewhat higher towards the end than the middle. They are long, yet not all alike, commonly three and sometimes four fathoms long. The height from the bottom to the top of the board (for the sides stand almost perpendicular) is from twenty inches to two feet, and the breadth in the middle about a yard and six inches."

Regular companies of men were organized to take charge of them, and for a particular description of the organization of these companies reference may be made to an order from William Shirley, Esq., General and Commander-in-Chief of His Majesty's forces, in the year 1756, which says: "That the battoemen be formed into companies of fifty men each, a captain and an assistant; each company to take charge and navigate 25 battoes, in the most expeditious and careful manner they can, in the stations they shall be placed. Each man to furnish himself with a good fusee or musket, and three pounds of suitable *balls*. Each captain to be allowed *eight shillings New York currency* per day; each assistant, *six shillings;* and each *battoeman, four shillings* per day, and to be found in the provisions according to the allowance of the army, and to be furnished with powder at the expense of the crown." They "are desired to send in their names to Sir John Sinclair, Deputy Quartermaster-General in New York."*

This market-place appeared to enjoy no particular name, either in the laws, records, or "old papers," and its location being in Broad Street, at the head of the Canal, near the foot of "Verlettenburgh Hill," afterwards more generally known as "Flatten Barrack Hill," or Street, I thought it not improper to designate it as the "*Flatten Barrack Market-Place.*"

The Laws of 1720, in noticing all the market-places, say of this: "At the north end of Broad Street, between the City Hall of this city and the cross street which leads from the Broadway to the Dutch Church, be and are hereby appointed one of the publick market-places of this city."

This hill or street is marked on Lyne's Map, 1729, as "Flatten Barrack," and at various periods afterwards, with both *Verlettenburgh* and *Flatten Barrack*, as the two following notices will show. In an advertisement (N. Y. Journal) of a house for sale, in the month of March, 1772: "The neat convenient house and lot of ground at the corner of *Flattenbarrack Hill*, near the old City Hall in Broad Street, occupied by Mr. John Coghill Knapp, (Attorney at Law,) and subject to the remainder of his lease, three years to come at May-day next. The rent twenty-nine pounds per year, and the taxes. A good title will be given by the executors to the estate of

* N. Y. Mercury, January 26, 1756.

Mary Lashby, deceased." John Jay, on the 3d of January, 1785, writes to Mayor Duane, and says: "As I intend in the spring to build on the east side of the Broadway, near *Verlettenburgh*, it is important for me to know whether the Corporation propose to leave that *street* in its present state, or by lowering it, render the streets leading from it to the river practicable for carriages. The present condition of the Broadway affords an opportunity for such a regulation which may never offer again, and the proprietors of the lotts in it, from near the Church *(Trinity)* to the Bowling Green, are exceedingly interested in knowing what to expect on that subject, because their houses ought to be accommodated to whatever plan may be adopted respecting the street. For my part, I am so fully convinced of the utility of such a regulation, that although my lott lies on the east side of the street, and I have no water-lotts to be filled up or benefitted by it, yet I would cheerfully contribute towards defraying any expense that might be occasioned by it. Yours, &c."

I am told that the name of *Flattenbarrack Hill* continued until within the last fifty years; and the *Old Boys* of New York, when they happen to meet together in conversation of their youthful pastimes, will eulogize the glorious sled-rides they ofttimes had down this once famous hill.

The part of this street running from Broad Street easterly was, at an early period, known as *Garden Alley, Garden Lane, Church Street,* and Garden Street, which at an early period led to Montayne's *Garden.* In 1794 the whole street through, from Broadway past the Dutch Church, was called Garden Street; and since the great fire of 1835, and the erection of the Exchange, it is known as Exchange Place.

"The canal in Broad Street went up originally to the hill called Verlettenburgh, since corrupted to *Flattenbarrack Hill;* the word *bergh* implied *a hill,* and verletten meant to stop. The ferry once there, at the head or stop of tide-water, furnished a means to bring country folks and marketing from Brooklyn and Gowanus, &c., up to the heart of the city,"* or rather to this market-place.

"This ferry-house," says Mr. Rammey, "was on the corner of Broad Street, at the northeast corner of Garden Street, where flat-bottomed boats used to come up to from Jersey." "To me," Watson says, "I confess, it seems to have been a singular place for a ferry; but as tradition is so general and concurrent, I incline to think it was so called from its being a resort of country boats coming there to find a central place for their sales. I have heard the names of certain present rich families whose ancestors were said to come there with oysters."†

* Watson, Annals N. Y., p. 188.   † Ibid., p. 182.

"Mr. David Grim told his daughter of there having been a *market* once held at the head of Broad Street. This agrees with what G. N. Bleecker, Esq., told me, (Watson,) as from his grandmother, who spoke of a market at Garden Street, which was in effect the same place."* No doubt this market-place was pretty well attended with market (ox) carts, country wagons, &c.; and near by, at the head of Broad Street, in front of the City Hall, were placed the implements of corporeal punishment—the *Whipping-Post, Pillory*, and *Stocks*—where occasionally the citizens assembled to witness the various punishments on certain individuals. Mr. Ebbets says: "He has seen them lead the culprits round the town, whipping them at the cart-tail."† "They also introduced the wooden horse as a punishment. The horse was put into the cart-body, and the criminal set thereon. Mary Price having been the first who had the infamous distinction, caused the horse ever after to be called 'the horse of Mary Price.'"‡ Many *fashionable* ladies of questionable character at that period gave the Public Whipper at times some delicate trouble, as they then wore unusually large *hoops;* and they were also worn by the negro slaves, and many other "slaves to fashion" at various periods, of which the following are instances: The first symptoms of the "hoop fever" appear to have broken out in London in the year 1711, when we find the "Spectator," July 26, uses language quite as *broad* as the bottoms of the ladies' dresses, and says: "The fair sex are run into great extravagances. Their petticoats are blown up into a most enormous concave. The women give out, in defence of these wide bottoms, that they are airy, and very proper for the season. Several speculative persons are of opinion that our sex has of late years been very saucy, and that the hoop petticoat is made use of to keep us at a distance. A female who is thus invested in whalebone is sufficiently secured against the approaches of an ill-bred fellow, and might as well think of Sir George Etherige's way of making love in a tub, as in the midst of so many hoops. The first time I saw a lady dressed in one of these petticoats, I could not forbear blaming her in my own thoughts for walking abroad when she was so near her time; but soon recovered myself out of my errour, when I found all the modish part of the sex as far gone as herself. Should this fashion get among the ordinary people, our publick ways would be so crowded that we should want street-room." The "Boston Gazette," in noticing the London news, June 17, 1724, says: "We hear that a young lady at Guilford, upon some discontent, took a lover's leap into the river, (Wey,) with a design to cure or drown herself; but

* Watson, Annals N. Y., p. 185.   † Ibid.   ‡ See Old Slip Market.

her large *hoop* keeping her above water, and she finding that element too cooling and uncourtly, screamed out for help, which was presently given her, and she was taken out alive."* Then the news from Boston, November 13, 1727, says: "The late dreadful earthquake was felt at Guilford, in Connecticut Colony, 160 miles from this place, where it was so violent that it shook down a chimney, threw open the door of the minister's house, tolled a bell, removed blocks in the chimney-corner and a chest about the floor, and shook the houses to a great degree. The shock lasted about a minute. A considerable town in this province has been so awakened by this awful providence, that the *women* have generally laid by their hoop petticoats."† "This great earthquake happened on the 29th of October, about twenty minutes before eleven in the evening. The noise was like the roaring of a chimney on fire; the sea was violently agitated, and the stone walls and chimneys were thrown down." "Another great earthquake took place on the 18th of November, 1755, at fifteen minutes after four in the morning, and continued about four minutes: walls and chimneys were thrown down, and clocks stopped." "On the same day Lisbon was destroyed."‡ This earthquake of 1727, although sensibly felt in New York and other States, did not discourage the continuation of wearing hoops, and more especially by some of the negro slaves. As late as 1732, I find one "Martin Jervis advertises his negro woman 'Jenny' as having ran away."§ "She had on when she went away a purpled-colored peticoat and a drab-colored waistcoat, a blue-and-white striped cotton and linen peticoat, and a yellowish dest-gown, roobed with red, a *hooped peticoat*, &c., and a bag of sundry linen." Some fifty years after, we find the remarks of a dissatisfied individual noticed in the Gazetteer, (January 4, 1785,) who says: "The article I mean to take notice of is the *hoop*, which is so universally worn, that it is impossible for a person to walk the streets without being frequently turned out of the way, and exposed to the annoyance of carts, coaches, &c. I think some method ought to be taken to check such an epidemic inconvenience, or to turn it to the public advantage. With this view, I would advise the Legislature to impose a tax on all *hoops*, which would add to the revenue of the State, and prevent the lower class from parading the streets enveloped with a *hoop* wide enough for a princess."

About the year 1855, in a very fashionable city of Europe, a very prominent individual again introduced the wearing of *hoops*, and it was strongly hinted that she wore them to cover her figure; but

---

* August 28, 1724.   † Upcott's Collections.
‡ History of Lynn.   § Weekly Mercury, Phila., June 11, 1732.

whether so or not, she wore them, and that was enough to set all the ladies, or rather females, of every description in every civilized country in the universe to wear them.   If this be so, it will be with her pleasure when *hoops* shall be out of fashion.

Reverting again to this market-place, we find, in the summer and fall of 1731, the markets were poorly supplied with provisions, in consequence of the great mortality of the *small-pox*.   A September number of the "Boston News Letter" of that year shows this fact, from a letter written in New York, of which the following is an extract: "Here is little or no news in the place; nothing but the melancholy scenes of little business, and less money; the markets begin to grow very thin; the small-pox raging violently in town, which, in a great measure, hinders the country people from supplying this place with provisions."   In the month of September, "41 out of 69 persons died of the small-pox; and in the first week of October, 61 died out of 70."

In the "Upcott Collection" of clippings, in the Library of the New York Historical Society, under date of September 27, 1731, the following appears: "The small-pox, fever, and flux prevail very much in this city, and many children die of the said distempers, as well as grown persons; and the country people are afraid to come to town, which makes the markets thin, provisions dear, and deadens all trade; and it goes very hard with the poor, insomuch that a charitable contribution for them is promoted, and one gentleman has given 20 pistoles, another £20 towards their relief, and other charities are thrown in, according to the circumstances of the benefactors."

"The following is an exact account of the burials in New York for three weeks, viz., from September 20 to October 11:

Of the Church of England,	108	Of Presbyterians, - -	5
Of the Dutch Church, -	99	Of Negroes, - - -	30
Of the French Church, -	6	(*Total,*)	248
Of those died of the small-pox,	-	- - - -	185
Of all *(other)* distempers, only	-	- - -	63

And for the succeeding fortnight, viz., from October 11 to October 25, 1731, exclusive of negroes:

Of the Church of England,	58	Of Lutherans, -	2
Of the Dutch Church, - -	56	Of Quakers, -	1
Of the French Church, -	2	Of Jews, - -	1
Of Presbyterians, - - -	5		125

"They write that most of these, and of the negroes, who were bury'd in this fortnight, died likewise of the small-pox.   As this distemper, therefore, is so very fatal in most of our colonies on the continent, where an increase of inhabitants is so very necessary, we can't but conceive, notwithstanding the casuistry of some, and the prejudices of others, that the practice of innoculation, skilfully introduced there, would be of no small benefit to prevent the ravages made by it, which sometimes depopulates whole provinces there, and frequently puts a stop to all manner of business, both public and private."

The "General Assembly" had previously been driven from their usual place of meeting, as appears from their proceedings on the 31st of August, the same year, in consequence of the prevalency of the small-pox. Their records say: "Upon information given to this house by some of the members, rumor were spread that a person is seized of the small-pox in the very house they now sit; the members who have not had the distemper (being about one-third of the whole number) are determined not to appear any more in the house during this session." They "Resolved, That the house be adjourned to the said City Hall accordingly."

Near this "market-place" was built the first engine-house to contain the first two engines used in this city, which were ordered in the month of May, 1731, through a committee, " to agree with some merchant or merchants to send to London for two compleat fire-engines with suction, and materials thereunto; that the sizes thereof be of the fourth and sixth sizes of Mr. Newsham's fire-engines." The Committee reported in the following month, that they had agreed with Mr. Stephen De Lancey and John Moore, merchants, at the rate of one hundred and twenty per cent. on the foot of the invoice, exclusive of commissions and insurance, and that the money be paid within nine months after the delivery thereof."

After their arrival, a room in the City Hall was temporarily fitted up to secure them; and no doubt they were first used at a fire noticed in the " Boston Weekly News," December 7, 1732, from the news from New York, which states: " Last night, about 12 o'clock, a fire broke out in a joyner's house in this city; it began in the garret where the people were all asleep, and burnt violently; but by the help of the two fire-engines, which came from London in the ship *Beaver*, the fire was extinguished, after having burnt down that house and damaged the next."

On the 2d of January, 1733, a Committee was empowered " to employ a person or persons forthwith to put the fire-engines in good order, and also to agree with proper persons to look after and take care of the same, that they may be always in good plight and condition, fitt for present use;" and in the month of April, 1736, instructions were given to a Committee to " cause a convenient house to be made contiguous to the watch-house in the Broad Street, (*which location was near this market-place,*) for securing and well-keeping the fire-engines of this city;" and it was also "ordered to pay to Mr. Anthony Lamb or order, the sum of *three* pounds *three* shillings and *three*-pence in full of a quarter of a year's sallary, as overseer of the fire-engines, for oil, tallow, and mending an iron hinge for the use of the said engines, as appears by his account."

After this period fire-engines were built and on sale here, as we find: "A fire-engine that will deliver two hogsheads of water in a minute, in a continued stream, is to be sold by William Lindsay, the maker thereof. Enquire at the *Fighting Cocks*, next door to the Exchange Coffee-House, New York."*

The appoinment of members, as well as the curious laws binding them, soon after took place; but the inefficiency of the power of these engines is shown when the Trinity Church was on fire in 1753, from a *communication* in the month of January, which says: "It hath more than once been observed that our engines are incapable of throwing water to such a height as is sometimes necessary. Of this we had a dreadful instance when the steeple of Trinity Church took fire. On that occasion, we observed, with universal terror, that the Engines would scarce deliver the water to the top of the roof. The spire, however, was far beyond its reach; and had not Providence smiled upon the astonishing dexterity and resolution of a few men, who ascended the steeple within, that splendid and superb edifice had in all probability been reduced to ashes. We are therefore in want of at least one engine of the largest size, which throws water about one hundred and seventy feet high.

"Another thing in which our present method of extinguishing fires is capable of further improvement is this: It is usual for people, in case of fire, to form themselves into two lines, the one to convey the full buckets to the engine, and the other to return the empty ones. Now it frequently happens that when the engine is full, word is given to '*stop water.*' This occasions a total cessation in the conveyance of more water to the engine, as well as the greatest confusion in the *ranks;* the consequence of which is, that the engine is empty before the *ranks* regain their former regularity, which creates a considerable intermission in its playing, and gives the fire time to resume its fury, and which, if often repeated, requires a much greater quantity of water for its total suppression. This inconvenience might be easily removed by supplying each engine with a large *tub,* of at least the size of an hogshead; which, being made of cedar, might be sufficiently strong, and at the same time light enough to be portable by two men. This vessel ought to be placed near the en-

* N. Y. Gazette, May 9, 1737

gine, and all the full buckets to be emptied into it. From this capacious *tub* three or four men might constantly and equally keep
the engine replenished, which would enable it to play an equable
and uniform stream."*

The success no doubt continued in this market-place, and the inhabitants near petitioned, on the 4th of May, 1738, "for liberty to
erect a publick market-house, at their own cost and charge, in Broad
Street, between the 'Watch-House' and the dwelling-house of John
Lashby;" which was granted, and a Committee was appointed "to
stake out the place." This Watch-House was located near the City
Hall, according to the report of a Committee on the 6th of August,
1731, in giving a description of the materials to build the Watch-
House, "at the upper end of the Broad Street, near the City Hall,"
and also from a Map drawn by David Grim, of this city, as it was
in 1742. No doubt the "house and lot" for sale, noticed before, of
Mary Lashby's, was the one here noticed as John Lashby's, at the
corner of Flattenbarrack Street.

I am inclined to think that no market-house was ever erected
here, as we find no notices of it in the laws, advertisements, &c.;
that if used as such after this period, it was principally as a market-
place where country people in their wagons and other vehicles stopped to sell their produce.

THURMAN'S SLIP MARKET-PLACE.

1733. A PETITION before the Council, on the 6th of April, 1733,
from "divers freeholders and inhabitants of the West Ward of this
city, showeth, that great numbers of farmers and other persons from
the Jersey side and up the North River do frequently land (with
their grain and other provisions for the market) at 'Thurman's
Slip,' which is a very convenient landing, but for want of a public
market-house there, are very often put to considerable expense and
great inconvenience for entering and carrying their goods for sale,
which very much tends to the discouragement of trade in general.
The petitioners humbly pray the leave and lycense of the Board to
erect and build, by voluntary contributions, a public market-house in
some convenient place in said slip." Although their petition was
granted, yet it was not built, as will appear from further proceedings.

* Independent Reflector.

The location of this intended market-place was between the present Liberty and Courtlandt Streets, on the line of Greenwich Street, and at that period just above Ellison's Dock. This was the great landing-place for many years, in fact, until the Crown and Bear Markets were established, for the market-boats of all sizes, and on their arrival a great deal of trading in wood, provisions, &c., was transacted, which in a measure made it a market-place, although no market-house was built, nor was it recognized by law.

Professor Kalm, in his Travels, says: "As he was sailing up the North River," in the year 1748, "all the afternoon (June 10) we saw a whole fleet of little boats returning from New York, whither they had brought provisions and other goods for sale; which, on account of the extensive commerce of this town, and the great number of its inhabitants, go off very well." "During eight months of the year this (Hudson) river is full of yachts and other greater and lesser vessels, either going to New York or returning from thence, laden either with inland or foreign goods." "The country people come to market in New York twice a week, much in the same manner as they do at Philadelphia:* with this difference—that the markets are here kept in several places."

"The water-melons, which are cultivated near the town, grow very large; they are extremely delicious, and are better than in other parts of North America; though they are planted in the open fields, and never in a hot-bed. I saw a water-melon at Governor Clinton's, in September, 1750, which weighed forty-seven *English pounds*, and at a merchant's in town another of forty-two pounds weight; however, they were reckoned the biggest ever seen in this country."

No doubt the wealthy baker, John Thurman, who owned considerable property in Crown (*Liberty*) Street, wished to improve it by having this market-place established near by. From his petition in 1735, asking for a water-lot in front of one of his on the North River, he says, " He was in possession of and in a certain messuage and lot of ground in the West Ward of the City of New York, fronting the North River, and extending to low-water mark, adjoining to Crown Street Slip, and lying on the north side thereof, of the breadth of one hundred and ten feet or thereabouts, and in consideration of the custom which this Corporation has always been pleased to observe in granting to the citizens and freeholders of this city the land or water-lotts fronting the several lotts of land of which they have been possessed."

Several years after, Mr. Thurman met with considerable loss here,

* See Philadelphia Markets, vol. ii.

by having *two lives* and his dwelling-house destroyed by fire, which is noticed in the N. Y. Mercury, March 24, 1760, as follows: "About 11 o'clock, on the night of the 17th instant, a terrible fire broke out in the loft of a back kitchen belonging to and adjoining the house of Mr. John Thurman, at the North River, in this city, occasioned through the carelessness of a negro wench, by her sticking a candle to a beam in the loft when she went to put her two children to sleep. The fire got to a great highth before it was discovered; soon consumed the kitchen, a store-house contiguous thereto, and Mr. Thurman's dwelling-house, with the greater part of his furniture; but the flames were prevented from spreading further, though the wind was pretty high, owing to the activity of the inhabitants. Mr. Thurman's loss is very considerable; the houses being his own property, as well as two negro children that perished in the flames."

In the early part of the year 1738, another petition was presented by divers of the freeholders and inhabitants of the West Ward, who state: "On or about the sixth day of April, 1733, preferred a petition to the then Common Council, wherein they prayed leave and lycense to erect and build, by voluntary contributions, a public market-house in some convenient place in 'Thurman's Slip.' It was ordered the prayer thereof should be granted, and that the then Aldermen and Assistants of the said ward should direct a public market to be made and erected in such convenient place thereabout as they should judge most requisite for the publick good. Your petitioners cannot assign reason for the neglect of the then Aldermen and Assistants in not directing a convenient place in the said slip for that purpose. Thurman's Slip is a very proper place, and hath a very convenient landing; that great numbers of country people, as well from Tappan and other places up the North River, as from the Jersies, do frequently land there with provisions and other necessaries for the markets, and we have great reason to believe that much greater numbers would frequent and come to it, if proper conveniences were made and provided for them. Your petitioners further humbly presume to beg that a committee may be appointed to direct and ascertain the place in said slip where a publick market-house may be erected," &c. This was signed by the following persons:

Harmanuis Schuyler,	Sarah Lyell,	John Thurman,
James Ackland,	Ann Huddlest	Petrus Rutgers,
Jacobus Stoutenburgh,	Elenor Morris,	David Abeel,
Evardus Brouwer,	Elizabeth Decay,	Johannes Brouwer,
John Peers,	Adam King,	Harme Stout,
Jacob Brouwer,	Mattys. Rack,	Johannes Van Orden,
Johannis Boogert,	Job Earle,	Jacob Hoonik,
Jacobus Montanye,	Benjamin Cain,	James Kenneydy.

A report on the above was made on the 12th of April, in the words following: "We have viewed the said slip and street, and find the same to be twenty-eight and a half feet wide. Unless the owners of the land bounding on each side of the said slip will leave so much land for the use of this Corporation, according to a draft made of the said street and slip signed by us, and have the same recorded accordingly, we find no conveniency there to build or erect a market-house." These refusals did not deter the "neighborhood," but caused them to look about for a new location, which they found at the foot of the street above, which had become, in 1742, known as Courtlandt Street. So in the month of July of that year, they again petition, that they "haveing an inclination to build a publick markitt-house, at their own cost and charge, in a slipp or street called and known by the name of Cortlandes Street, being in the above said ward, for the use of the inhabitants of this city. We humbly pray your worshipps to grant and release to us, the petitioners, the prevelidge for bulding such markitt-house for the use above said." This was also rejected on the 16th of July following; but thirty years after the Crown Market was introduced, to which the reader is referred.

In the year 1754, "Thurman's Dock" was noticed in the N. Y. Mercury, on the 16th of December, when "W. Wood" says: "The Albany Post will set out on the 17th instant for the City of Albany from his house on *Thurman's Dock* at the North River."

"BROADWAY MARKET."

1738. THE petition for the erection of a market-house in the Broadway, near Liberty Street, in 1738, is quite an original in style, but no doubt it was drawn up to suit the age. It was brought before the "Board" on the 13th of April of that year, of which the following appears on record: "Upon a petition which was presented by the chiefest part of the Inhabitants of the West Ward, and also great numbers of the North Ward, live at a great distance from any of the publick markett-houses, which makes it very unconvenient, and occasions a great loss of time for them and their servants to attend the marketts for their family provisions; and as there are great quantities of provisions frequently brought from Hackensack, Tappan, and other parts up the North River, as well as from the Out-Ward.—The petitioners are willing and desirous to erect and build at their own expense a convenient markett-house for publick use—of forty and two feet and twenty-five in breadth, in the publick street of the Broadway, in the middle of the same, fronting the street in which his Honor the Chief Justice lives, and opposite Crown *(Liberty)* Street—to be called the 'Broadway Markett-House;' that the same be a publick markett-place for all sorts of Corn, Grain, and Meal that may be brought down the Hudson River, and to be sold at no other market-place in this City except the publick Meal Market in Wall Street." It was ordered that "the prayer of the petitioners be granted, and to be finished within three months."

The position of this new market-place attracted all the produce, such as grain and flour, that came down the North River, as well as a great deal from Long Island; and those millers and farmers that came by water from a distance were obliged to have their slaves to assist them, rowing down to the markets and back, although they always took advantage of the tides. Many of these slaves brought along their perquisites, which they retailed around the streets, as it appears they had been in the habit of doing many years before. This had introduced an illegitimate sort of traffic with the Indians and many negro slaves of the city, who had spare, or stolen, time enough to make a little spending-money. It finally became so grievous to their masters, that a law was passed, in the month of August, 1740, which provided, "After the ringing of *three bells* and proclamation made for silence, was published, 'A Law to prohibit Negroes and other Slaves vending Indian Corn, Peaches, or any other Fruit within this City.' Whereas, of late years great numbers of Negroes, Indians, and Mulattoes, slaves, have made it a common practice of buying, selling, and exposing to sale, not only in houses, out-houses, and yards, but likewise on the publick streets, great quantities of boiled Indian corn, peas, peaches, apples, and other kind of fruit; which pernicious practice is not only detrimental to the masters, mistresses, and owners of such slaves, in regard they absent themselves from their service, but is also productive of increasing, if not occasions, many and dangerous fevours, and other distempers and diseases in the inhabitants: Therefore, Be it enacted and ordained, That any negro, Indian, or mulatto slave be convicted before the Mayor, Recorder, &c., of any of the above acts, shall be publickly whipped at the whipping-post, unless the master, mistress, shall pay to the person or officer informing of such offence the sum of six shillings, current money of this Colony: one-half thereof to such informer, and the other half to the Treasurer of this City."

Many of these slaves had become otherwise troublesome, as they held daily and nightly cabals, forming themselves into parties or clubs, thieving, &c. Some called themselves "Free Masons;" others after a liquor they were fond of—"Geneva Club;" others "Smith Fly Boys;" and others, again, as "Long Bridge Boys." We find their influence extended among the slaves of some parts of the country, and no doubt this came from the fact that their landing-place at the North River was near John Hughson's, the head-quarters, where originated the "great negro plot of 1741." Hughson's residence was near (the Cooper's, Gerardus,) "Comfort's Dock," and directly opposite Comfort's house. (The location now is between Thames and Cedar, on the line of Greenwich Street.) Near by was the then famous *well* which supplied many of the citizens with "Comfort's Tea-Water."

Hughson was a shoemaker by trade, says Horsmanden, but "kept a very disorderly house, and sold to and entertained negroes there" with "playing at dice"—frolicking; a witness says, "he saw a great many of them in a room, dancing to a fiddle, and Hughson's wife and daughter along with them." His house was open for the negroes, "and he entertained them at all times; those that had no money, at free cost." He employed "some of the head negroes as agents under him, to decoy other negroes. Comfort's negro *Jack*, one of the captains of these bands of fools, had so well approved his parts and capacity to Hughson and the rest, that he had a deputation for swearing such converts as he made, either abroad or at home; and in both cases had great opportunities of caballing with negroes; for his master was frequently absent from home for several weeks together, insomuch that Captain *Jack* looked upon the house as his own, and himself as his own master. To this *well*, every morning and evening, resorted negroes from all the quarters of the town, for 'tea-water,'" with whom he introduced this subject. There is no doubt but some of the country slaves, in their almost daily visits to the city, while landing so near these head-quarters, became acquainted with this contemplated conspiracy, as "many cabals of negroes had been discovered, particularly in Queens County, on Nassau (*alias* Long Island.) The negroes had there formed themselves into a Company about Christmas last; by way of play or diversion, had mustered and trained with the borrowed arms and accoutrements of their masters." These negroes were found out, and punished.

Early in the month of May, (1741,) "at Hackensack, in New Jersey, eight miles from this city, the inhabitants of that place were alarmed about an hour before day, and presented with a most melancholy and affrighting scene! No less than seven barns in that neighborhood were all in flames; and the fire had got such head, that all assistance was in vain; for in a short time they were burnt down to the ground. Two negroes, the one belonging to Derick Van Hoorn, the other to Albert Van Voerheise, were suspected to have been guilty of this fact; the former having been seen coming out of one of the barns with a gun laden, who pretended, on being discovered, that he saw the person who had fired the barns, upon which his master ordered him to fire at him; and the negro thereupon immediately discharged his piece; but no blood was drawn from any mortal, that could be discovered. The latter was found at his master's house loading a gun with two bullets, which he had in his hand ready to put in. Upon these and other presumptive circumstances and proofs, both negroes were apprehended, and in a few days tried, convicted, and burnt at a stake. The former confessed he had set fire to three of the barns; the latter would confess nothing." (See "*Old Slip Market.*")

This "Tea-Water Well" of Comfort's, as previously noticed, was somewhat famous, and frequently referred to in Horsmanden's Great Negro Plot. No doubt its water must have been superior to all the other public wells, as it was sought after morning and evening, and carried away in *kegs* by the slaves of many of the principal citizens, many years before this great negro plot took place.

The famous "Tea-Water *Pump*," which still lives in the recollections of some old citizens, was a different well, or rather a fine flowing spring in a well, which no doubt originally assisted in forming the "Fresh Water" or "Kolch Pond." This was located on or about the present northeast corner of Orange and Chatham Streets. Professor Kalm, while visiting New York in 1748, first notices this spring, and says: "There is no good water in the town itself, but at a little distance there is a large spring of good water, which the inhabitants take for their tea, and for the use of the kitchen." This, no doubt, soon became their chief source of supply for "tea-water;" and when it began to be carried in hogsheads on the carts, it was quite necessary to have a sort of *engine* to raise the water high enough to run into these hogsheads; and no doubt this *engine* was about the first common pump introduced here. Montressor, on his Map, (No. 6,) in the year 1775, notes it as the "Fresh-Water Engine, from which the town is supplied." In the Revolution it is advertised thus: "Proposals in writing will be received by the Vestry, at the Alms-House, on Monday, the 2d of April, (1781,) from such persons as may be desirous of renting the

'Tea-Water Pump' for the ensuing year."* Three years after, (1784,) "Abraham Revere committed suicide, who lately occupied the 'Tea-Water Pump;' "† and about the same period, " a correspondent recommends to the attention of the magistrates a nuisance generally complained of in this dry, warm season. A number of people assembled round the pond *(Collect)* from whence the tea-water is raised, and wash their dirty linen. It is unnecessary to expatiate upon the utility of preventing the continuance of a practice which has a manifest tendency to affect the health of the inhabitants of this city."‡ Then we find—"Eight or nine lots of ground, *(to be sold,)* of one hundred feet in length, and twenty-five in width, situate behind the *Tea-Water Pump*, between that and the fresh-water pond, *(Collect,)* with the buildings thereon—an excellent stand for a still-house, brew-house, or sugar-house, as there is the best of water all round it, and it is supposed the *Tea-Water Pump* feeds itself through said lotts."§

Winterbotham, in his general description of New York, written about the year 1790, also notices the " Tea-Water Pump," as follows: "Most of the people are supplied every day with fresh water, conveyed to their doors in casks, from a spring almost a mile from the centre of the city. This well is about twenty feet deep, and four feet *(in)* diameter. The average quantity drawn daily from this remarkable well is one hundred and ten hogsheads, of one hundred and thirty gallons each. In some hot summer-days two hundred and sixteen hogsheads have been drawn from it; and what is very singular, there are never more or less than three feet of water in the well. The water is sold commonly at three-pence a hogshead at the pump."

A few years after, the *Minerva* (December 10, 1796,) states—"A report having been in circulation that the water of the 'Tea-Water Pump' begins to fail, and also, that the proprietor will not allow any more water to be drawn from it than is absolutely necessary for the use of the citizens for *tea* and *drinking*, the subscriber begs leave to contradict the said report, and inform the citizens that notwithstanding the extremely dry season, the source of the *tea-water* has not in the least diminished; and so far from his refusing any demand for water, he hereby offers the citizens a plentiful supply for *washing* or other family uses. Any order for one or more hogsheads of water, directing the place where to be delivered, sent to the *pump*, will be immediately attended to. The price of the water is 4s. per hogshead, containing 140 gallons.

" WILLIAM C. THOMPSON."

* Royal Gazette, March 31.   † Penna. Packet, July 20.
‡ N. Y. Packet, August 19, 1784.   § Ibid., Oct. 25.

Two years after, (1798,) the reputation of this tea-water had become decidedly bad, if we should judge by the following article, which says: "The New Yorkers have no clear, cool water to slake the thirst—yet they pretend their city water is very pure and nice. The Collect behind the 'Tea-Water Pump' is a shocking hole, where all impure things centre together, and engender the worst of unwholesome productions. The water has grown worse, manifestly, within a few years. It is time to look out some other supply, and discontinue the use of water growing less and less wholesome every day. Some affect to say the water is very cool and refreshing. Everybody knows, from experience, the water gets warm in a few hours, and sometimes almost before it is drawn from the carter's hogshead. Can you bear to drink it on Sundays in the summer-time? It is so bad before Monday mornings, as to be very sickly and nauseating; and the larger the city grows, the worse this evil will be. Already it has been whispered by some vigilant travelers through our city, that the New Yorkers are like the dog in the manger—they will not provide aqueducts themselves, nor let anybody else do it. Take the matter into consideration, and resolve, every man for himself, to leave no stone unturned to have this grand object of watering carried through."* It was but a year or two afterwards when the "Manhattan Water" took its place.

Although this Broadway Market was originally ordained as a meal market, yet we find, on the 7th of November, 1741, by a LAW then passed, "giving priviledge to country people to sell or expose to sale in the Meal Market (Wall Street) and Broadway Market of this city, beef, pork, veal, mutton, and lamb by the joint, or by pieces, cut up the same in pounds or pound pieces, or in great or small quantities or parcells, as they shall see convenient—paying in the same manner and proportion that the butchers are to do." That is, "for each head of cattle, one shilling; for every hogg or shoat brought into or cut out for sale in any of the market-houses, the same; and for every sheep, calf, or lamb, two-pence."

The increasing amount of business done here induced the inhabitants of the West Ward, in 1745, to ask for "liberty to make an addition of twenty-one feet at the north end of the market in Broadway;" and soon after the like addition was added to the south end.

No doubt the city was in a prosperous condition at this period, as many improvements are noticed, especially by Kalm, who says: "In size it comes nearest to Boston and Philadelphia; but with regard to its fine buildings, its opulence, and extensive commerce, it

* Daily Advertiser, September 6, 1798.

disputes the preference with them." Of the streets he says: "Most of them are paved, except in high places, where it has been found useless. In the chief streets there are trees planted, which in summer give them a fine appearance, and during the excessive heat at that time, afford a cooling shade. I found it extremely pleasant to walk in the town, for it seemed quite like a garden. Most of the houses are built of bricks; and are generally strong and neat, and several stories high. Some had, according to old architecture, turned the gable end towards the streets; but the new houses were altered in this respect. Many of the houses had a balcony on the roof, on which the people used to sit in the evenings, in the summer season. The roofs are commonly covered with tiles and shingles. The walls were quite covered with all sorts of drawings and pictures, in small frames. On each side of the chimneys they had usually a sort of alcove; and the wall under the windows was wainscoted, and had benches placed near it. The alcoves and all the wood-work were painted with a bluish-gray color. New York sends many ships to the West Indies, with flour, corn, biscuit, timber, tuns, boards, flesh, fish, butter, and other provisions; together with some of the few fruits that grow here. Many ships go to Boston, in New England, with corn and flour, and take in exchange flesh, butter, timber, different sorts of fish, and other articles, which they carry further to the West Indies." "The goods which are shipped to the West Indies are sometimes paid for with ready money, and sometimes with West India goods, which are either first brought to New York, or immediately sent to England or Holland. If a ship does not choose to take in West India goods in its return to New York, or if nobody will freight it, it often goes to Newcastle, in England, to take in coals for ballast, which, when brought home, sell for a pretty good price. In many parts of the town coals are made use of, both for kitchen fires and in rooms, because they are reckoned cheaper than wood, which at present costs thirty shillings of New York currency per fathom." "New York has likewise some intercourse with South Carolina, to which it sends corn, flour, sugar, rum, and other goods, and takes rice in return, which is almost the only commodity exported from South Carolina." "The goods with which the Province of New York trades are not very numerous. They chiefly export the skins of animals, which are bought of the Indians about *Oswego;* a great quantity of boards, coming for the most part from Albany; timber and ready-made lumber, from that part of the country which lies about the river Hudson; and lastly, wheat, flour, barley, oats, and other kinds of corn, which are brought from New Jersey and the cultivated parts of this province. I have seen yachts from New Brunswick laden with wheat which lay loose on board, and with flour packed in tuns; and also with great quantities of linseed. At this time a bushel of linseed is sold for eight shillings of New York currency, or exactly a piece of eight. New York likewise exports some flesh *(salted meats)* and other provisions out of its own province, but they are very few; nor is the quantity of pease, which the people about Albany bring, much greater."

"There are several churches in the town, which deserve some attention. 1. The English Church, built in the year 1695, at the west end of the town, consisting of stone; and has a steeple, with a bell. 2. The new Dutch Church, (*Nassau St.,*) which is likewise built of stone, is pretty large, and is provided with a steeple; it also has a clock, which is the *only one* in the town. This church stands almost due from north to south. In this church there is neither altar, vestry, choir, sconces, nor paintings. Some trees are planted around it, which make it look as if it was built in a wood. 3. The old Dutch Church, which is also built of stone. It is not so large as the new one. It was painted in the inside, though without any images, and adorned with a small organ, of which Governor *Burnet* made them a present. The men, for the most part, sit in the gallery, and the women below. 4. The Presbyterian Church, which is a pretty large one, has but lately been built. It is of stone, and has a steeple and a bell in it. 5. The *German Lutheran* Church. 6. The *German Reformed Church.* 7. The *French Church,* for Protestant refugees. 8. The *Quaker Meeting-House.* 9. To these may be added the *Jewish Synagogue.* There are many Jews settled in New York, who possess great privileges. They have a synagogue and houses, and great country-seats of their own property, and are allowed to keep shops in town. They have likewise several ships, which they freight, and send out with their own goods. In fine, they enjoy all the privileges common to the other inhabitants of this town and province. During my residence in New York this time, and in the two next years, I was frequently in company with Jews. I was informed, among other things, that these people never boiled any meat for themselves on Saturday, but that they always did it the day before; and that in winter they kept a fire during the whole Saturday. They commonly eat no pork; yet I have been told by several men of credit, that many of them, (especially among the young Jews,) when traveling, did not make the least difficulty about eating this, or any other meat that was put before them; even though they were with Christians. Both men and women were dressed entirely in the English fashion."

We now turn to the Laws of 1748, and also those of 1762, where we find one of the t's at the end of the word "markett," which notices it "Broadway Market;" but the citizens had dropped this name, and adopted another, many years before. About the year 1740 the name of "Oswego" became one of the most prominent subjects before the people, and in their councils. The name came from a great trading-house and fortification, which Governor Burnet had erected in 1722, at the mouth of the then Onondagus River, on Lake Ontario. In a speech made by Governor Hunter to the "House," April 27, 1741, on the war with the French, he says: "The preservation of *Oswego* and the fidelity of the Six Nations (of *Indians*) is of more consequence to the province than any other thing whatsoever; and if we lose them, no part of the country will be safe."

Great preparations were made in this city for the defence and protection of that fortification. Enlistment of soldiers, battoes, provisions, all were mustered together here at intervals, and sent to the foot of "Crown Street," which was the general landing and starting place. Every article prepared for the expedition was sent or directed to the "Oswego Landing," at the foot of "Oswego Street," and the name soon reached this market-place, as it were, by acclamation of the citizens; the same manner as when Lafayette landed here in 1825—everything afterwards had Lafayette prefixed to it. "To be sold at public vendue, on Wednesday, the 7th of November next, at 10 o'clock, on the premises, a dwelling-house, bake-house, and lott of ground in Crown Street, commonly called 'Oswego Street.'"*

Horsmanden tells us, in his "Negro Plot," of the many valuable articles to be removed to Hughson's House: it "was become a mart of so great note among the negroes, that with them it had obtained the name of 'Oswego,' after the province trading-house.'"†

Among the numerous articles sent to the troops in the French war, at a late period, were enumerated in the "Patriotism of Queens County,"‡ Long Island, dated "*Jamaica, September* 25, 1755.— This day, 1,015 sheep, collected in three days in this county, were delivered at New York Ferry, to be sent to Albany *by water*, which were cheerfully given for the use of the army now at or near Crown Point." "The good mothers, also, in a few hours collected nearly 70 good large cheeses, and sent them to New York, to be forwarded with the sheep to the army." Sir William Johnson acknowledges, in the following month, that he had received "69 cheeses and 200 sheep, being a part of 1,000 raised in Queens

* Gazette, Nov. 5, 1759. † P. 353. ‡ Onderdonk's "*Olden Times*," Hist. Lib.

County as a present to the army. Though cattle and a few sheep had been sent by some of the provinces to this troop, yet your sheep were very seasonable, and highly beneficial. Your cheeses were highly acceptable and reviving; for, unless among some of the officers, it was food scarcely known among us."

This example induced Suffolk County, also, to send "50 head of fat cattle; of which a yoke of oxen was a special present for the late famous Hendrickson and his Indian adherents." "The women of the county are knitting several large stockings and mittens, to be sent to the poor soldiers in garrisons."

The name of "Oswego Market" continued in the "papers," petitions, &c., in connection with this market, until its final close. The "N. Y. Mercury," April 29, 1754, notices—"Reading, writing, and arithmetic are carefully taught at the corner house, near the Quaker Meeting-House, in Crown Street, near *Oswego Market*, by John Nathan Hutchins." This man was the first almanac-maker here, which was a smoky, dingy-looking pamphlet, with a string tied through the back and top; always found hanging up alongside of the old fire-place, in company with the bellows, iron-holder, a goose's wing, and other *fixings* belonging to the kitchen of all well-regulated farm-houses. Then, in the *same* paper, May 1—"Edward Willet, who lately kept the 'Horse and Cart Inn,' in this city, is removed into the house of the Honorable James De Lancy, Asq., Lieutenant-Governor, at the sign of the 'Province Arms,' in the Broadway, near '*Oswego Market*.'" The "Gazette," April 25, 1763, notices—"Peter T. Curtenius, opposite the *Oswego Market*, has, besides hardware, a parcel of the best black wampum *(Indian money)* to dispose of." Again, "Mercury," May 23d, 1768—"John Balthus Dash, tinman, acquaints his customers that he has moved from the *Oswego Market* into the corner house where Nicholas Stagg formerly lived." Marschalk, on his Map of New York, (1755,) gives it also the name of *Oswego Market*, which had then become the common one.

Grant Thorburn, in a letter to the Editors of the "Home Journal," says: "I have just parted with my old neighbor, Mrs. Van Antwerp, now residing at No. 48 Maiden Lane, in the ninety-first year of her age. She affirms that the *Oswego Market* stood in the very centre of Broadway. In her young days, her brother, Alderman Bogart, known as the best biscuit, tea-cake, and rusk baker in the city, and who, in past generations, on the west corner of Cortlandt Street and Broadway; there he daily fed the hungry, and yearly gave *cookies* to the Dutch Church charity scholars." In relation to this market's removal into Maiden Lane, Mr. Thorburn's evidence is wrong, as will be seen in the following pages.

Prior to 1762, hay was usually sold by the wagon, cart-load, or half-load; and it was found, by experience, the loads were very unequal, which brought many disputes and controversies between the boatmen and cartmen, and then, again, by the buyer and cartmen. It was thought there should be fixed certain weights and certain places to weigh the hay; this law established one of the places at this market. That "from and after the 20th of September, 1762, hay shall be sold by the hundred weight of 112 lbs.;" and it was also "Ordained, that proper and convenient machines, or engines, and scales and weights for weighing carts and waggons, and hay, shall be made, erected, furnished, and provided, at the three following places in this city, to witt: one machine or engine, with scales and weights, shall be made, erected, and set up and supplied, at or near the south end of the market, commonly called the *Broadway Market*, in this city; one other at the White Hall Slip; and the other at or near the dwelling-house of the Widow Van Keuren, in Montgomerie Ward. Isaac Van Hook is hereby authorized to take charge of the one at the *market;* Richard Weston at White Hall Slip; and John De Peyster, Jun'r, at or near the house of Widow Van Keuren. For the weighing of hay, one shilling and sixpence; one-half by the seller, and the other by the buyer. Carts and waggons to be weighed without charge; and the weight, in plain or legible figures, upon the after part of the shaft, by the above officers. The rates to be charged, 4s. if pitched into a stable; but if thrown down in the street, 3s., and no more."

From the above, we find this market-place noticed as the "*Broadway Market;*" and the next year, in a petition, it is found with another name. This states, "That the *Crown Market*, (more commonly called the '*Oswego Market*,') in the Broadway, is at so great a distance from the North River, that the country produce brought down and across the said river, to supply the markets of the city, must be carried in carts from the different ships and wharfs on the North River to the said *Crown Market*." They wish "a new market at the foot of Courtlandt Street or Messier's Dock."

An unfortunate occurrence took place near this market three years after, noticed in the "press" September 18, 1766. "On Monday last, a negro man was driving a chair, in which was a nurse and two small children of Mr. Verplank, of this city, merchant. As they were passing *Oswego Market*, a dog flew out at the horse, which occasioned him to start and fall down before, whereby the driver was thrown off, and the nurse and two children fell on the rump of the horse, and from thence to the ground. The eldest child. a little boy, escaped unhurt; the nurse was bruised with the fall; but unhappily, the little girl, about three years old, fell near the hind feet of the horse, who, struggling violently to recover himself, before the child could be taken away, gave it two mortal strokes on the head, of which it died in less than half an hour."*

At this period (1770) this market was doing a large business; but Broadway was so glutted up in business hours, that many vehicles could not pass and repass: this caused many complaints.

Several butchers are noticed on a petition, occupying stands here, from which we find the following:

William Norman,   John Faulkner,   Edw. Rack Wolff,
Jacob Otte,   William Fray,   Christopher Stamler,
Prantiz W. Cornell,   Julian Pine,   John Onderline.

The cost of the sweeping the *Oswego Market*, from a bill presented, from 19th September to the 16th January, 1770—123 days, at 6d. per day—by George Helbert, amounted to £3, 1s., 6d.   John Hagelman also swept it at the same price.

In the early part of the next year, (1771,) the records show this market was indicted as a nuisance.   "It represents that a certain street in the City of New York, commonly called the Broadway, situated and being in the West Ward, is a certain ancient street and highway of our sovereign Lord and the King, George the Third, &c., and used for all the liege subjects of our said Lord the King, their horses, coaches, &c., to go, return, pass, &c., at their will and pleasure.   That in the middle of the said common street and highway stands a certain building, &c., called the *Oswego Market*, which obstructs the street."

The Attorney-General moved for a writ to the Sheriff to prostrate without delay the *Oswego Market;* but it was afterwards "Ordered, that unless the said indictment is traversed within twenty days, that a writ be ordered to abate the same."   The Committee were ordered to employ Mr. Duane as counsel in defence of said indictment.

The indictment against this market-place created a great sensation with all classes, and more particularly with the owners of property around it; but, as they all thought it could not be retained in that location, they wished to have another as near it as possible. Some wished it near the North River; others, in Maiden Lane, near Broadway; but the largest number wished the location to be in the present part.   Broadway, at this time, from the Government House (Battery) to Vesey Street, was generally known as "The Broadway" and "Broadway Street;" and from Vesey Street up to sand-hill cross-road, (afterwards Art Street, now Waverley Place,)

* N. Y. Gazette, &c.

"St. George," or "Great George Street." This was, however, changed on the 24th February, 1794, by the Board, and "ordered one continued street, and that it be called 'Broadway.'"

In the month of March, (1771,) a petition from fifty-nine "of the neighborhood" was presented to the Common Council, "praying to grant them the priviledge to erect, at their own expense, a market-house in the Fields, (Park.") And "if the Oswego Market should be removed to the North River, it might be convenient for some few inhabitants, and the particular interest of others." But "if a convenient market was erected in a proper part of the *Fields*, it most certainly would answer many good and efficient ends—being more in the centre of the city; the city tenants residing at and about Incklan Barrack, the farmers and others, from all parts of the Bowery and Kingsbridge road, who pay considerable taxes, &c."

This was followed by another, signed by four hundred and forty-one of the "principal inhabitants," who state that, "We, the subscribers hereunto, join in humble petition, craving that if the Oswego Market is to be removed, that there may be a market erected in the *Fields* instead thereof." Among the signers were

Marinus Willet,	Nicholas Bayard,	Edward Burling,
Henry Kip,	Corns. Roosvelt,	William Ellsworth,
David Grim,	David Waldron,	John Minuse,

and others.

More than one hundred and twenty-five "carmen" also petition; and state, that "in case the *Oswego Market* should be removed, that you will be pleased to grant liberty to erect a publick market at a proper place in the *Fields*—being thoroughly convinced that it will not only tend to *their own maintenance*, but to the benefit and convenience of the publick in general, and the poor in particular." The "carmen" thought if the location was made at the "North River," a large share of their business would be cut off from carting the large quantity of produce that came by the water.

The owners of property around this market-place finding they were going to lose it, petitioned, on the 24th of April following, for aid to assist in erecting a market-house in Maiden Lane, near Broadway. They state that they "have purchased their estates at an advanced price, in confidence that a grant from the Corporation was a sufficient security to them for the market remaining where it now stands; but are fearful that the late indictment of the Grand Jury will prevail against it. They have concluded to purchase one-third of Conroe's lot, on Maiden Lane, to erect a market-house by the assistance of the Corporation." The Corporation, however, gave them no encouragement.

The question of the removal of the old "*Broadway*," alias "*Oswego Market*," was at last settled, by Mr. Samuel Jones, who, on the 29th of July following, " delivered his opinion, that it would be most advisable to remove *Oswego Market*, as the indictment found against it cannot be defended." The Board " therefore agreed to take down or remove the same," and soon after they adopted the site of the Bear Market, as the new location; but even after its erection we find a petition was signed by *two hundred and twenty-five* of the citizens, who had appeared on the 28th of October following, " who wish to erect at their own expense a market in the *Fields*." If this had been favorably received, and the erection of a building taken place, the " Park" would have been graced with an *institution* more useful than ornamental.

"WHITE HALL SLIP MARKET."

1746. THE location where this market-house was erected in the year 1746 was an old-established market-place. Near it, in 1656, " *The Market-Place at the Strand*" was established; then followed the " *Custom-House Bridge Market*," and a short distance above the "*Broad Street Market*" had ceased to exist some few years before; and the inhabitants of this neighborhood in the South Ward, being without a market-place near by, some *one hundred and forty-six* persons petitioned for " priviledge to erect and build a market-house at the east end of Pearl Street, and a slip at the west end, at their own expense. A convenient slip may be made for the receiving boats and canoes that may bring provisions to the same market."

Among the signers to this petition, we find

Paul Richards,   Philip Cortlandt,   Arch'd Kennedy,
Edward Holland,   Isaac De Peyster, and others.

At this period Pearl Street at the west end commenced on the shore, near where now runs State Street, and ran easterly, or at the east end of Pearl Street ended in Whitehall Street; from this the continuation was called Dock Street. The location of this market-house, accordingly, was at the corner of Whitehall and Pearl Streets, where it is seen on the original " South Prospect of ye flourishing City of New York," printed in London in 1746, (in the Society Library in this city,) and is also noticed in the Laws of 1748, as the "*Market-house at the end of Pearl Street*." The next year the Gazette (*August* 24*th*, 1749,) states: "At Mr. John Whiley's, the corner house almost opposite the 'White Hall Slip Market.'"

White Hall took its name from *White Hall*, London, and at an early day this name became attached to Colonel Moore's large white house, or hall, which stood close by this market, and no doubt gave this market-place the above name.

To further prove the fact, that the west end of Pearl Street began on or near the line of the present State Street, the N. Y. Mercury, September 7, 1767, says: "Yesterday morning the Coroner's inquest set on the body of one William Kieth, a soldier of the 16th Regiment, who was found drowned near the *end of Pearl Street*, under the wall of the Battery."

The "old landing-place at the Strand" was yet popular with the Indians, although there had been the basins and a bridge made there; and this part of the petition for a "slip at the west end" was to draw them away, "it being sometimes much crowded." "Those who knew," say: "I have seen in 1744, and after, several Indian canoes one after another come down the East and North Rivers, and land their cargoes in the basins near the Long Bridge, and take up their residence in the yard and store-house of Adolphus Philips, where they generally made up their baskets and brooms, as they could better bring the rough materials with them than ready-made baskets and brooms. They brought with them, when coming from Long Island or other sea-shores, a quantity of dried clams, strung on sea-grass or straw, which they sold or kept for their own provisions, besides the flesh of the animals they killed."

Adolphus Philips appears to have been a prominent and popular merchant, officer, and citizen in his day. Several years before this market-house was established, an election had taken place here, but it appears it had not been conducted as at the present time. The New England Weekly Journal, September 12, 1737, says: "On Saturday last came on the election of a representative to serve in General Assembly for the City and County of New York, in the room of Captain Garrit Van Horn, deceased. The electors appeared in the Fields (*Park, the usual place of election then,*) about 9 o'clock, with drums beating and colors flying, trumpets sounding, and violin playing. The two candidates put up were Mr. Adolphus Philips and Mr. Cornelius Van Horn. Most of the merchants and gentlemen of the place appeared for Mr. Philips, and seemed to be the greatest number; but a *poll* was demanded, and thereupon the candidates and electors repaired to the City Hall, (*Broad Street,*) where a poll was carried on all day, till about 9 o'clock at night, with great warmth on both sides." Mr. Philips received 413, and Mr. Van Horn 399 votes; the former was declared duly elected.

This market-place stood about four years, when we find, on the 26th of April, 1750, a Committee was "empowered to agree with several persons" "to remove the market-house near the Battery at the corner of Pearl Street."

"BURLING'S MARKET."

1746. ON the 28th of February, 1746, a petition was before the Board, "from sundry inhabitants of the Montgomerie Ward," praying "for leave to build a market-house in Rodman's Slip, at their own expense, was again read, (it having been before them at a previous meeting,) and the priviledge granted."

Rodman's Slip had been previously known as Lyon's Slip on Lyne's Map, 1729; but is found with both names in the records; and as Rodman's Slip on Ratzen's Map in 1767. Prior to this it was occasionally known as "Burlin's Slip," and afterwards they added G to *Burlin*, to correspond with the surname of the old Quaker merchant, Edward Burling, from whom this slip and market took their names. I might also add here, that a part of this family moved to New Jersey and settled "Burling-ton" in that State. He lived at the corner of the "Smith's Fly," (*Pearl Street*,) and Golden Hill, where "Edward and James Burling sold iron, hardware, and New York distilled rum."[*]

The law of 1748 notices this market-place as the "Market-House at Rodman's Slip," and the N. Y. Gazette, June 1, 1752, says: "By Samuel Bowne's, at *Burling's Slip*, near the *new market;*" another paper,[†] in 1754, notices "John Parsons, joiner, having lately set up in his business, between the *new market* and Fly Market;" and Maerschalck's Map of the city, 1755, marks No. 12 "Burlin's (*Burling's*) Market," and this was its general name, until it ceased to exist.

It never appeared to be a popular market-place, if we should judge from the contents of the following petition presented on the 4th day of July, 1760, from "John Riker and others, to the number of sixty and upwards, inhabitants on both sides of the slip, commonly called ' Burling's Slip, in the East Ward,' which was read, setting forth that notwithstanding the good intention of making or leasing that space for a slip, and the erection and building a *market-house*, then at the

[*] N. Y. Mercury, July 25, 1756.　　　　　[†] Ibid., April 29.

head of said slip, your petitioners conceive that not only the good ends and purposes which were expected in making the same have not succeeded for many years last past, chiefly from the almost disuse of the same." It had then been standing about fourteen years, and although it is marked on the map of the city by T. Maerschalken, 1763, letter Z, I think it did not then exist, except on that map. The Laws of 1762 do not notice it, nor can I find any further reference to it in the old papers, except a notice in the Weekly Gazette and Post Boy, July 3, 1766, that "On the evening of the 1st of July, Godfrey Haynes, who followed the business of lobster catching for *this market*, went in the waters to swim, near 'Burling Slip,' and soon after drowned." "*This market*," in the above, no doubt meant the New York markets in general.

"EXCHANGE," (IN BROAD STREET.)

1752. THIS building, no doubt, when erected, was intended for the principal use of the merchants and gentlemen of the neighboring vicinity, as an Exchange; but, as the lower part was used as a *market-place* many years after, it was but right to claim it as such for the time during which it was so occupied. The *Exchange* and the "Exchange Market" were two separate buildings, and, at one period, both existing at the same time, as will be shown.

In the month of June, 1752, several gentlemen subscribed towards erecting this building, at the lower end of Broad Street, near the "Long Bridge." "£100 was voted by the Common Council to assist in so laudable an undertaking." This location would now be nearly on a line of Water Street, in Broad.

The plan was proposed, and the building commenced; but, on the 4th of October following, a resolution passed the Board, "That the whole, or as much of the foundation on the east side of the Exchange now a-building and to be built at the lower end of Broad Street, as is necessary, to be taken up; and that five arches be made on each side, instead of six, with two at each end." Its erection proceeded very slowly, as I find it was not finished until 1754, when it was leased for one year to Oliver De Lancey, for £50; the lower part was used by the merchants, and the upper rooms were appropriated to various uses.

Notice was given on the 4th of February, in the "press,"[*] that "The new 'Exchange' being to be opened as a Coffee-Room on Monday, the 11th day of this present month of February. KEEN & LIGHTFOOT."[†]

"'The Beggar's Opera' and 'The Devil to Pay' to be performed by a Company of Comedians, from London, at the new Theatre in Nassau Street, this present evening, 18th March. To begin at 6 o'clock. Boxes, 6s.; Pit, 4s.; Gallery, 2s. Tickets to be had at Mr. Parker's and Mr. Gaine's printing-offices, at the *Royal Exchange*, at the King's Arms, at Scotch John's, and of Mr. and Mrs. Love, at the play-house."

Then, on the 6th of May—"The Post-Office is removed to the house wherein William Walton, Esq., lately lived, near the *New Exchange*."[‡] And then—"To be sold at publick vendue, to the highest bidder or bidders, at the *New Exchange*, in the City of New York, on Wednesday, the 29th of May next, at 11 o'clock in the forenoon, two certain lots of land; which said two lots lie three miles from the German settlement on the Walkill."[§]

Two years after, on the 19th of April, we find—"The proprietors of the 'New York Society Library' are desired to attend with their ballots at the *New Exchange*, on the last Tuesday in April, for the election of twelve Trustees."[||] Then, on the 10th of July, 1758—"Roper Dawson, at the Long Room over the *Exchange*, continues to sell green tea, coffee, &c."[¶]

In the month of February, 1760, the "Board" was informed that "Mr. Watts and others had sent to Europe for a *large clock*, which they intended as a publick one, and desired to know, that if the Common Council would take charge of it and erect it in the Exchange at their own expense, it was at their service;" which was agreed to. In 1763, the N. Y. Mercury notices "Tickets for the electrical experiments in the Exchange, which begins this day at 11 o'clock, are sold at the 'Gentleman's Coffee-House,' and by Hugh Gaine."

Trouble and hardship were now commencing, with business dull, and a great deal of suffering; which is first represented in a "communication" in Holt's N. Y. Gazette, &c., January 4, 1765, as follows: "The declining state of business in the city, together with high rents and prices of the necessaries of life, having reduced very many families and poor people to great distress, especially since the late severe weather, we hear several humane gentlemen of this city have made contributions for their relief."

[*] N. Y. Mercury.   [†] Ibid., March 18, 1754.   [‡] Ibid., 6th of May.
[§] Ibid., March 4, 1754.   [||] Ibid.   [¶] Ibid.

The infliction of the "Stamp Act" soon followed, which led a Committee of several prominent merchants and others, who advised and directed that the English merchants should ship no more *goods* to the Colonies until the repeal of the Stamp Act, and to decline selling on commission any such goods after the 1st January, 1766; which was generally carried out. This led to the establishment of a Fair or Market at the *Exchange*, for the sale of "home-manufactured goods." The following notice appears in the "papers,"* dated October 17, 1765: "We hear that the design of establishing a market, to commence on Wednesday, the 23d inst., under the Exchange." And on the 24th appears—"Yesterday was opened a market for home manufacture—supplied principally from the country"--"to be held on every 1st and 3d Wednesdays in each month." A notice on the 9th of December gives a more particular account of what was sold. "On Wednesday last was held the market for home manufactures; and though so late an institution, we have already the pleasure to see it attended with great success. Both sides of the Exchange were crowded with a variety of goods, which had a very quick sale, and many gentlemen furnished themselves with good warm clothing, &c. Cloth will continue to be in great demand, as all ranks are zealous to wear it." "To be clothed in homespun, or in garments which had been discarded, was now honorable and fashionable."† Again, on the 30th of the same month—"As the first Wednesday in January falls on New Year's Day, we inform the publick that the market which was designed for that day will be held on Friday, the third. There will be a considerable quantity of cloths for men's winter clothes, besides a variety of other articles—linens, stockings, mittens, men-caps, woolen checks, striped stuffs, linsey-woolseys, handkerchiefs, bellows, crockery-ware, combs, gloves, shoe-brushes, metal buttons, &c. Happy country! that can supply itself with these articles." Obadiah Wells was an agent for the sale of these goods, and received five per cent. for sales and remittances.‡

The odious "Stamp Act" passed on the 22d of March, 1765, and was received here with such a determined opposition, that the Government officers who had been appointed to distribute them were compelled to resign this office, and "declare they will have nothing to do with the stamps." It, however, was short-lived; in fact, it only existed, in a state of torpitude, one year, less four days, when its convulsive struggles ceased, on the 18th of March, 1766; and as soon as "the news of the repeal of the Stamp Act, caused a sudden joy through all ranks of people in the whole city; all the bells were set

* Weekly Gazette & Post Boy.   † Dunlap, p. 424.   ‡ Weekly Post Boy, April 24, 1766.

a-ringing, and continued till late at night, and the next morning until nine o'clock."*

This resistance to the "Stamp Act" had the effect of leading the farmers, mechanics, artisans, and others into more general habits of industry and frugality; in fact, it gave them a feeling of independence, that thereafter they could rely on their own resources.

"*Publicola*"† congratulates the public on the patriotic and frugal spirit that begins to reign in this province. "For, (he says,) 1stly. I observe that many of our most worthy citizens, and principal gentlemen, are clad in country manufacture or turned coats. 2dly. That spinning gets daily more in vogue, so that we rather want materials than industrious hands."

Under this latter head, (*2dly*,) no doubt, its remarks were or became true, if we should judge from the following: "On the 9th instant, three young ladies at Huntington, on Long Island—namely, Ermina, Liticia, and Sabrina—having met together, agreed to try their dexterity at the spinning-wheel. Accordingly, the next morning they set themselves down, and, like the virtuous woman, put their hands to the spindle, while their hands held the distaff; and at evening they had 26 skaines of good linen yarn, each skaine containing 4 ounces: all which was the effects of that day's work only. N. B.— 'Tis to be hop'd that the Connecticut ladies, who are so expert at their spinning-wheels, will not presume to think but that their equals may be found on Long Island, if not in Huntington."‡

Proceeding with "*Publicola's*" remarks, under the next head: "3dly. That the farmers are endeavoring to remedy this difficulty, by the large quantity of flax-seed sown more than usual, and their intention of keeping more sheep. 4thly. That little lamb now comes to market, as no true lovers of their country, or whose sympathetic breasts feel for its distresses, will buy it. 5thly. That sassafras, balm, and sage are coming greatly into use instead of tea, and are allowed to be more wholesome: this seeming trifling article greatly increases our debt to England. Lastly. The fashion of funerals and mourning is in general much altered from the late troublesome, ridiculous, and expensive method; for what could be more absurd than for a person, when in affliction for their dearest relatives, to be teased about dress and ceremonial, and perhaps involved in a large bill of costs, when their creditors are most apt to call upon them?" He further says, in a postscript, that "an effectual way to prevent lamb being brought to market would be, for all the well-affected to their country not to buy any *meat* from such butchers as killed any lamb."

* Weekly Post Boy, May 23, 1766.   † Ibid., May 30, 1766.
‡ Weekly Mercury, March 20, 1769.

But these exciting times have drawn attention from the *Exchange*, which the "Chamber of Commerce," at a meeting, February 7, 1769, were consulting about. They wished " to have a decent, large and commodious room to meet in, and that the room over the *Exchange* will be proper for that use." It was " Ordered, that a Committee do wait upon the Mayor and Corporation, and apply to them for the use of the room over the *Exchange*, and agree on such terms as they judge reasonable." This " Committee " reported at their next meeting, (*March* 7*th*,) that the Corporation " were pleased to say that the *Chamber* should have the use thereof for one year, free of rent, from the first of May next, if they would put it in such repairs as they required, and after that to pay £20 per annum."

Here they met, and while they discussed the " topics of the day," they also discussed their " bread and cheese, beer, punch, pipes, and tobacco, provided (by the Treasurer) at the expense of the members present, so that it doth not exceed *one shilling* each man, which each person is to pay to the Treasurer."

These " topics of the day " were worthy of grave discussion, not only by the members of this Board, but by all the patriotic inhabitants. The Revenue Act, with its onerous duties and taxes, and many others respecting domestic manufactures and foreign commerce, with the quartering and providing of a large body of an obnoxious and insolent soldiery, all tended to encircle them with rank oppression; but again they arose, as with the " Stamp Act," and strike such a blow as led to the separation of the Colonies from Great Britain. The merchants, traders and others again entered into non-importation associations; but not with the same unanimity as before, as we find several examples made of those who were not true to their agreement.

" A parcel of earthen ware, wrought iron, and a few other pack ages of goods, having been brought in here on Tuesday last, from New Haven, lately imported there from Liverpool, it was found, on inquiry, that they belonged and were consigned to persons in this city, save only fifteen crates of the earthen ware, the property of the master of the vessel in which they were imported, and by him sent here for sale. But we have the pleasure to inform the public, that the owners of said goods, so far from insisting on their delivery here, agreeable to the tenor of the bills of lading, did very cheerfully sign an order to the master of the vessel who brought them, to take them immediately back again to New Haven; there to lie in store until the act of Parliament imposing duties on paper, glass, &c., is repealed."*

" The Committee appointed to inspect into the importation of goods

* Penna. Chronicle, July 13, 1769.

in this city, contrary to the agreement subscribed by the merchants, traders and others, are, in consequence of the trust reposed in them, under necessity of advertising the public, that Thomas Charles Willet, milliner, in Wall Street in this city, having been at Philadelphia about six weeks ago, and suspected of having brought goods from thence, confesses that he did there purchase sundry goods to the amount of thirty pounds, which he exposed to sale in this city; that he exchanged in Boston, from whence he is lately arrived, some unsaleable goods he has had in his store, for others which were absolutely necessary for his business. He alleges, in his justification, that he did not know when he purchased the goods in Philadelphia, that it was contrary to the agreement of the merchants here, and that as those he brought from Boston were only in exchange for others less valuable, he conceived no injury done by it to the colony. How far these excuses will exculpate the conduct of the said Willet, must be submitted to the important public and to the *patriotic ladies* of this city, who will undoubtedly treat him accordingly."

"Saturday last, (*says the same paper, July* 14*th.*) an *amende honorable* was performed by Mr. Simeon Cooley, of this city, in the presence of a numerous audience, for a contempt and opposition shown the agreement of British America for non-importation of goods. He begged pardon of all his fellow-citizens; promised never to offend again in like manner, and engaged to send all the effects he had imported to the public store, there to remain till the *revenue acts* were repealed." They were soon after repealed, all except that on *tea*, which the people refused to use, or allow to be landed, or imported.

Among the first to suffer for acts of resistance was one of the prominent "Sons of Liberty," Captain (afterwards General) Alexander McDougal, whose prominent history with the "War of the Revolution" is not yet written, except in the pages of other histories, newspapers, &c. This patriot was arrested and imprisoned for a long time, but was upheld by the "people," who daily visited him in crowds; in fact, he was obliged to fix certain hours for visitors, many of which were ladies. Gaine says: "Wednesday last, the *forty-fifth* day of the year, *forty-five* gentlemen, real enemies to internal taxation, by or in obedience to external authority, and cordial friends to Captain McDougal, and the glorious cause of American Liberty, went in decent procession to the new goal; and dined with him on *forty-five* pounds of beef-stakes, cut from a bullock of *forty-five* months old, and with a number of other friends, who joined them in the afternoon, drank a variety of toasts," " to the number of forty-five."*

* N. Y. Gazette, &c., February 19, 1770.

We again turn to the "*Exchange*," where we find, "On Monday, the 14th inst., January, at six in the evening, will be held at the Long Room in the Exchange, the Annual Meeting of the *Marine Society* of the City of New York, in the province of New York in America, of which the members and those who incline to become members are desired to take notice. By order of the President.

"ROBERT BENSON, *Sec'y*."[*]

Then, in the month of June following, it was found in the possession of several *valiant soldiers*, whose grand attack on two peaceable countrymen is noticed, as follows: "On Tuesday, the 11th instant, we, the subscribers, Jacob Mills and Jeremiah Mulford, of Brookhaven, on Long Island, having taken lodgings at the house of Mr. William Milner, near the *Exchange* in New York, about 9 o'clock in the evening we went from his door into the *piazza-of the Exchange*, where three soldiers who entered immediately after us, and the centry, who stood there before, without the least provocation on our part, furiously attacked us with drawn bayonets, both by thrusting and striking, whereby we were both wounded in many places and one of us dangerously in the head, face, hands, and body, and then forcibly carried us away to the *guard-house*, and there confined us. We being at first ignorant of the cause of this outrageous behaviour, inquired the reason of it, and entreated the soldiers not to murder us, which we apprehended was their design, and which they often threatened both on the way to the *guard-house* and while we were there; they accused us with throwing stones at the centry in the *Exchange*, (placed there, we understand, on account of an entertainment made by the officers in the rooms above.) We declared and offer'd to prove our innocence of the charge—or to give security for our appearance to answer for our conduct the next day—but all in vain, we were hurried to the *guard-house;* and after several hours' confinement, were told that if we would pay 45s., they would release us; we expostulated on the injustice of the demand, but one of us being faint thro' loss of blood, and being in danger of bleeding to death, in order to get our wounds dressed, and out of such hands, we consented to deliver the money, which, when they had received, they suffered us to depart.

"Next day, being advised that the shortest means of redress would probably be by trial before a court-martial, we applied accordingly to advice, and on Thursday the 13th, a court-martial being called, the four soldiers were brought before them for trial. We had several witnesses to prove that we were not the persons who threw stones at the centry; that we had but just left the house

[*] N. Y. Journal, January 14, 1771.

of Mr. Milner, and had not meddled or concerned ourselves with them at the time they attacked us. On the other hand, three or four soldiers in behalf of the prisoners appeared as witnesses, who declared that we had thrown stones at the centry, and that the money paid for our release was not extorted from us, but voluntarily offer'd and press'd upon the soldiers in order to induce them to release us, that the affair might drop without further inquiry." "No oath was administered to any of the witnesses on either side. Upon the whole, we could obtain no manner of redress, and have since understood that the soldiers were cleared."*

The next year, (1772,) the cupola of the Exchange being much out of repair, an appropriation of £50 was voted for that purpose. The lower floor at this period was no doubt used as a place of meeting of the merchants, as the repeal of the *Act* on many of the "home productions" had withdrawn this sort of trade from here; however, there appears to have been business enough in the neighborhood to induce the Corporation to establish a ferry two years after at this slip, " or from a stairs directly fronting the Broad Street, at the east side of the Long Bridge, and on Long Island at a stairs built at the Dock of Mr. Remsen. This ferry will be called *Saint George's Ferry*. Passengers on the New York side will find the ferryman, if not at the stairs, attending either at the house of Mr. John Lee, the corner below the Coenties Market, or of Mr. James Cobham." Then " John Cornell gives notice that he has opened a tavern at his house on Tower Hill on Long Island, near the new ferry, called 'St. George's Ferry.' Companies will be entertained, if they bring their own liquor, and may dress turtle, &c., at said house on the very lowest terms."† In the month of August following he gives notice, " that there will be a *Bull baited* on Tower Hill, at three o'clock in the afternoon, every Thursday during the season."

The Corporation in the previous month of February had agreed to establish ferries " from Coenties Market to the landing-place of Philip Livingston, Esq., and Mr. Henry Remsen on Nassau Island; another from the Fly Market to the present ferry at Brooklyn, and a third from ' Peck Slip' to land at the place last mentioned."

We turn to the Exchange, and find "Rivington" (*March* 24, 1774,) says: "On Tuesday last the greatest and most respectable number of the inhabitants of this city ever known to be assembled on such an occasion, gave at the *Exchange* a very elegant entertainment to His Excellency the Governor, (*Tryon*,) on his approaching departure for Great Britain. True harmony and convivial mirth filled the heart of every one present, and the day and evening passed

* N. Y. Journal, June 30.　　　　　　† N. Y. Mercury May, 1774.

with the most uninterrupted concord and unanimity. When His Excellency took leave of the company, he thanked them for their genteel compliment; and added, that he went from them with reluctance, but that he expected soon to return, and hoped to find them in the same happy union in which he then left them."

The general introduction in the colonies of the manufacturing of woolen goods caused from the "Stamp Act" in 1765, no doubt tended to increase the breeding of sheep and lambs, but not to that degree which the demand called for. Prior to this "Stamp Act," sheep were raised more for exportation than for wool, as that article was but little used, and consequently at a low price, and not in demand. Mutton had but few admirers, and sheep were not allowed to increase above the demand for exportation; but in the "lamb" state, thousands were exterminated as food; and although associations were organized against the use of *young* lamb, yet this fact did not assist in the large demand for wool.* The Provincial Congress in 1774, however, passed a resolution prohibiting sheep from being exported; this, with the increased price of wool, gave more encouragement to the farmers, until destroyed by the "Revolution."

Soon after this resolution was passed by Congress, an attempt was made to evade it by one of the trading vessels. "On Monday last, (*said Gaine,*) a discovery being made that 18 sheep were in a sloop in the harbor bound for the West Indies, a number of citizens waited on the Captain, and informed him that the exportation of *sheep* was contrary to a resolution of the Continental Congress, and thereupon obtained his promise that they should be relanded, and not carried out of the harbor. The people were satisfied, and patiently waited till evening, when a report prevailing that the vessel was to sail that night, about 200 inhabitants assembled on the wharf, appointed and sent four persons to wait on the Committee of Correspondence, and request their advice concerning the measures proper to be taken. By their advice, the merchant to whom the vessel came consigned was sent for, and desired to cause the sheep to be landed and delivered to one of the Committee appointed on this occasion by the people, which person gave his promise to return the sheep as soon as the vessel sailed. Accordingly the sheep were landed, delivered, and soon after the vessel was sailed, returned to the proprietor; on which the people being well satisfied, peaceably dispersed."

These proceedings were not at all relished by "A Westchester Farmer," who says: "Had the Congress attended in the least to the farmers' interests, they never would have prohibited the exporta-

* See Fly Market, "Archives," p. 914, October 20, 1774, vol. I.

tion of sheep, after they came to a certain age. It is the exportation that keeps up the price of sheep; it is the advantageous price that encourages the farmer to feed them: take away the profit of selling them, and the farmer will keep but few. For they are not, and I am confident never will be, in this country, worth keeping for their wool alone. However, right or wrong, the Congress have passed the decree. *Thou shalt not export sheep* was pronounced at Philadelphia; and, right or wrong, the Committee of New York are determined to put it in execution; and *thou shalt not export sheep* is echoed back from New York. How this decree is to be supported in New York, may be learned from the following affair: A gentleman, an officer in the King's service, had purchased a number of sheep to carry with him to St. Vincent's: Mr. Gaine's *newspaper* says eighteen. The New Yorkers, probably afraid that they should lose their share of the mutton, assembled on the dock, sent for the Committee, and, in open violation of the laws of their country, obliged the merchant to whom the vessel had been consigned to have the sheep landed: the sheep were committed to safe durance till the vessel sailed, and then were delivered to the proprietor. I suppose to the person who had sold them to the officer; though how he could be the proprietor after he had sold them, I cannot see."

The next year, the subject of killing lambs in certain months of the year was brought before the Provincial Congress, and on the 23d of June a resolution was introduced by Gouverneur Morris, "That the inhabitants ought not to kill any lamb until the first of November next." This was referred to a meeting on the 29th inst., when "Mr. (Captain) McDougal offered a substitute, which was carried;" and they "Resolved, therefore, That no person in this Colony kill any lamb until the first day of August next."

In the month of August following, a public-house opposite the Exchange was much injured from a cannon-ball, the particulars of which are as follows: "On the night of the 23d of August, 1775, while the Sons of Liberty were removing cannon from the Battery, the *Asia* man-of-war began firing with cannon, and the balls struck a house next to Roger Morris's and Samuel Fraunces', at the corner of the Exchange: each had an eighteen-pound ball shot into their roofs."* This firing was the first cannonading the city received in the Revolution, and caused considerable alarm, especially among the women and children, many of whom hurriedly left the city.

Some of the "Sons of Liberty" soon after turned their attention to Rivington, whose "Gazette" had become very abusive; when one of their number, Captain Sears, brought into the city a small body

* Rivington's Gazetteer, August 31, 1775.

of Connecticut troopers, in the middle of the day of the 4th of December following, and demolished his press and printing materials, which stopped his paper, and he soon after went to England. However, he returned after the British troops had taken possession of the city, and his reception back again is thus noticed: "On Thursday evening last (26*th September*, 1777,) the house of Loosley and Elms, King's Head Tavern, was elegantly illuminated, to testify the joy the true 'Sons of Freedom' had on the arrival of Mr. Rivington from England. This gentleman, with unparalleled fortitude, having nobly disdained to usher to the world any inflammatory pieces, which might be productive of introducing anarchy, instead of constitutional authority, into this once happy country, felt in the severest degree the rage of popular delusion. Liberty he always firmly adhered to; licentiousness from his soul he ever detested. A person, in honor to free press, extemporary pronounced this:

> ' Rivington is arrived—let every man
> This injured person's worth confess:
> His royal heart abhorr'd the Rebel plan,
> And boldly dam'd them with his press.' " *

He came with the appointment of King's Printer for New York, and changed the former name of "Rivington's Gazette," to the "Royal Gazette," in which were afterwards found the Government's proclamations and orders.

William Butler, a British officer, says: "The inhabitants, from the arrival of His Majesty's troops till the evacuation of New York in November, 1783, were free from the payment of taxes of every kind, either for the purpose of lighting the lamps or cleaning the city, repairs of the pumps, streets, or roads, or the public works, as well as the maintenance of the poor." "The markets were raised above *eight hundred per cent.* for the necessaries of life. The landlords, from the demands for houses, raised their rents on an average of four times the sum such houses rented previous to the rebellion. And the vast number of merchants and others daily arriving in the city, was the cause of a constant increase in the article of house-rent."†

Some details of the scarcity of provisions in the city at this period are introduced in the history of Fly Market; but out of the city, the *Rebels*, as Rivington was much pleased to notice the Patriots, in his *Royal Gazette*, November 17, 1777—" By a flag of truce which arrived on Tuesday evening, which left Albany on the 4th inst., we learn that the necessaries of life have risen to such exor-

---

* N. Y. Gazette and Weekly Mercury, September 29, 1777.
† Tomlinson's Papers, in Mercantile Library.

bitant prices as make them almost unattainable to those not concerned in the *Rebel* Army." "The currency is reduced to the lowest ebb, and barter is substituted in the place of money. Those
who have not one commodity to give for another, must pay the following prices, viz.: Port wine, 8 dollars per bottle; rum, 12 dollars
per gallon; salt, 30 dollars per bushel; Bohea tea, 16 dollars per
lb.; sugar, 10 shillings per lb.; beef, 1 shilling and 4 pence per lb.;
indifferent linen, when to be had, 12 dollars per yard; and butter,
from 9 to 10 shillings per lb." The same, 24th inst., states that
such articles as "flour, rice, tea, and tobacco were brought by *land*
over the Middle Road, through York *Town* in Pennsylvania, and
Hartford in Connecticut, to Boston, where flour sells at 15 dollars
per hundred; shoes, 10 dollars; boots, 36 dollars; and trowsers,
(pantaloons,) such as are worn by negroes, 18 dollars a pair; a very
plain surtout coat, without lining, 60 dollars; ordinary beef, 1 shilling; prime do., 15 pence; pork, 18 pence; and not a single hat to
be purchased at any price."

We also find "Holt," the patriotic printer of the *N. Y. Journal*,
who, with the army under General Washington, had left the City
of New York, and afterwards was found publishing his paper along
at intervals, suffering with the rest, for want not only of means, but
also of the necessaries of life, which he proposes to take in the way
of trade. In the month of August he says: "And the printer being
unable to carry on his business without the necessaries of life, is
obliged to affix the following prices to his work, viz.: *For a quarter
of news*, 12 lbs. of beef, pork, veal, or mutton, or 4 pounds of butter,
or 7 lbs. of cheese, or 18 lbs. of fine flour, or half a bushel of wheat,
or one bushel of Indian corn, or half a cord of wood, or 300 wt.
of hay, or other articles of country produce, as he shall want them,
in like proportions, or as much money as will purchase them at the
time; for other articles of printing work, the prices to be in proportion to that of the *newspaper*. All his customers, who have to
spare any of the above, or other articles of country produce, he
hopes will let him know it, and afford him the necessary supplies,
without which his business here must very soon be discontinued."

The situation of the *Rebels* on the 12th of June, 1780, at the
Highland Forts, and the detachments that were sent to the north
from there, were noticed as follows: "They are obliged to carry
even provisions with them, which they can ill spare, living, as they
do at the Highland Forts, from hand to mouth; there being no
magazines anywhere, and the country already drained, and the
prospect respecting the ensuing harvest very discouraging."* "To

* N. Y. Gazette and Weekly Mercury.

supply the deficiency of meat, they are employed, in all the upper parts of the (North) river, in taking and salting fish for the Continental soldiers." From another source—"We are informed by a gentleman who lately left Albany, that the chief Continental butcher there is ordered to employ a number of the other butchers in catching fish, such as herring and sturgeon, for the use of the Continental Army, as their money is reduced to so low an ebb, that they cannot afford beef, and that they have a guard at the farm of General Schuyler at Saratoga, to prevent the inhabitants getting any share of the fishery."*

The next year, (1781,) in the month of July, we find General Washington at Dobb's Ferry, where he and his little army lay encamped; and, to encourage the farmers and others to bring provisions, clothing, &c., there for sale, he, by a "Proclamation," established a market-place, as follows:

"Be it known, That every day during the time the army remains in its present position, from daybreak until noon, two market-places will be open for the supply of the army: one near His Excellency's Head-Quarters, in the field first back of the house and near the quarters of the Adjutant and Quarter-Master-General; the other in the French camp, near the house of Henry Taylor, which is the Head-Quarters of His Excellency the Count de Rochambeau.

"All persons who will bring any article of provisions, and small supplies for the use of the army, may depend upon being protected in their persons and property; and shall have full and free liberty to dispose of the produce without molestation or imposition; and will receive no hinderance from the guards of the army on their passing to or repassing from the market-places. No person will be permitted to take any article without the full consent of the owner.

"It is expected, however, and will be required, that every person, on his or her first coming to market, will be furnished with a certificate of recommendation, shewing their attachment to the American cause and interest, signed by two civil magistrates, or two other respectable persons, of known and approved character, that no injury may arise to the army from the arts of designing and evil-minded persons. If the army should take a different position, other places will be named where the like liberty and protection will be given. Given at Head-Quarters, near Dobb's Ferry, the 10th day of July, 1781.   G. WASHINGTON.

"By His Excellency's command.
                "JONATHAN TRUMBULL, JUN'R, *Secretary.*"

In 1778, says the "*Royal Gazette,*" of the 2d of December, "Mrs.

---

* Royal Gazette, May 17.

Treville has just returned from the country, and opened the ' London Coffee-House' at the *Exchange*, where gentlemen may be entertained with breakfasts, dinners, and suppers, tea, coffee, &c. Those gentlemen who please to honor her with their company, as she is provided with a good waiter and cook;" and on the 2d of February, 1780, " the New York Marine Artillery Company are desired to meet this day, at twelve o'clock, at their *rendezvous* in the *Exchange*."

But the Exchange was not long after a *rendezvous* for the British soldiery, either to meet or feast; smiling *peace* stepped in and bade them depart, and give place to the tired and tried soldiers of freedom, that they might rest in the arms of liberty.

The first news of *peace*, says Butler,* in a letter, was " On the 6th day of April, 1783: a packet from England arrived at New York, and brought over the preliminary articles of peace; and on the 8th of the same month, His Majesty's proclamation, declaring a cessation of hostilities, was publickly read by the Town Major at the City Hall." The reception of this proclamation among the loyal citizens is thus described: " We are informed by persons who were present at New York when the proclamation for a cessation of hostilities was read in the presence of a great number of people, that at the conclusion, instead of the signs of approbation generally exhibited on such occasions, nothing but groans and hisses prevailed, attended by bitter reproaches and curses upon their king, for having deserted them in the midst of their calamities. The greatest despair is depicted in every countenance, and the little comfort they can possibly experience in the deserts of Nova Scotia will tend to heighten their distress. It is said that the number of persons last embarked for that country amount to near four thousand."†

This was followed with an " Order," dated " Head-Quarters, New York, 16th of June, 1783. The proprietors of houses or lands lately evacuated will apply to Lieutenant-General Campbell, for the possession of those on Long Island; to Brigadier-General Birch for those on York Island, and Brigadier-General Bruce for those on Staten Island. These general officers will be pleased to cause all such estates to be immediately delivered up to the proprietors or to their attornies, unless where they may see sufficient reasons for retaining them some time longer, which reasons they will report to the Commander-in-Chief. In like manner, all estates which shall hereafter be evacuated are to be surrendered up to the proprietors.

"(Signed,)   OL. DE LANCEY, *Adjt. General*."‡

---

* Tomlinson's Papers, in Mercantile Library.
† Penna. Packet, April 17, 1783.   ‡ Ibid., June 21.

A correspondent describes the manner in which these estates were delivered up to their rightful owners. He says: " On the publication of the ratification of the preliminary articles of peace, many of the old citizens of New York, who had fled from that place at the approach of the British, sold and disposed of their places in the country, (thinking, as all the world thought besides, that it was actually peace,) and went to New York, but to their utter astonishment, even of the loyalists, those people were not permitted to go into their own houses; the keys of all empty houses, and such as should be evacuated, being ordered to the Commandant's office, who out of his very great goodness condescended to let such houses, on the party hiring paying him down *three months' rent*. We need not inquire who pockets this three months' rent, with all other rents within the British lines, injustly detained from the rightful owners. The Commandant, General Birch, will not tell us, nor will any concerned in this very honorable traffick. Suffice to say, it has long been, and still is, lost to all *Whig* proprietors of houses, to subjects of the King of Great Britain."* Another says: " A number of houses in New York being now empty, many of the former owners have applied for leave to repossess them, but have in general been refused."† The wretched condition in which the houses, churches, and other property were also found, is thus described by another, who " observes that he has lately viewed the churches and houses in New York, and that all the churches are, except the Episcopal, the Moravian, and the Methodists, converted into store-houses or barracks, and appear in a very loathsome condition; the fences which encompassed the burying-yards being destroyed, the pews in all, and the galleries in some of them, pulled down; the windows broken and otherwise much abused."‡ " A person recently from Staten Island, relates that there is scarcely a pannel of fencing left in all that place; and others say the case is precisely the same on Long Island, the rails having been burnt by the soldiery. It is with the greatest difficulty the unfortunate inhabitants can keep a small inclosure for their cattle and flocks at night, which they are obliged to watch through the day to save their grain from destruction;"§ and no doubt, from the latter cause. " A melancholy accident happened (April 17) at the house of Leffert Lefferts, Esq., in Bedford, Long Island; his daughter, a very accomplished young lady, having observed to her mother that a loaded pistol, left by a drover who had been *watching his cattle* with it the preceding night, upon a chest of drawers, was rather dangerously placed, and that some of the chil-

* Penna. Packet, July 22, 1783.   † Ibid., August 23.
‡ Ibid., May 27.   § Ibid., July 3.

dren might be hurt by it, proceeded to remove and put it in a holster that hung close by; but in the operation the pistol discharged, the shot went through her body, and she expired immediately."*

Many other interesting facts are shown in a letter, dated "Hackinsack, August 30, 1783," of which the following is an extract: "This month completes seven years my family and self have lived in a state of exile from our wonted habitation in New York. What a scene, or rather what a tragedy, has been acted in our country since that time! I was lately over at New York, and though I did not meet with any considerable personal insults, I had the mortification to see some overgrown Tories stalking about, whose looks I did not altogether approve of. There is one Tilton I saw there in particular, whose practice has been these six or seven years to burn gristmills and meeting-houses without the lines. This fellow walks constantly with a spear-cane, and talks of nothing but rebels and rebellion, and such like stuff. As to the British, they are tolerable civil and polite; and though there are centries placed at almost every hundred yards distance, they molest no one who behaves himself with propriety. The poor Hessians will soon be all embarked and gone. In general, they have been very much inclined to desert, and several boatmen and *market people* are in goal, upon an accusation of having aided and assisted numbers of them in getting off. The fire-wood, to the amount of several thousand cords, laid in by the British army since last spring, at the expense of 50s. and £3 a cord, is now selling out at 25s. and 28s. per cord. I met with some of my old acquaintances here, who were, some of them, formerly very fat, stout men, that are now reduced to mere skeletons, at the prospect of leaving this place with the army. A certain Tory gentleman, who lives not a very considerable distance from the Brookland Ferry, will stay, in my opinion, without the consent of the Legislature, as I think he intends to fret himself into the grave in the course of a few weeks. You may remember that in 1775, when you and I were crossing over to Long Island, that we laughed to hear him and Parson Inglis *tête- -tête*, talking about the 75,000 Russians that were to come over to annihilate us, knits and lice. There is no end to auctions and vendues; everything is selling off, and I believe a great deal more than the venders can make a good title for. Amongst other articles, there are immense of household furniture exposed to sale, either new painted, or disguised in such a manner as to prevent the former proprietors from knowing it again. Few or no negro slaves are given up. My chief errand to town was to look up one of mine, and I saw the rogue, but found he had

* Penna. Packet, April 26, 1783.

formed such connections with a certain great personage that I could no longer look upon him as my own. He told me he was going to *Novy Koshee*. An American officer was lately in town, (I believe he was of the militia,) and having met with some ill-usage, complained to David Mathews. This Father of the City, it is said, treated him very roughly, and by way of shortening conversation, wished all d——d rascals in hell. The General then hurried away, and by a speedy embarkation narrowly escaped a good pelting with stones, with a volley or two of which he was complimented after the boat left the wharff. The meeting-houses are in a most deplorable condition, the receptacles of filth and nastiness. Except theft and pilfering, there is very little business carried on at present. The boat we went to town in had her sails stolen away in the night, although we lay on board purposely to watch them. We were thankful, however, that we were not stolen boat and all."*

Another report soon after states, that "Some nocturnal incendiaries made a *third* attempt to destroy the City of New York by fire. Six of the villians, we hear, are taken."† (The two first, viz., 1776 and 1778, are noticed in this volume.)

The communication on the rivers for market and other river craft was opened to and from New York in the month of April, and "We further learn that since the communication has been opened to New York, the *markets* there have fallen considerably, and it is expected that beef, flour, butter, &c., will be as low as ever in a short time."‡ Then the arrival of two sloops at Albany in the month following, from New York, is noticed, and before they were allowed to trade, a meeting of the inhabitants was called, when they decided to grant them permission to do so.§

In the month of October following, the news from New York states: "Last Monday (20th inst.) evening, Captain Stewart's vessel, lying in our harbor, with the colors of the United States of America flying, was boarded by the *Canaille*, who in a riotous manner tore them down and carried them through the streets in triumph, attended by a chosen band-itti of negroes, sailors, and loyal leather-apron'd statesmen. The injudiciousness of this shabby outrage, and the consequences that are likely to result from it, are too obvious to need any comment."‖

It was not long after, however, when the patriotic citizens were enabled to take down the *last flag* which had been flying above one hundred years over the City of New York, and in its place was hoisted the welcome *Stars* and *Stripes*, although some little difficulty

---

* Penna. Packet, September 18. 1783.   † Ibid., October 7.
‡ Ibid., May 6.   § Ibid., June 10.   ‖ Ibid., October 28.

was experienced in doing so, as appears stated in a letter from New York, dated 26th November, 1783: " Yesterday gave us our city. To the honor of Britain let it be published in every newspaper, that to add to their name, (which has already been branded with every kind of infamy,) they cut away the halyards from the flagstaff in the Fort, (formerly FORT GEORGE,) and likewise greased the post, so that we were obliged to have a ladder to fix a new rope. Inventions prevented any delay, for the glorious stripes were fixed in the sod, and a discharge of thirteen (*guns*) fired. The city has been remarkable quiet. A few days will, I hope. produce a little scrutiny, when the *Tories* take care."*

Soon after the Council of Appointment " ordered that all persons becoming inhabitants of this city do, within 24 hours after arrival, report their names, former places of residence, and number of their family to the Secretary of the Council; and that all inhabitants receiving inmates or lodgers, do in like manner report their names and former places of abode, &c."†

" When I look around me," says another, " and see the contrast between the Whigs and Tories, I am hardly able to contain myself; these despicable beings are basking themselves in the sunshine of affluence and ease, whilst those who have been wasting their constitutions and spending their fortunes in the service of their country, have hardly been able to support themselves with the necessaries of life during the winter. The distresses that have been exhibited here within the three last months are striking proofs of my assertion."‡ Another also writes, " that the distresses of the poor were never so great as at present."§ Added to this, when the Hon. JAMES DUANE was appointed Mayor of the City, " Instead of giving a public entertainment on the investiture of the mayoralty, as had been customary with his predecessors, humanely reflecting on the want and distress which are so prevalent at this severe season, he rather chose to present twenty guineas towards the relief of his suffering fellow-citizens, observing, on the occasion, that his liberality was limited by the shock which had affected his private fortune in the progress of the war."‖

Some two years after the evacuation, says Dr. Anderson, sheep had become tolerable plenty again, when a number of agents from the English manufacturers of cloths and other woolen goods came here and bought up nearly all the sheep and slaughtered them, stripped the wool from the skins, and sent it to England to be manufactured and returned. This experiment in a measure failed, as

* Penna. Packet, December 2, 1783.   † Ibid., December 4, 1783.
‡ Ibid., March 20, 1784.   § Ibid., March 13, 1784.   ‖ Ibid., March 20, 1784.

many of our farmers' wives had previously obtained the knowledge of making the *homespuns*, which they yet, and many years after, preferred to wear. The carcasses of this mutton were sold so cheap that thousands laid up their winter's provisions of this meat.

Not a market-house was found to have been altogether used for market purposes, except the Fly and Oswego; all below these were destroyed. The lower part of the Exchange was the only place unoccupied in a public building that could be used for a market, which the "neighborhood ask that it may be temporarily used" for that purpose. On the 14th of April, 1784, the authorities "do agree and order, that the lower part of the building commonly called the Exchange be used (until further order of this Board) as a public market-place." No doubt it was soon after taken possession of by butchers and others, and established a market-place; or so it appears in a notice for the sale of "that spacious, well-built freehold estate, situate in Great Dock (*Pearl*) Street, well known as FRAUNCES's TAVERN. The premises are extensive and well adapted to the uses of a numerous family; its vicinity to the *new market*, and the probability that new and elegant houses will soon be built in that part of the city."* The Hon. William A. Duer also notices the occupation of the *Old Exchange*, which, he says, was "a brick building standing upon arches in the centre of Broad Street, below Great Dock Street. Here our merchants once used to congregate; but the space under the arcade had been converted into a market of a different description, where, instead of uncurrent notes or fancy stocks, the more substantial articles of beef and mutton were bought and sold." Grant Thorburn, in one of his letters, says: "As I entered Broad Street, near its foot stood the old Royal Exchange. On the ground floor a butcher was cutting beef-steaks; a dozen or more of Bergen squatters' were trying to dispose of their stock of crabs, clams, and muscles; and all were talking together, and creating a compound jargon of High-Dutch, Mowhawk, and African, accompanied with laughter loud and long."

The butchers who resided in the city were obliged to use the old public slaughter-house, which had stood on Bayard near (now) Mulberry Street, until the summer of 1784, when it was ordered to be removed to Corlaer's Hook, and to be built over the water. Those who stood in this market, being so far from the new location, petitioned for liberty to kill their cattle in the slaughter-house at Whitehall, which had been used by the British troops while in possession of the city. They also, in their petition, say: "That we often want to slaughter beef, veal, and mutton in one day, and that the two lat-

* N. Y. Packet, September 9, 1784.

ter being allowed to be killed in the slaughter-house at the White-Hall; and if we are obliged to go to the Corlaer's Hook to slaughter our beef, it will put us to a great inconvenience; that we are willing to make Mr. Blanchard (*lessee*) ample satisfaction for it, so that he may not be a loser." (Signed by) John Jeremiah, butcher; Christian Miller, butcher; John Caple, butcher; William Hunter, butcher; and John McLaughlin, butcher.

John Jeremiah was very patriotic as well as somewhat remarkable in his business, having been the only butcher who conducted his whole business in the First Ward of the City of New York after the Revolution. He was a native of Saxe Gotha, Germany, and came to Philadelphia in the year 1773, where, on the breaking out of the war, he entered into the service of the Pennsylvania Militia, and was at the battles of " Mud Fort" and Trenton; after which he entered on board of the American privateer *Holcker*, and served the term of enlistment; when he returned to Philadelphia and entered into his business of a butcher for a short period, or until the close of the Revolution, when he immediately removed and became a citizen of New York. Here he again started into business, with a stand under a large tree near Coenties Slip, which is still remembered by some of the old citizens. The old market-house had been destroyed during the war, and no other place could be then assigned. He next moved in the *Exchange*, where we now find him; five years after the " Exchange Market" was finished, and he was transferred on stand No. 1, where he continued business many years after. He resided at No. 14 Water Street until his death, which occurred in 1816; having lived in this ward over thirty years. He was the father of the well-known old butcher and highly esteemed citizen, Thomas Jeremiah, whom we shall further notice in the " Washington Market."

The large rooms in the upper part were next taken for public purposes; the Legislature, Courts of Justice, and occasionally societies, held their sessions there. Governor George Clinton, by a proclamation of the 16th November, 1785, " required the Senate and Assembly of the State to meet at the *Exchange* in this city on Friday, the 6th of January next." To prevent the interruption from street noises, " chains were ordered to be fixed across the street" on the 23d October, 1789. The following month " the Federal Court, for the District of New York, met at the *Exchange*, and after forming the Court, the Judge was sworn, and several Attornies admitted."[*]

The St. Tammany's Society or Columbian Order obtained, through petition presented on the 10th of September, 1790, a privilege " to use the *Exchange Room*, weekly, as a temporary accommodation."

* N. Y. Packet, November 5, 1789.

This was signed by a committee consisting of

Melancton Smith,   James Ogden Hoffman,
William W. Gilbert,   James M. Hughes.

Three years after, the city (in fact, the whole country,) became violently agitated in consequence of the war between France and England. Two parties appear here much interested: the Federals for neutrality, and the Whigs for assisting the French.

The French Minister, *Citizen Genet*, arrived here and met with an enthusiastic welcome, having been brought from France in the French frigate-of-war *Ambuscade*, commanded by Citizen Bompard. A British frigate, called the *Boston*, of 32 guns, commanded by Captain Courtney, soon after appeared on the coast, anxious to have an engagement with the *Ambuscade;* and what follows is better told by the "Press," noticed July 31st, same year: "On the Coffee-House books on Monday, the 29th instant: last evening came up from Sandy Hook the revenue cutter, Captain Dennis, who at 4 P. M., two leagues E. by S. from Sandy Hook, spoke the British frigate *Boston*, Captain Courtney, who informed Captain Dennis he would be happy to see the *Ambuscade*. (Pinned under it immediately:) *Citizen Bompard will wait on Captain Courtney to-morrow, agreeably to invitation; he hopes to find him at the Hook.*"*

A number of parties of citizens (among which were several Whig butchers, who carried down a liberal stock of fresh meats, vegetables, &c.,) in different boats, to be eye-witnesses of the battle, and many bets are laid on the subject. (I am told by one of the party that several butchers were on board of the *Ambuscade*, and took an active part with them.)

"The action begun about half past five Thursday morning, at the Hook, (2d of August,) and lasted one hour and three-quarters precisely, during which time each frigate behaved with the utmost bravery. One shot from the *Ambuscade*, about the middle of the action, killed Captain Courtney and his first Lieutenant of Marines. The *Boston*, in the end, sheared off and ran away, the *Ambuscade* after her, but could not overtake her; however, she captured a British brig, and carried her into New York as a prize."

From an authentic translation I find —"Our ship's *(Ambuscade)* colors, torn as they were at the close of the action, have been presented to the Tammany Society of this city, as a token of that respect which those virtuous patriots merit, in our opinion, from their Republican brethren in France."

In 1795, "the Corporation generously granted the *Exchange* in Broad Street for the use of a 'Museum,' to the Tammany Society;"

* N. Y. Journal, &c., July 31, 1793.

and the latter, by a resolution on the 25th of June following, "relinquish and assign all their right in the Museum to Gardiner Baker, upon the following conditions: That the same shall forever hereafter continue to be known by the name of 'Tammany Museum,' in honor of its original founders and patrons; that each member of the Tammany Society shall, with their wives and children, forever hereafter have free access to the said Museum, free of any expense." "The room in which the Museum is contained is 60 feet by 30, with an arch of 20 feet high, on which is elegantly painted a sky-blue, and intermixed with various kinds of clouds, in some of which are naturally represented a thunder-storm, with flashes of lightning. The walls were covered with painted trees, animals, birds, &c. The natural curiosity was 'a perfect horn between 5 and 6 inches in length, which grew out of a woman's head in this city.' The living animals was a porcupine, from the East Indies; the ant-bear, from the coast of Patagonia; the American gray squirrel, and other smaller animals; and living birds, was the King of Vultures, from South America; the American Eagle, very large and gay; and two beautiful doves, from the Bahama Islands; besides preserved animals, birds, fishes, and artificial curiosities, coins, and medals."*

Gardiner Baker was a very eccentric, as well as a very small man; somewhat enthusiastic, but industrious and good-natured. At this early day he was the *Winskinsky* of the Order of St. Tammany. The Hon. William A. Duer† says of him: "The good little fellow was not only a collector of curiosities, but himself a greater curiosity than any in his collection. Not only his person and manner singular, but so were his address and conversation; and the experiments he made upon the vernacular tongue were not less cruel than ludicrous. He had been bitten, too, by a mad antiquary, and the unction with which he would descant upon some dilapidated vestige of local interest exceeded that of a monk in exhibiting an undoubted relic, or recounting some miraculous but well-attested legend. How he would luxuriate in describing one of the windows of his repository; the former course of the creek down Broad Street, under which it still ran; and pointing out the 'old ferry-house' at the corner of Garden Street, with the pettiauger-shaped vane on its gable! Then, as an object of special interest to myself, he would direct my attention to the house in which 'Old Madam Alexander kept her crockery-shop on one side of the Hall, and her husband, the lawyer, his office on the other.'" This notable couple (says Duer) were his (D's) great-grand-parents.

* Daily Advertiser, November 6. 1793.
From his Address before the St. Nicholas Society, December 1, 1848.

In the month of August, 1798, although the yellow fever had commenced to devour its victims, yet our little friend Baker was preparing a grand display at his Museum, which is thus editorially noticed in the "press:"* "We are informed that an elegant transparent view of Mount Vesuvius, showing the great eruption in 1779, will be shown to the public, this and to-morrow evenings, from one of the windows of the Museum, pointing up Broad Street." This, no doubt, was his last display at this Museum, as he was soon after taken sick, and went to Boston, where his sickness proved to be the *dreaded fever*, of which he died in the month of October of that year.

In the month of July a most distressing occurrence, says the *Commercial Advertiser*, (July 20, 1798,) took place this morning, at a French boarding-house on the corner of Pearl and Broad Streets, just opposite this "old market-place," the "*Exchange.*" It appears that two persons were employed in the Theatre, one of which was rather celebrated as an actress, named Madame Gardie, and the other, represented as her husband, were, with her child, about eight years of age, living here on rather slender means, and no doubt, in consequence of pecuniary troubles, he murdered her while asleep, and then committed suicide.

"Dunlap"† says: "The young man *(Gardie)* was in debt, and, as he himself thought, without resource—he was helpless and friendless. His wife importuned him to write to his father, (who is represented 'as a nobleman, the King's Receiver-General at La Rochelle.') He now resolved to return to him, and wished her to return with him; but she could not conquer her repugnance to the family which had rejected her, and the people who had chased her from the stage and the country. She refused to return. It appears a separation had been agreed upon, whether final or temporary, is not known. He had engaged his passage for France, and she had been the evening before her death at Mr. Hallam's, consulting as to the means of enabling her to return to St. Domingo. On the fatal and horrible night, Gardie removed the boy from his mother's bed into his own, in the same room, in which he soon again fell asleep; but soon starting at the sound of a groan, which he thought proceeded from his mother, the little lad, in great terror, called out, 'What is the matter, papa? What is the matter with mamma?' 'Hush!' was the reply: 'your mamma is not well—but she sleeps—don't disturb her.'

"Again the child slept; but a noise of falling, struggling, and groans, a third time awoke the boy; his calls were unanswered—

* Daily Advertiser, August 24. † American Theatre, pp. 404, 405.

all was dark and silent. His terror increased when he found that he received no answer. Wild with terror, the child reached the door of the chamber, and by his cries awakened the mistress of the house, who, not understanding him, 'sternly ordered him to go to bed.' The child, not daring to return to the dreadful chamber, sought the bed of one of the negro servants, and crept trembling to his side. In the morning they found the miserable murderer lying in the middle of the floor, weltering in his blood; his right hand above his head, still grasping the knife, with which he had been forced to inflict several wounds on himself before he fell. She had been killed by one blow, and lay as if asleep."

The Museum of Mrs. Baker in the Exchange was continued until the year 1799, when this old building was ordered to be taken down, in consequence of the complaints made against it. In a petition dated 20th of February of that year, signed by more than 100 persons, who stated: "Should it take fire, inevitable destruction and utter ruin must to the adjacent building ensue; it obstructs the passage of the streets contiguous thereto, and prevents the free circulation of air; and in short, to say the most of it, it is visibly a theatre of obscenity, and, instead of being a benefit, it is in every sense of the word a public nuisance, and that unless every nuisance is thoroughly removed, a return of the said malignant or yellow fever may be expected."

The building " is ordered to be removed between the 20th day of June next, (1799,) reserving for the public use the bell and stone-flagging in and about the said building; and that the Clerk notify Mrs. Baker, (*now widow*,) the present occupant, of the determination of the Board on this subject, and that she remove from the said building by the 20th of May next."

"PECK SLIP MARKET."

1763. THIS market-place was established by the action of the Common Council, at a meeting held on the 8th of March, 1763, on a petition from William Walton, Jacobus Roosevelt, Esq's, and sundry others, for liberty to erect a public market-house, at their own cost and expense, in or near Peck Slip, in Montgomerie Ward in this city, when it was unanimously resolved and ordered that their prayer be granted.

The inhabitants " subscribed large and generously towards defraying the expenses of erecting the brick market-house." This was the first one built of brick in the City of New York; it stood facing Water Street, on the westerly side, at the head of Peck Slip, which derived its name from Benjamin Peck, Esq., a wealthy and worthy citizen, who died several years previous to its erection.

It being in the neighborhood of the most fashionable dwellings, and the *élite* of the city, it soon drew around it a large trade. Sometimes it was known as the new "*Jersey Market,*" but usually as "the new market at Peck Slip," until after the Revolution, when it became known as "*Peck Slip Market.*" In 1767 we find, " to be sold at public vendue, on Thursday, the 15th instant, a good new brick house and lot of ground in 'Montgomerie Ward,' in Queen Street, facing the new *Jersey* Market at Peck Slip," &c.* Two years after, " Arnout Cannon has opened a vendue-house at Peck Slip, opposite the *market.*" Three years after, "John Arthur, on 'Cow-foot Hill,' near the *new market* at Peck's Slip, has just received a variety of goods, &c."†

The trade continued good until the " Revolution," when the attendants deserted it, but soon after it was taken possession of by the British troops, who used it as one of their store-houses, &c., until the 5th of September, 1783, when an order from the (British) Commandant says: " The market at Peck's Slip is now clearing, and will be reserved for the sole use of the country people, who may kill their stock to bring to market." It also gave " permission to all persons coming from any part of the country with live stock for the use of the markets to kill and dispose of the same, provided the stock is slaughtered at such places in this city as are set apart for that purpose, or on board the vessels in which it is brought, and carried to one of the public markets to be disposed of.

" New York, Sept. 5, 1783. J. BLUKE, *Secretary.*"

Soon after the " Evacuation " several butchers had stands assigned to them there, and these, with the other occupants, did considerable business, but it was never after so thriving as before the war. From the height of the arches, it was a very cold market-house in the winter, as will be perceived from a petition of the butchers on the 19th December, 1784, who stated: " That from the height of said market, in the winter season it is impossible to stand the cold north wind. We therefore pray that this Honorable Board would order that a few feet of each side towards the northwest end may be inclosed."

On the 1st of August, three years after, the Board " Ordered Al-

* N. Y. Mercury, January, 1767. † N. Y. Journal, December 10, 1772.

derman Hazard and Mr. Van Zant to be a Committee to examine and direct such repairs to *Peck Slip Market*, and the street adjoining it, as was needful; and on the 6th instant £15 was advanced for that purpose."

Two years after, General Washington became President of the United States, and soon after took up his residence near, in the old Mansion House which stood (until a few years ago) at the corner of Franklin Square and Cherry Street, one square from this market-house. In the month of May following, his steward caused the following notice to be published, headed, "*The President's Household.* Whereas all servants and others employed to procure provisions or necessaries for the household of the ' *President*' *of the United States* will be furnished with monies for these purposes. *Notice is therefore given*, that no accounts, for the payment of which the public might be considered as responsible, are to be opened with any of them. SAMUEL FRAUNCES, *Steward of the Household.*"[*]

In the month of December following, "A *Cook* is wanted for the President of the United States. No one need apply who is not perfect in the business, and can bring indubitable testimonials of sobriety, honesty, and attention to the duties of the station." Then, "A *Coachman*, who can be well recommended for his skill in driving, attention to horses, and for his honesty, sobriety, and good disposition, would likewise find employment in the family of the President of the United States."[†]

Washington was a rigid observer of punctuality, and he demanded it from his household as well as all whom he had dealings with. " It is also known that whenever he assigned to meet Congress at noon, he never failed to be passing the door of the Hall when the clock struck twelve." "A Captain Pease wished to dispose of a beautiful pair of horses to the President, who he knew was an excellent judge of horses. The President appointed five o'clock in the morning to examine them at his stable. The Captain, thinking the hour too early for so great a man to be stirring, did not arrive with the horses until a quarter after five, when he was told by the groom that the President was there at five, and was then fulfilling other engagements. Pease was much mortified, and called on Major Jackson, the Secretary, to apologize for his delay, and to request the President to appoint some new time"—when he was compelled to wait one week for delaying the first quarter of an hour.

" His dining hour was four, when he always sat down to his table, only allowing five minutes for the variation of time-pieces, whether his guests were present or not. It was frequently the case with

* N. Y. Packet, May 7, 1789. † Ibid., December 19.

new members of Congress, that they did not arrive until dinner was nearly half over; and he would remark, 'Gentlemen, we are punctual here; my cook never asks whether the company has arrived, *but whether the hour has.'"** His diet was also simple and plain, seldom partaking of but one dish. Judge Wingate, who was one of the guests, describes his first dinner after his inauguration. "The guests consisted of the Vice-President, the foreign Ministers, the heads of Departments, the Speaker of the House of Representatives, and the Senators from New Hampshire and Georgia, the then two most Northern and Southern States. It was the least showy dinner that I ever saw at the President's table, and the company was not large. The President made his whole dinner on a boiled *leg of mutton.* It was his usual practice to eat of but one dish. After the dinner and dessert were finished, *one glass* of wine was passed round the table, *and no toast.* The President arose, and all the company, of course, and retired to the drawing-room, from which the guests departed, as every one chose, without ceremony."†

Another anecdote, from a respected friend, William J. Davis, Esq., "is related of *Sam*, (as Samuel Fraunces was familiarly called,) who was always anxious to provide the first dainties of the season for the General's table. It appears that Sam, on making his purchases at the Old Fly Market, observed a fine *shad*, the first of the season; he was not long in making the bargain, and it was sent home with his other purchases. Next morning it was duly served up in Sam's best style, for the General's breakfast. The General, on sitting down to the table, observed the fish, and asked Sam what it was: he replied, that 'it was a fine shad.' 'It is very early in the season for them,' rejoined the General. 'How much did you pay for it?' 'Two dollars,' said Sam. 'Two dollars! I can never encourage this extravagance at my table,' replied Washington. 'Take it away—I will not touch it!' The shad was accordingly removed, and Sam, who had no such *economical* scruples, made a hearty meal on the fish at his own table."‡

Does not the mind of the honest reader naturally lead to some of the following reflections? Will this *high office* ever again, from among the millions of men, be filled with such a combination of examples— Wisdom, Honesty, Simplicity, Frugality, and Temperance? (leaving out the "Soldier.") No—would be the immediate response—although we have not the tongue to say, *we have them not;* yet, that class of men are not destined—cannot be placed in that exalted position—because the people are not the *power;* but there is the ma-

* Lincoln's Lives of the Presidents, p. 66.
Watson's Annals New York, p. 352.   ‡ Valentine's Manual, 1854, p. 551.

chine power, high above the people—who *grinds* the many, to serve a small and the worst portion of that people. If time would condescend to make it once more *fashionable* to select such men to guide and govern this nation, or any part or parcel thereof, what a happy people that generation will be—so filled with those feelings, so much enjoyed by all who lived under Our Washington's Administration!

And as to the amusements—more especially to the public assemblies—instead of eleven or twelve o'clock at night before it was *fashionable* to enter the ball-room, in "olden time" respectable people, who valued health and a vigorous body for the next day's duties, at these hours were preparing for rest. The hour *then* to be ready on the *floor* is better described by—"Mr. Picken respectfully informs the Ladies and Gentlemen of New York, that his public *Dance* will be on Monday next, at the 'City Assembly Rooms,' to begin *precisely at five o'clock* in the evening. Price of Tickets, *(not two nor five dollars, but)* six shillings, to be had at the City Tavern."*

The hour for starting on a sleighing party was one o'clock, P. M., when "away they went, animated by the jingle of one or two cowbells, to take a cup of hot tea and have a dance at Madame T——'s, at H——. Cæser, on their arrival, tuned his three-stringed fiddle; the gentlemen appeared in their square-toed pumps, and the ladies shook off their *pattens, (over-shoes,)* to display their little feet in peak-toed, high-heeled slippers; and at it they went, dancing and skipping for dear life, until eight o'clock, when they hurried to town—for to be abroad *after nine o'clock*, on common occasions, was then a sure sign of moral depravity."† Reader! if both customs were now fashionable, which would you prefer to enjoy, or wish your sons and daughters to patronize? But my reflections have carried me from my subject.

In the month of November, at a meeting of the "Board" on the 2d inst., they "Ordered, that the Public Hooks and Ladders be removed from the gangway of Mr. George Codwise to the market-house at Peck's Slip;" and the next year George Peck was paid £7, 4s., 6d. for repairs to this market-house.

When the "Catharine Market" was finished, in 1786, this market was almost deserted by its tenants; but few stands were occupied at that period, and it continued to grow worse, when, on the 7th of May, 1792, a petition was placed before the Board, stating it as "useless, and tends greatly to obstruct the street, and praying an order for its removal;" and was followed on the 22d of July, same year, with two petitions—one for and one against its removal;

---

* N. Y. Packet, Dec. 17, 1789.   † Watson's Annals, p. 212.

and finally, on the 26th of August, 1793, the Treasurer "was ordered to sell, at public vendue, the materials of the market-house
at Peck's Slip; the purchaser to remove the whole of the materials,
and fill up the street to a level, within fifteen days."

BEAR MARKET "

1771. WITHIN the recollections of the living, (1858,) this well-
known market-place and the "Fly Market" were the most prominent
public markets in the City of New York, although the "*Bear Market*" was not known until the Fly Market was more than seventy
years old.

In the month of August, 1771, the question of erecting this market-house was brought before the Common Council; and after a
spirited opposition, it was decided to build it on the west side of
Greenwich Street, between Fulton and Vesey Streets, then known
"at the Corporation lotts, to the northward of Die's Dock." Some
wished its erection at Mesier's Dock, others at Die's Dock; and others,
again, wished it to grace the present Park, the lower part of which
was then known as the "Fields," and the upper part the "Commons." The following shows the proceedings in relation to this subject: "At a meeting of the Common Council on the 19th of August,
1771, several petitions were presented by sundry inhabitants relative to the erection of a market at the respective places, as follows:
Mesier's Dock, Die's Slip, and at the Commons; and some of the
members of the Board were of the opinion that it would be most commodious and beneficial for the publick to erect the said market on
some of the lots belonging to the Corporation, lying to the northward of Die's Dock." The several places were respectively voted for.
First a motion was made, whether the market should be erected in
the Commons or at the North River, and after a long debate, the
question was put and carried against erecting it at the North River.
Then the resolution came up whether the market should be placed
in the Fields; that was also lost—eleven voting in the negative and
four in favor. Several other resolutions were also put and lost at
the several places; when the last resolution was put, "whether the
market should be erected at Mesier's Dock, or on the Corporation
lots, to the northward of Die's Dock, and carried for the 'Corporation lots,' viz., five voting for Mesier's Dock, and ten for the Cor-

poration lots." It was then further "Resolved and ordered by the
Board, that if a market be erected by the neighborhood at the place
now agreed upon, that the same do not exceed 210 feet in length and
30 feet in breadth; that a stone foundation be laid under the whole,
and that the building of the same be under the entire direction of
this Corporation."

The contemplated size was not satisfactory; it was too long, as it
would, when built, interfere with the street and shore where the market and other boats landed. The subject came up again three days
after, when a plan was shown: "Which is to contain agreeable
thereto 166 feet in length, and 28 feet in breadth, was exhibited to
this Board and approved of; and thereupon it was ordered that the
Aldermen and Assistants of the West, North, and Montgomerie Wards
be a Committee to superintend the building of the same, and see
that it be completed by the first of November next." One week
after, (29th August,) "it being represented to this Board that a
very considerable sum is already subscribed towards completing the
said market, and there being no persons properly authorized to receive the said subscription money when collected; this Board therefore, at the request of a number of the subscribers, do hereby appoint
'John Stagg,' of this city, bricklayer, to receive the same, in order
that it may be applied to the purpose for which it was subscribed."

Among the donors towards establishing this market-place, I find
"Trinity Church" contributed largely, as appears by the following
resolution: "Thereupon it is resolved and agreed that this Corporation will also contribute the sum of two hundred pounds towards
building the said market, and will release their right and claim to
the ground on which the same is proposed to be built for the use of
the market forever."

The building commenced, as appears from an editorial, which says:
"Saturday last, (30th August,) the first stone of the 'Oswego Market,' now erecting on the Corporation ground at the North River,
was laid by His Worship the Mayor, (WHITEHEAD HICKS,) and the
second by Mr. Recorder, (Thomas Jones,) and the market is to be
finished with all expedition."*

From this we find it was first called "Oswego Market," which was
caused from the fact that part of the materials of the "Broadway
Market-House," (known in its latter years as the "Oswego Market,")
when torn down, was used to assist in the erection of this market-
house, and it is probable they thought, in moving the materials, they
would also move the name; but whether so or not, it appeared to enjoy this name in some of the proceedings for above two years after.

* Gazette, September 2, 1771.

However, the main object in their *moves* did not immediately prove successful. The *trade* was not moved, as will appear from the various petitions, to introduce these facts.

Just after it was finished, (November 14,) a petition from George Stanton and Abraham D. Revier, praying a lease of two lots on the south side of the Corporation Dock, between the "Oswego Market and the North River."

This was soon after followed with a petition from the butchers in the "New Oswego Market," to be allowed to remove from it. They state: "Being butchers, exercising their trade in the new market-house, that on the removal of the Oswego (*Broadway*) Market and the erecting of the other, procured stalls and standings therein, hoping, in the honest exercise of their trade there, to gain a comfortable maintenance; that they have been greatly deceived in their expectation, but having usually exercised their trade in the western part of the city, and unwilling to lose their customers, and therefore have, to their great loss, hitherto continued their attendance in the new market. That the trifling resort of customers to that market frequently obliges them to carry their meat unsold home again, by which it depreciates upon their hands. That being no longer able to resist so manifest a loss and disadvantage without ruin to themselves and their families, are compelled to desert said market and seek some other place in which they may exercise their trade with some prospect of a subsistence, which they are confident they can never gain in their present situation. That from their certain knowledge of the supplies of provisions from the North River and the great resort of consumers at the Oswego (*Broadway*) Market, while it stood in the Broadway, they are convinced that a public market-house directly below that place and adjoining the (*North*) river will be attended with a great concourse of buyers and sellers, and tend much to promote the public convenience. That the persons who have erected, at their own cost, a large, convenient building there, (see '*Crown Market*,') are willing to devote the same to the use of a public market. They therefore pray, as they are very unwilling to abandon the western part of this town, that this worshipful Board will permit them to erect their stalls in said market-house." This was signed by

Nrs. Stakes,	Henry Spingler,	John Finck,
Francis Marmal,	Christof Tamplar,	Thomas St. Amore,
Jacob Ott,	Baltes Spingler,	Jacob Finck.

In the month of March, next year, was presented another petition from the Owners of Land and Gardeners in the "Out Ward," who bring their produce to the markets. They state, "That many of your petitioners, since the removal of the old Oswego Market, have brought their greens and other produce to the new Oswego Market. That upon tryal, they find, to their great loss, they are not able to sell one half the quantity of their truck they used to do in the old Oswego Market, which they conceive is owing to the remote situation thereof; it being no thoroughfare, and so far from the centre of the city, that few people frequent it; and those that do, come chiefly from the Church *(Trinity)* ground; and the bulk of these are of the poorer sort of people, who can't purchase much. Besides this, many of them have also gardens: of course they have no occasion to purchase any garden truck of us. Your petitioners have attempted to get relief by going to the 'Fly Market,' but it is so crowded that they can find no room to stand with their produce." They wish relief, " by giving leave to erect a public market on the lot commonly called Conroe's Lott, which they conceive would be convenient for the public and for themselves." Among the signers—above seventy—were

Cornelius Cozine, Sen'r,	Garrit Stryker,	Jellis Mandevill,
John Horson, (*Harsen*,)	James Stryker,	Peter Bussing,
Cornelius Horsen,	John Hopper,	Sam'l Delamater,
John Webbers,	Samson Benson,	Petrus Waldron.
Mathew Buyce, and others.		

Another followed from the farmers and others residing in the Counties of Orange and Bergen, signed by more than one hundred, which stated, they " bring to New York poark, butter, veal, and other country produce; all which they have brought hitherto (since the removal of the old) to the 'new Oswego Market.' That they find, by dear-bought experience, great loss and inconvenience in the sales of their produce in the present market, which is owing, as they conceive, to its standing in a place where there is no thoroughfare, and of course very few people pass and repass. That the Oswego *(Bear)* Market, which subjects us to great inconvenience and loss of time if we can't find a ready sale for our produce, because staying only one hour later in the tide puts us back often a whole day or more in our return home. Whereas, if the market stood in a place where there are many people passing it, it would enable us to make quick sales, and by that means it would save us time and expenses; all which we are convinced of by experience, having tryed both the old market in the Broadway and the one down to the North River." They wish the Corporation to give the inhabitants of the neighborhood of the old market privilege to erect a new one on "Conroe's Lott." *(See Oswego Market, in Maiden Lane.)*

After the establishment of the new market in Maiden Lane, and the Corporation had accepted the "Crown Market," many of the occupants of this were transferred into them, leaving but a few in this, although several were afterwards added; but a large part was left unoccupied.

In consequence of this, Alderman Blagge obtained permission, on the 26th of May, next year, to place a hay machine in the then called "Corporation Market at the North River." But on the 17th of the next month the Committee who were appointed to locate this machine stated, "they had fixed on the south end of the 'Oswego Market,' opposite the middle part."

However, the name of "Oswego" had been, by common consent, transferred to the new one in Maiden Lane, which act left this market without "name or fame;" but fortunately, just above this market, a fine large Bear, in attempting to cross the North River from the Jersey shore, was killed by a young butcher, from this market, named Jacob Finck, and some others, who went after him in a boat; they brought him to the market, where Finck dressed him, and where many went to see the "*Bear* down to the *market*."

These animals had been often seen and killed quite near the city, either while crossing the harbor or North River; and, at an early day, even in the city itself. " Woolley's Journal,"* written while its author was a resident of New York, about the year 1679, says: "I was one with others that have had very good diversion and sport with them, in an orchard of Mr. John Robinson's, of New York, *(now located ' in the heart of the Second Ward,')* where we follow'd a Bear from tree to tree, upon which he would swarm like a cat; and when he was got to his resting-place, perch'd upon a high branch, we dispach'd a youth after him with a club to an opposite bough, who knocking his paws, he comes grumbling down backwards with a thump upon the ground; so we after him again."

Advancing to the year 1732, I introduce a different animal into the city; the account of which is found in the *N. Y. Gazette*, July 24, which stated: " Last Thursday (20th) morning a creature of an uncommon size and shape was observed to break through a window of a store-house in this city, and jumpt into the street, where suddenly a number of spectators, who followed it till it jumpt over several high fences, and at last stuck between two houses, when they shot it. Many has had the curiosity to view it, and say it was 7 foot long. Most of them say it is a panther, but whence it came, or how it got into the store-house, we are at a loss to know."

The same paper, November 26, 1759, also notices the killing of a bear in the harbor as follows: "On Sunday week last past, a large

* Page 41, published by Gowan.

bear passed the house of Mr. Sebring on Long Island, and took to the water at Red Hook, attempting to swim across the Bay, when Cornelius Sebring and his miller immediately pushed off in a boat after him. The latter fired and missed, on which Mr. Sebring let fly and sent a ball in at the back of his head, which came out of his eye, and killed him outright."

Some four years previous, a man was killed by persons looking for a bear near this city. The account says: "Jacob Cole, an inhabitant here, being out a-gunning, on his return home saw something stir in a parcel of weeds, where, 'twas said, a bear had been seen that morning; upon which he repaired to a house nigh at hand, to get assistance in order to destroy him, when a white man and a negro, with a gun each, loaded with ball, came down to the place where he supposed the bear was, and on his arrival, he first fired, and after him the other two; they then proceeded nearer, when, to their great astonishment, they found one Cornelius Fonck shot dead on the spot, who, it was supposed, had laid himself down there to sleep."

I am told that, previous to the introduction of this bear-flesh by Mr. Finck, these animals were seldom or never brought to our markets for sale, and that but few would partake of their flesh except Indians, hunters, or slaves; but this animal, no doubt, being a fine one, and having been dressed and cut up nicely by Mr. Finck, induced many to try it, who pronounced it good eating; and from that time all the *bear's meat* that was brought to the city was carried and sold in this market, and it became known by the popular title of "*Bear Market.*"

Mitchell, Blunt, Hardie, and others, authors of Hand-Books of New York City, give this market the name of "*Bare* Market," in consequence of the sparseness of the population, business, and supplies, occasioned by the great fire which happened on the 21st of September, 1776. They state that, "in the progress of improvement, it happened that the market-house was finished long before the streets were rebuilt, or the generality of the inhabitants reestablished. As there were, for a considerable time, few purchasers, so it was seldom that a person who had provisions to sell would lose his time by exposing them there. In short, there was for a year or two, or more, a spacious building, with very little produce. This led the citizens, when they mentioned it, to distinguish it by the name of ' Bare Market,' or 'the market at which there is nothing for sale.'"

The name of "Bear Market," however, it bore years before the Revolution, and no doubt the evidence would have convinced either of those historians, were they now alive, or any others who may

read the following advertisements from the "Press:"* "All sorts
of meat to be smoaked at Bennett, Cox and Bennett's Red Herring
Manufactory, near the '*Bear Market*,' near the North River, by John
Bennett, in a peculiar method to himself, at three-pence per piece,"
&c.† The next year, "Samuel Ellis has for sale fat shad, lean shad,
and fat herring, opposite the '*Bear Market*,' at the North River."
Again, we find—"Taken out of the corner house near the '*Bear
Market*,' on the 26th of June last, the book belonging to the hay-
scale at the said market, containing the weight of all the hay at
that scale. Whoever has got said book in their possession, and
will deliver it to me, the subscriber, or give information about the
same, shall be very well rewarded for their trouble, &c. ISAAC VAN
HOOK, JUN'R."‡

The "War" soon after took place, and caused all the patriotic to
leave the several public markets; and this became almost deserted,
except in the continuation of the sale of hay, as we find noticed a
loss, or rather was "Dropped in the ruins, (*from the great fire of* '76,)
between St. Paul's Church and the *Hay Market*, a plain silver watch,
with a double plain steel chain, and one red seal set in silver, (the
impression of a bird.) Two dollars reward will be paid by John
Cox, at the sign of the King, in Cooper Street."§

We find that a great many of the public as well as private buildings were made use of for store-houses, barracks, &c. The city being under martial law, all proclamations and orders were usually
noticed in the press, and one in relation to the use of this market is
dated "Forage Office, New York, September 10, 1778. The
farmers on New York Island, Long and Staten Islands, are hereby
required immediately to thrash out their grain, as the straw is wanted for the use of His Majesty's troops, for which they will be paid
at the usual rates on producing certificates of the delivery from the
Deputy Commissioners at the different posts: at Brooklyn and
Flushing, on Long Island; at Cole's Ferry, on Staten Island; and
at Kings Bridge, Marston's Wharf; and '*Bear Market*,' on New
York Island, with the same allowance for transportation as they received last year. GEORGE BRINLEY, *Commissary Forage.*"

This agrees with what the centenarian, Mr. John Battin, told me
about this market. He said "it was used for a barrack and depot for hay, grain, and straw, and part of the time a troop of cavalry
was stationed there."

The War of the Revolution stopped the wheels of prosperity for

* N. Y. Gazetteer, December 23, 1773. † N. Y. Gazette, 1774.
‡ Constitutional Gazette, July 20, 1776.
§ N. Y. Gazette and Weekly Mercury, August 11, 1777.

many a long year; but at last a glorious peace came, and with it the oil of free government, which, after a time, set those wheels in motion again, and caused them to move more rapidly than before. A great change had taken place—many old faces had forever disappeared; the war, with its fruits—death—had driven and taken the patriotic tradesman, mechanic, and farmer from their once happy homes and prolific fields, while those who returned found almost nothing to trade with; their homes desolated, and their once beautiful fields without fences and turned into a common; and those who had acted the loyal part were, in their turn, obliged to depart for foreign shores, and some never again to behold the " land that gave them birth."

This market-house was found in a " dilapidated state and almost useless;" but it was soon after repaired by the neighboring inhabitants at their own expense.

The shore on the westerly side of this market-house ran almost up against it, when it was built, but after a period the wharf was docked out, so that " nine lots of 23 feet front, and from 60 to 90 feet in length fronting the river and slip," were sold at auction in 1784; a space of twenty-eight feet broad " should be reserved in the rear of and extending in length parallel to the market, from Partition (*Fulton*) to Vesey Streets."

About this period this market became usually known in the records as the " *Hudson Market*," which continued for many years, but the " press," in noticing the advertisements, still keep the name of "*Bear Market*." In the month of September, 1784, we find, " That the ferry across the North River, from the Corporation Wharf to Hoboken, be exposed to sale at public vendue to the highest bidder, on Wednesday, the 6th day of October next, at X o'clock in the forenoon, at the '*Bear Market*.'"*

This ferry to Hoboken was established in the year 1775 from this market, and by " Cornelius Haring, who begs leave to inform the public that he intends on Monday, the first of May next, to open the new established ferry from the remarkable pleasant and convenient situated place of William Bayard, Esq., at the ' King's Arms Inn,' from which place all gentlemen travelers and others, who have occasion to cross that ferry, will be accommodated with the best of boats of every kind, suitable to the winds, weather, and tides, to convey them from thence to the new (*Bear*) Market, near the Corporation Pier at the North River, opposite Vesey Street, in New York, at which place a suitable house will be kept for the reception of travelers passing to and from his house, and will have his boats

* N. Y. Packet, September 27.

in good order. And as his boats will always be ready to attend travellers, and those gentlemen and ladies from the City of New York, as well as those of the province *(New Jersey)* he lives in. The boats are to be distinguished by the name of the Hoobook (*noticed afterwards Hoebuck*) Ferry painted on the stern."*

In connection with the above ferry, " the flying machine that used to ply between Hackensack and Powles' Hook will, for the sake of a better and shorter road, begin on Saturday, the 13th day of May, and thenceforth continue to drive from Hackensack to Hoebuck, &c.   ABRAHAM VAN BUSKIRK."†

The same paper, two years after, (January 13,) notices—"A chaise was taken from the ferry near the Bear Market, about three weeks since; the body-carriage is painted cream color, with flower-pots on each side and back; in the latter is a cypher, O. T.; steel springs; the inside, light-colored cloth. Whoever gives information of said chaise, or will bring it to James Hallet, coach-maker, in Broadway, will receive five dollars reward, and no questions asked."

We turn again, and look in the N. Y. Packet of 1785, and find, on the 20th of January, the following notice: "To be sold by Samuel Ellis, No. 1 Greenwich Street, at the North River, near the *'Bear Market,'* that pleasant situated Island, called Oyster *(Ellis's)* Island, lying in York Bay, near Powles Hook." Greenwich Street, at that period, ended in Courtlandt Street.

In the year 1784, a strong and an unsuccessful movement was made to remove the "public slaughter-house," which stood upon a part of Bayard's Farm, in consequence of its dirty condition. Some butchers wished to kill in their own, or private slaughter-house, above a certain line; others, to the eastern part of the city; and Richard Deane, a distiller, then located just above this market, on the North River, wished to erect a public one, on and near his distillery. "That he will convey warm water from his distillery to keep it clean. The cattle can be landed at his dock from New Jersey, which may probably be an encouragement for more cattle to be brought from that quarter than has heretofore been done. That for every beast killed he shall receive the sum of two shillings, which is now the usual price paid; and that he shall have a lease for the same for thirty-one years, giving him an exclusive right." The following were the names of those butchers who signed the above petition, and no doubt they were the principal ones of this period:

Jotham Post,	John Perrin,	John Lovell,
Henrich Astor,	Henry Spingler,	Isaac Varian, Sen'r,
Jacob J. Arden,	Adam Finck,	Joseph Varian,
George Thompson,	Stephen Hilliker,	Isaac Varian, Jun'r,

* Rivington's Gazetteer, April 27.   † Ibid., May 4.

Joseph Mott,	Jacob Hilliker,	Michael Varian,
John Basley,	George Messerve,	John Pessinger,
Andrew Basley,	William Wright,	Nicholas Wethershein,
George Wilt,	Samuel Ellis,	James Manold,
Joseph Wilt,	George Hopson,	Edward Patten.

Among these, we recognize those who took a prominent part in the "Great Federal Procession" in honor of the Federal Constitution to form these United States, which took place in this city July 23, 1788. The whole was under the direction of Mr. Richard Platt, assisted by Colonel William S. Livingston, Colonel Aguilla Giles, Major Bleecker, Captains Fowler, Stagg, Dunscom, Morton, Messrs. John R. Livingston, Daniel Le Roy, Thomas Durie, Edward Livingston, Staats Morris, and John Lefferts. These gentlemen, by way of distinction, were all clad in a conspicuous uniform; that of Mr. Platt was designated by a blue coat, red sash, and white feather, tipped with black. His assistants or aids wore white coats, with blue capes and sashes, white feathers, tipped with blue, and carrying speaking-trumpets. The procession paraded at 8 o'clock, A. M., in and near the *Park*, then called the *Fields*. At 10 o'clock a salute of 13 guns was fired from the small Federal ship *Hamilton*, (which was in the procession on wheels,) as a signal to move. In the second division (of which there were ten) the butchers of this city were out in large numbers, and made a very fine display. They were headed by Mr. Jotham Post, Alexander Fink, John Lovel, and Jacob J. Arden. A flag of fine linen, neatly painted, displayed on the standard the *coat of arms*, viz., *three bullocks' heads, two axes* crossway, a *boar's head*, and two garbs, supported by an *ox* and a *lamb*, with the motto,

> "Skin me well, dress me neat,
> And send me aboard the Federal fleet."

A *slaughter-house*, with cattle dressed and killing; a *market*, supported by *ten pillars*, and another "partly up," under which was written, "*Federal Market*," supported by "*Ten*," in letters of gold; "*Federal Butchers;*" a ship, with smaller vessels. The standard was carried on a stage drawn by four bright bay horses, dressed with ribbons; a boy dressed in white rode and conducted each; on the stage a *stall*, neatly furnished; two butchers and two boys on the stage at work, splitting the lambs, cutting meats, and arranging this stall. This stage was followed by one hundred butchers, (mounted on fine horses,) with clean white aprons, and steels attached to their sides. Then came a band of music, followed with two banners appropriately painted, with their coat of arms and motto—"Federal Butchers." The one in front was supported by Mr. William Wright, and the one in rear by Mr. John Perrin.

The several trades, societies, and other large and small bodies
were numerously represented in the procession. After leaving the
Park, they proceeded down Broadway into Whitehall Street, turned
into Great Dock Street, (now lower end of Pearl,) up through Hanover Square into Queen, (now the part of Pearl above Wall.) Here,
at the corner of Wall Street, they passed an emblem representing
the "*Thirteen States,*" inclosed in a circle of about two feet in diameter—*Thirteen Stars;* ten of which were brilliant, *one* (designed
for New York) half illuminated, and two almost obscure, with the
initials of North Carolina and Rhode Island. On they went,
through Queen Street into Chatham, up Division into Arundel,
(Clinton;) turning to the left—

> "A clattering noise now strikes the ear,
> And lo! the Cooper train appear;
> The busy workmen hoop the useful cask—
> With hopes inspired, e'en toil 's a pleasing task.
> Read on their flag their future views described,
> In humble verse. *But see the Butcher tribe!*
> *Choice meat, already drest, the stall supplies,*
> *And many a figure on the canvass flies.*" *

into Bullock *(Broome)* Street, and through Bullock into Bayard's
Lane, to the high grounds known as Bunker's Hill or Bayard's
Mount, which lay east of Bayard's House, near Orange, Grand, and
Mulberry Streets.

On the eastern slope of this hill were ten extensive tables, loaded with provisions, waiting for these numerous guests. These tables
projected in direct angles from one common centre, which was a
little elevated, for the use of the members of the Congress, civil
and legislative magistrates, and strangers of distinction, who had a
complete view of the whole. The butchers on that day furnished a
capital bullock, weighing in the quarters *one thousand pounds*, which
they *roasted whole*, and presented to the procession in general.

Dr. Alexander Anderson, now eighty-six years old, who was then
a boy of some fourteen or fifteen years of age, told me "he then was
learning the art of engraving with Peter Maverick, who together
walked in this procession, each carrying engraved plates, and sat
down to the tables, which were filled with roasted beef, bread, besides
numerous casks of beer. There was an ox roasted on this occasion,
but a great part of it was unfit to be eaten, having become tainted
while in the process of cooking."

At the time of this procession, the Federal Constitution was before the Convention assembled at Poughkeepsie, and in two days
after was adopted by New York. Ten States had previously joined
under this Constitution, and the *butchers* in this procession, with

* New York Packet, August 8, 1788.

their emblems, were representing New York as *another pillar partly
up.* The broad foundation-stone had been permanently laid on the
imperishable rock; while the cautious and careful builders (among
whom was Hamilton) were examining every section of this mighty
constitutional pillar, which they in the end found perfect. These *one
hundred* patriotic butchers came forth as the common laborers to
assist, and did assist, in placing that *pillar* strong enough, that all
future ages and generations might stand and feel secure upon its
broad platform. And when the undermining, unconstitutional job-
bers or disunionists, with their *drilling tools*, attempted to bore,
break, blast, or divide a section or part of that glorious structure,
their stealthy noise was heard by the many patriotic descendants
and successors, who rose in their strength, and moved forward to
wipe them off from the face of our Republican soil.

There is another individual who has claims to notice, but whose
name does not appear in the preceding list of petitioners as his,
dated some two years after, from which I shall refer to, in sketch-
ing a few incidents of his life. It is no other than Ebenezer Winship, usually known in his day as Colonel Winship, who, on the
first battle-field of the Revolution, volunteered his services for his
country, and they were accepted. In the affair of Lexington, he,
with his kin, Simon, Thomas, and John Winship,* all farmers,
shouldered their trusty muskets, and stepped forth to fight our
country's battles. He followed on after the British troops, and was
received by Washington at Boston, where soon after he was appointed to office, and did his whole duty through the war. In 1783,
after the evacuation, he found himself in the City of New York,
with the poverty so common to all the soldiers of the Revolution,
and a large family, from whom he had been long separated. Having some knowledge of country butchering, he commenced selling
meat in this market from off the benches placed in it by the Common Council; and he continued until we find his petition, dated
January 16, 1786, before the Council, asking for certain privileges.
This petition "Humbly shews Ebenezer Winship, that being warmly
attached to the cause of America, in an early period took an active
part as an Officer in the American Army, and continued in the service during the contest; the which, being accompanied with other
misfortune, hath obliged your petitioner to follow butchering for
his and his family's support, which your petitioner hath followed
for two years past, and hath found great difficulty in killing his cattle at the *(public)* slaughter-house, agreeable to the Law of the
Corporation. As your petitioner lives two miles from the city, and
ofttimes his cattle being so wild it renders it difficult to drive them,

* Force's Archives.

and as it cannot be a nuisance to the city to kill his cattle at his house, your petitioner having no other alternative by his industry to procure a support in this city for him and his family, and the difficulty that attends his killing at the *(public)* slaughter-house, must consequently oblige your petitioner to remove from the city, unless your Honors, in your goodness, grant him this liberty, &c." His wish was not granted.

With a large family, and limited means and space to do his business, it required all his exertions to support them; but in 1794 he was successful in having a stall granted him, as will be shown in an editorial, which states he "was Colonel in the Revolutionary Army. He was in the affair of Lexington, and served his country ably and satisfactorily during the war."

It happened that in the year 1794, during the Mayoralty of Mr. Varick, a stall in *Bear Market* was given to Colonel Winship. This stall was held by the Colonel until his death, which occurred in the year 1799. It was somewhat remarkable that all six of his sons, Ebenezer, John, Samuel, Daniel, Thomas, and Jonathan, were butchers, and four of them were separately engaged in business in this market at one time, and all at different periods. His son Ebenezer was a "drummer-boy," and served under his father during a part of the war.

To give the reader an idea of the amount of fees collected at this period from the several public markets, a sworn return is made to the Mayor (who is known by the " Charter" as Clerk of the Markets) by two persons, or deputy clerks: one was Assistant Alderman Abraham Van Gelden, and the other Rynier Skaats. From the 1st of February, 1786, to the same date, 1787, these fees amounted to £583, 4s., 8d. Then, "from the Oswego, Exchange, and Hudson *(Bear)* Markets, from the 1st of February, 1787, until 31st January, 1788, both days inclusive," Rynier Skaats reports - - - - £176 9 6
From the "Fly," Peck Slip, and Catharine Markets, -   490 10 6

Total, - - - £667 0 0

In 1793, the Mayor reports having received from Rynier Skaats, for fees collected by him in the Oswego, Exchange, and Hudson Markets, - - - - - - - - - £ 404 14 10
From James Culbertson, collected in the Fly, Peck Slip, and Catharine Slip Markets, the sum of -   938 15 2

Making, in the whole amount, - - - - - £2,064 15 0

Meal and flour, after the Revolution, were sold in all of the public markets; but there were yet stringent laws attached to their sale, which perhaps can better be explained from the following petition, presented in the month of March, 1788, from fourteen dealers out of the markets. They state that, "in consequence of a law of the Corporation which prohibits our purchasing *flour* out of the market before four o'clock in the afternoon, your Honors will readily believe that it is but seldom to be bought at that time or hour; and if ever it is, then it is of such of the country people as stayes the night over, and tryes the market the next morning, and in that case always asks an extravagant price the evening before; so there is no chance for us to buy any at all, unless we pay higher than market price, unless we live in breach of the law; but in that case a freeman's liberty is taken away by his oath; and it is well known that there are hundreds, if not thousands, in this city, who cannot buy otherwise than by the *retail;* and whilst the hucksters are permitted to buy after eleven o'clock, who are no ways so serviceable to the publick as our calling, we therefore think it a hardship on us, and in some measure depriving us of getting a living for our families, besides the service we are to many others. We doubt not but your Honors will, after the considering the matter, at least put us on a footing with the hucksters, by permitting us to purchase after eleven o'clock, &c."

Two years after, (1790,) John Ackerman was "permitted to erect a scale at his door for the weighing of flour brought to market in bags," for which he was allowed a small fee. Six years after, (1796,) this office was sought after again, and at the same time the country people were accused of "imposition and fraud," and it was thought that another "weigh-master" might prevent them. James Hearn says in a petition: "The injury our fellow-citizens sustains by the unjust proceedings, it can be proved by several persons that in weight of meal a vantage of eight or ten pounds in the hundred weight has frequently taken place." He wishes this appointment, "furnishing himself at his own expense with just and lawful scales and weights thereto to weigh meal and other articles which may be brought to market, (upon oath.") He, however, was not appointed.

About this period, (1789,) Governor John Page, a delegate to Congress from Virginia, compares New York with Philadelphia, in a letter to his son. He says: "This town is not half so large as Philadelphia, nor in any manner to be compared to it for beauty and elegance. Philadelphia, I am well assured, has more inhabitants than Boston and New York together. The streets here are badly paved, very dirty and narrow, as well as crooked, and filled up with a strange variety of wooden, stone, and brick buildings, and full of hogs and mud. The College, St. Paul's Church, and the Hospital are elegant buildings. The Federal Hall, (*Wall Street*,) also, in which Congress is to sit, is elegant."

The hay machine or scale, which had been placed in the end of this market before the war, was reported on by Alderman Gilbert, October 7, 1788, that it "is improperly situated and greatly obstructs the street, and ought to be removed into the passage leading behind the '*Bear Market*,'" and it was done.

The next improvement here was the raising of the market-house "one foot six inches, and that the leasing of the cellars under the market be delayed until the said improvement be completed." The bill for this work was presented by Isaac Mead, June 2, 1792, and amounted to £69 18s. 6½d. The cellars were leased at auction on "the 3d of September, at 12 o'clock in the forenoon, on the premises, for a term of twenty-one years."*

At this period died at Brookfield, Mass., on the 3d of December, (1792,) Sarah Noble, in the 102d year of her age. "She was descended from the family of Drake in East Chester, State of New York. She remembered the time when the first sermon was delivered in East Chester, by an Episcopalian clergyman, who is supposed to have been the first missionary of that order in the State of New York. She was able to recollect when *knives* and *forks* were *first used* in the City of New York. She was the first person who brought *tea-cups, tea*, and *potatoes* in the town of New Milford."†

The increase of business here had been steadily advancing for many years, and the market-house on certain days of the week was overrun, so that many were placed outside without shelter, which gave much dissatisfaction. Petitions were presented for more shelter, and the citizens of the neighborhood asked permission to enlarge, by erecting another market-house of twenty feet in width in Vesey Street, between Greenwich and Washington Streets, which was granted.

The location on which this new building was erected is yet seen in the irregularity of this part of Vesey Street; the two market-houses appeared as follows:

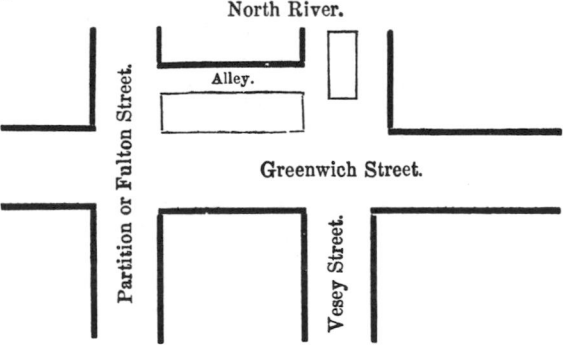

North River.

Alley.

Partition or Fulton Street.

Greenwich Street.

Vesey Street.

* N. Y. Journal, August 29, 1792.   † Phila. Daily Advertiser, February, 1792.

With a passage between them. On the north of the straight line of
Vesey is the part which Trinity Church granted "for the use of a
market forever."

This new *house* was usually noticed in some of the records as the
"Upper Hudson," and the other the "Lower Hudson;" but the
former was more generally known by the butchers and many of its
patrons as the "Buttermilk Market," in consequence of the great sale
of that article made into it, by the (Jersey) Dutch women, who daily
attended there. "Laurie Todd" says, in 1794, this market "was
supplied principally from Haverstraw, Hackensack, Bergen, and
Communipaw; and unless you could talk a good portion Dutch, it
was little use to go there to traffic."

Here, too, as at Catharine Market, the Jersey negroes would meet
on their "holidays," of which Pause or Pinkster was the principal
one, sell their trifles, crack eggs, sometimes engage in a break-down;
in this, however, they were not so early accomplished as their Long
Island friends, whom they occasionally visited at the Catharine
Market, as they were for many years placed "up head" in this great
and nimble art.

At this period the first notice of fat beef being offered for sale in
this market is placed to the credit of Samuel Winship, who says:
"Will be exposed for sale at the Hudson (No. 1 this) Market, by
Samuel Winship, on Friday and Saturday next, the finest beef now
in the city. It was fattened by Jonathan Varian. The connoisseurs
of this city and the citizens are requested to attend and partake of
the purchase, and please their tastes. Mr. Winship flatters himself
that a general and liberal attendance and purchase will be had on
those days."* Again, he says, in the same paper, on the 7th of June
following: "This day will be exposed for sale, by Peter Crawbuck,
at No. 5 Exchange Market, and by Samuel Winship, in the Hudson
Market, the finest beef now in the city. The bullock, in carved
meat, weighed 1,100 lbs., &c."

In the summer and fall of 1798, the yellow fever, as noticed before, was very fatal, more particularly on the eastern side of the
city; the North River side was more healthy, and usually furnished
less nuisances, in the way of dirty slips; but just at this market one
was found in a very filthy condition, and in the month of August it
was ordered to be filled up. Complaints were also made of several
venders of fruit and vegetables, who remained after market hours,
creating much noise until a late hour of the night. Among the complaints was one from a physician, whose name will not appear, as no
doubt his communication will be satisfactory, when read as original-

* N. Y. Journal and P. R., May 21, 1794

ly written. He addresses it to the Mayor, and says: "S^r—Our Intention is to show you the True State of bear Markett. We are Buisy filling up below, in Order to Keep Clear of filth, & M. Morrison Pays his attention in Seeing it Sweep. Mr. Culbertson (*Clerk of the Market*) also Pays his attention in Plasing the Huxsters. But when his Back is Turn^d they all Do as they think proper—they Make a Costom, When the Butchers is Gon, to Move in the Markett with their Coffee & Frute, and by that Means Collect Numbers of Idol, Drunken, & Durty Men Seting and Lying on the Stalls, So that the Butchers with Difficulty Can Scarcely make them Even Look Deasent, as the Huxsters, more or less of them, Stays until 9 or 10 O'clock at night, & their Frute Draws Large Gangs of unruly Boys, Disturbing the Peasable Inhabitants; this, S^r, you may Relye on as being Facts. New York, August 15, 1798."

The Deputy Clerks received orders to remove "all venders of fruit and vegetables from the public market-places and streets adjoining at sunset every day, except venders of vegetables on Saturdays."

This new (*Buttermilk*) market, after being finished, was wholly used by the country people and fishermen until 1796, when we find four stands in the end joining on Greenwich Street. The lower (old) market-house had received two additional stands, the year before, which increased their number to fourteen. No further additions were made to either until 1800, when two were added to the "Buttermilk Market," and soon after a Committee reported in favor of "adding six more stalls, and moving the fourteen now in up to the north end of the 'lower market.'" Making a total of twenty-six stands, occupied by the following butchers:

In the Old Market-House.

No. 1. Samuel Winship.   No. 2. Francis White.
  3. William Chivvis.   4. Daniel Spader.
  5. George Hutton.   6. John Hopkins.
  7. Jonathan Spader.   8. George Fash.
  9. Frederick Haws.   10. Henry Merkel.
  11. George Goodheart.   12. Lodowick Harpel.
  13. John Abeel.   14. Geo. Wash. Varian.
  15. Cornelius King.   16. Frederick Merkel.
  17. Christian Miller.   18. Ebenezer Winship.
  19. Francis Spicer.   20. Alexander Fink.

"Buttermilk Market."

  21. John Winship.   22. Thomas Winship.
  23. Adam Hartell.   24. John Graff, Sen'r.
  25. Anthony Rawlings.   26. Charles Gilman.

In 1802 the Market Committee, consisting of Philip Brasher, John Oothout, Winant Van Zandt, Jr., "Reported the propriety of increasing the number of butchers' stands, as follows: Catharine, 4; *Upper Hudson*, 8; *Lower Hudson*, 2; and Oswego, 4." This increased the number to thirty-six, and before they were removed, the numbers in both were *forty-eight* regular stands.

The two market-houses were again crowded, and more room was demanded, for the much-increased country visitors and the wants of the fishermen, whose number had also increased; they were accommodated by the erection of a new fish market in 1805, which we find "running at right angles with the lower (old) market, and on a line with the other (*Buttermilk*) market between Greenwich Street and the bulkhead." At the same time, "a bell of 60 to 80 lbs. weight, about the tone of G, was ordered to be hung on the top of the northwestern extremity of the "Hudson (*old*) Market, and to be protected by a small cupola."

In the face of the increased business and improvements, a Committee (without the appearance of being asked) reported on the 1st of July following, "That the ground on which Hudson (*old*) Market now stands is too valuable to be appropriated for a market, and is situated in a street too important for the purpose; that it is in a state of decay, and will be useless in two or three years. The Committee, therefore, are of opinion it will be for the public advantage to run a new bulkhead across the slip, and proceed to fill up the same, and to erect a substantial and commodious *(brick)* market on the ground to be filled up."

Although this report was confirmed, yet it was not carried out, in consequence of leases of several of the lots, which they proposed to use or sell, not having expired.

In 1807 chains were placed across Greenwich Street, to prevent interruption during market hours; they, however, were soon found to be more troublesome than useful, and the next year they were taken down.

The stalls or stands which butchers' meats were sold off, in " olden time," in many cases were mere rough-hewed benches, with a coarse tow or linen cloth laid on them. One old butcher told me that when his uncle *(John Aimes)* commenced business, he, with another, took from his house his dinner-table, and carried it down in the "Old Bear Market," from which he sold his uncooked meat for many months. Others, who were longer in business, and who felt themselves above a "bench or table," had a standing, which consisted of a narrow (wooden) *box*, without a bottom, setting down on the floor, with two upright posts, hewed (or "*axed*" out) square, pinned or nailed to the back, on which were nailed two or three bars across, filled with wrought nails as meat-hooks. These were, however, soon much improved, when they began to saw and plane the timber, and the blacksmiths to beat their hot iron into proper hooks. At this period their stalls (as they were now known) still were set on or very near the floor, and much filth collected under and behind them, which could not be got at without removal. To remedy this, the Board passed a resolution, "That each and every butcher who occupies a stall in any of the public markets shall, within six days from the date hereof, (*August* 28,) cause the said stall to be raised *eight inches* from the floor of the market, so that a broom may be admitted, to remove such dirt, filth, or rubbish. Should any refuse to comply, they will be fined five dollars, and also the further sum of two dollars for every day's neglect thereafter."

In the month of December of this year, Daniel Deavenport petitioned for stand No. 8, occupied at this period by George M. Patton; and one of his strong claims for it, he says: "His father, who is now an aged man, was in the service of his country during the Revolutionary War, and that he feels it a pleasure as well as a duty to support him." He was successful in obtaining No. 8.

Daily, though early in the morning, passing or among the crowds, at a later hour, were the sellers of hot coffee and muffins, for the tired and hungry marketmen; and these became so numerous as to draw a very large share of the trade from the victualing-houses around the markets, who complained to the Common Council. The report of a Committee on the subject, made on the 12th of March, 1810, is rather of a "flowery" nature, and deserves record here. It reads as follows:

"They say that they draw a crowd around them, such as to render business altogether impracticable." "The houses in the neighborhood of these markets are occupied principally by victualers, who calculate in the custom to be derived from market people, and have been induced to give very extravagant rents." "They are well provided with every description of viands, and can satisfactorily administer to the wants not only of the fatigued countryman, but even to the dainty appetite of the most squeamish. Everything appears inviting and nice, and the salutary beverage so much applauded for its vivifying efficacy, here flows abundantly. The early stirring and often chilled marketman can here quaff his ambrosial coffee at as cheap a rate, and with infinitely more comfort. Four cents a pint for coffee, and two cents for a muffin, is the usual price taken at the stands in the markets. So, also, in these houses they sell this, as well as every nourishment, at the same reasonable ratio." Which report was confirmed.

The subject of removing the market-house was often agitated, and in 1811 the appearances were so strong, that the butchers in it, in the month of June, petitioned the Board, "stating that, understanding a market-house was to be erected below them, praying that they may have stands assigned to them in the new market-house." Nothing, however, was done until the next year, in the month of February, when a Committee stated the reasons assigned by Major Fairlie, who was one of the Committee in 1805, why a new market-house was not erected at that period. "From him they learnt that the lots belonging to the Corporation on the west side of the new market, together with the ground in front of the line of Greenwich Street, were then considered as appropriated to the object; but that, in consequence of the leases on said lots having a long time to run, the necessary funds could not so conveniently be then raised therefrom as might be when said leases were about expiring. Your Committee, however, find that this difficulty is now obviated, and that the period is now arrived when this dormant subject ought to be revived, and the ideas of our predecessors carried into operation." "The leases on those lots will expire on the first day of May, 1813, and if it be intended to sell them, together with the ground in front, up to the line of Greenwich Street, for the purpose of erecting a new market-house, as was formerly contemplated, it will be necessary to have the same finished in season, so that the butchers who occupy stalls in the present market may transfer themselves without any interruption to that neighborhood." "They recommend that the former proceedings in relation to this subject be now carried into execution."

Before the new building was commenced, several claimants for damages presented themselves, and stated in a petition, on the 1st of February, 1813, that "Thomas Stagg and others had at their individual expense erected the market called Hudson *(old house)* Market; that, understanding the Corporation was about selling the property and removing the market, he prayed that the sale might be delayed, until compensation was made to petitioner and those concerned," which appears cost upwards of five hundred pounds. The Comptroller reported to the Board on the 8th of the same month, that "there was no reason to doubt the fact as stated. From information received from respectable sources, it was generally the practice, in former times, for individuals to contribute towards making public markets, thereby to increase the value of adjacent property, as well as to obtain other benefits accruing from such establishments. In a recent conversation with an old inhabitant in the vicinity of the Hudson Market, he mentioned that, shortly after the close of the Revolutionary War, the above-mentioned market was in a state of decay, and almost useless; that himself and others contributed to its repair, but that he did not expect the Corporation were to make indemnification; as a large, convenient, and ornamental market is erecting near the river in the vicinity of the present one; as the benefits derived in the space of forty years have probably equaled the advantages ever contemplated by the first contributors; as the precedent once made of refunding to individuals their voluntary donations, on similar occasions would open the door for a great number of ancient claims, and be the source of much difficulty and embarrassment." "The lots have already been sold, although this circumstance should have no effect on the merits of the question."

This report was agreed to, and this ended the matter; but before the new *(Washington)* market was finished, the old market-house was torn down, and the occupants were placed in or under a shed thrown up on the east side of Greenwich Street, directly opposite the former old market-house, until stands were assigned them in the newly-finished building, called the "Washington Market."

"CROWN MARKET."

1772. NEARLY forty years before the establishment of this market-place, the neighborhood had attempted to establish the "Thurman's Slip Market" on the spot where the next generation, in the year 1771, built this market-house.

We find on the 24th of January of this year a petition from the residents in the neighborhood of Thurman's Slip, asking the privilege to erect a large market-house at or near the old intended site, which was signed by Peter Mesier, John Thurman, Jr., Ralph Thurman, John Van Dalsen, Marcellus Gerbrants, Robert Leake, Abraham Bussing, Sering Lininseer, and Helena Rutgers.

The introduction of the Bear Market was then the prominent subject before the Board, but Thurman and Mesier, with the assistance of Assistant Alderman Abraham Mesier, wished to introduce their own instead of the "Bear" Market. They succeeded in obtaining permission, but no Committee was appointed to select the location;

so, on the 19th of February following, John Thurman, Jr., appeared before the Board, and offered sundry reasons to induce them to fulfill their promise. The Board agreed to leave it to some future Common Council. The petitioners, however, concluded, as they had the privilege granted before, to go on and erect a market-house; and on the 7th of Jan'y, 1772, Assistant Alderman Mesier "informed the Board that himself and others had erected a building as a market-house at the North River, and were desirous of conveying the same to the Corporation for public use." This was followed with another petition from John Thurman and others, on the 1st of March, "requesting the Board to accept this market-house," "provided the proprietors of the ground on which the said market stands do in some short period release the said ground to this Corporation and their successors." It was accepted by a large vote in favor, "and the Board do hereby establish the same building as a publick market-house accordingly."

After a time it became known as "Crown Market," after the street which ran alongside of it, although occasionally it is noticed as "Mesier's Market," and also "Thurman's Market."

In the following September, the election of the West Ward "was ordered to be held at the southernmost market, at the North River, commonly called 'Mesier's Market;'" and in the next year, same month, among the places to hold the polls, "that in the West Ward, at the 'Crown Market,'" which were the same. One other reference in an advertisement is given of it, but no name; this appears on the 14th of January, next year, as follows: "At publick vendue, on the premises, on Monday, the 24th day of January, or at private sale any time before, the dwelling-house and lot wherein Mrs. Helena Rutgers lately lived, (being a brick house two stories high,) fronting Queen (Pearl) Street, near the *Fly Market*, and almost opposite the Mayor's. Also, on the 26th January instant, three dwelling-houses and lots belonging to them, and one other vacant lot, wharf, and water-lot, (lately belonging to the estate of Petrus Rutgers, deceased,) situate at the North River fronting Thurman's Slip, near the *new market*.   "ADRIAN RUTGERS,
                                                    "RICHARD SHARP,
                                                    "JOHN MORIN SCOTT,
                                                    "BENJAMIN KISSAM."*

The name "Crown," after the emblem of royalty, the principal head ornament worn by sovereigns, was given to this street, about the year 1695, and afterwards to this market-place. The street continued with the name until about 1797, when it was altered to suit

* N. Y. Gazetteer.

an "emblem of our Republic," known as Liberty, or rather the Goddess of Liberty, as she is always represented with a *head ornament*, too, but which usually has a more democratic appearance than that of royalty in appearing in the form of a *cap*. The Goddess, no doubt, in her excessive exultation after the victorious Revolution, instead of putting the *cap* on her head, stuck it on a *pole*, in shouting independence for these United States.

There is no regular butcher noticed in connection with it, and there is no doubt that it never was much of a market-place. It ceased to exist some time during the Revolution, with the strong presumption that it was burnt up in the great fire of 1776, of which the following is a sketch: On the 21st of September, "the fire originated at or near Whitehall, soon extended to the Exchange, took its course up the west side of Broad Street, as far as Verlettenbergh Hill, (*Flattenbarrack Hill*,) consuming all the blocks from the Whitehall up. The flames extended across the Broadway from the house of Mr. David Johnson to Beaver Lane or Fincher's Alley on the west, and carried all before it, a few buildings excepted, to the house at the corner of Barclay Street, wherein the late Mr. Adam Vandenbergh lived, sweeping all the cross streets in the way. The buildings left standing on the west side of the Broadway are supposed to be Captain Thomas Randall's, Captain Kennedy's, Dr. Mallat's, Mr. John Cortlandt's sugar-house and dwelling-house, Dr. Jones's, Hall's Tavern, St. Paul's (Church,) Mr. Axtell's, and Mr. Rutherford's."* From Mr. David Grim's account: "The fire, he says, burned both sides of Beaver Street to the east side of Broadway, then crossed Broadway to Beaver Lane, and burning all the houses on both sides of the Broadway, with some few houses in New Street to Rector Street, and to John Harrison's, Esq., three-story brick house, which house stopped the fire on the east side of Broadway; from thence it continued burning all the houses in Lumbard Street, and those in the rear of the houses on the west side of Broadway to Saint Paul's Church; then continued burning the houses on both sides of Partition, (now Fulton,) and all the houses in the rear (again) of the west side of Broadway to the North River," which no doubt included this "market-house," as Hill's map of 1782 also shows the "burnt district" of 1776 as covering the part where the market-house stood.

* Philadelphia Evening Post, 1776.

"OSWEGO MARKET."

1772. THE "Old Swago Market," as it was usually called for shortness, is still green in the memory of some of our citizens. It stood for many years at the corner of Broadway, running down Maiden Lane to about Little Greene Street, on the south side, covering a part of the ground now occupied by the lower corner houses, with a wide carriage-way on the north side, and a narrow one on the south and east sides.

The "Broadway Market," commonly known as the "Oswego Market," in the last years of its existence, stood near this market-place, and was, as before noticed, indicted as a nuisance and torn down in the month of July, 1771. But a few months had passed when the inhabitants of the neighborhood, feeling the inconvenience, petitioned on the first of March (1772) following for permission "to erect a market-house on the lots of ground formerly occupied by Mr. Canaro (or Conroe's) on the east side of Broadway Street," which permission was given, "provided the proprietors release the said ground to the Corporation and their successors;" and this was the last market-place established before the Revolution.

Immediately after its erection it took the name of "Oswego Market," and the manner of raising the money to build it was by lottery. The N. Y. Journal of the 25th June, same year, says: "For raising the sum of three hundred pounds towards discharging the expenses of a market lately erected at the corner of Maiden Lane, near the place where the old Oswego Market stood in the Broadway. The lottery to consist of two thousand five hundred tickets, at two dollars each. N.B.—Not two blanks to a prize. Tickets to be had of Nicholas C. Bogert, Henry Roome, Jonathan Lawrence, and all the neighbors about the market."

The purchase-money paid for the ground, however, was not all raised in this manner, as we find several suits were commenced against Nicholas Bogert, Henry Roome, and others, who set forth in their petition in 1789, and say: "That the neighborhood, by subscription, raised a sum of money to purchase the lot of ground whereupon the Oswego Market is erected; that the monies raised fall short of the sum of £50, that yet remains due on the said bonds, for which a suit is commenced against some of the petitioners, who prayed for aid from the Corporation," and no doubt they received it.

Before the war we find the mail-rider for Albany put up in a "Taylor's shop," near this market. The "post-rider" states: "For the benefit of the public. Inasmuch as many persons frequently have business with the Albany post-rider, this is to inform them that he puts up at Mr. Joel Holmes', Taylor, fronting the south side of the Oswego Market, and is every body's very humble servant, if he is paid for it. N. B.—The printers are desired for the future to send all the papers as go by him to the above place."*

In the month of November, 1787, a butcher named Charles Dawson, in this market, "for having totally neglected his business at his stall or standing," was by resolution deposed of his license. Then, in the following month, the porters "stationed at the 'Oswaygo Market' complain, through a petition, that they have given every due attention to said place, with a desire to give satisfaction, but are latterly much deprived of our rights by many intruders who are not duly authorized, which prevents us of making a sufficiency to support our families." They pray the interposition of the Corporation, who soon after report a law to regulate porters.

One of the principal market-women, who daily attended at this market both winter and summer, was Mrs. Frances Banta, (usually known as "Aunt Frankey,") one of the daughters of Philip Minthorne, and a sister to Mangle Minthorne. On some eight or ten acres left to her by her father, near the present corner of Third Street and Bowery, she lived, and grew her produce or market truck. Her father, while living, had owned about 110 acres of land running along the east side of the Bowery Road, commencing from about First Street and running up to Fifth Street, thence in an easterly direction to the East River, taking in a part of the present "Tompkins Square," which then was a salt marsh. This property old Minthorne divided up into nine parts, and bequeathed it equally to his nine children, when it afterwards became known as the "nine partners," giving each one a *slice* or small front on the Bowery, which ran easterly, gradually increasing to a greater width, and ended in a Lane that ran parallel with and a little east of the First Avenue. The balance of this property on the east side of the Lane was at that period divided by another Lane which ran easterly, and was principally all meadow or marsh land. This was divided on the north side of the Lane into "nine parts," and on the south side into nine other parts, and these three divisions were numbered, so that each had an equal share of both good and poor land.

The Bowery division commenced with the first division on the south end, and the following will show who inherited them. No. 1,

* N. Y. Gazette, March 7, 1774.

Nicholas Romaine, son-in-law, who married Margaret; No. 2, Viert Banta, another son-in-law; No. 3, Philip Minthorne; No. 4, Samuel Hallet, married Sarah; No. 5, Paulus Banta, the husband of Frances, or "Aunt Frankey;" No. 6, Henry Minthorne; No. 7, Mangle Minthorne; No. 8, John Minthorne; and No. 9, Abraham Cox, another son-in-law.

In the month of March, 1775, Paulus Banta advertises, "To be sold, a lot of ground containing about 8 acres; one acre and three-quarters is salt meadow, being in the 'Out Ward' of this city, in the Bowery Lane, whereon is a good dwelling-house and barn, &c. If not sold by the 18th of April, to be then sold by way of public vendue on the premises."* A week after, another notice of a house and lot to be sold in " Dirick Dye's Street;" apply to Paulus Banta at the said house.

Each market-day found "Aunt Frankey" ready for an early start, with her produce placed in her market-cart over night, and before daylight next morning she was on her way down the Bowery Road, and into this market, ready to serve the then early risers, who were anxious to get the choice. Her surplus vegetation was housed or buried in the earth for the winter's sales and extra profits; and she raised a large family, two of whom were daughters, whom she taught the same *accomplishments*, or rather habits of industry so peculiar to those early days. No doubt one of these daughters even exceeded the mother, as will be perceived in a sketch of her history in the Union Market; the other is also noticed in the Centre Market.

The working ladies of that day, in their early rising, had but little fear of an attack of rowdies or robbers; and if so, they had self-possession and the advantage of an active out-of-door life, which assisted to give them strength enough to resist or conquer the assailant. Incidents would occasionally occur to these early-rising market-women, one of which is noticed as follows. The Press says: "A market-woman a few mornings since was coming to market very early, attended by a favorite dog. In passing the Bowery, the dog strayed from the road into an adjacent field; the woman repeatedly called the cur, but to no purpose; this surprised her, as he had hitherto been very obedient to his mistress's mandate; she at length left her cart, determined to see what attracted the dog's attention, when, to her astonishment, she beheld a living infant lying on the ground, apparently but a few hours old, with a bundle of clothes, and a purse containing 50 guineas. The woman took the infant, with its appendages, and conveyed it safely to her home, where she will doubtless humanely treat the little unfortunate innocent, as well

* Rivington's Gazetteer.

on account of the uncommon adventure as the reward which accompanied it."*

A few days previous, in the same month, a great excitement was created in this city, afterwards known as the "Doctors' Mob." It appears from the several accounts, that some persons, among whom it was thought several students of medicine, or young doctors, had at various times dug up from several of the cemeteries of this city a number of dead bodies for dissection, which had been conducted in so indecent a manner, that it raised considerable clamor among the people. They had not only taken up the bodies of blacks and strangers, but those of some respectable persons. These circumstances had considerably agitated the public mind; "and it was further provoked," says Judge Duer, "by the reckless and wanton imprudence of some young surgeons at the Hospital, who from one of the upper windows exhibited the dissected arm of a *subject* to some boys who were at play on the green below. One of them, whose curiosity was thus excited, mounted upon a ladder used for some repairs, and as he reached the window, was told by one of the doctors *to look at his mother's arm.* It happened, unfortunately, that the boy's mother had recently died, and the horror which had now taken the place of his curiosity induced him to run to his father, who was at work as a mason at a building in Broadway, (no doubt on Saturday, April 12,) with the information of what he had seen and heard. Upon receiving the intelligence, the father repaired to his wife's grave, and, upon opening it, found that the body had been removed. He returned forthwith to the place where he had been at work, and informed his fellow-laborers of the circumstances: their indignation and horror at the relation were nearly equal to his own. Armed with the tools of their trade, they marched in a body to the Hospital, gathering recruits by the way, in number amounting to a formidable mob." They could not have attacked the Hospital that day, as the N. Y. Packet states: "Last Sabbath (13th of April) afternoon, a number assembled and broke into the Hospital, where, 'tis said, some mangled bodies of the dead were found." "The mob attacked several young doctors present, and mauled them considerably; but the Mayor and Sheriff, with the help of some other gentlemen, got the population dispersed, but several of them were struck, and received much abuse and insult."

"On Monday morning, a number of people collected together, and commenced to search the houses of the suspected physicians, where they did much mischief and damage. The Governor, Chancellor, Mayor, and others, finding the passions irritated, went among them,

* Packet, April 25, 1788.

and endeavored to dissuade them from committing any excesses. They promised them every satisfaction the laws could give; this tended to allay the excitement upon many, who retired to their homes. But in the afternoon a mob of a different character, who were more fond of riot and disorder, went to the jail, and demanded the doctors who were there imprisoned. The magistrates were obliged to order out the militia, to suppress the riot and protect the jail. At dusk a party of armed citizens marched to the release of the jail, and as they approached it, the mob, huzzaing, began a heavy fire of stones, brickbats, &c. Several of the party were much hurt, and in their defence were obliged to fire, which killed three or four persons, and a number wounded, which finally dispersed the mob."

The Brigade under General Malcom and Colonel Bauman's Artillery were out several days and nights after in detachments; but the mob did not again collect, and the peace of the city was again restored. It appears from the following letter of General Malcom to the Mayor and Corporation, that he had one (at least) wounded man in his ranks. This was dated "*New York, September* 2, 1788.—The bearer is Ephraim Totten. As a good citizen, he turned (out) with me upon the volunteer party which rescued the goal from the rage of the mob in April last, and among many others who performed that unpleasant duty, received a severe wound, which has not only prevented him from pursuing his trade since that time, but has also involved him in considerable expenses. Such a case, I dare say, will be deemed a proper one for the interposition of the Common Council; and I am persuaded your Honor will cheerfully present and recommend it to the Board, &c. W. MALCOM. Mr. Totten is a sergeant in the militia."

Then follows a certificate from some of the officers. "Being officers of the Company in which Mr. Totten received his unhappy wound, justice and humanity induce us fully to concur with General Malcom in the preceding representation. Your Honor's most obedient, humble servants, NICHS. J. ROOSEVELT, Adj't 3d Reg't. JOHN WOODWARD, Capt. 4th Company, 3d Reg't." Two doctors' bills are also presented for services rendered to Mr. Totten. From Dr. William Moore: "For medicine, attendance, &c., from April 14 to June 15, 1788, £9, 19s., 0d." From Nic's Romayne, M.D.: "For attendance and consultation with Dr. Moore, &c., £3, 4s., 0d."

The business and growth of the neighborhood around this market at this period appears progressing, and the neighborhood "were for increasing the accommodations for the country people;" so, in 1792, permission was given "to extend the roof of the 'Oswego Market' over the side-walk, to shelter and accommodate them."

Some two years after, Grant Thorburn appears to have become almost a daily visitor at this market, as will appear from his letters published by General George P. Morris & Co. in the *New York Mirror and Home Journal.* He locates it with " the west end resting on Broadway, and the east end near No. 20 Maiden Lane; and there it stood in 1794, when I first saw it. At that time I was forging nails in Liberty, opposite Little Greene Street. At that time peaches were cheaper than potatoes. I used to go round after dinner, as the Bergen negroes were packing up, and get my apron nearly full for a three-penny Corporation bill. I think it was in 1796 that Mrs. Jeroleman set a table in the market to sell hot coffee for three-pence a cup, and dough-nuts for one penny each. Her table was the first of this description that I remember to have seen. She was a large woman, and reported to weigh two hundred and twenty-five pounds—a genuine *vrow* from the heights of Bergen. As she moved in the market with her broad Dutch face, the butcher-boys sung out, ' There goes the large dough-nut.' "

In another letter he says: " I often spent part of the hour that was allotted me for dinner in this market, in listening to the Bergen farmers and freemen of the city bargaining in the Dutch language. What a confusion of tongues! It appeared to me a perfect Babel. I could hardly prevail upon myself to believe that the Mynheers possessed a language; that they had a medium whereby they could exchange their sentiments, express their wants and wishes, and give utterance to those feelings which form a part and parcel of our nature; or, if so, they had pretty much the same mode of communicating their ideas as the wild-geese of my own country, as well as using a somewhat similar language; little thinking that my own native tongue must sound equally harsh and uncouth in the ears of my honest Dutch friends, who then, by-the-by, had the ascendency in the city, in point of numbers. For the benefit of the rising generation, be it known, at the time I am speaking of, there were more arrivals from Amsterdam than from Liverpool!"

" I have a distinct recollection of an ancient-looking colored man, who rejoiced in the *sobriquet* of ' Coppie Gillie.' He used to hang about the market, and perform such odd chores as were required of him by the butchers. It was said that he was the last of that unfortunate company who were engaged in the Negro Plot of 1741-2, and, from the participation in that affair, had acquired that nickname."

The additional accommodations, previously noticed, were soon taken up, and the business appeared to be approaching to the highest point of its history, which no doubt was between the years of

1795 and 1800; and there is no better sign than to find very many persons naturally anxious to crowd into a crowd. Here we find, in the month of November, 1797, a petition from the butchers of this market, stating, "They have been informed applications has been made by certain butchers for stalls in the said *(Oswego)* market." They humbly pray "that the upper end of the said market, above the stalls of Alexander Fink and Adam Fink, may be reserved for the country people resorting to the said market; and if any more stalls are allowed in the said market, that they may be placed in the lower part thereof." This was signed by

Alex'r Fink, Sen'r,	Adam Fink,	George Ship,
Jacob Appley,	George Haws,	Cornelius King,
Alex'r Fink, Jun'r,	Adam Hartell,	Francis Spicer,
John Boscawen,	John Lyons,	William Perrin,

and Peter Ritter.

The first name, Alex'r Fink, Sen'r, was an old butcher, who had formerly stood in the "Broadway Market," as had also his brothers, Adam, John, Jacob, and Abraham; and no doubt their father before them (who bore the name of Alexander) had there transacted the same business. Before and shortly after the Revolution, the name was spelled Finck, and so it was continued in some of the old Directories; but about 1790 many of the family changed it to Fink, as at present known.

Among the signers, also, is Alex'r Fink, Jun'r, a son of the above Alex'r, Sen'r, who lived within my recollection; in fact, they were a large family, many of whom were butchers. The above Alex'r, Sen'r, before he commenced business in the former "Oswego Market," was admitted a freeman, (then Jun'r,) which took place in the year 1765, and is noticed as follows: "By John Cruger, Esq., Mayor, and the Aldermen of the City of New York. To all whom these presents shall come, send *greeting*. Whereas Alexander Finck, Jun'r, butcher, hath made application to be made a freeman, and citizen of the same city. These are therefore to certify and declare, that the said Alexander Finck is hereby admitted, received, and allowed, a freeman and citizen of the same city; to have, hold, use, and enjoy, all the benefits, privileges, franchises, and immunities whatsoever granted or belonging to the same city. In testimony whereof, the said Mayor and Aldermen have hereunto caused the seal of the said city to be affixed. Witness, JOHN CRUGER, Esq., Mayor, the twenty-third day of October, in the fifth year of the reign of our Sovereign Lord, *George the Third*, by the grace of God, of Great Britain, France, and Ireland, King, defender of the faith, &c., and in the year of our Lord 1765. By order of the said Mayor.

"AUG. V. CORTLAND, *Cl'k.*"

George Ship, one of the butchers there, was somewhat a remarkable business man; although possessed of no education, or rather he could not read nor write, yet, with tact, he managed to transact a large business successfully. He was born in the Landgraviate of Hesse-Cassel, and on the commencement of the Revolution, he, with others of his Hessian countrymen, were hired to fight the battles of the British; but very early he left, or deserted, and entered into the service of the Americans, in which he continued until peace, first in the "Mrs. Washington Guards," a Regiment of Light Horse, under Lieutenant-Colonel Baylor, the story of whose surprise and massacre at Tappan formed one of the bloodiest episodes of the war; and then as wagon-master in the auxiliary French army. After peace he commenced business in this market, with Jacob Appley, with whom he continued several years: he, however, obtained stand No. 5, and although he was, at times, somewhat eccentric, with some humor, yet, by diligence and frugality, he obtained a large share of the business. Ofttimes he became the *butt* of several of the other butchers, of whom Haws, Appley, Fink, and King were most prominent in working up some practical or other joke. Ship was always anxious to hear the news, when a newspaper could be obtained, and invariably called on his friend Haws to read for him; which he would do, with the paper likely upside down, some great or horrible occurrence, which he knew would either surprise or annoy Ship, and in the end create a hearty laugh. But Ship sometimes managed to get even with them, when opportunity offered; and about the year 1802 a remarkable circumstance of an exciting nature did occur, when he outgeneraled them for quite a period, although he was not aware that he was the origin of what proved to be a wonderful ghost hoax, until preparations were made to "head the spectre off."

A watchman somewhat vigilant, as well as a strong believer in supernaturals, had occasionally seen after the midnight hours a swift-footed, mysterious-looking and noiseless phantom, which appeared like a horse and rider, who almost flew over the ground, and at every leap sparks of fire would be seen at both ends of this singular object while passing down Elizabeth Street, and disappear somewhere below the Bull's Head yards, which extended through to this street. In this neighborhood were also the residences and slaughter-houses of several of these butchers who stood in this market, as it was also Ship's. This watchman had told this marvelous story so often, that many had watched with him, and believed it was no other than a real *live ghost*.

Ship was the owner of an excellent swift racing mare, and, having belonged to a cavalry company, he was an expert rider; this animal he used some two or three times a week when he went to visit a very intimate friend, who lived in Spring Street, not far from the "Manhattan Well,"* and when he did so it was universally late, often in the small hours of the morning, when he started to return; his mare, then anxious to get home, would not allow the grass to grow under her feet, while passing through Spring to Elizabeth and down that street to her stable. After a time Ship found he was watched, but he also discovered that he was the "great ghost" that so many had seen, and not a few so much afraid of; and concluded that so long as they did not molest him, he would not allow them to grow the wiser; so on every light night he was disguised with a white sheet wrapped around him, and thus homeward he rode many a night; however, at last, some of his butcher friends got knowledge of it, and waited one night to see this flying ghost, when they soon came to the conclusion that it was Ship's mare. The next day they accosted Ship, but he *knew nothing* about it, and offered to assist in taking or stopping the ghost, by placing a barrier across the street, which was done. Ship, however, marked its lowest and weakest spot, where he knew his gallant mare could clear without trouble; so midnight came, and soon after the white rider and mare came flying down, and over she went and disappeared. This established the fact, when hundreds believed and reported all sorts of ghost stories; but Haws, Graff, and many other butchers, concluded to head the ghost off and adopt something that would put a stop or an end to many of the ghost-affrighted stories, which had now become quite current in many parts of the city; so they gathered together all the old carts, boxes, timber, &c., and erected a barrier high enough to stop *Old Nick* himself, if he should come that way. Ship had also willingly lent his aid to build this grand barricade, and, this being one of his visiting nights, he concluded not to disappoint *anybody;* so after dusk, all being yet quiet, he mounted his mare to take his usual ride and keep the ghost's great reputation up which it had now obtained. A little later hour than usual the clattering heels and streams of fire were heard and seen, and the noble steed came rushing down this haunted street, while many an eye and mouth stood open wide enough to take in this fearful sight; but just before the barricade was reached, a sudden turn to the left was made across the lots into the Bowery Lane, and down she went in Bayard Street and quickly disappeared into her stable; but some of the butchers were there waiting in the dark, and as soon as Ship had dismounted, two or three grabbed him; when he, having the advantage of strength and activity, slipped out of their grasp by leaving his coat and sheet

* See Spring Street Market.

behind, when he escaped to his house. The evidence, however, was overpowering, and "George Ship's Ghost" was for many years a laughing joke among the people of the neighborhood, and many of the old butchers of New York recollect it to this day.

Continued changes in the occupancy of certain stands were also taking place, as well in this as in every market-house in the city; in fact, it is the prominent trait in most of the human family usually to "keep the stone rolling that never collects the moss;" while a few others, again, will settle themselves down and remain fixtures on the spot once chosen, until forced by death to change. We find but five of the above petitioners of '97 left in 1802, and but nine of the stands occupied, as follows:

No. 1. Alexander Fink, Sen'r.	No. 2. Adam Fink.
3. Jacob Jeroleman.	4. Jacob Appley.
5. George Ship.	6. George Haws
7. Philip L. Luff.	8. Jacob Tier.
9. Vacant.	10. Vacant.
11. Vacant.	12. Henry Smith.

The occupant of No. 8, Jacob Tier, was in his day somewhat remarkable for great strength, endurance, activity and fearlessness, but withal of a quiet and amiable disposition. In an early day, for a large wager, he had performed a remarkable feat, by wheeling a common wheelbarrow from his house, corner of Bowery Lane and Grand Street, all the way (and it was a rough way at that period) up to Kingsbridge, within a given time, which he easily won.

He was always a friend to the aged or weak, and a foe to the *bully* or braggart, whom he detested, when they attempted an imposition. Perhaps this latter feeling was the cause of his having engaged, although at an advanced age, in a desperate battle, which is thus noticed: "A few days since, five or six armed soldiers took a fancy to march abreast on the side-walk in the Bowery, sweeping every man, woman, and child they met with into the snow. At length, coming up to a poor man who was sawing wood and piling it on the side-walk, they ordered him to remove his wood, that they might march without impediment. The sawyer not readily complying with the command, one of them struck him on the head with the butt-end of his musket, and cut his hat through to his head. They were proceeding to abuse him further, when Mr. (Jacob) Tier, a butcher and an aged man, between 70 and 80, interfered; on which the soldiers began to ill-treat him also. At this moment a sleigh with a number of butchers, friends of Mr. Tier, coming up, they immediately landed, attacked the soldiers in turn, disarmed them in an instant, and gave them such a drubbing that they soon ordered a retreat; and it is not probable this party will again be found abusing peaceable citizens."* I am told that William Vonck was one, and the leader of this party, who, after disarming them, took their muskets into the Bull's Head Tavern, where they remained until the soldiers made a suitable apology.

In the month of August, 1804, John Pintard, the Inspector, recommended that " so much of the 'Oswego Market' as is unoccupied by the butchers be taken down, and that the remaining part be repaired." The same year the Humane Society acknowledges the receipt of " 16 calves' heads from the butchers" of this market.

The building of a new and extensive *market* on the west side of Washington Street (afterwards "Washington Market") had been agitated for some years, and it was partially arranged that when this was built, they would do away with the *Oswego Market*, as it had now become old and dilapidated, although it had some repairs in 1807.

In the month of March, 1810, "will be offered for sale to-morrow (Saturday, 31st,) morning, at the stall of Alexander Fink, Sen'r, No. 1 'Oswego Market,' and at the stall of Alexander Fink, Jr., No. 22 Bear Market, the fattest beef that has been for sale this season, being twins, a steer and a heifer, fed by Mr. Hezekiah Howell, of Orange County, N. Y."

In the following month of May a resolution was passed to remove the present *Oswego Market-House* into Vesey Street, below Washington Street, and to erect such part of it as they may think proper. This, however, appears not to have been carried out at this time, as I find on the 3d of June a petition from the butchers in this market praying that stands in the new (Washington) market about to be erected may be assigned to them, equally advantageous in point of situation with those they now occupy; which was conformed to; and the next year, (1811,) on the 6th of May, a resolution was passed, " that the Street Commissioner ascertain the line of Mr. Binninger's property, and that the *market-house* and engine-house be immediately removed;" and no doubt the " *Old Swaga*" Market's sound *bones* and *ribs* were left in the present "Washington Market," which will in a few short years be again disturbed.

* Evening Post, February 10, 1813.

"CATHARINE MARKET."

1786. IN the year 1786, Mr. Henry Rutgers, with several of the prominent inhabitants in the vicinity of Catharine Street, "prayed permission to erect a public market-house at Catharine Slip, at their own expense." They were to furnish the ground and put it up forthwith. A Committee, however, was appointed "to determine the place and the manner of building the market-house." They located it on nearly the same spot where the present iron market-house stands, with the west end facing Cherry Street; the south side just cleared the north side of Catharine Street, and the east end not quite down to Water Street. In less than a month (June 28) Mr. Rutgers informed the Board that the market-house was ready for the reception and accommodation of butchers and country people. It took its name from the slip and street, which were named after the wife of Captain Harman Rutgers, whose residence was near where Catharine Street now connects with the Bowery.

Several of the butchers remaining in the *Peck Slip Market* were then, by their wish, removed into this market, when it soon commenced doing a good business, and yearly increased it; having a great many country people visiting it, both from Long Island and Westchester County, who were principally ranged on the north side, under temporary sheds and awnings.

The first fisherman introduced at this market was in the year 1797, when Mathias Wessels petitions, in the month of May, "to obtain liberty to erect a shed building on one side of Catharine Slip Market, for the purpose of exposing to sale all kinds of fresh fish brought to this city." The citizens in the neighborhood, to the number of sixty-eight, petition, and "beg leave to observe, that we should consider a fish market at Catharine Slip as a very great favor. The mode of establishing so desirable and valuable a privilege to the inhabitants of this quarter of the city we submit to your wisdom and discretion, hoping you will consider it an object worthy your immediate attention." This privilege was soon after granted.

In the following month of August a great commotion was created, from the finding of several parts of a human body in the slip at this market, by some of the market people, early on the morning of the 19th inst. The following account gives more of the details:

" Last Saturday morning, between seven and eight o'clock, the flesh
of the late unfortunate criminal (or some other man) was found
floating in Catharine Slip, which, with the last parts of his body, were
carried to Long Island, and there buried by John Bell. We are
credibly informed that this shameful exposure was not through the
wantonness of the surgeons, as supposed, but of the *porters* employed to sink them, being contained in a bag, with weights for that
purpose; but it seems the porters conceived the bag of value, and
by this means the parts were set afloat."*   This was proved to be
the body of the criminal, John Young, from the communication of
Drs. John B. Hicks and Richard S. Kissam, who say: " In order to
avoid any unnecessary injury to the feelings of the persons who had
assembled to see the execution, the body *(of John Young)* was conveyed to Potters Field, from whence, at a late hour of the night, it
was carried to the Anatomical Theatre, where we commenced and
finished the dissection, in as decent and secret a manner as the nature of the business would admit of. We have to regret that the
persons to whom the remains of the body were committed to be in-
terred, being apprehensive that, if buried in the yard, it might be
discovered, and lead to disagreeable consequences, deemed it expedient to commit the same to the bottom of the river. In their
alarm and confusion, they neglected to give the bag the necessary
weight to sink it, in consequence of which the following morning it
was found floating."

This "Young" had committed murder in the month of June previous, which was noticed in the "press"† as follows: "About sunset
last evening, (June 28,) as Mr. Robert Berwick, Deputy Sheriff, was
conducting one 'Young,' an English musician, *(bassoon-player at the
Theatre,)* to goal, Young shot him through the body, and he expired
immediately. He had him in custody for debt, and had been waiting on him to several places for the purpose of procuring bail, but
had refused to go to any ' other place.' Young found that he must
go to prison, sprang away from Berwick, drew a pistol, and shot
him. He was immediately secured, shortly after tried, condemned
and executed."

The steady increase of business soon found the market accommodations too small, and in the month of August, 1799, a petition from
thirty-five of the prominent citizens near by asked "for a new and
enlarged market-house at Catharine Slip;" and although the subject was postponed for a time, yet we find the market-house finished
in 1800. In the month of October, a Committee, consisting of Aldermen Richard Furman, John Bogert, Mangle Minthorne, Jotham
Post, and Philip J. Arcularius, reported, that they " are of opinion

* New York Journal, &c., August 23, 1797.   † Ibid., June 29, 1797.

that *sixteen stands* for butchers should be granted in the said market, and that the *nine* who held stands in the old market should have the preference; that the most proper disposition of the said stands would be, to affix an annual rent, in preference to selling them" at public auction. The public sale of stands in the Fly Market, in 1796, had been much regretted by the Corporation, who soon found out that, in departing from the old-established rule of disposing of butchers' stands in the public markets, had and would lead to favoritism or injustice, and in the end be extremely pernicious in its consequences. About two years after the sale of these stands, the Corporation appointed a Committee " to repurchase them, by refunding to the fourteen butchers the money they had paid for them, together with interest, if they would reconvey the stalls to the Corporation. The butchers, however, preferred to part with their money, and keep their stalls *in fee*. They would not reconvey; they found themselves independent with their stands, and they viewed them as estates for their children, &c." This fact is proven by the following certificate, made by Daniel Winship, August 15, 1806, who says: " The Corporation appointed a Committee to confer with the *fourteen* butchers of the Fly Market who had purchased stalls. I was one of the fourteen who had purchased: the butchers appointed a Committee to confer with the Committee of the Corporation. We met the Committee of the Board, who made several proposals to us, all of which I do not remember; but I recollect perfectly that they wanted to get the stalls back, but we would not consent. They then wanted us to agree that, after holding the stalls twenty years, they should return back to the Corporation. To this we objected. We objected because, according to the sale, we viewed them as our own property, and the property of our heirs.   DANIEL WINSHIP."

These no doubt were the prominent reasons that no more should be sold at public auction, but that an annual rent should hereafter be affixed to each butcher stand; and the balance of these sixteen stands in this market, after the " *old nine*" had taken their choice, the other seven should be drawn for, which left them occupying their stands in the following manner:

No. 1. Francis J. Dominick.	No. 2. Jacob Varian.
3. Andrew Paff.	4. Jacob H. Varian.
5. Mathew Goodman.	6. William Moore.
7. George Thompson.	8. John Lyons.
9. Smith Townsend.	10. Christian Hartell.
11. John Boscawen.	12. William Perrin.
13. John Waters.	14. Michael Nestler.
15. John Smith.	16. Isaac Wood.

Among these were several "regular jokers," full of life and fun, and fun they would have sometimes at considerable cost. The first introduction in this city of public "negro dancing" no doubt took place at this market. The negroes who visited here were principally slaves from Long Island, who had leave of their masters for certain holidays, among which "Pinkster" was the principal one; when, for "pocket-money," they would gather up everything that would bring a few pence or shillings, such as roots, berries, herbs, yellow or other birds, fish, clams, oysters, &c., and bring them with them in their skiffs to this market; then, as they had usually three days holiday, they were ever ready, by their "negro sayings or doings," to make a few shillings more. So they would be hired by some joking butcher or individual to engage in a jig or break-down, as that was one of their pastimes at home on the barn-floor, or in a frolic, and those that could and would dance soon raised a collection; but some of them did more in "turning around and shying off" from the designated spot than keeping to the regular "shake-down," which caused them all to be confined to a "board," (or shingle, as they called it,) and not allowed off it; on this they must show their skill; and, being several together in parties, each had his particular "shingle" brought with him as part of his stock in trade. This board was usually about five to six feet long, of large width, with its particular spring in it, and to keep it in its place while dancing on it, it was held down by one on each end. Their music or time was usually given by one of their party, which was done by beating their hands on the sides of their legs and the noise of the heel. The favorite dancing-place was a cleared spot on the east side of the fish market in front of Burnel Brown's Ship Chandlery. The large amount collected in this way after a time produced some excellent "dancers;" in fact, it raised a sort of strife for the highest honors, *i. e.*, the most cheering and the most collected in the "hat." Among the most famous in their day was "*Ned*" (Francis,) a little wiry negro slave, belonging to Martin Ryerson; another named Bob Rowley, who called himself "*Bobolink Bob*," belonging to William Bennett, and *Jack*, belonging to Frederick De Voo, all farmers on Long Island; (the latter owned a farm of 20 odd acres of ground in the centre of what is now Williamsburgh, fronting on the river, running easterly between 7th and 8th Streets.) Jack was a smart and faithful man, and when he was set free by the laws, he became, after a time, a loafer, and died at this market. He was brought up by Mr. De Voo, who thought a good deal of him, and on the day when he was made free, he fitted him out in a new suit from "top to toe," and then said to him: "*Jack*, if you go home with me, you shall never want; but if you leave me now, my home shall never more know you." *Jack* could not be persuaded to return home by many of the butchers and others, but would stay in the city. It was not long before his former master was importuned by several persons to take him back, but his answer was: "The laws set him free and he left me—now let the laws take care of him." Many New Jersey negroes, mostly from Tappan, were after a time found among them, contending for the prize, and oftentimes successfully too; they were known by their suppleness and plaited forelocks tied up with tea-lead. The Long Islanders usually tied theirs up in a cue, with dried eel-skin; but sometimes they combed it about their heads and shoulders, in the form of a wig, then all the fashion. After the Jersey negroes had disposed of their masters' produce at the "Bear Market," which sometimes was early done, and then the advantage of a late tide, they would "shin it" for the Catharine Market to enter the lists with the Long Islanders, and in the end, an equal division of the proceeds took place. The success which attended them brought our city negroes down there, who, after a time, even exceeded them both, and if money was not to be had "they would dance for a bunch of eels or fish." I have been often told that much of this dancing took place on Sunday mornings; but this was not so, although there were always large collections on that day with their trifles to sell, and their friends to meet or visit.

But few butchers at this period kept horses and carts, and only those who were doing a large business and lived some distance from the markets; their meats were brought to the markets before daylight, and after unloading the apprentice-boy was ordered to take them home for the day, and bring down the boss's breakfast. Those who had no horse or cart, and especially those who were known as "small-meat butchers," brought their *stock in trade* in wheelbarrows.

Andrew Paff, the occupant of No. 3, did so, and, having no *boy*, his "wife brought down his breakfast, and while he was eating she would attend, and after gathering up the gambrils and sets, with the breakfast-kettle" and something for dinner, put all in the wheelbarrow and trundle it home.

An apprentice had but little to do with carrying home the customers' purchases, except now and then for a boarding-house, or the captain of a vessel, when the wooden tray came into use. Those private families who could afford to keep slaves, brought them along for that purpose, and "the man in middling circumstances of life never scrupled to carry home his marketing, or even his cwt. of meal;" he then, however, had the advantage of distance, as the city was not so extended as at the present day.

Within my recollection, it was the fashion with many persons to carry their marketing home; as an example, Dr. Samuel L. Mitchell, who lived in White Street near Broadway, (about the year 1825,) generally carried from the Washington Market, almost daily, a well-filled basket in one hand, with sometimes a large fish in the other, or something else, to balance with; and, if questioned about it, I have heard him say: " The man who was ashamed to carry home his dinner from market, did not deserve any."

I am told that the first introduction of the use of the horse and cart for that purpose was made by Jacob Aimes, of Washington Market, after it became established; and at this market Smith Townsend (noticed as the occupant of No. 9) followed on after him, but it was not general until about the year 1820.

The whole business of a butcher was conducted quite different at that time from what it is now, being on a much less expensive system. Then the butchers calculated to bring to market just about what could be profitably sold for the day, and have it all *cut up*, sometimes hours before daybreak, ready for customers and others, who made it a practice to go early to market to procure the choice pieces, as at that time there was no *reservation*, and those who came late had to take such as was left; by ten o'clock the market was considered through, although many poor persons and others, who were looking for bargains, would come after that hour or late on Saturday nights to pick up the remnants; sometimes, however, a *bad market* in hot weather would catch the butchers, and cause to be sold " a big piece for a shilling," to have a clean stall, as meats were usually less than half the price they now range, and the butchers had no refrigerators or other convenient places to keep pieces over, as they now have.

The *modern* retail butcher, in the first place, does not generally rise so early in the morning, as the main business of selling seldom commences earlier than eight o'clock, and usually lasts only until ten o'clock; then, again, it is not only the *selling*, but the receiving and sending home the various other articles purchased, which requires two or three men around the stall, the same number of boys, with horses, carts, and wagons to carry baskets upon baskets of vegetables, poultry, fish, eggs, &c., which are usually sent to the butcher's stand, where space must be found for them, so all these various articles can be satisfactorily arranged before the purchasers will leave them. All to be attended to in two short hours. Then follows the trouble of sending all home correctly and in season, which certainly gives more anxiety to the butcher than it does to dispose or make the sale of his meats; and if the boy loses a head of salad, breaks an egg, or an apple gone, the master butcher is called upon to account for it, and very likely a scolding with it; and to sum all up, this modern custom needs *extra* help, *extra* space, *extra* carts and wagons, *extra* patience; and with all, and the worst of all, *extra expense.*

The refrigerators so generally used now came into use by the butchers and housekeepers about the year 1835, although I find they were introduced, in fact invented, in the State of Maryland, in the year 1801.

Thomas Moore, of Montgomery County, Maryland, says he " projected a refrigerator in 1801, for the purpose of carrying butter to market in hot weather. The machine is very simple and cheap; by the proper arrangement of one conductor and several non-conductors of heat, a comparatively small quantity of ice made use of is almost entirely prevented from receiving any heat, but what it extracts from the butter, and this it effects with great facility, without being brought in contact with it. Butter may be carried in this machine throughout the whole of a hot summer's day, and delivered at market as hard as it is usual to see it in the middle of winter. This, however, is only one of the uses it may be applied to; every family may be furnished with a vessel in their cellars, in which, by the daily use of a few pounds of ice, fresh meat, milk, butter, liquors, or any kind of provisions, may be cooled and preserved. It would be very useful to butchers, who often lose considerable quantities of meat in summer."[*]

Stands for the sale of coffee, cakes, and other eatables appear to be one of the fixtures of every well-governed public market, unless there are cellars under them for that purpose. This market having none of these accommodations, Elizabeth Kline, in the month of August, 1801, petitioned for "privilege of selling coffee and chocolate in the Catharine Market, where nothing of this kind is at present sold by any person;" which no doubt was granted.

The market-house was nearly filled with butchers, leaving but a small space remaining for country people and a few fishermen; the great demand for stands had induced the Common Council to consent to fill all up with butchers' stands in 1802, and of providing another market-house for the country people and fishermen. But the citizens thought the Common Council ought to provide another house first, and petition in the month of August, stating, "they were informed the Board have in contemplation to permit the lower end of said market-house, now made use of as a fish market and a shelter for country people resorting there, to be filled up with stalls for butchers; which measure, if carried into effect, will prove a serious

[*] American Citizen, September 16, 1802.

inconvenience, unless some convenient place near the said market can be provided for the accommodation of fishermen and country people."

This new market, however, was not then built, but in the month of May, 1805, another was ordered to be erected, at an expense not to exceed five hundred dollars: " the dimensions of which were 30 feet on Water Street, and 18 feet over the slip, that the market-boats might lie under the market, and stairs to accommodate the fishermen."

About the time this market-house was erected the yellow fever had made its fatal appearance, when the butchers of this market, on the 9th of September following, present a petition, stating " that there is a probability of the butchers of the Fly Market being permitted to remove their stalls into Chatham (*Square*) Street, near the new watch-house, in consequence of the appearance of the approaching sickly season, (and if so) it will considerably cut us off from our profit and privilege in business; that on a former removal of the butchers to the aforesaid place, we were placed at the lower end of the arrangement, very much to our disadvantage and loss. We pray on the ensuing removal to direct it so that we in our turn may have the privilege of setting our stalls at the upper end of the arrangement, next to the watch-house;" which was granted.

The accommodations for fish-cars at the Fly Market had, at this period, become objectionable, or at least many found fault with the sewer that emptied out among the fish-cars, and would not purchase their supplies there, but went up to this market, which produced a great change in the fish, as well as the whole market; and in a few years it became known as the " great fish market," where fish was brought from all quarters in wagons, boats, and skiffs from the Jersey shore and Long Island, and smacks from the eastward. From 1812 to 1822 it was the wholesale as well as the best retail fish market, and it still continues (in the latter trade) one of the best " Sunday morning fish markets." " To get a bunch of fresh fish, you must go to the Catharine Market," is an old saying; and where so much fish was kept, a great many were thrown into the slip, which added another prominent feature to this market.

There was an old man engaged in the market about the year 1815, by the name of *Sam Way*, a great " shark-catcher." The dead fish thrown out from the many fish-cars and smacks no doubt attracted many *shark* in our then quiet waters around this slip; and when *Sam* heard the cry of "*shirk* around the slip," he would drop his broom, have his " chain-hook" out and baited, and in a few minutes the cry was, " Sam's got one hooked;" then, being a large, strong man, he would soon lay the "*shirk*" on the dock; and he had been known to take seven in one day, some of them fourteen feet in length. One day he hooked "a big one," and he had got into a skiff which lay tied at the end of the slip; the shark took to pulling and broke loose the skiff with *Sam* in, and away he went down the river, at race-horse speed, nearly as far as Red Hook, before he tired out, or *Sam* could hold him up; he, however, mastered him and brought him back, and Sam after that concluded not to be run away with again. So he stuck to the raft or dock when he fished for "*shirk.*"

Part of this new market-house after a time, in consequence of the increasing business, was demanded, and six more butcher stands added. A bell was fixed up on the market in 1810, and the year after the cellars were leased for twenty-one years, and the chains which had been placed across Cherry Street were complained of, and ordered to be taken down.

The death of one of the butchers, Captain John Lovell, drowned in the slip, who occupied stand No. 22, shows the manner which their stands were disposed of afterwards for the benefit of their widows. It appears the Common Council had, by mistake or misrepresntation, granted this stand to John K. Floor, when the widow, Margaret Lovell, petitions for them to reconsider their vote, and says: "That usage had allowed her a claim on it, and that she wished to convey her right to his brother, Robert Lovell," (who had worked for him;) also presents a petition recommended by several citizens in favor of him. The subject was referred to a Committee, who reported in a few days after, "That they had made due inquiry in relation to the existence of a custom set forth in her petition, and are fully satisfied that said custom has long existed, and which your Committee consider as laudable and reasonable, and hope it may be continued. They have also ascertained that Mr. Floor was still in possession of another stand in Fly Market, and consider it will be unreasonable and improper to permit him to hold two stalls at the same time, and deprive the widow of the deceased Mr. Lovell of the benefit of the one held by her husband so shortly after his decease." They therefore rescind the former resolution granting to Mr. Floor, and now grant it to Robert Lovell, (it being understood that he shall make her suitable compensation for the relinquishment of her right under the said custom,) and a resolution was passed to that effect.

In 1816 another enlargement was asked for, and among the reasons given are, "that a supply of butchers' meats cannot be obtained, and particularly in the summer season, on Saturday evenings." So, on the 11th March, a Committee reported in favor, and say: "The market at present occupied as a fish market running east and west be turned so as to run north and south, and that an addition be built of about 80 feet running north and south, and the cost not to exceed five hundred dollars. This appears to have been finished on the fourth of July following, and the stands for butchers all occupied, many of which were represented by a Committee as doing business without licenses, and they reported in favor of granting such to the following persons:

No. 15. John P. Harmony.	No. 16. James Taylor.
17. Samuel Martin.	18. Joseph Conklin.
19. Joseph Hyde.	20. Benjamin Lovell.
21. Walter Durbrow.	22. Isaac Wood.
23. Sylvanus S. Townsend.	24. John K. Floor.
25. Jacob Varian.	26. Jacob H. Varian.
27. William Shot.	28. Richard Platt.
29. James Goodman.	30. Andrew Hutton.
31. Jonathan Skillman.	32. Thomas M'Cready.
33. James Cammell.	34. Jacob Odell.
35. George Stagg.	36. Andrew Smock.
37. William Messerve.	38. Albert Fisher.
39. James Reeves.	40. James Sullivan.
41. Jacob Acker.	42. Mathew Vogel.
43. John King.	44. William Appleby.
45. Nicholas Dean.	46. Thomas Marshall.
47. Thomas Place, Sen'r.	48. George W. Varian.

Some two months previous to the placing of the additional stands in this market, "the Street Commissioner was authorized to have the grounds round the new market raised, and a gutter to be paved on each side;" and at the same time the Clerk, Nathan Eizenhart, was removed, and John Bremner was appointed. Several of the Clerks were reported to the Board as having not settled their accounts of fees for several months past. The Comptroller "suggested that an order should pass, obliging all persons who have the receipts of public moneys to render accounts, and make payments to the Treasurer within a limited time." The former Clerk, Mr. Eizenhart, promised to settle within the week, and the other delinquents were ordered to be prosecuted if their accounts "remain unpaid at the beginning of next week," and that all should pay the fees monthly hereafter, to comply with the law.

Some six years previous, the fees collected and expenses for one week for this market in the month of April, as furnished by the Clerk, are shown as follows: "A return of the fees arising from the Catharine Market, for six days past, commencing Monday 2d, and

ending Saturday, 7th of April, 1810, both days inclusive, £7, 9s., 10d., or -   -   -   -   -   -   - $18 72
   Allowed for collection, commission of 10 per cent.,   1 87

                                                 $16 85
   To one week's sweeping, -   -   - $1 25
   To two days' short change in last month,   42   1 67

   WM. CHEVERS.   Balance, $15 18."

We advance now to the month of June, 1816, when the Clerk
reports the number of animals exposed to sale here, or at least those
which he received fees for, running through the months of January,
February, March, and April.

	Cattle.	Sheep.	Calves.	Hogs.
January, - - -	391	880	79	9
February, - - -	273	626	108	25
March, - - -	255	161	480	27
April, - - - -	180	28	1,114	32
	1,099	1,695	1,781	93

I also find the total amount sold in the Washington, Fly, and this
market, for the above months, was, 5,018 beeves; 8,763 calves;
7,333 sheep and lambs; and 1,629 hogs; which produced a revenue
of $2,000 to the city. It will be perceived the month of April
shows a great decrease in the number of cattle, and scarcely *one
sheep* a day for the whole market; while the numbers of calves
have taken their place. The collection of fees in this manner were
always very small, especially in the spring months, when, also, but
little country produce was brought to our markets, and of course
much less fees was obtained from them; but after the adoption of
letting butchers' stands for an annual rent, which appears to have
taken place in 1821, it was found much larger. The proceedings
show, in the month of April of that year, the passage of a resolution to "lease for one or more years the butchers' stands at the different public markets, the rent to be paid in advance; and in any
case where the occupants are not disposed to pay the price assessed
on them, to sell them at public auction. This arrangement is in
lieu of the fees paid for the articles that were exposed for sale."

Soon after, each butcher here was served with the following
printed "*Notice:*—SIR: The Collector of the Corporation Revenue
will attend at *John Vanderbilt's store, No. 3 Catharine Market*, on
the 4th day of May, between the hours of 10 and 12 o'clock, for the
purpose of receiving the first quarter's rent for the stalls or stands
occupied by the butchers in the Catharine Market. Such of the

present occupants as wish to retain them are requested to be punctual in calling upon him and paying the rent, as it will be presumed that those who neglect so to do intend to relinquish their stalls. New York, 3d May, 1821."

We will now travel back to the year 1817, and find the Clerk of this market, also the Clerks of the Washington, Duane, and Spring Street Markets, were placed on the same footing—" to be allowed, in lieu of any other compensation, one dollar per day."

In the month of June, 1819, John Bremner, the Deputy Clerk, addresses a note to the Market Committee, in which he says: "I have been repeatedly requested by the drovers that sell cattle to butchers of Catharine Market, that there should be a public scale; therefore, I hope that your Committee will grant the request that will be communicated to you by the bearer of this." Communication read as follows: "To his Honor the Mayor, in Common Council convened: The petitioner humbly sheweth, that this market needs a public scale; and the stall No. 43, occupied by me, I have willingly consented to have it transferred for a public scale, and satisfied with the compensation that the butchers have made me. New York, June 11, 1819.   BENJAMIN DAVIS."

The Market Committee reported favorably, and ordered " the said petitioners to pay the expense of said publick scale; which scale to be the property of the above-named market."

The next year, in the month of February, the fishermen, who were quite numerous, petitioned to the Board to allow the grocers to keep open their stores on Sunday mornings. They state, they " are fishermen by occupation, and daily supply their fellow-citizens with fish, and make their stand in the Catharine Market; that you are well aware of the exposed situation at all seasons of the year, and more particularly during the cold season suffering with cold, clothes wet, and frequently frozen; they can get no refreshment on Sunday mornings, the grocers not being allowed to open their shops. They pray to allow the grocers by said market to keep their shops open until market-hours are over on Sunday mornings, &c." (Signed by)

Jason Smith,	C. Simmons,	David Thomas,
William Chewick,	Peter Patterson,	S. Maynard,
Joseph Caywood,	Thomas D. Gildersleve,	Mace Adam,
Peter Ackerman,	Samuel Butler,	J. Gabriel Gantz,
Gideon Wonzer,	Benedict Hazard,	Thomas Harris,
Cornelius Bogert,	John S. Avery,	Joseph Keen,
Thomas Shard,	John Williams,	Jacob Monell,
James Woodruff.		

In 1821, we again find no shelter for the accommodation of the country people. A great many petitioners, in the month of October, say: "There is sufficient room for extending in the slip from the bulkhead; as it now stands, there is upwards of thirty feet to the permanent line, and ninety feet running east and west, which may be occupied for a fish market; and that part now used as a fish market be appropriated to the use of country people. As the 'Fly Market' is soon to be removed, a portion of it might be erected here at a small expense."

As soon as the Fulton Market was erected and opened for business, this market and several others felt its effect, in the reduction of the trade, but more especially this; for about two years a great many complaints were made, and petitions presented, and some with cause. On the 11th of January, 1823, the butchers petitioned, and complained that they "pay heavy rents for their stalls, but the practice of vending meats both by the saddle, quarters, and the whole of the carcass or body of such animals, are not permitted to be sold, but at a public market; and the practice in the Bowery, opposite 'Clark and Lewis's, (Tavern,) by speculators purchasing hogs, sheep, and calves, and offering them for sale there, and other places, contrary to the regular rules and laws of the Corporation, and defrauding the Corporation of their regular fees—if they were compelled to attend the regular and legal markets. Your petitioners therefore humbly pray that your Honorable Body will take this case into serious consideration, as it not only operates against the revenue of this city, as well as against the interest of your petitioners, who are paying a high rent for their stalls, and compelled to endure the grievance, unless your Honorable Body, by our humble prayer, will enforce an ordinance to cause this infringement removed, and the venders to attend with their produce at the public markets. It is with diffidence we approach the Board, but confident your Honorable Body will grant us such relief as the circumstances of the case will require."

The Committee reported a suitable ordinance for their protection on the 20th inst. following. Again, in the month of February, they presented a petition for the reduction of the rent on their stalls; which was referred, or "laid down to sleep." But a perceptible change was creeping on, as many of the old faces were turned again towards this market; and soon after it became one of the best country produce markets in the city. The testimony is of my own knowledge, as I often visited this as well as others, with an esteemed *uncle* from Westchester County, who usually brought his produce there, and sometimes as often as three times a week. The preference was given here for quick sales and good prices. The Saturday night markets were again also crowded, sometimes almost to over-flowing.

An interesting sketch, showing the large business of this market, and the prosperity of the working classes, is noticed in the *American* of April 6, 1825. It is headed, "*Proof of the Comfortable Situation of the Working Classes in our City.*—I took a station at Catharine Market, which is the great emporium for the mechanics and laborers on Saturday evening, to offer a 'joint and trimmings' to any one who appeared to be in want. At the end of two hours, I observed but one individual whose external appearance warranted my offer-ing the boon: he answered (in reply to my application) that he re-ceived ten shillings per day wages, and that he had in his pocket five dollars of the week's earnings to buy his Sunday dinner. I counted upwards of 870 men and women who passed me to buy at the market in the two hours." (Ten shillings per day at that time would be equal to twenty now, (1857,) with the high rents, pro-visions, and style of living.)

The next evidence of its increasing prosperity is in a numerously-signed petition from the inhabitants in the vicinity of this market, dated 20th June following, praying for better accommodations. They say, in relation to a former report of the Committee: " Hav-ing reported it so far decayed as not to be worth the expense of re-pairing, and that a new one ought to be erected." " We therefore pray your Honors to direct and appoint that the market to be erected be built of *brick*, similar to the one adjoining it; the ground where the decayed market stands being sufficiently firm and com-pact to sustain a building of that description." They also " submit to the consideration of your Honorable Body the expediency of building another market, for the better accommodation to the fish-ermen than they enjoy on the site where the market now stands, and to the butchers, as giving them more stalls, (the number of which is at present quite inadequate to the demand,) but would materially conduce to the public convenience and comfort." They conclude by wishing the Corporation " to visit the fish market of a Sunday morning, which, for the abundance and variety of its fish, is thought to surpass any of the kind in the United States." The Committee reported, on the 28th July following: " That the market established at Catharine Slip has become one of considerable importance; it is frequented by a great number of respectable butchers, country peo-ple, and fishermen, and supplies a large proportion of the inhabitants of the eastern and northern sections of the city. The public derive from it a larger revenue, in proportion to its cost, than from any other market, and your Committee are disposed to give it a full share of the disbursements now making by them." "On examination, it is found that the lower market is a mere shell, in a ruinous state, and not worth repairing; and its continuance in its present state would not only be unjust as it respects the butchers, who pay a liberal rent to the Corporation for their stands, but must become a nuisance to the neighborhood." They ordered a new building.

After the new building was finished, a space was allotted in it for country people, which was not satisfactory to all, as some would settle on their old standing-places in Cherry Street, in spite of the orders. However, the attempt to drive them in the lower market drove them from the market. This brought forth a remonstrance from the citizens, butchers in the upper market, and many of the farmers who had supplied this market for many years. On the 11th of August, 1828, they " wish the country people should not be confined with their produce to the lower end of the lower market; that last summer an effort was made to confine them to the *lower* part of the market, and the consequence was that the country people, who had before frequented there, left the market, and many of them did not return until the present system was adopted. That they are now daily returning, and should they be prevented from selecting their stands, they will no doubt again leave the same." Among the signers the following farmers and gardeners are found, principally from Long Island:

Jacob Van Alst,
Christopher Van Pelt,
Whinent Van Pelt,
John Van Pelt,
Teunis Van Pelt,
Henry Lewis,
Garrit Van Winkler,
Joseph Josline,
Samuel Van Brakle,
Daniel Van Cleve,
James Dunlap,
John Boyd,
John Meserole,
Walter Way,
David Van Alts,
William Boyd,
Peter Colyer,
Henry Stoolkeff,
George R. Vandeveer,
John Vestavelt,
and John Skillman.

Frederick Devoo,
John T. Van Cott,
Jacob Bennet,
George B. Kelly,
William J. Bennet,
William Melville,
Abr'm Boerum,
Evander Berry,
William Randell,
David Van Pelt,
James B. Colyer,
William Archer,
Isaac Trotter,
William Kelley,
Asa Remsen,
David P. Miller,
Abr'm Vandervoort,
John M. Roberts,
James Berrien,
Jacobus De Bevoise,

Isaac Lowsbury,
Cornelius Van Cott,
Walter Van Pelt,
Stephen Weeks,
John Van Houten,
Jacobus Lott,
T. T. Cowenhoven,
Thomas H. Bassett,
A. B. Selover,
William G. Heyer,
Chas. Debevoise,
J. Randel, Jr.,
William Paynton,
Henry Boerum,
Peter Bogert, Jr.,
Benjamin Berrant,
Cornelius Hubbard,
Henrick M. Heyer,
Peter Van Cotts,
Jervis S. Rockwell,

Jacob Van Alst, one of the above signers, was somewhat remarkable as a regular and steady visitor for a great many years, (I am told more than fifty,) and always came in a row-boat. His farm was near a place called the Dutch Kills, on Newtown Creek, where, at an early period, he was a large producer, but for the last ten or fifteen years (prior to 1857) a very small boat carried his products; habit, however, had made it necessary to present himself and cargo at this market on certain days, while many occasions of severe storms and rough sailing had given his old friends a thought of giving him up, thinking he would not venture in his frail craft, or if so, that he would be in great danger of being lost. He, however, seldom disappointed them, as he well knew the tides, currents, the time and place to cross, when to hug the shore, and at last the bow of his boat would come poking in the slip, sometimes to the astonishment of all present, when Uncle Jacob received an extra shake of his hard, dry, but warm hand. His last load, however, has been carried, and his *frail craft* is laid to rest.

At this period (1828) the market was doing an excellent and profitable business; the whole market well attended by country people, and the butchers' stands all occupied by the following butchers:

No. 1.	George Dominick.	No. 2.	John M. Smith.
3.	John P. Aimes.	4.	David Lyons.
5.	John Tier.	6.	George M. Hartell.
7.	William Phillips.	8.	Amos Wood.
9.	Christian Hartell.	10.	Samuel Martin.
11.	Isaac Valentine.	12.	Geo. W. Varian.
13.	William Messerve.	14.	Philip Romaine.
15.	John Moore.	16.	Caleb Conklin.
17.	Thomas Varian.	18.	Peter Wagner.
19.	John Scott.	20.	Jeremiah Tier.
21.	William Anderson.	22.	Henry Collins.
23.	John H. Tier.	24.	John K. Floor.
25.	Jacob Varian.	26.	Thomas Marshall.
27.	William Shoults.	28.	Richard Platt.
29.	James Goodman.	30.	Orville Nash.
31.	William M'Cready.	32.	John Sharp.
33.	Owen Manahan.	34.	John P. Barker.
35.	Abraham Rhoades.	36.	Mathew Byrne.
37.	John Phillips.	38.	John Wallace.
39.	Jacob Pessinger.	40.	Gilbert Griffin.
41.	Thomas H. White.	42.	Nicholas Goodman.
43.	*Scales.*	44.	William Appleby.
45.	Gilbert Cromwell.	46.	Bethuel Howard.
47.	George Pessinger.	48.	Joseph Conklin.

Very many of the above I personally knew, and although I have some knowledge of their general history, which no doubt would be somewhat interesting, yet not sufficient for an historical sketch; but I live in the hope that I or some one else may obtain such from their friends or relatives, that the merits of good men, and the examples of usefulness, patriotism, and honesty may live after them.

Colonel William Appleby, once the occupant of No. 44, has many years ago retired from active business, laden with years and a plentiful store. He was brought up in this city on a part of what was once known as Bunker Hill, or Bayard's Mount, a sort of fortification or raised embankment, thrown up on a very high hill, (near the corner of Mulberry and Grand Streets,) about the commencement of the Revolution. An extract of a letter from New York, March 16, 1776, says: "One-third of the citizens were ordered out to erect new works; they began a fort upon Mr. Bayard's Mount near the Bowery, and another all around the hospital. To-day another one-third is gone out. Every street in the city is to be barricaded."* Before this period, this mount was known as "Mount Pleasant," an attractive resort in warm weather by many persons for the pleasant breezes and fine views of the North River, the Kolch, and upper part of the city. Perhaps a few incidents connected with its history would not be out of place here, and the first to present was a fatal duel which was thus noticed in the Press. On the 25th of September, 1787, at 11 o'clock at night, says an editorial, "a duel was fought on the ground near Bayard's Hill, in which the noted Monsieur Chevalier de Longchamps was unfortunately killed. It is said that his antagonist was a Frenchman, (*Captain Verdier, late an officer in Count Pulaski's Legion,*) who had served in the late American army; he had thought himself much injured by some assertions made by the Chevalier, and meeting him in William Street on Tuesday (25th) afternoon, an affray took place, which in the evening terminated in the melancholy catastrophe above mentioned. The gentleman who killed him has since sailed in a vessel for the West Indies."†

The next year, on the 23d of July, the "Great Federal Procession" took place, and ended their march on this hill or "mount," where ten enormous tables laden with provisions were found ready for the use of all. The butchers also had a large dressed "ox, weighing one thousands pounds," which they had roasted whole and presented to the patriotic and numerous body of men.

In the year 1795, we find a very strong feeling against the Federal Governor (*John Jay*) of New York, on account of his neutrality treaty with England, which the Republicans looked upon as a repu-

---

* Penna. Journal, March 20, 1776.   † Daily Advertiser.

diation of our country's obligation to France. The feeling ran so high, that on the 20th of July, says the Press: "A body of war-worn soldiers of the late American Army paraded the streets, bearing a French and American flags, with the British flag *reversed* underneath them. They proceeded to 'Bunker Hill,' where they burnt a portrait of John Jay, holding a balance containing American Independence and British gold, the latter prepondering. They then gave three cheers and returned in triumph through the city about five o'clock, leaving behind a dozen *Tories* to snuff the ashes of the bon-fire."

Colonel Appleby, while a boy, recollects that upon the top of this "mount" was held bull-baits, flying-horses, and other exhibitions; and it was also a great place where antagonistical boys met to "fight streets," which occasionally took place between the "Broadway Boys and Bowery Boys." Sometimes *hard battles*, as they were considered by the actors, were fought by throwing stones at one another; and when it came to close quarters, the fists and sticks were brought into play, and what was remarkable, that seldom any very serious injuries were received on either side. Sometimes one party would have possession of the "mount," then again the other, but usually the greatest numbers took possession after a few bloody noses or bruised shins; both, however, were generally routed by the dreaded appearance of one or two constables.

"They commenced leveling this 'hill' about the year 1802, and in digging down, the earth was removed more than fourteen feet lower than the bottom of the well, which no doubt had supplied the garrison who quartered there during the Revolution. In this well were found old iron hoops and other relics, among which was an old cannon, (a nine-pounder)."*

Near the foot of this hill, on the southeasterly side, was the old family burying vault of the Bayards—then known as Bayards' Vault, which had been or was thought to be the last resting-ptace of the former generations of that old family; but in the march of improvement, which had begun here soon after the year 1790, its occupants were transferred to another resting-place, and the old vault became empty, or at least only for a short period, as there came a singular and miserable-looking specimen of humanity, and took possession of this much-dreaded "tenement-house." The marks of time, however, had left in it enough crevices and holes to insure ventilation, and here this hermit or ragman, as he was generally known, lived several years. He wore the cast-off clothing given him, and these he patched with pieces of various colored rags or carpet; the rags hanging

* Cozzens' Geological History.

in every direction, which gave him a sort of hideous and frightful appearance, which sometimes alarmed grown persons as well as the neighboring children, who would seldom go near him. Many thought he was an old robber or murderer; and as he would not converse or seldom answer questions, he was somewhat feared, and not much troubled with visitors. Young Appleby often carried him cold victuals, sent by his mother, Mrs. Baisley, and Mrs. Hopkins, when the hermit became quite friendly, and would occasionally talk of some troubles or disappointments in England, and that his name was Captain Dundas. Winter and summer he remained in this place, sleeping on his bed of rags, until at last he took his final sleep, where he was found buried in his filthy bed, the last tenant of the "Old Bayard Vault."

Young Appleby was apprenticed with Thomas Place, butcher in the "Fly Market," and served him faithfully; began business for himself in 1811, and entered this market in 1816, where, by early rising, diligence, prudence, and honesty, he became possessed of abundance of this world's goods; while he lived the life of a valuable citizen, friend, and father, and although of a social disposition, yet he enjoyed his family and fireside above all others. Public office had often sought him, but he invariably would not accept, as his wish was not to be conspicuous, except it was in some old-fashioned custom, in style of living, dress, and more particularly in the wearing of his hair done up in a cue behind. However, occasionally the strife of politics attracted his attention, when he would enter with all his power, especially for a friend of either himself or government, and his influence was considerable, as in the end he generally proved successful. So strong was his feeling of friendship, that upon one occasion, when his own interest was largely at stake in the passage of a measure, that he publicly said, " My friendship and esteem for Henry Eckford is superior to my interest, and I must drop my own to succeed with his." He did so, and never after regretted it.

He was generally known as Colonel Appleby, which title he came honestly by, although at a late period. Being somewhat patriotic in his early days, he joined the Horse Artillery in 1816, under Capt. Geo. G. Messerve, then attached to the 3d Regiment, was promoted in 1821 to Cornet, and the next year as Lieutenant, which position he held and performed the duty many years. About the year 1836 he removed on his farm in New Jersey, and in 1843 was elected *Colonel* of the "Middlesex Regiment," in which county he still resides, as one of the remaining "Gentlemen of the Olden School."

In the summer of 1830 the upper market-house was much complained of, in consequence of the almost useless cellars under it; and it was also much out of repair. Strong hints had been thrown out by interested parties to change the location, and now was thought the proper time to make the effort; so they presented a petition, praying to have this market-place removed, and a building erected 150 feet square, with fronts on South and Water Streets, between Catharine and Market Streets. The butchers and others strongly objected to its removal there, and also petitioned, "That they were opposed to the contemplated removal of Catharine Market, in the manner proposed in a petition heretofore presented to your Honorable Body; that the market, as at present located, is convenient enough for every purpose. All that your remonstrants wish is to have the upper market taken down and rebuilt on the same spot, in a different way: that is, made lower, without any cellars underneath, so that the disagreeable smell arising from those cellars may be done away in future." On the following 27th of December the Market Committee reported, and the following resolutions were adopted: "That that part of the Catharine Market lying between Cherry and Water Streets be taken down, and that a new market, conforming with the plan which has been made thereof, be erected in the place thereof." "That the Market Committee receive proposals for building of such new market, and that $4,000 be appropriated for the expense thereof." And in the month of February, next year, the new market-house was ordered "to be placed 8 feet easterly and 3 feet southerly from the old one."

In the month of September following, the butchers in the lower market complained of the "hucksters and country people standing on the side-walk opposite said market, between Cherry and Water Streets," when the Clerk was directed to "order them in the lower market which was assigned them."

In many of the markets about this period, the Market Committee, when exchanging or transferring butchers' stands, it was usually the practice to make them all "premium stands;" and if the stand was a "corner," or otherwise valuable, a high premium or sum of money was demanded, (see *Johnson's, Centre Market*, and others;) if it was not, a low sum, besides all unpaid back rent, left due by a former occupant. In the month of November, 1834, the "Committee" reported on the transfer of stand No. 46 in this market, from William N. Hedge to Edward Conklin; and they state, "That said stall is not a premium stand; that the person for whom the transfer is sought to be obtained is well recommended as a regular-bred butcher, and the Committee think *one hundred dollars* would be the fair premium value thereof." They offer a resolution to the above effect, and it was adopted. Then, in the month of April, 1835, they report on the petition of David Haight for stand No. 5, Goveneur Market, and Michael Phelan for stand No. 10 this market, and say, "That the petitioners come well recommended as regular-bred butchers, and your Committee see no reason why they should not receive license, although they do not wish to make a premium stand of No. 10 Catharine Market." A resolution was passed to license both. Then, a few days after, the Committee reported on several stands here, and state, they "have consulted with the butchers in the several markets as to the premiums to be paid by the petitioners, and report the result of their deliberations by the following resolution: *Resolved*, That butcher stand No. 6, Catharine Market, be transferred to George M. Hartell, on payment of $50 and back rent," *(held previously by his father.)* "Stall No. 38, do., be transferred to Lewis Jolley, on payment of $15 and back rent," *(formerly held by Jacob Somerndyke.)* "Stall No. 48, to Gilbert Underhill, on payment of $50 and back rent," *(formerly held by Joseph Conklin.)*

The next year the "second market-house," between Water and Front Streets, is reported as being in a dilapidated condition. Petitions were again presented for its removal to Pike's Slip and other places. The subject came before the "Committee" in 1837, when Sylvanus Miller advocated that it should be located at Pike's Slip, while Eldad Holmes brought forth the claims of those interested in having it remain in the old location. The latter prevailed, as the Committee reported in favor of the old site, and it was built accordingly. In this year the Committee also made a report in favor of appointing two suitable persons for "Superintendents of Markets," and in this report they present the following remarks: "The public markets are the resort of this whole community to procure the necessaries as well as the luxuries of life, and a weighty responsibility rests upon the Common Council to see that they are properly regulated; that such provisions only are exposed for sale there as are sound and wholesome, and that every arrangement be made that can contribute to the comfort, convenience, and health of the city. They recommend a law to appoint two suitable persons, to be known as Superintendents of Markets; the one for the east, and the other for the west side of the city; and it imposes upon them duties that, if faithfully discharged, will secure to our citizens well-regulated public markets, and sound and wholesome provisions at reasonable prices. The Committee have, in the proposed law, provided that the Superintendents shall be appointed by them to hold their office during their pleasure, with a view to the appointment of persons known to be capable of faithfully discharging the duties, and that in case they should not prove to be such, to substitute others in their stead.   The compensation of these officers, in the opinion of the Committee, should be eight hundred dollars per annum.   This sum will enable them to devote their whole time to their public duties." This law was adopted in the month of February of the above year. Two suitable persons, in William Vonck and John Triglar, two old respectable butchers, were strongly recommended by the butchers, and received the appointment to these offices; and I may say, without fear of contradiction, that they performed their whole duty, according to the binding oaths they took, and gave general satisfaction.

In the month of December, 1840, the Collector of the City Revenue (Thomas Lloyd) made a return of the occupants of the stands in this market, when we find them occupied as follows:

No. 1.	George Dominick.	No. 2.	Jacob H. Varian.
3.	Walter Anderson.	4.	David Lyons.
5.	Daniel Haight.	6.	William Pitman.
7.	William D. Floor.	8.	John Farigan.
9.	Henry Develin.	10.	Michael Phelan.
11.	George W. Martin.	12.	Samuel Cornell.
13.	William Messerve.	14.	Philip Romaine.
15.	John Scott.	16.	Edward McManus.
17.	Joshua M. Varian.	18.	John V. Eddy.
19.	Barnard Hanigan.	20.	John Conway.
21.	George W. Truss.	22.	Richard Conway.
23.	John W. Palmer.	24.	John K. Floor.
25.	Joseph C. Appleby.	26.	James Appleby.
27.	Orville J. Nash.	28.	Richard Platt.
29.	James Goodman.	30.	Richard H. Platt.
31.	Julius Johnson.	32.	John N. Hoofmin.
33.	Owen Monaghan.	34.	Mathew Byrne.
35.	John Davis.	36.	John L. Delahunt.
37.	Sylvester Pendleton.	38.	James Post.
39.	Unoccupied.	40.	James W. Cruise.
41.	Mathew W. Bird.	42.	Unoccupied.
43.	Scales.	44.	James Horton.
45.	Gilbert Cromwell.	46.	Joseph Conklin.
47.	Henry B. Taylor.	48.	Thomas Calhoun.
49.	Alexander Anthony.	50.	Benjamin Oakley.
51.	Andrew Lang, Jun'r.	52.	William Reynolds.
53.	Abraham Horton.	54.	Edmund Conckling.
55.	George Pessinger.	56.	William J. Omberson.

Nearly two years after, this "Collector of the City Revenue," Thomas Lloyd, was a large defaulter, and became exposed from a casual conversation of the occupant of No. 55 with a then prominent

Alderman. This Lloyd defalcated with the funds of the city to a very large amount, and fled the city in a brig called the *Hope*, supposed to belong to him, for Cape de Verds and a market. Says the "Brother Jonathan," of that date: "If this is his own vessel, Lloyd has certainly struck out a new path in defalcation; for a man's swindling the public treasury, buying a brig with his plunder, and sailing away in his own vessel, is something new under the sun, and develops a skill in financiering which introduces a new variety into the somewhat stale records of roguery." The Comptroller, in a report of this defalcation, says: "Without surprise of the integrity of the Collector, letters were sent, with my signature, to some of the tenants largely in arrears, requiring them to pay up forthwith; of their being sent the Collector had no knowledge; only one tenant made answer to me or my clerk, and he stated he had paid up; and when Lloyd was spoken to on the subject, he referred to his book, admitted he had received, and that he had omitted it, but would include it in his next return." He, however, was soon after fully exposed, from a conversation that took place between Mr. George Pessinger, a butcher in this market, and Alderman Elijah F. Purdy, who remarked to Pessinger, that the *butchers had paid no rent* for about three years past, and could prove it by the Collector, (Lloyd.) Pessinger said that was not so—that he and others had *paid up*, and would immediately produce receipts enough to satisfy him or anybody else, which he did. This, indeed, was a surprise to the Alderman, as well as to many of Lloyd's friends, he being such an excellent and generous politician, and also a strong party man, that it could scarcely be believed. The Alderman, however, immediately made it known to the Comptroller, Mayor, and others; but before Lloyd could be secured, he was off in his "brig," leaving behind him a letter, dated 28th March, addressed to the Comptroller, stating that "*he had abandoned the office;*" taking with him, as shown by the Comptroller, that he "should have returned, - $432,437 79
"Returned by him, - - - - - 314,989 62

"Leaving the amount by him 'defalcated,' - $117,448 17."

This defalcation no doubt led to the adoption of a different mode of collecting the rents and fees of the several public markets: "That from and after the first day of March next, the butchers in all the public markets pay the rent of their stalls daily to the Clerk of said markets, and the Clerk pay over said fees and rents to the Comptroller on Monday of every week."

In 1844 a report was made and resolutions adopted to erect a new fish market, to increase the accommodations here. The old fish market, the report stated, " has been built many years, very near a half a century, and little or no addition has been made, while the population has increased at least ten-fold in that section; during which period commodious and spacious markets have been erected in other parts of the city where the population in recent years has been materially diminished. The present *fish market*, in consequence of the filling up of the slip, has become a nuisance, which can only be obviated by erecting another to extend further in the river, as all the offal would then be carried off with the tide, and the old market could then be used for country produce, and would make ample accommodations for that purpose; the expense of its erection would not exceed, in the opinion of your Committee, $1,300, as a considerable portion of Fulton Fish Market could be used to advantage on its erection, that market being about to be torn down."

In the month of October, 1847, the " Committee" reported in favor of repairing the market-house, and " to be done forthwith. It requires new roof and other repairs indispensable to the wants of those doing business there, which will require an appropriation of 2,500 dollars to complete." There is no doubt this appropriation was all used; but if on the market-house, it does not appear to have been well applied, as we find but a very few years after petitions for a new market-house, which some few of the Press strongly oppose, and among the many objections, assert, (as appears, without any authority,) " that the market was a great loss to the city." If this was so, the " Committee on Markets," in the month of October, 1847, must have made a great mistake when they reported the " Catharine Market had been paying an interest of 40 *per cent.*" on its estimated value. Other portions of the " Press," however, looked at it with different eyes; among these is the following: " Statements have been made in some of the city papers that the business of Catharine Market has been declining for some years, and that some of the stalls are unoccupied, from a general indifference to rent them. To our vision and judgment these statements do the market injustice. It is true that, like all our markets, it has suffered from the unfaithfulness and negligence of the Common Council, but in every other respect it still sustains its old rank among our best city markets. Many of those who occupy stalls in it are among our oldest and most respectable citizens. The rent paid for the past year amounted to $5,490, and the receipts reached nearly a million of dollars. The market is a great convenience to the neighborhood in which it is located, and could not be dispensed with without great injury to the residents in that quarter of the city."* Another account, from a military editor,

* N. Y. Sun, April 10, 1853.

says:* "The old dilapidated, sombre-looking, rat-infested, and rat-undermined market-house is a festering sore on that part of the city, and yet it is a great place of thrifty business, where many of our active business citizens have acquired great wealth rapidly, and others are doing the same thing. A stranger visiting the street and market-place after business hours could hardly be induced to believe that it was a place of business at all. But yet it is one of the greatest thoroughfares in the city. The ferry, at present a nuisance, does a tremendous business; however, in a few months there will be two instead of one—they will be ornaments to the city. Notwithstanding the unhandsome and inconvenient state of the market, we find therein a most respectable, most thrifty, money-making class of butchers, occupying most of them high positions in private life, and we take pleasure in naming them. As we enter the upper market from Cherry Street, we find arranged on either side, and licensed, as follows:

"No. 1. William F. Warner.   No. 2. Jacob H. Varian, Jr.
3. William Forshay.   4. Alfred Varian.
5. George Tappan.   6. Joshua Martin.
7. C. W. Farrington.   8. William Pittman.
9. John Scott.   10. Michael Phelan.
11. William Messerve.   12. William Nugent.
13. Sidney Fish.   14. Richard Conway.
15. Jacob Varian.   16. James Valentine.
17. Joshua M. Varian.   18. John V. Eddy.
19. Abraham Vanderbeck.   20. Michael Conway.
21. George Levinus.   22. Charles Conway.
23. Silvanus Haight.   24. ⎰ Messrs. James Ap-
25. Joseph C. Appleby.   26. ⎱   pleby & Co.

In the Lower Market.

27. Edward Lynch.   28. Washington Romaine.
29. F. Samuel.   30. Sylvester Pendleton.
31. John F. Messerve.   32. Edward Pendleton.
33. Owen Monaghan.   34. Mathew Byrne.
35. John Monaghan.   36. Edward Byrnes.
37. William Pendleton.   38. Joseph Zanger.
39. Solomon Pearsall.   40. Peter Bowers.
41. Joseph Lawson.   42. Jeremiah Dowling.
43. Samuel Storms.   44. Walter Appleby.
45. Stephen Storms.   46. John Appleby."

From 47 up to 58 were not licensed in the year 1854. In the fish market are noticed Messrs. Allen Tinker, J. W. Masten, George

* Colonel William W. Tompkins.

Gordon, Wearing & Comstock, William Tucker, Seymour Brown, Cyrus Bisley, Crofts & Houston, Wagner & Son, A. Lockwood & Co., and William Clark.

Here we find the name of Varian strongly represented, and the oldest name now known in the profession in New York City. First, we have Isaac Varian, Sen'r, a butcher once in the Old Slip Market, about the year 1720; then Isaac Varian, Jun'r, a butcher in the Fly Market, about the year 1750; then his son, Richard Varian, a butcher, about the year 1770, in the same market, and at the same time keeper of the Bull's Head in the Bowery, and superintendent of the "Public Slaughter-House," under Nicholas Bayard, both before and after the Revolution, but *not* during that war, as will be seen from his petition, dated April, 1784: "That he had the superintendence of the said slaughter-house for several years before the late war, and flatters himself he conducted the same in such a manner that no well-grounded complaint was ever made of its being offensive; and if it had been otherwise of late, the same may be wholly attributed to the state in which it was left by the British at the Evacuation. That he has a large family to support, being sixteen in number, and has been in *exile* during the late war; and without presuming on his own merit, he begs leave to say, that he has ever considered it his duty to exert himself to the utmost of his power in the service of his country." His *exile*, or at least a large portion of it, was being engaged on board of a privateer, which had been quite successful; but near the close of the war, while bringing in a prize, they were overhauled by superior force, and both privateer and prize were taken, when the prisoners were sent to Halifax, where they remained in prison until peace was proclaimed, when he returned home to the Bull's Head, and found his wife in full possession. Turning again to trace the name of Varian down, we find the patriotic blood of Richard Varian is shown in his son, George Washington Varian, who occupied, in 1828, stand No. 12; who, in the war of 1812, was a Lieutenant in the "Columbian Volunteers," organized about the year 1806, and composed *wholly of butchers*. In this war they performed three months' duty on Staten Island, and then again three months more service in guarding the steam frigate "Fulton the First," while building; and then, again, we find his son, Joshua M. Varian, on No. 17, this market; the present Captain of the "First Troop of Washington Greys," and one of the best-drilled officers in the "First," or any other Division of citizen soldiers, as the drill of that splendid and fearless body of men can and have shown on several occasions, more particularly on camp duty at the Quarantine (Camp Washington) on Staten Island, in 1859. The Captain has always been quite as prompt in business as in the field; gentlemanly, correct, and highly esteemed by the many who know him, but none more so than those under his command, who have on several occasions not only given him "votes of thanks," but have left or presented to him so much, so valuable, and so beautiful worked gold and silver, that must be hereafter an incentive for his generations to follow on, and increase the fame as well as the name of Varian.

The "Public Slaughter-House," noticed above, stood, at that period, on the eastern bank of the *Kolch*, into which its drainings ran, and the "House," from long and neglected use by the British troops, had long been very unpleasant to some of the neighborhood. Although many of the butchers, in a petition, state, "That the said slaughter-house having by law been fixed and established for many years, and they were precluded from killing cattle at any other place to the southward thereof, they have purchased and built their dwelling-houses in the neighborhood for their convenience; and the said 'slaughter-house' being near the Bowery Lane, where droves of cattle are usually brought; that they have every reason to be satisfied with the conduct of Mr. Richard Varian, the Superintendent of said S. H., to render it of public utility, and from being offensive to the neighbours." This was signed by

George Messerve,	Stephen Hilliker,	Henrich Astor,
Jotham Post,	William Wright,	Joseph Varian,
Jacob Arden,	Samuel Ellis,	Michael Varian,
Nich's Wethershine,	George Hopson,	Isaac Varian, Sen'r,
Henry Spingler,	John Lovell,	Isaac Varian, Jun'r,
Joseph Wilt,	Andrew Basley,	George Thompson,
George Wilt,	John Perrin,	James Manold,
Edward Patten,	Jacob Hilliker,	Adam Van Derberck.

The "slaughter-house," however, was soon after removed to Corlaers Hook, and the right of slaughtering was purchased of Bayard by James Blanchard, who soon found the business quite disagreeable, and no doubt made so by the butchers, whom the law forced into it. In a memorial dated October, 1785, Blanchard says: "That George Messerve, a butcher, sued your memorialist before Alderman Bayard for a *cake of fat*, he alleged to have lost last winter out of the public slaughter-house; and last evening it was submitted to a Juory, who awarded him damages to the amount of his charge, with costs of *sute*. There was nothing alleged that the slaughter-house was left unsecured, but that the slaughter-house keeper was answerable for all the beef, heads, tongues, hearts, liver, fat, and everything whatever, to be delivered to the butchers when demanded, or

pay for it if lost; and for my own security, & until I could lay the
matter before the Corporation last evening, I directed the doors of
the Slaughter-House not to be opened 'till daylight, that every one
might distinguish his own property; but about an hour before day
the butchers came as usual, & being told the door could not be
opened 'till daylight, they instantly broke the locks, & went in &
took what they said was their own.   That under the present situation, your memorialist is subject to be sued for every mistake that
is made, whether designedly or inadvertently, and is informed that
the measure pursuing is to raise such disturbances as to oblige your
memorialist to abandon the Public Slaughter-House.   Wherefore
your petitioner prayeth that such rules & regulations may be established as to prevent the inconveniences he is exposed to, &c."

In the month of May following, Blanchard presented another
memorial, in which he stated: "That your memorialist's importuni-
ties to the magistrates have been incessant, but the uneasiness of
the butchers and their violence increases.   That all the care ever
known in a public slaughter-house is constantly adhered to on my
part; notwithstanding, they frequently & wantonly injure the implements, which I submit to, and make immediate repairs.   They
now refuse to pay their duty established by your law.   Joseph Mott
refuses, & when requested, returns indecent answers.   Henry Ashdore (*Astor*) also refuses, and laments his being obliged to take license under a pack of rebel rascals, with many other enormities
and evil examples.   Wherefore your memorialist begs leave once
more humbly to remonstrate and pray, that if there is no way to
compel a number of abandoned men to an observance of your laws
and a peaceable behavior, that I may have a reasonable compensation for the time of the slaughter-house yet to come."

The Public Slaughter-House was continued until the year 1789,
when the butchers bought out the remainder of the lease from Mr.
Blanchard, and the law was repealed.   But, to prevent nuisances,
the Board appointed butchers who were willing to serve without
compensation, to act as Inspectors of the private slaughter-houses,
and these were continued for many years; and in 1806, when the
Board appointed the annual Inspectors, they gave them additional
powers, in the following resolution: "That William Wright, Daniel
Winship, Jacob Tier, William Chivvis, David Marsh, Jacob Varian,
and Christian Miller, *(all butchers,)* be appointed Inspectors, to inspect the slaughter-houses in the city, and to carry into effect such
parts of the law for preventing nuisances as regards butchers, and
to punish transgressors of such regulations as the butchers may
adopt among themselves for the purpose of conducting their business with every possible propriety."

We turn to this "market" again, and find, in the month of May, 1854, an appropriation was made, plans drawn and accepted, and a contract entered into, to build the present substantial iron market-house. The stalls were moved out in the month of June following, the old market-house taken down, and the new one finished in the month of September, when it became occupied with many new stalls and stands, which added very much to its former unsightly appearance.

One mistake was, however, made many years ago, when the attempt to force the many country people who had so many years visited here, into the lower market-house; for since that period they have gradually left, until at last but a few visit it regularly; although occasionally it appears like olden times, when numerous country wagons are seen standing with the horses' heads turned into the front of the wagons, chewing the welcome fodder, and the walks crowded with baskets of fruit and vegetation of all sorts, looking so fresh and inviting.

One Sunday morning in the month of August (1859) I strayed down there about five o'clock, and found the butchers just opening their stands, to deliver their sold meats and dispose of their "odds and ends," as they are allowed to do in this market. On the wharf above the "ferry-house," alongside of the "fish market," were drawn up several fish-wagons, which had come from along the bays and shores of Long Island, containing, as appeared, the "week's catch" of clams, muscles, eels, lobsters, shrimps, small sand-porgies; and mixed up among them, were seen several fishermen's boys and "hangers on" from other markets, with the refuse pieces of stale halibut, weak-fish, bunches of herring, &c.; the latter persons making a considerable noise and bluster in the sale of their stock.

On the cross-walk were several stands of smoked eels, with heads and skins on, smoked halibut, tripe, pigs' feet, plates of boiled lobsters, crabs, and other delicacies of that stamp. On the walk, hanging on the awning-posts, were several cages of baby-robins, bobolinks, and other birds, the owner of which was asking 12 shillings for a young robin, which he guaranteed the buyer "he would not touch $3 for in three months' time." Then, on a partial covered floating scow, were two or three persons attempting to hold a sort of prayer-meeting, which was now and then interrupted by an individual who did not appear to admire their style of getting converts; and directly opposite, while I stood listening to the address, a couple of white loafers (if their faces had been washed) were pitching into each other in the "rough and tumble" style. Close by and along the front of two or three closed stores was represented the last of the "Long

Island negroes," some of which had for the last fifty years visited this market on Sunday mornings. I asked the oldest woman, who had her roots and herbs displayed for sale on a cellar-door, " How many of the old colored persons (once slaves) are there now left, who yet come here?" Her answer was, that " there was only about *four* who occasionally came—*the rest are all dead;*" and the last five words came forth with a good deal of feeling. After a few moments she began to name some of those who had died, disappeared, and gone away, she did not know where. Knowing something of the history of their former generations, although slaves, when all were instructed, well-fed, and dressed, with the merry laugh, song, and dance, and withal trusted with their masters' business and the proceeds of their sales—and then turn and look on these poor, squalid, dirty, half-dressed, ill-fed and bred, and some no doubt with a strong inclination to be thievish—by their looks—I felt that when Government made them free, Government should have removed some of the obstacles which interfered with the intellectual progress and the domestic comfort of the newly liberated African race—that they might have appeared not only here on a Sunday morning, but any day and anywhere, and be a useful and respectable body of people.

"EXCHANGE MARKET."

1788. THIS appears to have been the fourth and last public market-place established in Broad Street, and nearly on the same spot where the " Broad Street Market-House" stood fifty years before, extending across Front Street and ending at or near the slip.

The first movement made towards erecting this market-house was in the month of October, 1788, when a large number (121) of the " neighborhood" asked for the privilege to erect a market-house " on the Long Bridge, in the South Ward," leading from the Exchange to the river, " at their own expense." " That its dimensions should be one hundred and thirty-three feet in length and twenty feet in breadth." " That to erect a market in any of the streets now unoccupied will darken, obstruct, and injure the city. But that the Long Bridge, which is already taken up by oystermen and others, only tends to increase the dirt, without benefiting any but individuals." A committee of five reported in favor of building this market-house, and the building progressed, but at a cost which exceeded their funds in hand, and they petition in the month of June, next year, "for aid of the Corporation in the finishing of the market-house lately erected; to which the Board granted £15 towards its completion."

Soon after a Committee was appointed "to remove the butchers out of the (*old*) Exchange in the new (*Exchange*) market lately erected;" when the business was greatly increased, beyond what it had been in the old market-place. The principal part of which was with the shipping and other water craft.

Into the slip at the foot of this market came the sloops from Albany and other places, with small boats from Staten Island, Bergen, &c.; and, after a time, it became known as the "Albany Basin," and of later years as the "Old Albany Basin." In consequence of the scarcity of small change at this period, the Common Council, in the year 1790, began to issue "Corporation tickets," of which we learn from a report of the "City Treasurer, Daniel Phoenix," that "from the 16th of April, 1790, to March 5, 1798, there was emitted for small change, - - - - - - - £15,471 6 0
The amount canceled up to March 5, 1799, - 9,025 5 0

Leaving a balance of - - - - - £6,446 1 0."

Grant Thorburn notices these Corporation paper bills in the following "sketches of the past." He says: "About the year 1794 the fire-engines in the city were of a very inferior quality; we had no water except from wooden-handle pumps, which stood on the corner of every street; by a law of the Corporation every owner of a dwelling was obliged to procure a fire-bucket for every fire-place in the house, or back kitchen; these buckets held three gallons, made of sole leather; they were hung in the passage near the front door; when the bell rang for fire, the watchmen, firemen, and boys, while running to the fire, sung out, 'Throw out your buckets;' they were picked up by men, women, and boys running to the fire. Two lines were formed from the fire to the nearest pump; when the pump gave out the lines were carried to the nearest river; one line passed down the empty, the other passed up the full buckets; if a person tried to break through the lines, he was compelled to fall in or get nearly drowned by buckets of water thrown over him; the buckets were marked with the name and number of the owner; every morning after a fire, the Corporation carmen went to the streets near the fire, picked up the buckets, and dumped them in the lobby of the old City Hall, which then stood where now stands the Custom-House; people then sent their children or servants to bring home the buckets, when they were hung up in the front entry to await the next fire. At that time we had no water except what we procured from the town pumps; they were unable to wash clothes with the pump water; therefore every yard was furnished with a cistern or a large hogshead to catch rain-water for the women to wash their clothes; we were unable to make tea with the town pump-water. In the rear of 126 Chatham stood a pump, denominated the tea-water pump; every day (Sabbath excepted) a carman called at our door with a large cask full of tea-water, for which we paid him one penny a pail; (we had no cents in those days—our small currency consisted of 'Corporation paper bills,' from *one* to *twelve pennies*.) If my memory is correct, I saw this tea-water pump in use in the store 126 Chatham—the water from the well was brought in the store by leaden pipes, then mixed at the counter with Irish whiskey and Yankee rum, and sold for six cents per half-pint tumbler. In 1798 the Manhattan Company was incorporated; they dug a well deep and broad near the *Kolch*, now denominated the *Collect;* here was a well whom none could *pump dry*, being fed from the *Kolch*. A large pump was placed in the well, which was kept in motion night and day by a powerful steam-engine; wooden pipes were laid from this Manhattan well through every street between the well and the Battery; thus every householder had the water conveyed into his yard or cellar, by paying a small sum annually. This Manhattan water was soon found inadequate to supply the growing population, so the Croton River is brought to our doors, where it may rest while woods grow and water runs.

"When digging to lay the pipes for the Manhattan water in 1798, one day, in passing the corner of Broadway and Wall Street, I saw a number of people collected around the men who were laying the pipes; they were curiously examining a large log they had just dug up; it was ten feet round, though much decayed; no one could tell what could have been its use. Old David Grim, then over ninety years, told me, when he was a boy, his father told him one of the city gates stood there, and that a strong wooden wall, ten feet high, ran from the East River up Wall Street, crossing the city and terminating in the Hudson River. It was thus that Wall Street derived its name.

"In 1807 I stood on the wharf at the foot of Cortlandt Street and saw the first steamboat start for Albany; after she left the wharf a few minutes, she stopped; the crowd began to murmur; 'I told you so,' said one; 'I wish I had my money out of her,' said another; she began to move upwards—the crowd gazing till she was out of sight; they dispersed, predicting she would never see Albany—she reached Albany in *thirty hours*."

We turn back to the year 1793, when the Philadelphia Daily Advertiser, August 7th, notices, "All sorts of provisions bear a high price at our (*New York*) markets daily; flesh and fish of all kinds, poultry, butter, cheese, vegetables, &c.;" and in the following month the same paper (18th September) presents a proclamation from Governor George Clinton, "to prevent market-boats and others going on board or approaching too near vessels which may be performing quarantine, below the point of Governor's Island. Notice is hereby given that the Health Officers will cause a *black flag* to be constantly displayed at the mast-head of such vessels respectively," who had on board the yellow fever.

The visit of the yellow fever two years after (1795) drove the butchers from this market, as well as from all the others located in the infected district, when they obtained permission from the Common Council to remove anywhere above it, many of whom sold meat at their residences.

From letters of Dr. E. H. Smith to Dr. W. Buel on the yellow fever in this year, we learn that "Every one knows that the summer and autumn of 1795 were excessively sultry and excessively wet. Meats spoiled in the market-place uncommonly quick, and those which were brought home, apparently fresh and good in the morning, were often found unfit to be eaten when cooked and brought upon table. Esculent vegetables in general, and especially fruits, were usually poor, tough, and tasteless. The peach, particularly that of the clingstone, was scarcely digestible, and often occasioned temporary illness, quite severe, while it doubtless aided in the production or aggravation of the fever."

Of the *fever* of '98, some account has been given in the history of the "Fly Market," and that of '99 made its appearance early in the spring, and continued until October, but not of so fatal character as the year previous; the butchers left the markets as usual, and appeared not very anxious to get back again, as many of them staid out after being ordered in by the Mayor. So on the 28th of October, the Common Council, by resolution, "ordered the butchers who had not complied with the order of the Mayor, to do so on or before the first of November next, or they will be suspended; and to render accounts of the number of the cattle, hogs, calves, sheep, and lambs they had killed during the prevalence of the epidemic, or between the 1st of May last and the 31st day of October inclusive, before the 15th day of November next."

In 1797, David Markler (*Merkel*) petitioned for a stand in this market, which we find was granted; but he was not noticed among the occupants in 1800. At that period the stands were occupied:

No. 1. John Jeremiah.   No. 2. Peter Crawbuck.
    3. Isaac Beyea.   4. Vacant.
    5. John Deavenport.   6. Vacant.
    7. H. Conrad.   8. Godfrey Crawbuck.
    9. Vacant.   10. Vacant.

In 1805, Nicholas Boyce was found on No. 4; and the year after, James Bradley occupied No. 10.

In the month of May, 1804, Richard Smith, the Deputy Clerk of several of the public markets, writes to the Common Council, soliciting them "to add to the fees of John Butler, sweeper to the Exchange Market, two shillings, as he receives but *six shillings per week*, and receives no amoliment from the butchers and hucksters, as the other sweepers do." They consent to allow the additional sum of two shillings, making " 8*s*. per week to be given to Mr. Butler."

The continual changes in the occupancy of the stands showed the business of the market at this period was not in a prosperous condition, and the merchants had been complaining of its being much in the way; these combined caused the City Inspector, John Pintard, to recommend its removal, which no doubt would then have been accomplished, had not two hundred and seventy-eight petitioners on the 28th of September following, " praying that the Exchange Market may be removed near the slip, instead of a total removal." Nothing, however, was done this (1804) year; but the next, the dreaded *fever* again appeared, and the Board, on the 9th of September, "*Resolved*, That the butchers of the city be authorized to remove to such position south of the three-mile stone as may be assigned to them by the Market Committee."

After the fever had abated, and in the absence of the occupants of this market, the market-house was sawed through into three pieces or sections, and were separately moved on the spot where the "Old Exchange" had stood several years before, between Water and Front Streets.

The change of location was not much, but it somewhat enlivened the trade for two or three years. Then, again, we find several of the stands vacant, and an application made, and permission given to John Butler, (who had changed his business,) in the early part of the year 1809, to occupy part of the lower end of the market for a grocery-store and stage-office, for Amboy and New Brunswick, N. J.

At this period we find the price of beef, as made out by Peter Crawbuck, butcher, of this market, against the Commissioners on the Fortifications at the Narrows, from the month of July to September, 1809, ranged from eight-pence up to one shilling per pound.

The old inhabitants and many merchants, at this period, had begun to withdraw their residences and places of business up town: the former in Broadway, Beekman, and other streets near the Park; and the latter in Pearl, Wall, Maiden Lane, &c.; which placed them nearer the attractive "Fly" and "Bear" Markets; and the "Exchange Market" is represented, "That from the scanty supply of meats, fish, and vegetables which is invariably found in that market, and from its being situated so far on the southeast end of the town, &c., it ought to be removed." This was not, however, accomplished until the 9th of May, 1814, when a Committee reported in favor of removing it. They say "that said market is useless; and it appears that two-thirds of said market is generally made a deposit for coarse merchandise and lumber, to the annoyance of the stores and merchants around said market." The Board ordered its removal, under the direction of a Committee.

"SPRING STREET MARKET."

1800. THIS public market-place, like many of the others preceding it, had several names attached to it, during its existence; the one at the head appears, after it had been erected several years, to have been officially given to it, and which it enjoyed as long as it stood. Several attempts had been made to introduce a public market-house where this stood, prior to 1800, but all had been unsuccessful. In this year, on the 22d of July, a report was made, on the petition of Aaron Burr and others, on the subject of a new market-house in Brannon Street. They state, "That Brannon Street is sixty-five feet in width; that Lewis Lorton and Joseph Watkins are the owners of the lots on the north and south sides of said street; that they propose, if leave is granted, to erect a market; to throw in the street each two feet, making said sixty-nine feet. The market-house they intend twenty-one feet wide and fifty feet long." The Board concluded that the street would not be wide enough, and therefore would not grant permission. So, on the 22d September, Hugh Gaine offered, or rather solicited, "permission to erect a market-house on his ground opposite Leonard Lispenard, Esq's, *(below Canal in Greenwich Street,)* upon the same terms and under the same restrictions they have done to those that have lately applied." The next day following, the first petitioners "beg leave to say, that the street wherein the market was pro-

posed to be built, called Brannon Street, is made to the width of
eighty feet;" and that they "have been favored with considerable
success from the Corporation of the Trinity Church, of the sum of
one hundred pounds." Consent was now obtained, and we find the
market-house built, with the name of the "Market-House in Brannon *(now Spring)* Street."

"Brannon" was the keeper of a noted public-house and a beau-
tifully-laid-out garden, located at the present southwest corner of
Hudson and Spring Streets, where yet stands the old house. Here,
Judge H. Meigs told me, about the years 1803, '4, and '5, he used
to visit, when it was known as the "Washington Garden," kept by
a very clever comedian and his son, named "Tyler," which led
some to call it "Tyler's Garden."

In 1801, we find the name of this market-place changed, in a no-
tice of the butchers who first occupied the stands in "*Greenwich
Market.*" On No. 1, Arnest Fink; No. 2, William Chivvis; and
No. 3, Henry Tenbrook.

Early in the year 1805, a bell was ordered to be hung in the
eastern end, and "to be protected by a neat temporary cupola."
The next year, the building was raised, and a cellar put under it,
and also three more butchers' stands placed into it. On No. 4,
Jacob Aims; on No. 5, John L. Fink; and on No. 6, Blaze Tenbrook.

In consequence of changing the name of Brannon Street, the next
year, to Spring Street, the same resolution again altered the name
of this market-place, and it "be known hereafter as 'Spring Street
Market;'" named after the many springs on the line of the street,
which was known or laid out in 1797; but it then ran quite a
crooked course, leading from Broadway down to and past an excellent spring, now located just above the present line of Spring
Street, between Greene and Wooster Streets; then this street or
lane continued westerly, to about Sullivan Street, where it crossed
a ditch; and on the other side was another large, fine spring, lying
at the foot of a hill; then the lane turned north between two hills,
and ran down westerly into the "Road to Greenwich."

The first of these two springs became quite famous, a few months
prior to the establishment of this market-place. The "Manhattan
Company," in searching around the city and suburbs for water,
found this spring, when they caused it to be dug out several feet,
and made it into a well, with the intention of using it; but they in
the end concluded it would not answer their purpose, so they left it
curbed and covered, and from that period it became known as the
"Manhattan Well." I am, however, informed from a highly re-

spectable source, that the other, near Sullivan Street, was the old Manhattan Well. (The "Press" also notices it—see below—as "a little east of Mr. Tyler's;" but then there were no other landmarks near to designate it by.) This evidence comes so strong as to almost shake me; but the evidence on the other side appears stronger, and I must yield to the first "spring." This latter information was obtained from five or six persons who often passed it; two others were brought up near it; and one other, when a child, was taken to it just after a most inhuman murder of a beautiful young Quakeress was committed, on a cold winter's night, the 22d of December, 1799, the last time this poor girl was seen alive. Although she was missed the next morning, it appears there was but little effort made to find her, as she had informed her friends and family that she was going to be married privately, and it was several days before any efforts were made to look after her; no doubt from the fact that the authorities and citizens were making great preparations for the funeral procession of our "Washington," then the all-absorbing topic, which took place in this city on the 31st December—the last day of the last month, and almost the last year of the last century.

Dr. Anderson's recollection also corroborates the "first spring," as he says "he visited it, as did many hundreds, immediately after the body of the murdered girl was found."

The missing girl was not noticed by the "Press" until the body was found, when we find in the *Mercantile Advertiser*, 4th January, 1800: "On Thursday afternoon the body of a young woman by the name of Juliana Elmore Sands was found dead in a well, recently dug by the Manhattan Company, a little east of Mr. Tyler's, *(who then kept the Washington Garden, noticed before.)* The circumstances attending her death are somewhat singular. She went from her uncle's house in Greenwich Street last Sunday *(week)* evening, with her lover, with the intention of going to be married; from that time until Thursday afternoon she had not been heard of. Strong suspicions are entertained of her having been willfully murdered."

Another account says: "As a young man (*Levi Weeks*) of respectability residing in the house in which she lived, with a relative, had, for a considerable time, paid his addresses to her, it was the general expectation of her acquaintances that the celebration of their nuptials would shortly take place; and this opinion was strengthened by their seeming reciprocal attachment, and her telling a confidant on the fatal day that terminated her existence, that that evening was appointed by them for the performance of the ceremony, which it was their wish to be done as privately as possible. The uncertainty of her fate for so considerable a length of time naturally excited the solicitude of her connections, and the peculiar kind of uneasiness of mind displayed by her lover, together with the supposition of their having went to be married, drew suspicion of his having been the cause of her murder and consequent secretion; insomuch that some gentlemen, immediately on the discovery of the body and before his knowledge of it, had him apprehended; on which he asked, Was he the man? He said it was hard to accuse him—and asked whether she was found in the *Manhattan Well.* The body, on first sight, bore evident marks of violent hands, and it was attested to the inquest, that between eight and nine of the evening of her departure, shrieks and cries had been heard near the fatal pit into which she must have been most inhumanly hurled. The Coroner's inquest, in order to obtain all possible evidence, prolonged their sitting from Friday morning until Saturday night, when they brought in their verdict, *Willful murder.*"*

The trial of Weeks took place in the month of March following: he having for his counsel Messrs. Alexander Hamilton, B. Livingston, and Aaron Burr; and for the people, Cadwalader D. Colden, Assistant Attorney-General. It continued two days; that is, from Monday morning, (the 31st day of March,) at 10 o'clock, until half past one the next morning, when it was adjourned until Tuesday, 1st of April, same hour. "At 25 minutes past 2 o'clock (Wednesday morning) the examination closed, seventy-five witnesses having been sworn. The Counsel for the prosecution wished that the Court would adjourn, as they had done the preceding night; he stated that he had not slept since the morning that the cause opened, and had then been without repose *forty-four hours;* that he found himself sinking under this fatigue." "The Court, however, said it would be too hard to keep the Jury together another night without the convenience necessary to repose, and they therefore could not think it proper." No summing up took place on either side, but the Chief-Justice, Lansing, charged the Jury, who soon after brought in a verdict of "*Not guilty.*"

This market in its early years seldom supported more than four or five stands with butchers; in fact, the population did not increase in this part of the city so fast as in the eastern and central parts. In the summer months a very good business was done here, while many of the citizens were residing and boarding in this neighborhood, (then known as the "lower village of Greenwich.") Many of the old mansions were taken for this purpose, which were once

* N. Y. Journal, &c., January 8, 1800.

famous as country-seats for many of the old Knickerbocker families. The cold weather, however, was sure to drive them into town again, and in winter business became very dull here.

The cold winter of 1817 was unusually severe, or so it is represented in the Press; as late as the 15th of February, I find "The North River is frozen over opposite the city, so that people pass and repass on the ice from shore to shore." "Several gentlemen set out for a sleigh-ride on the ice, from Flushing to Riker's Island, where they arrived in safety. This was the first sleigh that was ever known to visit the Island, and, as it passed down the Bay, drew forth numbers of people on the shore to view so singular an event."* The next year, about the same time, "Long Island Sound was entirely closed with ice between Cold Spring and the Connecticut shore."† The North River was also so firmly frozen that teams crossed over to the Jersey shore; many tents were also pitched, where they sold liquor, roasted clams and oysters, and, I believe, some persons attempted to roast an ox, but it failed; from the heat in roasting clams, &c., the ice became quite weak near the furnaces, which occasioned their removal to new locations near by. Alongside of the tent of Jeremiah Butman, the ice had become thin and quite rotten from the effects of a furnace and several days of mild weather, which led him and others to think it almost time to be off. However, many were passing and repassing, which kept business good, and he held on; but a man happened to step upon a weak spot outside of his tent, where the furnace had stood, broke through, and was struggling in the water, when a friend put his head inside of Butman's tent, saying, "Jerry, there is a man gone down your cellar!" "Is it so?" said Jerry; "then it is about time for me to leave these premises." The man was got out, the tent struck, and with a sled all were safely removed to *terra firma*.

In the month of December previous, the prices of provisions were quoted as follows:

"Best Beef, per lb., 12½c.

    do.   per cwt., 7 to 12c.

Pork, per lb., 10c.

    do. per cwt., $8.

Veal, per lb., 10c.

Mutton, do., 8c.

Turkeys, apiece, (good) $1.56.

Fowls, per pair, 56c.

Geese, per piece, 50 to 56c.

Butter, fresh, 33c.

    do. in firkins, 23 to 26c.

Potatoes, per barrel, 56c.

Turnips,   do.,   31c.

Cabbages, per 1,000, $6 to 7.

Wood, oak, per load, $2.25.

    do. walnut, do.,   3.50.

    do. pine,   do.,   1.62½."‡

* Evening Post, February 15, 1817.
‡ Columbian, December 5, 1818.

† Long Island Star, February 16, 1818.

On the following 14th of March a communication says: "The exorbitant prices demanded for all description of provisions is a serious and alarming difficulty, that has long occupied the attention of all classes of citizens. Provisions are now sold at higher prices in this city than in any part of the world."*

In 1819 the business in this market took quite a start, as many new buildings had gone up around it, and others in the course of erection. The market-house had become quite old and very much out of repair as well as crowded, and a new one was asked for, or the old one repaired and enlarged. This was followed on the 24th of May (same year) with a report "to extend and repair the old house," at a cost of about 160 dollars. This, however, answered but for a short period, as the yellow fever of 1822 not only filled all the houses, but many more, which were run up in a few days, and greatly increased the business; so much so, that the neighborhood petitioned "to further enlarge the same with another extension." The Market Committee, on the 28th of October, report, "That they have examined said market-house, and find the whole occupied by butchers and hucksters, to the entire exclusion of country people. The expense of building an addition thereto being very small, as nearly all the materials are now in the public yard from the 'old Fly Market,' they recommend that an addition of *fifty feet* be built from the present market towards Washington Street," not to exceed two hundred dollars, which was by resolution adopted.

A few years previous several violators of the law had managed to escape conviction, in the selling of meat in the markets without a license or permit. John Jenkins, however, had been convicted in the month of September, 1821, of selling "meat on the stall of Mr. Jeroleman in Spring Street Market," and fined twenty-five dollars and costs; and at the same time Isaac Varian had also been convicted and fined for selling "sheep and lamb in the lower Fly Market without a permit, and in consequence of not paying the fine, were imprisoned." They both petition for relinquishment of fine. Varian states: "That he is in very impoverished circumstances, and has a wife and two children (all of whom are sick) dependent on his daily labor and industry for their support and maintenance. Should your honorable body be pleased to release your petitioner from said fine and judgment, it will be the means of rescuing himself from imprisonment and want, and his family from suffering, &c." The Market Committee, in the following month of October, state, "That as the conviction of persons is frequently attended with great trouble and difficulty, and as the laws should not be violated with impunity,

* Columbian, December 5, 1818.

your Committee report against both Varian and Jenkins;" when it was resolved, "that it will be inexpedient to grant the prayer of the petitioners."

This enlargement appeared to answer but few years, as it was again reported as being crowded; and we find in 1828 twelve butchers' stands occupied by the following persons:

No. 1. Arnest Fink.   No. 2. Abraham Lozier.
    3. John A. Fink.   4. Jacob Siler.
    5. Henry Cornell.   6. John Miller.
    7. Charles Reeves.   8. James Reeves.
    9. Aaron Woodruff.   10. James H. Haws.
   11. Lawrence Martin.   12. James Reeves, Jun'r.

The occupant of No. 1, Mr. Arnest Fink, deserves a much better sketch of his life than I am able to give; but a rough notice will, I hope, keep his many virtues living after the present generation has ceased to exist. He was one of the sons of Adam Fink, and first entered in business on No. 1, where he remained until this market was taken down. He then purchased a stand in the Clinton Market, where his name will be noticed again. He was one of the really good, honest, kind-hearted gentlemen, whose memory and examples should always live; never rough, boisterous, nor showy, but always the plain, pleasant, smiling individual, whose heart, hand, and purse (which was large) were always open to the unfortunate, or the young business man, whose means were smaller than his character. To such he would render assistance to start in the world; lend his money, and when paid, he would have *no interest*, not a cent above the principal—"it was not lent as a broker or a bank, but as a friend," he would say; and if they were behind or unfortunate— "pay me when you can;" and he was seldom taken advantage of. I knew him, almost from the time of my first recollection, and his memory still lives, respected, not only by his old associates, but by all those who were fortunate enough to have dealings with him.

One of those yet living friends, universally known and respected, says in a letter to me, of this gentleman: "I was intimate with *another*, whose manners were gentle, habits of proper virtue and religion, who, in a long period of steady industry, became wealthy—who never displayed it in any mode of living—who lent money most liberally, but thought it wrong to take interest on such loans, and never did. A better man has never come to my knowledge than this—he has been dead many years—his name was *Arnest Fink*." Such is the evidence of the Hon. Judge Henry Meigs, and is worthy of record on any page.

In the year 1829 Clinton Market, which was to take the place of this market, appeared nearly finished, and the butchers in this market petitioned for stands to be assigned to them in the new market. They were told by the Corporation: "If you want stands in the new market, you must buy in competition with others." They then, on the 16th of February, remonstrate against having all the stands sold, "as they consider that, as they are to be removed from the stalls they at present occupy, they are entitled to a preference of the stands in Clinton Market." They were, however, not noticed with their remonstrance; and those who had money were obliged to purchase at very high prices. This, no doubt, was the cause of the establishment of the "meat-shops" in our city, as the taking away of one of the butchers' stands, (Henry Cornell's,) who was unable to purchase, led him to establish himself in a "meat-shop," where he was supported by many of the citizens, who thought the Corporation had deprived him of his just rights, encouraged him in his then unlawful acts; and although often convicted, yet his friends assisted him to baffle the Corporation, and, in fact, to make it appear that our "public markets," as then conducted, were a monopoly. This led on others to open "shops;" and although some were fined and imprisoned, yet they succeeded, and a law was established in their favor in 1843.

This old market-house was cleared and offered for sale, and on the 4th of May following (1829) the Market Committee reported "the sale of the old Spring Street Market for $53 cash;" after, however, appropriating 35 feet to be removed to the Greenwich Market for a shed, and 35 feet more to the Grand Street Market for the same purpose.

"STATE PRISON MARKET."

1806. IN the early part of the year 1804, two butchers, by the name of John Chivvis and Francis White, Jun'r, put up a shed under some large trees on the Greenwich Road, just below Christopher Street, where they commenced selling their meats; it was not long before several butchers in the Spring Street Market sent in a petition, and on the 22d of April it came before the Board, "praying that the butchers at the State Prison may be removed." This petition does not appear to have been noticed; so, on the 6th July following, the "Spring Street butchers remonstrate against the selling of meats at

Greenwich." This was referred to a Committee, and with it a petition from several of the inhabitants, for the establishment of a public market-place, and one also from the two butchers, to sell meat at "Greenwich, near the State Prison." A favorable report was made on the 6th of May, 1806, and the Alderman and Assistant of that (8th) Ward were empowered to assign the new market-place. They removed these squatters from their first location, down below Christopher Street, on the road leading to the *Prison* and De Klyn's Ferry to Jersey. The ferry started from about the present corner of Hammond and Washington Streets, where this road then ended, on the north; on the south it ran along the shore of the Hudson River and entered into the old "Road to Greenwich," about where it crosses Clarkson Street.

The butchers in this "shed market" occupied stands, No. 1, John Chivvis, and No. 2, Francis White, Jun'r; and as to vegetables and fish, the first were plenty around among the gardeners when in season, while potatoes, cabbages, dried herbs, and salt fish were retailed at old "Tine (Valentine) Kettleman's grocery," just above the prison. Fine fish were caught, sometimes in great plenty, off the prison, in the Hudson River, or the villagers were obliged to go to the city, at the Catharine or Fly Markets, to procure them at certain seasons of the year.

In 1810, Henry Merkler, in a petition, says, "he lately held stand No. 2 in the market at the State Prison, wishes a stand in the Duane Market," which was granted to him.

Near by was also kept the "Greenwich Hotel," somewhat fashionable as a summer resort, where the stages run several times a day to and from the city. "A few gentlemen may be accommodated with board and lodging at this pleasant and healthy situation—a few doors above the State Prison. The Greenwich stage passes from this to the Federal Hall and returns five times each day."*

The State Prison, from which this market-place derived its name, was built, or rather it was begun in the summer of 1796 and finished in 1797, as appears from a part of the Governor's (John Jay) proclamation, dated November 25, 1797, in which he says: "That the State Prison, to be built in the City of New York, shall be considered as the State Prison for the whole State;" "and whereas the State Prison in the City of New York is ready for the reception of prisoners." He also directs all Sheriffs to convey criminals to the same.

The building and grounds occupied about four acres; that is, it took in the space commencing from the present corner of Christopher, and ran up Washington Street to about half way between

* Columbian, September 18, 1811.

Charles and Perry Streets, and then ran westerly to West Street, (with a break in the north line,) down West Street to Christopher, and up that street to the corner of the starting-point. The whole being surrounded with a heavy, high stone wall, and on the corners of this wall were always to be seen the guards in uniform, marching to and from with guns at a "support;" and for protection from storms, small round sentry-boxes were so placed that the whole inside yard was in view.

Part of the main building, with the cupola, may yet be seen from West Tenth (formerly Amos) Street, below Washington Street; there is also a part of the north wing, which fronts on, and is known as No. 676 Washington Street. The first prisoners admitted into it is noticed in the Daily Advertiser, December 1, 1797, as follows: "We announce the opening of the new State Prison. The prisoners, to the number of 70, were removed thither last Tuesday (28th of November) night." Among the first State prisoners was one which Grant Thorburn thus describes: "One day I went up to the Park to see a man hung; after gazing two hours at the gallows, the rope, and the iron ring in the end of the rope, the Sheriff announced a reprieve; I must own I was disappointed; the man's name was Noah Gardner. He kept a large shoe factory in Maiden Lane; he was found guilty of forgery, at that time a capital offence; as the State Prison was nearly finished, the Society of Friends induced the Governor to remit the sentence. So he was sent to the State Prison for life. Being a shoemaker, they found him a stool, leather, wax, knives, lasts, and awls. Here commenced the State Prison manufactory of shoes, which threatened to fill the country with convict boots and mouse-traps. The masters, journeymen, and apprentices petitioned the Assembly at Albany, who forbid the boot and shoe making, and commenced the making of birch-brooms and mouse-traps.

"Noah and I were on social terms when he kept store in Maiden Lane; after he had been three years in the prison, I paid him a visit; he remarked, the first month he was in prison, he sat alone—after the first criminal court, he welcomed three apprentices; he learned them to work, as they could steal no more. Every court sent him a fresh supply; now there were over 300, they sat in ten large rooms. Noah being boss, superintendent, and master, he walked from room to room with a stout cane in his hand, up one row and down another among the stools, punishing the evil-doer and praising them who done well; thus having served the public seven years, the Friends induced the Governor to grant an unconditional pardon. 'Now,' said they to the Governor, 'you have saved a useful life; he is a reformed man.' They hired a store for him in Pearl Street, near Peck Slip, bought his shoes, lent him money, endorsed his notes, &c.; his shoes were made by men who wrought in their own houses. He joined the society, said thee and thou with the best of them. He was now in the full tide of successful experiment. One day he cut out a pair of boots; on handing them to the journeyman, 'Friend,' said Noah, 'thee must bring them boots on second day evening; I promised them to a customer.' 'You shall have them,' said the man. The boots did not come home till third day evening. Noah was wroth; he put forth a long lecture on the horrors of disappointment. Says the culprit, 'I am a poor man, have a wife and three children; my wife is sick, I had to nurse her and cook for the children—I was unable to finish them sooner.' Noah would hear no excuse, but continued the lecture; the man waxed wroth; he struck his hand on the counter, and exclaimed, 'I know it is a terrible thing to be disappointed; I remember going up to the Park to see you hung; when the Sheriff read the reprieve I never was so disappointed in my life.' Noah was dumb; he opened not his mouth, he paid the man for the boots, gave him another pair to make, and ever after treated him kindly.

"Noah went on prospering and to prosper; one day he borrowed some extra sums, and got a number of extra endorsements; these he cashed in Wall Street; that night he fled to parts unknown, taking with him (to cheer him on the way) a beautiful young sister, the daughter of one of his Friends; he left a wife and children in New York. After fifty years' inquiries, I never could find that any one knew whither he went. Thus ended the first specimen of State Prison reform."

There were seldom more than 250 convicts during the first ten years after the prison was built, many of whom were employed by the city on the roads, sewers, &c. Their summer dress was a jacket and trowsers, made of linen cloth, of a brown color. The dress worn in winter was of the same color, and made of woolen and linen cloth. These clothes were all made in the prison; and when a convict was imprisoned a second time, he appeared distinguished by a dress one-half red and the other half blue.

The composition and cost of their daily meals may be seen in the following tables. For breakfast in the month of August, 1800, for 235 persons:

Ingredients.	Cost.
1 peck of rye,	$0 25
6½ quarts of molasses,	1 02
130 lbs. bread, of rye and Indian,	1 95
Fuel used in cooking,	0 08
	$3 30

Dinner in July for 225 persons, same year:

17 ox hearts, - - - - - -	$1 63
7 ox heads, - - - - - - -	1 09
6 lamb plucks, - - - - - -	0 19
1 peck potatoes, - - - - - -	0 15
3 lbs. of Indian meal, - - - - -	0 04½
¼ lb. pepper, - - - - - - -	0 10½
Fuel and herbs, - - - - -	0 24
	$3 45

Supper in August for 218 persons, same year:

	$	c.	m.
36½ lbs. of Indian meal, for mush, - -	$0	54	7½
1½ lbs. salt, - - - - - - -	0	3	0
61 lbs. bread, - - - - - -	0	91	5
2 gals., 3 qts., and 7 gills molasses, - -	1	79	0
Fuel, - - - - - - -	0	8	0
	$3	36	2½

At its first opening, the convicts were principally employed in making shoes, which were sold in this city at its warehouse, which is thus noticed: "*State Prison Warehouse, No. 1 Beekman Slip.*— A large and general assortment of shoes, made in the State Prison, are now ready for sale, and offered to the public, wholesale and retail, at prices cheaper than have been common for many years past."*

For several years after it was organized, several desperate attempts were made to break out; and the first noticed was attempted by the shoemakers, in 1799. The "Press" states: "On Thursday (13*th June*) afternoon a most daring attempt was made by some of the convicts in the State Prison to make their escape. It originated with the shoemakers, who, to the number of 50 or 60, work in the room called the Mechanics' Hall. They seized upon their keepers and some of the prisoners, who they found not disposed to join in the attempt; but they were soon discovered by the guards and fired upon, wounding several, and the rest gave up."†

The *Gazette* says: "The Companies of the First Battalion of Artillery were forming for review; information came that the prisoners were forcing the gates and making their escape. The Companies formed instantly, marched out to the prison on the run, and were soon followed by many other uniformed companies;" but the tumult was quelled before their arrival.

Three or four days after, seven prisoners, however, did escape,

* Commercial Advertiser, July 16, 1798.   † Patriotic Register, June 15.

" under the cover of the darkness and storm; but by what means, we have not learned. They were confined in separate cells, and we are told were naked when they left the prison walls behind them."

A desperate attempt to escape was made by about 40 of them in 1803, in the month of April. They rose on their keepers, secured them, and made their way into the main yard, where they attempted to get over the wall by placing board and other material together, something in the form of a scaffold; and, to create a greater confusion, they set the prison on fire. However, the sentry observed them in time to give the alarm; the bell was rung, the guards assembled, and the prisoners persisting, were fired upon, when several were killed and badly wounded, before they would retire in their cells. The fire was in the mean time put out by the keepers."[*]

The next year, however, they succeeded in destroying the north wing by fire. The "Press" notice this, from which the following is taken: "On the 7th of May, 1804, the city was alarmed by fire, which proved to be the State Prison, and was not got under until the north wing had been burnt down to the lower story; damages laid at 25,000 dollars. It was set on fire by some of the prisoners, who, after locking up the keepers, went to the garret and set it on fire: however, one, more humane than the rest, released the keepers. Many of them at this time escaped."[†] Several other attempts were made, and some successful, before their removal to "Sing Sing," which took place with the male prisoners in the year 1828, and the females in the spring of 1829. I am indebted for much of the above information to Mr. Joseph Crowell, (since deceased,) who bought part of this property, when it was sold in the month of May, 1829.

We now turn to this "old market-house," to find that when the "Greenwich Market" was erected, (in 1812,) the butchers and others were transferred from this *shed* into it, and the "State Prison Market" ceased to exist as a public market-place.

"CORLAERS HOOK MARKET."

1806. ALTHOUGH this market-place and house were named "*Grand Street Market*" when it was ordered built, yet it was afterwards commonly known as "*Corlaers Hook Market*," and "*Corlaers Market*;" and as there was another market-house built many years

[*] Evening Post.   [†] Ibid.

after near this place, generally called and known in the Records as "*Grand Street Market*," I have adopted for the former market the common name, instead of the proper one; however, it may have been altered to "*Corlaers Hook Market*" soon after it was built, without that fact appearing in the Records.

Corlaers Hook took its name from Jacobus Van Corlaer, (somewhat famous as a trumpeter under Governor Van Twiller,) who owned a plantation located at this point.

On the 19th of May, 1806, the Board gave permission to Abraham Cannon and others to erect a market-house, at their own expense, at the foot of Grand Street, (facing the present Goerick Street,) and to be called "*Grand Street Market*." A cellar was built under it, at an expense of three hundred dollars.

In consequence of the market-house being placed too far on the north side of Grand Street, the line of this street was changed at this place; but it was done by the then owners of the property, who were anxious to have a public market-place located there, even at a loss of the most valuable portion of their lots, some fifteen feet of their fronts.

When the market-house was finished, butcher stand No. 1 was granted to Thomas Winship, Sen'r; and a short time after, stand No. 2 came in possession of his brother, Samuel; and the proceedings show, after this period, it enjoyed the name as above designated. We find, in 1808, another stand was allowed William Shott; and two years after, George Hepburn and Samuel B. Kline were permitted to have stands in "Corlaers Market;" then, the same year, a Committee reported "that it would be proper to fix a bell in 'Corlaers Hook Market;'" and the next year, "stand No. 3 in Corlaers Hook Market was granted to Samuel Raymond."

On the 25th of May, 1812, hand-bells were, by a resolution of the Board, introduced in all the public market-houses, and "the Deputy Clerks of the several markets, who shall ring the same, one-quarter of an hour previous to the time" *(which was fixed at 2 o'clock, P. M., each day throughout the year,)* "for the butchers to leave their stalls."

In 1814, permission was granted to James Hunter, William Vail, and others, to erect a fish market—to be attached to this market— at their own expense; but to be done under the direction of a Committee, who had it placed, by the influence of Mr. Hunter, before his property; the west end on a line of Mangin Street, and the east end on the shore of the East River." (See *Grand Street Market*.)

The business here, at that period, was not sufficient to profitably employ these two market-houses, and for a length of time the occupied stands were reduced to two; and afterwards this old market-house was leased to Samuel Winship, for many years, at a nominal rent, where he sold his meats; and in the cellar below (which was almost level with the street at this period, which had been previously dug down,) he kept a bison, or buffalo, for several years, principally for "baiting." In those days bull and bear baiting was in favor of the law, and quite fashionable among a certain class of citizens.

Mr. Winship had many years before introduced this cruel sport on "Bunker Hill," which he had inclosed inside the fortification, a very high fence, and arranged seats like a circus, capable of seating two thousand persons, without a cover, and charging each person a "quarter of a dollar for admittance;" and it was always full, they being regularly advertised. In the centre of this "circus" was a large cleared circle, where the animal was brought into, and chained or tied fast to a large swivel ring fastened in the ground, with a rope long enough for him to run around this circle. Then bull-dogs were brought forth to worry him, and ofttimes were immediately killed by the bull. But enough of these *baiting* particulars.

After Bayard's Hill was dug down, Winship built another open "circus" at the northwest corner of Broome and First *(Christie)* Streets, where he continued the same cruel performance several years; and finally he fitted up another near this market, where he occasionally baited this buffalo.

Mr. Winship was one of the sons of Colonel Ebenezer Winship, noticed in the Bear Market, and a very large man, seldom weighing less than 250 pounds, very fond of sport, jovial and free-hearted, or rather benevolent.

After the streets had become regulated around this quarter of the city, this old market-house stood so as to interrupt the travel past it. A petition from the owners of property near by, in the month of August, 1819, wish it removed; and others, again, petition for it to remain, and state they "have, in consequence of the advantage of this market, given up the front part of their lots in order to have a wide space for that purpose." The Market Committee, after examining the whole matter, reported on the 6th of September following: "That there were two small market-houses at the lower end of Grand Street, near the East River; that the old market-house near Goerick Street, built long before the streets in the vicinity were regulated, occupied a necessary part of the carriage-way, and was useless, while the (*Grand Street*) market erected a few years since, near the river, would accommodate the neighborhood." The Board adopted the following resolutions, which were submitted by the Market Committee: "*Resolved*, That the Street Commissioner be instructed to sell at public auction the *old market-house;* and that the same be removed, and the street filled up and leveled on or before the 10th day of September next.

"*Resolved,* That the butchers who are licensed for stands in said market be permitted to occupy stands in the market near the river, and that the Market Committee be instructed to designate such stands."

The cupola and bell were taken down and placed in the other market-house, and the old materials were sold for $43; "the purchaser removing the same, and filling up the cellars by the 20th instant;" and so ended the "Corlaers Hook Market."

"DUANE STREET MARKET."

1807.   IN the early part of the year 1805, nearly two hundred of the inhabitants and freeholders of the Fifth Ward subscribed to a petition to the Board, for a market at the foot of Duane Street.   In their petition they state, "That the Corporation of Trinity Church, having some years ceded to your Honorable Board certain lots of ground, with a view that a public market should be erected at the lower end of Duane Street; that when it should cease to be used for that purpose, it should revert to the donors.   The petitioners have for some time past been in the expectation of seeing some measures adopted towards the accomplishment of that object, but have been disappointed.   That the population of this part of the city having of late years greatly increased and still continuing to increase with great rapidity, your Honorable Board must no doubt see the propriety of extending to the inhabitants of this district an equal facility of procuring the necessaries of life as their fellow-citizens enjoy in the other wards.   They beg leave to state that this vacant space remains entirely unoccupied, and they can conceive no purpose to which it can be applied with equal propriety as to that of a public market."

On the 13th of May following a Committee reported in favor of allowing the petitioners to erect a market; and further say, that "Trinity Church having declared and reserved this place for a market, the present proprietors of the property around it purchased at an advanced price in consequence, and the improvements in the neighborhood will warrant a market to be erected—they recommend that the inhabitants be permitted at their expense, agreeably to the plan to be adopted." But it was not until the early part of the year 1807 when the Board concluded to have a market-house built on the west side of Washington, between Duane and Reade Streets, and " that five hundred dollars be appropriated for making a cellar under it."

In the month of October of that year, the market-house was ready for business, and the Market Committee placed eight butchers' stands, which were occupied by the following:

No. 1. Jacob Jeroleman, (S. side.) No. 2. Jacob Tier, Jr.,(N. side.)
    3. William Mooney,   do.   4. John Ludlum,   do.
    5. Thomas White, Jr., do.   6. William Gibson, do.
    7. Henry Hoffman,   do.   8. James Owens,   do.

Hoffman declined to accept, and No. 7 was granted to Caleb Conklin. The cellars were leased to John J. Westervelt, for five years and six months, at the rate of 300 dollars per annum, and the exclusive privilege was granted to Joseph Page for twelve months to sell *fish* here.

It was the intention of the inhabitants around here to have named it the "Washington Market," but it was never recognized as such by the authorities; however, John Low, in his " *Tables*" at this period, gives it this name, and locates it "between Reade and Duane, in Washington Street." This was several years before the present Washington Market was built or located.

In the month of February, 1809, William Mooney said, in a petition, "That in December last (1808) he relinquished his stand in Duane Market, with the intention of leaving the city; that circumstances have since altered that intention, and he is now desirous to resume his former occupation; that understanding Mr. George Cuthbert has applied for permission to sell *small meat* in the Fly Market, which, if granted, the stand No. 7, occupied by him in Duane Market, will become vacant, he prays that it may be granted to him, more especially as towards the building thereof (*this market*) he contributed the sum of fifty dollars, as will appear from the receipt of the Collector;" which was reported in favor.

Susanna Brookins, in the month of March, 1810, petitioned for permission to sell coffee in this market, and said, " Previous to her being burnt out of the house in which she then occupied near Duane Market, she had a license *(permit)* to sell coffee, &c., in the said market; that from the conflagration, your petitioner had to save her life by jumping out of a window, and lost every article she then possessed; in consequence of which she was obliged to leave the said market. That she has a large family to support, and prays for a permit to sell coffee as heretofore;" which was granted to her.

As a place of business, after the year 1813, this market almost proved a failure, as most of the stands were changing their occupants, or were often empty; and no doubt the cause was from the erection of the Washington Market, which soon attracted a large share of the public patronage.

In 1816 a bell was placed on the top of the market-house, a favorable report having been made some six years previous to that effect. Then we find two years after, (1818,) in the month of August, one John Varick petitions for the office of Deputy Clerkship of the Duane, Greenwich, Centre, Essex, and Goveneur Markets. He says, "he has been a regular-bred, and accustomed to the employment of a butcher, for nine years." His petition was referred to the Committee, who found him honest, sober, and fit for the office; and they reported in his favor.

Only imagine that *one man* should be satisfactorily performing the duties appertaining to *five public market-places*, when a large business was done in them; where now, in the same number of small market-places, we have some eight or ten Clerks, Collectors, and also two Superintendents, who are paid very high salaries for *not doing* what they ought, but doing a very *great deal* what they ought not to do!

Never were our public markets conducted in so expensive and disgraceful manner as they have been under the present system. But I am straying from my subject, and stepping along too fast into a more corrupt age.

The business in 1818 had so much decreased, that the returns of this year showed but two butchers who occupied stands in this market: John R. Tier, on No. 1, and Robert his brother, on No. 2; the latter remained with it until it ceased to exist.

The only part of the market in which any considerable business was done was the grocery store under it, where a great deal of spirituous liquors were sold, which the Common Council objected to, and denied Mr. A. Buckman, the lessee, the privilege under his lease to do so. He then petitioned to sell liquors, but a Committee reported, "to return him his money, and in future no license be granted for this purpose under any public market."

About the year 1825 bale hay was introduced in our city, and a few years after William Civill, the keeper of the public hay scale, then located at the foot of Duane Street, leased the under part of this market-house to store bale hay, which he used until it was taken down.

After the "Clinton Market" was established, the business grew still less, and but one butcher is found occupying a stand, the market-house in a state of decay; and in the month of February, 1830, a communication from Thomas Hertell, Elbert Herring, and others, owners and occupants of property in the vicinity, "consenting to a removal of the market, and that the same should remain open as a public square, until the Corporation should think proper to rebuild a market there." This was acted upon, and a Committee "reported, April 19th, same year, to remove the market-house, and the ground be regulated and paved."

Soon after the market-house was removed, Trinity Church claimed and took possession of the land, which, according to the terms, reverted to them again; and for the further disposition, I am much indebted to the Rev'd Jesse Pound, formerly of "St. Matthew's," (*Christopher Street*,) who writes me that Trinity Church then gave it "to the Church of St. George the Martyr, then in charge of the Rev'd Moses Marcus, and designed for the accommodation and benefit of English emigrants. The Church edifice, which it was contemplated to erect thereon, was never built. Mr. Marcus exchanged the old market site in Duane Street, with the City Authorities, for about 20 lots of city property, which that noble institute, St. Luke's Hospital, now occupies."

"GRAND MARKET-PLACE."

1807. In the year 1807, a large, or "Grand Market-Place," was laid out by the Commissioners, Gouverneur Morris, Simeon De Witt, and John Rutherford, and enacted by the people of the State of New York, represented in Senate and Assembly, on the 3d of April of that year.

This "Grand Market-Place" took in Tompkins Square, and ran to the East River; or bounded on the north by Tenth Street, south by Seventh Street, east by the East River, and west by the First Avenue.

The Commissioners, in their remarks, say: "Another large space —which in no distant period will be required for a public market. The City of New York contains a population already sufficient to place it in the rank of cities of the second order, and is rapidly advancing towards a level with the first. It is perhaps no unreasonable conjecture, that in a half a century it will be closely built up to the northern boundary of the '*Parade*,' (*this** '*Parade*' ex-

* Map of the City of New York, by William Bridges, 1807.

tended from Twenty-first Street up to Thirty-fourth Street, west by Seventh Avenue, and east by the Third Avenue,) and contain 400,000 souls."

Of the produce brought to our market, such as butchers' meat, poultry, fish, game, vegetables, and fruit, they say: " The dealers in those articles will also find it convenient, and so will those from whom they purchase, to meet at one general mart. This has a tendency to fix and equalize prices over the whole city. To a person engaged in profitable business, one hour spent in market is frequently worth more than the whole of what he purchases; and he is sometimes obliged to purchase a larger quantity than he has occasion to use, so that the surplus is wasted. Moreover, the time spent by those who bring articles of small value from the country, in retailing them out, bears such great proportion to the articles themselves, as to increase the price beyond what it ought to be. In short, experience having demonstrated to every great aggregation of mankind the expediency of such arrangement, it is reasonable to conclude that it will be adopted hereafter, and therefore it is proper to provide for it now. The place selected for this purpose is a *salt marsh*, and, from that circumstance, of inferior price, though, in regard to its destination, of greater value than other soil. The matter dug from a large canal through the middle, for the admission of market-boats, will give a due elevation and solidity to the sides; and in a space of more than 3,000 feet long, and upwards of 800 wide, there will, it is presumed, after deducting what is needful for the canal and market, be sufficient room for carts and wagons, without incommoding those whose business or curiosity may induce them to attend it."

On the 12th of March, 1812, a resolution was passed to petition to the Legislature for power to reduce or discontinue this market-place, which I think was not immediately done; although we find three years after, on the 6th of March, (1815,) " the bill for the alteration of this 'Grand Market-Place' was approved, and directed to be duly authenticated;" which no doubt was to reduce it, by taking two avenues off of the west end.

In 1817, Poppleton's Map of the City shows this market-place as laid out, where we find (which is also within my recollection) a natural creek ran up nearly to the First Avenue, directly through the centre of it; the mouth of which lie between *"Manhattan Island"* below it, and " Burnt Mill Point" above it. *"Branda Munah Point,"* we boys used to call it, was a great fishing, and also a swimming-place. " Manhattan Island" was a small knoll, containing perhaps an acre of land, lying near Avenue D, just above

Houston Street. When I first knew it, several creeks were crossed on small wooden bridges to reach it.

This "reduced" market-place now stood bounded on the west by Avenue C; the others remaining same as before. Nothing was done with it until 1823, when we find, on the 7th of July, a petition from Thomas L. Ogden, Nicholas Fish, and others, before the Board. "They wish the Corporation either to take the property thus placed at their disposition, or to renounce altogether the right of doing so. Justice requires that they should make the election, and that private rights and interests should be no longer suspended and sacrificed upon the mere speculative anticipations of the Commissioners, without any ascertained benefit to the public. They pray that the land designated as a public market-place may be taken by the Corporation, upon a just equivalent to the proprietors, or that the right to it may be removed and renounced. That your Honorable Body will be pleased to make such application for the purpose to the Legislature as may be requisite."

A Committee reported, and in the end *Resolved*, "That all right and claim of the Corporation to the land on the East River, between Seventh and Tenth Streets, appropriated for a market-place, ought to be released to the owners of the said land."

This was followed, on the 15th December following, with a report from the "Committee on Applications, to whom was referred the draft of a memorial and law for regulating the market-place in the meadows near Stuyvesant's land." They find it to agree with the report of the Committee, and *Resolved*, "That the memorial be executed; that, together with the law, be forwarded to the Legislature, at their next session."

Their action deprived the people of this valuable market-place, if it had been carried out as originally intended.

"COLLECT MARKET."

1809. NOT far from Broadway, near Cortlandt Alley, on the south side of Walker Street, once stood a long wooden shanty, dignified with the name of a market, established through the instrumentality of Dr. Samuel L. Mitchell, who, with several of the citizens, had early wished for a public market in that neighborhood, but the Board had refused their sanction. However, in the year

1809, the Doctor induced two butchers, or rather one was a butcheress, with as many hucksters, to locate here. For further information I am much indebted to that highly-esteemed gentleman, the late Dr. John W. Francis, for the following communication:

"Associated with the origin of the 'Collect Market' may be cited an instance of the zeal and efforts of the late distinguished philosopher, Dr. Samuel L. Mitchell, in the furtherance of that undertaking. He had announced to several of his friends the contemplated project, and in order to facilitate the measure, he had engaged certain butchers and hucksters to occupy places on the selected site. Thither he repaired at early morn daily, for the purchase of supplies; and, with that singular indifference to public remark which so eminently characterized him, burdened himself with his basket of vegetables and his meats, and proceeded through Broadway to his residence in White Street, announcing to all inquirers the new organization, and its admirable and ample accommodation for the thrifty housekeepers of that section of the city. He was admitted to have proved an excellent advertisement for the new institution. At this time he was deeply engaged with his 'History of the Fishes' which may be found in the bay and rivers of New York; and public curiosity being alive to his researches on that branch of natural history, not then much explored, he enhanced the importance of the Collect Market as a fish market. The learned Doctor unquestionably drew many customers to that, as a convenient and responsible mart."

The success of the butcher and butcheress—Joseph Blackwell and Elizabeth Crawbuck—and others, induced the Common Council to recognize it as a "public market;" and the introduction of other butchers—the brothers William and Thomas Mook, John Graham, Cornelius Vanderburgh, Mathew Bird, George Paff, and Mathew Buchannan.

Unfortunately for the butchers, Dr. Mitchell was deceived as to the ownership of the grounds chosen; for, after the erection of the sheds, the selected spot was found to belong to Peter Jay Munroe, who, as soon as it was fairly established, demanded of the butchers "ten dollars apiece for the use of the grounds, and threatened to prosecute them unless the sum was not forthwith paid;" and they were obliged to pay this sum, which at that period was considered a *tall* transaction, when many owners of such kind of property would have been glad to have given sufficient space for the benefits of having a public market near them. Several of the occupants of the stands left, whether in consequence of the demands of Munroe or not, I do not know; but other applications soon followed; one of which, named William Dusenberry, petitions "for stall No. 4," near the Collect, or "Collect Market," and wishes to occupy it in his own name. But the butchers "pray of your Honors not to grant unto William Dusenberry a stand in the temporary market by the Arsenal, as the said subscribers can prove he is no butcher, nor ever was." Signed by

No. 1. John Parcells.   No. 2. Joseph Blackwell.
     3. Mathew Flagar.   4. Formerly Mrs. Crawbuck.
     5. John Simonson.   6. Martin Lemon.
     7. William Lowree.   8. John Fitzgerald.
     9. Isaac Beyea.   10. William Mook.

We find this market-place is sometimes called the "Arsenal Market," "Mosquito Market;" but usually known as the "Collect Market." In an advertisement,* April, 1813, headed "EXTRAORDINARY! *To all Lovers of Fat Beef*.—Joseph Blackwell, 2 'Collect Market,' near the Panorama, Broadway, takes the liberty of informing them that he will have on Saturday, the 10th inst., in said market, beef of the most superior quality ever offered for sale in this country." This animal proved to be the heaviest ever known before in New York City—the weight of his four quarters, in beef, was near 1,900 pounds.

The next year, also, in the month of April, is found in the Press: "*To the Lovers of Fat Beef*.—This is to inform the public that there will be offered for sale, by Joseph Blackwell and Jeremiah Tier, at No. 1 and No. 11, in the market, near the Circus, in Broadway, (*corner of White Street*,) on Saturday, the 30th instant, beef of a superior quality than any ever offered for sale in this city, and it is believed never has been equaled in the United States. This steer is only six years old, and was bred and fatted by Mr. John Seabright, near Albany, in the State of New York. It is allowed by old experienced butchers that this steer will weigh eighteen hundred weight, and have more fat than any beast has ever produced in the United States. N. B.—This is the ox that was exhibited through the streets on the 27th instant."

Many years before this market-place was established, Mr. Blackwell commenced business in a temporary shed in Broadway, near the corner of White Street, but was induced to move by Dr. Mitchell, as was also Mrs. Elizabeth Crawbuck. She, after losing her husband, (Godfrey Crawbuck,) petitioned to the Common Council in 1809, representing "she had permission to sell meat in a vacant lot fronting to Broadway, near Reade Street; that a building is shortly to be erected on the ground; she will have to remove. She can obtain leave from the owner of a lot of ground above the *Arch* in Broad-

* Daily Gazette.

way (*Leonard Street*) to put her stall on, and she has no other means of supporting her helpless family, among whom is a crippled son." The Common Council granted her permission to remove; but she did not remain long here before she again removed in the Collect Market. She was an excellent saleswoman, and succeeded in supporting her family while in business.

The name of "Collect" originated from the Dutch of "*Kalck Hook*,"* given to a point of land on the shore of the (*Colleck*, or Kolck,) pond, the site of an old Indian village. This location was near the Halls of Justice in Centre Street; but all the low grounds extending above to the "Stone Bridge," corner of Canal and Broadway, were filled in, and within my recollection was called the "Collect," and this "The Market on the Collect."

In the month of March, 1817, a petition was before the Board from more than seventy-five citizens residing in the vicinity of this market-place, who wish to have it removed to some other part of the Collect grounds, as the old market shed is in a falling-down condition, and the grounds were wanted for other purposes. A Committee reported in favor of the above in the month of June following, and state, "That after due investigation, they have fixed on a site along Collect (*Centre*) Street, from Anthony to Leonard Streets, on the grounds belonging to the Corporation. This piece of ground is in length on Collect Street 183 feet, averaging about 110 feet deep, and by taking 25 feet for a market and 25 feet for a street or passage in front of the remaining grounds, will leave sufficient depth for buildings adapted to the purposes for which they would be occupied. It is believed a market-house of 75 feet in length would answer all present purposes, leaving sufficient room to extend it as circumstances may require. An area of 108 feet by 50 feet, together with a part of Collect Street, (which is 60 feet wide,) presents ample room for the purposes of a vegetable market."

The whole cost to be about $2,000. The project was not carried out, however, by the Board, as the majority were in favor of having it established above Grand Street. The butchers, with several others, were opposed to its removal above this street; but when they found the report and resolution in favor, they again petitioned for stands in the new market. This was signed by

Thomas Harrison, on No. 1.	Joseph Blackwell, on No. 2.
William H. Gross,	" 3.	John Hilliker,	" 4.
John Simonson,	" 5.	William Reeves,	" 6.
Thomas Mook,	" 7.	William Bowen,	" 8.
James Simonson,	" 9.	William Mook,	" 10.
John A. Besler,	" 11.	Mathew Boscawen,	" 12.

* Valentine's New York.

Some little changes were, however, made before they left the old market; but all were removed according to their wish, and the old shell was soon after torn down.

"GREENWICH MARKET."

1812. IN the month of April, 1812, a petition from the inhabitants of the "Village of Greenwich," for a public market-place, was presented to the Common Council, and this, with a proposition from the Corporation of Trinity Church, and also a communication from Mr. Garrit Gilbert, containing a liberal offer of a "lot of ground 25 feet on Greenwich Street and 50 feet on Henry (*Perry*) Street, and the building of a market-house thereon," were all referred to the Market Committee, who reported, on the 5th of October following, on the proposition made by the Corporation of Trinity Church, which met their approbation. "The Vestry of the Church offer to make a cession of a piece of ground, to be used for a public market, 50 feet wide on the south side of Christopher Street, extending in length on a line of the said street from Greenwich to Washington Streets; on condition, however, that when said ground shall cease to be so used, it shall then revert back again." The proposition was considered very liberal, and recommended the acceptance thereof; and also an offer of one hundred and fifty dollars, formerly made towards building on the property of Mr. Gilbert, be applied towards erecting a market-house on the ground now offered to be ceded. This report was approved, and the market was built, with the west end on a line of Washington Street, running up on the southerly side of Christopher Street towards Greenwich Street. On the 18th of June, 1813, the building was reported finished, and the Market Committee recommended the following butchers for stands in "*Greenwich Market;*" "but previous to taking possession thereof, they shall ascertain by lot who shall be entitled to the choice," which resulted as follows:

No. 1. James Reeves.   No. 2. Adam Tenbrook.
3. Frederick Glasshorne.   4. Adam Fink.
5. George Patten.   6. John Tenbrook.

The name of "Greenwich," we find, was applied to "Spring Street Market" at an early period; but as it was not the proper one, we did not introduce the origin of the name in its history; and as this market-place was never known by any other name than "Greenwich Market," it was thought proper to introduce such evidence here.

The name of "Greenwich" is taken from a very old town, some four or five miles from London, on the south bank of the River Thames. Here are many public establishments, among which are the famous and noble Greenwich Hospital, Greenwich Observatory and beautiful parks, and where many families of wealth reside, besides being a favorite resort of holiday seekers from the great City of London.

Not less than eight towns in the United States have been named after it: we have *Greenwich* in Hampshire Co., Mass.; *Greenwich*, Fairfield Co., Conn.; *Greenwich*, Washington Co., N. Y.; *Greenwich*, Warren Co., N. J.; another *Greenwich* in Gloucester Co., and still another *Greenwich* in Cumberland Co., same State; *Greenwich* in Berks Co., Penn.; and *Greenwich* in Huron Co., Ohio.

" Greenwich " was given here to a collection of country-seats on the North River about the year 1750, which included " Lady Warren's,"* (the present residence of Abraham Van Ness, which originally comprised nearly the whole of the present 9th Ward,) J. Jeauncey's, William Bayard's, and Oliver Delancey's estates, measuring about one mile in extent, commencing from about Hamersley and running up to Seventeenth Street. Greenwich Street was a part of the old " Road to Greenwich," afterwards "Greenwich Road," finally changed to "Greenwich Street."

The visits of yellow fever in 1798, '99, 1803, and '5, tended much to increase the formation of a village, near the " Spring Street Market," and one also near the "State Prison;" but the " fever of 1822" built up many streets, with numerous wooden buildings, for the uses of the merchants, banks, (from which Bank Street took its name,) offices, &c.; and the celerity of putting up those buildings is better told by the Rev'd Mr. Marcellus, who informed me, that "he saw corn growing on the present corner of Hammond and Fourth Streets on a *Saturday* morning, and on the following *Monday* 'Sykes & Niblo' had a house erected capable of accommodating *three hundred* boarders." Even the Brooklyn ferry-boats ran up here daily.

"Hardie," in his account of the fever of 1822, says, " Saturday, the 24th August, our city presented the appearance of a town besieged. From daybreak till night one line of carts, containing boxes, merchandise and effects, were seen moving towards 'Greenwich Village' and the upper parts of the city. Carriages and hacks, wagons and horsemen, were scouring the streets and filling the roads; persons with anxiety strongly marked on their countenances, and with

* Her husband, *Sir Peter Warren*, died in Dublin, 29th July, 1752, aged 48 years.

hurried gait, were hustling through the streets. Temporary stores and offices were erecting, and even on the ensuing day (Sunday) carts were in motion, and the saw and hammer busily at work. Within a few days thereafter, the Custom-House, the Post-Office, the Banks, the Insurance Offices, and the printers of newspapers located themselves in the village, or in the upper part of Broadway, where they were free from the impending danger; and these places almost instantaneously became the seat of the immense business usually carried on in the great metropolis."

In order to designate these two villages or places, the one at the State Prison was usually known as the "Upper Village of Greenwich," and the one about Spring Street, near the North River, was called the "Lower Village of Greenwich."

In the year 1819 this market-house was enlarged and a cellar wall put under it, at an expense of $575, which gave those doing business in it much more convenience, and the means of preventing their meats and vegetables from freezing.

In 1822 Jacob Seiler (Syler) petitioned for a butcher's stand in this market, and the Market Committee reported in his favor; and they also "beg leave to represent that, in their opinion, the public interest would be promoted by vesting His Honor the Mayor with power to license all persons as butchers, who may be from time to time recommended by the Market Committee. It frequently happens, as in the present (*Seiler's*) case, that nearly a month elapses after a petition is dated before the applicant is informed whether the prayer of his petition is granted, during all which time the stall remains unoccupied, and the public lose the rent; whereas, if the power to license was in the Mayor, it would require but a very few days to decide on every application;" and they offer the following: "*Resolved*, That His Honor the Mayor be authorized to license all such persons as butchers as may be recommended by the Market Committee, and that he be requested to report from time to time the names of all such persons as he shall have licensed;" which was adopted.

So particular were the Corporation in granting licenses to young butchers, that they were not only required to serve a regular apprenticeship, but their conduct and morals were also particularly considered; and I have met with but one case where a license was granted under age, and this was a partnership in one stand. In the case of Samuel S. Cornell and William P. Munson, who apply for stand No. 52 "Fly Market," in the month of May, 1821, after they had proved regular apprenticeships served, the father of one of them stated, that "one of the above applicants is my son. As he is not quite twenty-one years of age, knowing that it is contrary to the laws of the Corporation to grant permission to any butcher under age, I take the liberty to state, that should the Committee give the stall above alluded to, I shall consider it a favor particularly done to me. Mr. Cornell is about three-and-twenty years old; I know he has served a regular time to the business. I will obligate myself to pay the rent of the stall, and to see that their *conduct is good*." The Market Committee "*Resolved*, That they be licensed for stall No. 52 Fly Market."

Prior to the year 1825, one Clerk of the Market attended to the duties of collection of moneys, and in fact had the whole charge of this market, and five others, without the aid of a "Superintendent of Markets," viz.: Greenwich, Spring Street, Centre, Essex, Grand Street, and Goveneur Markets. Peter Ammerman performed this duty when a large business was done in all of them, but it was found too much for the old man, and in the month of April of the above year the Market Committee "*Resolved*, That the office of the Clerk of the six upper markets be divided, and that Peter Ammerman continue to perform the duties of Clerk of the Essex, Grand Street, and Goveneur Markets during the pleasure of the Board, and that a new Clerk be appointed for Centre, Spring Street, and Greenwich Markets;" and the pay less than *one dollar per day*, as we find that the Market Committee, in the month of October, 1827, reported in favor of allowing Mr. James Gilbert, of Spring Street, Centre, and Greenwich Markets, *one dollar per day*—every day commencing 1st of August of that year.

At this period we find six markets attended to by one man, at likely less than *one dollar* per day—is 365 dollars; while at the present day we are *saddled* with a Clerk to each market, besides Collectors and a Superintendent, at a cost of not less than $8,000 to the city, besides the enormous sums that are made—*nay, demanded*—from occupants. Comment is unnecessary.

In 1828 this market-house was again enlarged, and soon after ten butchers' stands are found occupied, and but one of the original six is found among them. They appeared as follows:

No. 1.	Dennis Valentine.	No. 2.	Hebron Hurd.
3.	Bussing Valentine.	4.	Joseph Jacacks.
5.	William B. Mirrick.	6.	William Searles.
7.	Jeremiah Kilpatrick.	8.	Caleb Angevine.
9.	Charles Gilman.	10.	Gabriel Duryea.

From the establishment of this market-place, the business was generally good, more especially in the summer season, as many persons moved and boarded in Greenwich Village; and after 1822 it continued to grow better; in fact, so much so, it increased to ten stands in 1828; and in 1832 fourteen stands are found occupied, and but one of those left, as noticed in 1828. They were then found on

No. 1. Daniel S. Hyde.	No. 2. Henry Pray.
3. William B. Mirrick.	4. Milton Jacacks.
5. James Reeves, Sen'r.	6. James H. Houghtalin.
7. Thomas Reeves.	8. Jared Goodheart.
9. Weigh scales.	10. William Piercey.
11. Andrew Foshay.	12. George Goodheart.
13. Isaac Valentine.	14. William Goodheart.

The occupant of No. 1, Daniel S. Hyde, in an advertisement, claims to have sold the first pair of Premium Cattle in Greenwich Village. He says: "These oxen are six years old, and raised by J. M. Meeker, Esq. They obtained the first premium at the Orange Cattle Show, New Jersey; and he feels a pride in having the honor of presenting to the Village of Greenwich the *first pair* of 'Prize' steers ever exhibited in this part of the Island."

After this period the trade began to fall off; and when the establishment of Jefferson Market took place, (in 1833,) the butchers' stands began gradually to be unoccupied, and finally reduced down to the number of two; in fact, the business had fallen off so much, and the market-house became so uninviting, in consequence of neglect and its age, that the Common Council, on the 28th of May, 1835, ordered it to be taken down, and "the grounds paved, and appropriated for market purposes;" fearing that, if it was not so "*appropriated*," Trinity Church would claim possession, because of the violation of the contract made with that "Church," that the grounds should be always used for market purposes.

I feel, however, satisfied that if the inhabitants and owners of the property in the neighborhood should, at their own expense, erect thereon a small, neat market-house, petition to have it made a public market, without the incubus of a public officer attached to it, and allow butchers and others to go in free of rent, except so much as to keep it in repair, it would tend greatly to increase the business, as well as the value of their property.

"G O V E N E U R   M A R K E T."

1812.   At a meeting of the Board held on the 20th of July, 1812, a Committee reported in favor of allowing Christian Berg and several residents and owners of property in the vicinity of Goveneur's Slip to erect a market-house at their own expense.   They immediately proceeded with it, and in less than six weeks it was ready for occupation.   The Market Committee recommended stand No. 1 be granted to William Mooney, in consideration of its being the wish of all those who contributed towards building the said market; and that five next succeeding numbers be granted to the following applicants, as they may respectively draw them by lot, viz.: Richard Ford, Charles Myers, Stephen Smack, James Goodman, and Richard Kennah."

This market-house was a small affair—in fact, the smallest in the city at that period; its location was a little north and east from the present one, and its cost but $357.$\frac{75}{100}$; two hundred and twenty of which was raised by subscription, and the balance was paid by Mr. Berg; but who afterwards petitions to the Corporation to have them refund the money.   On the 29th of March, 1813, it was ordered that the Comptroller pay $137.$\frac{75}{100}$ to Christian Berg, to reimburse him this payment.

The name of "Goveneur" was taken from a family of that name who owned a large estate here, and which also gave the name to "Goveneur Street," which ran through this property.

Its business commencement was rather flattering, but after a few years it began to decrease; the stands were vacated and occupied alternately; seldom above three stands of the butchers were occupied or doing business there until about 1820, when that part of the city had greatly increased with tenement-houses, ship-building, &c.

In 1824 a petition was before the Board from the citizens near this location, asking for a new market-house, "or the old one moved fronting the street and repaired ; for as it now stands it is too low, and a considerable distance from the street;" "and a great inconvenience, especially in the winter season."

Another and a more numerously signed petition was before the Board on the 31st of July, 1826, which states: "That it is in a bad situation, in consequence of the length of time it has been standing without any repairs, and its situation on the slip.   A part of the floor is below the surface of the pavements; the roof leaks; one or more of the corner posts are entirely gone; every heavy rain overflows the floor, and renders it almost impossible to stand in the market; holes are bored through the floor to drain off the water; that water collects under the market, stagnates, and becomes in warm weather almost insupportable. The consequence is, butchers will not locate there, and the inhabitants are put to great inconvenience, and are obliged, in many cases, to go to Catharine Market for supplies." The Market Committee reported: "They find it the same— in a very decayed state, and totally unfit for use. That in consequence of the rapid improvement in that part of the city, a new market is very much wanted at that place, and the probable expense of erecting about five hundred dollars." The Board resolved to build accordingly, and the new market was finished in the month of January of the next year.

On the 12th of February following, the Market Committee reported the sale of four stands at public auction, and two by private contract, as follows: " That on the second day of February, stands Nos. 3, 4, 5, and 6, in the new Goveneur Market, for the sum of one hundred and fifteen dollars for the whole, for fifteen months, from 1st inst.; and have, by private contract, let stand No. 1, at the yearly rent of $60, and stand No. 2 at the yearly rent of $45, for the same period; making altogether two hundred and twenty dollars per annum, or equal to *eleven per cent.* on the cost of the market, estimated at $2,031.$\frac{86}{100}$;" and when the grounds ceased to be used for public market purposes, they were to revert back to the original owners. The six stands were then occupied by the following butchers:

No. 1. Henry Hyde.	No. 2. William P. Varian.
3. Adolphus Odell.	4. Joseph B. Smith.
5. John Crawbuck.	6. Joseph Ferdon.

The terms were, " the first quarter's rent on each stand paid in advance;" and the old market building was soon after sold to Henry Hyde, for the sum of forty dollars.

Although there were six stands leased, yet the business was not again enough to support them, as the next year the returns showed but two occupied, one by Henry Hyde, and the other by John Boscawen.

Henry Hyde, the occupant of No. 1, was long established here, and as a butcher he was among the best in his day, being an excellent judge of stock, and while in business he always sold the best and choicest meats. He was extensively known on Long Island among those who raised and fatted stock, and they had so much confidence in him, that many fine animals were sent to him, without first making the price, as he always gave them satisfactory returns; and of course " there was no butcher like Henry Hyde," and they were not far from the truth.

In the year 1834 the business was again quite promising; we, however, find but one of those noticed in 1827. On

No. 1. Henry Hyde.	No. 2. John Mills.
3. Alex'r J. Brown.	4. John Cornell.
5. Gabriel Duryea.	6. Christian Truss.

This reputation of prosperity was not of long duration, as the trade was attracted to the numerous " meat-shops" in the neighborhood, and the market became almost deserted, with, I believe, one exception, for a long time. However, in 1848 four stands are occupied by the following butchers:

| No. 1. Henry Hyde. | No. 2. Andrew Storms. |
| 3. Stephen Storms. | 4. John Cornell. |

Soon after a petition for a new market was presented, and in 1852 the proper officer was directed to have the new market at Goveneur's Slip completed forthwith; but soon after the old market-house was sold at public auction for the sum of $127, and immediately after removed.

The new market-house is now occupied with two or three butchers, one fisherman, and one huckster; the upper part as a police station for the Seventh District, with prison cells beneath.

"WASHINGTON MARKET."

1812. THE question of erecting a large market-house on the site now occupied by the main market building, running along on the west side of Washington Street, with wings down Fulton and Vesey Streets, was strongly advocated in the year 1805, after certain improvements had been made in the making a bulkhead and filling it up. Before they were finished, a Committee was appointed " to prepare a plan of a substantial and commodious market to be built on the said site, and to report the same to the Common Council without delay." It was, however, delayed, and for nearly six years afterwards, in consequence of the leases of several lots not expiring before the year 1813, and the unusually large but necessary funds to be raised under the circumstances, it was concluded to defer it until a more suitable opportunity.

On the 10th of February, 1812, the subject was again reported on by a Committee, who " recommended that the former proceedings of the Board in relation to this subject be now carried into execution, and that the propriety of appropriating the ground above referred to for building said market, as also the producing a plan on which the same shall be constructed, be referred to some proper Committee;" which were appointed, and the subject disposed of.

This Committee, on the 1st of June following, reported the plan, which is still seen in the present old building, " forming a hollow square;" and the market-place was to employ the " whole block bounded by Washington, West, Partition (Fulton,) and Vesey Streets, for market purposes." The building was immediately commenced; and on the 5th of October following a report from the Committee stated, that " the plan as agreed upon by the Board has been substantially adhered to; but as, in the opinion of your Committee, the compleating of one-half of said plan will answer all purposes, their contracts as yet have provided for laying this fall the foundation only along Washington Street, and fifty feet thereon down Vesey Street and Partition Street." They " moreover propose making a contract for the stone pillars which may be required, in order that the superstructure may without interruption progress early in the spring." The next year, on the 31st of May, the Committee reported, that " Washington Market" was not in a fit state to receive the butchers from the "Old Bear Market," which had been torn down, and temporary sheds were ordered to be erected for that purpose, near where the " Bear Market" had stood.

The name of "Bear Market " was applied to this new market, and continued for many years; I may say that it was so designated by many of our old citizens, who could not consent to give up or change the old association for the more modern one, although the latter, if not so venerable, is more revered.

Before the close of the year 1813, the new market-house was fully established; the butchers from the old Bear Market were all placed in on the stands allotted them with satisfaction, and business commenced with highly flattering prospects, although the prices of provisions were very high, in consequence of the war with England. The first victories by sea and land obtained over that great power, by General Harrison and Commodore Perry, were the cause of a general illumination throughout the city, which took place on Saturday evening, the 23d of October. The Evening Post of the 25th instant says: " It deserves attention that the butchers of the city distinguished themselves on this occasion, by illuminating their stalls in the various markets, with a profusion of lights placed in such a manner as to produce the most striking effect. They, too, had their transparencies with '*Free Trade and Butchers' Rights.*'"

I have previously noticed that one part of the "Old Bear Market" was called "Buttermilk Market," where the "Jersey Dutch" women, dressed in linsey-woolsey short gowns and petticoats, came in great numbers with their butter, pot-cheese, curds, and buttermilk; and great quantities of the latter were brought here in their well-scoured (or *boondered*) churns and sold. This trade was transferred into this new or Washington Market, and continued until about the year 1830, when the last one of these specimens of "Olden Times" disappeared forever. Their last location was at the corner of Washington and Fulton Streets, at the corner of the market.

The "old Jersey Dutchmen," who came down with them in their skiffs about this time, (1813,) usually divided their stock in trade; they took the products of the farm and part of the dairy, *i. e.*, the butter, which was the most valuable part, into the country market, where butter was a quick sale at 3s. and 3/6d. per pound; and these prices continued throughout the season. Great quantities were gathered up in several of the counties along the North River by speculators, as appears from the following "communication" in the Gazette, November 1, 1813, headed "WINTER BUTTER."—"It is certain that full seven-eighths of the article is in the hands of a company of speculators in Newburgh, and the different towns in the County of Orange. It is therefore recommended to the citizens of New York, who are to be the ultimate consumers, to suspend their purchases for the winter's supply for at least one month, rather than to gratify those gentlemen by giving them the moderate price of 2/6d. and 3s. per pound."

Many of the principal grocers held meetings in relation to this subject, and passed certain resolutions; one of their meetings is noticed in the Evening Post, as follows: "A large meeting of grocers was held at Harmony Hall, on the 11th of November, (1813,) in relation to the price of butter, when it was stated that large quantities were held by several monopolizers and speculators in this city and Orange County. They passed resolutions that they would not purchase of them, but would purchase or give higher prices to others from neighboring counties and sister States. They also recommended to all grocers not to take any of the *notes* of the banks in the County of Orange, during the present season. Signed by '*James Smith, Chairman,*' and '*N. T. Hubbard, Secretary.*'"

In 1820, the "Agricultural Society," for the purpose of encouraging the making of choice butter, which was usually brought to market in one and two pound rolls, gave notice to those who were in the habit of bringing this article to this and the Fly Market, that they would give premiums for the best brought on the first days of June in each year. A Committee from the Society was appointed in June, 1821, to examine the butter in these markets. In this market, "the first premium, a silver cream pitcher," was awarded to Mrs. Hopper, of Hackensack, N. J., and the second prize, "a silver cup," to Mr. J. Coon, of Greenbush, opposite Albany, N. Y. In the "Fly Market," the first prize was taken by Mrs. Stewart, of Jamaica, L. I., and the second prize to Mrs. Morris, of Morrisania, Westchester County, N. Y. In the same month, in the following year, at this market, Mr. Cornelius Terhune, of *Hackensack*, carried away the first premium, a silver pitcher, valued at $15; Mr. Josiah Austin, *Seconicus*, the second premium, a silver pitcher, valued at $10; and Mr. Thomas Brown, *Westchester*, the third premium, silver cup, valued $5. This encouragement continued for several years, producing, it is said, a decided improvement in that necessary article of consumption. There were, however, a few countrymen, who had the reputation of making the most they could out of their productions, whether honestly or dishonestly, they cared not; but it generally fell under the latter head.

One morning a respectable-looking and quite a wealthy farmer, who was generally known as a very close shaver, or, in other words, as fond of cheating whenever he had a chance, brought his butter handsomely done up in pound rolls. This was at a time when it was scarce and worth 3s. and a quick sale at that price, which no doubt had induced him to scant the weight in each roll. Unexpectedly the weigh-master (whether he mistrusted the farmer or not) saw his butter opened for sale, (which the farmer could not quickly cover out of sight,) when he prepared his test scale to weigh it; while doing so, the farmer, in his anxiety, quick as thought, slipped a guinea out of his vest pocket, and while the weigh-master's back was turned, thrust it into the top roll, as he thought unperceived by any one. The roll was taken up, and it weighed full weight, which satisfied him without weighing any other; but while he was putting up his scale, a Quaker gentleman, who had been standing off a little distance, and had seen the whole transaction, came up and inquired the price of his butter. "Three shillings," said the farmer. "Put me that roll in my kettle," says the Quaker, pointing to the "*guinea roll.*" *Farmer.* "I have that roll sold to a friend." *Quaker.* "No, thee has not—thee can give thy friend another roll, if they are all good and weigh alike;" and turned to question the weigh-master; who said to the Quaker, "He was entitled to the roll, or any roll he choosed to take, if they were priced to him." With this the Quaker took up the guinea roll and placed it in his kettle, then laid down three shillings; and as he was going, he coolly told the farmer: "Thee will not find cheating always profitable."

We will now look back in the year 1815, when we find the centre part of this market on Washington Street was two stories high, on which stand the cupola and bell. These upper stories were appropriated for a watch-house for the "First District Watch," which now to look at would appear very small accommodations, but in those days they were ample for the necessary numbers of "Night Watch" required for the protection of this large portion of the city. Our good citizens were not then annoyed with such numbers, *both in and out of public office*, of drunkards, rowdies, rioters, thieves, garroters, robbers, and murderers as are now out of such confinement as their several cases would seem to demand; and as for sellers of unwholesome provisions, they were immediately brought up to the bar of justice, where political influence would not save them. We find one John Fanton, a blacksmith, petitioning to be released from the fine and imprisonment in the month of November of this year. He says, he "was committed to the goal of the City and County of New York, for a breach of one of the Ordinances or By-Laws; your petitioner's son, a lad about thirteen years of age, for exposing unwholesome provisions for sale, to wit, two geese, as was alleged, which the Clerk of Washington Market said were *blown*. If they were *blown*, it was not with the consent or knowledge of your petitioner. Further, your petitioner is a blacksmith by trade, resides in Greenwich Village; he has a family consisting of a wife and ten children; that he has always supported his family heretofore; but owing to misfortune and losses, he has become reduced, and some time since his property was sold on execution, and stripped of everything excepting what the law allows him. Your petitioner is destitute of any ways or means of paying the forfeiture or penalty, or any part thereof. Further, if he should be confined for thirty days, your petitioner's family will become greatly distressed, as the only support for them is his earnings from day to day." He prayed a discharge from prison, but his prayer was denied.

I have previously noticed the prices of provisions as being very high on the commencement of the war of 1812; they continued so for five or six years, and the price of neat cattle ranged from £5 to £7 4s. per cwt.; pork, £4 to £4 8s. per cwt.; poultry, 12 to 15 pence per pound, and very scarce.

In the month of June, 1816, a report was made by Richard Smith, Clerk of this market, of the numbers of cattle, sheep, calves, and hogs which he had received fees for in the previous months of January, February, March, and April; and it also shows the greater amount of business done in the Fly Market during the same months, by the larger numbers of animals reported. In this market they appear as follows:

	Beeves.	Sheep.	Calves.	Hogs.
January, -	491	858	202	371
February, -	394	575	296	242
March, - - -	447	319	948	102
April, - - -	312	222	1,719	152
Total, - - -	1,644	1,973	3,165	867

The high prices of all kinds of provisions, and more especially that of cattle, was the cause of introducing cattle from Ohio. The first drove was brought on here in the month of June, 1817, by a drover named " Drenning." The " Press" gives us the following account: " They appear as fresh as if just taken off one of our Long Island farms. When it is recollected that they have been driven nearly one thousand miles, this fact will be considered a very remarkable one. Several of our leading butchers have made an offer of *twelve dollars* a hundred for the beef of this drove, which was refused; but it is supposed *twelve dollars and a half* will purchase them." Mr. Drenning had started from Chillicothe, Ohio, with about 200 in the drove, driving them very slowly, and only a few miles per day; he arrived here with more than 100, having sold many of them on the way." The "old butchers" recollect them, and say they looked well, having been strongly fed on whole corn daily from the time they started.

I have previously noticed that the Common Council had regretted the selling of butchers' stands at public auction. More than ten years had now elapsed, and with the several changes of the members of this body, these regrets had been forgotten, or they intended to adopt another system of leasing these stands. The Market Committee reported, December 2, 1816, on the stand No. 10 in this market, and stated, that " it is now vacant; and as there is a great many applicants for the same, they recommend to the Corporation the propriety of selling the same at auction, for —— years, to the highest bidder, who shall be a regular butcher, and the purchaser to be approved by the Board, at an annual rent, payable quarterly; and the rent shall be considered including all market fees."

This reported arrangement, the butchers thought, was, if anything, worse than the former, and more than forty of them, from this market, presented a memorial, and stated their reasons, on the 23d of the same month. They stated, " That the petitioners are informed that this Honorable Board intend, in future, to sell all such stands as may become vacant, for a number of years, at auction, to the highest bidder; which measure will be productive of great inconvenience and distress to butchers who may purchase such stands, and by their industry and attention establish a profitable trade to the same, which they will probably have to quit at the end of their term, not being willing to bid for the same perhaps more than it is worth, and the same be purchased by some adventurer, who will receive the benefits arising from the industry of the former holder of said stand; and, as persons of capital can alone bid for the stands, those butchers who are poor will not be able, during their lives, to procure a stand to follow their business at; and further, persons who are not butchers may hire persons who are butchers to hire such stands, and share the profits of the same, to which they ought not to be entitled; by which means, many regular-bred butchers will be deprived of the means of getting a living for their families," &c. This memorial, and several petitions on the same subject, from the butchers of other markets, were referred; and finally, these vacant stands were drawn for by lot, under certain restrictions, which gave general satisfaction.

The anxiety of butchers to procure stands in this market, at this period, shows the fact that it was prosperous, and advancing in favor with the citizens, who began to desert the Fly, and betake themselves to this market; and in the year 1818, there appear to have been fifty-five regular stands, which numbers commenced from the centre of the market on Washington Street, and advanced or counted to the right adjoining, (and not opposite.) They were occupied as follows:

No. 1. John J. Fink.	No. 29. Francis Spicer.
2. John G. Graff.	30. Christian F. Hartell.
3. Chas. Weatherspoon.	31. John Hutton.
4. Thomas Starr.	32. Corn's King, Jr.
5. Nicholas Dean.	33. Adam Hartell, Sr.
6. John Shane.	34. Doorway.
7. George Haws.	35. John Davenport.
8. Simeon Travis.	36. Lawrence Wiseburn.
9. Charles Gwyer.	37. Jacob Aims.
10. Benjamin Davis.	38. Henry Wicker.
11. John Henning.	39. John Brewer.
12. Isaac Vaughn.	40. George Hutton.
13. George Vaughn.	41. William Passman.
14. William Vonck.	42. William Chivvis.
15. Jacob Flagar.	43. John Chivvis.

No. 16. Michael Hillman.
17. James Owens.
18. J. L. Fink.
19. Hugh Goble.
20. Jacob Harriot.
21. Christian Harriot.
22. Charles Gilman.
23. Charles Gilman, Jr.
24. Thomas Collister.
25. Bartholomew Granger.
26. John Pessinger.
27. Isaac Boyce.
28. Samuel White.

No. 44. Henry Owens.
45. William Hopkins.
46. John Hopkins.
47. Jacob Acker.
48. James Chivvis.
49. Philip L. Luff.
50. Cornelius Chivvis.
51. Ludowick Harpel.
52. Ernest Keyser.
53. Thomas Jeremiah.
54. Abraham Vermylia.
55. John Fink.
56. Alex'r Fink, Jr.

Many of these, who were principally old butchers, had disappeared ten years after, when the occupants of these stands are again noticed; from among these were several whose memories are worthy of further and future record.

The occupant of No. 42, William Chivvis, was born in Richmond, Virginia; and when the Revolution took place, he enlisted for *three years*, or "during the war," under Captain Eno's, but was transferred to Captain John Champe Carter's Company of Artillery, where he became one of the gunners. He was in the battles of White Plains, Saratoga, Monmouth, Stony Point, and Yorktown, and served under Lafayette (when he came into command) until the end of the war. While his Company lay encamped at Valley Forge, in June, 1778, he became acquainted with Farmer *Doty's* daughter *Jane*, engaged himself to her, and as soon as the war was over, and he discharged, he sought her, was married, and for a few years turned farmer, until business began to move in New York, when he proceeded there, and about 1790 commenced business as a butcher, of which he had gained some knowledge in the victualing department while in the service. In this market, on some benches, he began the business, and continued it until 1819, when the Market Committee had, or were about, depriving him of his stand. In the month of March we find the following petition from him before the Board. He stated: "That your petitioner is now *seventy years old*, and by misfortunes has become destitute of property; while he has a large family to support. That he *was a soldier engaged in his country's cause the greater part of the Revolutionary War, and* during that time was engaged in several of the most sanguinary battles; which facts are at this day in this city susceptible of proof. That your petitioner, altho' almost borne down with age, & with the troubles incident to his embarras'd situation, with a large family,

& to seek daily for their support, has been informed that an *order*
or arrangement has been made by which the stall which he has occupied, No. 42 Washington Market, for *upwards of twenty-four
years*, is about to be taken from him & given to *another*, while the
profits of said stall, through his own exertions & the aid of his
sons, who are butchers in the same market, is the only vestige of
hope for the support of himself & family in his declining years.
Your petitioner has been enabled for the last two years to carry on
his trade in a limited manner, but yet in a way to enable him to sustain his family & himself. That the person who is seeking for the
stall occupied by your petitioner has, as your petitioner is informed,
represented that the stall has not been occupied by me in *two years*,
& that he served his time out with Mr. L. Harpell; which representation is totally untrue. The stall has been occupied to the best
purpose by your petitioner during the most of that time, with the
aid of his sons, to the accommodation of the public, & to produce a
revenue to your petitioner & his family, for their support.

" WILLIAM CHIVVIS."

Numbers of merchants and others recommend him, " as an aged,
respectable citizen, believing, as we do, that the facts set forth in
the foregoing petition is in all respects true." This was signed by

A. Stagg,	William H. Ireland,	William Ross,
Joseph Ireland,	John McKesson,	Isaac Graham,
Jackson Haines,	John Hunter,	Benjamin Stagg,
M. Allison,	James L. Bell,	Francis V. Many,
Rd. Allison,	John Salisbury,	Benjamin Ferris,
Wm. Allison,	James Hopson,	A. Labagh,
James Warner,	Chas. Denison,	Eben'r T. White,
John Connor,	Smith Cutter,	Daniel D. Smith,
Samuel Burns,	Jno. Neilson,	Wm. Hardy,
John Disbrow.		

Richard Smith, the Deputy Clerk, was directed to make a report
of the above case. He says, (May 3,) in a note to Alderman Buckmaster: "*Sir*—You sent by the bearer to know how long William
Chivvis has been absent from his stall. He has been absent near
two years, I believe, but am informed he has got his license by some
butchers, and had a *side of beef* this morning." On the 7th he says:
"One circumstance did not occur at the time I wrote it. I have
since recollected that he was at his stall with meat personally,
some time in December last. His stall has been occupied since,
more or less." His stall was restored to him.

He had a large family, among whom were several sons; five of
them were butchers, viz., John, William, Cornelius, James, and

Peter. His children were brought up in a respectable manner, giving them a liberal education, which at that period was a large item in the many family expenses. He, however, lived and died an honest man, being called away in the year 1823, then eighty years of age.

The occupant of No. 18, John Lawrence Fink, known as Captain Fink, from the fact that he held that office during the war of 1812, and gallantly performed his duty. Previous to the commencement of this war, he was an officer in a troop of horse called the "Flying Artillery," which was composed principally of butchers; but, wishing for more active service, he sought and was commissioned a Lieutenant, with rank from 6th of July, 1812, in the 13th Regiment of Infantry, Lieutenant-Colonel Chrystie, and was soon ordered to the Canadian lines. In the battle of Queenstown, says an eye-witness, "Early on the morning of the 13th of October, 1812, Lieutenant Fink commanded the advanced guard, consisting of seven non-commissioned officers and twenty-four privates, who, at half past three o'clock, embarked on two small boats to cross the river, accompanied by Lieutenant-Colonel Chrystie and Lieutenant Steakes. When approaching the enemy's shore, within about forty yards, they commenced firing upon the boat which contained Lieutenant Fink— it being the *first fire* which had been made upon our troops—and killed and wounded about half of the men in his boat. In a few minutes the starboard oar was shot away, and several holes through the boat, which rendered it useless. The current setting strongly towards the American shore, and having but one oar left, it was utterly impossible to effect a landing on the British shore, against this current. They were forced to return to the American side, when the boat sunk as they neared it. Lieutenant Fink found another boat, and with Lieutenant McCarty and five men, again embarked, and soon effected a landing, and with a few others, to the number of about twenty men, marched up the heights, where they found Captains (afterwards General) Wool and Ogilvie, Lieutenant Kearney, and other officers, with about sixty men, partly under cover of a bank, (formed by cutting a road,) who were without ammunition. They concluded to charge the enemy. Lieutenant Fink charged the main body on the left, while Captains Wool and Ogilvie charged on the right; which threw the enemy into confusion, and they fled, when the heights were taken possession of by the American troops. Lieutenant Fink had his epaulette shot away, several shot through his clothing, one of which tore off the tassel of his boot, and another through his hat." Lieutenant-Colonel Winfield Scott having, meanwhile, crossed the river, and assumed the command, relieving Captain Wool, in the latter part of the day an increased reinforcement of the British and their Indian allies moved against the little party. At the same time information was received from General Van Rensselaer, on the American side, that he could not give them any assistance, but would cover their retreat, and furnish boats for them to recross the Niagara River, and induced them to resolve upon a retreat; which they performed in good order, without losing a man, to the margin of the river; but, to their extreme mortification, not a boat was there, nor did any arrive; and they were surrounded with five times their number, and taken prisoners. They were sent to Quebec, and after a confinement, sent to Boston on parole; whence Fink was brought sick, by his friends, to New York—he being yet on *parole*.

The Adjutant-General wrote to Fink, on the 24th of March, (1813,) " It has been determined by the Secretary of War, that commissioned officers on *parole* may be employed on the recruiting service, and I am instructed by him to order you to report yourself to the superintending Field Officer of the district in which you reside, for this duty." This remarkable order, however, was countermanded on the 14th of April following, by the Secretary of War, who said: " You are released from the orders of the 24th of March ultimo, and the orders you may have received in consequence. You will not enter upon any military duty until your exchange be duly notified."

Governor Daniel D. Tompkins took quite an interest in Lieutenant Fink, and intimated to him, that he would intercede to have him exchanged or promoted, if it was his wish. Lieutenant Fink answered him on the 31st of May following: " I beg leave to state that nothing but an earnest wish to serve my country ever induced me to accept the appointment (of *Lieutenant*) which the President (*of the United States*) has conferred upon me, and it is the same consideration that now induces me to wish that I might be exchanged, should it be possible. My present inability is not suited to my disposition, and I feel anxious to assume my station in the army, in order to endeavor to retrieve the mistakes of Queenstown, in which affair I had the misfortune of being taken. My wishes also are, if such arrangement can be made with propriety, to be transferred to the cavalry,* it being a corps with which I have for years been in the habit of doing duty, from which circumstance I am attached to it in preference to the infantry."

His wish, however, was not gratified, for we find the Adjutant-General, in a note to him, dated 9th of November following, detail-

* He had previously belonged to the " Troop of Horse " known as the " Flying Artillery."

ed him as a " Commissary of Prisoners of War :" " You will collect
all the prisoners of war, who have been furloughed to remain in the
district. Quarters will be provided for them on Staten Island.
You will have them provisioned with every article of clothing and
provisions which they may be entitled to ; they must not be allowed
to leave the Island, but under a written *pass*, and that given but to
those you can depend upon."

Here he remained until the month of July, when he received a
commission for captain, dated 25th of July, 1814, and soon after enrolled a company, which he marched on to Plattsburgh. While on
the march several officers had spoken slightingly of his conduct at
Queenstown, and had also cast certain imputations upon his character ; he mistrusted who it was by their keeping aloof from him ;
finding they were the individuals, he marched into their quarters,
and demanded immediate satisfaction ; they, however, in effect denied they were the originators. The subject began to assume a
serious aspect—challenges were sent and accepted ; but the commanding officers had become in possession of the whole facts, and
immediately took such measures as to bring satisfaction to all.
Captain Fink refuted it from witnesses who took part in the battle,
and the officers offered such apologies as were satisfactory. Captain Fink's appeal was answered by General Scott as follows : " On
the road near Batavia, August 14, 1814.—Lieutenant J. L. Fink : *Sir*
—By a letter I have received from you, it appears that certain imputations have been cast upon you, in relation to your conduct at Queenstown on the 13th October, 1812. Though I knew not your name
at the time, your person was familiar to me on that day, and during
the period of my command, your deportment appeared equal to that
of any other subaltern of your regiment. In passing by water from
Queenstown to Boston, in company with the officers captured with
me, you were frequently the subject of their conversations, and I
heard not from either of them a syllable to your dispraise. I am,
sir, respectfully, your most obed't,　　　W. SCOTT, *M. General.*"

Captain S. W. Kearney says, on the same subject, " The part you
bore on that day was creditable to you as a soldier, and assisted to
reflect honor upon our old regiment and country. It was in character with your conduct whilst we served together in the regiment,
and, I believe, was so considered by all who belonged to it."

At the close of the war, he was entreated by many of his military
associates to remain in the service ; but he replied, " that inasmuch
as his country no longer needed his services in the field, he could
not become a *pensioner* on the Government."

He soon after became possessed of a farm on the great bend of the Susquehannah, in Pennsylvania, where he turned his attention to agriculture, and afterwards changed his location into the State of New York; but not succeeding, he came to the city about the year 1836, when he was appointed keeper of the "Magazine," in 64th Street, near 5th Avenue; then, afterwards in the Custom-House, and then again at the City Hall.   In 1850, his death was thus announced in the Press: "Died, on Friday last, the 1st (November) inst., Captain John L. Fink, formerly of the Thirteenth Regiment United States Infantry, commanded by Colonel Chrystie, in which, during the war of 1812, he ranked as the bravest of the brave of New York's gallant sons, who composed the officers and privates of that regiment, and whose heroic deeds at Queenstown Heights, Plattsburgh, &c., are matters of our country's history."   His funeral took place from his late residence at Greenpoint, Long Island, on Sunday, the 3d inst., with military honors, as will be perceived by the following: "First Brigade New York State Militia: Special Brigade Order. New York, November 2d, 1850.   Colonel Spicer, of the Second Regiment, is hereby directed to detail Captain Darrow, Company D, Washington Continentals, to perform funeral honors to the remains of a gallant soldier of the war of 1812, J. L. FINK, to-morrow (*Sunday*) at two o'clock, P. M., from his late residence, Greenpoint, Long Island.   By order of HENRY STORMS, *Brig. General.*"

After the month of August, 1814, specie payments had been suspended by all the banks, and the Corporation, for the purpose of facilitating trade, had again issued paper bills for small change, representing $6\frac{1}{4}$, $12\frac{1}{2}$, 25, and 50 cents, signed by John Pintard, Thomas Franklin, and William McNeal, to the amount of one hundred thousand dollars.

They were currently passed until February, 1817, when the banks resumed paying specie, and the "Press" says: "The butchers, and those who sit in the vegetable market, will sell for one week *twelve per cent.* cheaper than they have done, by way of welcoming the recommencement of the silver age.   Silver is silver, and chaff is chaff, say they."

But they, as well as other tradesmen, were at times annoyed with another evil; country bank bills, some of which stood upon very *weak foundations*, flooded the city, and at intervals, the butchers and others were caught with printed paper representing bank bills, which were much like the Western "Wild Cat" of the present day.   Meetings were held by many tradesmen, who denounced this kind of money.

The Press notices a general meeting held by the butchers, at the house of S. Raymond, Bowery Road, on Tuesday evening, 22d, when they resolved, " That after the 30th day of the present month, we will receive no country bank-notes that are below par in New York," and " that all who feel an interest for the prosperity of the city and the protection of the poor, be requested to assist in carrying the above resolution into complete effect, by refraining from offering any of the above description of notes, and by promptly refusing to take them. DAVID SEAMAN, *Cha'n.* T. GIBBONS, *Sec'y.*"*

The butchers of this market met the next day at " Robbins's " public-house, in Vesey Street, and subscribed to the above.

Two years after, (1821,) in the month of March, some little excitement was occasioned by the introduction of 64 head of fat cattle at the spring show of the New York County Agricultural Show, held at a place called " Mount Vernon," on the East River, just above Cato's and the Shot Tower. Twenty, which took the first premium, were taken to the " Fly Market," and noticed in that market.

Thirty-two, part of which had taken the second premium, were fattened by Mr. Philip Fink, of Orange County, New York, who was much disappointed in not receiving the first premium, as it would have made considerable difference in their sale; but as he found there was a spirit of rivalry between the butchers of this market and the Fly Market, he concluded he would arrange with the butchers here to have the thirty-two head to be disposed of as they pleased, and none should be the loser; all but two or three accepted the proposition, and arranged their business accordingly.

The " Press" says this lot of cattle (64 head) " was finer than any collection of the like number that have ever been seen in this country, and it may safely be said that Philadelphia cannot furnish at this season 64 head of fat cattle superior to those now offered at our fair." The judges on fat cattle at this fair were Messrs. David Marsh, Arnest Fink, James Owens, George Hawes, Sen'r, and George Thompson; and on fat calves and sheep, Messrs. John Doughty, Thomas Starr, and James Perrin.

We also find, from a " card," Mr. Philip Fink informs the citizens of New York, that he will expose for sale at the Washington Market, on Saturday next, (17*th* *inst.*,) the beef of thirty-two head of cattle which he yesterday exhibited at the fair, and which obtained the second and third premiums. Mr. Fink requests his friends to view the beef to-morrow, from 2 to 6 o'clock, P. M., at slaughter-houses No. 166, 172, and 174 Mott Street, where he will be ready to attend them.

"P. Fink hereby offers Mr. Ebenezer Stevens, of Dutchess County, a bet of 1,000 dollars, on the production of 20 head of the largest

* Columbian, June 23, 1819.

and best cattle at the next March fair in New York. The cattle to be raised and fatted in the State of New York, and to be kept at least eight months on our respective farms." Two days after, " Mr. Ebenezer Stevens begs leave to inform Mr. P. Fink, that he is no gambler, but does not apprehend any difficulty in beating him at any future time, as he has done in his twenty premium cattle; and besides, he does not believe that the New York County Agricultural Society was established for the encouragement of that art; and he further begs leave to say, that if Mr. P. Fink thinks that his rage will influence any wise man in his favor, and by that means insure him a market for his opposition cattle, he may perhaps find himself mistaken. Another thing Mr. Stevens thinks, that if he had acted towards Mr. Fink as Mr. Fink has done towards him, he would have expected to have been excluded by the Society from offering cattle again for any premium.   E. STEVENS."

The carrying of this beef to market was the finest and largest display of the kind that ever took place in this city. The " Press" says: "About 60 carts, accompanied with music, and flags and streamers, conveyed through the streets the 32 head of cattle fatted by Philip Fink, of the Washington Market." These cattle averaged 188½ pounds of rough fat each. Those of Stevens, 182½ pounds each; showing that Fink's cattle yielded the best.

The various stalls and meat were beautifully dressed, and the market for it was satisfactory. Then, to close the affair, the prisoners in the debtors' prison acknowledged " a donation of excellent steaks from P. Fink, Esq., of Washington Market They also offer sincere thanks to Jonas Humbert, Esq., (*baker*,) for repeated supplies of bread. ' *He that giveth to the poor lendeth to the Lord.*' Debtors' Prison, March 17, 1821."

The next year, in the month of March, (30th,) the " Press" notices "*Fat Beef.*—The beef of the twelve cattle which were exhibited through the city on Monday last will be offered for sale by the subscribers, on Saturday, 30th instant, (exclusively in Washington Market;) the south wing, fronting on Fulton Street, will be appropriated for that purpose. Lawrence Wiseburn, John Brewer, Daniel Spader, John Trigler, and Christian Harriot." An editorial says: " We were much gratified yesterday on viewing the procession of butchers' carts containing the quarters of the 12 cattle raised by Mr. (*Philip*) Fink, of Orange County. There were in all thirty carts, which were ornamented with flags, containing appropriate devices. The beef will be for sale this morning in the Washington Market, and we have no doubt the whole of it will be sold at handsome prices." Another grand display of " fat beef," mutton, &c.,

occurred in the Fulton Street wing of this market on the 20th of March, 1824. In this lot of superior cattle, two were fattened by William Slocum, of Rensselaer County; five oxen and one calf by Ebenezer Stevens, of Dutchess; four oxen by Philip Fink, of Orange County, New York. Six of these cattle were sold by Messrs. Wiseburn, Harriot, and Burtnett; and five oxen, one calf, and three sheep by Messrs. Spader and Hill. Messrs. Burtnett and Harriot were located on the Washington Street side, but on this occasion they changed, to have the show together. Since that period, " fat beef" exhibitions have often taken place, and some of them were got up in the most imposing, as well as the most expensive manner.

The sale of stands at public auction in the new Fulton Market, a few years before, had taken place; the year after, the Common Council had the subject under serious consideration of disposing of the stands in this market in the same manner, which soon after brought forth the following, and I may say truthful, petition, dated April 15, 1822, from the licensed butchers of this market. In it they state: " That understanding that it is in contemplation by your Honorable Board to dispose of the stalls now occupied by your petitioners, as has been done with those in *Fulton Market*, and humbly conceiving that the situation of their respective markets is different from that alluded to, they have ventured to submit, with all due deference, the propriety of adopting another system, which would be equally productive to the *revenue* of the city, more consistent with that equity which should exist in every department of society which has been attached to public markets. On these points they would urge that the collection of the *revenue* arising from public markets would be always more certain when imposed in manner and degree consistent with justice, and equal to the value of the privileges enjoyed; and when this is not so, industry is paralyzed, and the inclination, as well as ability to be punctual, taken away. With this view, your petitioners, full aware that by exposing their stands to *public sale*, by suffering an unrestrained competition where neither the character nor circumstances of purchasers are tested by security, and by having no recourse to your petitioners, should they not purchase under these disadvantages, you will oblige them to hold their stands at a rate beyond their real value, and ultimately to abandon them altogether. And your petitioners would further respectfully urge, that the interests of the community cannot require the sacrifice of any particular part thereof, but that its true interest consists in the equal support of all; and they humbly conceive, that should your Honorable Board persevere in the *sale of stands at auction*, no permanency, society, nor character will ever attach itself to the profession. Justice also requires that your petitioners, who are established in business, and whose whole dependence is on that business, should be permitted to pursue it. But can they, when opposed by men who care not what they bid for stalls, because no guarantee is required, and they have neither character nor property to sacrifice—can they, if defeated in purchasing stands in a public market, buy elsewhere, and of whom they please? No—for the law confines them to public markets, and they must act agreeable to that law. Under all these circumstances, your petitioners trust that they have not presumed too far in addressing your Honorable Body, and they confidently hope that this subject, which has only been proposed, will receive your deliberate attention; and your petitioners, as in duty bound, will ever pray, &c."

This petition satisfied the well-disposed of the "Council," who successfully opposed the contemplated measure, and there it rested.

The small shed in the rear of the main building, which accommodated the country people and fishermen, had now become much decayed, and altogether too small for its increasing trade; so, in the month of July, the Market Committee recommended, and the "Board" resolved, "That that part of the 'Washington Market' called the country market be rebuilt and enlarged, so as to accommodate the country people and fishermen resorting to that place;" but before it was finished the yellow fever again visited the city with great severity, and drove all the residents from the lower or infected portion of the city, which was fenced in. All the occupants of the stands in the infected parts were, by a resolution passed in the month of August, ordered from them to certain designated places. Those from this market were placed at "Hudson Square," or rather St. John's Park, in Hudson Street; those on the east side made Chatham Square their market-place; but in consequence of the great diminution of the population, there were but few who remained, and they required but few to serve them. Some idea may be formed of the desolation of the infected district from the following: "We have seen green beans at Mr. Bruce's store, which were plucked this morning, by one of the watchmen, from vines growing in Liberty Street, which had not been touched by the frost. Mr. Bruce has some musk-melons, of from two to three inches in length, which grew upon the pavements in Greenwich Street. The beans, which are about three inches in length, grew also in the street, and, as in the case of the musk-melons, are the product of the seed thrown out by the inhabitants before they were driven thence by the pestilence, and which took root in the scanty soil between the paving-stones. What a striking evidence is this of the utter desertion of that part of the city by all human beings and domestic animals! And what a picture of desolation and germ does it exhibit!" Cold, frosty weather, however, at last appeared, when the butchers and others returned to the markets.

In the month of November following, "Jane Simpson," an old huckster, complained, through petition, of being overcharged; she says, "That she is now seventy-eight years of age and upwards, and that she has for twenty-five years of that period been a vender of fruit and vegetables in said market, and has always punctually paid her fees. She pays a tax of about nine shillings weekly, whereas others in said market, many years younger, occupying, perhaps, double the space, and perhaps having fifty times more wealth, pay but three shillings weekly. She wishes to have the stands equalized."

The next year, (1823,) in December, all the hucksters ask for a reduction to six cents per day, instead of 12½. This was signed by

"Mary Rose,	Barbary Wiseburn,	Jane S. McColleck,
Elizabeth Gilman,	Margaret Sharp,	Susan Palmer,
Mary Mills,	Mary Folar,	Bridget Banks,

on behalf of all the hucksters;" but their request was not acceded to. Several of these women I well knew, when an apprentice, and must notice one or two of them.

Mrs. Barbary Wiseburn, or rather "Aunty Wiseburn," was a very close neighbor; her stand being just behind my boss's, where I occasionally held conversation with her, and now am almost ashamed to confess that at times I was guilty of playing some joke upon her. To hear—yes, I can yet remember her scolding me in her crooked English, " *You debil, Tom!*"—especially when her favorite "pussey cat" was suffering from an extra pinch or a pulled tail. But I thought a great deal of her, as she was a good, motherly, honest woman, who had no doubt seen a good deal of trouble, as well as hardships, in her early days. She was once the wife of Daniel Wiseburn, who came to this country with the return of Lafayette in 1780, then joined the army, afterwards transferred to the "Light Infantry Company" under Lafayette's command, fought in several battles, and closed with Yorktown; and when the General took leave of them, he said, "he wished once more to express his gratitude to the brave corps of Light Infantry, who for nine months past have been the companions of his fortunes."

After peace, Wiseburn returned to Germany, married Miss Barbary ———, and remained some five years, when they both, with their infant child, "Lawrence," came and settled in New York. The business of his trade at this period did not afford him a living; and having leased a house, which then stood near the corner of Fourth (*Allen*) and Rivington Streets, with several acres of ground attached, they commenced raising garden truck for market. The wife attended the Bear Market, when they had truck to sell, while he worked at his trade, (tailor,) or the raising of vegetables. In this way they succeeded in laying up a small store; but unfortunately, in the year 1799 Wiseburn died, and left this widow with several small children; although one or two of her boys were now large enough to assist her in the gardening, and she became obliged to daily attend this market, until it was torn down, when she moved into the new Washington Market, and there remained until she died, in 1837.

Next to her sat quite a young, rosy-cheeked girl, who is yet living. At that time she appeared a sober, sedate person; always known for strict business habits, combined with integrity and frugality; and the result has been, a success. She last year (1858) made an excellent as well as an elegant show of the various sorts of pickles, &c., at the Fair of the American Institute, held at the "Crystal Palace," which, with all the other very many valuables, were destroyed in that "public calamity." Jane S. McColleck & Co's pickles, &c., are seen for sale in numerous places throughout the country.

Previous to the petition of the hucksters, the fishermen from this market asked, through the same source, for a law to restrain fish-peddling in the streets; and this gives us the following names of those who occupied those stands at that period, viz.:

Reuben P. Wells,	Jeremiah Haley,	Aaron Carter,
Samuel Chappell,	Nathan Rathbun,	Ira Darrow,
Samuel Hiscox,	Thomas Jeffray,	Daniel Eldridge,
Percer W. Grant,	Rufus W. Main,	Thomas Wells,
Benedict Wells,	William Rogers,	Thomas Avery,
Lodowick Latham,	William Oliver,	Francis Sison.

From another petition presented the next year, (1824,) "to have a plank floor laid, instead of brick, to the Fish Market," the following additional fishermen's names appear, viz.:

Samuel Chappell,	A. Hicks,	James Jeffray,
Wm. G. Cochran,	Robert Wilson,	John Washington,
Ebenezer Fisk,	Robert Jeffray,	Erastus Mitchell,
L. P. Morris,	Asa Willis,	William Grant,
Henry Wallace,	Ben'n S. Penniman,	James Annett.
Smith Hicks,		

The new country market, after its erection, was almost daily filled with those who pretended to be agents for farmers and country people, but who were in reality forestallers; and, as the laws were then carried out, when the individuals were caught, it was a very difficult matter to fasten it on them. They were not then allowed a regular location, but they usually managed to take up the best stands before the arrival of the country people, who, with their produce, were driven into the street. The "Press" often notice these facts; and among the cases reported, says the *Evening Post*, was the following: "A few days ago, a woman from the country with a basket of ducks, not being able to get a stand in the poultry market, set her basket down on the side-walk, out of the run of the market custom. Here she was met by one of these great fat *he-forestallers*, and offered *three shillings* a pair for her ducks. Not being able to get any nearer the market, and despairing of a better offer, she consented that he should have them. The basket, with the ducks, were immediately taken to the forestaller's stand in the poultry market, and while he was in the act of removing the ducks from the basket to the coop, a gentleman came up and inquired the price of them. '*Four shillings* a pair,' was the answer, and the gentleman agreed to take the whole; much to the mortification of the poor countrywoman, who stood by waiting for her pay at *three shillings* a pair."

Several months after, an especial invitation was given, through the "Press," to the "Authorities," to pay a visit to this market on a particular morning, where, it was said, "they will find nearly the whole of the spacious building lately fitted up at the public expense, for the accommodation of the country farmers and market people, occupied by hucksters and forestallers, while the others are driven on the streets."

There are many who think that all who have regular stands in our markets are forestallers; but such is not the fact; many of them sell on commission, or have their agents North, South, East, and West, procuring many early or rare productions. The forestaller of former days is he who kept or occupied a regular stand, under the disguise of an agent, with an assistant or partner, while he was prowling around the market, watching every article brought to it by the country people, or to meet them coming to it in their wagons on the roads or boats, and from them purchase all he could; and if the producer, in his anxiety to ask price enough, or more than the forestaller could get or sell it for, the forestaller's plan was then to "*set him*," by not offering, but ask him if *he won't take*—maybe a trifle less. Then the producer imagined it to be a genuine offer; and often it had the effect of having him think he had not asked price enough; so he refused, and proceeded on to the market, where he held his produce until his chance of even getting "market price" was gone; and he told all who inquired his prices, that he had been offered this *(fictitious)* price for his produce. If, however, he concluded to take the false price first offered, he was told by the forestaller that he "hoped he would find somebody fool enough to give it to him." This was but a small part of their operations: their "arts and sciences" were, and are still, numerous, and sometimes almost indescribable, as they work all together, both men and women, in this unlawful practice; and after a successful bargain, they divide the spoils. I must say it is not so common now as it was several years ago; not because there are no forestallers left, but because there is not so much opportunity. Our markets would not be half so well supplied with early vegetables, fruits, &c., if it were not for speculators, who enter into it because they find it profitable; as we find them in everything else where capital can be advantageously used.

About the year 1830 the Market Committee attempted to stop forestalling by the male hucksters, by imposing very high fees on each. To get over this, they turned, or represented themselves, as agents for countrymen; and what made it worse, some countrymen lent their names to shield them. The Clerk of the Market, in his report in July, states, "That the men-hucksters have all turned agents for the countrymen, by which means there is a decrease of market fees." The Market Committee directed the Clerk "to allow the women-hucksters to purchase vegetables, &c., at any time of day from country people." "That no person be permitted to sell vegetables as agents in this market, unless the owner or owners of the property first apply to and procure from the Chairman of the Market Committee a permit for such agent." The regular commissioned dealers, however, soon after came in, and now many farmers and producers from the North, East, South, and even the "Far West," consign their productions to them, with a great deal of satisfaction.

Forestalling, and many other unlawful practices, is, however, known to many of the public officers, who are sworn to prevent them, but who either do not understand the nature of the oath they took with their office, or they are so much engaged in "political patriotism," that they have barely the spare time to attend to anything but make what "pocket money" they can, or, I should have said, pockets, as their general rule is to keep *two*—a *very small one* for the use of the city, and an *exceedingly large one* for themselves; and I believe there are sometimes conditions made, when a division must necessarily be made with some of the "appointing powers" from the large *pocket*, when it becomes suddenly "well filled." These, with other *onerous* duties, a fast horse or team to exercise every day, is as much as could be expected by our good-natured citizens, who are so willing to pay heavy rents, taxes, assessments, &c., for the very worst help they could possibly secure; and I suppose all that can be said on this subject will hardly create even a *wish* to have better men; instead of a determination to stop this collusion or peculation, by placing good, honest, practical men, or such as you, *Mr. Reader*, would trust to conduct your own business, where thousands upon thousands of untold or uncounted *dollars* were received by them, or passed through their hands, as is the case in this market.

There were exceptions at an early period, when *men* were recommended by the stand-holders of the various markets for their honesty, fitness, &c., and were chosen or appointed by the authorities. Such a man, the first Deputy Clerk I knew in this market, was Leonard Baum. The Market Committee, in a report made March 15, 1824, tends to prove this fact by the following: "That the salary of this officer was fixed, before the building of the new country market, at $312 per year; that since that time the business of that market has greatly increased; indeed, so much so, that since the appointment of the present Clerk, (*Leonard Baum*,) the collections made by him has been about equal to those of Fulton Market, and nearly *double* what was received last year in the corresponding months." They recommend that his salary "be increased to that received by the Clerk of the Fulton Market, viz., $500 per year."

One month previous, the Superintendent of Repairs was directed to fit up the centre building, (where was formerly held the watchhouse,) "as a dwelling for Mr. Baum, the Clerk." He held this situation until the month of September, 1836, when he resigned it, "an honest man," after holding the situation about *thirteen years.*

In the year 1824, on the 13th of December, the Market Committee recommended, " a suitable fish market be erected immediately in the rear of the country market, over the head of the slip, in conformity with the plan," being thirty feet wide and forty long, on a line of Vesey Street, some forty feet west of the country market, on the river—the whole expense not to exceed seven hundred dollars; which was adopted.

In the erection of this fish market, the passage-way for carts, wagons, &c., had been stopped on the west side of the market, and caused a great deal of travel, and at times crowding, through Washington Street. West Street had not been opened, or rather the slips had not been filled to form that street. A report in the early part of the year 1828 had been before the Board, and laid on the table, upon this subject, which kept growing worse every day. However, on the

17th of November, in the same year, it was again called up and read; part of which is as follows: "The said street now extends from the Albany Basin to the State Prison in one unbroken line, except at Spring Street Basin, across which it has been ordered to be continued, and at Washington Market Basin, and it will shortly be extended from the State Prison so as to unite with the Tenth Avenue above Fort Gansevoort; when that shall be done, and the street continued across the Washington Market Basin, and the Tenth Avenue be opened, it will form a direct and uninterrupted communication from the Albany Basin to Kingsbridge, at which place the said avenue terminates.

"Washington Market Basin, in its present state, is a great impediment to the free intercourse which ought to exist between the upper and lower parts of the city along the North River, as all persons passing from one to the other, along West Street, are under the necessity of going round Washington Market into Washington Street, which, during the business hours of the day, is so much obstructed by market carts and wagons as to render the passage of other carriages almost impracticable.

"The proposed improvement is, in the opinion of your Committee, necessary for the accommodation of the Washington Market. At present there is but a few feet of street between the market and the bulkhead, on the west side, which is barely sufficient for the passage of a cart, and that only as far as the middle pier; there being no passage whatever for carts or passengers from the middle pier to the north side of the basin. The basin, if West Street should be extended across it, would still be sufficiently large for the accommodation of market-boats, as well as such others as would have occasion to resort to this place—there would remain of said basin a space of 327 feet by 192." A resolution was passed "to cause West Street to be extended across the slip at Washington Market, between Fulton and Vesey Streets."

In this year the cupola was also ordered to be built on the market-house, at a cost of $425, according to the original plan, in place of the temporary shed previously built.

We have shown the occupants of all those who occupied regular butchers' stands ten years previous; they are introduced again at this period, and those who then are noticed are marked with a star at the end of their names:

No. 1. William Vonck.	No. 29. Jesse T. Spicer.
2. John G. Graff.*	30. Cornelius V. Gibson.
3. John A. Graff.	31. Mathew Harpel.
4. John L. Starr.	32. Thomas Jeremiah.*
5. Andrew Seaman.	33. James W. Hartell.

No. 6. Nicholas Dean.*
7. John F. Haws.
8. Simeon Travis.*
9. Charles Gwyer.*
10. William Hanshe.
11. Christopher Gwyer.
12. James Wood.
13. George Vaughn.*
14. George Camerden.
15. Hugh Goble.
16. George Goodheart.
17. Joseph Leviness.
18. Thomas W. Stanton.
19. John Shain (Shane.)*
20. Jacob Harriot.*
21. Christian Harriot.*
22. John Keyser.
23. Garrit Sentis, Jun'r.
24. Martin Borowsan.
25. Bartholomew Granger.*
26. Francis Granger.
27. James Byrnes.
28. John Harvey Lyon.

No. 34. No stand.
35. John Deavenport.
36. Lawrence Wiseburn.*
37. Jacob Aims.*
38. Philip L. Luff.*
39. Henry Wicker.*
40. George Hutton.*
41. Adam Hartell, Jun'r.
42. Owen Geary.
43. Ernest Keyser.*
44. Effingham W. Marsh
45. John D. Spader.
46. John Andarise.
47. George W. Ewen.
48. Joseph Hill.
49. William Moore.
50. Joseph Pell.
51. Lodowick Harpel.*
52. Jacob H. Ridabock.
53. David Brown.
54. William Webber.
55. Robert Gwyer.
56. Daniel Burtnett.

At this period I became an apprentice with the occupant of No. 48, Joseph Hill, a driving business but a generous man, and withal a practical Christian, one of the few who " do unto others as they would wish them to do unto themselves," and he was prosperous; with him I labored many long days, and never worked for any other in the same business. His benevolence and charitable doings were proverbial; he was almost daily called upon, either by the unfortunate, or those who were engaged in assisting them; it was either *meat* or *money* at market, in the morning, or his personal attendance on the sick or meetings, in the evening. My recollections recall an instance which happened at a time when, I may truly say, that friend deserted friend, and, in some instances, even the ties of relationship appeared to have no claim to humanity. In the first cholera, in the year 1832, when it appeared in its most fatal character—when thousands had left the city—when I have repeatedly rode in my employer's cart, in the broad daylight of an early summer morn, from Houston Street down Broadway to Fulton Street, and on several occasions met but one or two persons, and those were watchmen; although some mornings, in glancing up and down the cross streets, there were occasionally to be seen a butcher's or milkman's cart; and on one occasion a near relative, who lived in Amity Street, went out and returned twice, at the breakfast hour, to get milk, and after waiting some time, looking up and down, not a cart to be seen, and but few persons in the street.

It was at this time when my employer said to me one morning: "Thomas, I am much wearied, and need some rest; last night has quite overcome me, in sitting up with a Captain ——, who has the cholera; and being a very large, heavy man, his situation requires strength and attention, although I have been assisted by his two affectionate daughters, who have attended him day and night, but are unable to lift him. He is a Christian friend of mine, without any others, except these two devoted daughters," &c.

Quite near the "Methodist Church," in Allen Street, I went the same night, and sure enough found a large, heavy man, who had received that unmeasured attention and careful nursing, which no doubt was the means of saving him; either one or the other of these daughters, through the night long, was on a continued watch, to perform the slightest wish of their only parent, while the other, in a chair alongside, was taking repose, and my assistance was only occasionally wanted.

That Methodist Church lost one of its best members when Mr. Joseph Hill died, which took place the next year, leaving an interesting family and many friends behind.

In or through the course of five years, I became intimately acquainted with many of the other butchers here, and have never forgotten the impressions which some of them left on my memory—the mirror of a well-spent life cannot be looked at too often—their several histories would be interesting and instructive, but too voluminous for me to attempt; however, a brief notice of a few of them cannot be out of place here.

Thomas Jeremiah, once the occupant of No. 32, held a stall in this market twenty-two years, or until the year 1835, when he was elected, "County Clerk;" since which time he retired from the business, and is yet living, the respected President of the "Bowery Savings Bank." He was elected Assistant Alderman of the 10th Ward for the years 1828, '29, and '30; Alderman in 1831; then, again, in 1838 of the 17th Ward, and in 1844 a representative to the Legislature. In all these public offices he never represented the partisan, but the *man*, for the good of the whole; and to place his name before the people, he was sure to be elected on any ticket, always receiving the respect and confidence of his fellow-citizens.

In his business he always found something to employ himself with: if not cutting up or selling meat, he was informing his mind; and a singular fact was, that he learned the French language perfectly while attending at his stall in this market.

The Hon. Judge Meigs says of him in a letter to me, of which the following is an extract: " With his occupation one hardly expected the best traits of a gentleman with literary accomplishments—my comrade, a man of delicate frame, and yet unvarying health and temperament—was well read in French literature as well as English —as fine manners as any Parisian gentleman—of unstained reputation, public and private—it was Thomas Jeremiah."

Jacob Aims, recently the venerable President of the Butchers' and Drovers' Bank, occupied stand No. 37 from the year of the erection of this market until about 1840, when he was called to preside at this bank. From a poor and almost uneducated boy, he has, with determination, industry, integrity, and promptness, accumulated a fine property; and we might also add to these, great sagacity and financial abilities, which have rendered him one of the most successful of our bank presidents.

The same I may say of Daniel Burtnett, the President of the Citizens' Insurance Company, whose stock now ranks with the very best. He also has lately (1860) had additional honors as well as duties placed upon him, by being elected the President of the " Citizens' Bank," which duties he is now performing so well and with great satisfaction. His ready mind, quick perception, and gentlemanly manners have given him great advantages, and placed him foremost in the profession, while doing business on stand No. 56.

While young and an apprentice, the war of 1812 called forth his patriotism, as well as many other butchers, both old and young: this, however, is shown in the following graphic and interesting sketch furnished by him in answer to questions on this subject. In the month of May, 1858, he says: "Aware that you are actively engaged in compiling a history of the public markets of the City of New York, together with the leading men of the profession that occupied them, I deem it a duty, as much as I feel it a pleasure, to give you a little, though gratifying, incident that occurred during the late war with England, showing not only the patriotism of the master butchers, but parallel with them the spunky national feeling that pervaded the ranks of the apprentices.

" The master butchers held a general meeting, at which it was resolved to tender their services to the General Government, for the purpose of aiding in the erection of fortifications—at that time deemed necessary at various places, both for harbor and inland defence: the old gentlemen selected Brooklyn Heights as the field of their labor, and a right good jolly time they made of it.

"The apprentices, not to be outdone by their masters, held a meeting in Bayard Street, at which the attendance was very large and enthusiastic; your humble friend was elected to preside, and in presenting to the meeting for their consideration the exposed situation not only of our inland passes, but seaboard towns, the necessity for prompt action, &c., &c., my suggestions were not only met by outbursts of applause, but boy speeches were made in profusion, which, if they were not of the Clay and Webster order, the terrific cheers more than atoned for the absence of oratory in the speeches.

"The meeting resulted in the appointment of a Committee of three, consisting of the following boys: Valentine Merkle, Henry Spurling, and Daniel Burtnett, who were clothed with full power to make such arrangements as would not only meet the demands of the Government officers stationed here, but exhibit (to what was then called the 'War Committee,' who met daily at the City Hall,) the fact that if it was necessary to drop the shovel and grasp the musket, they might find *one hundred boys* who were ready at the beat of drum.

"The Committee accordingly met on the following morning, and, after deliberating on the course to be pursued, called on Major Horn, who then had charge of the working parties, who very cheerfully accepted our service, and assigned us a location on the right of 'McGowan's Pass.'

"Our next important object was to furnish such quantities of edibles as would satisfy the appetites of those who never declined a good dinner or refused a hearty supper. A fine horse and tasty wagon was obtained, which was filled with hams, tongues, roasted beef, etc., etc., and an early day was fixed for a start; and at 6 o'clock in the morning away we went, with a fine band of music, colors flying, hearts beating, and in one and a half hours we were on the ground. (The prompt action on the part of the boys allowed them six more working hours than other *parties*, who left the dock in the city in old boats, which very seldom reached the place of operations before 12 at noon, and left at a very early hour by the same conveyance, in order to reach their homes before night.)

"We then adjourned to a beautiful green field in the immediate neighborhood, partook of a hearty breakfast, and went to work with a good will; and you, my dear Colonel, know enough of our physical capacity to admit, at least, it was such a day's work as the present boys of the profession might attempt, but would not likely perform. At this time the militia from the upper counties, that were mustered into the service, were encamped on the heights at Yorkville, to guard that and other passes to the city. I merely mention this well-known, although unimportant fact, to show the military gallantry of the officers in command on our return to the city. We quit work about sundown, after having thrown up a breastwork of about one hundred feet in length, twenty in breadth, and four feet in height, sodded complete; the material for which was carried in hand-barrows from the foot of the hill and adjacent grounds.

"After having received the thanks of Major Horn, together with 'three times three' from idlers, non-combatants, &c., we formed in order of march by sections of three, and on reaching the heights, the whole command stationed there turned out to receive us, with colors flying, drums beating, and every other demonstration of approval. After passing the heights, we marched quietly but rapidly down to the Bowery, where we were met by a delegation of butchers from one of the public markets, who had prepared a sumptuous supper, which was tendered to us in a few appropriate remarks by the chairman of the delegation, but very respectfully declined on our part, solely on account of excessive fatigue. After arriving at head-quarters, the boys were dismissed to their respective homes, where, in the arms of Morpheus, they sought the much needed repose.

"Thus ended the first patriotic demonstration on the part of the butcher boys, many of whom, soon (by age) to become men, were called on to man the defences they had so recently aided to construct; among the number, your humble friend was drafted, and, he trusts, done his whole duty as a soldier, until honorably discharged. But afterwards served ten years in the military, and is now almost, if not quite, the only survivor of that little band of boys who gave, as an humble offering on the altar of their country, one hard day's work at least.

"I had almost forgotten one little event that caused much merriment, with any quantity of enthusiasm, viz.: a flag with a white ground and black letters, with this inscription:

'Free trade and Butchers' rights,
From Brooklyn's Fields to Harlem Heights.'

When the pole of the flag was stuck in the adjoining breastwork, and its folds wafted to the breeze, it was hailed with nine hearty cheers. Having thus performed my promise, to give you some idea of the butcher boys of that day, permit me to offer you my sincere congratulations, &c."

If the reader will enjoy the same amount of information and pleasure that I have in reading the above historical sketch, then my respected friend will not only receive my hearty thanks, but I hope many thousands more.

But I must now turn to speak of an old gentleman, and a most valued friend, who greatly assisted me when I most needed it: a plain, quiet, unpretending, honest, and truly a Christian man; without display, he frequently assisted many unfortunate and deserving poor, who will miss his benevolence and kindness when his pleasant face and words shall no more be seen or heard here. Such a man was Henry Wicker, many years the occupant of No. 39.

Lawrence Wiseburn, another, whose varying fortunes has produced no change—the same honest, and also the Christian man to-day, as when the occupant of No. 36; but not now so rugged, or capable of battling with the more modern times. In former years, patriotism, inherited through a father who fought in the Revolution, was somewhat strongly developed in him; as the duties of a private, then non-commissioned officer, were by him performed prior to and during the war of 1812, and since that period was many years Captain of a fine troop of horse. Two or three times he has been chosen and faithfully performed the duties of public office with satisfaction, and not one *man* can say aught against him.

Then Ernest Keyser, on stand No. 43, who became one of the largest dealers in this city. He commenced in the Bear Market, in 1802, with John Graff, and from strict attention to business, he succeeded in establishing a large trade before that market was torn down; this was further increased in this market, and for many years he did one of the largest and most successful butchering businesses in New York, which he continued until the year 1844, when he retired from active duties. He was also one of the pioneers in the ice-trade in this city; through hot and cold, night and day, he was ever busy at work, and by promptness and frugality, he has filled his "cream-pots" (as he called his earnings) full to overflowing.

His brother John, or Captain Keyser, (on No. 22,) as he was usually known, from the fact that he was Captain of the "Old Blue Troop," once called the "Flying Artillery," and composed principally of butchers, (and it is now the oldest military organization in the city,) in 1825, and many years after; then he was among the first exempts to assist in organizing the FIRST TROOP OF WASHINGTON GREYS, and in 1837 became its Captain. His social qualities were extraordinary—always full of pleasant wit and humor, and occasionally curious, practical jokes; one of which I shall here introduce. One of the other butchers in this market, who belonged to the latter "Troop," had forgotten to pay, as promised, for a small article, valued at *about ten cents*, purchased of the Captain early in the morning. After the morning's business was through, the Captain sent for his "*Orderly*," who also stood in this market, and ordered him to notify every member present (about twenty) to appear at his stand in five minutes' time, with whatever weapons they could lay their hands on. They all appeared punctually, with knives, choppers, gambrils, &c., when he at once, without any explanation, ordered them into line, and put them on the march to the front of this individual's stall, where he halted, and faced them; then stepping in front of the *culprit*, who was greatly surprised at this unusual and strange visit, the Captain addressed him by name, in a loud but determined tone of voice, proceeded with a lecture on a soldier's first duty—the importance of punctuality and promptness—and closed by demanding the immediate payment of *ten cents for the kidney*, and the taxable costs! The gathering and marching of this body through the market caused a large collection of outsiders; then followed the sober character of the address, and its final conclusive demand almost "brought down the (market) house." Such a laugh had not been enjoyed by the market people in many years.

Still living is Bartholomew Granger, once the occupant of No. 25, who, in his day, was one of the neatest and the cleanliest butchers, and also one of the best salesmen in this market. His meats were always of the best quality, cut up with remarkable skill, very smooth and handsome; and his stalls, fixtures, and tools showed that they were daily attended to, with plenty of "elbow grease."

Then there were the Graffs, (both father and son,) on Nos. 2 and 3; both gentlemen of modest and retiring habits. The Gwyers, Harpels, and many more excellent men, who have followed on, some of which, and their generations, are now prominent before the citizens who visit there.

On the 16th of December, 1833, a report was made, and a resolution adopted, "to erect a building, in extension of this market, on a line of West Street," at an expense estimated at about three thousand dollars, which was approved by the Mayor, on the 1st of January of the next year, (1834;) and in the following month of March an appropriation was made, showing the cost of this building at $3,325. This is the present market-house, directly on the east side, and adjoining West Street, running from Vesey to Fulton Street, afterwards known as the Country and Fish Market; as the fishermen were moved out of the old fish market, (built in 1824,) in the south end, and country people in the north end of the new one. The old fish market being now much out of repair, and disconnected from the old market buildings, it was concluded in the month of July following, that, as its "removal and repairing would cost more than the sum of five hundred dollars," which was the extent of authority for repairs as fixed by law, the Board therefore "*Resolved*, That the Superintendent of Buildings be, and he is hereby, authorized and directed to cause the Washington Fish Market to be removed and repaired, at an expense not exceeding the sum of fourteen hundred dollars; the amount to be paid out of the general appropriation for markets, and the application for money to designate this particular object." The removal and re-building of this old market-house caused a connection of the old market-houses with this new "Country and Fish Market" only on the Vesey Street side; and on the Fulton Street side a large vacant space, for country wagons, carts, &c., was left for their accommo-dation.

About the year 1825, the system of making "premium," or stands which the proprietors or their families, in case of death, would have the right to dispose of, commenced. These were not those which had been sold at public auction, but the many in the old markets which had been either drawn for or gifted. Many butchers wished such right of disposal, so that they might get some value for their fixtures, as well as for the trade, custom, and business.

By introducing several instances, no doubt the system will be better understood. In the month of January, 1825, the Market Committee reported in favor of the following transfers, on certain conditions: Stand No. 52, this market, held by Daniel D. Tomp-kins, be transferred to George W. Campbell; and that stand No. 36, same, held by John H. Tier, be transferred to James Valentine. "That the petitioners are well recommended, and that the stalls *(stands)* have never been sold for a *premium*. Your Committee have consulted with the butchers and others as to the premium value of said stalls, and have come to the conclusion that stand No. 52 is worth $100 '*premium*,' and stand No. 36 is worth $300 *premium*, which the petitioners are willing to pay." They offer a resolution " to grant the above, on their paying the amount into the City Treasury."

Several other cases of the same character followed in some of the other public markets, one of which will be noticed in the history of Centre Market, as demanding of a very large sum, under pecu-liar circumstances. However, we will introduce a few more, which took place in this market in the year 1834.

On the 1st of January of that year, a report was adopted " on the petition of William Hutton, for John L. Heyer's stand, No. 53, this market." They state, " It is not a *premium* stand, but Mr. Hutton has agreed to pay the Corporation one hundred dollars, which is supposed to be a fair compensation for the right of said stall."

Then, on the 7th of the same month, a petition from Mr. Joseph

Hill (presented after his death) was before the Committee, who state, "That they have examined the state of this case, and find it to be one of a peculiar character, owing to the death of the petitioner subsequent to asking leave to transfer said stall. Your Committee, therefore, under existing circumstances, deemed it proper to have the said stand appraised, *(by butchers,)* which appraisement amounts to $700." They offer the following resolution: "*Resolved*, That the butcher's stand No. 48 Washington Market, lately in the occupation of Joseph Hill, deceased, be transferred to Samuel Hill, on payment of $700 to the Corporation, &c.;" which was complied with, and his brother took possession. Then, in the month of July, the following resolution was also passed: "*Resolved*, That stand No. 21, *(this market,)* now occupied by Christian Harriot, be transferred to Thomas P. Way, on his paying into the City Treasury $700 as premium for said stall, and on his complying with the law to regulate the public markets in this city, &c." In the same month they again "*Resolved*, That a butcher's license be granted to William Harrington for stand No. 5, *(this market,)* on his paying $300 to the Collector of the City Revenue, for the use of the city."

Another peculiar case (where the occupant had died) is that of a petition from the wife of Robert Gwyer, before the Board, in the month of October, which shows, "That the deceased, husband of your petitioner, was a licensed butcher, occupying stand No. 28, *(this market;)* that application was made a short time previous to his death for the transfer of his stand in the usual way; that said application was withdrawn, by consent of parties, on the ground that there was no actual necessity for it at that time. Circumstances have since occurred in the death of my husband, as to make it a matter of necessity; and your petitioner therefore humbly prays your Honorable Body will transfer said stand to John S. Boyce and Samuel Holden, &c." This was referred to a Committee of butchers, selected by the Market Committee, who report: "We, the subscribers, being a Committee appointed by the Honorable the Market Committee to fix on a *premium* for stand No. 28, have duly considered the subject, and unanimously agreed on five hundred dollars. Daniel Burtnett, Ernest Keyser, Jacob Aims, Thomas Jeremiah, Jesse T. Spicer, and George Vaughn." The Market Committee accepted this report, and "*Resolved*, That his Honor the Mayor be requested to grant butcher's license to John S. Boyce, for stand No. 28 Washington Market, on exhibition of a receipt that five hundred dollars has been paid into the City Treasury for *premium* for said stall, and on his complying with the market laws, rules, &c." This was approved by the Mayor, November 4, (1834,) following.

The action or proceedings of the Market Committee, since the year 1831, were made legal by a law then passed, which read as follows: " A Law constituting a Market Committee of the Common Council. Be it ordained by the Mayor, Aldermen, and Commonalty of the City of New York, in Common Council convened, that from and after the passage of this ordinance, the members of the Board of Aldermen who now are or who may hereafter be appointed members of the Market Committee of said Board of Aldermen, and the members of the Board of Assistants who now are or who may hereafter be duly appointed members of the Market Committee of the said Board of Assistants, be, and they are hereby, jointly constituted the Market Committee of the Common Council for all legal purposes." " Passed the Board of Aldermen November 14, 1831; passed the Board of Assistants November 21, 1831, and approved by the Mayor November 22, 1831."

This Committee had been greatly assisted in their various duties by consulting with some of the principal butchers of the several public markets, who were ever willing to give such information or propose such measures as would tend to the general good. The Committee, in view of these advantages, in the month of June, 1835, sent notes of invitation to the following butchers to appear before them: " Messrs. Aims, Burtnett, Reeves, Scott, Phillips, Pessinger, Winship, Hanshe, Pray, and De Voe."* When it was mutually agreed that the licensed butchers in the several public markets should meet and appoint an " Executive Committee," to consult with the " Market Committee" on all important subjects relating to markets, which may be referred to them, by petition or otherwise.

Soon after a meeting was called, and one from each of the thirteen markets was elected, who were called together at the house of Andrew C. Wheeler, 261 Bowery, when he was elected the Chairman, and *ourself* the Secretary. From this body the " Executive Committee," consisting of three, viz., Daniel Burtnett, Andrew C. Wheeler, and George Pessinger, were appointed to meet with the Market Committee at their regular meetings.

Some of their proceedings will be noticed in the histories of other markets, and their assistance was politely requested from year to year, until those market laws were abrogated in 1843.

The many changes in the occupancy of the butchers' stands, from 1828 to 1840, has induced me again to give them at the latter date: those marked with *two stars* were occupants in 1818, and with *one star* of 1828.

No. 1. William Webber.	No. 29. Jesse A. Marshall.
2. John C. Chamberlain.	30. Pierson S. Halsted.

* See Union Market.

No. 3. John A. Graff.*
  4. John L. Starr.*
  5. William Harrington.
  6. Alfred Smith.
  7. Ernest Fink, Jun'r.
  8. William W. Bennett.
  9. Christopher Gwyer.*
  10. Freeman P. Bird.
  11. Dennis Valentine.
  12. William J. Valentine.
  13. Edward Roblin.
  14. George Camerden.*
  15. Hugh Goble.*
  16. George Goodheart.*
  17. Joseph Levinus.*
  18. John Phillips.
  19. Benjamin Jacacks.
  20. William Smith.
  21. Thomas P. Way.
  22. John Keyser.*
  23. Garrit Sentis, Jun'r.*
  24. William H. Halsted.
  25. Bartholomew Granger.**
  26. Francis Granger.*
  27. Charles Cadwell.
  28. Samuel Holden.

No. 31. Jacob Hanshe.
  32. James S. Halsted.
  33. Mathew H. Chase.
  34. No stand.
  35. Walter Durbrow.
  36. James Valentine.
  37. Jacob Aims.**
  38. John P. Aims.
  39. Henry Wicker.**
  40. John Harris.
  41. Edward Revere.
  42. Bethuel Howard.
  43. Ernest Keyser.**
  44. Effingham W. Marsh.*
  45. John D. Spader.*
  46. John Andarise.*
  47. William Moore.
  48. William Mook.
  49. Samuel Hart.
  50. Peter Valentine.
  51. Ludowick Harpel.**
  52. George W. Campbell.
  53. Adam R. Palmer.
  54. George Jacacks.
  55. James Stewart.
  56. Daniel Burtnett.*

Many of these, as well as a large number of the licensed butchers of the City of New York, have histories which would be interesting and instructive, but as they could not be condensed in this volume, I have concluded to give sketches of their history, or at least such as I am in possession of, and what I expect will be furnished me, will be ample to form a separate volume. There is one, however, among the new occupants, since the last period of their being noticed, who appears to have been quite prominent in and about the period of the war of 1812, as well as one of the many sufferers of the once well-known "Dartmoor Prison Massacre."

Bethuel Howard, for many years the occupant of No. 42, when about 20 years of age, in the year 1812 enlisted for one year in the "New York Volunteers," under the command of Colonel Andrew Sitcher, when he received the bounty money of $34, and after being in service about nine months the regiment was disbanded, on account of some informality. Soon again he entered aboard the privateer "Governor Tompkins," Captain Shaler, which vessel carried 15 guns and 115 men for a three months' cruise, taking several valuable prizes, burning some, and sending others into the various ports.

On one occasion they discovered what they thought a large merchant vessel in the evening of one day, and thought she would be a valuable prize; they bore down upon her, and by daylight next morning found themselves almost in the clutches of a British frigate, who, on seeing the movement of the "Tompkins" to get out of her way, began to send several unpleasant messengers to bring her to. The wind being very light, Captain Shaler concluded not to stop, but ordered out his ten sweeps on each side, and five men to each sweep put so much life into the "Tompkins," that a safe distance was soon made between them.

The fife and drum also much assisted in enlivening the motion as well as the *spirits* of the men, although the sailing-master, John Atkinson, was sometimes very generous and liberal with the latter, in another form, when the occasion demanded; then an extra allowance was presented them in a more acceptable form, *i. e.*, the liquid state. But usually the sailing-master was rather unpopular with those who were not fond of duty—they called him "Speaking Trumpet Jack," which name he enjoyed, from the fact that whenever he found a man asleep on his post, or neglectful of duty, he invariably placed his trumpet somewhat heavily over the head of the culprit, which generally led him to believe that it was not done in fun.

Mr. Howard, with three others, after taking the "Young Husband" as a prize, were put on board to run her into the nearest port, but being overtaken by a severe storm, were obliged to lay-to three days at Block Island, watched by the British cruisers; however, they got away and made for the shore, and succeeded in reaching Newport. After reaching New York, three other prizes, the "Myriad," valued at £75,000; the brig Henry, valued at £50,000, and another not recollected, were the spoils of this cruise; and Howard's share amounted to about $600—and the "Governor Tompkins" never returned; many supposed she foundered at sea.

Again Mr. Howard, in the month of August, 1814, entered aboard the Baltimore clipper schooner "Amelia," Captain Adams, who took several prizes, among which was the brig "Nancy Howard," into which Howard, with three other Americans and four of the British crew, was placed aboard to be sent in; but this prize was unfortunately retaken, with these men as prisoners, by the frigate "Hamadryad," Captain Chatham, where Howard and the others were kept about two months, then taken to St. Johns, N. B., placed on board the frigate "La Loin," thence sent to Plymouth, England, and put on board the prison ship "Impregnable;" from thence, after a short period, to "Dartmoor Prison," which lies about 17 miles from Plymouth, where he was kept from the month of October, 1814, to July, 1815.

In this prison they were stowed among the thousands of both French and American prisoners; many of the latter were American seamen, taken from merchant vessels; all kept in a filthy and dirty condition, often on short allowance, through the instigation of Captain Shortland, the keeper, who gave orders to the contractors to serve them with bad bread, sour meat, &c.; but the worst is yet to be told. On the 6th of April, while a number of American prisoners were playing ball in yard No. 7, where a small hole, the size of a large pane of glass, sufficiently large to admit a boy or small man to pass through, had been made by some persons for the purpose of obtaining the ball, when it flew over the wall into a large yard inclosed by high walls, wherein the soldiers or guards were stationed in their barracks.

The ball happened to pass over the wall, and they were trying to get it, when Captain Shortland entered the gate with about 300 soldiers, and ordered them to fire on the prisoners and those who came out of the prison to learn the cause of the firing. The soldiers pursued and shot down the flying prisoners, and also fired through the windows and doors inside of the prison. Some seven or eight were killed on the spot, and thirty-eight wounded, three of whom died two days after. Howard was released and conveyed from this murdering hole on board of a cartel, and arrived in New York, where he commenced his business again, and in 1821 obtained stand No. 46 Catharine Market, which he held until 1832, when he removed to the above stand in this market. Several years ago he retired from the active duties of his business, but he occasionally is found at the Bull's Head, procuring *stock* for his son, who has taken his place on No. 42.

Again we refer to the market-houses, which we find in 1842 well filled, in fact, overflowing, as numerous complaints were made by the country people of the want of room under shelter. The large market space, both in the Vesey and West Street sides, which had been appropriated and used by the country people so many years, had at this period been all taken up by the forestallers, agents, &c. So many individuals wanted stands *just among* the country people— and when certain people want there is always a way to get; honestly if they can, but whether so or not they must have them; and those *very honest* officers in charge allowed them to get and get, until the countrymen were again driven or got out. They had been driven out so often, that many of them gave up bringing their produce themselves, but employed agents to sell for them; while others, more persevering, would set down their produce in the gangways, in front of these individuals, where sometimes *warm words* would be used by both parties. However, the "country people" concluded to try what effect another petition, showing the whole facts, would produce in the Board, which we find before them in the month of October, next year, reading as follows: "The petitioners, farmers, bringing the produce of their farms to 'Washington Market,' would respectfully call the attention of your Honorable Body to the inconvenience to which we are subject there; if we go into the market, called the country market, with our things, we are in danger of being assailed, and our things upset, and in some cases destroyed by the speculators, who occupy every spot with their boxes, and will not allow us to stand them on or before them, as they say that they have to pay for their stands; if we go on the *side-walk* opposite the market, we are liable to be driven off by the occupants of the stores; and if in the street, we are in danger of being run over by the carts and exposed to all kinds of weather, after riding *fifteen or twenty*, and some of us *thirty* miles at night; it is vain that we apply to the Clerk of the Market, as he says there is no room, and we must find a place where we can. These are the inconveniences, to say the least of them, under which we labor; and we humbly trust that your Honorable Body will remove them as far as you may deem it necessary; all we ask is a place to ourselves, where our things are not liable to be destroyed, and ourselves threatened with personal violence if we take them in the market, &c." New York, May, 1843.

Peter C. Westervelt, Jr.	Peter Huyler,	Jacob J. Hopper,
Jas. H. Brinkerhoff, Jr.	Richard Berdan,	Teunis Van Pelt,
Jacob J. Brinkerhoff,	Sam'l P. Demarest,	Gilbert D. Blauvelt,
John G. Speer,	William A. Bogert,	Jacob A. Brinkerhoff,
John J. Banta,	Mathew M. Bogert,	John Ackerman, Jr.
John J. Van Wagonen,	John G. Banta,	Nicholas A. Voorhis,
Andrew C. Colman,	Isaac D. Demarest,	Albert Voorhis, Jr.
John S. Demarest,	Cornelius R. Haring,	Cornelius J. Haring,
John Wanamaker,	Philip Brinkerhoof,	George Vreeland,
Jacob Van Winkle,	James Herring,	William H. Zabriskie,
Peter P. Westervelt,	Peter R. Terhune,	Garret H. Zabriskie,
John M. Hopper,	Henry H. Voorhis, Jr.	Cornelius Vanvale,
John P. Westervelt,	James Y. Demarest,	Abram Debaun,
Cornelius Van Winkle,	John Voorhis,	Garret Oldis,
John A. Demarest,	Jasper Cadmus, Jr.	John P. Outwater,
John S. Berry,	Lomas Bickell,	Peter T. Wortendyke,
John H. Ackerman,	Benj. Bogert,	George C. Demarest,

Richard Van Winkle, Henry A. L. Voorhis, Stephen Vreeland,
Lawrence Vreeland, John Van Buskirk, Garret Vreeland,
James H. Brinkerhoff, Simon Van Antwerp, John D. Peack,
Aaron H. Westervelt, Albert J. Terhune, Chas. A. Fellows,
Lawrence Mann, Peter H. Ackerman, Jacob M. Meescles,
Daniel J. Haring, John R. Romaine, Mathew Demarest,
C. A. Debaun, Frederick Croute, Jas. P. Westervelt,
John N. Hoppin, Oliver P. Smith, George Vreeland, Jr.
Martin Sishhult, Jacob P. Mowerson, William D. Haring,
William Sexon, Richard Terhune, Peter S. Bogert,
Cornelius C. Holdrom, Levi Sherwood, David J. Christie,
Christian Van Horn, Henry Ferdon, Ab'm J. Van Voorhis,
Isaac J. Haring, Frederick B. Mabie, Alb't A. Brinkerhoof,
Abraham Vreeland, Martin Hennion, Peter Howard.
John A. Hopper, Mindert Van Horne,

The Committee on Markets reported on the above petition, viz.:
"That they have long been impressed with the necessity of providing more extensive accommodations at the above-named market, and have only been deterred from suggesting the present proposed addition in consequence of their anxious desire to lessen as much as possible the expenses of the city; but, upon a thorough investigation, they find that, by inclosing the vacant space on Fulton Street adjoining the *fish market*, which is now used only as a receptacle for rubbish of every description, the fees arising therefrom will in one year more than pay the whole expense of the outlay, and at the same time be a very great accommodation both to the buyer and the seller, as at present many of the farmers, for the want of room in the market, are obliged to occupy the side-walks, a long distance above the market. As an evidence of the propriety of erecting the addition proposed, your Committee would state, that an offer has been made to erect the *shed*, and to pay $2,000 per annum for its use. With these facts before them, they feel that they would not be doing justice to the public did they not urge the commencement of the work. With this view, they offer for adoption the following resolution: *Resolved*, That the vacant space at Washington Market fronting on Fulton Street, and adjoining the fish market, be inclosed with a proper roof, and a floor laid down, under the direction of the Committee on Public Offices and Repairs, and that twelve hundred and fifty dollars be appropriated for that purpose. The same to be done by contract."

This shed was put up accordingly, and gave accommodations only for a short period to the country people, as other *individuals* again wanted; and their having but the Superintendents of Markets (after this period) and a Clerk or two to *convince* of their superior rights to take the countrymen's allotted space, they were usually successful, especially if their *arguments* were weighty; and then one stand after another were *given* away to these "*proper persons,*" as the law directs, until at last the countrymen had again to fill the gangways, side-walks, and streets.   Even on these places they were followed by others, who wished to represent or be considered "countrymen," to those citizen purchasers who sought for the originals; and when any petitions, reports, or other movements were made for additional room, it was always presented as being for the accommodation of that wronged class—the *country people.*   The following resolution and report, made in the months of May and June, 1847, in making additions on the West Washington Market ground, on the west side of West Street, will show this fact:

"*Resolved,* That the Committee on Markets report to this Board the propriety and expediency of erecting a suitable market on the ground recently *filled in,* and *now being filled in,* between Fulton and Vesey Streets, and fronting on West Street, with a view of affording more market accommodations for *country people* and *others* attending the Washington Market, and also of *removing* the *sheds* and other obstructions on the side-walk of said streets adjoining the said market, and adjacent thereto, so that the free and proper use of the said streets may be enjoyed as of right appertains, together with the cost of said building and improvement."   This Committee reported, on the 7th of June following, "That they have had this subject under consideration, and, with a view of obtaining correct information as to the necessity of the proposed improvement, your Committee personally examined the premises, and are fully satisfied of the necessity which exists of some improvement being immediately made.   This plot of ground is at present occupied by a *few wooden shanties,* which pay to the city only about *three or four dollars per day,* and is otherwise used as a place of general deposit for all kinds of rubbish, filth, &c., and is consequently an intolerable nuisance, not only to those doing business in the vicinity but to our citizens who may have occasion to pass through this section of the city.   Your Committee deem it inexpedient to recommend the erection of a permanent market-house on this ground at the present time, inasmuch as the same having been but recently filled in, is constantly settling, and therefore renders the same impracticable; but to obviate this objection, and to afford the required facilities for the constantly increasing business done in and around this market, would recommend that *two sheds* be built thereon, which your Committee estimate can be done at an expense of from three to four thousand dollars, and, according to the plan on which your Committee propose building them, will produce a revenue to the city of from twelve to fifteen dollars per day, this almost paying the construction in one year." A resolution was passed to comply with the above, and appropriating $4,000 for their erection.

The erection of these two market sheds, and the continued filling up of the slip, gave cause to the captains of the regular market-boats to present the following petition, which appears before the Board in the month of August following: " The undersigned, doing business in and about *Washington Market*, and engaged in bringing produce to said market, *respectfully represent*, that, in consequence of the extension of the pier at the foot of Vesey Street, and the filling up of the slip between Vesey and Fulton Streets, immediately in front of said market, they are apprehensive that vessels, other than those engaged in bringing produce to the Washington Market, will use and occupy the pier and slip in front and adjacent to the same, to the exclusion of the *market-boats*.

" The undersigned therefore beg leave to state, that vessels bringing produce to the said market have heretofore enjoyed the exclusive use and occupation of the piers and slip immediately in front and adjacent, and they respectfully request that the said vessels, in view of the new arrangement now in progress, may be continued in the exercise of their rights and privileges, to the exclusion of all other vessels. The undersigned regard a compliance with this request as of the highest importance to the market as well as to the undersigned, and as in no respect interfering with the just rights of other vessels.   (Signed,)

Thomas Morford, sloop *Cyrus.*
Amos Tilton, schooner *Columbus.*
John Price, sloop *Merchant.*
Hiram Seeley, sloop *Exchange.*
Jacob W. Fountain, sloop *Ware.*
William Lee, sloop *Fashion.*
John Jacobs, sail-boat *Telegraph.*
William Wayman, sloop *Mary Elizabeth.*
William C. Wilson, schooner *Jersey Blue.*
John T. Walling, sloop *General Taylor.*
Charles H. Miles, sloop *Yarice.*
Joseph Ketcham, sloop *Revenge.*
Daniel Van Brunt, sloop *Cybele.*
John Gould, Captain of sloop *Trader.*
Bernard Saryelere, Capt. sloop *C. Whitey.*
John Dubois, sail-boat *Gazelle.*

W. S. Horner, sloop *Oregon.*
Clarkson Price, sloop *Herald.*
James Seely, sloop *Tribune.*
Haddock Whitlock, steamer *Argo.*
Jas. M. Walling, sloop *Wake.*
William Smith, sail-boat *Major Ringold.*
John Bennett, Jr., pettiauger *Washington.*
Rich'd R. Bennett, pettiauger *Ocean Child.*
Thos. M. Leonard, sch'r *George & William.*
John Seely, sloop *Exceed.*
Thomas Adams, sloop *Suffolk.*
James Bowne, sloop *President.*
John Holmes Van Brunt, *Sop of the Dread.*
Abraham Bogart.
Simon Wardell, Capt. of sloop *Sylphide.*
Abel Sammis, Captain P. R. *Herald.*"

Early in the year 1849, a favorable report was acted upon by the Board, who wished authority from the Legislature to erect a large new market-house on these new-made grounds; which Mayor Havemeyer vetoed, and gave the following reasons for so doing. This is dated March 5, and reads as follows: "After a careful consideration of the resolution of your Honorable Body, directing the Counsel of the Corporation to apply to the Legislature for authority to build bulkheads in the Hudson River, from the pier foot of Dey Street to the pier foot of Vesey, a short distance of 362 feet from the present line of West Street, to fill in the space behind said bulkhead, and to erect upon the ground there to be made.a building or buildings for public market purposes, I am unable to give it my approval, and therefore respectfully return it, for reconsideration.

"The law makes West Street the exterior street along this portion of Hudson River, and prohibits the making of any additional ground or the erection of any additional buildings west of said street.

" It appears, however, that in 1844 the Common Council built a bulkhead across the slip, between Fulton and Vesey Streets, about 200 feet west of the exterior street, and filled in the space thus inclosed, without having obtained the authority from the Legislature, and that the ground has since been occupied for market purposes. It is now proposed to obtain the authority to enlarge this ground, so as to enable the Corporation to dispense with the block of ground between Washington and West Streets, now occupied by the Washington Market.

" The report of the Committee does not allege the want of an additional market accommodation as the ground of the reconsideration, but urges the proposed improvement with the (expectation) of realizing, by the disposal of the ground on which the present market stands, a considerable sum above what the improvement will cost. My objection to the proceedings recommended is, that it is partial in its character, and not designed with reference to any given plan of improvement along the Hudson River; and although in this particular instance it might result in pecuniary benefit to the city, it is calculated prospectively to interfere with the adoption of a proper general system of improvement beyond the line of West Street, and also to affect injuriously the large pecuniary interest which the city has in its numerous wharves and piers along said river. If it should be deemed necessary to make provisions for a new exterior street, beyond the line of West Street, a proper and general plan should be adopted for that purpose, not only to insure the best arrangement for commercial accommodation, but to indemnify the Corporation for the loss of property in wharves and piers which they would thus sustain, and also to define the relative rights of the Corporation and private owners to the wharves and piers to be made beyond or along said exterior line. W. F. HAVEMEYER."

This put a stop to the erection of a market-house on this new-made ground. Then we find some good suggestions made by the Comptroller, in his report in 1853. He says: " In the course of the last year or two land has been gained from the North River by constructing a bulkhead from pier No. 20 to No. 23, between Vesey and Dey Streets, and covering an area equal to *ninety full lots*. The new land is entirely outside of West Street, which at that point is the exterior line of the 400 feet granted to the Corporation by the Charter of 1730, usually called the ' Montgomerie Grant.' The bed of the river, beyond the line of West Street, and of the four hundred feet embraced in the Charter, belongs to the people of the State of New York, and before the land is sold, or any erections made on it, it is advisable to have the title settled by an act of Legislature. This will undoubtedly be granted on a memorial from the Common Council. The duty assigned to the Comptroller to take charge of the real estate of the city, and prevent encroachments thereon, has convinced him that rigid measures should be taken to prevent encroachments on the water as well as on the land. The great value of lots in the lower part of the city is such, that instead of dredging out the slips, they are allowed to fill up, and when complaints are made in regard to the want of water, a bulkhead is constructed across the slip, the piers are extended out, and land is made; and whether the fee of the soil is in the City, the State, or ' unknown owners,' is not material to the manufacturers of land, provided a few lots can be gained out of the rivers or the bay."

The Common Council, however, instead of applying directly to the Legislature, as suggested by the Comptroller, placed it in the hands of a Committee, who after a time caused it to be used for market purposes, by allowing it first as stands for country wagons, and soon after *certain individuals* were able to obtain " permits" to erect permanent sheds, until at last we find the whole of this new-made land covered over with such structures, and the country wagons crowded off. The manner in which these permits were obtained led to some unpleasant exposures of the market officials, of which the following will give some idea.

A correspondent in the " Leader," of March 13, 1858, gives more " fact than fancy" in the financial collection of this market by the officials, who says: " There is a fortune sufficient to sustain a Newcastle or a Cornwall in the revenue derived from a *three years' term* of the market property. To manage the matter properly it requires a degree of dexterity and shrewdness that is possessed by a few on their entrance into office; but an accommodating conscience will soon adapt itself to the necessities of the position, and become as imaginative in corruption as the elder Dumas or Charles Dickens are in composition. They are gallant fellows, too, these expert Clerks of Markets; clever—aye, generous in their hospitality; and their professed friendship to men in position can only be equaled by the devotion of Damon and Phythias." "They are cautious, too —so cautious that the world cannot 'say they did it,' and, when questioned, are dumb—' dumb as a clam.' "

There are nearly if not more than five hundred stands in the old Washington Market, the lowest rental of which is two dollars per stand, and advancing from that figure until it reaches eight, and perhaps ten dollars per week. This is only for stands in the market proper, while on the side-walk a weekly rental of one dollar and a half is exacted from every person exposing goods for sale. It is generally fully occupied, and on my visit during the past week, in the coldest weather we have had this winter, I found the side-walks crowded with dealers in every description of merchandise. In my judgment, it would be a safe calculation to set down the amount received from the old market proper in round numbers at twenty-five hundred dollars weekly. This is rather below the mark, but I desire to keep within bounds, and speak only what I conceive to be the truth.

"There are over four hundred stands erected on the made ground known as West Washington Market, each of which pays nearly a like amount, and consequently it may be called, say two thousand dollars weekly—not to lead the public to believe that I exaggerate in the most remote degree. This will make, in the aggregate, *forty-five hundred dollars* weekly from stands alone in both markets.

"At this season (*March*) of the year the market wagons from the surrounding country are of course not as plenty as during the summer and fall months, but it can be safely estimated that even now at least three hundred market wagons can be found every morning at Washington Market. During the business season, when garden produce is sold by every man who raises it for the city, there are no less than sixteen hundred to two thousand wagons which pay daily for the privilege of selling their vegetables, &c. The rate charged by the Clerk of the Market for this permission is twenty-five cents per day; and I do not think it at all extravagant to suppose that twelve hundred dollars is received weekly throughout the year from this source. There are other parties who occupy any vacant space they can find in the vicinity, who pay a daily rent; but of this I will not speak, as no definite amount can be approximated to such floating tradesmen and operators. It must be large, nevertheless, as numbers are engaged there daily to my knowledge. Let me reflect, and see how much this would amount to annually, as the revenue of Washington Market. The gross amount I have estimated at *fifty-seven hundred* dollars weekly. I will call it *five thousand* dollars; and at this rate, which I know is far below the real figure, *the amount annually received from Washington Market alone is over two hundred and fifty thousand dollars.* It is astonishing—it is almost beyond belief—that this immense sum is collected; but I am prepared to show that it is not only a stern reality and fact, but that it is beyond the amount I have named. How much of this finds its way into the City Treasury, let me examine and see.

"The returns from Washington Market for stands and fees for the past six months, as appears from the Comptroller's books, is as follows: For butchers' stands, - - - - $1,665 64
For market fees, - - - - - 25,862 36

$27,528 00

" *Twenty-seven thousand five hundred and twenty-eight dollars*, in round numbers, for six months' receipts of Washington Market, making for the whole year, at the above ratio, *fifty-five thousand and fifty-six dollars!* A singularity exhibits itself in the returns made to the Comptroller, that the amounts for fees are the same in January that they are in September and October. Curious, very, that the same amount of business is done weekly throughout the whole year, the only variation in the weekly returns not amounting to over ten dollars in the average. The facts which I have presented are not all the sources of revenue derived from Washington Market. During the past five years, the large block of vacant land now known as West Washington Market has been built over with sheds to accommodate the increased business drawn to that neighborhood. There cannot be a shed erected unless by permit from the City Inspector, (through and under the direction of the Superintendent of Markets,) and the sheds are erected and paid for in a very *peculiar* way. It is said that only *one* man has the patent right for this work at the present time, and the remarkable appearance of his edifices have christened them with the euphonious name of Cata-*Moran*.

"The sheds and permits included are sold to whoever will give the highest price; and instances have been known of eight hundred dollars having been paid to secure an eligible location. At this, or even a much less figure, what an amount of money has the city been swindled out of by corrupt and thieving officials!"

Additional testimony to the above I find in the columns of the *New York Atlas*, April 4, 1858, which appears quoted from a petition presented to the Common Council, in which the names given I have excluded, as my object is to present one of the plans by which large sums of money are collected never finds its way into the City Treasury. This sets forth: "That (a certain person) has been allowed to erect about *seventy stands* upon the grounds west of Washington Market, originally set aside for the occupancy of farmers' wagons, which have been sold for upwards of $35,000, no part of which was paid to the city. That within the last six years about five hundred stands have been erected in connection with the public markets, which have been sold for *several hundred thousand dollars!* not a penny of which has been paid into the City Treasury. That Mayor —— commenced an investigation into the abuses connected with the markets, and that after he had obtained positive evidence that upwards of six thousand dollars had been illegally paid for *permits* and *stands*, he mysteriously abandoned the investigation. That while only about $1,000 a week is paid over to the Chamberlain of the City for stand fees collected at Washington Market, there are upwards of one thousand stands in the market and upon the grounds around it, which pay a rent to the Clerks of from two to six dollars a week, besides a large amount collected from persons who sell produce on the side-walks in West Street, and the streets adjacent, who pay from twelve to sixteen shillings each per week. In addition to all this, market fees to the amount of twenty-five cents each are collected from about five hundred farmers and gardeners daily. That while the market managers profess to have a rule that no person can have more than one stand, Mr. ——, Clerk of the Market, swore before the Market Committee, last fall, that he gave (a certain person) *fifteen permits* for stands. He states that (this person) is only an agent of the market plunderers to erect stands at a cost of about $30 each, which are afterwards sold at prices ranging from $400 to $1,000."

To continue the history of this "new-made ground," we find in the month of May, 1858, in Board of Councilmen, a message was received from the Mayor, announcing the lease of the West Washington Market property in the following language: "I am informed that a lease has been executed by the people of the State of New York to James B. Taylor and Owen W. Brennan of the property situated on the westerly side of that street, north of Dey and south of Vesey Street, in this city; being the ground now used by the Corporation for market purposes, west of the ground on which Washington Market stands. In pursuance of this lease, notices have been served on the lessees and tenants of the Corporation now occupying portions of this property, similar to the annexed: 'NOTICE.—All persons in possession of lands owned by the State, situated on the westerly side of West Street, north of Dey, and south of Vesey Streets, in the City of New York, and now leased to Messrs. Taylor and Brennan, (and being on these without any right from the State,) are notified to surrender possession of said land and premises immediately, or legal measures will be at once taken to remove them therefrom.

'LYMAN TREMAINE, *Attorney-General.*'

"James B. Taylor and O. W. Brennan, No. 48 Pine Street, New York, Lessees. Albany, April 24, 1858." The matter was referred to a Special Committee of the Board of Councilmen.

"Taylor and Brennan soon after commenced a suit of ejectment against the city, and one hundred and eighty-six persons, tenants of the Corporation, who occupied stands for market purposes on the land, as well to recover the possession thereof, as for the rent of the premises. The proceedings were, however, afterwards amended by adding the people of the State as complainants.

"An application was also made by the complainants before Justice Davies for the appointment of a receiver of the rent of the tenants. This was opposed on the part of the city; but the motion was successful, and the receiver, (Cyrus Curtiss,) who was thereupon appointed, subsequently took charge of the rents.

"From the decision thus made by Justice Davies, an appeal was taken to the full Bench of the Supreme Court, which, as I am (says Mayor Tiemann) informed, reversed the decision of the Justice; but, as Taylor and Brennan afterwards discontinued their action as against the city, no formal order was entered of such reversal.

"The suit having been discontinued against the city, their tenants were left as the only defendants therein. In consequence of this, they requested, in a letter to me, which I transmitted to the Common Council in the month of January last, that the city should take upon itself their defence. In this communication, deeming the city the only party actually interested, I recommended that the Counsel to the Corporation be directed to take charge of such defence, and a resolution to that effect was promptly adopted by your Honorable Body. Before, however, the Counsel to the Corporation was substituted in the suit, a default was taken about the 12th of May last against all these tenants, and a judgment was entered against them for over sixty-nine thousand dollars. A writ of possession was thereupon delivered to the Sheriff, who proceeded, about the 23d of May, to remove the parties in occupation. It was only then that the Counsel to the Corporation learned of the rendering of the judgment. He at once took vigorous measures to open the default, and set aside the judgment; and after an able argument by him, on the motion made for this purpose, assisted by William

Curtis Noyes and John McKeon, Esq's, as associate Counsel, a decision was rendered on the 9th instant, (July,) by Justice Roosevelt, setting aside the inquest, and all the subsequent proceedings of the complainants." He " also shows that the lease of the State to Taylor and Brennan was entirely void, as the State officers had no authority to make the same. The learned Judge, besides, orders that the Receiver shall account for all the sums received by him, and that they be paid over into the City Treasury. He also orders that an injunction issue to prevent the tenants from paying to, or the Receiver from collecting any rents from the premises. They are to be paid, as heretofore, to the agents only."*

While this portion of the market property was agitated by law, a destructive fire took place, which consumed and destroyed nearly all the sheds that covered the entire space. The fire broke out about fifteen minutes to eleven o'clock on Wednesday night, July 11, 1860, in a shed occupied by Thomas Waterman, a dealer in eggs, located at the corner of (what is called) Centre and River Row. The wind at the time was blowing strongly from the west, and in consequence of the inflammable nature of the small wooden buildings, or sheds, the flames spread with great rapidity. Apprehensions were at one time entertained that the flames would extend to the old market buildings on the east side of West Street, but, by the energetic exertions of the firemen, it was confined to those on the west side. About twelve o'clock the fire was at its height, when the whole number of sheds (nearly two hundred) were blazing away, which presented a brilliant illumination, and could be seen at a great distance. Above two hundred agents, commission, and other dealers in produce sustained losses, which it was thought would average about $400 each, on their stock and buildings; and but three are reported as being insured. The origin of the fire was not known. About two weeks after the burnt space was again covered with sheds, but of a more attractive appearance than their predecessors, and business appeared as thriving as ever.

In the early part of January, 1861, an adjustment of the long-standing controversy between the city and the State authorities, concerning the ownership of what was called the "West Washington Market property," which appears in the form of a compromise, between the Comptroller and Corporation Counsel on the part of the city, and Messrs. Taylor and Brennan, lessees of the State. The latter are to be paid $300,000, in consideration of which they agree to discontinue the suit which has been so long pending, and also all claims for rent in the past and present. The question of title to be settled between the city and State.

* Communication from the Mayor, July 11, 1859.

"The result," says *The World*, January 9, 1861, "to Messrs. Taylor and Brennan cannot be set down otherwise than as an eminently profitable speculation. Their net profits may be deduced from the following figures of receipts and disbursements:

Rent collections from Dec. 29, 1859, to Sept. 23, 1860,						$ 53,000
Premiums for stands,	"	"	"	"	-	10,000
Paid as compromise by city,	-	-	-	-	-	300,000
						$363,000
Salaries,	-	-	-	-	-	$ 5,000	
Legal expenses,	-	-	-	-	20,000	25,000
Net profits,	-	-	-	-	-	$338,000

"Who will not say that this has been a brilliant speculation for Messrs. T. and B.?"

About eight years ago (1851) a strong effort was made to displace the old market-house, by the erection of a splendid new structure; as we find a resolution in favor of advertising for proposals to build the Washington Market had passed the Board of Aldermen on the 4th of June, 1851. This advertisement read thus:

"Sealed proposals will be received at the office of the Commissioners of Repairs and Supplies until Saturday, August 9, 12 o'clock M., at which time they will be publicly opened, for the erection, in sections, of a new market on the site of the present Washington Mardet, according to and in pursuance of the plans, &c."

Among the estimates for doing the entire work complete,

John B. Corlies appears the lowest, viz., - - $375,500
Benjamin F. Camp   next,   "   - -   433,933
Peter J. Bogart   next,   "   - -   443,693

And here it rested until the next January, when it was again agitated, or shaken up a little; and then again, in the month of October following, a resolution was offered to have the market built according to a plan prepared by Frederick A. Peterzen, and the contract be given to John B. Corlies, the lowest bidder. This, in the end, was laid on or under the table, where it was found again in 1854, and brought forth in a favorable report from a Committee to rebuild the whole market according to the former plans and estimates. However, the contracts were ordered not to be signed, as the Mayor had vetoed it; and so they stand at the present day.

The present old dilapidated market-houses here are certainly a disgrace to the City of New York, and have been for the last fifteen years, and there is now no encouragement even to attempt to better them, in the erection of new buildings, while we have inefficient public officers to direct or superintend. Nothing can be done to accommodate the public, without there is a chance to make *something* out of it; as these public offices, when obtained, cost large sums, and the mere salary of a thousand or two of dollars is no consideration at all, as either amount would hardly pay for a nomination. If a movement for public accommodation is suggested, out comes the conservative or opposition press to show that what would legitimately cost 150,000 dollars would, if conducted by these inefficient officers, cost the city 250 or 300,000 dollars.

The Grand Jury has, within a space of three months, presented this market-place a nuisance no less than three times: once in the month of November, then in December, 1858, and the last time in January, 1859, when they state, they "also endorse the action of a former Grand Jury, in presenting as a nuisance Washington Market, and the grounds attached thereto, with a recommendation that those in favor give the matter immediate attention."

This market is without doubt the greatest depot for the sale of all manner of edibles in the United States; it not only supplies many thousands of our citizens, but, I may say, many of the surrounding cities, towns, villages, hotels, steamers, (both ocean and river,) and shipping vessels of all descriptions. The great business done here certainly demands better accommodations for both buyer and seller, and they should have them. Here we find almost an endless variety and vast amounts of meat, poultry, fish, vegetables, fruits, &c., which daily concentrate here, and not room enough to receive and properly display them for sale, much less room enough to accommodate the thousands who purchase here. There is, however, one great advantage and relief here—that the greater part of the business is principally done by wholesale, between the hours of twelve and seven o'clock in the morning; and those who generally purchase here go well prepared for any and every emergency.

In concluding the history of this market, no doubt many will think, and think truly, that the great mass of confusion and corruption, the crowded state, and especially the want of system, which now, and for a long time, have disgraced some of our public markets, and more especially this one, has been produced by the selection and appointment of inefficient public officers to govern them; who have no idea of the demanded duties, or the wants of a public market. In an unlawful manner, they have taken possession of and allotted all the stands or spaces reserved for the country people; encroached on the passage or gangways, and so reduced the room for the necessary business transactions of both buyer and seller, that it has driven a great portion of the retail trade from this market.

Ofttimes the small passage-ways are so obstructed, that to pass through is almost impossible; and if the attempt be made, the person must be prepared to receive a greasy, dirty, or torn coat or dress, besides being crowded or pushed, or the danger of having his pocket or basket relieved of anything valuable. But on the other hand, if all the display was made in proper market-houses, where every article was systematically arranged and kept in proper order, what a sight! an attraction! an accommodation, and an ornament to our city, would be the great " Washington Market!"

"GRAND STREET MARKET."

1814. WE have sold and removed the " Corlaers Hook Market," in the year 1819, and in another location, at an earlier period, (1814,) erected the *Fish Market*, (see " *Corlaers Hook Market*,") which afterwards became known as " *Grand Street Market*."

No doubt the object Mr. Hunter had in view, in erecting this market-house, was to draw the business of the Corlaers Hook Market near, and to benefit his property. He succeeded in getting two butchers, George Paff and Joseph Bull, with several other stands, besides those who sold fish in it; but the butchers and many others left, after a short stay, as they could not succeed; but as soon as the " Corlaers Hook Market" was torn down, the occupants were transferred into this, and after a time it became a good, although a small, market for business.

After the transfer, the following butchers occupied the following stands: On No. 1, Henry Hoffman; on No. 2, Thomas Winship; and on No. 3, John Winship.

" Grand Street" took its name from a grand, wide street laid out in 1767,* to connect on the east and west sides of the " Great" or " Delancey's Square," bounded on the north by the present Broome, on the south by Hester, on the east by Orchard, and on the west by Eldridge Streets. Grand Street commenced from the Bowery Lane, (on the west side it was called Judith Street,) and ran to this *Square;* then, on the east side, it continued on to Mr. Jones's country-seat, " *Mount Pitt;*" and when the high hills were dug down, it ran to the East River.

This market-house was very poorly built, with but few accommo-

* Ratzan's Map City of New York.

dations, and no cellar under it; as one of its patrons (James P. Allaire) induced several of the butchers to petition for privilege to place an ice-house under it; which was before the Board on the 7th of August, 1820, and leave obtained; so Mr. Allaire, at his own cost, built it, and filled it with ice, that he might, he said, "now and then have a good piece of corned beef through the warm weather."

The next winter produced more ice than was needed; in fact, it was the most steady cold weather that had been known for many years. The Press says: "The weather, after 21 days of steady cold, began to moderate on Saturday afternoon, (the 20th.) On Saturday morning Long Island Sound was crossed upon the ice from Sands' Point to the opposite shore, distance eight miles. The price of oak wood was up to $5 a load on Saturday."* Three days after: "The cold still continues intense; both the North and East Rivers were crossed on the ice, and the bay is nearly filled with floating ice, which will probably be closed by another cold night, and our harbor shut up for the first time in 40 years."† The next day: "The North River continues to be crossed with safety on the ice; the distance between the two shores has been measured, and found to be a mile from Cortlandt Street to Powles Hook. The Hoboken ferry-boat, with 57 persons and 23 horses on board, drifted on Wednesday evening below Governor's Island and was inclosed in the ice, where she now remains. The people suffered much from the cold during the night, although none were frozen."

The news from Bridgeport, dated 24th, said: "On Thursday night last the cold was so excessive that Long Island Sound, opposite the west chop of this harbor, was completely closed over by ice; the distance at this place is about 30 miles. Such an event, it is believed, has not taken place during the last 40 years."

The Press of the 27th says: "More than a thousand persons crossed the North River yesterday on the ice; produce of every kind was taken over in sleds, &c., and hundreds were seen skating in the middle of the river." I well recollect the sight, as an elder brother and myself were *enjoying* a walk on the river at the same time, but it was the first and last walk on this river the latter ever cared for.

Then, there "came up from Staten Island yesterday, on the ice, a boat and seven men, viz., John Vanderbilt, A. Lawrence, William Drake, Robert Davis, Lewis Farnharm, and Mr. Wainwright." "The mail for Staten Island was yesterday taken down over the ice by Daniel Simonson and Joseph Seguine. Many persons walked yesterday from Long Island to Staten Island—such a circumstance

* American, January 22, 1821.　　　　　　　　† Ibid., January 25.

has not been witnessed before since the year 1780, when heavy ordnance were conveyed on the ice from New York to Staten Island."

This long and severe cold weather caused much suffering among
the poor, and led to the establishment of soup-houses, through the
generosity of many of our butchers. Collections were also taken
up in the churches for their benefit, one of which is noticed on the
30th as amounting to $2,106.46.

In the month of February, 1829, " the East River was completely
closed with ice, from Riker's Island to Sands' Point, a distance of
about 18 miles. Six gentlemen who left New Haven on Sunday
morning at 10 o'clock reached this city at 10 next morning, almost
exhausted, having labored very hard for 24 hours to get here. They
were obliged to walk the greatest part of the way, the snow drifts in
many places being so formidable that no vehicle could surmount or
work through them."*

A most remarkable long winter and deep snow, more especially
in the Eastern States, took place in the year 1836. In the early part
of April the *New Hampshire Courier* says: "At the close of March
the snow was not only two feet deep, but it is as solid as ice, and
the Merrimack is passable on the ice for sleighs and teams, the snow
being about as thick on the ice as it is on the land. We learn that
in many parts of the State great want of hay, and the dying of almost whole stocks of cattle, attending the winding up of the winter.
It is now going on *five months* since the snow first covered the
ground, and we have had constant and pretty good sleighing all the
time. Such a winter as the past, or perhaps we should say present,
has no man living among us ever before seen, and the like he probably never will see again." At this time, "the ice on the River
Schuylkill, Pennsylvania, is said to be from 22 to 24 inches thick."

In the month of March, " oak wood was selling in New York at
$16.50 per cord, and pine at $11.25," with a small supply.

We turn to this market, and find a petition from the butchers and
sellers of fish, on the 16th of September, 1822, "requesting a platform and shed at the east end of the market," which was granted.

The arrangement of stands in this market in 1824 was somewhat
different from other markets; the vegetable and fruit stands came
first, or on the west end; the eight butchers next, and the fish stands
on the east end. The butchers stood:

No. 1. William Degraw.	No. 2. Thomas Winship.
3. John Varick.	4. Alexander Brady.
5. Benjamin Ward.	6. Walter Byrnes.
7. Stephen Doan.	8. Hugh Harrigan.
9. Vacant.	10. Vacant.

* Evening Post, February 25, 1829.

Many of the above butchers were business men and of good repu-
tations, which, no doubt, gave character and a successful trade here
for many years. The occupant of No. 1, William Degraw, succeeded John A. Martin in 1820, and held it until his death in 1826, when
his widow, Susan Degraw, in the month of March, petitions and
says, that "she has been left nearly destitute and without any means
of supporting herself, and prays the Board would grant her a license
for the said stand during pleasure." The Market Committee report
in favor on the 24th of April following; when the Board "*Resolved*,
That a *license* be granted to Susan Degraw for stall No. 1 Grand
Street Market."

Thomas Winship, on No. 2, was also a very prominent man, not
only in this market, but in his (13th) Ward, of which, as an Alderman, he served his constituents both faithfully and honestly, and his
vote was always cast conscientiously on all subjects which came before him.

In the year 1827 this market was represented as having become old
and much crowded, from the fact that it was doing an excellent business; some wished it removed out of the street; and others, again,
that a large plot should be purchased to erect a very large market-
house. The butchers, with above one hundred of the inhabitants of
that district, petition for stands in the new Manhattan Market, then
erecting close by. They state, "It will be injurious to have two
markets so near together, as there is one at present building on
Manhattan Island. They wish to resign their stands which they at
present occupy, and allow them to report back to your Honorable
Body." This was signed by the following:

No. 1. William Shelton.　　　No. 2. Thomas Winship.
　　3. George Nash.　　　　　　4. Alexander Brown.
　　5. Benjamin Ward.　　　　　6. Walter Byrnes.
　　7. David Perrin.　　　　　　8. Edward Smith.
　　9. John Kent.　　　　　　　10. John Varick.

In the month of May, next year, a numerously signed petition was
before the Board, asking for a new large market. "They represent
that the population of this part of the city has increased with great
rapidity, so much so, that the present *market* cannot long afford the
necessary accommodation for *victualers* in proportion to the increase
of inhabitants; and, therefore, that additions will have to be made
to the present *market*, or a new one erected. They would further
observe, that the number of stalls regularly occupied is *ten*; while
the number occupied in the *Spring Street Market* is *twelve*; and as
it has been deemed necessary to purchase ground at a great expense
for the purpose of removing and replacing the market at the foot of

Spring Street, your memorialists hope and believe that your Honorable Body will purchase a *piece of land* in the vicinity of the *Grand Street Market*, in order that it may be removed and a more convenient one erected," &c.

On the 19th instant following a formidable *remonstrance* appeared before the Board, which suggested the "impropriety of building a market as petitioned for, there being now *three markets,* besides the *present one,* in the vicinity of from *one-half* to three-quarters of a mile;" "that the *Manhattan Market,* distant not to exceed *three hundred yards* from the Grand Street Market, is conveniently located on *thirty-two* lots, which cost about forty thousand dollars, and that a market cannot be built as petitioned for in Grand Street for less than from twenty to thirty thousand dollars." The Market Committee, on the 11th of August, report, "The present market at the foot of Grand Street *is old* and in a very decayed state, and ought to be removed, and a new one built in its place, at a cost 'estimated at one *thousand' dollars.* They therefore resolve to erect *one seventy-five feet in length* and twenty-seven in breadth."

The next year the new market-house was finished, and the old building sold for $49.75, when the former occupants of the butchers' stands were informed by the Common Council, that they intended to sell the ten stands at public auction, which drew a petition from a large number of the inhabitants of the 7th and 13th Wards, and one also from the butchers, which was before the Board on the 26th January, (1829,) "praying that the stands may not be sold at public auction, but renewed to the old occupants." Before, however, they had advertised the sale, the butchers came forward and offered them large and liberal rents, much more than they had paid before; the Committee, however, would not accept, but on the day of sale, which took place at the new market-house, these ten butchers had agreed among themselves to purchase their several numbers as occupied in the old market-house. Many other butchers who had come to bid, on hearing the facts, agreed not to interfere or bid. The first stand set up, the original proprietor bid $10, and not another bid could the auctioneer get, so it was knocked down to him; the next was started, when some person bid against the original; he was seized and hustled out of the market, and came near being thrown into the dock. The Committee stopped the sale, and agreed to accept the liberal terms offered. Here, at least, was one instance where the butchers assisted each other in an attempt to deprive them of their rights in equity, if not in law.

The rapid growth of this neighborhood began soon after 1830, when this market felt its effects, and soon all the stands were filled, and an excellent business continued there up to the period when the old market was displaced for a new one.

In the year 1835 we find many changes in the occupancy of the butchers' stands, which appears as follows:

No. 1. Andrew Storms.   No. 2. Thomas Winship.
    3. John Pendergast.   4. George Scott, Jun'r.
    5. Mathew Bird.   6. Walter Byrnes.
    7. George Cummings.   8. Samuel J. Pittman.
    9. John Kent.   10. Benjamin Ward.

The business of the market, with that of the street and ferry, demanded more accommodations than there was room in this (Grand) street to give, without blocking it up. So the authorities purchased a plot of ground upon which the Monroe Market was built in 1836, into which the occupants of this markst were transferred, and the old " Grand Street Market-House" disappeared.

"CENTRE MARKET."

As early as 1812 a proposition was made to establish a public market on a piece of ground between Orange and Rynders (*Centre*) Streets, fronting on Grand Street. This location, before the earth of a very high hill was removed, had been known as "Bunker Hill," and "Bayard's Mount," and it was the highest and steepest elevation on the south end of New York Island; supposed to be about 100 feet higher than the present level of Grand Street.

The proposition to establish a market-place here, at the above period, was referred to a Committee, but as the war of 1812 became the all-absorbing topic, the matter was laid over until it was again revived by the inhabitants of the Sixth, Eighth, and Tenth Wards, who presented a formidable petition to the Common Council on the 14th of July, 1817, for the above location and object; and on the 25th of August following, a Committee reported in favor of buying this plot, bounded by Grand, Orange, Rynders (*Centre*,) and Broome Streets, which, they state, "could be purchased much below its value." Mr. Morris Martin, the owner, agreed to sell it to the Corporation, if it was to be always used for public market purposes, for the sum of five thousand dollars. The Committee also proposed to build a market-house, measuring eighty feet by twenty-five, running along Grand Street, at an estimated cost of one thousand dollars. This report was accepted and passed by the Board.

In the month of November it was reported ready for occupation, when a resolution passed, "that it be called 'Centre Market,'" and the butchers holding stands in the Collect Market were, with several others, recommended to be licensed; when they were placed in the new market, in the following order:

No. 1. Asa W. Wesson.	No. 2. Joseph Blackwell.
3. William H. Gross.	4. John Hilliker.
5. Jacob Tier.	6. William Reeves.
7. Stephen Hilliker.	8. John Fash.
9. Thomas Mook.	10. William Bowen.
11. James Simonson.	12. John A. Beslar (Basely.)
13. William Mook.	14. John Triglar.

The market was opened with a good business, and the first meat sold in it was by Thomas Mook, the occupant of No. 9, who claimed to have sold a fine steak to Daniel Spader, an old butcher of Washington Market, who resided in Mulberry, near Spring Street. Mr. Mook was (and is yet) a true type of this family, of which several were butchers; all were gentlemen of good education, but of retiring disposition, and most worthy, honest men.

Among the other occupants removed from the "Collect Market" into this were two remarkable sisters, daughters of Mrs. Frances Banta, (noticed in the "Oswego Market,") who early taught them to know how to earn their livelihood, instead of *not to know how*, as is the fashion of the present day. They were early in life left widows, with families to support on small incomes; and although they had wealthy relatives, they felt not like receiving dependent charity, but rather preferred to call their early teachings into action, and earn an independent livelihood.

A sketch of the life of one of the daughters will be found in the "Union Market," and the other, Mrs. Fanny Watson, or rather "Aunt Fanny," was long known in this market; in fact, until her death, which occurred in 1841. She was a large, well-formed, as well as a well-informed woman, very sprightly, quick, and a general favorite here, where she spent many years in accumulating a property, of which a part was unfortunately destroyed by fire. She, however, succeeded in bringing up her family in such a manner as to give her pleasure; and when she died, she left a snug property and a good name for industry, intelligence, and honesty.

In the month of May, 1821, a petition was before the Board, signed by Philip C. Ruckel, foreman, and thirty other firemen belonging to fire-engine No. 40, then located in Mulberry, below Broome Street, "stating that they were residing in a thickly populated part of the city, and wish to have a bell placed on the steeple of this market-house, at a cost of $55," to which a favorable report was made and afterwards adopted.

A successful trade continued here, and it being the only *central market* in the city, (from which no doubt it took its name,) it was continually adding to its business as the neighborhood increased. This increase demanded more room, especially for country people and the fishermen, which led a Committee, in the month of July, 1822, to report on building an addition with the materials from the " old Fly Market," which had been taken to the public yard, and which it was thought were sufficient for that purpose, so they recommended the following : " *Resolved*, That a market-house be built on the public square at Centre Market, not to exceed seventy-five feet in length." In this addition, after it was finished, we find two additional butchers' stands placed, and but few changes in the occupancy of the other stands are found in the year 1824. Nicholas Goodman then occupied No. 3; Francis O'Neil, No. 4; William Borden, No. 7; Thomas G. Harrison, No. 12; and on the new stands George Clinch, No. 15, and John B. Smith on No. 16.

About this period there were several butchers in this as well as one or two other markets engaged in, or who at least encouraged an affair which perhaps was one of the most ridiculous as well as one of the most perfect " hoaxes" ever introduced to the public, originating in a few playful remarks made by a near relative, in a joking conversation.

In the neighborhood of Mulberry and Spring Streets almost every afternoon congregated a number of butchers and others, to learn and talk about the current news of the day. Among the number was an old retired carpenter, whom we shall call *Lozier*, (a name that he afterwards assumed in carrying out his " hoax,") who was full of fun and " dry sayings," and his equal was seldom found in carrying a long face with them.

In the year 1823 or '4, one fine afternoon, this old carpenter, as usual, sought the current news of the day of this relative, whom we shall call Uncle John. " Well," says Uncle John, " we have had a long conversation about New York Island, and have come to the conclusion that the island is getting too heavy on the Battery end, where it is altogether too much built upon, and we therefore consider it dangerous; so our intention is to have it sawed off at Kingsbridge, and turn that end down where the Battery is now located. But the question is, how shall it be done, as Long Island appears in the way? Some think it can be done without moving Long Island at all; that the bay and harbor are large enough for the Island of New York to turn around in; while others say, Long Island must be detached and floated to sea far enough, then anchored, until this *grand turn* is made, and then brought back to its former place." "Lozier" at once took hold of this enormous job, and daily he was in consultation with the many visitors in relation to it, which generally took place before strangers, who, of course, overheard the conversation, usually appearing to be carried on in great earnestness; and, poor frail human nature! they would believe, and ofttimes suggest an opinion on some difficult point.

This subject, for some two or three months, appeared to be the question of the day—"*sawing the Island off;*" and "Lozier" having the job, was waited upon by numerous persons, and among them were several mechanics. Some were engaged to build barracks, which were to accommodate the hundreds of workmen; others to make the large sweeps, about twenty-four in number, of 250 feet in length, which were to be used on the opposite sides of the extreme ends of the Island, to sweep it around after it was *sawed off*. The iron-work on these sweeps was to be made in a peculiar but substantial manner, and an excellent neighboring blacksmith was very anxious to do the work, as he said, "There was no work in his line that he could not do;" and although his wife had no faith in this job, he every few days presented himself to Lozier to receive the dimensions of each part or piece, that he might properly estimate on it. Laborers and others who were seeking work, and happened to meet those who were acquainted with this job, and more especially with some of the butchers in this market, sent them to "Lozier," who questioned them particularly as to their being *long-winded*, as he wanted a good many "pitmen," or those who could *go below, to saw;* he having engaged sufficient *sawyers* for the work above. They very generally would engage, and even assert that they could stay *below* as long as they might be wanted.

In this manner a great many were engaged, who soon became anxious to be set at work; but "Lozier" had not engaged a sufficient number, and he could not think of going on with this large job until he had. This led those who were engaged to seek others, and at last the numbers became so thick and pressing, that it got too warm for "Lozier." He was forced to name a certain day, and thought it best to divide them; and on this particular morning one party were directed to be at the "forks of the Broadway and Bowery," near the present Union Park; and the other portion to be at *No.* 1 *Bowery, corner of Spring Street,* where a large number of live hogs was expected to be ready, which they were to drive up. Others were to carry provisions, tools, &c., in wagons and carts; and a few wagons were to carry up the wives of several of the workmen, who were to do the cooking, washing, &c., for all.

The day came, when great numbers presented themselves, but "Lozier" was nowhere to be found, and more particularly at *No. 1 Bowery, corner of Spring Street.* Soon, however, some of the more knowing ones got hold of the merits of this great job, and felt as if they had been "handsomely sold." Yet they desired to appear as if they had not engaged in it, and began to cast ridicule upon the excited and angry ones, and very soon there were but few who would confess they had been engaged "to saw the Island off." "Lozier," in the mean time, lay quietly housed up; and so he staid several weeks, not daring to venture forth even to the "rendezvous;" and when he did so, he was disguised into the general appearance of a different person, and assumed his *proper* name; as some of the most excited had not only used hard words, but also threatened, if they ever got hold of "Lozier," they would "saw him off."

Previous to the year 1825, the Common Council usually sold the street manure or sweepings at public auction, which yielded to the city a pretty round sum. This year, however, when the time arrived to offer it again, which was on the 25th of April, says the press, "It seems that yesterday, when the sweeping and cleaning the city was offered at public sale, it was found that a combination was formed among those who were presumed to stand ready to bid a fair price for the privilege, and instead of paying anything, they demanded to be paid; and the least they would consent to take was $5,000 for the first district, and $10,000 for the second, and so on; thus prostrating the whole plan."

This combination or company had the "sweeping" years before, and were prepared with horses and carts, which a new party or company would have to furnish; and therefore they could dictate terms.

Street cleaning, however, was not so profitable then, as a few thousands would satisfy; but now a few hundred thousands are taken or got rid of; the *politicians* now-a-days being of a more hungry set.

In 1826, on the 4th of August, another addition or extension to this market was ordered to be built on Rynders *(Centre)* Street, and four new stands, Nos. 15, 16, 17, and 18, were reported sold at auction on the 19th of March of the next year, (1827,) and the stands previously known as 15 and 16 were moved up, and changed to Nos. 19 and 20. The numbers began on the Orange Street side, or east end of the market-house, on Grand Street. On the north side stood No. 1, occupied by John Triglor; on the lower side, next to Grand Street,   No. 2. William Mook.

No. 3. Thomas G. Harrison.

5. William Bowen.

7. John Fash.

9. William Reeves.

11. James B. Dominick.

13. John M. Seaman.

15. Sold to John Lyons, for $1,355.

17. Sold to Ephraim B. Bolander, for $1,476.

19. George Clinch.

4. James Simonson.

6. Thomas Mook.

8. William Borden.

10. Jacob Wiggins.

12. George Deitz.

14. Joseph Blackwell.

16. Sold to John Valentine, for $1,410.

18. Sold to William P. Varian, for $1,400.

20. William A. Smith.

For several years past the market people had become annoyed, and had also petitioned against "allowing persons from the country, who were daily in the practice of bringing down provisions in their wagons and selling the same in the Bowery, between Division and Bayard Streets:" they considered that this produce ought to be sold at the public markets. Then, again, in 1828, several butchers had located themselves in the Bowery, above Prince Street, which was the cause of a memorial being presented from the butchers in this market, who state: "That for some time past there is a number of men that have located themselves in the Bowery as butchers, very much to the annoyance of your petitioners, as it is from that quarter that they draw their chief support." They wish to have their stalls removed.

These butchers referred to were John Deavenport, Daniel S. Hyde, Joseph Townsend, and John Flock, who reply soon after, and state: "That they have been regularly brought up to the butcher's trade, and duly licensed. They have hired situations in the upper part of the Bowery, which they have occupied for some time past, and where there is no public market near them." Several of the inhabitants also petition for them to remain, which was followed up by another from this market, recapitulating the same grievances; and they also say: "That some of your petitioners have had frequent conversations with some of the members of the said Market Committee," and have understood from them, "that a law had been passed" "to remove said stands north of Tenth Street, to take effect on the first day of the present month, (May;) but on referring to said law, they find the same does not compel the occupants of the said stalls to remove, although well convinced that the meaning, spirit, and intention of said law is to remove said stalls beyond the limits." A law was passed to have them removed on the first of November following. However, before they were removed, the inhabitants were before the Board with the subject of erecting a new market on the corner of Second Street and the Bowery, which the butchers of the Centre Market strongly opposed with a petition, asking the Common Council " to keep their promises with them." " That about two years since, some of your petitioners purchased stalls *(stands)* in the Centre Market, and owing to an understanding between them and the Chairman of the Market Committee that there should be no meats sold by certain butchers in the Bowery after said stands were disposed of, they were induced to pay a very great price for said stands, fully believing that the market limits were to be extended. That your petitioners sent a petition to your Honorable Body, requesting the *limits* might be extended. That your Honorable Body saw fit to grant their prayer, and passed a *law* to extend said *limits*, but owing to some mistake made in describing such *limits*, they were only extended *one street*, when your Honorable Body meant that they should be extended *ten streets*. That your petitioners, seeing the error, petitioned to have the same corrected, and extend said *limits* as originally meant and intended; and that such petition was granted, and a *law* passed to extend said *limits* to Tenth and Thirteenth Streets, northward. That certain butchers, who stand on the corner of the Bowery and Second Street, are daily exposing *meats* for sale, contrary to said *law*, and have been so doing since the first day of November last. That they have complained over and over again to the Corporation Attorney to prosecute said butchers, but your petitioners can get no redress in that way."

" Your petitioners most ardently ask of your Honorable Body to protect them in *their rights*. Many of your petitioners are young men, just commencing business, with nothing to depend upon but their *stands* for their livelihood. They therefore pray that your Honorable Body will take it into mature deliberation before they conclude where to locate a market; and though the inducements to build it on the spot proposed may be great, your petitioners beg your Honorable Body also to take into consideration the great and irreparable injury will be to your petitioners, as well as your Honorable Body, &c."

This petition, and the unwearied efforts of several of the prominent butchers, among whom were John M. Seamen, George C. Clinch, and John Triglar, had the effect, at least, to change the location farther above the site of the Tompkins Market, and to accept the liberal proposition of Charles Henry Hall, noticed in the history of that market.

The occupants of the butcher stands, as they appeared in the month of March of this year, appear to have been changed considerably since the last notice made of them. They were occupied as follows:

No. 1. John Triglar.	No. 2. William Mook.
3. Thomas G. Harrison.	4. James Simonson.
5. William Bowen.	6. Thomas Mook.
7. John Fash.	8. William Borden.
9. William Reeves.	10. Jacob Wiggins.
11. James B. Dominick.	12. George Deitz.
13. John M. Seaman.	14. Joseph Blackwell.
15. John Lyons.	16. John Valentine.
17. Ephraim B. Bolander.	18. William P. Varian.
19. George Clinch.	20. William A. Smith.

Soon after, a somewhat remarkable incident took place with the butchers here, which proved there was a strong unanimity of feeling for the general advancement of business here, which perhaps seldom or ever occurred before in this city. In their anxiety to establish or keep up the reputation in the sale of the choicest meats, all promised to withdraw from business on a certain day, if either one or two of them would purchase the celebrated ox *"President,"* and have his beef sold in this market. George Clinch, on No. 9, and William P. Varian, on No. 18, concluded to purchase this then wonderful animal, estimated to weigh above 4,000 pounds alive; they had him slaughtered, and found his dressed weight less than 1,900 pounds. This, with several other fine cattle, (one pair of which, called the "Mitchell Steers," from Long Island, yielded 651 pounds of rough fat,) were dressed and paraded through the streets in procession, with numerous banners, &c. The principal motto was, *"Centre Market against the World,"* which took place on Friday, the 6th of February, 1829, and the next day it was offered for sale. All the stalls were not only gayly dressed with banners and flags, &c., but their usual occupants gave their services gratis on this occasion.

A large quantity of the prime parts was sold at *one dollar per pound*, which produced an excellent market for the whole, and gave general satisfaction. A very choice piece of the Ox President was sent " to Andrew Jackson, President elect of the United States," with the following letter:

"NEW YORK, *February* 10, 1829.

"*Sir*—The undersigned Committee, in behalf of the butchers of Centre Market, of the City of New York, take the liberty of presenting you with a piece of the *Ox President*, lately slaughtered at this market, (said to be the fattest ever raised in this country,) which they beg you to accept as an humble tribute of their gratitude for the eminent public service you have rendered our country, and as a mark of their esteem for your private virtues.

"We are, very respectfully, your obedient servants,

"GEORGE CLINCH,
"JOHN M. SEAMAN,
"J. B. DOMINICK."

The reply of President Jackson read as follows:

"WASHINGTON CITY, *February* 16, 1829.

"*Gentlemen*—I have received the piece of beef of the large and fat ox lately slaughtered by the butchers of the Centre Market, of the City of New York, which you have been pleased to present as a token of their respect for my character. I accept it with pleasure, and promise to-morrow to give it a place on my table, as not an inappropriate emblem of the hospitality and solid prosperity of your citizens. Have the goodness to accept for yourselves, gentlemen, and offer to the butchers of the Centre Market, assurances of my grateful regard.   Your ob'dt servant,

"ANDREW JACKSON."

In the month of February, 1831, the brick pavement in the butchers' market was ordered to be replaced by a wooden one, and the crowded state of the market induced an appropriation of $300, in the month of September following, " to erect an addition of 48 feet to the east end immediately." Then, in the following month of January, (1832,) a resolution was passed to sell four additional stands at a " premium," at public auction, for cash, which took place on the 15th of February. Four stands, from 17 to 20, were moved up and numbered 21, 22, 23, 24, and Nos. 17, 18, 19, and 20 were sold to the following persons, and at the following prices: No. 17 to Thomas Varian, at $1,725; No. 18 to Charles De Voe, at $1,480; No. 19 to George A. Fink, at $2,150; and No. 20 to William Hays, at $1,850. At the same time there were sold Nos. 11 and 12 in the Essex Market, Nos. 3 and 6 in Tompkins Market, Nos. 8 and 48 in Fulton Market, No. 27 in Catharine Market, No. 27 in Washington Market, and No. 5 in Grand Street Market, which netted a premium of $12,510.

On the 28th of May following, the Joint Committee ordered licenses to be granted to all those who purchased stands; " and they take this occasion to say, that owing to the indefatigable industry and perseverance of Mr. Smith, the Collector of the City Revenue, they have brought the markets to what they deem a healthy state, whereby the city revenue has been much enhanced, and the butchers fully protected in all their rights and privileges."

A petition was before the Board in the month of June, in the next year, from Frederick Johnson, stating that he was a "native of the City of New York, and has served a regular apprenticeship with Joseph Blackwell, a butcher, and for some time has conducted the business—for the account of Mr. Blackwell in this market—and he is willing and desirous of transferring his stall No. 14 to your petitioner." Mr. Blackwell signs his willingness, and also states, "he has occupied this stand ever since the erection of this market-house. That he has now living with him a young man named Frederick Johnson, who has been regularly brought up to his own calling, most exemplary in his deportment, of most industrious and strictly moral habits; and as he is without natural protectors, having early lost both of his parents, and has a brother and sister looking to him for protection, he is desirous of placing him in a situation where he can be useful to himself and become a valuable member of society." However, before action had been taken by the Market Committee, Mr. Blackwell died, and the Committee soon after reported in favor of selling this stand at public auction; but the Chairman of the Committee gave Johnson permission to occupy it until the 1st of May. Johnson felt disappointed, as were many others in the market, who thought the decision of the Committee had been changed after the death of Blackwell had taken place; as they expected it would be transferred by paying a fair premium, as was done in the other markets.

Mr. Johnson then addressed them the following communication:

"*Gentlemen*—Having learnt, with much surprise, that it was contemplated to sell my late uncle's stall by auction, I have considered it prudent to lay before your Committee some facts which I trust will induce you to report favorably, and relieve me from a suspense which tends greatly to paralyze my efforts in business. That stall was obtained by my uncle in like manner with those formerly held by John Triglar, William Gross, Asa Wesson, John Fash, John Hilliker, and others, in the same market, all which have been sold or transferred by authority of the Corporation: that of Mr. Hilliker being disposed of by his widow; permit me, then, to suggest, that after so many precedents, I could entertain no doubt of obtaining the conveyance applied for, especially under the facts which I now detail, and which, I trust, you will see presents a stronger claim to your favor than even the case of John Hilliker. In the year 1829, my uncle, by reason of divers responsibilities for others, became insolvent; this soon .... rendered him unfit for business, so that I took charge of his stall, assumed his debts, then amounting to about $1,000, which I have since paid to the uttermost farthing; took upon myself the support .... of his family, ... who were dependent upon him, and who are to this day maintained by me. I have paid faithfully the rent of the stall, and kept it so supplied as to do my full share in keeping up the reputation of the market. I think, gentlemen, these facts will convince you that the prayer of my petition ought to be granted; and that in contrast with those to whom the same favor has been extended, I present a claim upon your liberality and justice too strong to be passed by. In addition to the assurance of my statements being correct, given below by my friend P. W. Engs, I can, if necessary, prove to you the truth of them by numerous other persons, &c." Mr. P. W. Engs vouches for all the above facts, after stating that he had "resided for about fourteen years near Centre Market, and during all that time have dealt at Blackwell's stall. He could by verbal statement add further evidence of the justice of Mr. Johnson's claim."

The report of the Committee was made, and finally adopted on the 5th of November, same year; in which they state they were "of opinion that said stand should be transferred to said Frederick Johnson, and that he should be duly licensed for the same, on his paying into the City Treasury the sum of twenty-five hundred dollars;" and they "*Resolved*, If the Board of Assistants concur, that the butcher's stand No. 14 Centre Market, lately occupied by Joseph Blackwell, be transferred to Frederick Johnson, on his paying into the City Treasury $2,500, and in all other respects conforming to the laws regulating our public markets." Johnson's many friends assisted him, and he became the occupant of his uncle's stand.

At this period this market was among the best in the city, the business profitable, and the patrons numerous, but with many complaints of not having room enough to transact the ordinary business in a satisfactory manner; with many it was useless to attempt an increase, because the Common Council had placed them in such a compass or space, that a business or enterprising man must stop there; in fact, it was saying, "You may do so much—but no more," even if you are willing to pay for further accommodations. These oft-repeated complaints induced the Market Committee, on the 6th of June, 1834, to report, " that the public markets should be sufficiently capacious to accommodate all who resort to them, both buyer and seller, with ample room for their mutual accommodation." " The Centre Market and ground cost the public $10,000, and is now paying 30 *per cent*. on the investment, as appears by the Comptroller's books; it is contemplated to enlarge this market by taking 14 lots of ground in the centre of the adjoining block, which is bounded by Orange, Broome, Mulberry, and Grand Streets; which space being 175 feet by 200 feet, will not cost over $60,000, which is about one-half of the sum that any other location could be had for in the vicinity of the present market.

This contemplated " scheme," however, did not take place, and some few did not line their pockets, as they expected to have done; nor did any relief accrue from this truthful report of the enormous per centage it exposed; which, however, was exceeded in another report, made in the following November, on the same subject, showing that it " pays the Corporation, on the present investment, between *thirty and forty per cent.*"

Some little temporary relief was given by the addition of a shed on the outside, and as a new building had been promised and would soon be erected, it had the means of somewhat quieting the stand-holders; but the Market Committee, in the mean time, had resolved to crowd four more stalls in, and to have them sold at auction on the 17th of March, 1835, for a " premium." This was more than the butchers could bear, so they employed " Counsel," and obtained an injunction from the Vice-Chancellor, restraining the Comptroller from selling them. This was followed with a report in the month of April, from the Counsel to the Corporation, R. Emmet, stating, " that a bill was filed in the Court of Chancery, by George C. Clinch, William P. Varian, John Phillips, Ephraim B. Bolander, William Spencer, and George A. Fink, to that effect. The Common Council passed a "*resolution*, that the Counsel of the Board be directed to answer, that the same be discharged." He, however, on the 23d of July following, advised a settlement; and the Committee " directed him to settle the same according to the terms proposed by the Counsel for the butchers," and the stands were not sold.

The butchers' stands at this period were occupied as follows:

No. 1. Henry Resler, Jun'r.	No. 2. William Mook.
3. Thomas G. Harrison.	4. James Simonson.
5. William Bowen.	6. Thomas Mook.
7. James I. Titus.	8. William D. Borden.
9. William T. Ryer.	10. Jacob Wiggins.
11. James B. Dominick.	12. Moses E. Arment.
13. John M. Seaman.	14. Frederick Johnson.
15. Joseph Hill, Jun'r.	16. John Valentine.
17. Thomas Varian.	18. Charles De Voe.
19. George A. Fink.	20. William Spencer.
21. Ephraim B. Bolander.	22. John Phillips.
23. George Clinch.	24. William P. Varian.

The building of the present brick market-house had been some time under consideration, but it was not favorably reported upon until the early part of May, 1838, when resolutions were passed to re-build this market-house on the grounds intended for its occupation; these were represented as being " 88 feet, 6 inches, on Grand

Street; 35 feet, 7 inches, on Broome Street; 389 feet, 6 inches, on
Orange Street; and 382 feet, 10 inches, on Centre Street." An appropriation of $50,000 was made for its erection; the estimates
adopted, however, were made by John Thompson, on the 18th of
June, for $39,390 ; although an additional sum of $980 was added,
to "strengthen the truss-girders, change the cellar-doors, alter the
steps, &c., which, with the original estimate, was equal to $40,370."

In the month of January following the new building was ready
for its occupants, and the opening of it for business was celebrated
by a grand ball and supper, given by the butchers belonging to this
market, in the large rooms now occupied by the military. This
was announced in an advertisement, as follows:

"A Butcher Ball and Supper,

"In commemoration of the opening of the new Centre Market,
will take place on the 17th of January, in the spacious rooms over said
market. Tickets, $5, to admit a gentleman and two ladies, can be
had on application to either of the following Committee, at the
market or their residences:

"JAMES B. DOMINICK, 93 Mercer Street.
JAMES WHINNEY, 184 Ludlow Street.
WILLIAM H. MOOK, 3d Avenue, near 24th Street.
T. H. MOOK, 3d Avenue, near 24th Street.
H. J. RYER, 145 Centre Street.
MOSES E. ARMENT, 171 Rivington Street.
FREDERICK JOHNSON, 28 Second Street.
FREDERICK CLINCH, 56 First Street.
JOSEPH W. CLINCH, 56 First Street.
WILLIAM T. RYER, 145 Centre Street.

"The New York Brass Band is engaged. Leader of the Cotillon,
Mr. BROWN. Leader of the Brass Band, Mr. LOTHIAN."*

Two days after, an editorial says: "The whole world—that is, the
eating world—will be there, and a great affair it will be. Not sir-
loins or rump steaks only, but all the delicacies of the season will
be displayed in the most tasteful and fashionable style."† The
tickets were soon disposed of, and before the ball took place $25
apiece were offered and refused for them. The ladies' tickets were
beautifully got up, with an engraving representing the new market
building, with Terpsichore, Cupid, wreaths, and the names of the
Managers—all printed in gold.

The day after the ball an editorial says of it: "The ball in honor
of the opening of the new Centre Market was quite a brilliant affair

* Evening Star, January 8, 1839.   Ibid.

last night, and all the ceremonies of reception, ladies' saloons, gentlemen's retiring-rooms, &c., &c., were arranged with as much taste and fashion as they could have been at Almack's. It should be known that this market, after the design of Mr. *(Thomas)* Thomas, the architect, is the first in this country which may be deemed a complete building. Faneuil Hall, Boston, is something like it, but the London markets of the first class come nearer to it. The saloon fronting Grand Street was fitted up with much taste with banners, portraits, and various decorations. Not having time to introduce the coal-gas, the saloon was lit up with spirit-gas, which burnt but dimly, owing to the heat of the rooms.

"The dancing to a splendid band, which played all the fashionable airs and waltzes, was kept up with great spirit; the ladies, who were numerous, and splendidly dressed, entered fully into the spirit of the scene; but the supper, or banqueting-rooms, created surprise and admiration. The long corridors over the market, from Centre to Broome Street, were thrown open, and brilliantly illuminated; each saloon had four tables, covered with all the delicacies of the season, in the very best style, by Mr. and Mrs. Niblo, who, with an army of waiters, were in attendance; and, when a thousand persons were seated at the tables, with all the brilliancy of dress and joyous hilarity, the *coup d'œil* was really beautiful. His Honor the Mayor, and the members of the Corporation, were of course all present, with a number of invited guests; and when it is recollected that giving a grand ball by a Committee of the Butchers is not an every-day affair, they deserve great credit for the manner it was carried through."*

There were very many handsome ladies present, and the greatest order and decorum were observed. They are a class of rich, substantial citizens, and all have received good educations, with the usual accomplishments.

On each plate was the following, printed on vellum **paper**:

"BUTCHERS' BALL—JANUARY 17, 1839.

"*In Commemoration of the Opening of Centre Market.*

"Music and Mirth, and beaming eyes
   Of peerless Beauty, here unite,
To gild each hour as it flies,
   And every joyous heart delight;

While fitly, 'neath this festive dome,
   Circe and Plenty shall provide,
To dedicate her chosen home,
   Our City's ornament and pride."

I might also add another incident or two which took place at this ball. The saloon being lighted, as above stated, with spirit-gas, created so much heat, and the window-frames worked so badly, that they would neither shove up or down; when the President of the

* Evening Star, January 18, 1839.

Board, who was present, ordered the panes to be knocked out, which soon gave relief. About twelve o'clock, P. M., when all were on the floor, many of whom were dancing, some of the Committee heard a creaking noise, and discovered the floor in one end of the room had settled some three or four inches; they quietly went down in the market-room, and put up a few studs or timbers, to make sure that it should not settle further, at least that night.

The excellence of the supper and arrangements called forth a letter of thanks to Mr. and Mrs. Niblo; and one of the Committee thought he never saw before, or since, so much taste, elegance, and tempting luxuries displayed, as was shown on those tables.

This ball was so successful, and gave so much satisfaction, that another was finally agreed upon, to take place in the month of February, 1842, which appeared in the advertisements as follows:*

"Butchers' Ball.

" The butchers of Centre Market will give their second grand ball and supper at the four spacious rooms of the Apollo Saloon, on Tuesday evening, 15th February, 1842. Those wishing tickets are requested to make early application, as the number is limited. Tickets to be had at Centre Market, or any of the following Committee:

Joseph W. Clinch,	Moses E. Crasto,	Frederick Johnson,
William Wood,	Henry J. Ryer,	Sam'l L. Arment,
Samuel H. Denton,	Thomas H. Mook,	Wm. D. Kirschbaun,
William T. Ryer,	James S. Egbert,	Cornelius M. Cregier,
John E. Dean.		JAMES B. DOMINICK, Chairman.

JOSEPH C. PINCKNEY, Secretary."

The ladies' tickets bore the same engraving as those of the first ball, except the date. The Managers on this occasion were:

J. B. Dominick,	Joseph W. Clinch,	William T. Ryer,
Thomas H. Mook,	Joseph C. Pinckney,	James S. Egbert.

This also was a well-arranged and conducted ball, but not quite so successful as the first. The supper and arrangements were not so satisfactory, although quite as good as were usually given. Each gentleman, on sitting down, found the following verses on his plate, which he was expected to digest first:

" To the Apollo the butchers have come one and all,
To enjoy the delights of an Annual Ball ;
They have *fare* for the palate, and *fair* for the heart,
And a bumper they 'll drink to the fair, ere they part.

Sure Apollo of old was a pattern of grace,
While modern Apollos wear a round, jovial face :
He of old was unsocial ; while these relish life,
Feast, drink, and make merry, love home and a wife.

* Evening Post, February 15, 1842.

While we drain, then, the bowl, filled with nectar divine,
And enjoy the rich feast, and quaff the red wine,
We'll live in the love, and rejoice in the light
Of bright sunny eyes which beam on us to-night.

Our host, tho' but one, sure a host we may call,
For a host of good cheer has he given us all :
Let the host, then, partake of the host we have here,
And cheer the good host, for his host of good cheer."

Previous to the finishing of the new market-house in 1838, the question came up before the Board about the occupancy of the large rooms, and in the month of December the subject was brought before the Board, of appropriating the large rooms over the market for the use of the military; when the following resolution was passed: "*Resolved*, That it be referred to the Committee on Public Offices and Repairs to inquire into and report the propriety of appropriating a suitable portion of the second story of *Centre Market*, now in progress of being built, for the use of the several *uniform* military companies of the city." This Committee reported as follows:

"Petitions have heretofore been presented to the Common Council, asking to have a building erected for the purpose of accommodating the militia. The project has been favorably spoken' of, though no report has been made on the subject. The Committee have had several interviews with the officers commanding the different Divisions of Militia, for the purpose of ascertaining whether the rooms are large enough to accommodate the whole. From information thus derived, the Committee is satisfied that they are sufficient for all the purposes for which they are intended to be used. There are four rooms connected together, by openings of twelve feet, which can be closed at pleasure, and used separately or otherwise, as may best suit their convenience. There are two separate entrances from the street, which will permit the Artillery and Infantry to occupy separate apartments, without incommoding each other. The arrangements made by the Committee have been submitted to the officers, who have expressed themselves as being perfectly satisfied. The Committee propose the following resolutions:

"*Resolved*, That the room fronting on Grand Street, in the second story of Centre Market, and the room next adjoining, be given to *(Major-General Sandford)* the officer commanding the Division of Artillery of this city, for the purpose of drilling and exercising the men under his command, under the following regulations, viz.: no arms, ammunition, or accoutrements shall at any time be kept in these rooms; meetings for any other purpose than those mentioned above shall not be allowed.

"*Resolved*, That the use of the two remaining *rooms*, extending up to the keeper's apartments, be given to *(Major-General Doughty, Major-General Stryker, Major-General Jones,* and *Major-General Lloyd,)* the officers commanding the several Divisions of Infantry in this city, for the accommodation of their several Divisions, for the purpose and under the restrictions mentioned in the preceding resolution.

"*Resolved,* That the rooms referred to in the two preceding resolutions may be occupied for the purposes therein named until otherwise ordered by the Common Council." Adopted and approved.

These "rooms" were divided up among the several Regiments composing the eight Brigades, to be used as drill-rooms, meetings, &c. The necessary arrangements were made by a Committee called the "Drill-Room Committee," consisting of one Colonel from each Brigade, organized as follows:

Colonel GEORGE H. BIDDLE,   59th Brigade.
"   THOMAS F. DE VOE,   63d   "
"   WILLIAM MITCHELL,   45th   "
"   H. M. SCHIEFFELIN,   58th   "
"   JOHN EWEN,   10th   "
"   S. JONES MUMFORD,   63d   "
"   NICHOLAS CARROLL,   3d   "
"   ROBERT C. MORRIS,   64th   "

For several years the commandants of regiments ordered their officers and non-commissioned officers to drill on certain evenings assigned to them, which tended much to increase their efficiency and usefulness.

On the 27th February, 1839, three fish-stands were drawn for in this market, viz.: No. 1, Willis Hall; No. 2, James Linsey; and No. 3. Elstein Tucker; and in the month of June following a shed was "ordered to be built at Centre Market, to accommodate country people."

In the previous month of April, after the Harlem Railroad Company had laid down their track along Centre Street, it was found to interfere with the butchers' carts, whose owners could not back to the curb-stone. They ask, through petition, to have the curb " set in for this purpose;" and " that they do not wish to be considered as unfriendly to the laying down of the railroad track, by presenting their petition." The Committee, in their report, state that they "have examined the premises, and are of opinion that public accommodation will be promoted by setting in the *curb-stone* six feet, which will then leave twelve feet for side-walk next the market, a width ample for all purposes. The width proposed to be taken from the side-walk is now occupied in some places by *fish-cars,* which in such situations have not the merit of ornament or utility. The Committee have conferred with the officers of the Railroad Company, who express their willingness to go to the expense of altering the *curb-stone*, and to lay the space between the rails and the curb with *wood pavement*, for the benefit of the horses standing at the market. The Committee offer the following resolution: *Resolved*, That the *curb-stone* on the easterly side of Centre Street, in front of the market, be set *six feet* into the walk from its present line: *Provided* that the same be done at the expense of the Harlem Railroad Company; and *provided* that the said Railroad Company pave the space between the rails and the said curb-stone with *blocks of wood;* the value of stone pavement to be allowed to their credit, in the assessment for paving the street, on so much of the said pavement as does not legitimately belong to them to make."

In the month of May following, what was formerly known as Orange Street, on the east side of this market, was changed by the following: "*Resolved*, That the new street east of and adjoining 'Centre Market,' and between Grand and Broome Streets, be known and designated as 'Centre Market Place.'"

At this period the heaviest and finest ox then known in the States was sold by the occupant of No. 27, Joseph W. Clinch, in company with Mathew H. Chase, of No. 33 Washington Market, who together had purchased this extraordinary animal of Erastus Jeffers, Esq., of Waterville, Oneida County, N. Y., by paying $600 for him; and this amount, with other numerous expenses for advertising, ribbons, music, help, &c., ran up his cost to a large amount. But being well sold, they made, instead of losing money, as is usual on these occasions. About one-third of the beef of this animal was sold at *one dollar per pound*, and all the other parts were also well sold, clean off, on Saturday, the 25th of January, 1840.

Since that period several other fine animals have been sold here, and no doubt the largest and heaviest bullock ever produced in the United States (perhaps in the world) was exhibited and sold in this market by William Lalor, who gave general satisfaction by having this monstrous animal fairly weighed alive, rightly dressed, and the quarters weighed under the supervision of some of the best and most reliable men; although I must admit the quarters were hung drying too long (10 days) in the slaughter-house before the beef was weighed, which no doubt was a loss of some 50 pounds—the usual time being from two to four days.

This enormous animal, called *Union*, was purchased of E. Haxton, Esq., Beekman, Dutchess County, N. Y., by Mr. Lalor, for the great sum of $850. He weighed at home 3,452 lbs.; the day before he was killed he weighed 3,419 lbs., and after his beef had been hanging *ten days*, the four quarters weighed 2,319 lbs. It was, with several other fine cattle, displayed in carts, forming a large procession, which proceeded through many of the principal streets to this market. The prime cuts were sold at *one dollar a pound*, and the other portion at high prices; the whole of the sales amounting to above $1,000, which, after deducting expenses, left a fair profit, but a great deal more credit to the purchaser, for the manner in which he conducted the whole exhibition, and the taste he had displayed in dressing his stall and meats.

In the latter part of the year 1853, an addition of an average of thirty feet wide and thirty-five feet high was inclosed and joined to this market, on the street or "Centre Market Place" side, at an expense of about $5,000.

Some of the rooms in the upper part of the market-house were several years occupied as a station-house for the Fourteenth Ward Police, and afterwards as the Fourteenth Patrol District, which the police held until the year 1857, when the military again obtained possession of all these rooms, and since have repaired and made them more safe, by raising and strengthening the floors, which had been in a dangerous situation many years. This has been followed by introducing additional rooms in the place of the shed erected in 1853, the ceilings of others raised, partitions and walls removed; so that it now accommodates the Sixth, Eighth, and Seventy-first Regiments for drill and company meeting rooms.

Since 1850 the occupants licensed for butchers' stands in this market have been as follows:

No. 1. William Hays.	No. 2. William Kinner.
3. Samuel T. Williams.	4. William D. Borden.
5. Thomas Mook.	6. James Wilson.
7. Mook & Sheldon.	8. Mook & Sheldon.
9. Charles Hellen.	10. Jacob Lettice.
11. William Seal.	12. William Mook, Jun'r.
13. Timothy Lawrence.	14. Bryan Lawrence.
15. Frederick Johnson.	16. David Kehoe.
17. James Keating.	18. William Reid.
19. James Reid.	20. Henry Diffenbach.
21. Philip Reid.	22. John E. Dean.
23. Joseph Jantzen.	24. John B. Jantzen.
25. Joseph W. Clinch.	26. Frederick Clinch.
27. Joseph Flynn.	28. James Simonson.
29. Widow Harrison.	30. Augustus Fink.
31. William Lalor.	32. Andrew Reid.
33. Widow Varian.	34. John M. Seaman.
35. David Seaman.	

"ESSEX MARKET."

1818. THE wants of the inhabitants of the Tenth Ward, in the year 1818, for a market-place near the present location of the Essex Market, were, by a petition, laid before a Special Committee, who, on the 29th of June, reported in favor of the accommodation requested, in which it was stated that "a large proportion of the inhabitants of this section are mechanics and laboring men, who reside from half a mile to one mile and a half from any of the markets now established; the inconvenience experienced by these citizens, whose time is of the utmost importance to them, may be easily conceived; that more accommodations of the kind can be afforded at a moderate expense; they ought to be granted, and which will only cost about seven hundred dollars." The Board adopted a resolution to build "a market-house 40 by 20 feet, in the centre of Grand Street, between Ludlow and Essex Streets," which was finished in the month of September, and the Market Committee reported in favor of placing the several butchers on the following stands:

No. 1. Thomas Place.   No. 2. Henry Spicer.
    3. Henry N. Disbrow, (1819.)   4. Samuel Piercy, Jr.
    5. Thomas Bockover,   do.   6. Andrew Van Dusen.
    7. Stephen Doan.   8. John Ackerly.

This was followed in December with a resolution, "That the market lately erected in the centre of Grand Street be known by the name of 'Essex Market.'" The name *Essex* was no doubt taken from the street on the east side of this market-house, laid out and known about the year 1765,* then running on the east side of the "Great or Delancey's Square,"† located near the centre of Delancey's Farms, which extended from Division (the line of Division between this and Rutgers' Farms) up to about Stanton Street, and from the Bowery to the East River.

The street no doubt received its name from the county of that name in England, and likely the giving of this name to this market-place may have had an impetus from the victorious career of Commodore Porter in the frigate *Essex*, in which he swept the Pacific Ocean during the war with Great Britain, as it also had in giving the name to several counties and towns in several of the United States.

* Ratzan's Map, 1766.   † See "Grand Street Market."

The business of this market began with more than ordinary good prospects, and having been well conducted, it soon drew numerous patrons to it, as well as to assist in the erection of numerous buildings on the large quantities of vacant ground, some of which had to be leveled from a great height before it could be used for that purpose.

On the east side of this market-place, before the hills were dug down, was the favorite place on which the well-known and eccentric Johnny Edwards, the "scale-beam maker," held forth to sometimes large numbers of persons about once a week. From his residence, in Greene below Prince Street, he rode over to this place in his business cart, and getting on his favorite rock, he would entertain his hearers by his singular and sometimes pointed remarks.

About the period of the establishment of this market-place, a colored girl, named Rose Butler, was convicted and sentenced to be hung, for setting her master's house on fire, with the intention of burning her mistress to death. Johnny Edwards exerted his whole energies in her cause; in the streets, markets, and churches his whole saying was, "Blood for blood—but not blood for fire." On one occasion, being in a meeting-house of the Baptist Church, of which the Rev. A. McClay was pastor, situated in Mulberry Street, near Chatham, Johnny arose and commenced aloud with his exhortations; the sexton requested him to be quiet, as it disturbed the congregation; to which Johnny answered, "Glad on it—they ought to be disturbed."

Rose Butler appears to have been convicted of arson by the verdict of a jury, at an Oyer and Terminer, held on the 19th of November, 1818, before Justice Thompson, and sentenced to be hung on the 11th of June, 1819. The "*Evening Post*" of that date says: "This morning there were collected a concourse of two or three thousand people to witness the execution; but the Sheriff received a respite from the Governor till the 9th of July, stating one of the reasons, as I am informed, to be the insanity of the prisoner; but it is said that the inducement is the hope that she may make a disclosure of the names of some accomplices. That she had accomplices is pretty certain, though she denied it to one of the clergymen who attended her; for, after she was confined in prison, the house was again set on fire, and burned to the ground; and we hear that threatening letters (*of the rising of colored people*) have lately been sent to the Mayor, if the execution should be carried into effect."

"On the day when the execution took place, a large crowd of people, with the guard, assembled at the Bridewell, from whence she was taken in a carriage to then Potters Field, (*Washington Parade Ground or Square.*)

" Mr. Bell, the Sheriff, performed his duty in person, in his official full dress. She made no disclosures of accomplices, and her last words were, ' I am satisfied as to the justness of my fate—it is all right.'

" We are happy to learn that the colored people of this city, being convinced of the enormity of the crime, are generally reconciled to the fate of Rose Butler, and it is hoped that no offence of a similar nature will ever again occur."* The witnessing of this execution still remains in my memory, as being one of the most prominent transactions of my boyhood.

Three years had hardly passed, when complaints were presented, in petitions, of the narrowness of the street on the sides of the market-house, which much interrupted the increased business, and praying for the removal of the market, " when another one shall have been built in that vicinity."

Several reports were made for relief, but nothing was done until the month of October, 1823, when a Committee reported in favor of purchasing seven lots, and soon after seven additional lots were added to the first, lying on the north side of Grand Street, opposite this market, belonging to Nicholas Goveneur; all of which were purchased, and the Corporation Counsel reported as having obtained a deed for them in the month of December.

The erection of a new one-story building, extending from Ludlow to Essex Street, was commenced in 1824, and finished in the early part of the next year, when the stand-holders in the old were removed into the new market-house. The Market Committee, in answer to a petition of Henry Marsh for a stand in this market, in the month of April, state: " The number of stands at present is *ten*, which were leased for the ensuing year, with an express reservation of the right to establish *four new ones*, if, in the opinion of the Common Council, the convenience of the public should require it." They are now of the opinion that " it ought to be done, but that the new stands should be sold at auction, in the usual way;" and recommend the following resolution: " *Resolved*, That four new stands be erected in Essex Market, and the leases sold at auction."

On the first of August, 1825, these four stands were sold, for a premium of $1,790; which money was paid in, and licenses ordered for the following purchasers, in the month of July:

No. 5. Stephen Jordan.   No. 6. Philip H. Underhill.
7. John Palmer.   8. Henry Resler, Jun'r.

The city a few months after was relieved of a nuisance, which had been a great eye-sore to many of the citizens, and more especially

* Columbian, 9th and 10th July, 1819.

on the public thoroughfares. This was done by the introduction of the "hog-cart," as the laws appeared not sufficiently stringent to keep those animals out of the streets. Many *scrimmages* have I seen in some of the localities where the negro hog-catchers, and also the officers who attended them, were either cheated out of their prey, or obliged entirely to desist, especially in the neighborhood of St. Patrick's Cathedral, where almost every woman, *to a man*, was joined together for common protection in resisting their favorites from becoming public property.

In the month of November, (1825,) the Press appears pleased to notice this fact, when one says: "We are glad to learn—and the reader will be both surprised and gratified at the information—that the hog-cart, so long a desideratum here, is making a tour of sequestration through the city, and collecting the unsightly and ferocious quadrupeds which have hitherto enjoyed free commons on our streets. Since the task is undertaken, we trust that, although they amount in all to squadrons, a general gathering will be made, and that none will be left for the annoyance of the public hereafter."

"The efforts of the 'catchers,' however, have occasioned several ludicrous scenes. Among the rest, the passengers in Broadway, the thoroughfare of fashion, taste, and beauty, were on Wednesday entertained with a well-contested, and for some minutes doubtful, race. A good-sized pig was observed to be quietly discussing the remains of some offals, which not unfrequently adorn our principal promenades, when the cart, of course, stopped, and the catchers, four stout blacks, approached the animal with hostile intent and fearful note of preparation. They had 'clipped him round about,' and one had actually laid violent hands on his ears, when the creature, disapproving of their proceedings *in toto*, wheeled about, and held his course down the street; the three 'darkies,' yet on their legs, pursuing at a round pace. The animal now began to pull harder, and the hunters stretched themselves to their utmost, so that the trial of speed became every moment more and more interesting. The bipeds, however, succeeded in overtaking the quadruped; but just as they were again laying ungentle hands on his body, he bolted, turned, and steered 'bock again' in full cry. Finally, the pursued, almost exhausted, was taken by the pursuers, seized by all-fours, and introduced, to the tune of his own music, into the car. The vehicle moved onward to get other, and, we trust, less difficult prey."

The "hog-cart" was not at all a popular "institution" with a good many, and it only occasionally appeared in the streets, when it was sure to attract a crowd of leaders or followers, who were ready to assist in depriving it of animal occupants. "If the laws are to be put in force (says an editorial) in relation to hogs, the driver of the cart must be protected in discharging his duty. Yesterday afternoon, as some dozen of the swinish multitude were driven in the vehicle appropriated for the accommodation up the Bowery, a mob of perhaps four or five hundred sympathizing individuals, who thought the hogs were ill-used, followed the equipage, with a determination to effect their deliverance. It may be proper to state, that the hog-cart is a kind of Noah's Ark, upon small wheels, with interstitial apertures, to give the pigs a free circulation of air, and enable them to look out, and enjoy the prospect on their route to the Alms-House. It was driven yesterday afternoon by one person, and followed by an out-rider on horseback, as an escort. Against this unfortunate guard the attendant company of ragamuffins, idle boys, and sweeps, hurled all the rotten apples, pears, and other missiles they could muster. They knocked off his hat two or three times, and rendered the color of his jacket, which had been white, altogether *unintelligible*. The man, of course, was clamorous, and the porkers squealed terribly.

"The assailants at last exhausted their ammunition, upon which some of them rushed into a fruit-shop and laid unlawful hands upon its contents, not without the violent remonstrance of an old lady, who was the proprietor. With this supply, the poor protector of the hogs was again pelted sadly. The determination of the mob was to upset the cart; and very probably they may have eventually succeeded, as we did not mark their further progress. As this sort of mischief may be always anticipated, it is surprising that a more efficient escort is not provided for the removal of these nuisances."*

The continuation of the hog-cart was not of long duration, and in the latter part of its existence it was forced to adopt an early hour in the morning when it appeared in the streets, or it was sure to be attacked.

In this market-house, at this period, the fourteen butchers' stands were placed in the centre part, and the fish and vegetables in the ends; this arrangement, however, was changed in 1832, when four more stands were added, and the end on Ludlow Street was filled by them, by moving the original stands down to the corner, where the numbers began, and occupied as follows:

No. 1. William Winter.	No. 2. William Graham.
3. William Neilson.	4. John Singer.
5. Adam H. Chappel.	6. Philip H. Underhill.
7. William Kellinger.	8. William L. Reeves.
9. Thomas K. Kellinger.	10. Jacob Patterson.

* Evening Post, September, 1826

No. 11. William De Forest.   No. 12. John Tier.
   13. Samuel Piercy, Jr.   14. John Monaghan.
   15. Alexander Brown.   16. Peter Valentine, Jr.
   17. Gilbert Graham.   18. Walter Briggs.

In the month of February, 1834, a resolution was adopted relative to the extension of this market, Grand Street and Centre Markets, and the taking of a piece of ground in the 11th Ward for a Union Market-Place. The "Joint Committee on Markets" reported the estimated cost of

Grand Street Market, $32,000   Essex Market, - - $50,000
Centre Market, - - 60,000   Land in 11th Ward, 8,000
for Union Market. Making a total of $150,000.

"By a law, making provision for the redemption of the city stocks, all market fees and market rents are appropriated for the extinguishing of said stocks.

"The annual receipts from the markets, and applied to this purpose, have been very large, and it is believed there is no property held by the Corporation netting so large an amount on its cost as that derived from the rents and fees of the markets. The following are the receipts during the last year:

For premiums on butchers' stands, -   -   - $10,857 28
Interest on premium stands, - - - -   1,951 83
Market fees, - - - - - - -   19,484 17
Market rents, - - - - - -   30,218 65

Making a total, - - - - - - $62,511 93

"There are thirteen markets in this city, from the rents and fees of which the aforesaid income is derived. The cost of these several markets in the aggregate, according with a calculation entered into by your Committee, amounts to the sum of $640,000, consequently the receipts of the last year was nearly *ten per cent.* on the cost."

In the following month of October, Alexander Brown petitioned for a transfer of his stand, No. 15, to Samuel N. T. Kellinger. Both of these gentlemen desired that this stand should be made a "premium stand," to which the Market Committee agreed, that if, "in case a new market shall be built next to the Essex Market, on the grounds lately purchased by the Corporation, the proprietors of this stall, and all other stalls in the Essex Market, which have paid a *premium* to the Corporation, shall be allowed the amount of premium so paid on any purchase they may make in the new market; but in no case shall any amount of premium be paid back, either when a purchase is made for a less sum than the premium paid in the present market, or where a proprietor or proprietors of stalls sold for premium in the present market."

The grounds purchased by the Corporation, noticed in the above, were additional grounds adjoining, formerly belonging to Robert Tillotson, which had been purchased in the month of June previous, with a view of erecting a much larger and more commodious market-house.

In the month of October, 1836, the old market-house was ordered to be taken down and the materials to be used in building a market for country people at the "Tompkins Market," and another more commodious market-house erected, which was commenced and completed in the month of January, 1837, when 44 butchers' stands were resolved upon to be let for that purpose, and those who occupied in the old market were allowed to appoint a Committee to select their stands in the new one. This left twenty six to be drawn for by ballot. The "Executive Committee of Butchers," after examining the numerous applications, selected those who were entitled to draw. On the 2d of February following the Committee proceeded to draw, when the following were the successful butchers:

No. 3.	William Dunham.	No. 4.	George Leviness.
5.	Andrew C. Wheeler, Jr.	6.	Thomas Sybert.
7.	William Lawrence.	10.	John Kling.
9.	Cornelius M. Cregier.	16.	John H. Nash.
17.	William A. Jackson.	18.	Stephen Jordan.
19.	Marvin R. Underhill.	20.	James Waters.
21.	Jacob Boyce.	26.	James Valentine.
27.	William Carstang.	28.	William H. Halstead.
29.	William Winter.	30.	Samuel Compton.
32.	Levi Duryea.	36.	John Brewer, Jr.
39.	Robert Piercy.	40.	Cornelius F. Borden.
41.	James Leach.	42.	Nicholas Cromer.
43.	Richard Miller.	45.	Samuel Arment.

The numbers ran to 46. Two of the stands, Nos. 10 and 38, were afterwards taken for the public scales.

In the month of June, 1839, the Board adopted the following: "*Resolved*, That the Superintendent of Buildings advertise for estimates for the construction of a cupola on the Essex Market, now fitting up for the accommodation of the Second District Watch, agreeable to the plans and specifications, &c.; and that $1,100 be appropriated for the same." This year also was first introduced " ice-boxes or refrigerators" into the public markets, and in 1843 the Croton water.

In the year 1840 we find many changes in the occupancy of the butchers' stands, but all are full, and occupied as follows:

No. 1. John Singer.
3. William Dunham.
5. Stephen Brower.
7. Daniel Lawrence.
9. John Finn.
11. Francis M. Dominick.
13. William Graham.
15. Philip H. Underhill.
17. William A. Jackson.
19. John Brewer.
21. William N. Hedge.
23. E. Harrison Reed.
25. John W. Tier.
27. Harman Baisly.
29. William Winter, Jr.
31. Samuel Piercy.
33. Jacob L. Dodge.
35. Samuel Kellinger.
37. Alexander Brown.
39. James L. Leach.
41. Richard Miller.
43. Samuel Arment.
45. William Lawrence.

No. 2. Thomas K. Kellinger.
4. Vacant.
6. William Rhoades.
8. John Hickey.
10. Scales.
12. Charles Campbell.
14. Hugh Killin.
16. George I. Manolt.
18. William H. Cornell.
20. Jacob Boyce.
22. Levi Duryea.
24. David M. Tier.
26. George W. Hopkins.
28. Daniel Harmony.
30. William H. Hopkins.
32. Jacob R. Reed.
34. Walter Briggs.
36. William L. Reeves.
38. Scales.
40. John W. Hyde.
42. Mathew Bird.
44. Nicholas Cromer.
46. Jacob Pessinger.

For several years a very fair business was done in this market for about 30 butchers' stands, and, of course, there were but few of the 46 which were those who did well; this kept continual changes on some of the other stands; in fact, after 1844 many were unoccupied, and so remained many years, when the authorities, anxious to have rents for them, gave to those who occupied adjoining stalls, permits to occupy them, if they paid the rents; which is the cause why so many butchers occupy two stands, not only in this, but in many others of the public markets.

This market-house remained until the spring of 1852, when it was decided to erect a large, handsome brick building, at an estimated cost of about $50,000, for market and other purposes. In the month of December following the exterior was completed, but the interior was not finished until the 23d of March, 1853, when it was opened for business. The second and third stories were to be occupied by the Police Court, Justice's Court, Eastern Dispensary, and the Tenth Ward Station-House. It stands on the old site, with a front reaching the entire length of the block, 175 feet on Grand Street; the depth on Essex and Ludlow Streets is 83 feet, 4 inches. The rear building is one large room, lighted by several windows on the sides and roof, intended for fish, poultry, vegetable, and other stands. The front building has three stories and a deep basement; the latter appropriated for stores. The upper rooms are used for public purposes, Police Station and Prison, offices for the Superintendent of Streets and Lamps, and Markets, and for the drill-rooms for military. On the market floor there were appropriated 24 butchers' stands, 20 vegetable and poultry stands, 8 butter and cheese stands, 6 fishermen stands, 2 for smoked meats, 2 for coffee and cakes, and one tripe stand.

The butchers who occupied them in 1853 were as follows:

No. 1. William H. Graham.   No. 2. William Graham.
  3. Conrad Briel.   4. Thomas H. Brown.
  5. Daniel Briel.   6. Joshua Mesur.
  7. Charles Campbell.   8. Jacob Straus.
  9. Leopold Lederer.   10. E. A. Wheeler.
 11. J. C. Palmer.   12. Levi Duryea.
 13. Philip R. Haight.   14. David M. Tier.
 15. Aaron Haslacker.   16. B. Krouse.
 17. Thomas T. Hudson.   18. William H. Hopkins.
 19. John C. Hooper.   20. Stephen Carpenter.
 21. Philip Friedman.   22. William Craft.
 23. Walter Briggs.   24. Henry S. Carpenter.

This market has been most fortunate, for more than twenty years, in having an honest and most worthy man for a Clerk. Mr. Allan Thomas has been that man, and through the whole of that period he has never missed but one Saturday night (that night he was sick) in being the last man to close the market doors after business hours. It is a remarkable instance of one man being held in office where the changes of party deem it necessary to remove the worthy as well as the unworthy. His returns in the collection of market fees and rents have never been questioned; in fact, I heard it said by respectable men, that he returned to the Corporation more than he collected; it was, however, explained that he made good all that he could not collect from the delinquent stand-holders. He had otherwise strong claims on the public, he having lost one of his legs in the performance of his duty as a fireman.

However, at last, in the winter of 1858, an attempt, whether successful or not, was made to displace him, at the instigation of a man who, it was said, was much better qualified to keep a " grog-shop," as he always carried a suitable sign, than to be a public officer. He wanted to palm off upon the stand-holders and the citizens a man, or a being in the shape of a man, who had enjoyed prison quarters for quite a term; but whether so or not, we find the following in the *Express*, January 13, 1859: "This morning Mr. Allan P. Thomas, twenty years Clerk of Essex Market, was presented by the butchers of that market with an elegant gold-headed cane, valued $50, in testimony of his general integrity, urbanity, and obliging conduct during the period of his incumbency." I have since learned that this worthy man was turned out.

"FULTON MARKET."

1821. THE subject of establishing a market-place in the vicinity of the present Fulton Market was before the Board as early as the year 1815; it was also strongly agitated the year after; and finally, by an act of the Legislature, passed on the 14th of March, 1817, the Common Council was authorized to take possession of the land which is now occupied by that edifice. The land, however, lay in an uncertain state, until 1820, when it was decided to sell it; but the resolution was afterwards rescinded, no doubt from the following circumstances. Early in 1821, a large fire took place in Fulton Street, Front Street, and Crane's Wharf, which destroyed all the wooden buildings on this site. This induced the Mayor to call a meeting of the Board on the 29th of January of that year, for the purpose of deciding the question, " Whether or no a public market shall be erected on this site." The *Gazette* of that date says: " The late conflagration has exposed to view this beautiful spot of ground, which has so universally been considered as the most eligible situation for a market, and which has already been actually vested in the Corporation for the purpose of a market. Its vicinity to the ferry, by which the marketing from Long Island will be saved the expense of cartage, a basin for smacks and fish-cars, unequaled in its purity, from its depth of water and the rapidity of its current, being decidedly in its favor for keeping and having good fresh fish, which the waters at the Fly Market could not furnish, in consequence of the large sewer entering the slip, and, in the summer season, so offensive as to be prejudicial to health."

Several petitions, editorials, and letters appeared in favor and against it. The *Long Island Star*, February 7, 1821, says: " The people of Brooklyn are interested in the removal of the Fly Market to Fulton Slip. We despair of obtaining on this side of the water a concentrated market, where should be sold meats, vegetables, and poultry in all their varieties. It appears to suit the *genius* of this people to have little 'meat-shops' scattered throughout the village; and the *eating* part of the people must submit to 'Hobson choice' in the selection of their meats. Hence many of our people go almost daily to Fly Market. The new location, being situated adjoining the (*Fulton*) ferry, will be to us a great convenience."

The farmers and marketmen were also strongly in favor of a new market at this place, and, in a petition, they represent "numerous circumstances which make it important not only to us, but to the citizens of New York, that a new and convenient market-house should be built there, as there would be a great saving in not having to cart our truck, nor pay frequently from four to six cents on a bag or basket of vegetables to get it carried from the ferry to the present (*Fly*) market, which we must add to what would otherwise be our price, and the citizens must pay it. We could afford to sell cheaper if we had better accommodations, for it cannot be expected that we should go to the present (*Fly*) market, remain out all night, without shelter to protect our *marketing*, and to obtain a stand, without being well paid for it. Many of us bring our truck to market in boats, and are obliged, on account of the tides, to come in the evening; and on this account we are obliged to remain out until morning, without covering or shelter. And we contribute, gentlemen, to a large amount in fees to the Clerk of the Market. Some of us pay one-fourth of a dollar for the privilege of standing in the street unprotected, and selling a single calf or sheep, and on other things in proportion; and we ask if we are not entitled to some little accommodations from this payment to the Corporation."

"We hope, gentlemen, that in your deliberations, you will give particular consideration to our want of shelter and other comforts in the present Fly Market, and erect a new and spacious market at Fulton Slip."

A favorable report from a Special Committee was made on the 12th of March following, on the subject of erecting this market, and it was favorably received and adopted; when a Committee of *five* was appointed to procure plans and estimates, and superintend its building. The contracts were made with Messrs. Gideon Tucker, Thomas S. and Philetus H. Woodruff, who commenced its erection. In the mean time the Common Council had given notice to the butchers of the several markets that they intended to dispose of all vacant stands in the several markets, and also a large number in this would be sold at public auction; the latter of which they expected would be wanted and eagerly sought after; but in their avarice or anxiety, or rather want of practical knowledge, they had adopted such stringent terms and conditions as were anything else but acceptable to the butchers or the future prosperity of this market-place.

In answer, however, to the proposed terms and conditions, several of the Fly Market butchers held a meeting, and appointed a Committee to present their views in a petition through their chairman, Thomas Gibbons, who was authorized as "a Committee to confer with such Committee as in your wisdom you may deem proper to appoint, relative to the report of the Committee on the subject of publicly selling the stalls of the several markets. We, in compliance with our instructions as well as our own impressions, do herein humbly solicit such attention to our prayer, and the prayer of our constituents at large, as may lead to some further explanations on the part of your Committee, and that a reciprocal interchange of sentiments may be allowed, &c." A Committee from the Board met with that from the butchers, but it had no effect, as the Market Committee had determined to sell, as before reported; but they concluded to wait until the sale of the stands in the new or Fulton Market were made.

The new market building was rapidly progressing, and by some much admired, but by the old butchers it was thought it would be very inconvenient, on account of the high steps. This no doubt led to an article in the *Gazette*, September 1st, headed: "*Premium.*— The butchers in the Fly Market, who expect to remove to the *new market* at the foot of Fulton Street, about the first of November next, desirous of doing all in their power to accommodate their customers, particularly the aged and infirm, hereby offer to supply with meat for one year, any person who may construct the most easy and best method of *hoisting* from the street up into the market all such as find it inconvenient to ascend the lofty steps of said market. The inventor is requested to submit a model of his machine to a Committee of butchers, on or before the first of October next, as it would be desirable to have at least two erected before they commence business in said market."

We find the market-house so far finished in the month of December as to have the bell hung, and the publication of the stringent "terms and conditions," noticed before, which read as follows:

"1*st*. The stands shall be rented at public auction, on the 18th December instant, at 10 o'clock, on the premises.

"2*d*. No person except a regular licensed butcher can be permitted to rent any of the said stands.

"3*d*. The stands will be rented on a lease of five years from the first day of January next, for the highest rent per annum they will bring; but no stand shall be disposed of at a less rent than one hundred dollars per annum.

" 4th. The rent of the said stands shall be paid quarterly in advance, as follows: the first payment to be made on the first day or January aforesaid; the second on the first of April thereafter; the third on the first day of July thereafter, and the fourth on the first day of October following; said payments to be made at the times aforesaid in each and every year during the continuance of the lease.

" 5th. Should default be made in any of the aforesaid payments, and the rent remain unpaid ten days after it shall become due, the stands on which such default is made shall revert to the Corporation, and the lease for the same be null and void.

" 6th. The persons renting the aforesaid stands are to be exempt from the payment of all fees for all permitted articles sold at the same.

" 7th. No stand can be transferred from one person to another except by a written permit from the Common Council; and no person can sell at any stand except the one for which he is licensed.

" 8th. The stalls to be placed on the aforesaid stands must be constructed agreeably to the direction of the Market Committee.

" 9th. Every person who may rent any of the aforesaid stands shall in all things conform to the rules and regulations prescribed by the ordinances of the Corporation which now are in force, or which may hereafter be passed for regulating the said market; and also to the provisions and conditions of the lease to be given, a copy of which may be examined by those concerned at the Comptroller's office, City Hall.

"*Resolved*, That the Market Committee be authorized to lease the butchers' stands in Fulton Market, subject to the above terms and conditions.

"*Resolved*, That his Honor the Mayor be authorized to license such butchers as may be recommended to him by the Market Committee, previous to the next meeting of the Board.

"Any butcher holding a stand under the Corporation, in any of the other markets, shall be at liberty to relinquish the same, in case he should rent a stand in the Fulton. If Fulton Market is not completed and ready for the reception of the butchers by the 1st of January next, the rent of the stands will not commence until such time as the Market Committee shall decide that the market is in a situation to be occupied."

These " terms and conditions" became known to the butchers immediately after they had passed the Board, who at once called a meeting, when the following resolutions were passed:

"At a numerous and respectable meeting of butchers, held at the Bull's Head, *(Bowery,)* on Tuesday evening, 11th inst., *(December,)* the following resolutions were passed unanimously:

"*Resolved*, That the sum of $100 a year for the stands in the Fulton Market is more than many butchers will be able to pay, and consequently will not only disgrace them, but make them objects of perpetual prosecution.

"*Resolved*, That the method adopted by the Corporation, in fixing a yearly rent on the stands, and at the same time selling them at public auction, is novel, without precedent, and prejudicial to the peace and harmony of society.

"*Resolved*, That the resolutions now passed by the Corporation are calculated to *set one butcher against another*, and finally to make them the instrument of their own persecutions.

"*Resolved*, In our opinion, that after a butcher has purchased a stand, and by an honorable conduct has improved it, that at the end of every five years the Corporation should, for their own benefit, sell those improvements to the highest bidder, is a scheme so repugnant to every principle of justice, that none but the most abject could submit to.

"*Resolved*, That these resolutions are not the offspring of a premeditated and wicked opposition to the Corporation, but an honest expression of our feelings for our violated rights and privileges.

" WILLIAM MESSERVE, *Chairman.*

" T. GIBBONS, *Secretary.*"

The butchers had, through committees and individuals, advanced every honorable means and arguments to convince the Corporation of the injustice and wrong they were about entailing upon them, but the majority would not be convinced; so the butchers made up their minds not to bid on any stand offered for sale, and several of them, from the injustice and illiberal usage of several of the most prominent members of the Board, when approached with petition or otherwise, had reason and just cause to feel not only indignant, but to harbor a spirit of retaliation.

In this position, they went to the sale, which took place on Tuesday, the 18th of December, 1821, at the Fulton Market, conducted by James Bleecker, Auctioneer. The stands were offered for sale. The *Gazette* the morning after, in an editorial, says: " Yesterday was the day fixed on for the sale of the stalls *(stands)* in the Fulton Market, and a considerable crowd was assembled on the occasion, drawn together, no doubt, by the late contention between the Honorable the Corporation and the butchers. We do not pretend to be judges of the existing differences, but we are sorry to learn that but few of the stalls were sold, in consequence of the adherence of the butchers to the late determination not to purchase agreeably to the *terms of sale.* We still hope that some arrangement will be made, satisfactory to the parties, and beneficial to the public."

At the sale, the butchers stood their ground; but one individual, named *Leonard*, (a dealer in cigars,) who, not being a regular butcher, and in opposition to the announcement made by the butchers, bid and bought the first stand offered; but when his name was announced by the auctioneer, he was seized, and dragged or hustled towards the dock, when he was thrown in the river, and came near being drowned. A few more stands were offered, and sold, at such offers as the butchers had arranged should be given for them, when the sale was stopped, and postponed.

The butchers again petitioned, which came before the Board on the 24th, (of the same month,) "praying that the three first sections of the law passed on the 10th December, inst., be so altered and amended," " that instead of selling the stands at auction, the Corporation should affix a rent upon their respective stands as they should deem just, and that the numbers of the stalls be put into a box, and be drawn for by the butchers; and the number each one draws, let him occupy during the will and pleasure of the Corporation. We humbly pray that you will see that it is calculated to place the poor butcher upon a nearer footing to his more prosperous neighbor; while selling the stands at auction, and a repetition of sales, must, in our opinion, in its very nature, have a direct contrary operation. Another very important consideration in our plan is its moral tendency, by preventing those angry feelings, the natural offspring of violent opposition; and by preventing the wealthy from obtaining a dangerous influence over the poorer part, which a repetition of sales must undoubtedly produce," &c. The Board, however, laid this petition *on the table,* and adopted the following coercive resolution: "*Resolved,* That the Market Committee be authorized to rent the butchers' stands in Fulton Market, at auction or otherwise, *to any person* who will give the highest rent for the same, *whether they be licensed butcher or not;* but no stand shall be rented *for a less sum than* $100 *per annum:* Provided, however, that if the licensed butchers shall, on or before the 29th day of December, instant, either personally, or by a deputation from their body, signify to the Market Committee that they will bid for the said stands, and comply with the regulations of the Common Council on that subject, that the said stands shall be rented to none but licensed butchers."

This caused another meeting of the butchers, on the 27th inst., when they appointed a committeè of seven, viz., Messrs. Thomas Gibbons, Jacob Aims, Thomas Jeremiah, Cornelius Schuyler, David Marsh, James Reeves, and David Seaman, who were instructed to confer with the Corporation, and to "use all honorable means to remove the difficulties between them and the Corporation." They met together, and after a consultation, some of the worst features were stricken off; and as they could not accomplish all, the Committee of Butchers agreed to report favorably at their next general meeting, which was held on the following Wednesday. At this meeting, after their report, a resolution was adopted, "that the difficulties being removed between them and the Corporation, they were ready to rent the stands at the place and time appointed."

The second sale was held on the 3d of January, 1822, in a "large Court-room in the City Hall, in the presence of the Mayor and Market Committee, and a great number of citizens; which was conducted with good order and propriety." The sales commenced with No. 1, located at the corner of South and Fulton Streets, and reached to No. 88; although but 86 were sold, to the following purchasers, and at the yearly rents:

No.	Purchaser	Rent	No.	Purchaser	Rent
1.	George Manolt,	$455	No. 2.	Eliphalet Wheeler,	$400
3.	Albert Fisher,	410	4.	William Ponsford,	290
5.	Cornelius Schuyler,	275	6.	Daniel Burtnett,	225
7.	Mathew Byrnes,	240	8.	David Marsh,	205
9.	John Rudman,	200	10.	Andrew C. Wheeler,	165
11.	Joseph O. Bogart,	200	12.	Andrew Fisher,	200
13.	Lanning Ferris,	220	14.	John Perrin,	205
15.	Jacob Fisher,	305	16.	George G. Messerve,	310
17.	*Stairway.*		18.	George Messerve,	300
19.	David Tier,	100	20.	J. D. Crawbuck,	220
21.	Cornelius V. Gibson,	200	22.	William Messerve,	175
23.	Elnathan Underhill,	240	24.	Wm. Messerve, Jr.,	205
25.	William Reynolds,	340	26.	Isaac Rhoades,	225
27.	George W. Varian,	230	28.	George S. Messerve,	260
29.	Thomas McCready,	375	30.	Daniel Winship,	480
31.	Samuel Larned,	110	32.	J. McCready,	250
33.	Christian Stamler,	400	34.	John Fisher,	210
35.	Daniel Winship, Jr.,	265	36.	Daniel Rhoades,	205
37.	Andrew Smock,	230	38.	Thomas M. Jenkins,	205
39.	John D. Kent,	260	40.	M. Lemmon,	200
41.	Michael Crawbuck,	220	42.	James Titus,	210
43.	John Stamler,	300	44.	David Seaman,	325
45.	Thomas G. Harrison,	300	46.	Peter Valentine,	300
47.	William Patten,	250	48.	G. Messenger,	200

No. 49. Christian Truss, $200 No. 50. Edward Fitzgerald, $200
51. John Harriot, 180   52. Valentine Merkel, 150
53. William P. Munson, 150   54. John Simonson, 160
55. Effingham W. Marsh, 215   56. Carman A. Simonson, 150
57. John Carpenter, 290   58. Nathaniel Underhill, 155
59. George Thompson, 320   60. Thomas Gibbons, 330
61. John Lyons, 230   62. Isaac Schuyler, 150
63. Francis O'Neil, 250   64. William Foster, 145
65. Mathew Smith, 165   66. Peter Wilt, 145
67. William R. Batt, 140   68. John Doughty, 135
69. William Messerve, 200   70. Thomas Dunning, 135
71. *Reserved.*   72. Nicholas Stael, 195
73. William Graham, 230   74. Richard Dark, 170
75. John Fearnley, 135   76. John Bridle, 120
77. G. C. Goodwin, 135   78. E. C. Pell, 115
79. David Perrin, 140   80. Burdet Striker, 120
81. J. R. Striker, 130   82. R. Ten Eyck, 115
83. Frazier Broadway, 125   84. Mathew Vogel, 115
85. Frederick Hawes, 145   86. William Warlow, 130
87. Jonathan Skillman, 235   88. Ephraim Bolander, 220

The sale of these stands figured up to the large sum of $18,865; and this was followed with a resolution by the Board to sell the cellars under the market, on the following Monday, the 7th inst., for three years, viz., from the 1st of February, 1822, to 1st of May, 1825. Twenty-one cellars were offered, and the following sold. (No. 1 commenced at the same corner as the butchers' stands.)

No. 1. Wm. L. Degraw, $1,060 No. 2. Catharine Miller, $510
3. Isaac Fairchild, 325   4. Joseph W. Howard, 500
5. Joseph O. Bogart, 360   6. Thomas Gentle, 450
7. Smith & Maintain, 810   8. Abner H. Parker, 350
9. Stewart Elder, 300   10. Serval Cutting, 300
11. Henry J. Hassey, 490   12. Daniel Vanduestir, 300
13. Francis Ogsbury, 280   14. John Crowley, 290
15. John D. Keating, 550   16, 17, 18, 19, and 20, fronting
21. Abiel Brown, 900   "Crane's Wharf," not sold
Whole amounting to $7,775.   then.

On the 15th the poultry, vegetable, and fruit stands were also sold at auction, on a lease of three years. Thirty-four stands, which were under cover, with the conveniences of a cellar to each, brought a yearly rent of $1,320. The lowest brought $30, and the highest $60. Sixteen outside stands brought $365, at an average of $23 each; and four sausage-stands brought $83.

Besides the above, a very large sum was expected to be collected from the stands reserved for country people.

The *Gazette* of the 21st January says: "The public are informed that Fulton Market will be opened on Tuesday, the 22d instant, and that the sales at the '*Fly Market*' will be discontinued after Monday, the 21st instant. J. MORTON, *Clerk, (C. C.)*"

The editor also says: "The Fulton Market, take it in the whole, is the most spacious and costly one in the country; and as it is to be a productive one to the city, may it also be so to the butchers, and other occupants of this market, in proportion to their respective merits." *To the butchers* this afterwards proved rather an unfortunate speculation for many of them, as will be hereafter shown.

The same newspaper of the 23d again says: "This market was opened yesterday, and it was ornamented with the handsomest exhibitions of beef, mutton, pork, &c., ever presented to the public. We passed through it in company with several gentlemen from Europe, who were unanimous in the opinion that they had never seen anything of the kind to equal it, in all respects. One man appeared in market with *ninety-two pairs* of fine canvas-back ducks, which he brought in a wagon from the Susquehannah. They were selling from 16 to 18 shillings a pair."

"It is gratifying to learn that those miserable wretches, commonly called '*Fly Market sharks,*' *(shirk butchers,)* will not be permitted to infest the Fulton Market."

In the month of November previous, Ezra Frost was appointed the Deputy Clerk, and allowed a salary of $500 per annum, with privilege to occupy the upper part of the eastern front of the market; and in the following month of February Isaac Asten, previously appointed the sweeper, petitions for an increase of pay.

The Market Committee say, "That the pay allowed by the Corporation was $4 per week; that he also received, in addition to this, *one cent* per day from each butcher and huckster who occupied said market." They agree to allow him 75 cents per day for his own attendance and duties, and $15 per month for the payment of an assistant sweeper, and $9.37 per annum to defray the expenses of shovels, hoes, brooms, &c.

The five reserved cellars under this market were offered and sold on Saturday, the 26th of January, (inst.,) for a period of fifteen months from the 1st of February following, viz.:

No. 16. Isaac Fairchild,	-	-	-	-	$330
17. Abigal Blakely,	-	-	-	-	285
18. Prior & Bayard,	-	-	-	-	415
19. John O'Bryan,	-	-	-	-	320
20. Abel Brush,	-	-	-	-	450
Making a total sum of	-	-	-	-	$1,800

Four hucksters' stands were also sold at the same time, for a term of three years: Nos. 56 and 57, at $24 per annum; Nos. 58 and 59, at $26 do. These several amounts would add the receipts, so far, to about $30,000; then the fees from the country and outside stands, about $15,000 more, would make a total annual income of about $45,000 !!

However, the attempt to collect this large income, by the wrong system adopted by the Common Council, in the disposition of more stands than wanted by the public, then forcing the many into "promises to pay," that they might become the possessor of a stand, was the sure means of not only breaking down the business of the market, but also of the many who had ventured and lost their all. If the Common Council had been guided by the knowledge they obtained, and placed about one-half the number of stands, with the *terms* of encouragement then presented to them, how easy it would have been to have gradually increased the number and the future prosperity of this market! But their course was a death-blow, from which it never recovered. The butchers had truly said, in their *resolutions* adopted at a meeting held on the 11th of December, 1821, but a few months before, that the amount was "more than many butchers will be able to pay, and consequently will not only disgrace them, but make them the objects of perpetual persecution."

But few months had passed when the butchers of this market petition "for a reduction of rent," which was barely noticed. However, when the second monthly payment (*1st of April*) became due, it was found that many of the butchers had deserted their stands, and others of them unable to pay their rents. The Mayor, on the 29th of April, laid before the Board a list of stalls vacated and unpaid; the Comptroller also reported a list of the lessees "who had failed to comply with the terms of their leases, several of whom, in the opinion of the Comptroller, *were unable to pay;*" and a resolution passed, "that the stalls of such persons as were unable to pay should be vacated." This "resolution" had also the effect of driving several more out.

When the Common Council were about to inflict on the other public markets the same system as they had adopted with this, as previously noticed, these butchers, with an unselfish view, arose, and through petition . . . . . "Certify, that they *are not averse* to having the stands in the other different markets placed under regulations different from those of Fulton Market. But they perfectly acquiesce in the propriety of departing from such regulations, as they conceive them, notwithstanding their own situation, to be pernicious, and destructive of all regularity and equality in the profession, and therefore impolitic."

Petitions from several of the other markets, on the same subject, led the Common Council to reconsider their former acts, and on the 10th of June following they "*Resolved*, That the stalls in all the markets of this city, except the Fulton and Old Slip Markets, be leased at *private contract*."

In this month, a Committee of the "Agricultural Society" awarded premiums for the best butter brought to this market. The first premium, a silver pitcher, valued at $15, was awarded to Mrs. Commodore Morris, of Morrisania; the second, a silver milk pitcher, valued at $10, to Mrs. Edward Leveridge, of Newtown, L. I.; and the third, a silver cup, valued at $5, to Mrs. Ray, of Westchester. And about the first of July, "twenty thousand, four hundred and forty-five baskets of raspberries are certified by the Deputy Clerk of Fulton Market as having been sold in one day." Also, on the 11th of this month, "the poor debtors in prison were enabled, by the generosity of the butchers, fish-dealers, and sellers of vegetables in this market, to partake of an excellent dinner." "It affords the editor of the *Long Island Star* great pleasure to state, that the butchers sent them 200 lbs. of the finest beef, the fish-dealers 100 lbs. of fresh fish, and the women four baskets of the best vegetables."

Several of the prominent butchers were doing a good business, and could well afford relief to the poor prisoners; but very large numbers were not even paying expenses, and were obliged to appeal to the Common Council for relief " . . . . from their said leases, and placed in said market on such principles that they can pay their fees and maintain their families." And the next month after, they again are "praying they may be permitted to give up their present leases." At last, the Comptroller was "authorized to cancel all leases *of those* who should pay up back rents, and surrender their stands, on or before the 1st of September;" which but few were able to conform to, especially the *paying up*.

The yellow fever at this time was raging in the lower parts of the city, especially in the vicinity of the Fulton Market, which put an end to business there; so leave was granted the stand-holders to remove to the vacant space in Chatham Square. There they staid until the cold weather set in, when they returned; but many of the stalls were deserted by their former occupants, in consequence of the decreased trade, the effect of improper management. Some of these persons were prosecuted and thrown into prison, where everything of value was squeezed out of them or their friends, before they were allowed to depart from the prison walls; but the unfortunate and friendless were kept closely confined during the pleasure of the Common Council.

John McCready petitioned for relief, saying, he " lately held the stand No. 32 Fulton Market, and is in debt to the Honorable Board for rent to the amount of one hundred dollars or thereabouts, for which he has been sued; and being unable to pay the same, is now confined in jail, by which means he is entirely thrown out of his business, and his mother, who is dependent on him, is left destitute of support." That " he is willing to give his promissory note for the sum, payable in two years, in quarterly payments, with an endorser, if this ..... Board will be pleased to liberate him from confinement, &c." The Board accepted his proposition, and released him.

Then we find, in the month of November, (inst.,) several butchers also praying for relief, in .... " being confined in the City Jail, and on the jail liberties, at the suit of your Honorable Body, beg leave to represent to you our situations, and pray that we may be enabled to do something for the support of ourselves and families. The majority of us have large families dependent on us for their daily bread, which we are unable to give them, in our present situation, except by the charitable assistance of our friends. By granting the petitioners their discharge from imprisonment, you will confer, &c.   (Signed,)

" Mathew Vogel,   Edward Fitzgerald,   John Hyde,
    Wm. P. Munson,   David Perrin,   Geo. S. Messerve,
    Robert P. Denike,   Frazier Broadway,   John D. Crawbuck."

Previous to the opening of this market, the hucksters were not allowed to sell certain articles, among which were eggs. Here, however, they had obtained consent to sell eggs with their fruit and vegetables, through petition; and they, as well as the butchers also, petitioned for a reduction of rent, which was not allowed them. Many of them had *widow* attached to their names, as appears from their petition.

Margaret Knapp,	*widow.*	Catharine Simonson,	*widow.*
Elizabeth Arnold,	*widow.*	Mary Leyack.	
Margaret Boyce,	*widow.*	Abbey Moore.	
Mary Holly,	*widow.*	Hannah Valentine.	
Mary Hoxey,	*widow.*	Elizabeth Gansey.	
Catharine Briskow,	*widow.*	Mary Singer.	
Mary Ackerman,	*widow.*		

The disposition of the vacant butchers' stands, and the lessening of their numbers, with further accommodations for the fishermen,

were before the Board in the month of October, (inst.,) when that
" body" concluded "that the east wing *(Beekman Street)* be appropriated for the use of the sellers of fish;"...."that the Comptroller
be authorized to receive a surrender of the butchers' leases, without
payment of rent, provided it will not prejudice our claims on them;"
and "that the Market Committee dispose of such number of butchers' stands, by auction or otherwise, until the first day of May next,
as they may deem proper; not, however, to exceed sixty."

Among the first fishermen here, I find the names of

Elisha Baker,	Samuel Coit,	Daniel Baker,
William Latham,	William Young,	Daniel Maynard,
Joseph Potter,	John Williams,	David Loper,
William S. Wright,	Palmer Clark,	Jonathan Smith,
Thomas Eldredge,	Cyrus C. Curtis,	William Carter,
Elisha Lyman.		

In relation to the "surrender of the butchers' leases," *forty-five*
stands were surrendered on the 1st, and *twelve* on the 11th of November; being *fifty-seven* of the stands, which were rented for *five
years*, on the 3d of January previous.

The manner afterwards adopted for disposing of the "sixty
stands" was usually by private contract, some few by auction, and
others, again, as follows: When a *vacant* stand was wanted, or an
exchange or transfer called for, the applicants were informed that
all the back rents were to be paid, and in some instances a *premium*
besides; so that in the end the Common Council lost nothing by
their forcing operation of—*what one can't pay, another must.*

In the latter part of the year 1823 all the butchers' stands on the
east or Beekman Street wing were vacated, except one, which was
removed, as will appear from the report of the "Committee" made
on the 15th of December, upon the application of John Bridle, the
occupant of No. 76, who wished to be transferred on a vacant stand
on the Front Street side. The report states, "That the above is
the only stand occupied in the east wing, and that a portion of the
main market on Front Street is also unoccupied. It is probable
that the west wing and the main market will be as much as ever
may be wanted as a butchers' meat market. It is therefore thought
advisable to recommend that a surrender of the above stand be received, and that a stand be granted as requested, at such rent as
may be deemed just."

After the removal of all the butchers' stands from the "east
wing," it was taken for the use of the fishermen.

In the month of August previous, the Market Committee made
several additional regulations, which were somewhat onerous to the

Deputy Clerk, by which he was called upon to perform "watch duty" at this market. As a conscientious man and Christian, he would rather worship his Maker than watch this market on the Sabbath-day, and preferred to resign his post, in the following singular *communication:* "To Stephen Allen, Esq., Mayor of the City of New York, and President of the Common Council.—*Exodus*, 20th chapter, 8th verse, it is written, '*Remember the Sabbath-day, to keep it holy.*' First Samuel, 15th chapter and 22d verse: '*Behold, to obey is better than sacrifice, and to hearken than the fat of rams.*' In the new law of the Common Council, they have made it my duty to watch Fulton Market after the closing of said market until 10 o'clock at night, and every Sunday till 10 o'clock, P. M.; which duty I cannot, on any consideration, consent to comply with. How can I do such work on the first day of the week, and sin against God? Under these considerations, I forthwith hasten to inform the Corporation of the City of New York that, if I may continue as I was when first appointed Deputy Clerk of said market, I have concluded to remain, and serve the public to the best of my abilities; but, if I cannot hold the office as Deputy Clerk without serving as watchman, as the law directs, I beg leave to return my warrant, with thanks to the members of the Common Council for favors past, and pray them to accept the same, and to appoint some other person to fill my place as soon as it is convenient. Pardon this your servant's freedom of communication, as I hope I am dictated by conscience, in the love of truth and righteousness.

"NEW YORK, *Sept.* 1, 1823.   EZRA FROST."

The Market Committee had this communication before them, and reported: "That the salary paid was sufficient compensation for all the duties demanded; and the Board *Resolved,* That the resignation of Ezra Frost be accepted." Soon after appeared a "communication" from some person, who thought "the Honorable Corporation are entitled to the thanks of the butchers and inhabitants in the vicinity of Fulton Market, and the citizens generally, for appointing to the Clerkship of Fulton Market that industrious and worthy man, Mr. George Duryee, whose unremitted attention, both as to cleanliness and good order, far surpasses any market in this city."[*] (See *Franklin Market*.)

In the year 1825, a sensible change for the better appeared in the business here, which gradually kept improving, and for the following ten years it continued to do an excellent and profitable business; every article of a choice and superior quality could be obtained here in its season. Then we had no "Southern steamers"

---

[*] American, March 23, 1824.

or "iron horses" to bring the early products from the sunny South; but we had Long Island and Southern Jersey, who were rivals, that strove for the fabulous prices paid for their first rarities and finest productions, which they invariably brought to this market. Occasionally, however, a late or poor season found the market poorly supplied in the spring months.

In the month of June, (1826,) next year, vegetables are noticed as being very high and scarce. The press says: "For several days past the prices of vegetables in our markets have been as follows: Potatoes, 15 to 25 cents per half peck; peas, 25 to $37\frac{1}{2}$ cents per do.; turnips, 12 to 20 cents per bunch of about 6; onions, equal to $12\frac{1}{2}$ cents per pound; cabbages, containing 3 or 4 leaves, without any head, 10 to 15 cents each; beets, radishes, cucumbers, &c., none; lettuce, 4 to 5 cents per head; cherries and strawberries scarce, dear, and of poor quality. At these exorbitant rates, the market is not half supplied, and every green thing it contains is bought up at an early hour in the morning." This was before the introduction of early vegetables from the South.

In 1828 every butcher's stand was occupied, many of them doing a good business; but we find only about one-half of those who commenced in 1822. Some had withdrawn to other markets, others broken down, disheartened, with debts due to that *power* who, by their wrong policy in the outset, had assisted in the overthrow of many of them; and when those who attempted to lift their heads again, in seeking to obtain a stand in some other market, the city's officials were in readiness with a demand for the *old back rents*, which must be paid before a license could be granted to them for a new location.

Among the occupants of these "sixty stands," we find but *ten* of the eighty-six purchasers occupying their original stands, although there are many more on other stands who were among the original purchasers. In the following list, these *ten* are marked with a star:

No. 1. James Johnson.	No. 2. Gilbert Underhill.
3. Mathias Smith.	4. William Wells.
5. Joseph B. Smith.	6. Jacob Vogel.
7. Richard Hunt.	8. Charles Kent.
9. Simon Seaward.	10. Tobias Boudinot.
11. Abraham Valentine.	12. Elias B. Messerve.
13. Lanning Ferris.*	14. George Brown.
15. Jacob Fisher.*	16. Nicholas W. Messerve.
17. *Stairway.*	18. David Marsh.
19. Andrew C. Wheeler.	20. John Rudman.
21. Peter Wilt.	22. Robert Elder.

No. 23. Cornelius Schuyler.
25. Elnathan Underhill.
27. George Haws, Jr.
29. Thomas Gibbons.
31. Daniel Winship.
33. Christian Stamler.*
35. John Evans.
37. William Jenkins.
39. John D. Kent.*
41. Jonathan Wilt.
43. Carlysle Weeks.
45. William Patten.
47. William J. Boyce.
49. John Brewer.
51. George Hoyt.
53. Henry Smith.
55. Joseph Alden.
57. James I. Titus.
59. John Bridle.
61. Elias De Forest.

No. 24. John Perrin.
26. Isaac Rhoades.*
28. George Beck.
30. Eliphalet Wheeler.
32. William Foster.
34. William P. Woodcock.
36. Daniel Rhoades.*
38. Thomas M. Jenkins.*
40. John Post.
42. William S. Callender.
44. Jacob A. Stamler.
46. Peter Valentine.*
48. David Reynolds.
50. John Henning.
52. John Slote.
54. James Van Arsdale.
56. Carman A. Simonson.*
58. Nathaniel Underhill.*
60. John Chappel.

Among these were several usually known as "small-meat butchers," who slaughtered and sold only sheep, lambs, and calves; and at this period, in consequence of the market laws giving the country butchers, or rather "shirks," more advantages than they possessed, a petition for relief was presented in the month of April, when they state, "Butchers that have served regular apprenticeships to the business, residing in the City of New York, are prohibited selling meat by the quarter in the country market, and have been entirely excluded from that part of the market, while the butchers from every part of the country, residing in the country, are permitted to stand in the country market to vend their meats, at the rate of one shilling per day. The inequality existing between the country butchers above mentioned and the licensed butchers of New York are these: *First*, That the country butchers have to pay only when they come to market, while the licensed butcher has to pay whether he has *meats* in market or not. *Secondly*, That the country butcher does neither fireman's, military, nor jury duty; or subject to any tax whatever to the City of New York—only *one shilling* per day when they attend market; while the tax of licensed butchers is very great, perhaps more so than any other mechanics in the city. To exercise our profession, to vend our *meats*, to procure a livelihood, we are compelled to go to market." They state, "On Saturday, March 29, 1828, there were *one hundred and sixty-three calves* offered for sale in the country market by the country butchers before mentioned, which would occupy twenty-four stands, at one shilling per stand, which would amount to three dollars. A licensed butcher, selling the same quantity of calves, would pay at least twenty dollars to the Corporation of New York, while the country butchers only pay three dollars. In speaking of the above country butchers, we do not mean the country farmer that raises his own produce; we only refer to those who buy their stock, slaughter and vend it in the market, and sell their skins by the season, and keep a regular *tally, (account on wood,)* the same as licensed butchers."

The Board laid the matter over, through the influence of a few of the prominent members. The butchers felt they were not properly treated, and they concluded they had strength enough to have a representation in the Board. So at the next election, from the Tenth Ward, in 1828, they elected Thomas Jeremiah Assistant Alderman; and in the two next following years David Marsh was elected Alderman, while Jeremiah was continued in the lower Board. Their combined assistance brought forth a repeal of the ordinance, which is shown in their report made in the month of April, 1830, just two years after the date of the above petition. This report states, after reviewing the petition and the "ordinance," " The Committee have carefully considered how the alleged grievance to the city butchers should be remedied, and after much deliberation, they have arrived at the conclusion that the law, as it existed previous to the passage of the amendatory ordinance above mentioned, was sufficiently liberal, and that neither the convenience of our own citizens, nor any other consideration, requires that the privilege which farmers and countrymen have of selling meats in our markets should be extended by the express terms of an ordinance, beyond their own produce; and when it is considered that, under color of the amendatory ordinance, an abuse of the intended privilege has crept in, highly injurious to a meritorious class of our citizens, and which cannot, in the opinion of the Committee, be effectually restrained, but by confining this privilege within its original limits, no better remedy can be applied than the repeal of such ordinance; by which measure, every farmer will still be allowed to sell in our markets such small meats as he may have raised and slaughtered himself, while country butchers will no longer be sanctioned in buying stock wherever and in whatever quantities they may think fit, and by exposing it for sale in this city, rival our licensed butchers upon very unequal, and, to the latter, very disadvantageous terms.

"In this view of the subject, the Committee beg leave to submit the draft of an ordinance, hereunto annexed, and they offer the following: *Resolved*, That the ordinance, entitled 'A Law to amend a Law to regulate the Public Markets,' passed 7th May, 1827, be repealed, and that an ordinance, of which a draft is hereunto annexed, be passed for that purpose." (*Passed April* 19, 1830.)

At this period an English traveler, by the name of Fowler, in his "tour," paid a visit to this market, and thus speaks of it, and of the prices of provisions: " · · · · I have repeatedly visited, and have no hesitation in saying, that for the richness and abundance of its supply, it surpasses any I ever saw, especially in fruits and vegetables; and in fish, flesh, and fowl there is every profusion and excellence. I have been frequently asked by my American friends whether I considered their *beef* equal to 'the roast beef of Old England'— but I would confess myself not epicure enough to tell the difference."

The prices of provisions of the following kinds are as follows:

For beef, (best cuts,) from 8 to 12 c. Do., common pieces, 4 to 8c .
Mutton, lamb, and veal, 6 to 8 c. Pork, "   " 5 to 7 c.
Turkeys, 75 c. to $1.25. Geese, per piece, 50 c. to $1.
Ducks, per pair, 75 c. to $1.25. Chickens, per pair, 50 to 63 c.
Butter, per lb., 15 to 18 c. Eggs, per dozen, 12 c.
Apples, per barrel, $1.50 to $2. Potatoes, per bushel, 30 to 38 c.
Turnips, per bushel, 25 to 38 c.

In this market, at this period, were many butchers who are worthy of more than a passing notice; and as my intention is to still further collect such information as may be both interesting and profitable as examples, I shall defer it for some future period. Perhaps, however, a few words of one or two who passed away soon after will not be out of place here.

David Marsh, once the occupant of No. 18, was an old "Fly Market" butcher, very much respected for his public and private worth. In 1822 and '23 he held the office of Assistant Alderman of the Eighth Ward; and again, in 1829, '30, and '31, the office of Alderman of the Eleventh Ward, and gave general satisfaction. He was a gentleman of the "old school," plain, unpretending, of a most pleasant and social turn, and strictly an honorable man. In the Fly Market he was patronized by many of the leading men of the day, some of whom, for a joke, succeeded in perplexing and annoying him. They had previously agreed to meet at his stall at a certain busy hour on a Saturday morning: they came on him suddenly, and all claimed to be waited on first. It was Uncle *David* here, and Uncle *David* there; we want our meat, and we want to pay for it. They bothered him so, that at last he went and sat down on his chair. "Now, (says he,) if you don't all leave the market immediately, not one of you shall have an ounce of meat from my stall." It was said that it was the first time they ever saw him annoyed.

Thomas Gibbons, the occupant once of No. 14 Fly Market, and of No. 29 this market, was another most worthy, generous, and public-spirited gentleman. A man of decided talent, which he often displayed in defence of the profession; always on the lead to encourage agriculture, more particularly that of breeding fine stock, in getting up fairs, offering premiums, paying liberal prices for premium cattle. In public or private meetings, benevolent societies or celebrations, Thomas Gibbons was always found, or placed in the front rank; and perhaps no event was so conspicuous with the butchers (except the "Federal Procession" in 1788) as that of the "Canal Celebration," when his skill and liberality stood out boldly and bountifully, although greatly assisted by many other leading men. The following sketch will give the reader some idea of it, and of those butchers prominently engaged in carrying out its parts:

In the months of September and October, 1825, the butchers held various meetings, when they appointed for "Managers" Messrs. Arnest Fink, Thomas Gibbons, Jacob Aims, James Reeves, and John Trigler; and for the "Committee of Arrangements,"

Thomas Gibbons,	Thomas Jeremiah,	Lawrence Wiseburn,
Eliphalet Wheeler,	Frederick Hawes,	John Trigler,
Daniel Spader,	Robert Tier,	Albert Fisher,
Joseph Blackwell,	Barth. Granger,	Walter Durbrow,
Philip Luff, Jun'r,	Elias De Forest,	John Varick,
James Simonson,	John Perrin,	Jacob Ridabock,
Thomas Syberts,	Jacob Syler,	James Weeden,
Joseph Jacots,	John Wallace,	Christian Harriot.

The "Delegates to confer with the Corporation" were Messrs. Walter Durbrow and John Perrin, who, on the 6th of October, reported the butchers ready to parade with the procession, which took place on the 4th of November, 1825.

The several societies were ordered to form a line at 9 o'clock, A. M., on the west side of Greenwich Street, with the right resting on Marketfield Street. "At 11 o'clock the procession, under the direction of Major-General Fleming, who acted as the Grand Marshal, began to countermarch, or wheel and pass; the whole line moving at the same time, so that all might see each other; it then passed up Greenwich Street to Canal Street and Broadway, up

Broadway to Broome Street and to the Bowery, down the Bowery to Pearl Street, down Pearl Street to the Battery."*

The whole line marching six abreast, except the butchers, who were on horseback, and (*being No. 6*) formed and marched four horses in front, headed by Thomas Gibbons as Marshal, assisted by Lawrence Wiseburn, John Perrin, John Trigler, and Daniel Spader. Then came two trumpeters mounted, followed by "a car handsomely decorated with laurel, drawn by four horses; on the car a farmer represented with his stock, consisting of a live calf and several sheep; in front of the car two boys, in appropriate dresses, supported a banner, exhibiting on one side the emblem of the profession— a knife and steel crossed; above, the poll-axe; below, on one side, the saw, on the other the chopper; in the circle, an ox and sheep: inscription, ' We preserve by destroying.' On the reverse a pastoral scene, flocks and herds grazing, the plough, harrow, and other implements of husbandry, grain, &c., &c.: inscription, 'Agriculture our Nation's Wealth.' Twenty boys followed the car; they were dressed in white frocks, and carried in their hands the different implements of the trade. A white standard, inscribed 'The Butchers' Benevolent Society,' followed by fifty of the profession in white aprons and check sleeves, mounted on gray horses. Next, a large car, drawn by six horses; on a platform in the centre was a stall, at which a handsome *white ox* was feeding; the ends of the platform were inclosed by white palisades, and sodded, intended to represent a field and shrubbery, sheep feeding, &c. Another palisaded platform surmounted the stage, in which was placed the full form of an ox, handsomely prepared for the occasion, dressed with ribbons and other appropriate embellishments, attended by four boys in white frocks, decorated with ribbons—the whole intended to represent the process of grazing and feeding, until the animal is prepared for the knife.

"One hundred and fifty of the profession, dressed as before, with four standards, at equal distances, followed on black horses: on the first standard a heart is represented—inscription, ' Is devoted to our Country;' on the second, the form of an ox-head—inscription, ' Liberty is our Head;' on the third, the figure of a steak—inscription, ' To all we divide a part;' on the fourth was inscribed the words, ' Internal Improvements are Chains to strengthen the Union of the States.' Then followed the ' Butchers' Benevolent Society,' headed by its President, Lawrence Wiseburn; John Perrin, Vice-President; John Graff, Treasurer; Thomas Jeremiah, Secretary; Christian H. Hartell, Assistant Secretary."

* Colden's Account.

When the procession passed the corner of Broadway and Canal Street, where I, then quite a boy, stood, it appeared to me to be wonderfully grand and imposing, especially that part which was represented by the butchers. This was several years before I had any idea of becoming one of the profession, and I may say, I much less thought of recording the above incident; more especially that part relating to Thomas Gibbon , who at this period was considered very wealthy, but his generosity afterwards to a false friend, named *Sykes*, ruined him, and struck him down even to death's door. One who knew him intimately thus speaks of him in a " Communication," found in the press, at the time of his death:

" Died on the 17th (*November*, 1832,) instant, of a short but severe illness, Thomas Gibbons, an old and respected butcher of this city. As an old friend, we cannot permit his name to go down to the tomb without paying a small tribute to one whose acts of benevolence when living were calculated to draw forth the admiration and praise of society at large. But a few years since, possessed of an ample fortune, his only ambition was that of bestowing it on the needy without distinction, and it may be truly said, that owing to his extreme liberality may be attributed his misfortunes; and we may add, that his fine feelings of humanity led him into acts that prudence forbade, or self-preservation could not justify, which eventuated in poverty, but not dishonor ; and we can bear testimony that he bore up against accumulated difficulties with that spirit of Christianity that truly belonged to him. Persecution alone would occasionally compel poor frail nature to yield, but it was momentary. To say aught that could be said against this good man's life, it was only tarnished by misfortune.—B."

In the month of October, two years after, a petition was before the Board, praying for a new fish market to be erected at the head of the slip opposite the main market. The Market Committee reported in favor of it, after stating their " opinion that the fish market (or stands in the east wing) should be removed," " as it had become necessary by the increase of people frequenting said market." The water and other nuisances from the fish market descend into the stores below, causing it to be a nuisance. The estimated expense for building one 195 feet long was about $3,000. They offer a resolution to that effect, and it was adopted. In the month of May of the next year, a report from the Superintendent of Buildings shows that this new fish market cost $3,223.63, although contracted for $2,847.75 to James Phillips.

By the removal of the fishermen from the east wing it was again left vacant, except occasionally when the country market was crowded, and country people were placed in there. As the system of selling butchers' stands for a premium had been discontinued, and that of "drawing by lot" had been adopted, a great many applications had been made, and continued until the Market Committee, in the month of May, 1836, reported in favor of placing eighteen stands in the east end again, which were drawn by the following butchers:

No. 62. Elias B. Messerve.	No. 63. Marsden Shapter.
69. Wm. Van Benschoten.	70. Thomas Kirkpatrick.
71. Wm. H. Hopkins.	72. F. S. Flander.
73. James King.	74. Daniel Rich.
75. Robert Shark.	76. John Chappel.
81. Francis Dupont.	82. Edward Youngs.
83. George Winship.	84. Cornelius Kent.
85. Francis Degez.	86. Josiah Reynolds.
87. Albert Fisher.	88. Jacob Acker.

They then "*Resolved*, That the Collector of the City Revenue be directed to collect the rent from the above-named persons from the date of the passage of this resolution, the first day of August, the usual quarter-day."

It was not long before several of these began to vacate their stands; in fact, before one year had passed but four or five were occupied, and finally they were all deserted or exchanged for some other in the market.

A few years after the occupant of No. 35 was sued for debt, when, among other things which he assigned, was this stand, in the month of November, 1839. The Court of Chancery ordered it to be advertised and sold, which was done at public auction on the 31st of December of that year, to Christian Stamler, for $350, who paid down the auctioneer's fees and ten per cent. of the purchase-money, and as soon as the assent for transfer from the Corporation took place, he would pay the rest. This subject was before the Board, who referred it to a Committee, of which were Aldermen Caleb S. Woodhull and James Ferris, who reported that "there are two kinds of butcher stands in the markets of this city: those which are known and distinguished as *premium stands*, and those which are not—this is a *premium stand*." They further state, "In conclusion, your Committee are constrained to admit that these stands have always been recognized by the Corporation as salable property. The Corporation have themselves in the first instance sold them for large sums of money, and have been in the constant practice of assenting to and approving of their sale and transfer to others. It is a practice, therefore, that it cannot be controverted or disguised, that subject to certain rules and regulations necessary to be observed in conducting the business, these stands have been constantly sold for a valuable consideration, and that the Corporation have always been in the constant practice of giving effect to such sales by assenting to the same."

They offer a resolution, which was adopted, "That his Honor the Mayor be requested to issue a butcher's license to Christian Stamler for the transfer of butcher stall No. 35 Fulton Market, on his complying with the market laws and the regulations of the Market Committee."

In the month of December, 1840, many of the butchers' stands were found deserted, and others again only occasionally occupied, but of which the rents were paid by those whose names are found opposite to them. Those deserted are noticed as *unoccupied* in the following list:

No. 1.	James Johnson.	No. 2.	Carlisle T. Weeks.
3.	Eugene McCarty.	4.	Denton Pearsall.
5.	Peter Mencilliot.	6.	David H. Gould.
7.	Richard Hunt.	8.	Benjamin Mathewson.
9.	Unoccupied.	10.	Unoccupied.
11.	Abraham Valentine.	12.	David W. Piercy.
13.	Lanning Ferris.	14.	Ebenezer G. Ferris.
15.	John Perrin.	16.	Albert W. Smith.
17.	Entrance.	18.	Charles Gwyer.
19.	Andrew C. Wheeler.	20.	Francis Godine.
21.	Benjamin E. Ewen.	22.	Robert Elder.
23.	George W. Schuyler.	24.	Thomas Eicleton.
25.	Elnathan Underhill.	26.	Isaac Rhoades, Jun'r.
27.	George Haws.	28.	Jacob H. Ridabock.
29.	William Warner.	30.	H. H. Valentine.
31.	George Montgomery.	32.	Wm. B. Woodcock.
33.	Francis Spicer.	34.	William Chivvis.
35.	John McCarty.	36.	Daniel Rhoades.
37.	Marvin R. Underhill.	38.	Thomas M. Jenkins.
39.	John D. Kent.	40.	John Post.
41.	Jonathan Wilt.	42.	G. W. Vandenburgh.
43.	Benjamin T. Weeks.	44.	Jacob A. Stamler.
45.	Charles Kent.	46.	Peter Valentine.
47.	Cornelius Kent.	48.	B. W. Valentine.
49.	John B. Wilt.	50.	John Henning.
51.	William Hayward.	52.	John Sloat.
53.	Henry Smith.	54.	John Simonson.
55.	Joseph Alden.	56.	Carman A. Simonson.
57.	Stephen Williams.	58.	William Myers.

No. 59. Peter T. Valentine. No. 60. John Chappel.
  61. Elias T. De Forest.   62. Mathew Harpell.
  63. Joseph L. Henning.   64. Unoccupied.
  65. Unoccupied.   66. do. 68, 70, 72, do.
  67. do. 69. do.   74. do. 76, 78, 80, do.
  71. William Myers.   82. do. 84, 86, do.
  73. Rufus Rowe.   88. Jacob Acker.
  75. Unoccupied, also 77, 79, 81, 83.
  85. James P. Stanton.   87. Francis Degez.

For many years this market had been constantly increasing in the sale of fish, principally at wholesale, which led to the gathering of great numbers of fishing smacks in the slip at certain seasons; these, with other market craft, occasionally crowded so much as to be the cause of great complaint.

On the 28th of March, 1842, a petition was before the Board, stating, that "Your petitioners, boatmen, fishermen, marketmen, and others, trading to and with said city, beg leave respectfully to represent to your Honorable Body, that *Fulton Market Slip* has for a long time past, and until recently, been set apart for the sole use of *fishing smacks* and market-boats, and that during the business seasons of the year the whole of the said *slip* is barely sufficient to accommodate the numerous craft of the above description; that soon there will be from *ten to fifteen* vessels daily laden with *shad* for this market, and during the season vessels are plying from Long Island and the country adjacent laden with *vegetables* for the supply of the city daily.

"That it is absolutely necessary that that portion of your petitioners occupying the *fish market*, now yielding a revenue to the city, in order to be able to supply the market with fresh and healthy *fish*, that they should enjoy the uninterrupted use of a part of the slip adjoining the market for fish-cars, thus keeping their fish in the water until required for use.

"That, as your petitioners are informed and believe, a lease was granted of the *west side* of said slip, restricting the occupancy thereof to *two steamboats;* instead whereof, the lessees have *three,* and ofttimes *four steamboats* there at a time; and in addition to that, introduce other large vessels, to the great detriment and endangering of the smaller craft of your petitioners. That as the steamboats lie blocking up nearly the whole entrance to said slip, when the smaller craft are endeavoring to effect an entrance into the slip in a strong *ebb-tide,* they are inevitably borne by the current under the steamboat guard, breaking their stanchion, and carrying away their chain-plates, and otherwise injuring them; and in many instances the slip has been so much occupied with steamboats and other large vessels, that the smacks are unable to obtain entrance, and are compelled to go elsewhere and discharge.

"That great inconvenience and ofttimes great damage are experienced from steamboats, in this: that inasmuch as a long time before starting their wheels are put into motion, by which the small boats are driven against each other with such force as sometimes to damage them, the mud is raised in such quantities from the slip as to kill the fish, and not unfrequently the cars are turned over, and the fish lost out. They therefore pray that your Honorable Body will be pleased to exercise the power in you vested, in restraining the lessees of the west side of the slip, during the time said lease has to run, to the occupation of the same according to the terms thereof; and that after the expiration thereof, they pray that no steamboat, registered or sea vessels, be suffered to use the said slip." The deserved relief, after a time, was granted to them.

The removal of the fishermen from the "east wing" to the shed built for the fishermen along the slip had given some reason to think that the business, or rather the rapid decline of it, was the consequence; but no doubt the high prices of provisions along in the years 1837, '8, and '9; then followed the introduction of the "meat-shops" over the city, with the "hue and cry" of the press against the public markets, was the main cause. However, a numerously signed petition, dated August 2, 1843, asked the Common Council to remove the fishermen back into the "east wing;" and further state, that "the immediate removal of the fish market over the head of Fulton Slip, as being the only means by which the business of Fulton Market can be restored. We are satisfied, from facts that we can produce, that the building of the fish market has been the entire cause of the loss of the business of Fulton Market, and that its removal will be the means of restoring it, in a measure, to its former prosperity.

"We would call the attention of your Honorable Body to the fact of the almost entire neglect of the public authorities to our market, while we have been unable to get the needful repairs done; and we would now respectfully ask that some favors may be granted us, if only to preserve the value of the public property; for if some measures are not taken, the *income* of the Fulton Market property must be largely reduced every year."

The fishermen then followed with a remonstrance, dated April 1st, 1844, and say: "The undersigned, being fishermen and oyster-men, doing business in the Fulton *Fish* Market, understand that your Honorable Body contemplate removing them to the east wing of the Fulton Butcher Market, which to them would be a serious inconvenience.

" They wish your Honorable Body to take into consideration why they were first removed from that east wing—which was on account of the nuisance they were said to create, by their being compelled to use a great quantity of water, &c. They cannot now see any advantage they can have more than they had then, to obviate such complaints. They therefore do trust that your Honorable Body will take their case into serious consideration, and not remove them from their present location until they can have a permanent location, and that for their better accommodation," &c. Signed by

Willard Phelps,	Charles Royael,	John Durie,
Daniel Fowler,	Walter Pearsall,	Jared Baker,
Elisha Baker,	Albert Rogers,	Aaron Kingsland,
Elisha A. Baker,	Silas Manwaring,	Ebenezer Cutler,
Anson Ryno,	Thomas Mansfield,	William B. Storer,
Jeremiah H. Racket,	S. Dayton,	P. S. Griffin,
S. B. Tuthill,	Z. Moon,	John Comstock,
Daniel H. Racket,	Maxen Rogers,	Truman Lamphier,
Geo. F. Rogers,	William Brown,	Charles Rankins.

On the 25th of March the Report of the Committee on Markets upon this subject appeared before the Board of Aldermen, stating:

" That upon an examination of said fish market, they find it in a very dilapidated state, and requiring a considerable amount to be expended for repairs, which amount can be saved by transferring the fishermen to the east wing of Fulton Market, that portion having been originally intended for that purpose, and was so occupied for some years after the market was erected. The business of said market has been declining since the fishermen have been removed to their present location, owing to the great inconvenience experienced in crossing the street from the meat to the fish market, on account of vehicles of every description being continually congregated at that place; and the result has been, that many persons (especially females) who formerly purchased at this market, in order to obviate this difficulty, have gone to Washington and other markets, and it consequently has tended materially to affect the business of those who are located at this place, while the object for their removal has never been accomplished, which was, to have the places thus vacated occupied by butchers. The trial has frequently been made, but, after occupying a stand for a short time, finding no business could be done, it has been abandoned; and there are now but two butchers in that wing, both of whom can have their choice of the vacant stands in other parts of the market.

" Your Committee have had this subject a long time under consideration, and, after mature deliberation, are convinced that, by transferring the fishermen from their present location to the east wing of the meat market, will be a great convenience to the customers of that market, will benefit both butchers and fishermen, and tend to increase the revenue from said market. They therefore offer for adoption the following resolution :

" *Resolved*, That the fishermen holding licenses for the sale of fish at Fulton Market be transferred to the east wing of the meat market, and the present fish market be appropriated to country people bringing produce for sale." This report was adopted and approved.

In the month of April following the fishermen were removed into the east wing of the main market ; the shed which had been used by the fishermen, although it had been appropriated to the use of the country people, was not so used, and was taken down ; and the slip was ordered for the use of the fishing-smacks, market-boats, and fish-cars.

For several years a rapidly-growing wholesale fish-trade had been established from off the "smacks" on their arrival, and when the finny tribe were not in demand, they were emptied into the large cars, where they awaited the demands of ofttimes buyers, who then began to pack them for other cities; which, after a time, established a large trade in this manner.

In the month of September of the next year, a petition for inclosing and repairing the inside or country market was before the Board. It stated, "That the country part of the market is extremely dark ; and if sky-lights were placed in the roof, it would be a great benefit to those coming to and doing business in the market."

This was reported on, on the 21st of the following month, as follows: "That they have considered the same, and had plans and estimates made of the expense of said inclosure and sheds. They find that Fulton Market is the only market in the city that is not inclosed. The expense will be about $3,000 for inclosing the market in a proper manner. Your Committee feel satisfied that the outlay will be a good investment for the city, as the fees that will be collected from the part inclosed cannot be less than ten per cent. They would further state, that if the market is not inclosed, there will be considerable expense, as the market is old, and wants considerable repairing. They would therefore recommend that the prayer of the petitioners be granted, and offer the following resolutions for consideration :

" *Resolved*, That Fulton Market be inclosed, according to the plans herewith presented.

"*Resolved*, That the Superintendent of Repairs advertise for estimates to have the above inclosure completed, under the direction of the Market Committee, at an expense not to exceed $3,000."

Two years after, (1847,) in the month of June, another new shed was ordered to be constructed, extending along the whole width of the market on the South Street side, from Beekman to Fulton Street, and projecting "eight feet outside of the side-walk," which it was thought would "improve its appearance and increase its revenue." This shed was erected, and for a short period it was legitimately occupied; but now we find a part, at least, is converted into small eating saloons, while many other sheds have been put up on the walks around on the other sides, from which are sold shoes, stockings, hats, knives, pistols, flashy jewelry, books, pamphlets, papers, pictures, cigars, &c. In establishing these sheds, no doubt the *revenue* of some of the office-holders was much increased, who by this means put large sums of money, which should have gone into the City Treasury directly, into their own. A great many honest people may say that the manner of obtaining this money is unlawful and dishonest; but the unscrupulous politician, or rather the workers of the *political machine*, claim that "to the victors belongs the right to plunder."

The same Committee who reported on the erection of this shed on the east side of the market also reported on the necessity of making suitable accommodations for wholesale dealers in fish, which, at this period, had grown into a very large business.

Great quantities of fish were now brought by the Long Island Railroad daily to this as well as the Washington Market—(the latter yet sold considerable at wholesale.) The Fulton, however, had the natural advantage of being more favorably located; having much better water and slip accommodations. Favorable reports had been previously made for erecting suitable accommodations, but had not been carried out. This Committee, however, wished to erect it on the bulkhead where the old fish market stood, fronting on the main market, extending nearly the whole length of the same, at an expense of not exceeding two thousand dollars. Resolutions were passed to that effect, and the present fish market was soon after built.

This wholesale fish market is separated from the principal building by South Street, on which it fronts, and is merely a wooden shed; in length from dock to dock, with the rear over the basin, into which are the cars floating, usually full of live fish; and outside of these lie the smacks, which have just arrived, or are preparing to depart.

The lower end of this fish market is occupied by dealers in all kinds of live poultry, (and other animals,) which are used or sold principally for shipping, to adorn the farm-yards, or to ornament a park; and I have occasionally seen here some of the choicest breeds and the most beautiful poultry I ever saw on sale.

The wholesale fish-trade, for many years, has been constantly increasing, and now, hours before daylight every morning of the week, may be found here fish-wagons, carts, and other vehicles, from the various public markets, meat-shops, and street peddlers, from this and the neighboring cities, towns, and villages, for their daily supplies; which part of the business is generally over by seven o'clock, A. M. Then large quantities of salt-water fish are packed in boxes, and sent to the interior cities and towns.

The stands at which fish are sold by retail are located in the main building, on the north, or Beekman Street wing, where large quantities are disposed of daily.

Since the year 1850, the butchers' stands have had many changes in their occupancy; several of which were occupied only for short periods; others, again, have been totally deserted; and, again, there are some who have done a very large business, but principally in supplying large steamers, packets, and other vessels, large hotels and boarding-houses. Private residences have almost deserted this part of the city, and there are but few families who now patronize this market; I may, however, except several from Brooklyn. Between the years 1850 and 1855, the butchers' stands were occupied as follows:

No. 1. James Johnson.	No. 2. Ebenezer Kline.
3. Benjamin Mathewson.	4. Denton Pearsall.
5. Jacob Fisher.	6. Zophar Pearsall.
7. Richard Hunt.	8. Charles H. Hawkins.
9. Lawrence Clinton.	10. Unoccupied.
11. Abraham Valentine.	12. John C. Valentine.
13. Unoccupied.	14. Oliver Valentine.
15. John Perrin.	16. Henry Smith.
17. Stairway.	18. William A. Smith.
19. Arnest Aims.	20. Frederick Robertson.
21. Albert Fisher.	22. William Fisher.
23. Elnathan Underhill.	24. Thomas Eicleston.
25. George Haws.	26. John Ketchum.
27. George Haws, Jr.	28. James Tilby.
29. Charles Cooper.	30. William H. Valentine.
31. Isaac Anderson.	32. Cornelius Cooper.
33. Joseph Hayward.	34. William Sager.

No. 35. William A. Remer.
    37. Pearson S. Halsted.
    39. George Castell.
    41. Samuel Weeks.
    43. Benjamin T. Weeks.
    45. Abraham Leggett.
    47. Cornelius Kent.
    49. John B. Wilt.
    51. William Hayward.
    53. John Alden.
    55. Joseph Alden.
    57. Stephen Williams.
    59. William H. Cornell.
    61. Elias De Forest.
    63. Joseph Henning.

No. 36. John C. Chamberlain.
    38. James Parr.
    40. John Post.
    42. John Stamler.
    44. Jacob A. Stamler.
    46. Peter Valentine.
    48. Peter Valentine.
    50. John F. Henning.
    52. John F. Henning.
    54. John Simonson.
    56. Carman A. Simonson.
    58. Stephen H. Cornell.
    60. John Chappel.
    62. Charles Brower.
    64. J. P. Stanton.

From No. 64 to 68, which composes principally all the Beekman Street wing, is taken up with retail fishermen; and, to sum up in a few words, the Fulton Market is capable of being made much more convenient, cleanly, attractive, and profitable, both to stand-holders and the city.

"FRANKLIN MARKET."

1821. THE inhabitants in the neighborhood of Old Slip were about to lose the "Fly Market," which had accommodated and supplied them with provisions since the "Old Slip Market," that stood above forty years before in this Old Slip, at the corner of Pearl Street, was taken from them; and they wished for a nearer market-house than the new "Fulton;" so they petitioned, and the Board, on the 1st of October, 1821, agreed to the report then presented to them by the Market Committee, in which they state: "That it will be found necessary to erect a market somewhere in the lower part of the city; that it can be done at much less expense when the *Fly Market* is taken down than at any future period, as the materials may be so advantageously used, that for a very small sum a *new market* may be built, whereby a public revenue will be derived, as well as great convenience afforded to the inhabitants of that part of the town." They recommend the prayer of the petitioners for a market to be erected at Old Slip be granted, and therefore offer the following resolutions:

"*Resolved*, That whenever the Corporation shall deem it expedient to remove *Fly Market*, that part thereof known as the *fish market* be carefully taken down, and the materials removed to the *Old Slip*.

"*Resolved*, That a *market* be built at Old Slip, between Water and Front Streets, under the direction of the Market Committee, and that such part of the above materials as are suitable be used in the construction thereof."

In the month of February following, George Duryea applied, through petition, for the "Clerkship" of this market, in which he says: "That he is an old citizen of this place, in reduced circumstances, from misfortune, and unable to procure a maintenance for his family by manual labor, from the loss of one of his arms. That he was in the service of the United States, employed as a wagoner, during the late war; but having taken a load on his own account, was at that time wounded, and deprived of his arm, and therefore not entitled to a pension from the Government. He understands a new market is to be erected at Old Slip, for which a Deputy Clerk will be wanted," and he solicits the appointment. It was granted.

This market was reported finished in the month of June, when the inhabitants were anxious to have a fire-bell on the market. In consequence of its being a considerable distance from any church or fire bell, they "solicit that a cupola may be erected—as there is a gentleman in the neighborhood willing to present a bell suitable for the same;" which was ordered to be carried into effect, and a resolution soon after was passed, that this market be hereafter known by the name and style of "Franklin Market," after the great philosopher, Benjamin Franklin.

The *Gazette* of the 27th of June, 1822, says: "The market, though small, is still neat and airy. The stalls are, or will be, all taken up; and as it is situated in the centre of a wealthy neighborhood, it will be well attended. The market in that vicinity will be a benefit to the property, and those old wooden rookeries on the right of the market should be pulled down, and a row of neat houses and shops built, which would bring a good interest."

On the 8th of July following, eight butchers' stands, with two cellars, were rented at public auction, for a premium, during a period of nine months, with the privilege of renewals, to the following butchers and others, for the sums set opposite their names:

No. 1. Peter Crawbuck,	$535	No. 2. Rufus Gilbert,	$570
3. Elias B. Messerve,	295	4. Jacob H. Ridabock,	280
5. James Weeden,	265	6. Jacob Manolt,	270
7. George Merckle,	445	8. Charles Hopper,	430

No. 1. Cellar,   Samuel W. Kelly, - - - - - $150
    2.   "   Mead Darrow, - - - - - 180

                    Whole amount,   - $3,420
The whole cost of erecting this market was - - - 2,070

Which shows the city overpaid, on its cost,   - - $1,350

The "market" opened for business on the 27th of the same month, with flattering compliments from the "Press." They say: "The general display of meats was as handsome as anything we ever saw, in the early part of the morning. It was sold rapidly, and the butchers had no cause to complain of their first day's work;" and "there can be no better stand than the 'Franklin Market' for the sale of choice articles."

This encouragement, however, was of short duration, as the much-dreaded yellow fever, a few weeks after, made its appearance, and drove the stand-holders from its shelter; a few of whom located themselves in Chatham Square; but the others quit business for about two months, when they all again returned to the market. The butchers, in the month of November, petitioned for a remission of rent of stands for the time which had not been used by them, but the Board laid their claims to rest. This, with a decreasing business, as the same amount had not returned with the occupants, was anything but favorable to their future prospects.

Again, in the month of February, 1824, the butchers petition for a reduction of rent. They say: "They have been obliged to pay heavy rents therefor, which were enhanced by the existence of the yellow fever, (they being thrown out of employment,) and for which no allowances were made." The Committee laid the subject over, to be considered at the time of renting the stands for the next year. Several of the butchers became much dissatisfied after this period with the small amount of business done, which caused them to dispose of their stands, some of which were sold or exchanged several times, in the course of a few years. In the year 1828 the stands were occupied:

No. 1. Peter Crawbuck.   No. 2. Rufus Gilbert.
    3. Orman Broadway.   4. Thomas Glover.
    5. James Weeden.   6. James Ferdon.
    7. George Merkle.   8. Charles Hopper.

The number of butchers appeared to be more than was required for the business here, and several of them, after a time, began to drop off, one by one, until four or five were able to accommodate all that visited there. The principal inhabitants began deserting and tearing down then old, but once fashionable, dwellings, and fine large stores were erected in their places. This soon increased a large mercantile business about here, and with it came complaints against the market-house, of blocking up the street. Petitions for and against its removal were presented, and considered, but no action was taken until the year 1833, when we find, in the month of December, a report from a Joint Committee on Markets, with the Wharves, and Public Lands and Places," relative to filling up the "Old Slip" to South Street, the removing of this market-house, and erecting a new one in lieu thereof; which was finally adopted. In this report it is stated: "*First*—In respect to filling up Old Slip as far out as the line of South Street. The Committee have had no difficulty in arriving at the conclusion that the measure is a proper one. South Street is by law the exterior line of the city on the East River, and the expediency of filling up all the slips inside of that line as soon as may be practicable under the circumstances cannot be doubted; and *Secondly*—On the subject of removing the present Franklin Market, there appears a diversity of opinion. It is undoubtedly true that many families have removed their residences from the First Ward into the upper parts of the city, but the number of those that remain, and that will hereafter reside in that section of the city, is far too great to have their rights or conveniences disregarded; and perhaps no better argument could be adduced in favor of continuing a market in this location, than the fact that Franklin Market *has* been a source of profitable income to the city, and that the occupants of it, from whom such income has been derived, are desirous of remaining, and continuing their business there. The Committee, therefore, are of opinion that the remonstrance against the removal of the market ought to prevail to a certain extent: that is to say, that if the Common Council should direct the slip to be filled up to the line of South Street, and should think fit to take away the present market-house between Water and Front Streets, they ought to erect a suitable market-house on the ground to be so filled in fronting on South Street, in like manner with Fulton Market." The Committee submit resolutions, agreeing with the above; among which were, "That a new market be laid out and established on the ground to be filled in," between Front and South Streets; "that after the completion of such new market, the old market-house now fronting Old Slip be removed."

However, before the grounds were filled in and prepared for the new site, the "great fire" of 1835 took place, and saved the city the expense and trouble of removing this old market-house, as it left not a vestige of this wooden building behind.

This terrible calamity commenced in Comstock & Andrews' store, in Merchant Street, on the night of Wednesday, the 16th of December, when it spread in every direction, and burned furiously for sixteen hours before it was stopped, and this was done by blowing up several buildings with gunpowder; although the firemen worked like heroes, yet the weather was so freezing cold that the water congealed in the hydrants and fire-hose, rendering them useless. Several fire companies from Philadelphia, Newark, Elizabethtown, Jersey City, Brooklyn, &c., came promptly to assist, and did good service. Nearly *six hundred* buildings, with the ancient Dutch Church in Garden Street, the splendid edifice known as the Exchange, with the fine statue of Hamilton, placed a few months before in the centre of its rotunda by the merchants, were all destroyed. The shipping near the line of the fire were quickly forced to leave the docks, as the devouring element soon reached the wharves and destroyed the wharf logs, posts, and timbers, and caught and injured several of the flying vessels. The whole loss was variously estimated from *twelve* to *seventeen millions* of dollars.

Public thanks were tendered to several officers of the army and navy, among which were Commodore Ridgely, General Swift, Captains Mix and Walker, Lieutenants Temple and Nicholls, with the seamen and marines under their charge, who performed various efficient services; they were afterwards relieved with the old Third (now Eighth) Regiment, under then Colonel George P. Morris, and other military bodies, who were several days on guard duty.

On the 21st of the same month, the Board of Assistant Aldermen brought before· them and adopted the following: " Whereas the Franklin Market at Old Slip has been destroyed at the late fire, and the butchers having stands therein been deprived of the same;" therefore it was resolved, that " a temporary shed be erected in the Old Slip or Broad Street, for the accommodation of" all stand-holders, " until other provisions shall be made."

In the month of January, next year, it was ordered to be built on the site of the old one, and the following October the Market Committee reported on rebuilding this market as follows: " That your Committee deem that it is due to the inhabitants of the First Ward that an accommodation of this description should be granted to them, as the same has existed for several years past, and its existence at Old Slip has been a public convenience, and it is required by many individuals residing in the neighborhood." They recommend the following resolution, which was adopted: "*Resolved,* That Franklin Market shall be rebuilt at Old Slip on a line with South Street, and extending not exceeding one hundred and twenty-five feet towards

Front Street, with a width not exceeding thirty feet, to be so formed as to accommodate on the ground floor or basement a hose-cart
or engine, and the second story to be adapted to a sub-watch-house,
if it should be found necessary." The plan was reported, and " the
estimated cost, it was said, will not differ much from nine thousand
dollars, and will not exceed ten thousand dollars:" so said Charles
B. Tappan, then the Superintendent of Buildings; and the Committee on Markets, who were composed of the following, John B.
Schemelzel, William Hall, and Isaac Merritt, recommended such an
appropriation, which was adopted.   However, before the commencement of its erection a suit was brought against the Corporation, to
oppose its rebuilding, which was not decided until the summer of
1837, when petitions and reports were before the Board again, favorable to its completion.   They state, " that strong but selfish doubts
were entertained by a few touching the right of the Corporation to
rebuild said market in any part of Old Slip, and a powerful opposition was consequently maintained and prosecuted, which resulted in
a late decision in the Court of Chancery in favor of the Corporation.   Your petitioners were always aware that the plan finally
adopted of said market was entirely inadequate to the wants of the
community who were to be benefited by it, inasmuch as it is to be
six feet shorter than the *old one;* and in addition to which, sixteen
feet is very properly set apart and appropriated for an engine and
hose company, leaving a space to be occupied for market purposes
some 20 feet less than the old market.   Your petitioners have learned, with pleasure, that in addition to the great public necessity of
an engine and hose company in the burnt district, a sub-watch-house
is to be established, all of which is highly necessary in the midst of
a district where so much valuable property is nightly exposed to the
torch of the incendiary and the wiles of the burglar.   Your petitioners are strongly impressed with the opinion that the present plan
is entirely too circumscribed to answer the objects intended; and
also, that since the decision of the Chancellor in favor of the Corporation, no reasonable objection exists even among those who formerly opposed it *in toto.*   Your petitioners would therefore pray your
Honorable Body so to alter said plan as to extend said market north
upon a line with *Front Street,* or at least so far as may be deemed
expedient or necessary for the object desired; believing, as before
stated, that no reasonable objection now exists to such extension,
and believing also that such enlargement is imperiously demanded
by the public wants; that it will increase the public revenue in a
ratio beyond the expenditure thus incurred; and they would further
beg leave to state, that the ground proposed to be occupied for said

addition will ever be entirely useless for any other public purpose, the street being 50 feet wide on either side of the proposed addition. All of which is respectfully submitted," &c.

On the 30th of July following the Committee on Markets reported, that "since the passage of the resolution by the Common Council, directing the rebuilding of *Franklin Market* at Old Slip, it has appeared that a large number of the inhabitants of the First Ward are desirous that said market should be extended, in order to afford sufficient accommodations to the inhabitants of said Ward, as well as the supplying of the wants of the large shipping interest that must be necessarily supplied with provisions, &c., in that vicinity; and whereas by complying with the request of the inhabitants of said Ward it would afford an opportunity of furnishing several stands to many enterprising butchers who are anxious to commence business in any of the public markets.

"Therefore, be it *Resolved*, That the Superintendent of Buildings be authorized to contract for the extension of the Franklin Market fifty feet from the northerly end thereof, running towards Front Street; such addition to be built agreeable to the present plan, under direction of the Market Committee.

"*Resolved*, That the sum of $4,700 be appropriated therefor."

The present brick market-house was soon after erected; the butchers and others removed into it, where but few succeeded, as its day for furnishing private families had gone by; and but little other business was done than the supplying the increasing vessels which crowded the various slips in that vicinity. Here the occupants were prepared to furnish every article of human food, whether "fish, flesh, or fowl," animal or vegetable, in the living, dressed, or cured state; and much of this kind of business is now conducted here.

In the month of June, 1838, we find the butchers' stands occupied by the following persons:

No. 1. William Granger. No. 2. George Merkle, Jr.
3. Abraham Warner. 4. Thomas Glover.
5. James Weeden. 6. William Glover.
7. Unoccupied. 8. James King.
9. George Merkle. 10. Charles Hopper.

The basement under the market was leased to John E. Hunt, at $1,500 per annum, and the large room above was appropriated for the use of the "Society for the Promotion of the Gospel among the Seamen of the Port of New York."

Since this period the business has gradually left this market, and with it, of course, its occupants. In 1853 there were but three butchers licensed : on No. 1, Thomas Glover; No. 2, William Watts; and No. 3, Thomas Merkle, whose business is principally with the shipping.

"MANHATTAN MARKET."

1827. The proceedings of the "Council" show that on the 26th of March, 1827, the following resolution was adopted: "That the square or block of ground, bounded by Goerick, Rivington, Stanton, and Mangin Streets, belonging to the Corporation, be appropriated for a public market-place, and that the Market Committee erect thereon a market, (*house,*) not to cost over $2,000."

Perhaps there was no individual who worked harder to have this market established here than Colonel Appleby, who, although never an "office-seeker," yet his political influence at this day with many of the public officers was of the most successful kind. He was a personal friend of Henry Eckford, the once great ship-builder, who owned a large property around here; and although it was the interest of the Colonel to have the market near his own property, yet his particular intimacy with the wish of Eckford prevailed, and he worked with a will, although, to be confessed, it was of the most trying kind. Step by step, it was interest against friendship; he was, however, successful; friendship continued through life—even the grave has left no change in the yet active mind of Colonel William Appleby.

In the following month of September, the "Committee" reported its completion, at a cost of $1,975, and recommended it to be called "Manhattan Market;" and also to fix an annual rent for six butchers' stands, which were sold at public auction for the highest premium, on the 23d of October following, to the following persons:

No. 1. John Vandewater,	$505	No. 2. Hyatt Lyons,	$510
3. David Johnson,	340	4. Leonard Smith,	315
5. Nathaniel Cromer,	350	6. Mathew Vogel,	360

The name "Manhattan" was in this instance taken from a high knoll of land which, within my recollection, existed at that place, usually known and called Manhattan Island, it being surrounded with creeks and salt marsh; and at very high tides it was partly covered with sea-water. Its location was between Houston and Third Streets, and Lewis Street ran about through the centre of it.

In the month of July, 1829, an ordinance was before the Board creating a law for the inspection and measurement of vegetables and fruits, which was referred to a Committee, who afterwards reported in its favor. In the mean time, several applications for the offices were presented, through petitions. The first, Obadiah Newcomb, said, "He is a native of the United States; has been a resident of this city for twenty years past, and assisted, in the latter part of our Revolutionary War, in establishing the independence which we now enjoy." He appears to have been unsuccessful.

Samuel L. Feeks also represents, "That at the commencement of the late war, he entered the service of his country as a private soldier, in the regiment commanded by Robert Bogardus, Esq., and when peace took place obtained an honorable discharge. Subsequent to which, your petitioner obtained two several commissions in the regiment commanded by Samuel S. Dunscomb, Esq., and actually performed the duty pertaining to such office until his means compelled him to resign." He was also unsuccessful.

Isaac B. Van Duzen makes still a stronger appeal, through several citizens, who set forth, "That they have known him for a long time, and put the utmost confidence in his abilities and integrity. He is a gentleman, a native of this city, and a son of J. Van Duzen, Esq., one of the strugglers for our independence. Ambitious, in his youthful days, to defend his country's flag, he entered on board of the American brig *Catharine Ray*, and on the 1st of May, 1812, off 'New Rochelle,' was captured by the British squadron, and in the engagement had the misfortune to lose his leg. After having remained a prisoner six months, was exchanged, and on his arrival at this city was appointed a master's mate in the flotilla under the command of Commodore Lewis; remained in that situation until the Corporation accepted of his services on board the gun-boats provided by them for the safety of the harbor, and remained in that situation until the steam frigate (Fulton) was launched, when his services were no longer required." He, also, was not successful.

In the month of September, 1831, permission was given to James Dobbs, Isaac Hadden, and associates, to erect and inclose a frame sufficient to suspend a large bell, at their own expense, at the north-western part of this market square.

This market-place, however, proved a failure in business, it being not sufficiently patronized to support one-half of the stands placed in it. The butchers were deceived by the acts and promises of the Common Council made at the time of the sales of the stands, which fact is fully shown in a petition before the Board in the month of January, 1832, from the butchers, who ask for relief, and state, "That

Abraham M. Valentine, then one of the Aldermen and Market Committee, with the auctioneer, did expose for sale and sell the stalls in said market, from one to six inclusive; and further, that Abraham M. Valentine and the auctioneer did avow and declare, as an inducement to purchasers at that sale, that said 'Manhattan Market' was to be the only market in that section of the city, assigning as a reason that the Common Council had that square of ground on which the market stands *ceded* to them for that purpose only, and that a branch of the Williamsburgh Ferry should come to said market, which representation induced your petitioners to pay for said stalls sums of five hundred dollars and upward each; and further, that said A. M. Valentine and the auctioneer did at the above sale state that the 'Grand Street Market' was an obstruction in the public highway, and should be removed in one year and done away with; but, to the astonishment of your petitioners, the said A. M. Valentine did in a very short time after use all his influence to have the said Grand Street Market rebuilt within about 300 yards from said Manhattan Market, which renders the custom in said market about sufficient for the living of *two* butchers, and after all this duplicity did assist and effect the replacing the butchers of said Grand Street Market on their original stands for the simple sum of ten dollars each, and to the destruction of your petitioners. Now your petitioners humbly pray your Honorable Body that as we, your petitioners, were poor when we commenced, and did involve our friends as our surety, under prospects from assured authority, that your Honorable Body would relieve us, by such reductions as in your wisdom and justice may think proper, and place us on equality with our brother butchers; and as to the truth of the above statements, we have the affidavits of two respectable citizens of this city, namely, E. Townsend, Teller of Butchers' and Drovers' Bank, and Abraham Hatfield, 11th Ward Inspector." This was signed by

No. 1. William Wells. No. 2. Hyatt Lyon.
3. David Johnson. 4. Leonard Smith.
5. Nathaniel Cromer. 6. Mathew Vogel.

The Board recommended the taking off the back rent, which amounted to $394.50 up to May 1st, 1832.

After this period but two changes were made in the occupancy of these stands; they were on No. 3, Felix Quin, and on No. 6, William D. Atkins.

In 1835 a Committee reported the completion of the "Union Market," and soon after the stand-holders of this market were transferred into the Union Market, and this market building was taken for other public purposes until taken down.

'CLINTON MARKET."

1827. THE building of a market-house on the present site of the " Clinton Market" was strongly agitated many years before it was consummated. In 1821 an unfavorable report was presented to the Board from a Committee, which, for a time, allayed the hopes of many memorialists who wished it established at that early date. This report stated, " that the Common Council had lately been compelled to take measures for the removal of the ' Fly Market,' at the enormous expense of $200,000, exclusive of the expenses which may arise out of that measure other than the cost of the market;" and that one of the principal reasons assigned for that removal was, " that it stood over a sewer." " Your Committee cannot perceive why the presence of the mammoth sewer of Canal Street should not be as valid an objection against building a market on the site alluded to as the little sewer under the Fly Market was a good reason for removing it." They " cannot but think it would be the most extreme folly to carry into effect the project of the memorialists, that individual speculations ought not to be encouraged by misapplication of public money, and the building a market in the Canal Street Basin would be, under existing circumstances, any other than a wanton waste of public treasure; they therefore recommend the following resolution: That it is inexpedient to comply with the prayer of the memorialists."

In the early part of the year 1826, at a meeting of the Board, a Committee reported in favor of locating a new market-house on the present site of the " Clinton Market;" but it being intercepted by a numerously signed petition of about 650 citizens, who wished it to be erected near the North River, at the foot of Hubert and Laight Streets, was the means of deferring it, as the latter place was not favorably received. However, in the end, the present site was adopted, after the Legislature had passed a law to take possession of these grounds. The next year the plans were reported and adopted. They " propose to erect a new market-house between Spring, West, Washington, and Canal Streets, embracing 190 feet on Washington, 191 feet 10 inches on Spring, 50 feet on West, and 280 feet on Canal Streets, containing 23,154 square feet." " The cost will not be one-fourth of the cost of Fulton Market, and the income deriving from this market will doubtless justify all the expense that will be required in its erection;" and they resolve "that from and after the establishment of the said proposed market, the old (*Spring Street*) market be discontinued and taken down." In the month of August of that year a jury was summoned by the Sheriff, consisting of Joseph Ireland, A. P. Maybie, and James N. Wells, to value the property taken for the erection of this market. They reported the total amount to be $38,400; and the next year, in the month of April, the proposed cost (of $20,450) was presented, but it was thought it could be built by contract for a less sum, when it was resolved to advertise for contracts, to be built under the direction of the Market Committee. This was done, the market-house commenced, and on the 8th of December a resolution was adopted, giving it the name of "Clinton Market," after the former Governor, De Witt Clinton.

Early in 1829 it was finished, and a resolution was passed "to sell at public auction twenty-four butchers' stands, beginning at No. 15 and ending at No. 38, to be advertised as follows: "*Public Sale.*— On Tuesday next, April 14, 1829, at twelve o'clock, in one of the public Court-rooms in the City Hall, under the direction of the Market Committee, twenty-four stands in the new market recently erected on the North River, known as Clinton Market. *Terms and conditions* made known on the day of sale."

These "terms and conditions" were stated by the auctioneer, who commenced the sale; and after the sale of the first stand, no bids of any amount could be obtained; one stand stood at $15 a long time." The butchers were anxious to know what they were buying—" whether a lease of a stand *for one year*, or a right, which shall be now guaranteed to them for their disposal, or, in case of death, be for the benefit of his family; and also to be protected in their business?"

Alderman Cebra, the Chairman of the Market Committee, got upon the platform with the auctioneer, and stated, "that if the butchers did not bid freely the sale would be stopped, as the stands must sell for sufficient to pay for building the market." He at the same time stated, "that they need have no fear in bidding liberally, as *no meat* was hereafter to be sold south of Fourteenth Street, except in the public markets; and by purchasing a stand, it would be a living for them, and their children after them."

Upon this announcement being made, all the stands were bid off very rapidly, at prices varying from $700 to $3,000 each, to the following purchasers:

No. 15.	Samuel Hill,	$1,220	No. 16.	Charles Lozier,	$1,510
17.	Isaac Valentine,	840	18.	James H. Haws,	810
19.	James Reeves, Sr.,	810	20.	William Haight,	700

No. 21. Tho. E. Broadway, $1,000
No. 22. James Reeves, Jr., $1,090
23. Abraham Lozier, 2,700
24. Jacob Syler, 3,000
25. Arnest Fink, 2,600
26. John A. Fink, 3,000
27. Jacob Vogel, 1,010
28. Thomas Varian, 1,600
29. Samuel Piercy, 940
30. John Sharp, 1,130
31. William Austin, 900
32. John Miller, 1,010
33. Solomon Kipp, 1,000
34. Alex'r Underhill, 950
35. Adolphus Odell, 950
36. James Boyd, 1,020
37. Lawrence Martin, 2,150
38. William Hyatt, 2,310

The total amount adding up to the enormous sum of $34,250

All the purchasers paid down the ten per cent. of *premium* money, as was required by the terms of the sale, and were allowed to commence business on the follòwing Saturday, (18th of April.) Several of the butchers soon after gave acceptable notes for the balance of the premium, while others could not; others, again, were not satisfied with the Common Council in not immediately performing their promises, among which was the stopping the sale of meats below Fourteenth Street. So that, at the meeting of the Board held June 15 following, the Market Committee reported that but " thirteen of the butchers have complied with the terms of sale;" and the Board " *Resolved*, That butchers' licenses be granted to the above thirteen butchers, upon the usual terms, and to such others as comply with the terms of sale."

We find several of them forfeited their *ten per cent.* paid down, and vacated; and some, again, transferred their rights to others, which was made acceptable to the Common Council.

It, however, appeared that the business was not really sufficient to sustain so large a number, being double the number that occupied the "old Spring Street Market;" so, on the 7th of December following, the butchers petitioned for relief, and the Committee reported in favor of a reduction of twenty-five per cent. from the premium notes. This proved no relief; the Corporation had not fulfilled their promises, and the butchers claimed that they had no right, *in equity*, to ask them to fulfill theirs. Thus matters stood for two years, when several had left their stands; and others could not pay up, or even *twenty per cent.*, when demanded. The City Collector, however, by threats of prosecution, succeeded in collecting from some in full; others renewed their notes; and others, again, declined paying, until the Corporation performed their promises. The latter were proceeded against, and obliged to settle up, or were deprived of all which they had paid, which in some instances was of large amounts.

In the month of April, 1830, the following persons received permits to occupy stands as hucksters: Ann Parkman, Mary Shears, Elizabeth Anderson, Elizabeth Allison, Eliza Hunt, Sarah Murphy, Eliza Young, and Ann Bray.

Soon after, a building for a country market had been petitioned for, which brought a report from a committee, which was adopted, on the 22d October, 1833, to use the triangular block of ground bounded by Canal, Hoboken, West, and Washington Streets, for that purpose. It was the property of the city, having been filled up and gained from the North River many years before, and at this period it was used for public purposes. A part for a place of deposit for fuel, to supply the necessities of the poor during the winter, and the other part with paving-stone.

A resolution was passed to appropriate this ground for a country market, "for the accommodation of persons bringing articles, the produce of their farms, for sale." But the building of the market-house was not proceeded with until the latter part of the next year, as we find a resolution passed in the month of September, "that a market-house be built on these grounds, to extend the whole length of the Canal Street line, in conformity to the plans;" and "that the sum of three thousand five hundred dollars be, and the same is hereby, appropriated for carrying the foregoing resolution into effect." A further sum of nine hundred and fifty-five dollars was appropriated for the same purpose on the 24th of November following. It was soon after erected, and for many years after, on certain days of the week, was filled with country people and their productions, with great satisfaction to its patrons; and no doubt this addition, with the performance of the duties of that energetic Corporation Attorney, the late N. B. Blunt, had much improved the business here. He was ever successful, and all delinquents feared his sudden and overpowering attacks in sustaining those laws. He honored the office more than the office honored him.

Previous to the erection of this country market, in the month of April, a resolution was passed to sell at public auction, on the 29th inst., stands Nos. 1, 2, 3, and 4, and possession of them on the 1st of May following. The sale took place, and stand No. 1 was sold to William Anderson, for the sum of $4,200, with a rent of $100; No. 2 to Walter Anderson, for $3,600, rent $100; No. 3 to Arnest Fink, Jr., $2,000, with $60 rent; and No. 4 to William Lawrence, for $1,380, with a rent also of $60—making a total of $11,180 *cash paid* for four stands, was certainly a large amount, although Nos. 1 and 2 were thought to be the best stands in this or any other market, being both corners on Canal Street, and the nearest to the country market. This amount, added with the first sale, would make a total of $37,470 paid for twenty-eight stands, with a fixed yearly rent on each stand besides. This amount, within a trifle, would pay what the whole grounds*cost; leaving nothing but the interest of the cost of the buildings and repairs, to be annually paid, to keep it from being a tax on the city.

There were yet *ten* vacant stands left, between Nos. 4 and 15, located on the Washington Street side, which numerous applications were made for through petition, and the Market Committee had the subject up before them at various intervals, of the propriety of disposing of them by auction; the matter, however, was deferred until the premium system had become unpopular, and in 1837, on the 2d of February, they made arrangements to have them drawn for; " which was done openly, and in the presence of such of the butchers as wished to be present, and, as the Committee believe, to their entire satisfaction." In the month of June they "*Resolved*, That his Honor the Mayor be requested to issue butchers' licenses to the following persons in Clinton Market, viz.:

" No. 5. Daniel Sammis. No. 6. William H. Crary.
7. John H. Groshon. 8. Alexander Berryman.
9. George Starr. 10. Edward Norris.
11. Samuel Pheasant. 12. James Day.
13. James Darby. 14. Richard Valentine.

"*Resolved*, That the above-named butchers pay two months' rent forthwith; such renting to be for one year only, from the 1st of May, 1837."

In 1840 the stands were occupied by the following persons:

No. 1. Thomas E. Broadway. No. 2. Jacob R. Reed.
3. Robert Beaty. 4. Henry M. Valentine.
5. Christopher Allen. 6. William H. McCreery.
7. Morris Haight. 8. Alexander Berryman.
9. George Starr. 10. Vacant.
11. Samuel Pheasant. 12. James Day.
13. James Darby. 14. James Valentine.
15. Samuel P. Patterson. 16. Charles Lozier.
17. Isaac Valentine. 18. Edwin Roblin.
19. William Valleau. 20. George Gillet.
21. Edmund Broadway. 22. James Reeves, Jun'r.
23. Henry Cook. 24. Theodore L. Fink.
25. Arnest Fink. 26. Jacob H. Fink.
27. Alexander Underhill. 28. Edward Phillips.
29. Lawrence Wiseburn. 30. George H. Keyser.
31. George A. Wilt. 32. Alfred Smith.

No. 33. Charles Reeves.　　　No. 34. Lyman Seely.
　　35. Adolphus Odell.　　　　36. William Haight.
　　37. Lawrence Martin.　　　　38. William E. Hyatt.

The market laws, for many years, had attracted considerable attention, both for and against them; and although the premium system of selling stands had been given up, and the gift or drawing of stands had been established, yet some of the principal public officers thought or concluded it unpopular to prosecute the offenders, and would not perform their duty. This, no doubt, assisted in calling forth the following petition from the licensed butchers, dated January, 1837:

"That your petitioners hold and occupy stands or stalls in the public markets of the City of New York, which have been heretofore granted to them by the Corporation of the City, and for which stands your petitioners have paid large sums of money into the City Treasury in rents and premiums.

"That your petitioners, in the occupancy of said stands, and in the conducting and management of their business as licensed butchers, are subject to various laws, ordinances, and regulations which the Corporation of the City has from time to time found it necessary or expedient to establish for the public benefit and convenience, and which your petitioners are bound to observe under heavy penalties, and the risk of forfeiture of their stands and licenses.

"That believing these laws and ordinances, although in many instances subjecting your petitioners to great expense and inconvenience, are calculated and intended to promote the interests of the public and to secure the citizens an abundant and reasonable supply of sound and wholesome provisions, your petitioners have at all times submitted thereto without complaint.

"That the most prominent of these laws forbids the sale of butchers' meat at any place or places in the city except the public markets; upon which law the whole of our system of public markets depends, and upon faith of the observance and enforcement whereof many of your petitioners were induced (under the former regulations for the sale of stands) to pay large sums to the Corporation for the stands they still occupy, and to embark their means in their present business. But your petitioners have seen with the utmost astonishment that this salutary law has been permitted to be evaded from year to year, with so little attention on the part of the constituted authorities of the city, notwithstanding the repeated remonstrances of your petitioners, that it is at length openly violated and disregarded, and meat-shops are now established in almost every part of the city with perfect impunity. That these shops, being out of the control and in open defiance of the public authorities, and not under the inspection of public officers, or the wholesome restraints of competition, are calculated to become the vehicles of vending bad and unwholesome provisions, and the flesh of animals which have died from accident or disease, and which could not be exhibited in the public markets and exposed to experienced observers without detection. And your petitioners further show, that an attempt has been made to enlist the sympathies of the public on behalf of the occupants of these shops, by the allegation that all butchers who are unable to purchase stands are excluded from the public markets, although it is well known to all engaged in the business that the selling of butchers' stands has been discontinued by the Corporation, and that all the new stands in the public markets, appropriated during the last year, according to the system now established, were granted to the holders without premiums, and that all butchers of respectable character were given an equal chance for the vacant places.

"And your petitioners further show, that the occupants of the meat-shops prefer their illicit trade to an open and fair competition in the public markets, where the quality of their meats and the fairness of their dealings would be subject to inspection, and be brought into comparison with others; and if these shops were suppressed, the vacant stands, of which there are a great number in the public markets, could be filled without injury to your petitioners, and with increased benefit to the public. And your petitioners further show, that inasmuch as these vacant stands would be granted, according to the present system, without premiums, the occupants would not be under as heavy expenses as the keepers of shops who pay rents; the rent of the market stands being from ten to one hundred dollars, while the shop rents vary from one hundred to four hundred dollars per annum. And your petitioners further show, that they have viewed with the deepest regret the encouragement given to these open violations of the law by individuals in our public bodies, who have in many instances interposed to prevent the enforcement of the law, while the individuals complained of were still setting the institutions of the city at defiance.

"That your petitioners, while engaged in the lawful exercise of their business, and submitting to those regulations which the Fathers of our City have seen fit to establish for the public good, have been assailed with obloquy and abuse by those who have grown bold enough in their impunity to claim as a right what they first practiced by stealth, and who stigmatize as aristocrats and monopolists those citizens who respect the laws which they are daily violating. Your petitioners do not deem it necessary to answer these absurd charges; if they are monopolists, so are all our citizens whose occupations are the subject of regulations for the benefit of the whole community.

"Neither do your petitioners deem it necessary to set forth the advantages derived by the community from the establishment of public markets, in opposition to private shops. The open and direct competition of the whole trade, as well as the incidental competition of the country people, and the variety of supplies of all kinds which the public markets bring together, have always been considered as best calculated to keep down the prices of provisions to the lowest state which the general demand and supply of the whole city will admit, and no possible advantage can be gained by the community in destroying the public markets, and preventing this wholesome competition. Nor can any just ground of complaint be set up by the keepers of shops, that they are excluded from the markets, while a large number of vacant stands could be filled advantageously if these shops were suppressed, and which can be obtained upon much cheaper terms than the shops themselves, by any persons of good character, who are qualified for licenses. Your petitioners therefore pray that the laws and ordinances of the Corporation to regulate the public markets, and the sale of butchers' meat, may be enforced, and that the meat-shops throughout the city may be suppressed; that Superintendents of the Public Markets may be appointed, whose duty it shall be to enforce the market laws generally, and more particularly those relating to the sale of butchers' meat out of the public markets; and that these Superintendents may be compensated by a suitable salary, but not by any portion of the fines and penalties to be received upon prosecutions, of which, in the opinion of your petitioners, they should be entirely independent; and that, upon the suppression of such shops, that the unoccupied stands in the public markets may be granted to such persons as may be duly qualified, without premiums, in the manner recently pursued by the Market Committee—giving all applicants of good character an equal chance."

No relief, however, was obtained by the licensed butchers. Sometimes some of the members of the Board would attempt assistance, but it was either for show, or they were not encouraged by their associates. Several resolutions were introduced before the Board, by different members, on the 16th of December, 1839, which were intended for relief; they were, however, laid over; they appear as follows: "*Resolved*, That it is expedient to amend the ordinances relative to public markets in such manner as to permit meat to be sold in other places than the public markets, and so that persons may bring into and sell in any of the public markets meat, beef, mutton, veal, or lamb not killed in the city, although not raised or slaughtered on their own farms, subject to such inspection or regulation as may be prescribed.

"*Resolved*, That such provisions shall be made as may be reasonable and just for the repaying of those butchers who may have paid *premiums* to the Corporation for stalls within the last ten years, such parts of said premiums as they may be justly entitled to."

"*Resolved*, That the Market Committee be requested to report such amendments to the *ordinances* relative to the public markets as will extend the privilege to licensed butchers to sell at other places than the public markets, under suitable regulations, and as shall give just and adequate relief to such butchers as may have paid premiums to the Corporation for stalls purchased by them."

"*Resolved*, That the Comptroller be, and is hereby, authorized to refund all money, with interest, which has been paid into the City Treasury for premiums on butchers' stands in the public markets, and that *one hundred and fifty thousand dollars* be, and is hereby, appropriated for that purpose."

"*Resolved*, That it is expedient so to amend the market laws as to permit sales of meat at private stalls; and that the amount paid by the licensed butchers for the purchase of their stalls be refunded to them, and said stalls be rented yearly, by public auction."

These were referred, reported upon, and again, in the month of January, 1840, at another meeting, it was

"*Resolved*, That the report of the Market Committee of the 2d inst., together with the accompanying documents, and the resolutions presented to this Board on the 16th inst., on the subject of markets, be referred to a Select Committee of five members from each Board."

"*Resolved*, That it be referred to the Joint Special Committee, appointed in relation to the market laws, to inquire into and report upon the expediency of submitting the repeal of the existing market regulations to the people at the ensuing election, with a condition of fully indemnifying the butchers for the amount of moneys paid by them into the City Treasury for premium stands, and that the question be decided by the electors, by voting *yes* or *no*."

This Select Committee of ten from both Boards, on the 2d of March following, reported on the above resolutions as follows:

" REPORT.—The subject referred to your Committee is one that seriously affects the interests of our constituents! The public health, the comfort and convenience of our constituents, and the revenue of the city, are matters of too much importance to be subjects of careless or hasty legislation. Your Committee have therefore maturely considered the whole question in its leading aspects, and respectfully state the following as the facts which have appeared before them, and the conclusions to which they have arrived.

"The whole number of markets in the city is twelve; the value of which in fee is about one million of dollars. The revenue annually accruing from market rents, butchers' licenses, and sources of a similar character, may be safely estimated at about the sum of sixty thousand dollars. It is true that the whole amount of these rents is not regularly or punctually collected, and that many of the occupants of stalls have refused the payment of their rents in consequence of the numerous violations of the market laws, which they state exist to such an extent as to deprive them of their usual and ordinary business, whereby they have heretofore been enabled to pay their rents; and that the officers under the Corporation, whose especial duty it is to complain of such violations and prosecute the same to judgment, have either neglected or refused to protect them against these violations. The greater part of the sum thus accruing from markets either has, or (there is reason to believe) in a short period of time will be collected into the public treasury.

"The annual expense of maintaining the present markets, including the salaries of the officers charged with their superintendence and other necessary expenses, may be stated at about eighteen thousand dollars, which will leave the net revenue of the markets about forty-two thousand dollars per annum.

"The questions to which the Committee particularly directed their attention were the following: Have the Common Council, under the Constitution of the State and the Charter of the City, any right to enact laws similar to those now in force for the regulation of the public markets? How would the repeal of the existing laws affect the public health and convenience, or pecuniary interests of the city?

"The first question raised by this Committee has been fully and ably discussed in the report of the Market Committee of December 2d, 1839. With the views of that Committee the undersigned (after a careful investigation, and under the impression that the arguments therein contained might be found untenable,) are constrained fully to concur. The exercise of the power is almost universally admitted in this country, as in other enlightened governments, to be necessary for the protection of the public health, by preventing the nuisances of badly-regulated slaughter-houses in crowded parts of a large city, and by preventing the sale of unwholesome meats.

"It is unnecessary to enter into a full discussion of the effect on an unregulated pursuit of the business of butchers upon the public health and convenience. The experience of many cities has given rise to the creation of legal restraints upon the exercise of that business, (which in themselves considered appear arbitrary,) but have proved the necessity of some judicious restraints in all densely-populated communities. The restraints upon the exercise of any business should not be greater than public necessity requires. In this case some restrictions are undoubtedly necessary; and could an amendment to the existing system be proposed which would adequately secure the public interests in this material respect, and at the same time increase the accommodation of the public and give a greater opportunity to others to enter into the business of butchers, it would meet the approval of your Committee. No amendment, however, that fully meets the views of your Committee has been proposed, and the subject is surrounded with so many difficulties that your Committee are not prepared to suggest one to the Common Council.

" Your Committee entertain no doubt that the existing market laws are not in violation of the Charter of the City, or the Constitution of the State, although in some particulars they appear to be oppressive; yet it is confidently believed that the Common Council and all good citizens will agree with the Committee, that under the existing difficulties in which this subject is involved, and by a careful perusal of the arguments to which your Committee would respectfully call their attention, so far as it relates to the public finances, that no material alteration can now be made without a violation of the faith of the city to the public creditors.

" The debt of the City of New York is at this time large, and, by necessity, must be gradually increased, until the final completion of the Croton Water-Works. Under these circumstances, your Committee believe it to be the duty of the Common Council to take all legal and proper measures in their power to protect the public from further burdens. The taxes of the city are now sufficiently onerous to create much anxiety in the public mind. The ordinary revenues of the city, independently of taxation, are not adequate to the payment of its current expenses, and will not be sufficient for that purpose for many years. Whatever portion of the revenue other than the annual taxes is taken away, a deficiency in the annual receipts will be created, which can be supplied only by a resort to new loans, or to taxation. The annual net revenue from markets, as hereinbefore stated, amounts to about forty-two thousand dollars. That a repeal of the existing market laws will have the effect of greatly diminishing, and perhaps entirely destroying that branch of the public revenue, your Committee entertain no doubt.

" Independently of the necessary evils of a diminished revenue, to which your Committee have already adverted, it is a matter of great doubt whether the Common Council have not placed it beyond their power to repeal the existing market laws. By reference to Title 2 of Chapter 17 of the Laws and Ordinances of the Common Council, entitled 'A Law providing for the Redemption of the City Debt,' it will be seen that 'the net proceeds of all sales of real estate which belonged to the Corporation on the first day of January, 1825, and sold since that date, or hereafter to be sold, and all moneys heretofore received, or hereafter to be received, for market fees and market rents, are pledged, appropriated, and applied to, and constituted and form, a fund, called "The Sinking Fund of the City of New York," until the whole of the present stocks of the city shall be finally and fully redeemed.' Also, by reference to Title 3 of the same Chapter, amendatory of the aforesaid law, it will be seen that 'the Commissioners of the Sinking Fund are authorized to invest so much as may be necessary of the balance of the said fund standing to their credit, or which may stand to their credit hereafter on the books of the Comptroller, in the purchase of a piece of land in the Eleventh Ward, between North and Second Streets, and in the purchase of land for extending and improving the Grand Street, Essex, and Centre Markets; and the whole of the rents, fees, and income of the said markets, in their improved state, and land thus purchased, is hereby appropriated and pledged for the payment of principal and interest of the sum that shall be thus *drawn* from the said fund.'

" As these ordinances were severally passed prior to the creation of the stocks, the Committee deem the faith of the city as pledged to the holders of the stock; and that all the proceeds of the sales of real estate, and the moneys received for premiums, rents, and fees of the several markets, should be applied to the extinguishment of the debt; and that no part of these revenues can be taken from that fund, justly or legally, for other purposes.

" If this view of the subject is correct, no premiums can be refunded to the butchers from the revenues of the markets, and no portion of the premiums received can be withdrawn from that fund, as it has been expended in the purchase of other lands, and the erection of other market-places; and this, again, pledged back to the sinking fund. Whatever amount it may be necessary to repay them, in case the present market laws are repealed, must be procured by loan or taxation; none of the public property can be sold for that purpose, as it is all pledged to the public creditors; and until their claims are satisfied, no money can or ought to be raised from that source for other purposes. Your Committee believe that it is generally admitted that, provided the present market system is abolished, the butchers ought to be paid the whole, or a fair and equitable proportion, of the amounts they have severally paid into the City Treasury. If the Corporation would not legally, they would in equity, be bound to refund some portion, if not all, the moneys received in that way. If this be so, to effect the proposed repeal, or make any important amendments to the law, in which damage would be sustained by the butchers, a new debt must be created, or additional taxes must be imposed upon the people.

"The market revenues and real estate of the city, including market-houses and the ground on which they stand, are pledged, as hereinbefore stated, by a solemn act of the Common Council, as security for the public debt. With the wisdom or propriety of this course your Committee have nothing to do. The contract has been made, and your Committee have only to inquire at this time how far that contract is binding on the city.

"The debt secured by this pledge of real estate and the revenues of the markets was contracted in the exercise of the ordinary and legal powers of the Common Council. This debt cannot be repudiated by the Common Council, nor can they in justice to themselves, without the consent of the public creditors, withdraw the security which has been offered on the one part and accepted on the other, nor do your Committee believe the Corporation can equitably do any act which will tend to decrease the value of the security. That a reduction in the amount of revenue from markets, and a decrease in the value of the real estate devoted to market purposes would have that effect, is evident. The faith of the city cannot be violated without the consent of the people.

"These are important considerations, and your Committee have no doubt that the public, upon a full consideration of the matter, will submit to any inconvenience which many of them deem they suffer under the existing system, rather than cause an additional burden of tax to be imposed upon themselves, or submit to a violation of any contract with the public creditors made by their former representatives.

"Some members of your Committee were informed that the journeymen and apprentice butchers were advocates for a repeal of the market laws. This Board and the public will be enabled to judge of the correctness of this information from the petition hereunto annexed, received by your Committee while in session, signed by three hundred and eighteen of the journeymen and apprentice butchers, (being all in the city, with the exception of two or three, as your Committee are informed,) which is as following, to wit:

" 'The petition of the journeymen and apprentice butchers *respect-fully represents*—That your Honorable Body, some fifty or sixty years since, enacted laws regulating the public markets, and under the authority of that law established such rules and regulations as were deemed necessary to their perfect operation; one of which rules exacted an apprenticeship of seven years, but since modified to four years, to qualify your petitioners to obtain a stand in any of the said markets; and your petitioners have been further assured by every consecutive Board, that said rules and regulations should be continued, have been seriously induced by said assurances to learn the business, and have now arrived at that time of life at which they had a right to believe, under said assurances, their rights would not be violated; and although we are now without stands, we are not without hope that the time is fast approaching when we can obtain them honorably, and commence our business, either without asking your Honorable Body to violate or abolish, as we believe, the best-regulated public markets in the world, or feel a disposition to do so ourselves; and we further believe that those who are now engaged in shops, and are continually soliciting your Honorable Body to abolish said laws and regulations, would not hesitate to ask you to break down every barrier and destroy every guard that the law has erected for the preservation of peace, health, and morality, to con-summate their wishes.

" ' We therefore respectfully request your Honorable Body to sus-tain the market laws as they now are, believing that the public good would be best served thereby.   New York, 5th February, 1840.'

" The Committee deem it proper to state, that when they first en-tered upon the discharge of the duty assigned them, a majority of their number were of the opinion that some amendments might be made to the existing system, which would be satisfactory to our citi-zens, secure the public interests, and be acceptable to the butchers; under the peculiar circumstances of the case, however, and in view of all the arguments presented, your Committee deem it advisable to recommend to the Common Council, that until some other ar-rangements can be made to pay the existing public debt, they will refrain from any legislation which may be construed as a violation of the public faith, or which may expose our citizens to new and un-expected burdens, and possibly endanger the health of our city.   The system of disposing of stalls in the public markets for premiums your Committee believe to be erroneous.   Had markets been erect-ed of a less size, and at less expense than those now in existence; had they been increased in number and more equally distributed throughout the city, the public convenience would have been greatly advanced; and in addition to this, had the stands (instead of being sold for premiums) been disposed of at short intervals, by leasing them at public auction to the highest bidder, more opportunities would have been offered to those desirous of procuring stalls for the transaction of business, greater competition in the sale of meats, and the revenues of the markets increased rather than diminished.

"Your Committee would call the attention of the Common Council to this branch of the subject, if any legislation in relation thereto, at the present time, would result in any improvement without materially affecting the public treasury, or violating the faith of the city to the public creditors, or the holders of the premium stalls. The Committee, in conclusion, respectfully recommend the adoption of the first and second resolutions accompanying the Report of the Market Committee, hereunto annexed. Signed by the Committee."

Two years after (1842) the subject of paying back to the butchers the amounts by them paid as premiums came up again, but this time it was referred to the then Comptroller, D. D. Williamson, who not only reported unfavorably to the paying back of the premiums, but also says, the butchers "have no claim on the city, either in law or equity, for a reduction of rent, or for a return of money heretofore paid by them as premiums for a choice of stands in any of the public markets."

This report of Williamson's was deemed both unreasonable and illiberal, according to the evidence presented. However, one of the occupant butchers on No. 28, Edward Phillips, prepared the following in answer to the Comptroller's Report, which was read by Alderman Davis at a subsequent meeting of the Board. This appears addressed:

"To ALDERMAN DAVIS:

"*Dear Sir*—In the interview I had the pleasure of having with you on the subject of the memorial adopted at a meeting of the butchers, in relation to presenting the same to the Honorable the Board of Aldermen, you then stated to me that the subject of markets and market laws was a subject on which you had thought but little, but was desirous to hear all that could be said for and against, that you might be better enabled to make up your opinion understandingly; and believing the Report of the Comptroller calculated to prejudice your mind against the memorialists, above referred to, unless some of its absurdities should be pointed out, is the only apology I shall offer for troubling you with this scrawl at present.

"What the Comptroller says in relation to the reduction of

rents I should pass by in silence, were it not for some statements, which I am at a loss to account for the manner in which they found their way in said Report, unless they have been received through second hands. But then, sir, from the high opinion I have entertained for the Comptroller, I am still at a loss to account for the use of language as follows: 'It is well known that the butchers have refused, and still refuse, to pay rent,' &c. Now, sir, when this Report made its appearance, the butchers of Clinton Market were called together for the purpose of hearing said Report read; and among that whole assemblage there was none found who had refused to pay rent, while many are ready to testify that the former Collector—*and far be it from me, sir, to disturb the ashes of the dead* —repeatedly told them they ought not to pay while shops were permitted unmolested. He then goes on to say the Attorney of the Corporation had often been foiled in his efforts to sustain the market laws, and assigns the causes that produced the failure, and then proceeds with an attempt of odium on the butchers for not leaving their business to become informers against violators of the market laws, by asking, with some degree of triumph, as it appears, who ever saw a licensed butcher in evidence against meat-shops, &c. Now, sir, the fact is notorious, and I am surprised at such a statement coming from the Comptroller, that butchers have time and time again, not only individually, but collectively, complained of these violations of laws, and have appeared in court as witnesses in behalf of the city—but, sir, the Attorney has been foiled, this we acknowledge—but deny that his failures are attributable to the causes stated in the Report. The facts in the case are notorious, and I would refer you to Mr. TOMLINSON, who has tried the most of these cases for the last three years, who will state to you, as he has to me, that the causes which have created prejudices in the public mind against markets are, first, by the selling of stalls in the manner as the public understand it. *The Comptroller's opinion to the contrary notwithstanding*—your markets have become private instead of public markets, and as such ought not to be sustained. This, sir, together with the custom long in practice, that all persons must first serve an apprenticeship at the business before they were permitted to hold licenses for the purpose of carrying on the same, are the monopoly features connected with your market laws; and I think the Comptroller might have informed himself, had he taken a little trouble to inquire what public sentiment is on this subject. But the Report goes on to say that the butchers have not taken out licenses for the last four years, and are therefore not in a situation to claim protection. Now, sir, what are the facts in this case? It is true that the first license received costs one dollar, and but twenty-five cents for every renewal; whilst it was for many years customary for the Superintendents of Markets to come to the different markets at the expiration of each license year, with a renewal of the same; and I think, yea, I know, the Comptroller can point to no period when such renewal, presented as above stated, has been refused. Then, sir, it is not the fault of the butchers that they have not had their licenses renewed, but the fault of the city authorities, whose duty, it appears to me, was first to continue the custom established by themselves, or to give notice of the adoption of some new regulation. The Report goes on to say that the age has gone by when a market monopoly will be tolerated. This, sir, I fully agree with, and would only refer you to the memorial adopted at the meeting of the butchers, to show you that such is the opinion of a large majority of them. But the Report recommends a change in the manner of collecting the revenue from the markets. This, sir, I also believe to be preferable, for two reasons: 1st. In order that your markets should be what they ought to be—public markets—where all and every person may go to vend their meats, and by the adoption of this system will pay in proportion to the amount of business they do; and 2d. That this system, carried out, will produce a greater amount of revenue than ever has yet been received from public markets. But the Comptroller now, sir, assigns a reason for the payment of fees—that all persons vending meats should be amenable to the city authorities, in order that the community should have good and wholesome meats, and should not be liable, as he more than *intimates*, to the imposition which is now practiced, in the manner meat-shops now exist. But it strikes me, sir, that the Comptroller did not, when he penned that part of his Report, see that he was *advancing* one of the strongest arguments in favor of public markets, or he would, judging from the general spirit of his Report, have omitted it. But here, sir, there is not a hint dropped as to how this security, which he admits to be so necessary, shall be preserved to the community, by the system of shop-butchers. No, sir, not even a suggestion; and, as I think, sir, wisely, too; for if the health of the community requires all the security contained in the Report here referred to—and I, knowing something of the business of a butcher, believe it does—I would ask, and ask, sir, with some emphasis, how it is possible to receive it with so much safety as by the system of public markets, where the public have not only the security of a public officer, whose duty it is to inspect all that is there *exposed* for sale; but, my word for it, they have still a better security in the fact that it is there brought in competition with whole-

some meats—which fact alone would deter any who are base enough
to vend meats, died of disease, privately, as they have now an opportunity to do. Here they could not escape detection; while it is
here, and here alone, sir, that the community has what the Comptroller thinks they stand so much in need of, and which I can, from
facts within my knowledge, subscribe to.

"But, sir, perhaps all that I have said in relation to reduction of
rents might have been omitted, as such reduction was not asked for
by the memorialists, and I assure you, sir, would have been, were it
not, as I stated in the outset, for some statements there made calculated to mislead a mind, as, sir, I have every reason to believe
you was honestly seeking for truth on this subject. But, sir, in relation to refunding the amount paid into the City Treasury for premiums, we have from the Comptroller strong language, by saying,
1st. Has the Corporation sold any stall or stand to the butchers?
I answer, No. And 2d. Has any butcher ever paid for any stand
in the public markets? I answer, No. And finally conclude the
whole by giving his OPINION that they have no claim on the city,
either in law or equity. Now, sir, to propound a question of law, I
acknowledge my entire incompetency, and will therefore leave that
with the learned Comptroller. But, sir, when some of the facts in
relation to the matter, now pending before the Honorable the
Board of Aldermen, are stated—and facts, sir, which the Comptroller himself could not be ignorant of—I am at a loss to account
for the school of morals in which the Comptroller learned the
meaning of the word 'equity.' For Walker defines it justice,
right, honorable. And now, sir, I will confine what few remarks I
have to make to Clinton Market, believing this will be sufficient to
give you a general idea of the whole. Then, sir, to the facts.
Some fifteen years ago—for I shall not be particular about dates—
there stood at the foot of Spring Street, in the centre of the street,
one small market-house, running from Greenwich Street to the
river, built by the inhabitants, and ceded to the Corporation, which
afforded ample accommodation for twelve butchers and hucksters;
but it is true these butchers went in said market by having their
stalls granted them prior to the passage of that law for the putting
up at public auction. Well, sir, in this state, the wants of the
neighborhood, in the wisdom of the Common Council, required a
larger market, which resulted in the erection of Clinton Market.
Now, sir, when this was completed, the butchers then standing in
the old market-house asked for places to be assigned them there to
do their business; but they were told that the old market-house
would be torn down, and if they wanted to carry on their business

they must buy a stand in competition with others; that the law prohibited the sale of meats south of Fourteenth Street elsewhere than in public markets, and that said law would be enforced. And now, sir, for the result: these twelve butchers, with twelve others, making twenty-four, bought the number of stalls that was then sold, when, some three years after, the Common Council sold four more, making in all twenty-eight stalls. Now, admitting the bills then posted did state that the good-will or choice of stands, as the Comptroller understands it, would be sold for one year, for it is so long since I read them, I have forgot how they did read. I say admit, and what is proved, for certainly it appears to me, first, that the butchers were driven out of the place where they were doing business by the very power that placed them there. 2d. They were compelled to purchase a stand, in order to carry on their business, on such terms as the Common Council pleased to propose, as the law prohibited them from selling meat south of Fourteenth Street except in public markets. And, sir, I think you will perceive, from this simple statement, that the butchers have been, in all this premium business, mere creatures of the power of the Corporation, and in no instance were permitted to act their own will, if they would carry on their business. And now, in the face of all these facts:

" 1st. Being driven from their place of business;

" 2d. Compelled to go to another place under such rules and regulations as the Common Council pleased to propose, and these terms involving the amount of money now asked to be refunded;

" 3d. After selling 28 stalls in Clinton Market for more than one-half of the whole amount received in the City Treasury for premiums; and,

" 4th. After such sales, to place 10 stalls in said market without paying any premiums, and these better stalls than many that were sold, thereby bringing those who were compelled to buy in unjust competition, as the rents of the stalls thus given away were no more annually than those who paid large premiums were compelled to pay:

" I say, sir, with these simple facts staring the Comptroller in the face, and they are not half that might be told, I am at loss to know the school of morals he was educated in, when he asserts we have no claim in equity. But, sir, it is not to the Comptroller that we are now looking for a redress of our grievances long complained of; it is to the Honorable the Board of Aldermen that we look. Yea, I may say that *all* eyes are looking for an honorable adjustment of this matter, and for a prominent disposition of your markets and market laws. Yours, with respect."

"When the above letter was read in the presence of the butchers of Clinton Market—for it was in compliance with their request it was written—they resolved unanimously that Alderman Davis be requested to cause the same to be read in the Board of Aldermen this (Monday) evening, December 12th, 1842, if the same be in accordance with his feelings, and not in violation of the rules of the Honorable the Board of Aldermen.

"After the above had been read before the Honorable the Board of Aldermen, at their meeting on Monday, 12th instant, the author regretted his omission to state one fact among the many he omitted, which should have been stated as a reply to another part of the Comptroller's Report, which deserves a passing notice, viz.: On page 413 of said Report, after asking, Has any butcher ever paid for any stands in the public markets? and answering it negatively, he goes on to state that the choice of stalls has been sold, and the premium for such choice has been received by the city and placed to the credit of the Commissioners of the Sinking Fund, and says, 'I challenge any butcher in the City of New York to show any right or title whatever, that he derived from such payment, except it was a license from the Mayor to occupy said stall for a year or a part of a year—it is all idle for any one to say that the city is to pay back or return any moneys thus received; it cannot come out of the Sinking Fund, and I trust the citizens will not allow themselves to be taxed $80,000 for this purpose.' Well, prior to the passage of the law before referred to, of selling the good-will or choice of stands, as the Comptroller understands it, it was the custom, as it now is, to grant stalls gratuitously; now, under these laws, A had a stall granted to him, or A held a license from under the Mayor to sell meat at a certain number Washington Market, at a yearly rent of $70. Well, B is compelled, under the laws that then existed, to buy a stall in Clinton Market, or to buy the choice of stands, as the Comptroller understands it, at a cost of $4,000 premium, subject to a rent of $100 per year. Well, B receives the same kind of a license as A received; after a lapse of a few years, from the general expression of public opinion, strengthened by the acts of the Common Council in relation to premium stalls such as B holds, A feels a desire to have his stall made a premium stall, and makes application to the Market Committee to know what amount of money they will charge to make his a premium stall; the Market Committee, after taking the matter into consideration, agree to take $500 or $1,000, as the case may be. Well, A pays the above-mentioned sum, the amount is handed over to the Comptroller, and A rejoices to himself that he now holds a premium stall. Well, does A receive any new right or title from, that which he held before? Most certainly not; he held the license from the Mayor before he paid the above sum. Well, does he pay the above sum for the choice of stands? No, for he was in quiet possession before; but does he pay any less rent in consequence? No, his rent is the same; well, perhaps some person may be ready to ask, For what, then, did A pay $500 or $1,000? Kind reader, if I answer you in the words of the Comptroller, I must say—for nothing! And yet the Comptroller says ' it is all idle for any one to say that the city is to pay back or return any moneys thus received—it cannot come out of the Sinking Fund; and I trust that the citizens will not allow themselves to be taxed $80,000 for that purpose.' But this case of A's I would not have the reader believe an individual case, by any means; for many such might be stated. Nor yet would I have undertaken a task to which I am so incapable to do justice, had not the public mind, in my opinion, at this particular time, while the subject of markets and market laws appears one of the most exciting topics of the day, needed some light, however feeble the effort might be to diffuse it."

In the month of January, 1844, we find again a report of the Committee on *Finance* and *Markets*, on a petition from the butchers of this market, for a return of the premiums, which stated as follows: They " considered the subject one of much importance; they have given it a careful and thorough investigation; but feeling satisfied of the impropriety of allowing the butchers of any one market to receive back the amount paid by them for premiums, without extending the benefit to all who are disposed to comply with the terms required, they have endeavored to ascertain what amount has been paid into the City Treasury from its source, and find that 137 stands have been sold, and the amount paid is seventy-seven thousand, five hundred and eighty dollars and seventy-six cents, in the following markets, viz.:

51 in Fulton Market,	- - - -	$2,222 88
12 in Washington,	- - - -	4,362 00
7 in Greenwich,	- - - - -	550 00
11 in Catharine,	- - - -	2,274 88
8 in Centre, -	- - - - -	15,721 00
8 in Essex,	- - - - -	4,500 00
28 in Clinton,	- - - - -	37,170 00
6 in Tompkins, -	- - - -	4,065 00
6 (9) in Jefferson, -	- - -	6,715 00

$77,580 76

"From an examination of the books in the Comptroller's office, no stands appear to have been sold for a premium in either Monroe, Franklin, (a mistake,) or Union Markets. It is impossible, however, to state with precise accuracy the amounts received, in consequence of the *imperfect* manner in which these accounts have been kept." To my knowledge, there were many others made premium stands not noticed in the above.

Another set of resolutions on the same subject were passed in the Board of Assistant Aldermen, in the month of May, 1845, as follows: "*Resolved,* That the Comptroller be directed to notify all persons owning stalls in the various markets for which *premiums* have been paid to the city to present the several amounts paid for the same, and when purchased. *Resolved,* That the Comptroller and Finance Committee of both Boards be directed to ascertain the amounts for which these various claims can be settled, and report the same to the Common Council."

All these reports, resolutions, &c., tend to show the justness of the claim of the butchers who paid premiums for these stands; which question is yet to be settled, and it is a large amount the Corporation obtained from the butchers by promises which they have never performed, although I admit they have tried; but failing to do so, they are bound in honor, equity, and law to appropriate immediately a sum large enough to pay this righteous claim back, that all standholders may be placed on the same footing with others who occupy stands in our public markets.

In 1848 it was represented that the business in this market had considerably increased in consequence of several market sloops making it their depot, which formerly landed their produce at other places. They wished more shed-room. "The open space on the southwest side, from the outer edge of the present inclosure, should be shedded over to the line of Canal Street." "They have ascertained that these can be erected at an expense not exceeding the sum of one thousand dollars;" which was passed, and the money appropriated.

This shed, after being finished, attracted the country people under it, and they quite deserted the country market on the other side of Canal Street. The Hudson River Railroad Company, who had been waiting to procure this country market for its purposes, had now an opportunity, and in the latter part of the next year it leased it and the grounds for ten years, at an annual rent of fifteen hundred dollars.

The next year the Superintendent of Streets and Lamps, (Heman W. Childs,) in a report, states, "We have filled up every stand, and have numerous applications for more; I would recommend building a shed on the side-walk, on Spring Street, adjoining the market, about two hundred feet in length by fourteen or eighteen feet in width, which can be erected for about one thousand dollars, and would pay a good interest, and is indispensably necessary in order to accommodate the business that will centre at that market." This was done, and the flagging replaced with a plank "floor" in the month of October, 1852.

The next year, 1853, licenses were given to the following butchers:

No. 1. Thomas E. Broadway.   No. 2. Jacob R. Reed.
    3. Thos. E. Broadway, Jr.   4. Jacob R. Reed.
    5. Ellis D. Eddey.   6. Harman Bazley.
    7. Ellis Eddey.   8. John A. Bennett.
    9. Abraham Brewer.   10. Isaac Valentine, Jr.
  11. Samuel Farren.   12. John Black.
  13. James White.   14. James Valentine.
  15. John Kinner.   16. Charles Lozier.
  17. Isaac Valentine.   18. Samuel Valleau.
  19. John Rice.   20. William Valleau, Jr.
  21. William Valleau, Sen'r.   22. James Haywood.
  23. B. Rice & H. Cook.   24. James Haywood.
  25. Jacob H. Fink.   26. John Fink.
  27. John Akley.   28. John Vanice.
  29. Henry Keyser.   30. Zophar Hawkins.
  31. James Hawkins.   32. Zophar Hawkins.
  33. James Hawkins.   34. Charles Reeves.
  35. Adolphus L. Odell.   36. William Hanshe.
  37. Lawrence Martin.   38. William E. Hyatt.

There is considerable business done here in selling meat by the quarter, and at wholesale ; and there is also a large trade in oysters, clams, &c., in the slip adjoining.

The lease of the Hudson River Railroad Company for the building known as the "country market" having expired, we find in the *Tribune*, May 5th, 1860: "The Old Clinton Country Market—the old rotten building in the centre of the triangle of Clinton Market, at the foot of Canal Street, for many years a landmark—has become too dilapidated to answer the purposes of the marketmen, and yesterday the work of tearing down was begun. The space left is to be appropriated as a stand for the wagons of country marketmen."

"TOMPKINS MARKET."

As early as 1826 a report was made in favor of locating and erecting a market-house at the juncture of the Bowery and Third Avenue, but it was not sanctioned by the Board. On the 15th of December, 1828, however, it was decided to establish one on the present location, from the favorable report presented before them by a Committee, of which the following is a part: "That in the opinion of your Committee, a market is much wanted in that vicinity, and they have been some time in search of a proper site for the purpose; they have at length fixed upon one which, in their opinion, combines more advantages than any other in the neighborhood. It is situated on the east side of the Third Avenue, nearly opposite to its intersecting with the Bowery Road, and is bounded in front by the (Third) Avenue, on the north by Seventh, and on the south by Sixth Street. It comprises eight lots of twenty-two feet eight inches each, making a front on the Third Avenue of 181 feet 8 inches by 100 feet in depth along Sixth and Seventh Streets. Mr. Charles Henry Hall, to whom the property belongs, offers to sell to the Corporation for ↖ 2,500 per lot, making an aggregate sum of $20,000; should the Corporation purchase, he will cede to them a street 40 feet wide, in the rear, running from Sixth to Seventh Street, (now called '*Hall Street*;') he will also cede to them so much of the triangular piece of ground between Third Avenue and the Bowery Road (lying directly opposite to these lots) as belongs to him, which is the whole of the said triangle, with the exception of one lot of 50 feet in breadth on the Third Avenue; the same to be kept open as a public square forever. The site above mentioned is situated opposite two great leading avenues to the city; and as it is probable that this market will be principally supplied by country wagons, the square opposite to it will afford greater accommodations for them, as well as hay wagons, than any place in the neighborhood."

The contract was ordered to be made with Mr. Hall by a Committee, who reported on the 22d instant following, that he had "given 50 feet (instead of 40) on the east side for a street, and a relinquishment of a lease of 23 years in favor of the Corporation, and the contract agreed and signed."

In the month of September, in the next year, the Committee were empowered to erect a suitable market-house, not to exceed 100 feet in length and 30 in breadth, on this plot, which was commenced and finished early in the year following, when six stands were reported sold to the following butchers, at the prices set opposite their names, viz.:

No. 1.	John Flock,	$400	No. 2.	John Deavenport,	$400
3.	Jacob Evans,	250	4.	Asa W. Wesson,	250
5.	John Boscawen,	350	6.	Romeo Thompson,	350

Which amounted to the total sum of $2,000, with an annual rent of $280. The market opened for business on the 8th of May, 1830, with prospects of being one of the best up-town markets in the city, as its position was excellent for intercepting country wagons, and at that period it was thought the Harlem Railroad Company would have a turn-out near by, and make a depot for the reception of country produce. It attracted but few country wagons, however, and the Railroad Company concluded to establish a market depot between 27th and 28th Streets, in the Fourth Avenue, where it was afterwards held many years.

In the month of August following, the Superintendent of Repairs was directed to build a small shed on the side of this market for the use of the fishermen, who had become already necessary from its numerous patrons, no doubt in consequence of its excellent location, and also from the fact that its occupants furnished the best quality of provisions—two important points to secure patronage.

In the month of December, 1831, two new stands were ordered to be sold at a premium, which, however, did not take place until the 15th of February following, (1832,) when they were sold at public auction for cash. No. 3 to William J. Valentine, at $425; and No. 6 to Jacob L. Dodge, for $800. Two years after, in the month of April, two additional stands were sold at public auction for cash to the following butchers: No. 5 to William Harrington, at $365; and No. 6 to John C. Perrin, at $475. These were placed on those occupied by the old numbers, which were moved up and their numbers changed; when all the stands were found occupied as follows:

No. 1.	John Flock.	No. 2.	John Wallace.
3.	William J. Valentine.	4.	Charles L. Carpenter.
5.	William Harrington.	6.	John C. Perrin.
7.	Nicholas Romaine.	8.	George W. Peterson.
9.	John Boscawen.	10.	Romeo Thompson.

Near this market, which was about opposite the "forks of the road," was for many years the termination of the once famous "Third Avenue Trotting Course," where every fine afternoon (Sundays included) the tired, panting, and foaming steeds, before all sorts of vehicles, came rushing in from Harlem, or Cato's, in two's, three's, five's; and I have seen more than twenty, often appearing as if they were " all in a heap." There was no such road in the United States as the Third Avenue for a " trot." From almost one end to the other, through the centre of it, a smoothly-graded Macadamized road was laid, while on each side appeared a well-beaten track, usually preferred by the " knowing trotters," and the whole kept in the most perfect order. It was, however, a dangerous one for a pleasant family ride, as there were many—especially when quite late in the day—half-drunken fast men and boys, in their crazy excitement to get ahead, who made no bones (or rather, sometimes broken ones,) of driving a shaft into your horse, or their wheels against or even over you, and curse you in the bargain for being in their way.

Some distance above this market, at an early period, was a regular standing-place, where many went towards evening to see the " fast ones come in." Then, on looking up towards the rising ground, now about 28th Street, a cloud of dust suddenly rising denoted the coming of the " steeds," and it was not long before a well-known butcher of Fulton Market, having, well in hand, a gallant black horse, usually before a sulky, could be seen; and on the opposite side, a large, heavy man, who (some called " Larry") sat in a low, light, Brooklyn-built cart, before which was an excellent stepping, short-tailed bay horse; both teams head-and-head usually a long way before the " crowd," which was trailing on after them. Soon afterwards they all came in a body with such a shouting or hallooing of " Heigh!" " Heigh!" " Go-a-long!" " What are you about!" " Now-I-got-you!" " No-you-aint!" " Get out of the way!" with many like expressions, all commingled together as they rushed by, and which appeared as if a thunder-gust, or all the furies, were let loose at once. Some on a full run, sawing and pulling their horses first on one side, then on the other; others plying the whip most unmercifully on all sides; others, again, yelling like demons, who were trailing on behind; and these exciting scenes were repeated at intervals, until darkness closed the " trot" for the day.

Not many years passed before the " cobble-stone" pavement began to creep up; then followed, to Yorkville and Harlem, the heavy-ladened omnibus—to tear up; and finally appeared the " Third Avenue Railroad," which entirely used up, and totally exterminated, the far-famed " Third Avenue Trotting Course."

In 1836, a resolution was passed " to take down the old Essex Market building, and with the materials build a country market-house on the east side of Tompkins Market, and an appropriation of one thousand dollars be used for that purpose." This addition was soon after completed, which added much to its appearance, as well as the facilities and accommodations.

Then followed an accession of stands, among which were six to be occupied by butchers. These, under the new system, were drawn for in a fair and satisfactory manner; but, at this period, these additions were found too numerous, as several were destined to either break down or quit their stands, which again reverted back to the city.

There were several in this, as well as other markets, who claimed the same right to dispose of gift or drawn stands, as those who held premium stands.

About this period,* Richard Valentine petitioned for transfer of stand No. 14 Clinton Market, but was denied "the same, not being a *premium stand.*" This case, and one or two more, settled the question. The Committee, in the month of March next year, also passed a *resolution,* "That whenever any stall or stalls in the different markets become vacant hereafter, it shall be the duty of the Clerk, together with the Superintendent of Markets, under the direction of the Joint Market Committee, to cause a written notice to be placed on said stall or stalls, for at least one week, giving notice that said stall or stalls are vacant." Then followed, on the 12th of April, a *resolution,* "That stall No. 5 Tompkins Market be declared vacant;" and on the 8th of May following, Ambrose P. Rikeman drew this vacated stand. The next year, in the month of April, William Webber drew No. 15; and in the month of December, same year, (1840,) the butchers' stands were found occupied by the following persons:

No. 1. John Flock.	No. 2. John Wallace.
3. Lemuel Valentine.	4. Charles L. Carpenter.
5. Ambrose P. Rikeman.	6. John Rikeman.
7. Nicholas Romaine.	8. George W. Peterson.
9. Norris Hicks.	10. Romeo Thompson.
11. William V. Leggett.	12. Joseph Churchill.
13. Philip Webber.	14. John C. Perrin.
15. James Webber.	16. John C. Perrin.

About this period a very good business was found to be established here; so much so, that but few changes in the occupancy of stands were made for several years. To be sure it was in a measure somewhat paralyzed by the opening of the "meat-shops," but it did not last long, nor was it so much affected as some of the other public markets, as there were only two or three vacant stands at any one time, and these remained so but a short period.

* November 16, 1838.

Its patrons generally stood by the market, and those who left afterwards came back, with many others, who began to occupy the many first-class buildings which were so rapidly improving the neighborhood. Those butchers who remained and attended to their business received an excellent, as well as a successful, trade; and in times of scarcity of "small stock," they had peculiar advantages over all other butchers, being in view of principally all the stock driven to Browning's Bull's Head, (located just below, on Sixth Street,) which passed this market; when these butchers, of course, were there in time to meet, and obtain their supplies.

In advancing to the year 1850, some changes in the occupancy of the butchers' stands, since those last noticed, appear. We, however, find them all occupied, or licensed, as follows:

No. 1. Lemuel Valentine.		No. 2. William P. Woodcock.
3. Do.		4. John H. Woodcock.
5. George Hirleman.		6. William Corbitt.
7. James Kent.		8. Nicholas Romaine.
9. William Doubleday		10. Romeo Thompson.
11. Philip O'Neil.		12. George W. Martin.
13. John Doane.		14. Joseph H. Farrington.
15. Geo. A. Vogel.		16. Geo. W. Farrington.

Nearly opposite this market soon after was erected the magnificent edifice known as the "Cooper Union," by one of the most humane, generous, and benevolent of men. His object in this enormous building is fully described in the First Annual Report of the Trustees, which says: "Peter Cooper, a mechanic and merchant of the City of New York, having become satisfied early in life that the working classes of this city required greater opportunities for instruction and rational recreation than were afforded by existing institutions, determined, if he could command the means, to found an institution designed especially to supply the needs, of which he himself had been conscious. Having by industry and enterprise gained the necessary funds, he purchased the entire block of ground at the intersection of the Third and Fourth Avenues, and proceeded in 1854 to erect thereon a massive building of stone, brick, and iron, six stories in height, and completely fire-proof, at a cost, as shown by his books, of over $630,000 for the land and building." An act of incorporation having been procured from the Legislature at their last session, Mr. Cooper, in accordance therewith, on the 29th of April, 1859, executed a deed in fee simple of this entire property to the undersigned trustees, without reservation of any kind upon the trust specified in the act of the Legislature, the first of which is, " that the above-mentioned and described premises, together with the appurtenances, and the rents, issues, incomes, and profits thereof, shall be forever devoted to the instruction and improvement of the inhabitants of the United States in practical science and art."

This princely donation of Mr. Cooper, under all the circumstances, is destined to become—in the annals of philanthropy and benevolence—one of the greatest events of historical interest and example; and long may he live to enjoy the fruits of his opulence and benevolence.

In the month of May, 1858, a Committee waited upon Mr. Cooper to seek a room in this building suitable for an address. After hearing who the parties were, and the nature of the address, he said " he had dealt with the butchers for the last forty years, and felt under some obligations to them," and he finally concluded that "this address must be read in his room without any charge." The room, however, had not been seen by one of the Committee until the liberal offer had been made and accepted; and when the spacious hall was opened and entered by the expected and uncultivated orator, its enormous size and grand appearance somewhat changed his idea of holding forth; but Mr. Cooper was not to be changed; so he desired this orator to go to the extreme end and hold a conversation in a moderate tone of voice, which was done and distinctly heard, which of course settled the reading and the acceptance of the generous liberality of Mr. Cooper.

I must here repeat what was said on that occasion of Mr. Cooper: that "wealth has not added to his height, changed his appearance, nor affected his conversation; and in the erection of this immense and magnificent building, he has erected a *monument* and bequeathed his name to the future generations, who will bless and revere him for having given them a refuge from the many and severe storms of an early life."

In the month of December, 1856, the Common Council adopted a resolution to advertise for plans and specifications for building a three-story iron market; the upper part to be made suitable for the use of the Seventh Regiment, for drill-rooms, armories, &c., during the pleasure of the Common Council, and that premiums be allotted therefor, in three classes, viz.: first class at $200, second at $100, and third at $50. Several plans were presented, but those of Bogardus & Lafferty were adopted, and on the 31st of December a contract was concluded with Theodore Hunt, by which he was to erect the market-house, according to the plans, for the sum of $155,371.

The work of demolishing was commenced, the old building was torn down, and a range of low wooden sheds were put up around

"Hall Square," in front of the "Cooper Union," for the accommodation of the stand-holders of the old market-house.

The foundation of the new building was proceeded with, and the walls and columns of iron began to show themselves on its four sides above the level of the street, when the Common Council, in the month of April following, came to the conclusion that the building as it was then progressing would not be strong enough for the use intended and the support of its great weight; when they ordered it to be stopped. Some wished different materials to be used in its erection; and thus, I may say, it stood for more than two years before matters could be arranged, and the last contract be completed, by which iron was to be used in certain parts, instead of brick and stone.

The building, or at least the market part, was promised to the stand-holders in the course of the summer of 1860; but before this event took place, there had been some intimations and hints thrown out that it was the intention of the City Inspector to deprive some of the old stand-holders of their rights, or crowd them into smaller spaces. What this was done for there were various opinions; however, a few days before the opening an unfit official, who kept a public-house near by—and whether officially or not—informed the stand-holders that such was the fact. This appeared to them to come straight enough; but not being satisfied, they sought Mr. Irving, the Superintendent of the Markets, when he informed them, that all of them should have their rights, and plenty of room to transact their business; which he appears to have fully and satisfactorily carried out, as we find noticed in the *New York Atlas*.* " *The New Tompkins Market*.—The market portion of this building is so far completed as to admit of occupancy by the butchers and others doing business therein. On Monday last (6th) the occupants of stands removed from the unsightly building which they have occupied during the construction of their new quarters, to the new market. The removal was made under the superintendence of James Irving, Esq., Superintendent of Markets, whose magnanimous and disinterested allotment of positions has given the utmost satisfaction to all those having stands in the market. We are pleased at this manifestation from those citizens who have business connections with Mr. Irving, and congratulate him in thus executing impartially the trust imposed on him. Mr. Irving, having been a butcher, made the allotment with a view to priority of claim and possession while in the old market.'

The floor used for market purposes presents a space of nearly 180

* August 12th, 1860.

feet long by 96 wide. The side front, facing the Third Avenue, is entirely devoted to the sale of butchers' meat, on two ranges of stalls, between which runs a fine passage-way of about eighteen feet wide, left for the accommodation of those who go to market, that they may not be in danger of having their clothes spoiled, or of being crowded against greasy blocks or corn-beef trays, which are usually drawn too far out into these passage-ways in most of our market-houses.

The middle of this floor is used for the sale of vegetables, poultry, and game, and the other portions for the sale of hams and bacon, butter and cheese, fresh fish and shell-fish, &c., and a portion reserved for country people. One or two other stands will bear particular notice, on account of being something new in our public markets.

Under the south stairway are located stands Nos. 43 and 45, kept by two Frenchmen, (F. A. Bailly and J. G. Torrilhon,) who keep, besides, pork in every conceivable form, boned turkeys, capons, larded bird-game, *filet de bœuf*, &c., many of which are cooked ready "for parties, breakfasts, dinners, or suppers, cold or warm."

Then, on the eastern side of the same stairway, on stands Nos. 46, 48, and 50, are found L. Bonnard & Co., displaying numerous canisters, containing "Alimentary Preserves"—such as beef, mutton, veal, poultry, game, fish, &c., besides vegetables, truffles, fruits, and the celebrated *pates de foie gras*, or large *geese-livers*.

The two rows of butchers' stalls number twenty-eight, of which eight have a front of 12 feet each; eight more, a front of $11\frac{1}{2}$ feet; and twelve a front of 9 feet; all of which I found occupied, or represented as being in the possession of, the following persons:

No. 1. Lemuel Valentine.	No. 2. William P. Woodcock.
3. Do.	4. Do.
5. Dieffenbach & Co.	6. Alonzo Osborne.
7. John McChain.	8. J. M. Farrington.
9. Vacant.	10. James Larkins.
11. John Byrnes.	12. Landers & Co.
13. James Irving.	14. Isaac D. Hammond.
15. Do.	16. Do.
17. James Mooney.	18. Vacant.
19. John Donovan.	20. James S. Hall.
21. Do.	22. Do.
23. William Doubleday.	24. William T. Blair.
25. George A. Vogel.	26. George W. Farrington.
27. Do.	28. Do.

"JEFFERSON MARKET."

1832. SEVERAL years prior to the establishment of a public market on the grounds where the Jefferson Market now rests, the inhabitants of the neighborhood were anxious to have such an accommodation; and were willing to give the ground, *in fee*, necessary for that purpose, in a certain location near, but their offers were not accepted by the Corporation.

One location, however, had been selected, which it was thought would be accepted, by the encouragement given to those most active in the enterprise, and also the small amount of cost that would be required to erect a suitable market-house, by using the old materials of the "Duane Market," which was about being removed. Under these circumstances, these inhabitants, in the month of October, 1829, presented a petition, in which they state: "The undersigned understand that it is contemplated by your Honorable Body to remove the market-house at Duane Slip. They therefore pray your Honorable Body to direct the same to be placed on the *gore of ground* corner of Greenwich Lane and Twelfth Street, (on Seventh Avenue,) which, they are authorized to state to your Honorable Body, will be granted gratuitously for that purpose by the proprietors thereof. Your petitioners respectfully state, that the population thereabouts, and far above it, will be greatly accommodated thereby; and your petitioners are ever bound, &c. Signed by

"John Rodgers,   Caleb Cole,   George P. Rogers,
  John F. Adriance,   John Harris,   Wm. C. Rhinelander,
  Charles Oakley,   Frederick Naugin, Thos. P. Vanderhoff,
  Moody Cummings,   John Devlin,   Peter Blondell,
  Freeman Cole,   Richard Cromwell, Thomas M. Blakely,

and many others." This liberal offer, however, was not accepted, which disappointed many of the property-owners.

In the month of July, 1831, "sundry of the inhabitants of the Ninth Ward were again asking for the establishment of a public market in or about the centre of said Ward."

They then represented, that "the Ward, comprising a population of near 25,000, has at present no market within its bounds, except one at the foot of Christopher Street, on the borders of the North

River, with six or eight stalls; and no other near it except 'Tomp-kins Market,' on Third Avenue, which has but six stalls, and the access to which is cut off from a thickly-settled part of the Ward, by there being no communication between Broadway and the Bow-ery from Fourth to Eighth Street." They request "your Honor-able Body to cause a public market to be erected on the Sixth Avenue, at or near its junction with Greenwich Lane."

The subject was laid over until the month of September, when a remonstrance was presented against its erection here, and again it was postponed until the next month, (October,) when a Committee was appointed to treat with the owners of this property. In the month of January, 1832, this Committee reported that they could purchase the whole grounds for $30,500; and after several meet-ings, a Sub-Committee, in the month of February, were instructed to close the bargain, at this large sum.

The procurement of this plot of ground appeared to have given considerable trouble, as it was owned by several parties who were anxious to get a round sum for it, and the course they adopted with the Committee appeared to succeed. The sum of $32,500, in the year 1832, was paid for this gore of about twelve lots of land, when several thought it ought to have been purchased for a much less sum.

In the following month of June, the subject of building a brick market-house according to a plan then proposed was presented, which, after its approval, was ordered to be advertised for con-tracts. The estimate for its building was awarded to Messrs. Smith & Roome, for the sum of $6,576; and the building was com-menced, and finished in the month of November; when a resolution was passed, "that the new market in Sixth Avenue be called 'Jefferson Market,' after the third President of the United States, Thomas Jefferson."

Six butchers' stands were also ordered to be sold at public auc-tion, on the 14th of December following, at premiums, for cash; they were offered, but only two were sold on the 14th, and the other four on the 19th instant, to the following persons and prices:

No. 1. James C. Lyons, $1,250 No. 2. Alfred Lyons, $1,405
    3. Benjamin Oakley, 575   4. Benjamin Ward, 510
    5. Jas. H. Houghtalin, 980   6. Thos. F. De Voe, 880

There appears a considerable difference in the prices paid for these six stands; those four, Nos. 1, 2, 5, and 6, brought the highest prices, were sold as corner stands; the first two as "outside corners," and the last two as "inside corners."

The market was opened for business on Saturday, the 5th of January, 1833, but the anxiety of *one person* in making the first sale in this new building, led him to be guilty of making that sale the night before. The business, however, opened with bright prospects as a retail market, especially in that of *coarse meats*, as there were but few in proportion in that neighborhood then who purchased the *prime cuts*. Many of the wooden buildings in the neighborhood were those so suddenly put up in 1822 to accommodate bankers, insurance, and other companies, merchants, &c., who left them tenantless, after the dreaded yellow fever had subsided, which were at this period filled with weavers, laborers, and others who sought low rents.

The next year, (1834,) two more stands were ordered to be sold, to take place on the 15th of April, and to be placed between Nos. 3 and 5, and 4 and 6, and the old Nos. of 5 and 6 were to be altered to Nos. 7 and 8, which were then to be known as the *inside corners.* These two inside stands were sold as above, to the following:

No. 5. Samuel Sims,   -   -   -   -   - $550

    6. Samuel Van Wart, -   -   -   -   565

Which swelled the whole amount of cash paid to $6,715.

Soon after the establishment of the market, on a part of this market ground, on Amos Street, near Sixth Avenue, a large well was dug and a steam-engine was put up to pump and force a supply of water into the building called the " New York City Reservoir," which had been erected in the year 1829, by the Corporation, for the purpose of supplying the city with water in cases of fire.

It stood in Thirteenth Street, between the Third and the present Fourth Avenues. The large tank or cistern was formed of cast-iron plates united by screws and cement, resting on a foundation of solid stone masonry, forming an octagon of forty-four feet diameter and seventy-five feet above the ground to the top of the tank, surmounted by a cupola, making in all one hundred feet high. The well of this reservoir was bored through a rock one hundred and thirteen feet in depth by seventeen feet in diameter, with two shafts extending in opposite directions.

It was calculated to furnish about eight hogsheads of water per hour, which was raised into the tank by a steam-engine of fifteen horse-power. This water was conducted through pipes and discharged through hydrants.

In the month of April, 1835, by resolution, " this public ground and building at the new well at Jefferson Market, not used or occupied for the purpose of the well and water-works," were appropriated to the water purveyor for a work-shop. " The size of the ground unoccupied is 180 feet on Amos Street, 119 feet on Sixth

Avenue, and 75 on Greenwich Lane; room for storage of water-pipes, gas lamp-post, and also the hydraulic press for proving pipe, which, with the steam-engine there, he would be enabled to prove three pipes in the same time that it now takes to prove one." This space of ground has always been used for public purposes, and has never been a loss to the city.

In the month of March, 1836, was adopted and approved the Report of the Committee on Markets, on the subject of building a country market on the public ground adjoining this market-house, in which they state, that " they have carefully examined this subject, and find a market for country people and country produce is much needed there. Buildings are rapidly erecting in that vicinity, and a large population are now supplied from this market, and it is constantly increasing. It lacks a place where the producers of the soil can be accommodated, and when done it will be as good a market to procure supplies at as any other which is not on the water. Your Committee are of opinion that a country market should be built north of the present market, twenty feet distant therefrom, of one story in height, ninety-eight feet, four inches, in length, and thirty feet in width. The cost of which is estimated at a sum less than two thousand dollars." This market-house was built, and the fishermen, poulterers, and hucksters were removed into it from the old or butchers' market, where they had occupied just one-half of it. This space being now vacant, the next year, on the 10th of March, the Market Committee concluded to fill it with eight more butchers' stalls; but, as the system of selling stands at public auction for premiums was abolished, they were drawn for, beginning from No. 9 to 16, by the following butchers, with the yearly rents set opposite their names:

No. 9. James Watts, rent $100 No. 10. Henry Wiseburn, $90
11. Dan'l Lawrence, " 60 12. John Hanshe, 60
13. Henry T. Krowl, " 60 14. Gerard P. Hopper, 50
15. Samuel Jaques, " 100 16. Peter B. Marks, 90

The rent placed on these drawn stands was considerable more than that of the other eight " premium stands;" it being intended by the Corporation, as the owners of these drawn or gifted stands had paid no purchase-money down for the benefit of the city, they should pay an equivalent in this shape; and also to restrict them from the right to sell or dispose of their stands when they left them, either by death or otherwise, these stands should revert to the Corporation; while those who bought theirs at public auction, years before, had such rights and privileges guaranteed to them by the Corporation as to amount to *property in fee* in these premium stands.

On the 31st of March, 1836, a resolution was adopted directing

the Superintendent of Repairs "forthwith to make a passage way
for a thoroughfare in Jefferson Market, between Nos. 7 and 9, and
8 and 10, for the accommodation of the butchers." These eight
drawn stands were placed with the ends on a line with each brick
pillar, from the centre, in the same manner as the old or premium
stands were originally placed.

The same year these stands were added to this market, Mr. Charles
Oakley erected a long wooden shed fronting on Jones Street, between Bleecker and Fourth Streets, expressly for the accommodation
of those persons who at that period had no regard for the market
laws and ordinances. Mr. Oakley promised all who rented stands in
his market, that he would protect them from all suits brought against
them; but before one year was passed they all were forced to vacate,
and his market was closed up by the prompt and energetic action
of the Corporation Attorney. One of his tenants, by the name of
John Hilliker, resisted for some time, upon the assurance of Mr.
Oakley that he would protect him; but his petition and a report on
the subject showed that the promise was not fulfilled. Hilliker's
petition was before the Board in the month of October, when he solicited "to be released from a penalty obtained against him in the
Marine Court, on the 8th of September last, for selling fresh meat
in Mr. Oakley's market in Jones Street; that he has and did stop
selling after the said date; that he has a family to support, and is
unable to pay the said penalty, and that it was on Mr. Oakley's word,
pledged to him, that he did sell fresh meat, after your Honorable
Body put the market laws in force." The Committee reported, in
the month of November, "that Hilliker has shown no disposition to
contest this matter, except for the purpose of testing the legality of
the said *fine*, and was prompted to do so by the positive assurance
of Mr. Charles Oakley that he would indemnify and save him harm-
less against the same, which he has thus far failed to do," &c. A
resolution was passed that the judgment be canceled, on Hilliker's
paying the costs and fees.

The two (Jefferson) market-houses being separated by an unpaved
space of a little less than twenty feet, was at times, especially in
stormy weather, so as to be unfit to pass and repass from one market-house to the other; which called forth a petition to have it covered with a shed, which was done in October, 1839, and also a floor
of flagging laid; but it still continued to be a nuisance until it was
partially floored with plank, at private expense, when a few stands
were introduced on the north side of this space; and finally it was
wholly floored over, the sides of the two market-houses taken out,
and inclosed in one, as it now stands.

In the month of December, 1840, these sixteen stands were occupied by the following butchers:

No. 1. Daniel S. Hyde.	No. 2. Edward N. Romaine.
3. William H. Farrington.	4. Henry Goodhue.
5. Samuel Sims.	6. John De Voe, Sr.
7. James H. Houghtalin.	8. Thomas F. De Voe.
9. Michael Cox.	10. Moses De Voe.
11. Frederick M. Silber.	12. John Hanshe.
13. Henry T. Krowl.	14. George Glashan.
15. George Fink.	16. Peter B. Marks.

Many of those who attended to their business did very well for several years; but the agitation and the licensing the "meat-shops" appeared, and for a time it was almost a death-blow to many of the public markets. Those who occupied stands in them, finding their business deserting them, gave up their stands, and engaged in "meat-shops," where some prospered, whose rents and expenses were not large; but soon an indiscriminating licensing of all who applied (and great numbers did business who were not licensed, through the neglect of the city officers,) caused but few to succeed. However, in a few years a reaction took place, after the meat-shop system had been pretty thoroughly tried by many of our citizens, who found, in the end, that their wants could be better supplied where the public markets were within a reasonable distance, and they returned to them; and now those same markets, (or nearly all,) so nearly deserted at that time, are again fully occupied, although some have since had extensive additions.

I may say here, that this market has been unfortunate in its late additions, by the improper arrangements of some of the public officers; who, when a shed was added to the country market on the north side, made it cost the city about $2,200, when the author's carpenter estimated it would cost less than $500. Then, instead of having the stands (to the number of about twelve) drawn for, or some other fair disposition made of them, they were otherwise disposed of. Now, I will not state how they were disposed of, but how they and many others could be, if our Superintendents and Clerks of Markets were inclined to be dishonest, and wanted to make a great deal of money out of them.

New additions in buildings or sheds, in any of our public markets, will of course create additional stands, when these dishonest officers, not wishing their acts seen, or their conversation overheard, could meet at such market on a *Sunday*, lay out the size, number, and location of such stands, put certain prices on each, according to location; and then, as these *genteel men* have always some willing friends, who are either bailsmen, keepers of prisons or rum-shops, or those who " travel on their muscle," ready to render any assistance for a small share of the *income*, they are put in possession of all such "stands," and instructed what prices to ask and take, when applications are made for them. In the mean time, some may have been sold, or, I should have said, *given away*, (as the law strictly forbids the selling for money, or receiving any *valuables*, as a consideration for market stands, by the Superintendent, Clerks, or other public officers,) prior to the finishing of such additions, &c., to such persons as would wish to engage in business as soon as possible. The other stands, however, may remain idle, until some anxious person, with a *little money*, seeing the vacant stands, naturally will inquire of the Clerk if he cannot give him *one*. " No," the Clerk can say, " they are all *given* away long ago; but (in a whisper) he guesses that *Jack Cox*, the prison-keeper, will sell his stand"—so off the *anxious person* can go to see Mr. Cox. Mr. Cox, however, can talk *offish;* he expects he will put his *cousin* on it, when " he comes to the city "—as it is one of the best in the market, and worth at least $1,000 cash—any how, he won't sell it, without he gets its worth; and he cautions our *anxious person* not to let any person know he has offered it for sale. Well, if our *anxious person* is at all bright, he begins, by this time, to mistrust how the game is playing: he knows that this prison-keeper has no business with a stand, as " *a proper person;*" and he also knows that a stand cannot be obtained in our markets, under the present system, without it is got in this rascally manner. So an offer is made of 500, 600, 700, or 800 dollars in cash, and with it promises of secrecy; which is received, or passed, very likely by another party, who hands him a *permit* to occupy such stand; and when this *anxious person*, who, before this transaction, had worn a clear and quiet conscience, is accosted by some intimate *friend* with " How did you get your stand?" " Why, I got it *fairly*," he would say; but his conscience would say, " I got it *foully*." Then, again, if this *transaction* is noised about, or becomes known, our *anxious person* is waited upon by those engaged, or some of the public officers, who inform him, if he is called under oath, he must deny the whole, or he will have his *permit* revoked, or suffer some bodily harm. But to introduce all the improper acts which have, or could have, been transacted here, and at the other public markets, by such officers, would not reflect any credit on the citizens who elected those who appointed these inefficient and dishonest officers to these important trusts, where none ought to be placed but such practical, honest men as would be sought after and employed in a person's own business, and who also knew more of the duties required of them than they knew of political knavery.

The present laws regulating public markets are most injurious, expensive, and inefficient for the city, citizens, or stand-holders, and open to many abuses, impositions, &c., as I have previously shown. The whole system should be changed; and no doubt many would ask, How can we make it better? My answer would be, that you would not employ a shoemaker to make you a watch, nor a dishonest politician to conduct your affairs, or a business he knew nothing about, let alone the collection of large sums of uncounted money. No, you would go and get the assistance or knowledge of honest, practical men, who would give such services or information as could be embraced into proper laws to govern either mercantile, maritime, public markets, or any other subject demanding them.

Several years ago I, with several other stand-holders, were called upon to assist the authorities in the better conducting of the public markets; when an organization was perfected, which represented principally the business of every department in them, but before it was called into action several office-holders became incensed at the idea of having their rights or *perquisites* interfered with, and by their superior influence and oft-repeated threats (on a few) rendered this organization ineffectual.

The most prominent feature was to establish a law to do away with all paid officers attached to them, except so far as the appointment of a few collectors, whose time would be fully occupied, and of whose honesty there should not be the least doubt, and to be wholly under the direction of a "Board of Trustees." Perhaps, however, the following will give the reader some idea of a law which was then drawn up, but which now could be improved upon:

"An Act to repeal part of the ordinance organizing the departments of the municipal government of the City of New York, passed (1849,) known as ' the *Bureau of Markets*,' and also to establish a *Board of Trustees*, (or delegates,) who shall undertake the duties of conducting and superintending the several public markets in the City of New York.

" The Trustees or Delegates from the several public markets, who now are, or may be hereafter elected, shall be the occupants of stands lawfully *licensed*, or the holders of *permits* properly granted, shall give their services gratis, or without pay or reward, in superintending the public markets of the City of New York. They shall be elected from the several or such public markets as they represent, by the several occupants of stands also lawfully *licensed*, or the holders of *permits* properly granted to them in their several public markets, every one or two years, beginning from the *third Monday* in March, 18—; which election shall take place on that day every second year thereafter, in the following manner: *Four* Delegates from Washington Market, consisting of one butcher, one poulterer, one fruit and vegetable dealer, and one fisherman.   *Three* from Fulton Market: one butcher, one poulterer or vegetable dealer, and one fisherman.   *Two* from Catharine Market: one butcher and one fisherman, or other.   *Two* from Centre Market: one butcher and one fisherman, or other.   *Two* from Clinton Market: one butcher and one fisherman, or other.   One butcher each from Essex, Jefferson, Tompkins, Union, Gouveneur, Franklin, and all other public markets which may be hereafter established, which shall contain not less than twenty occupied stands.   They shall be known as a *Board of Trustees* of the public markets of the City of New York, and shall elect from their body a Chairman, Secretary, and an Executive Committee, who shall represent their body when empowered so to do, and who, in case of vacancy, either by death, resignation, or expulsion, shall have the power to order an election from the occupants of stands of such unrepresented public markets to fill such vacancy; but for such other public markets which may not be represented, shall be under the supervision of such Delegates as may be appointed from the *Board of Trustees.*

  " They shall from time to time examine the condition of the several public markets, and also advise and direct the Clerks or Collectors with respect to the regulation of the same; to examine the provisions, vegetables, and all other articles of food brought in and around their public markets respectively, and any article which may be suspected to be unwholesome; stale, blown, stuffed, or diseased meat or measly pork, or young, poor, and unfit veal or calves, or the flesh of animals died by accident or disease, or known or suspected to be diseased at the killing of the same, or spoiled poultry, game, fish, or stale vegetables or fruit, or any improper article of food, shall be taken and examined by these practical dealers, (where there is doubt,) which may be called on by either Delegate, Clerk, or Collector, (who may be present;) and if the article or articles prove to be unwholesome and unfit for human food, then the same shall be destroyed, and the seller conveyed before the nearest police magistrate, to be there dealt with according to law.   And no person or persons shall hinder, obstruct, or molest any Clerk or officers of the police from seizing and causing the same to be removed and destroyed, or any duties which may be enjoined on them, under the penalty of not less than ten, nor more than fifty dollars for each offence.

  " They shall recommend for *license,* as butchers, such persons as may be proper; and upon such recommendation the Mayor may from time to time issue licenses under his hand and seal to the persons named therein to exercise and carry on the trade and business of a butcher, in such places as may be designated, but not elsewhere. They may grant permits in writing to such persons as may be proper to sell meat by the quarter, who shall be known as *permit butchers;* and also permits to such other proper persons whose occupations are suitable for the public markets, who shall personally occupy such stands in and around the several public markets as may be designated, (within ten days) after receiving such permits, at such daily rates to be mentioned therein. And they may also, for good and sufficient reasons, annul such *permits.* They may *transfer butcher stalls, or grant permits* to allow *licensed* butchers, or *permit* stand-holders to combine their stands and business together for their mutual benefit and the accommodation of the public; but no stalls or stands, or any improper thing, shall be allowed on, or be so placed as to obstruct or infringe on the rights of another, or on a public passage-way. All *permits* granted shall, after having been fully examined and sanctioned by the Board of Trustees, be signed by their Chairman and Secretary. They shall have the power to appoint honest, practical, and suitable persons for Clerks (not more than three) for the large public markets, and one *Collector* for the small public markets, who shall, before entering upon the duties of their offices, execute a bond with sureties satisfactory to the Board of Trustees, and also approved by the Comptroller, in the penal sum of two thousand dollars, conditioned for the faithful performance of the duties of their respective offices. And they may also have the same power to remove either Clerk, Collector, or other persons under their direction, from their offices or places, if found guilty of neglect or dereliction of duty, after having their cases examined before the Board of Trustees. They may appropriate certain parts either in or outside of the several public markets for the use of country people for their produce, and also designate places for market wagons, carts, &c., that may bring proper marketable products to the several public markets. They may, with the like consent, when placing new or other stands in the new public markets which may hereafter be built, or others which may be enlarged, altered, or rearranged, charge such additional fees or rents as shall be an increase to the present revenue (18—) from the public markets as shall be deemed just and proper for the interest of the city and the prosperity of the public markets. All stands which may be kept vacant *ten days* (except in consequence of sickness, death, or other good and sufficient reasons,) shall be declared vacant, of which notice of such vacation (and the amount of fees due, if any, to the city revenue,) shall be placed or posted on such vacant stands for the space of three days; and if more than one proper applicant shall present themselves for the same, then the same shall be drawn for; the *drawer* shall pay the back fees due, and also a fair valuation for fixtures, (if left on;) and in case the *drawer* of these and all other new stands which shall be hereafter drawn for shall cease to occupy for the space of ten successive days, then they shall be declared vacant; and such stands, whether new or old, shall, in the above same manner, be drawn for the benefit of the former occupant or heirs, and the *good-will* or right of custom, if any there be. They may appoint proper persons to remove all dirt, filth, shells, garbage, or anything considered a nuisance, daily, and to perform such other services about the public markets as are necessary to cleanse the same, at a specified compensation; and may, for cause or neglect, at any time, remove them, and appoint others in their stead. They may cause and superintend the removal, building, or rebuilding, enlarging, repairing, alteration, and addition of the public market buildings, where it would be an advantage to the city revenue and the accommodation of the public. They may recommend suitable compensation to the Clerks, Collectors, Weighmaster, or Weighmasters, (if more than one be required,) and such other persons as may be employed to keep in order and cleanse the several public markets, who shall be subject to the control and supervision of the *Board of Trustees.* For the purpose of defraying the expenses to be incurred in pursuance of the last section, the *Board of Trustees* may, by a requisition, draw upon the Comptroller for a sum not exceeding two hundred dollars. They may in like manner renew the draft as often as may be necessary; but no such renewal shall be made until the money paid upon the previous draft shall be accounted for to the Comptroller by satisfactory vouchers for the expenditure of the money paid thereon; and when such draft or drafts shall be made upon the Comptroller, in conformity with the last two sections, he shall draw his warrant in favor of the *Board of Trustees* for the amount thereof. The Clerks of the large public markets shall collect the market fees and rents daily which shall become due in their respective markets; and the Collector shall collect the fees and rents weekly from all the small public markets respectively; and both Clerks and Collectors shall on Thursday in each week render a full account thereof, under oath, of the several individual names, amounts of fees and rents received by them from each numerically numbered stand under their appropriate heads, which shall also contain the whole amount received, and when paid; and shall thereupon pay over the amount so received to the Chamberlain. They shall also thereupon respectively receive from the Chamberlain a voucher for the payment thereof, which they shall forthwith, on the same day, exhibit to the Comptroller, and shall at the same time leave with him a copy thereof. The Clerks or Collectors may for good and sufficient reasons have the power to suspend any person having a stated stall or stand in a public market, to which they are respectively attached, or occupying a part thereof, or of the street adjoining the same, from occupying or using any part of the market or street, whether a licensed butcher or not; and immediately upon such suspension the Clerk or Collector shall report the same to the *Board of Trustees*, who shall hear the same, upon sufficient notice to the person suspended, and an opportunity afforded him to be heard in his defence, and whose decision upon the matter shall be final.

"The provisions of Chapter 12 of the Revised Ordinances respecting the duties of Deputy Clerks of the markets shall apply to the Clerks and Collectors; and the duties of the Weighmasters shall also apply to those hereby created, except where they are inconsistent with this act. The private markets (commonly known as meat-shops) shall not be under the supervision or direction of this *Board of Trustees*, but shall be under such laws, ordinances, and resolutions as may be recognized or passed by the Common Council. The *Board of Trustees*, Clerks, and Weighmasters are specially charged with the enforcement of all laws of this State, and all ordinances and resolutions of the Common Council not inconsistent with this act regulating the public markets; and they are also required forthwith to report to the Corporation Attorney all violations thereof."

We will now turn back again to the history of this market, and find, in a report made in the latter part of the year 1849, by Colonel Heman W. Childs, then "Commissioner of Streets and Lamps," in which he stated an *estimated* loss by the public markets in 1848 to the city, over and above receipts; and that this (Jefferson) market lost some $3,984.14—with "no prospect of business in the place, and its appearance of falling off."

After reading this report, I thought it could not be possible; but, to satisfy the public and myself, I set to work, and from the various public officers obtained the whole value of this property, including the various buildings; then the amount of lawful interest on the whole; from this was deducted the amount of receipts, charging the city such rents for the use of such buildings, &c., as were placed upon them by the officers in charge—that is, for the accommodations for the "Ninth Ward Police;" the "Police Courts;" the Prisons; two places to test water-pipes; yard-room for these pipes; the tower for the fire-bell; three stores, and a large hall above them, &c. These receipts having been cast up, left an income above seven per cent. advantage to the city, of $2,915.86. And as to the decrease of the business, I quoted from the reports of 1844, which stated, that the "butchers' stands and market fees were $1,048.04, and in 1848 $1,425.44;" showing a gain in four years of nearly $400, and the amount of business one-third more. This account was prepared for the "Press," as the "Press" had published this unlooked-for report. Being, however, intimate with Colonel Childs, I waited upon him with this evidence, and satisfied him that there was not such a loss, or any loss, but a large gain. He, however, wished it not to be answered by the "Press," but would refer to it in his next Annual Report; and I became satisfied that it would be best to assume this form; but it was not acknowledged.

So it rested until the early part of the year 1854, when Mr. A. C. Flagg, then Comptroller, again brought forth this same, I may call it, *false report*, and gave it to the public in a printed document. To counteract it, I soon after prepared an article on "The Public Markets," which was printed in the *New York Daily Times*, January 23, 1855, in which, in detail, is proven that this market paid "the snug sum of *seven thousand, five hundred and eighteen dollars and seventy-eight cents* above lawful interest, and all its expenses."

Now we turn to notice a report of the "Police Committee," made on the 3d of June, 1851, to allow the use of a part of this market property on Amos Street for prison purposes. The Boards "*Resolved*, That permission be given to the Governors of the Alms-House Department to erect a prison upon the vacant lot of ground belonging to the Corporation, situated in Amos (*West Tenth*) Street, adjoining the Second District Prison; being twenty-five feet front on Amos Street, and between the present prison and the engine-house."

The large fire-bell tower, built of wood, several years ago, which stood nearer the point of Sixth Avenue and West Tenth Street than the present one, was destroyed by fire on the afternoon of the following 29th of July, 1851. The large bell, weighing about 9,000 pounds, was cracked and ruined by the heat and fall. Another tower was soon after erected, of the same material, but nearer, and adjoining the country and fish market-house, on the northwestern end; this, a few years ago, had an addition made to its height, and much beautified; with also a fire escape-ladder, running from the upper floor or lookout to the roofs of the three-story building, containing two energetic fire companies: one, the Guardian Engine Company, No. 29, who have lately procured a fine steam-engine; and the "Gulick Hose Company," No. 11.

Next to this building stands the prison, which has been much enlarged and improved, as are also the court-rooms over the large building on the corner of Greenwich Avenue and West Tenth Street. In this are several stores and offices, and a communication with the large hall over the old market building, which had previously been used by the Ninth Ward Station-House, but now by several military companies, and other public purposes. While in the possession of the Police, in the year 1851, this Hall was the scene of a most heart-rending character, when near fifty little children lay upon the policemen's beds, bunks, and floor, nearly all dead or dying, occasioned by the terrible calamity which befell Ward School No. 26, in Greenwich Avenue, (located just above this market,) on the 20th of November, 1851, on a Thursday afternoon, about two o'clock.

One of the teachers in the female department was suddenly attacked with "a stiffening of the tongue, and a contraction of the muscles of the face," which frightened some of the children, who commenced screaming. Water being called for to use on the fainting teacher, raised the supposition of fire, and the next moment the cry of "Fire!" was echoed through the building. Subordination was at an end; the children rushed to the stairways, which were soon filled, and the pressure against the balustrades was so great that they gave way, and down, down the "deep well-hole" they were hurled to the bottom, where hundreds continued to follow and fall on those below, until they were piled up—a mass of children—eight feet square and about twelve feet high, principally little girls. In the boys' department, the resolute teacher, Mr. McNally, stopped the boys by placing his back against the door, and forbade any one to go out, which no doubt was the means of saving many lives; but the excitement was so great, that one bright, smart boy, (who I knew,) in trying to jump from the window to the roof of the house adjoining, fell short, and down he went, to be immediately killed. Being deeply interested, I hastened to the school-house, to see the last of these little ones carried to this Station-House Hall, where I quickly followed, to behold—Oh! what a dreadful scene!

The first person I saw was a friend, the father of a beautiful little lifeless girl, whom he was holding, while sitting on the floor, and calling to her by name. We hurried on, and stopped a moment to pick up a poor suffering boy, who, in his painful delirium, had thrown himself off the *bunk* upon the floor.   On we went, twice around that Hall, to examine each one a second time, to find those whom we thought, at the time, were lost.

The Press of the day, however, gave all the names, residences of the dead and severely injured, with the evidence taken before a Coroner's Jury, and other particulars; and we will leave this intensely painful subject to one of humanity.

On the Sixth Avenue side, under the eaves of the country market, may be daily found the "Blind Man of Jefferson Market," Henry McNerney, once an assistant clerk in the Navy Department at Washington, under the Honorable James K. Paulding.

Every morning, except the Sabbath, may be seen the little prattling daughter leading her blind father, threading her way through the carts, wagons, baskets, &c., to his little inclosed stall, where she leaves him with a " good-morning," and back home again she returns for her school; in the evening the same duties are regularly performed by her to take him home again, and on Saturday night late, between ten and eleven, his wife or son performs that duty.   As soon as he arrives at the market he opens his small store of goods, by taking down the shutters, dusts off his exposed wares, and tastefully, as well as *feelingly*, puts all in order ready for his scanty sales. Behind and before him are arranged his crockery, candies, cake, and cord; shoe-strings, sewing-thread, suspenders, sugar-plums, and many other little articles, make up his stock in trade, where all can be reached, cases opened, any article selected, and change given; and, I believe, but few have been heartless enough to steal or take advantage of him.

His trade, however, is quite slow, but patiently he waits for the sometimes few shillings, and then again an exceedingly good business day will bring him in a few dollars: he says, " I did pretty well when I first came here; then I took in three, four, and five dollars— now I seldom take in as many shillings."

So well do his eyes appear, that fifty persons might pass him and with a casual glance at him would not suppose those orbs were sightless—that he was a blind man; but if they drew near and looked at him a moment, they would discover the vacant stare, which for twenty long years have not been able to discover the least glimmer of light—all is darkness—one long dark night has he had, and so it will continue, no doubt, until his life's end.

He has been located here since 1852, by the kindness and intercession of some of the authorities who gave him a stand here, without rent; but I am sorry to record that at times, when any amount of sales were made by him, one of the Clerks demanded fees; however, within the last five years business has been so dull with him, that no fees have been collected from him. Year after year he has faithfully striven to obtain an honest living for his little family of five—and with the assistance of his wife, who occasionally performs house-labor, they have lived on—their joint earnings, however, were sometimes not sufficient to keep this little household together, if some kind friend had not assisted them.

About the year 1840, while engaged in his duties at Washington, which he well and faithfully performed, he became suddenly almost blind, and was obliged to come to this city for assistance. Having some means, he sought the best physicians, but with little immediate success; unfortunately, however, he, in his anxiety to get well soon, changed for a famous *quack oculist*, who with caustic burnt and killed the main nerve of the eyes, and no doubt it also for a time shattered the intellect. So anxious was he to obtain assistance, that the quack took advantage of it, and increased and received his enormous demands at every operation, which soon found all his means expended. But his former services and good character were not forgotten; his old employer sought him out, and on him displayed his kindness and benevolence: "As long as I have you shall not want." James K. Paulding never allowed him to suffer while he lived, nor will his generations, some of whom he has dandled on his knee while children—they never, nor have they, forgotten the "Blind Man of Jefferson Market."

To the year 1856 we turn, to introduce a sort of serio-comic article from the Press on some of the daily occurrences and sights which at that time took place at this market. It may appear somewhat egotistical in these pages; yet its pleasantry may assist to subdue this reflection, when the attention of the reader is drawn to one to whom the American people owe so much for the many brilliant and successful services which have been lavished upon them by the wisdom, gallantry, and generalship of Lieutenant-General Winfield Scott, and which have placed his name among the great men of the world.

The article, after alluding to a specimen of military nobility of the "mother-country," turns to introduce the following: "On any morning of the five days out of the six of our weekly calendar, Jefferson Market—in this emporium of the New World—represents a lap of luxury—the glory of a bountifully supplied and plenteous land. Here are gorgeous avenues of flesh, all garnished with masses, and quarters, and ribs, and loins of the finest beef, in streaks of mellow meat imbedded in layers of golden fat. Interspersed are columns

of the whitest marbled-fatted mutton.   In beautiful relief milk-white
veal and porcine carcasses fill up the intervals, with flowers and
greens of our forest lands, arching the roof—all so pure, clean, and
inviting that the poor man sighs, from the deepest depth of his
empty stomach, as he wonders why such plenty so persistingly hangs
so far beyond his reach; while the rich man's eyes feed with epi-
curean delight, and his mouth streams with watery, luscious ecstasy
as he casts his longing and far-reaching sight down these inviting
vistas of 'animal food,' and contemplates them in connection with
his own culinary department of his household.   On either side are
other avenues gracefully festooned with wreaths of 'Christmas ivy'
and of 'evergreens,' pendent from which full swelling-breasted turkeys droop their heads in melancholy nuidity; by their side, in cold
death's embrace, hang innocent ducks and sinless chickens, and fowls
of every size, form, and hue, with fore and hind quarters of game,
with clean bushy tails, all so beautifully and gracefully with succu-
lents interlaced, and so temptingly presented.   All looking so in-
vitingly entreating to be purchased, sent home, dressed and eaten,
that any man must be a perfect monster Graham-misanthrope that
could resist such an appeal as here is made upon his senses and
gustatory nerves by this Cornucopia of the meats, the fruits, and the
granaries of this fructiferous land.

    " In the recess of one of the avenues we speak of is situated the
excellent and abundantly supplied stand of Colonel De Voe—a noble
specimen of an American citizen, military as well as civil—whose
stall emphatically teams with the 'fat of the land.'

    " On. the opposite side to the Colonel's position is a young isolated
Cornucopia of the fruits of the earth, mixed with wild-fowl of the
air, all belonging and under the imperial sway of the 'Queen of the
Market,' a very smart and pretty woman, named 'Mrs. Mingay.'
Between these two stands a cane-bottom stool, especially devoted to
a distinguished American chieftain, upon which every morning seated
may be seen the martial, giant figure of *General Winfield Scott*.   By
his side stands Colonel De Voe, respectfully conversing with his distinguished friend, and taking his orders for the finest and best cuts.
At a respectful distance, with military submission, are the General's
two male servants, his *aids-du-market*, who ever and anon bring
tidings of their success from the distant portions of this camp of supplies.   This completed, the greatest military chieftain living sits
with classic dignity, like a martial Colossus of Mars, quietly smiling
to his friends, and patiently waiting for the attention to his wants
on the part of the renowned Mrs. Mingay.

    " Butcher-boys pass and repass the General with no more thought of the Hero of Mexico than they do of the lambs they have slaughtered. Old women and ragged children brush against the old gentleman, and, treading on his cloak, thrust their wares of tape, blacking, matches, &c., in his face, and shout in his ear, demanding of him to become a purchaser of their merchandise. Gaunt men, with awkward baskets of oranges, bawl in his face, 'O-rangis!' and the folks pass heedless on, thinking of nothing but their business, and paying no more attention, courtesy, or respect to *the presence* of the greatest of American warriors, than they would were he plain Mr. Scott, ship-chandler.

"But there sits the General, with his martial person, with his calm but eagle eye, as indifferent and as unconcerned as if he were no more than a living statue erected there by the love of the people, but whose accustomed presence had destroyed all novelty or interest in the living being. During all this time, the celebrated Mrs. Mingay aforesaid has been serving some dozens of 'biddies,' niggers, gentlemen and lady housekeepers and boarding-house keepers, when, breathless with exertion, she *hails* the General with, 'Now, General, what can I do for you?' The General, with stately humility and deference to the queen of esculents, through his *aids-du-market*, gives his orders, which being executed with alacrity and smiles, the fair Mrs. Mingay coquets with the money she is receiving, and the General replies to her pleasantries with unmixed affability. This completed, the Colossus Mars rises to his feet—no salutation, no look, no wonderment, no nothing greets him from the busy crowd, and, as plain Mr. Scott, the Lieutenant-General Scott, of the United States, quietly takes his departure for his home. But in case of war? Ah! then 23,000,000 of people would be at his feet—*à les Anglais*—shouting forth his praise, and calling upon him to destroy Columbia's foes, to be again dropped when the work was done, and refused back pay, and again represent the picture we have drawn, representing Mars on a market-day, smiling at the call of Mrs. Mingay, 'Now, General, what can I do for you?' Democracy is ungrateful—*sich* is life—and long life to Lieutenant-General Scott!"[*]

The last licenses for butchers' stands in this market appear on record as follows:

No. 1. John Hanshe.

No. 2. Bartlett Smith.

3. John De Voe.

4. George S. Starr.

5. George W. De Voe.

6. John De Voe & Son.

7. Frederick De Voe.

8. Thos. F. De Voe.

9. William Leary.

10. Moses De Voe.

11. James Waters.

12. Alexander Van Wart.

[*] N. Y. Mercury, March 9th, 1856.

No. 13. John Davidson.   No. 14. Robert Fleming.
    15. David B. Reed.   16. Jacob Bernheim.

There are several other butchers in this, as well as in many other of the public markets, who have not been regularly "licensed" for the stands they occupy; having obtained them under another head, and also in *another manner*, by the alteration of the Market Law: these are usually known as "permit butchers."

The business here has much increased within the last ten years, and now, no doubt, it will rank among the best of the up-town markets; the buildings, however, are much out of repair, and the supposition is that it will require the influence of a Seventh Regiment, or a chance for a large speculation, to obtain a new market-house on the present site of the Jefferson Market.

"WEEHAWKEN MARKET."

1834. THIS market-place, although known in the "Records" and "Maps" as the "Greenwich Market," was commonly called, and it was known, as the "Weehawken Market," by way of difference, when spoken of, from the old Greenwich Market building, which stood some time after this was erected. The name "Greenwich Market" had also been applied to the old "Spring Street Market," in its early years; besides this, the new street on the easterly side of this new market-place was named Weehawken Street. These several facts led me to adopt the name of "Weehawken," after an Indian name of "Weehawk," which gave the name to a place nearly opposite, on the "Jersey shore," from which, years before, a ferry-boat went to and fro, landing on this side, just above this market-place.

The first notice of the want of a market-house at this place was by a resolution made on the 23d of March, 1829, "that the front ground on West Street, between Christopher and Amos Streets, to the depth of thirty feet, be, and the same is hereby, reserved for the purpose of erecting a public market-house thereon." In the month of May following, the "State Prison grounds" were advertised to be sold, reserving and displaying on the maps this "market-place," which it was represented would soon after be established; and when the sale took place, this fact was again particularly noticed by the Corporation, which induced the buyers to advance the prices for portions of this property near this market-place.

Among the numerous buyers was the lamented Stephen Allen, once the Mayor of the City of New York, who lost his life by the burning of the steamboat *Henry Clay*, just below Yonkers landing, on the afternoon of the 28th of July, 1852. Two years the ex-Mayor had waited, without any signs of the erection of this market-house, although petitions and communications had been sent to the Common Council; but, as the "Jefferson Market" was in contemplation, some of the members thought it would accommodate this part of the city without this market, and they put in a plea that they were not bound, by word or print, to erect this "*Wee-hawken* Market."

The ex-Mayor soon after sent in a communication, in which we find the following: "Can any good reason be urged why the Corporation should not perform their implied contract with the purchasers of these lots? It will not merely be urged that the designation of the market on the 'map' did not imply a promise to erect one, and that no written stipulation was entered into. Reasons like these may answer when bargaining with individuals of a proper cast, but not with the agents of a public body like the Corporation of the City of New York."

In another petition, at the same time, from Abraham Van Nest and others, who "remonstrate against any market being erected in Greenwich Village, before the *(Weehawken)* one alluded to, and to which we are entitled by a public promise." "If the rapid growth of this city, and the increasing population, call for a market in the Sixth Avenue, *(Jefferson,)* we cheerfully say, grant it, but not until the one is erected which has actually been promised us."

Their communications and petitions were unheeded by the Common Council; the "Jefferson Market" was erected, and this subject was *staved off* until the month of November, 1833, when another petition was before the Board; and again they state, "At the time of the sale of sundry lots formerly belonging to the State, they consider the public faith was pledged to erect a market on the site as marked on the map." The Report of the Market Committee was also before the Board now, favorable to the petitioners, in which they state, "that many persons were induced to purchase lots fronting the said market square at a considerable advance over other lots in the neighboring streets, owing to an implied pledge that a market-house would be erected thereon." This Report was adopted and approved in the month of January, 1834, and a resolution, some time after, was passed to build "on Christopher Street 30 feet, on West 197 feet, 10 inches, on Weehawken 197 feet, 10 inches, and on Amos Street 30 feet." Then followed an appropriation of $3,475 for that purpose. The market-house was erected, when fourteen butchers' stands, and the necessary vegetable and fish stands, were ordered to be placed in it. From No. 5 to 14 were designated to be occupied by the butchers of the old ("Greenwich") market, reserving Nos. 1, 2, 3, and 4, on Christopher Street, to be sold at public auction, which took place on the 21st of October following, to the following persons and prices:

No. 1. Adam H. Chappel, $170 No. 2. Orville Toby, $120
    3. Laban C. Style,   30   4. Milton Jacacks,   25

The premiums were reported paid in, and the purchasers had produced a recommendation from licensed butchers of "their being fit and proper persons to receive butchers' licenses."

The other *ten* stands were occupied in the month of July, 1835, as follows:

No. 5. James Reeves, Sen'r.   No. 6. James Ford.
    7. Thomas Reeves.   8. Jared Goodheart.
    9. Scales.   10. William Tallet.
    11. Andrew Forshay.   12. Vacant.
    13. Mat'w Van Benschoten.   14. William Goodheart.

James Reeves, Sen'r, the occupant of No. 5, was somewhat remarkable looking as eccentric, especially (in his latter days) while doing business on this stand. About this period I became acquainted with him; then a very large, stout, but active man. He stood quite erect, except the head inclined a little forward, with a profusion of long, white silken hair hanging around his shoulders, and when at business in market he went usually without a hat, which gave him a peculiar and venerable appearance. Of a social disposition, and a large fund of varied information, his conversation was attractive, agreeable, and interesting, and in business he was an excellent salesman.

About the year 1818–19, he was doing business in the Catharine Market, when a "hue and cry" broke out against Jacob Barker's money, the Exchange, and Washington and Warren Banks, which money was at this period largely in circulation. An extract from a letter, dated June, 1819, will give the reader an idea of the excitement: "Jacob Barker's Bank (*Exchange*) is shut up this day, in consequence of a heavy run upon him yesterday to meet the Washington and Warren Bank notes, which he met in specie at 30 per cent. discount; there is a great mob around his *closed bank*, and constables are fixed to prevent its being gutted, as many fear will be the case. The people, however, dispersed peaceably, and several store-keepers and others advertise that they will receive Mr. Barker's notes in payment for goods."

Mr. Reeves, however, had so much confidence in Mr. Barker's honesty, that he continued taking his money until he had in possession $1,000, and finding he could not buy stock or pay it away, he began to think it was about time to do something with it; but as he had become somewhat excited in consequence of having his whole means in money that he could not use, he wished one of his sons to write Barker a note, informing him that "all he possessed, in fact, the earnings of years of labor, was in his money." His son waited on Mr. Barker at his house, and presented his note, when Mr. Barker told him to come to his office the next day. Reeves went himself, and Mr. Barker said, he knew him (*Reeves*) as a poor but honest man; that his confidence in him should not be changed, and forthwith drew him a check for the whole amount, at the same time told him to put over his stall—"*Jacob Barker's money taken at 50 cents on the dollar for meats*"—and all he took in that way he would redeem for the value it represented. Reeves done so, and Barker kept his word, by which Reeves made a large business, and in a short time money enough to buy a small property in Jane Street, which he held until its rise in value gave him enough to live comfortably upon, and something for his children after his decease.

This market-place was never a successful one, although for three or four years business enough was done there to have supported about four or five butchers; but after that period the "meat-shops" attracted certainly one-half of its trade, which left plenty of untenanted stalls and stands, although several paid the rents for them and did business elsewhere, in hope that the market laws would be enforced, when they might return, but that period never came.

Several changes had taken place in their occupation in the course of five or six years, and in 1840 these stands are found not all occupied, but in the possession of the following butchers:

No. 1. William O. Ford.   No. 2. James Ford.
3. Laban C. Styles.   4. Unoccupied.
5. John E. Reeves.   6.   do.
7. James Reeves.   8. Robert Piercy.
9. Thomas Reeves.   10. Samuel Piercy, Jun'r.
11. Unoccupied.   12. William Tallet.
13. Henry Pray.   14. William C. Goodheart.

In the month of March, 1842, a resolution was passed to lease this market to "George M. Buel for the term of three years, from the first of May next, at an annual rent of three hundred and twenty-five dollars, payable quarterly. Said Buel to reserve twenty feet of the south end of said market for the accommodation of *two butchers,* two hucksters, a fish and clam stand."

These remained only about three years longer, when it became at times deserted, and at last wholly so, when several of the owners of the property on Weehawken Street petitioned for leave to purchase this market property, which brought forth a favorable report from the Finance Committee in January, 1846, in which it was stated that these grounds were "sold under an implied pledge that a market was to be established in front, which induced them to give a much greater price for the property than they otherwise would have given; that the market was built and their property improved by the erection of buildings, and the petitioners in the receipt of a fair income, but that for the last year or two the market has been abandoned, and the market-house occupied for other purposes; in consequence of which their property has become greatly depreciated, and is much exposed to damage by fire, from the nature of the business conducted in said market-house. They pray to have it removed or sold to them at a moderate price, in order to be remunerated by the loss sustained."

About half of the old market building is yet (1857) standing, occupied with a depot for the Hudson River Railroad Company, small stores, and "dram-shops," and the other half with other buildings for various other purposes.

"UNION MARKET."

1835. ON the 6th of January, 1834, a Committee reported in favor of a site, which, they said, they "have selected for the erection of a market in the 11th Ward: is bounded by North (now *Houston* Street) and Second Streets, at the junction on Avenue D, and comprises a plot of ground containing 198 feet 6 inches on North Street, 202 feet 10 inches on Second Street, 46 feet 6 inches on the west end, and 21 feet 3 inches at the east end on Avenue D, which plot has been appraised at $8,000. which your Committee think is a very reasonable price, as it is situated in a very commanding position for the public market, and that it is a primary duty of the Common Council to render every facility to their constituents in the enlargement of the public markets in the upper and rapidly increasing portion of the city, as our public markets most unquestionably produce much the largest revenue to the City Treasury of all public property. For example, take the Fulton Market, which cost $200,000, the annual revenue arising from which is $19,077.10; or, in other words, over 9½ per cent. on the investment."

This truthful report, however, was not acted upon until the next year, in the month of March, when we find a *Resolution*, "'To contract with Charles Overton for building a 'market' on the ground lately taken for market purposes in the 11th Ward, of the same dimensions as the Jefferson Market, for the sum of $5,961," which was passed, and in the following month of May it was named the "*Union Market*," no doubt from the fact that the Corporation intended to *unite* the Manhattan Market with this, as that market-place had proved a failure.

As soon as this market-house was finished, the Market Committee decided to place the six butchers who had purchased stands in the "Manhattan Market" in this new building, and giving them from No. 1 to No. 6 inclusive. Then, on the 23d September following, they "Resolved that six new stalls be put in the upper end of 'Union Market.' The stands to be *drawn for by lot;* none but regular butchers be allowed to draw. No butcher having a stall in the markets, nor any butcher who may have within three months disposed of his stand in any of the markets, will be allowed to draw. Persons wishing to draw for a stand will make application to the Market Committee in writing, with the proper recommendations appended, &c."

Numerous petitions with recommendations were, on the 8th of October, put into the hands of the "*Executive Committee of Butchers*" for examination; and before proceeding further, it would be well to state how this "Executive Committee of Butchers" became recognized by the Common Council.

On the 16th of June previous the Market Committee invited the following licensed butchers to meet with them for consultation: Messrs. Jacob Aims, Daniel Burtnett, James Reeves, John Scott, Edward Phillips, George Pessinger, Thomas Winship, William Hanshe, Ebenezer Pray, and Thomas F. De Voe. "It was mutually agreed, that the licensed butchers in the several markets should meet and appoint an *Executive Committee* to consult with the Market Committee on all important subjects relating to markets which may be referred to them or otherwise." The butchers held an election, when it appeared that all the public markets returned a representative, and from these representatives an *Executive Committee of Three* was elected to meet with the Market Committee. These consisted of Messrs. Andrew C. Wheeler, Daniel Burtnett, and George Pes-

singer, who were in attendance at their meetings for many years.
Although changes were made at the annual election of the members
of the Common Council, yet the assistance of this *Executive Com-*
mittee was of so much importance or assistance to them, that they
yearly "*Resolved*, That the Clerk of this (*Market*) Committee give
notice to the ' *Executive Committee* of butchers,' requesting their action as formerly;" and so it continued until just previous to the
adoption of the laws of 1843, licensing the "meat-shops."

On the 8th of October *seventy-nine* petitions for chances to draw
by lot these six stands in this market were approved of, and Daniel
Burtnett, the Chairman of this Executive Committee, was appointed
to draw the tickets. The prizes and blanks were all put together,
and drawn by their numbers, and the numbers put on each ticket
when drawn by the Comptroller; after the whole was drawn, the
numbers and tickets were opened by the Chairman, and were compared with the numbers on the petition by him and the Comptroller.
This was the first *drawing* of butcher stands by *lot*. The result was
as follows:

No. 7. Jacob Vogel.   No. 8. John Trigler, Jun'r.
    9. John Palmer.   10. Duncan Campbell.
    11. Henry Cornell.   12. David Jaques.

The market was opened for business on Saturday, the 24th of the
same month, (*October*,) with excellent prospects; but it was soon
found there was not space enough to transact the business without
interfering with each other. So a Committee reported to the Board
on the 9th of November following, recommending that an open market of 63 feet in length by 21 feet one end and 30 feet at the other,
be built at the east end of the present brick market, at an expense
not exceeding $450.

In the month of May following (1836) a fire broke out in a cabinet-
maker's shop, in a large building located in the centre of the block
north of the market. The fire spread in every direction with great
rapidity, burning and destroying some twenty buildings on Avenue
D, Second and Third Streets. It crossed Second Street and reached
this market-house, totally destroying the roof and interior, leaving
the walls standing. The stalls, fixtures, and meats, &c., were saved,
and for a day or two the occupants were obliged to remain out-
doors. However, they set to work, cleared the rubbish out of the
burnt market-house, and again located themselves on their stands,
using canvas for covering; but the watchmen, who occupied the upper part, were obliged to seek other quarters until it should be
rebuilt.

It was at this fire, while it was raging, the firemen in a body turned their "fire-caps," by wearing the front to the rear, and refused to perform duty. The *Herald* says: " While the firemen were engaged in suppressing the fire, accounts were brought them of the removal of Mr. James Gulick, the Chief Engineer, by the Corpora-- tion. This caused an extraordinary sensation in the *corps*, and they struck in the midst of the raging element, which caused an extraordinary excitement in the neighborhood. The people were highly exasperated, and hard words were bandied about.

" When it was known that the firemen had struck, the Mayor started in his gig to the spot, and remonstrated with the firemen, but it would not effect their return to duty till Mr. Gulick was reinstated provisionally. When this was announced the firemen cheered, as if victory had been obtained, and then went to work. About dark the fire was subdued, but not till about $300,000 worth of property had been utterly lost by this quarrel between the Corporation."

It appears, previous to this, the firemen had the privilege of choosing an Engineer who would suit them, and the Common Council sanctioned it; but in the appointment of one of their own selection, they not only took away this right, but also took from them a man whom they all respected, and who was considered the best Engineer who had ever held the office.

On the same night of the fire, " near ten o'clock," says the *Herald,* "J. R. Riker was appointed Chief Engineer, in the place of Mr. Gulick, who is now removed entirely. The Corporation justify their conduct on the insubordination of the firemen during the engineership of Mr. Gulick."

Another fire broke out on the evening of the 6th inst., in Prince Street, when " a number of engines were not taken out at all, and every fireman had his *'cap turned;'*" and this continued for quite a period, or until Mr. Gulick was elected to a public office.

To rebuild this market-house, an appropriation of $3,000 was made, in the month of June following.

Some five months after, a report was adopted relinquishing one quarter's rent, on account of the loss and damage sustained by this fire. It stated, that " this market was greatly damaged by fire, in such a manner as to greatly injure the interests of the butchers occupying said market, although every exertion was made to repair the same, notwithstanding a considerable time did elapse before it was completed. Under the circumstances, your Committee believe it to be just to allow a deduction of *one quarter's rent* to the butchers in said market."

In the month of December, 1840, the following persons occupied the butchers' stands, or were licensed for them, as follows:

No. 1. William Wells.	No. 2. Felix Quin.
3. Felix Quin.	4. Charles S. Glover.
5. Henry Lang.	6. James Shaff.
7. Cornelius V. Borden.	8. Peter H. Stagg.
9. John Cromer.	10. William D. Atkins.
11. Jacob Vogel.	12. John Trigler.
13. John D. Farrington.	14. Nathaniel Cromer.
15. Paul Laundry.	16. Arnold Smith.
17. John Marshall.	18. David Johnson.
19. Henry Cornell.	20. Henry Latham.

For several years this market proved to be an excellent up-town market-place, until the "meat-shops" began to gather around its neighborhood, in defiance of the laws, although they were, in an early period, promptly prosecuted; but these prosecutions appeared to have become distasteful, either from political or a manufactured opinion, to many of the public authorities, whose immediate duty it was to uphold the laws, and consequently these violations remained unnoticed. Not only the occupants of this market, but the neighborhood, felt aggrieved, and once more appealed through petition, in the month of November, 1842, in which they state, "that the violations of the market laws have become so general—meats, fish, &c., being sold in shops, groceries, &c., and hawked through the streets, by persons of all descriptions and occupations, many of whom are not even citizens—that it has become imperatively necessary for the undersigned to appeal to your Honorable Body for redress, and to ask for the enforcement of those laws in relation to the public markets which were made and adopted for wise and salutary ends. In consequence of the general infringement of those laws, the sale of meats, &c., in the public markets is reduced to that degree as not to be sufficient to meet the expenses incident to the same, and is continued to the daily loss, and in many cases to the ruination, of the regular butchers."

After the licensing of the "meat-shops" became a law, this market was at intervals almost deserted, and so it remained until about the year 1845, when a change began to be perceived; the better class of citizens returned slowly to the market, and of course business sensibly increased. The vacant stands were gradually being taken up; some by old occupants, and others by new faces, and all were in hopes of better times.

Among these new faces here was one, a most remarkable character, previously noticed in the "Old Fly Market," in connection with her husband, John Barr, who died of yellow fever in the year 1798. "Aunt Katy Barr" was known to many of our old citizens for the last half-century: first as an occupant of the "Collect Market," when that first opened for business in 1810, in which she sold her vegetation for seven years, or until the occupants were transferred into the "Centre Market," in 1817, where I, while going with my *mother* to this market, became acquainted with her and her sister, "Aunt Fanny Watson," both market-women, or hucksters, whom I thought, in my boyhood, stood in that relative relation to me, and everybody else who addressed these remarkable women. I lost sight of, and had forgotten her, from about 1825 to 1857, when I heard of the "old market-woman" in the "Union Market," whose recollections of the past were most wonderful; and when I visited her, and first heard the sound of her voice, and quick answers, told me it was the same "Aunt Katy Barr." Then, although almost ninety years old, she recollected my *mother* and her "*wild boys.*" She had stood in the "Centre Market" from its first opening, when, soon after, she received a printed *permit*, with an engraved "Arms of the State" on the top, and which read:

" *To the Deputy Clerk of Centre Market :*

"In virtue of the authority given to the Market Committee by the ordinance of the Mayor, Aldermen, and Commonalty of the City of New York, entitled, 'A Law to regulate the Public Markets,' permission is hereby given to Catharine Barr to occupy a stand in said market, for the sale of vegetables, and the Deputy Clerk of said market is authorized to assign a suitable place for such purpose. New York, 12th day of May, 1818. By order of the Market Committee. G. BUCKMASTER, *Chairman.*"

About the year 1835 she removed into one of her houses in Second Street, near Avenue C, with her married daughter, (her only child,) which created a longer distance to travel, at an earlier hour in the morning. She was, however, among the first in the market, always ready for business; and on Saturday nights, after a long, tiresome day's work, sometimes as late as twelve o'clock, found her traveling through deep snows and cold storms towards her welcome home. This active life she continued up to 1850, when she in sorrow parted from the old associations in the Centre Market, and entered again upon new ones in this (*Union*) market. Here she passed eight years in her business, and on Saturday night, the 17th of October, 1858, she left here for the last time; as she, after a short illness of only four days, expired, and her body was borne to that final resting-place where she just *sixty years* before had followed her only husband; being a wife for a few short months, and a widow of *sixty years*, always treasuring in her memory her young and loving husband.

Since the rebuilding of this burnt market-house, it became settled and cracked, and continued to grow worse, so that it was thought dangerous, which deterred many from visiting it. The neighborhood concluded it would be best to petition for a new one erected on a larger scale, as well to accommodate the "Police" as the occupants of the market proper. Their petition was answered in 1853, by the rebuilding of a much larger and finer market-house; and in the month of May, 1854, the occupants who had been located under sheds, on the vacant ground east of the market-place, were removed in, numbering some 18 butchers, and 26 hucksters, fishermen, and butter dealers.

The following persons were about this period or afterwards licensed for the butchers' stands in this market, (ranging from 1853 to 1856:)

No. 1. George Hirleman.	No. 2. J. J. Cape.
3. Abraham Atkins.	4. Jacob Wilde.
5. Isaac Oberdorfer.	6. Isaac Menaber.
7. George Keets & Co.	8. Charles Summers.
9. John McElroy.	10. William D. Atkins.
11. Louis Oppenheimer.	12. David Jaques.
13. Henry Altheimer.	14. Thomas Healy.
15. Vacant.	16. Vacant.
17. Patrick Smith.	18. do.
19. Vacant.	20. John J. Cape.

The rooms above are used as a station-house for the Eleventh Precinct, and have been so used for many years.

"MONROE MARKET."

1836. The "Grand Street Market," which had stood more than twenty years in Grand Street, near where this new market-place was about to be located, had of late years become an obstruction to the business, especially to those who were passing with carriages, wagons, and carts to and from the ferry, which induced the Market Committee to report on this new location on the 6th of January, 1834, in which they state, that " the site which your Committee have selected for extending the 'Grand Street Market' is bounded on the north by Grand Street, on the south by Monroe Street, and on the east by Corlaers Street; comprising the eastern section of said block, and containing on Grand Street 140 feet, on Corlaers Street 119 feet, on Monroe Street 125 feet, and 225 feet on a line running through to the centre of the block." "Such ground, with the improvement, has been appraised at $32,000; your Committee are unanimously of opinion that the above site is the most eligible that can be procured in that section of the city." Although this report was favorable, yet the plan for building the market-house was not agreed upon until the month of January, 1836, when it was proceeded with, and a worse adapted building for the purpose could not have well been erected. The butchers remonstrated against its plan; some thought it more suitable for a livery-stable; others, again, that it would tumble down the first strong wind.

In the month of September following, the Committee agreed to name it "Lafayette Market," but before the expiration of the month it was changed to "Monroe Market," from and after James Monroe, the fifth President of the United States, who died on the 4th of July, 1831.

The following butchers from the old "Grand Street Market" were transferred into this market-house:

No. 1. Andrew Storms.   No. 2. Thomas Winship.
    3. John Prendergast.   4. George Scott.
    5. Richard Ellis.   6. Walter Byrnes.

On the 23d of February, next year, the Market Committee drew six more stands, to be occupied by the following butchers:

No. 7. Henry Latham.   No. 8. William Vandewater.
    9. Henry Mangles.   10. H. A. Beck.
   11. Geo. W. Hopkins.   12. Stephen Brown.

The occupant of No. 2, Thomas Winship, was the grandson of Colonel Ebenezer Winship, noticed in the "Bear Market," and a son of Thomas Winship, who many years before occupied a stand in the "Corlaers Hook Market." He was ever known as a worthy and an honorable man, and although an *Alderman*, (13th Ward, in 1844,) with and amongst the many scenes of bribery and corruption, yet he passed through his term with only pecuniary losses; a considerable portion of that article which is most sought after by the corrupt office-holder, who sometimes manage through a brief term or two to get in possession of enough to live, after their retirement, an independent life, and to be looked upon by some as worthy and respectable. But the honest Alderman would not touch the "thirty pieces of silver," by selling out his integrity or self-respect, and his constituents felt, in electing him to this once honorable position, they had given the right ballot for the right man.

On the 31st of March, 1837, the Superintendent of Buildings was, by resolution, "authorized to make such alteration in this market-house as he may deem necessary, to make a way or passage into the market from Monroe Street," which gave the rear stalls some more advantage for business; but there was never enough to support all the stand-holders, as we find after the first year or two many of the stands were unoccupied, although held by the owners, who paid the rents, in expectation of better times. In 1840 the following butchers held licenses for the stands as follows:

No. 1. Andrew Storms.   No. 2. Thomas Winship.
3. John Prendergast.   4. George Scott, Jun'r.
5. John Deal.   6. Benjamin Ward.
7. George Cumming.   8. William Nesbet.
9. Philip Weeks.   10. Richard S. Davenport.

The existing market laws at this period were not put in force; and as the neighborhood had a great number of "meat-shops," the proprietors of which defied the authorities, the consequence was, this market was injured, although it lingered along until the year 1847, when, on the 12th of July, a Committee reported in favor of selling the ground and premises at public auction.

In this year we find five butchers licensed for the following stands:

No. 1. John Prendergast.   No. 2. Thomas Winship.
3. William Nolan.   4. George Cumming.
5. John Masterton.

Soon after part of this market property was sold; one of the lots was purchased by Winship and Prendergast, who remained about one year after, when it was deserted.

A part of the old market-house yet (1853) stands on the corner of Grand and Corlaers Streets, almost ready to tumble down.

"HARLEM MARKET."

1840. THIRTY-THREE years (1807) prior to the establishment of the "Harlem Market," which we are now about to introduce, there was granted to a butcher, named Thomas Dunning, a privilege to erect a temporary shed as a market-house, near what was then called the "Five Corners," now located about 200 feet west of the Third Avenue, near 120th Street. This was established as a public market-place, to be under the same rules and regulations as all the others; but Dunning did not so understand it, and therefore paid no market fees for the space of two years, although repeatedly called upon to do so. The Mayor directed his Marshal, on the 27th of February, 1809, to suspend and commence suit against him, which had the effect of causing him to pay over £30 18s. 3d., the amount of the fees then due.

Another butcher at the same place, named William Perkins, also refused to pay his fees, when proceedings were also ordered against him. From that period up to the establishment of this "Harlem Market," there had been kept a sort of a market-place at or near the same location; but at times very indifferently supplied, which no doubt was in consequence of the meat-wagons, who, after a period, visited this place on certain days of the week. The neighborhood, however, was dissatisfied, and petitioned on several occasions, which do not appear to have been noticed until the month of May, 1838, when a report on taking ground at Harlem to build a market-house was read, as follows: "That a piece of ground should be taken somewhere in the vicinity of 120th and 121st Streets, near the Third Avenue, for a public market, and they think this a suitable location. The ground to be taken consists of two irregular triangles on both sides of an old road, 100 feet in width, running diagonally through the whole plot. The piece fronting on the Third Avenue has several low, wooden buildings on it, of not much value, &c.; the piece fronting on 121st Street has also two wooden buildings on it. Your Committee are of opinion that the value of the whole is not more than $5,500, and that the owners of the part fronting on the Third Avenue are so situated that a clean title could not at present be obtained. The property thus taken will be a suitable place for a public market and for engine-houses."

"Resolved, That application be made to the Legislature for a law authorizing the taking of a plot of ground on the Third Avenue, between 120th and 121st Streets, and running back two hundred and seventy-five feet, for public purposes, by Commissioners to be appointed by the Supreme Court;" which was adopted and approved.

Two years after another report on the subject was before the Common Council, stating "that by an act of the Legislature, passed at its last session, the Corporation have become possessed in fee of a plot of ground bounded" as above, "and designed for public purposes. During the investigation of the subject referred to your Committee, it has satisfactorily appeared that to no purpose could a portion of the land alluded to be more appropriately or advantageously used than for the erection of a public market thereon. It would afford very great accommodations to the inhabitants at Harlem and in its vicinity for a vast number who now have to procure their marketing in the city; and, in truth, it would be doing great injustice to the citizens there to deny them so reasonable a request," &c.

A resolution was also offered, directing the Superintendent of Public Buildings " to advertise for proposals for the erection of a market-house at Harlem, in conformity with the plan, and appropriating the sum of $1,500 for the purpose;" which was adopted.

But in the face of this, the Superintendent " contracted the building of it for $2,100," six hundred more than was authorized; and *extras* besides were demanded by the builder after it was finished, as will afterwards appear.

The building having been erected, it was soon occupied by four butchers, one fisherman, and a vegetable stand. The butchers were Philip Hardenbrook & Brother, Thomas Quinlan, and Henry Cook; the two latter, however, gave up their stands soon after.

In the month of August, 1842, a petition was before the Board, stating, " that several years since, that portion of the block of ground lying between 120th and 121st Streets, and extending from the Third Avenue and the Old Road, was set apart by the Honorable the Corporation for the purpose of a public square, and erecting a market-house thereon; that the said building has been completed, but that no steps have as yet been taken for the removal of the incumbrances from said grounds, &c." This, with others, after a period of several months, brought forth the following from the " Finance Committee:" "*Resolved*, That the Comptroller be, and he is hereby, authorized and directed to sell at public auction all the old buildings in Harlem Square, with the exception of the one on the corner of the Third Avenue and 120th Street, and to pay the proceeds of said sales into the City Treasury." This was adopted and approved in the months of September and October of the above year, (1842.)

At the time of the establishment of this market-place, the law favorable to meat-shops was not yet a law, only so far that no prosecutions took place, and they were allowed almost any and everywhere; and this was not all, as all sorts of flesh were carried in carts and wagons, and peddled around the suburbs; and Harlem was not excepted. From this cause, the business of this market declined, until not more than one or two butchers could be supported.

In the month of March the Brothers Hardenbrook made an application to lease it for a term of years; which was referred to a Committee, who reported favorable, stating, " that the market in question is not bringing the city anything, and no probability of its making any revenue for some time to come, unless it be in the way proposed." "*Resolved,* That a lease be granted to William Hardenbrook, for three years, of the building known as the 'Harlem Market,' at an annual rent of one hundred and fifty dollars; subject to a termination of said lease at any time during the term, should the Common Council take the same for public purposes."

In 1857 I found the Hardenbrooks yet in possession of this much-neglected market-house, although a resolution had passed many years before "to have it taken down and removed."

Since the establishment of this last public market-place in our city, there have been several others brought to the notice of the public; some of which have received favorable reports to establish them, but, for reasons unknown, (or at least strongly suspected,) they were "laid on or under the table;" while others, again, were defeated, mainly in consequence of the exposure of some of the rascalities shown up by a watchful and an honest PUBLIC PRESS, which could not be bought, nor brought "into the ring."

We owe a great deal to an honest "PRESS," whose great power and benefit, more especially in the saving of thousands of dollars, by its timely exposure and expression, its forming and informing the public mind, and its truthful daily historical events, which time makes more interesting and valuable. But this crowded volume has brought upon me the thought of its conclusion, that another more useful one may very soon appear, to redeem my promise made in the beginning.

Having thus passed through the several public market-places which have been established, from time to time, in different parts of the City of New York, I have at least noticed some of the incidents connected with their respective histories; and in taking leave of the markets, I do so with a hope and expectation of re-entering them at no distant day, for the purpose of noticing the various articles which are offered for sale therein; and I trust, should I be permitted to do so, that as much satisfaction will be experienced in a perusal of the more practical information which I will then have to offer, as there has been in its collection and compilation.

END OF THE FIRST VOLUME.

INDEX TO BUTCHERS.

Note.—The number of butchers (both of the olden and modern times) noticed in this volume is found so great, (being about 1,200,) that it has induced me to place them under the above separate head; leaving, however, the subject found connected with each individual for the General Index.

The surnames of many of the same name are also, at various intervals of time, found differently spelled or connected: thus, *Ensley, Enslee, Insley, Inslee,* or *Inslow; Outenbogart, Outen Bogert,* or *O. Bogert; Trigleth, Triglar, Trigler,* or the middle name or letter of certain persons left out altogether

It appears to have been the custom or fashion, in the "olden time," for individuals to write names or words according to the common pronunciation or sound; which, no doubt, is the cause of the change in the spelling of so many of the names of our old families; this has led me to introduce some of the different styles, as found in the originals.

A.

Abeel, John, 232. 323.
Acker, Jacob, 350, 413, 509, 511.
Ackerly, John, 479.
Ackerman, Samuel, 212.
Aims, Arnest, (*Aimes,*) 516.
Aims, Jacob, 346, 376, 412, 429, 431, 437, 438, 439, 494, 506, 581.
Aims, John P., 356, 439.
Aimes, John, 324.
Akley, John, (*Ackley,*) 549.
Alden, John, 517.
Alden, Joseph, 503, 510, 517.
Allen, Christopher, 531.
Altheimer, Henry, 586.
Andarise, John, (*Andarese,*) 429, 439
Anderson, Isaac, 516.
Anderson, Walter, 362, 530.
Anderson, William, 356, 530.
Angevine, Caleb, 402.
Anthony, Alexander, 362.

Appley, Jacob, 336, 337, 339.
Appleby, William, 350, 356, 357, 358, 359, 524.
Appleby, James, 362, 365.
Appleby, John, 365.
Appleby, Joseph C., 362, 365.
Appleby, Walter, 365.
Arden, Jacob, (*Arding,*) 149.
Arden, Jacob J., 315, 316, 367.
Arden, Francis, 212, 218.
Arment, Moses E., 471, 472.
Arment, Samuel L., 474, 485, 486.
Arnold, George, 160.
Astor, Henry, (*Henrich,*) (*Ashdore, Ashdoor,*) 159, 160, 184, 185, 210, 211, 212, 315, 367, 368.
Atkins, Abraham, 586.
Atkins, William D., 526, 584, 586.
Austin, William, 529.

B.

Bahanan, Alexander, (*Buchanan,*) 214.
Bahanan, Mathew, 214.

Baisley, Andrew, (*Basley, Bazley, Beslar, Beasly,*) 316, 367.
Baisley, Harman, 486, 549.
Baisley, John, 211, 316.
Baisley, John A., 461.
Barker, John P., 356.
Barr, John, (*Bear,*) 201, 206, 207.
Batt, William R., 495.
Batten, Philip, (*Battin,*) 91.
Bayea, Isaac, (*Beyea,*) 201, 212, 374, 379.
Beatey, Robert, 531.
Beck, George, 503.
Beck, George R., 200, 212.
Beck, H. A., 587.
Beck, John, 157.
Bennett, John A., 549.
Bennett, William W., 438.
Bernheim, Jacob, 576.
Berryman, Alexander, 531.
Bird, Charles, 212.
Bird, Freeman P., 439.
Bird, Mathew, 396, 460, 486.
Bird, Mathew W., 362.
Black, John, 549.
Blackwell, Joseph, 396, 397, 398, 461, 465, 467, 469, 470, 506.
Blair, William T., 557.
Blank, William, 206.
Bockover, Thomas, 479.
Bogart, Joseph O., Jr., (*Bogert,*) 200, 210, 212, 222, 233, 241, 494, 495.
Bogert, Abraham, 200.
Bogert, Joseph Outen, Sr., (*Outenbogert,*) 155.
Bolander, Ephraim B., 465, 467, 471, 495.
Borden, Cornelius F., 485.
Borden, Cornelius V., 584.
Borden, William, 462, 465, 467.
Borden, William D., 471, 478.
Borowsan, Martin, 429.
Boscawen, John, 336, 343, 405, 551.
Boudinot, Tobias, 502.
Bowen, William, 461, 465, 467, 471.
Bowers, Peter, 365.
Boyce, Jacob, (*Boice, Byce, Bice,*) 485, 486.
Boyce, John S., 437.
Boyce, Isaac, 413.
Boyce, Nicholas, 374.
Boyce, William J., 503.

Boyd, James, 529.
Brady, Alexander, 457.
Brewer, Abraham, 549.
Brewer, John, Jr., 485, 486.
Brewer, John, Sr., 412, 420, 503.
Bridle. John, 232, 495, 500, 503.
Briel, Conrad, 487.
Briel, Daniel, 487.
Briggs, Walter, 486, 487.
Broadway, Edmond, 531.
Broadway, Orman, 519.
Broadway, Thomas E., Jr., 549.
Broadway, Thomas E., Sr., 529, 531, 549.
Broadway, Frazier, (*Frazior, Zavier,*) 232, 495, 499.
Brower, Charles, 517.
Brower, Evardus, 131.
Brower, Stephen, 486.
Brown, Alexander J., 406.
Brown, Alexander, 458, 484, 486.
Brown, David, 429.
Brown, George, 75.
Brown, George, 502.
Brown, Samuel, 93, 115.
Brown, Stephen, 587.
Brown, Thomas H., 487.
Buchannan, Mathew, 396.
Bull, Joseph, 455.
Burk, John, 214.
Burtnett, Daniel, 232, 421, 429, 431, 432, 437, 438, 439, 494.
Byrnes, Edward, 365.
Byrnes, James, 429.
Byrnes, John, 557.
Byrnes, Mathew, 356, 362, 365, 494.
Byrnes, Walter, 457, 458, 460, 587.

C.

Cadwell, Charles, 439.
Calcutt, Jeremiah, 68, 70, 82.
Calhoun, Thomas, 362.
Callender, William S., 503.
Camerden, George, (*Camerding,*) 429, 439.
Cammell, James, 350.
Campbell, Charles, 486, 487.
Campbell, Duncan, 582.
Campbell, George W., 436, 439.
Campbell, James, 210.
Cape, J. J., 586.
Cape, John J., 586.

Caple, John, 298.
Carby, John, 201.
Carpenter, Charles L., (*Carpender*,) 551, 553.
Carpenter, Eliza, 93, 94.
Carpenter, Henry S., 487.
Carpenter, John, 148, 149, 157, 158.
Carpenter, John, Jr., 495.
Carpenter, Stephen, 487.
Carr, James, 212, 232.
Carstang, William, 485.
Castell, George, 517.
Chamberlain, John C., 438, 517.
Chappel, Adam H., (*Chapple*,) 483, 578.
Chappel, John, 232, 503, 509, 511, 517.
Chase, Mathew H., 439, 477.
Chivvis, Cornelius, (*Chivers, Chives*,) 414.
Chivvis, James, 413, 414.
Chivvis, John, 382, 383, 412, 414.
Chivvis, Peter, 415.
Chivvis, William, (*1st*,) 321, 323, 368, 413, 414, 415.
Chivvis, William, (*2d*,) 376.
Chivvis, William, (*3d*,) 510.
Clasen, William, 37.
Clinch, Frederick, 472, 478.
Clinch, George, 462, 465, 466, 467, 468, 471.
Clinch, Joseph W., 472, 474, 477, 478.
Clinton, Lawrence, 516.
Coleman, Henry, 60.
Collins, Henry, 356.
Collister, Thomas, (*Corleys*,) 413.
Compton, Samuel, 485.
Conckling, Edmund, 360.
Conklin, Caleb, (*Concklin*,) 356, 391.
Conklin, Edward, 360.
Conklin, Joseph, 350, 356, 361, 362.
Conrad, H., 374.
Conway, Charles, 365.
Conway, John, 362.
Conway, Michael, 365.
Conway, Richard, 362, 365.
Corbey, John, 199.
Corbitt, William, 554.
Cornell, Benjamin, 201, 212.
Cornell, Henry, 381, 382, 582, 584.
Cornell, John, 406.
Cornell, Prantiz W., 274.
Cornell, Samuel, 362.

Cornell, Samuel S., 401, 402.
Cornell, Stephen H., 517.
Cornell, Whitehead, 201, 212.
Cornell, Willet, 232.
Cornell, William H., 486, 517.
Cook, Henry W., 531, 549, 590.
Coope, Jesse, 228.
Cooper, Charles, 516
Cooper, Cornelius, 516.
Cooper, Giles, 102.
Cox, Michael, 562.
Cox, Thomas, 95, 96, 115, 131.
Craft, William, 487.
Crasto, Moses E., 474.
Crawbuck, Elizabeth, 396, 397, 398.
Crawbuck, Godfrey, 374.
Crawbuck, John D., 405, 494, 499.
Crawbuck, Michael, 232, 241, 494.
Crawbuck, Peter, 322, 374, 518, 519.
Cregier, Cornelius M., 474, 485.
Cromer, John, (*Crommer*,) 584.
Cromer, Nicholas, 485, 486.
Cromer, Nathaniel, 524, 526, 584.
Cromwell, Gilbert, 356, 362.
Crosby, Henry, 68.
Cruise, James W., 362.
Cumming, George, (*Cuming*,) 460, 588.
Cuthbert, George, 39
Curtis, Abner, 212.

D.

Darby, James, 531
Dark, Richard, (*Dart*,) 495.
Davenport, Daniel, (*Deavenport*,) 325.
Davenport, John, 201, 211, 374, 412, 429, 465, 551.
Davenport, Richard S., 588.
Davidson, John, 576.
Davis, Benjamin, 214, 352, 412
Davis, John, 362.
Davis, Widow, 93.
Dawson, Charles, 130, 249, 331.
Day, James, 531.
Deal, John, 588.
Dean, John E., 474, 478.
Dean, Nicholas, 350, 412, 429.
De Forest, Elias, 503, 506, 511, 517.
De Forest, William, (*De Foreest*,) 484.
Degez, Francis, 509, 511.
Degraw, Susan, 458.
Degraw, William, 457, 458.

Deitz, George, 465, 467.
Delahunt, John L., 362.
Denike, Robert P., 499.
Denton, Samuel H., 474.
Develin, Henry, 362.
De Voe, Charles, (*de Veaux*,) 468, 471.
De Voe, Frederick, 575.
De Voe, George W., 575.
De Voe, John, Jr., 575.
De Voe, John, Sr., 563, 575.
De Voe, Moses, 563, 575.
De Voe, Thomas F., 438, 476, 559, 563, 574, 575, 581.
Dick, William, 212.
Diffenbach & Co., 557.
Diffenbach, Henry, 478.
Disbrow, Henry N., 479.
Doan, Stephen, 457, 479.
Doane, John, 554.
Dodge, Jacob L., 486, 551
Dodomit, Richard, 54.
Dominick, James B., 465, 467, 468, 471, 472, 474.
Dominick, George, 356, 362.
Dominick, Francis M., 486.
Dominick, Francis J., 343.
Donovan, John, 557.
Doubleday, William, 554, 557.
Doughty, John, Jr., 197, 200, 202, 212, 232, 419, 495.
Dowling, Jeremiah, 365.
Dunham, William, 485, 486.
Dunning, Thomas, 495, 588, 589.
Dupont, Francis, 509.
Durbrow, Walter, 350, 439, 506.
Duryea, Gabriel, (*Duryee*,) 402, 406.
Duryea, Levi, 485, 486, 487.
Dusenberry, William, 397.

E.

Eddey, Ellis, 549.
Eddey, Ellis D., 549.
Eddy, John V., 362, 365.
Edsall, John, 214.
Egbert, James S., 474.
Eicleston, Thomas, 510, 516.
Elder, Robert, 502, 510.
Ellis, Richard, 587.
Ellis, Samuel, 313, 315, 316, 367.
Ensley, Daniel, Sr., (*Enslee, Insley, Inslee, Inslow*,) 157, 158, 212.

Ensley, Daniel, Jr., 201.
Ewen, Benjamin E., 510.
Ewen, George W., 232, 429.
Evans, Jacob, 551.
Evans, John, 503.
Everitt, William, Sr., (*Everet, Everett, Everit*,) 202, 212.
Everit, William, Jr., 200, 206.

F.

Farigan, John, (*Ferrigan*,) 362.
Farren, Samuel, 549.
Farrington, C. W., 365.
Farrington, George W., 554, 557.
Farrington, John D., 584.
Farrington, J. M., 557.
Farrington, Joseph H., 554.
Farrington, William H., 561.
Fash, George, 323.
Fash, John, 461, 465, 467, 469.
Faulkner, John, 274.
Fearnley, John, 495.
Ferdon, James, (*Furdon*,) 519.
Ferdon, Joseph, 405.
Ferris, Ebenezer G., 510.
Ferris, Lanning, 233, 241, 494, 502, 510.
Finck, Adam, (*Fink, Fincke*,) 315, 336, 339.
Finck, Jacob, 309, 311.
Fink, Alexander, Sr., 316, 323, 336, 337, 339, 340.
Fink, Alexander, Jr., 336, 340.
Fink, Arnest, Sr., 376, 381, 419, 506, 529, 531.
Fink, Arnest, Jr., (*Ernest*,) 439, 530.
Fink, Augustus, 478.
Fink, George, 563.
Fink, George A., 468, 471.
Fink, Jacob H., 531, 549.
Fink, John, (*1st*,) 200, 202, 212, 213, 214, 309.
Fink, John, (*2d*,) 413, 549.
Fink, John A., 381, 529.
Fink, John J., 412.
Fink, John Lawrence, 376, 415, 416, 417, 418.
Fink, Theodore L., 531.
Finn, John, 486.
Fish, Sidney, 365.
Fisher, Albert, 233, 239, 241, 350, 494, 506, 509, 516.

Fisher, Andrew, 232, 494.
Fisher, Jacob, 494, 502, 516.
Fisher, John, 494.
Fisher, William, 516.
Fitzgerald, Edward, 495, 499.
Fitzgerald, John, 200, 211, 397.
Flager, Jacob, (*Flagar*,) 412.
Flager, Mathew, 397
Flander, F. S., 509.
Fleming, Robert, 576.
Flock, John, 465, 551, 553.
Floor, John K., 212, 349, 350, 356, 362.
Floor, William D., 362.
Flynn, Joseph, 478.
Ford, James, (*Foord*,) 578, 579.
Ford, Richard, 404.
Ford, William O., 579.
Foster, John, 102.
Foster, William, 233, 241, 495, 503.
Foshay, Andrew, (*Forshay*,) 403, 578.
Forshay, William, 365.
Fox, Mathew, 201.
Fray, William, 274.
Friedman, Philip, 487.
Fullewever, Gerrit, 45.

G.

Garrison, John, 212.
Geary, Owen, 429.
Gibbons, Thomas, 211, 232, 237, 238, 419, 492, 494, 495, 503, 506, 507, 508.
Gibson, Cornelius V., 428, 494.
Gibson, William, 391.
Gilbert, Rufus, 518, 519.
Gilman, Charles, Jr., 402, 413.
Gilman, Charles, Sr., 323, 413.
Gillet, George, 531.
Glashan, George, 563.
Glasshorne, Frederick, 399.
Gleaves, Mathew, (*Gleves*,) 157, 158.
Glover, Charles S., 584.
Glover, Thomas, 519, 523, 524.
Glover, William, 523.
Gobel, Hugh, (*Goble*,) 413, 429, 439.
Godine, Francis, 510.
Goodheart, George, (1st,) 199, 323.
Goodheart, George, (2d,), 403, 429.
Goodheart, Jared, 403, 578.
Goodheart, William, 403.

Goodheart, William C., 578, 579.
Goodhue, Henry, 563.
Goodman, James, 350, 356, 362, 404.
Goodman, Nicholas, 356, 462.
Goodman, Mathew, 343.
Goodwin, G. C., 495.
Gould, David H., 510.
Graff, John A., (*Groff*,) 428, 439.
Graff, John G., 323, 412, 428, 434, 507.
Graff, Joseph, 212, 338.
Graham, Gilbert, 484.
Graham, John, 396.
Graham, William, 483, 486, 487, 495.
Granger, Bartholomew, 413, 429, 435, 439, 506.
Granger, Francis, 429, 439.
Granger, William, 523.
Green, Richard, 130.
Griffin, Gilbert, 356.
Groshon, John H., 531.
Gross, William H., 461, 469.
Gwyer, Charles, 412, 429, 510.
Gwyer, Christopher, 429, 439.
Gwyer, Robert, 429, 437.

H.

Haight, David, 361, 362.
Haight, Morris, 531.
Haight, Philip R., 487.
Haight, Sylvanus, 365.
Haight, William, 528, 532.
Hall, James S., 557.
Hall, Thomas, 211.
Halsted, Pearson S., (*Halstead*,) 438, 517.
Halsted, James S., 439.
Halstead, William H., 438, 485.
Hammond, Isaac D., 557.
Hanigan, Barnard, 362.
Hanshe, Jacob, 439.
Hanshe, John, 561, 563, 571.
Hanshe, William, 429, 438, 581.
Hanshe, William, Jr., 549.
Harck, William, 37.
Hardenbrook, Philip, 590, 591.
Hardenbrook, William, 590, 591.
Harmony, Daniel, 486.
Harmony, John P., 350.
Harpel, Lodowick, (*Ludvik, Loudavic*,) (*Harpell, Harple*,) 323, 413, 414, 429, 439.

Harpel, Mathew, 428, 511.
Harrigan, Hugh, (*Harrigen*,) 457.
Harriot, Christian, 413, 420, 421, 437, 506.
Harriot, Jacob, 410, 429.
Harriot, John, 495.
Harrington, William, 437, 439, 551.
Harris, John, 439.
Harrison, Thomas G., 462, 465, 467, 471, 498.
Harrison, Widow, 478.
Hart, Samuel, 439.
Hartell, Adam, Sr., (*Hartle,*) 160, 323, 336, 412.
Hartell, Adam, Jr., 429.
Hartell, Christian F., 412.
Hartell, Christian H., 343, 356, 507.
Hartell, George M., 356, 361.
Hartell, James W., 428.
Haslacker, Aaron, 487.
Hawkins, Charles H., 516.
Hawkins, James, 549.
Hawkins, Zophar, 549.
Hawes, Frederick, 323, 495, 506.
Hawes, George, Sr., 336, 337, 338, 339, 412, 419.
Haws, George, Jr., (2*d*,) 503, 510, 516.
Haws, George, Jr., (3*d*,) 516.
Haws, James H., 381, 528.
Haws, John F., 429.
Hays, William, 468, 478.
Hayward, Joseph, 516.
Hayward, James, 549.
Hayward, William, 510, 517.
Healy, Thomas, 586
Hedge, William N., 360, 486.
Hellen, Charles, 478.
Henning, John, 412, 503, 510.
Henning, John F., 517.
Henning, Joseph L., 511, 517.
Hepburn, George, 388.
Heyer, John L., 436.
Hickey, John, 486.
Hicks, Norris, 553.
Hill, Joseph, 421, 429, 430, 436, 437.
Hill, Joseph, Jr., 471.
Hill, Samuel, 437, 528.
Hilliker, Jacob, 316, 367.
Hilliker, Jacob, 316.
Hilliker, John, (1*st*,) 211, 461, 469.
Hilliker, John, (2*d*,) 562.

Hilliker, Stephen, 200, 212, 315, 367, 461.
Hillman, Michael, (*Hilaman*,) 413.
Hirleman, George, 554, 586.
Hoffman, Henry, 391, 455.
Holden, Samuel, 437, 439.
Hoofmin, John N., 362.
Hooper, John C., 487.
Hopkins, George W., 486, 587.
Hopkins, John, 323.
Hopkins, William, 413.
Hopkins, William H., 486, 487, 509.
Hopper, Charles, 518, 519, 523.
Hopper, Gerard P., 561.
Hopson, George, 316, 367.
Hopson, Samuel, (*Hopsen*,) 93.
Horsefield, Israel, (*Horsfield*,) 93, 94, 131, 132.
Horsefield, Timothy, 93, 94, 132.
Horton, Abraham, 362.
Horton, James, 362.
Houghtalin, James H., 403, 559, 563.
Howard, Bethuel, 356, 439.
Hoyt, George, 503.
Hudson, Thomas T., 487.
Hunt, Richard, 502, 510, 516.
Hunter, William, 298.
Hurd, Hebron, 401.
Hutton, Andrew, 350.
Hutton, George, 323, 412, 429.
Hutton, John, 412.
Hutton, William, 436.
Hyatt, William E., 529, 532, 549.
Hyde, Daniel S., 403, 465, 563.
Hyde, Henry, 405, 406.
Hyde, John, 232, 499.
Hyde, John W., 486.
Hyde, Joseph, 350.

I.

Inslow, Daniel, (*see Ensley,*) 158.
Irving, James, 556, 557.

J.

Jacacks, Benjamin, 439.
Jacacks, George, 439.
Jacacks, Joseph, 402.
Jacacks, Milton, 403, 578.
Jackson, William A., 485, 486.
Jacots, Joseph, 506.
Jantzen, John B., 478.
Jantzen, Joseph, 478.

Jansen, Pieter, 45, 48.
Jansen, Roelof, 45, 49.
Jaques, David, 582, 586.
Jaques, Samuel, 561.
Jenkins, John, (*Jinkers*,) 380.
Jenkins, Thomas M., 494, 503, 510.
Jenkins, William, 503.
Jeremiah, John, (*Geremiah*,) 298, 374.
Jeremiah, Thomas, 298, 428, 430, 437, 494, 504, 506, 507.
Jeroleman, Jacob, (*Gerroleman*,) 339, 380, 391.
Johnson, David, 524, 526, 584.
Johnson, Frederick, 360, 469, 470, 471, 472, 474, 478
Johnson, James, 502, 510, 516.
Johnson, Julius, 362.
Jolley, Lewis, 361.
Joosten, Symon, 51.
Jordan, Stephen, 481, 485.

K.

Keating, James, 478.
Keets, George & Co., 586.
Kehoe, David, 478.
Kelly, Edward, 94, 95, 96, 130.
Kellinger, Thomas K., 483, 486.
Kellinger, Samuel N. T., 484, 486.
Kellinger, William, 483.
Kennah, Richard, 404.
Kent, Charles, 502, 510.
Kent, Cornelius, 509, 510, 517.
Kent, James, 554.
Kent, John, 458, 460.
Kent, John D., 494, 503, 510.
Ketchum, John, 516.
Keyser, Ernest, 413, 429, 434, 435, 437, 439.
Keyser, George H., 531.
Keyser, Henry, 549.
Keyser, John, 429, 434, 435, 439.
Killin, Hugh, 486.
Kilpatrick, Jeremiah. 402.
King, Cornelius, 323, 336, 337.
King, Cornelius, Jr., 412.
King, Edward, 206.
King, John, (1*st*,) 350.
King, John, (2*d*,) 485.
King, James, 509, 523.
Kinner, John, 549.
Kinner, William, 478.
Kipp, Solomon, (*Kip*,) 529.

Kirschbaun, William D., 474.
Kirkpatrick, Thomas, 509.
Kline, Ebenezer, 516.
Kline, Samuel B., 388.
Kline, William, 211.
Knapp, Gilbert, 206.
Krouse, B., 487
Krowl, Henry T., 561, 563.

L.

Lalor, William, 477, 478.
Landers & Co., 557.
Lang, Andrew, Jr., 362.
Lang, Henry, 584.
Langstraat, Vande, (*Langstreet*,) 45.
Larkins, James, 557.
Larned, Samuel, 494.
Latham, Henry, 584, 587.
Laundry, Paul, 584.
Laurier, Widow, 130, 131
Lawrence, Bryan, 478.
Lawrence, Daniel, 486, 561.
Lawrence, Timothy, 478.
Lawrence, William, 530.
Lawrence, William, 486
Lawson, Joseph, 365.
Leach, James L., 485, 486.
Leary, William, 575.
Lederer, Leopold, 487.
Leggett, Abraham, 517.
Leggett, William V., 553.
Lemon, Martin, (*Lemmon*,) 397, 494.
Letice, Jacob, 478.
Leviness, George, (*Levinus*,) 365, 485.
Leviness, Joseph, 429, 439.
Levy, Asser, (*Ashur*,) 45, 46, 47, 50, 55, 242.
Lovell, Benjamin, (*Lovel*,) 350.
Lovell, Henry, 201, 212.
Lovell, John, Sr., 200, 202, 212, 315, 316, 349, 367.
Lovell, John, Jr., 212.
Lovell, Margaret, (*Widow of John*,) 349.
Lovell, Robert, 349.
Lowree, William, (*Lowrey*,) 397.
Lozier, Abraham, 381, 529.
Lozier, Charles, 528, 531, 549.
Ludlum, John, 391.
Luff, Philip L., Sr., 339.
Luff, Philip L., Jr., 429, 506.

Lynch, Edward, 365.
Lyon, Hyatt, 524, 526.
Lyon, Harvey, 232.
Lyon, John Harvey, 429.
Lyons, David, 356, 362.
Lyons, John, (1st,) 336, 343.
Lyons, John, (2d,) 465, 467, 495.
Lyons, Alfred, 559.
Lyons, James C., 559.

M.

Maacker, Veeter, 45.
Manahan, Owen, 356.
Mangles, Henry, 587.
Mann, David, (Man,) 201, 212.
Manold, James, 316, 367.
Manolt, George, (Manold, Manault, Mainault,) 201, 212, 233, 239, 241, 494.
Manolt, George I., 486.
Manolt, Jacob, 518.
Markler, Frederick, (see Merkel, Merkle,) 323.
Marks, Peter B., 561, 563.
Marmal, Francis, 309.
Marsh, David, (Mash,) 212, 221, 232, 368, 419, 494, 502, 504, 505, 506.
Marsh, Effingham W., 233, 429, 439, 495.
Marsh, Henry, 232, 481.
Marsh, James, 200, 212.
Marshall, Jesse A., 438.
Marshall, John, 584.
Marshall, Thomas, 356.
Martin, George W., 362, 554.
Martin, John A., 458.
Martin, Joshua, 365.
Martin, Lawrence, 381, 529, 532, 549.
Martin, Samuel, 350, 356.
Mason, George, 211.
Mathewson, Benjamin, 510, 516.
Masterton, John, 588.
McCarty, Eugene, 510.
McCarty, John, 510.
McChain, John, 557.
McCready, John, (McCrady,) 494, 499.
McCready, Thomas, 350, 494.
McCready, William, 356.
McCreery, William H., 531.
McElroy, John, 586.
McLaughlin, John, 298.

McManus, Edward, 362.
Meinderzen, Egbert, 45, 46, 48, 49, 51.
Menaber, Isaac, 586.
Mencillot, Peter, 510.
Messenger, G., 494.
Merkel, Frederick, (Merkle, Merkler, Markler,) 323.
Merkle, George, Sr., (Merckle,) 199, 518, 519, 523.
Merkle, George, Jr., 523.
Merkle, Thomas, 524.
Merkle, Valentine, 432, 495.
Merkler, Henry, 323, 383.
Messerve, Elias B., (Messarve, Messervy,) 502, 509, 518.
Messerve, George, (1st,) 206, 316, 367.
Messerve, George, (2d,) 494.
Messerve, George G., 199, 201, 212, 233, 241, 359.
Messerve, George S., 232, 494, 499.
Messerve, John S., 365.
Messerve, Nicholas W., 502.
Messerve, William, (1st,) 212, 233, 492, 494.
Messerve, William, (2d,) 350, 356, 362, 365.
Messerve, William, (3d,) 495.
Messerve, William, Jr., 494.
Mesur, Joshua, 487.
Miller, Christian, 221, 298, 323, 368.
Miller, John, 381, 529.
Miller, Richard, 485, 486.
Mills, John, 406.
Mirrick, William B., 402, 403.
Monaghan, John, 365, 484.
Monaghan, Owen, 362, 365.
Montgomery, George, 510.
Mook, Thomas, 396, 397, 398, 461, 465, 467, 478.
Mook, Thomas H., 472, 474, 478.
Mook, William, Jr., 439, 478.
Mook, William, Sr., 396, 397, 398, 461, 464, 467, 471.
Mook, William H., 472, 478.
Mook & Sheldon, 478.
Mooney, Edward, 200.
Mooney, James, 557.
Mooney, William, (1st,) 168, 200, 206.
Mooney, William, (2d,) 212, 391, 404.

Moore, John, 356.
Moore, William, (1st,) 343.
Moore, William, (2d,) 429, 439.
Mott, Joseph, 316, 368.
Munson, William P., 401, 495, 499.
Myers, Charles, 404.
Myers, William, 510, 511.

N.

Nash, George, 458.
Nash, John, 232.
Nash, John H., 485.
Nash, Orville J., 356, 362.
Neilson, William, 483.
Nesbet, William, (Nesbit,) 588.
Nestler, Michael, 343.
Nicholls, Jacob, 212.
Nicholls, Richard, 54.
Nolan, William, 588.
Norman, John, 200, 212, 232.
Norman, William, 274.
Norris, Edward, 531.
Nott, Joseph, 200.
Nugent, William, 365.

O.

Oakley, Benjamin, 362, 559.
Oberdorfer, Isaac, 586.
Odell, Adolphus, (Odle,) 405, 529, 532, 549.
Odell, Jacob, 350.
Omberson, William J., 362.
Onderline, John, (Underline,) 274.
O'Neil, Francis, 462, 495.
O'Neil, Philip, 554.
Oppenheimer, Louis, 586.
Otte, Jacob, (Ott, Utte,) 274, 309.
Outenbogart, Joseph, (see Bogart,) 155.
Owens, Henry, 413.
Owens, James, 391, 413, 419.

P.

Paff, Andrew, 343, 345.
Paff, George, 396, 455.
Palmer, Adam R., 439.
Palmer, John, 481, 582.
Palmer, J. C., 487.
Palmer, John W., 362.
Parcells, John, (Parsells,) 214, 216, 397.
Parr, James, 517.

Passman, William, 412.
Patchen, Jacob, (Patchin,) 228.
Patten, Edward, (Patton,) 212, 232, 316, 367.
Patten, George, 399.
Patten, William, 232, 494, 503.
Patterson, Jacob, 483.
Patterson, Samuel P., 531.
Patton, George M., 325.
Peacock, Alexander, 202, 212.
Pearsall, Denton, 510, 516.
Pearsall, Solomon, 365.
Pearsall, Zophar, 516.
Pendergast, John, 460.
Pendleton, Edward, 365.
Pendleton, Sylvester, 362, 365.
Pendleton, William, 365.
Pell, E. C., 495.
Pell, Joseph, 429.
Pell, John, 199, 201, 212, 233, 241.
Perkins, William, 589.
Perrin, David, 458, 495, 499.
Perrin, James, 419.
Perrin, John, (1st,) 315, 316, 367.
Perrin, John, (2d,) 232, 494, 503, 506, 507, 510, 516.
Perrin, John C., 551, 553.
Perrin, William, 336, 343.
Pesinger, George, (Passinger, Pessenger, Pessinger,) 208, 356, 362, 363, 438, 581.
Pesinger, Jacob, 356, 486.
Pessenger, John, Sr., 157, 159, 160, 161, 162, 163, 211, 222, 316.
Pessenger, Andrew, 160.
Pessenger, John, 160, 200, 201, 212, 413.
Peterson, George W., 551, 553
Pheasant, Samuel, 531.
Phelan, Michael, 361, 362, 365.
Philips, Edward, (Phillips,) 438, 531, 581.
Philips, John, (1st,) 211.
Philips, John, (2d,) 356, 471.
Phillips, John, (3d,) 439.
Phillips, William, 356.
Piercy, David W., 510.
Piercy, Robert, 485, 579.
Piercy, Samuel, Jr., (1st,) 479, 484, 486.
Piercy, Samuel, Jr. (2d,) 529, 579.
Piercy, William, 403.

Pinckney, Joseph C., 474.
Pine, Julian, 274.
Pittman, Samuel J., 460.
Pittman, William, 362, 365.
Place, James, 206.
Place, Thomas, 350, 359, 479.
Platt, Richard, 214, 350, 356, 362.
Platt, Richard H., 362.
Ponsford, William, 494.
Post, James, 362.
Post, John, 503, 510, 517.
Post, Jotham, 315, 316, 342, 367.
Post, William, 200, 212.
Potter, Simmons, 206.
Pray, Ebenezer, 581.
Pray, Henry, 403, 438, 579.
Prendergast, John, 587, 588.
Pullis, William, (*Pulis,*) 232.

Q.

Quinn, Felix, (*Quin,*) 526, 584.
Quinlan, Thomas, 590.

R.

Rawlings, Anthony, (*Rowlings,*) 323.
Raymond, Samuel, 388.
Raynor, John, (*Rayner,*) 212.
Redding, James, (*Reading,*) 201, 212.
Reed, David B., (*Read, Reid,*) 576.
Reed, E. Harrison, 486.
Reed, Jacob R., 486, 531, 549.
Reeves, Charles, 381, 532, 549.
Reeves, James, Jr., (*Reaves,*) 381, 529, 531.
Reeves, James, Jr., 350, 381, 399, 403, 438, 494, 506, 528, 578, 579, 581.
Reeves, John E., 579.
Reeves, Thomas, 403, 578, 579.
Reeves, William, 461, 465, 467.
Reeves, William L., 483, 486.
Regler, Andreas, 159.
Reid, Andrew, 478.
Reid, James, 478.
Reid, Philip, 478.
Reid, William, 478.
Remer, William A., 517.
Resler, Henry, Jr., 471, 481.
Revere, Edward, 439.
Reynolds, David, (*Raynolds,*) 503.
Reynolds, Israel, 228.
Reynolds, Josiah, 509.

Reynolds, William, 232, 362, 494.
Rhoades, Abraham, (*Rhodes,*) 356.
Rhoades, Daniel, 494, 503, 510.
Rhoades, Isaac, 494, 503.
Rhoades, Isaac, Jr., 510.
Rhoades, William, 486.
Rich, Daniel, 509.
Rice, Bernard, 549.
Rice, John, 549.
Ridabock, Jacob H., 429, 506, 510, 518.
Rikeman, Ambrose P., 553.
Rikeman, John, 553.
Ritter, Peter, 336.
Robertson, Frederick, 516.
Roblin, Edward, 439, 531.
Romaine, Edward N., (*Romane,*) 563.
Romaine, Philip, 356, 362.
Romaine, Nicholas, 551, 553, 554.
Romaine, Washington, 365.
Roos, Gerrit Jansen, 37, 45, 55.
Roper, John, (*Raper,*) 212.
Ross, Andrew, 201, 212.
Row, Michael Christopher, 93.
Rowe, Rufus, 511.
Rudman, John, 232, 494.
Ruffhead, James, 131.
Ryer, William T., 471, 472, 474.
Ryer, Henry J., 472, 474.
Ryer, William T., 471, 474.
Ryerson, George, (*Rierson,*) 211, 232.

S.

Sager, William, 516.
Sammis, Daniel, 531.
Samuel, F., 365.
Schuyler, Cornelius, 199, 201, 212, 233, 241, 494, 503.
Schuyler, George W., 510.
Schuyler, Isaac, 495.
Scott, George, Jr., 460, 587, 588.
Scott, John, 356, 362, 365, 438, 581.
Seal, William, 478.
Seaman, Andrew, 428.
Seaman, David, Jr., 478.
Seaman, David, Sr., 197, 201, 212, 233, 238, 239, 241, 419, 494.
Seaman, John M., 238, 465, 466, 467, 468, 471, 478.
Searles, William, 402.
Seaward, Simon, (*Seward,*) 502.
Seely, Lyman, 531.

Sentis, Garrit, Jr., 429, 439.
Shaff, James, 584.
Shapter, Marsden, 509.
Sheane, John, (*Shane, Shien,*) 412, 429.
Shark, Robert, 509.
Sharp, John, 356, 529.
Shelton, William, 458.
Ship, George, (*Shep,*) 336, 337, 338, 339.
Shop, Henry, 232.
Shotts, William, (*Shot, Shoults, Schotts,*) 350, 356, 388.
Siegler, Goodheart, 157.
Silber, Frederick M., 563.
Silber, Martin, 232.
Simonson, Carmon A., 495, 503, 510, 517.
Simonson, John, 397, 398, 495, 510, 517.
Simoson, James, 461, 465, 467, 471, 478, 506.
Sims, Samuel, 559, 563.
Singer, John, 483, 486.
Skillman, Jonathan, 350, 495.
Slote, John, 503, 510.
Smack, Stephen, 404.
Smart, Nicholas, 201.
Smith, Albert W., 510.
Smith, Alfred, 439, 531.
Smith, Arnold, 584.
Smith, Bartlett, 575.
Smith, Edward, 458.
Smith, Henry, (*1st,*) 339.
Smith, Henry, (*2d,*) 503, 510, 516.
Smith, John, 343.
Smith, John B., 208, 212, 462.
Smith, John M., 356.
Smith, Joseph B., 405, 502.
Smith, Leonard, 524, 526.
Smith, Mathew, 495.
Smith, Mathias, 232, 502.
Smith, Patrick, 586.
Smith, William, 439.
Smith, William A., 465, 467, 516.
Smock, Andrew, (*Smack*), 350, 494.
Somerndyke, Jacob, 361.
Spader, Daniel, 323, 420, 421, 461, 506, 507.
Spader, Jonathan, 323.
Spader, John D., 429, 439.
Spencer, William, 471.

Sperry, Henry, 214.
Spicer, Francis, (*1st,*) 323, 336.
Spicer, Francis, (*2d,*) 412, 510.
Spicer, Henry, 479.
Spicer, Jesse T., 428, 437.
Spingler, Baltes, (*Springler,*) 309.
Spingler, Henry, 186, 202, 309, 315, 367.
Spurling, Henry, (*Sparling,*) 432.
Stagg, George, 350.
Stagg, Peter H., 584.
Stakes, Nicholas, (*Steakes,*) 309.
Stamler, Christian, (*Semler,*) 212, 213, 232, 274, 494, 503, 509, 510.
Stamler, Jacob A., 503, 510, 517.
Stamler, John, (*1st,*) 232, 494.
Stamler, John, (*2d,*) 517.
St. Amore, Thomas, 309.
Stanton, James P., 511, 517.
Stanton, Thomas W., 429.
Starr, George, 531, 575.
Starr, John L., 428, 439.
Starr, Thomas, Sr., 412, 419.
Steel, Nicholas, (*Stael,*) 211, 232, 495.
Steenwyck, Cornelius, 45, 46.
Stewart, James, 439.
Stockford, John, 130.
Storms, Andrew, 406, 460, 587, 588.
Storms, Samuel, 365.
Storms, Stephen, 365, 406.
Straus, Jacob, 487.
Striker, Burdett, (*Stryker,*) 201, 495.
Striker, J. R., 495.
Styles, Laban C., 578, 579.
Sullivan, James, 200, 202, 350.
Summers, Charles, 586.
Syberts, Thomas, 485, 506.
Syler, Jacob, (*Siler, Seiler, Ceylor,*) 381, 401, 506, 529.

T.

Tallet, William, 578, 579.
Tamplar, Christof, 309.
Tappan, George, 365.
Taylor, Henry B., 362.
Taylor, James, 350.
Tenbrook, Adam, (*Tenbroeck,*) 399.
Tenbrook, Blaze, 376.
Tenbrook, Henry, 376.
Tenbrook, John, 399.
Ten Eyck, R., (*Den Eyck,*) 495.

Thompson, George, 212, 315, 343, 367, 419, 495.
Thompson, Romeo, 551, 553, 554.
Tier, David, 494.
Tier, David M., 486, 487.
Tier, Jacob, Jr., 391, 461.
Tier, Jacob, Sr., 221, 339, 340, 368.
Tier, Jeremiah, 356.
Tier, John, 212, 356.
Tier, John H., 356, 436.
Tier, John R., 392.
Tier, John W., 484, 486.
Tier, Robert, 392, 506.
Tilby, James, 516.
Titus, James I., 471, 494, 503.
Toby, Orville, 578.
Tompkins, Daniel D., 436.
Tourneur, Daniel, 45, 47, 48.
Townsend, Joseph, 465.
Townsend, Smith, 343.
Townsend, Sylvanus S., 350.
Travis, Simeon, 412, 429.
Triglar, John, Sr., (*Trigler, Trigleth,*) 203, 212, 362, 420, 461, 464, 466, 469, 506, 507.
Triglar, John, Jr., 582, 584.
Truss, Christian, 232, 406, 495.
Truss, George W., 362.

U.

Underhill, Alexander, (*Sandy,*) 529, 531.
Underhill, Gilbert, 361, 502.
Underhill, Nathaniel, 233, 241, 495, 503.
Underhill, Elnathan, 233, 241, 494, 503, 510, 516.
Underhill, Philip H., 481, 483, 486.
Underhill, Marvin R., 485, 510.

V.

Valentine, Abraham, 502, 510, 516.
Valentine, Benjamin W., 510.
Valentine, Bussing, 402.
Valentine, Dennis, 402, 439.
Valentine, Henry M., 531.
Valentine, H. H., 510.
Valentine, Isaac, (1*st,*) 356.
Valentine, Isaac, (2*d,*) 403.
Valentine, Isaac, (3*d,*) 528, 531, 549.
Valentine, Isaac, Jr., 549.
Valentine, James, (1*st,*) 365, 436, 439.

Valentine, James, (2*d,*) 485, 531, 549.
Valentine, John, 465, 467, 471.
Valentine, John C., 516.
Valentine, Lemuel, 553, 554, 557.
Valentine, Oliver, 516.
Valentine, Peter, (1*st,*) 494, 503, 510, 517.
Valentine, Peter, (2*d,*) 439.
Valentine, Peter, Jr., 484.
Valentine, Peter T., 511.
Valentine, Richard, 531, 553.
Valentine, William H., 516.
Valentine, William J., 439, 551.
Valleau, Samuel, (*Valloo,*) 549.
Valleau, William, Jr., 549.
Valleau, William, Sr., 531, 549.
Van Arsdale, James, 503.
Van Benschoten, Mathew, 578.
Van Benschoten, William, 509.
Van Borckeloo, Willem Jansen, 48, 51.
Van de Beeck, Paulus, 45.
Vandenburgh, Caleb, 199.
Vanderbeck, Abraham, 365.
Vanderbergh, Adam, (*Vandenbergh, Vandenburgh,*) 206, 367.
Vanderburgh, George W., 510.
Vanderburgh, Cornelius, 396.
Van Dusen, Andrew, 812, 479.
Vandewater, John, 524.
Vandewater, William, 587.
Van Gunst, Jan Hendrickson, 54.
Van Haerlan, Jan, (*Harlaem,*) 37, 45.
Van Hooghten, Jansen, 47.
Vanice, John, 549.
Van Meppel, Roelef, (*Mepplin, Jansen,*) 40, 48, 115.
Van Wart, Alexander, (*Van Wert,*) 575.
Van Wart, Samuel, 560.
Varian, Alfred, (*Verian, Berrian,*) 365.
Varian, George W., 323, 350, 356, 366, 494.
Varian, Isaac, (1*st,*) 94, 95, 130, 249.
Varian, Isaac, (2*d,*) 186, 200, 212, 315, 366, 367.
Varian, Isaac, (3*d,*) 315, 366, 367, 380, 381.
Varian, Jacob, (1*st,*) 221, 343, 368.

Varian, Jacob, (2d,) 356, 365.
Varian, Jacob H., Jr., 365.
Varian, Jacob H., Sr., 343, 350, 362.
Varian, Joseph, 315, 367.
Varian, Joshua M., 362, 365, 366.
Varian, Michael, 199, 212, 316, 367.
Varian, Richard, 199, 212, 366, 367.
Varian, Thomas, 356, 468, 471, 529.
Varian, Widow, 478.
Varian, William P., 405, 465, 467, 471.
Varick, John, 392, 457, 458, 506.
Vaughan, George, (Vaughn,) 412, 429, 437.
Vaughn, Isaac, 412.
Vermylia, Abraham, 413.
Vinton, David, 214.
Vogel, George A., (Vogal, Vogell, Vogle, Fogel,) 554, 557.
Vogel, Jacob, 502, 529, 582, 584.
Vogel, Mathew, 201, 206, 207, 208, 211, 350, 495, 499, 524, 526.
Volkersen, Hendrick, 45.
Vonck, William, (Vonk,) 341, 362, 412, 428.

W.

Wagner, Peter, 356.
Wallace, John, 356, 506, 550, 553.
Ward, Benjamin, 457, 458, 460, 559, 588.
Warlow, William, 232, 495.
Warner, Abraham, 523.
Warner, William, 510.
Warner, William F., 365.
Waters, James, 485, 575.
Waters, John, 343.
Watts, James, 561.
Watts, William, 524.
Way, Thomas P., 437, 439.
Weatherspoon, Charles, 412.
Webber, James, 553.
Webber, Philip, 553.
Webber, William, 429, 438.
Weblin, William, 82, 88.
Weeden, James, 506, 518, 519, 523.
Weeks, Benjamin T., 510, 517.
Weeks, Carlysle, 503, 510.
Weeks, Philip, 588.
Weeks, Samuel, 517.
Wells, William, 502, 526, 584.

Wesson, Asa W., (Wessen,) 461, 469, 551.
Wethershein, Nicholas, (Wethershine,) 316, 367.
Wheeler, Andrew C., 232, 438, 494, 502, 510, 581.
Wheeler, Andrew C., Jr., 485.
Wheeler, Eliphalet, 212, 213, 219, 220, 232, 494, 503, 506.
Wheeler, E. A., 487.
Whiney, James, (Whinney,) 472.
White, Francis, 216, 323.
White, Francis, Jr., 382, 383.
White, James, 549.
White, Samuel, 413.
White, Thomas, Jr., 391.
White, Thomas H., 356.
Whitehand, John, 212.
Whitehead, John, 232.
Wicker, Henry, 412, 429, 434, 439.
Wiggins, Jacob, 465, 467, 471.
Wilde, Jacob, 586.
Willet, Thomas, 37, 41.
Williams, John, 212.
Williams, Samuel T., 47.
Williams, Stephen, 510, 517.
Wilt, George, 316, 367.
Wilt, George A., 531.
Wilt, James, 211.
Wilt, John B., 510, 517.
Wilt, Jonathan, 503, 510.
Wilt, Joseph, 316, 367.
Wilt, Peter, 232, 495, 502.
Wilson, James, 478.
Winter, William, 232.
Winter, William, Jr., 483, 485, 486.
Wiseburn, Henry, 561.
Wiseburn, Lawrence, 412, 420, 421, 429, 434, 506, 507, 531.
Winship, Daniel, Jr., 233, 241, 494.
Winship, Daniel, Sr., 199, 201, 212, 221, 233, 241, 319, 343, 368, 494, 503.
Winship, Ebenezer, Jr., 323.
Winship, Ebenezer, Sr., 318, 319, 389.
Winship, George, 509.
Winship, John, 319, 323, 455.
Winship, Jonathan, 319.
Winship, Samuel, 216, 227, 319, 322, 323, 388, 389.
Winship, Thomas, Jr., 457, 458, 460, 581, 587, 588.

Winship, Thomas, Sr., 323, 388, 455.
Wolff, Edw. Rock, 274.
Wood, Amos, 356.
Wood, Isaac, 343, 350.
Wood, James, 429.
Wood, William, 474.
Woodcock, John H., 554.
Woodcock, William P., Sr., 503, 510.
Woodcock, William P., Jr., 554, 557.
Woodruff, Aaron, 381.
Wright, James, 232.

Wright, William, 200, 212, 221, 316, 367, 368.

Y.

Young, George, 130, 131.
Young, James, 201, 206.
Youngs, Edward, 509.

Z.

Zanger, Joseph, 365.

GENERAL INDEX.

ABEEL, David, petition in 1738, 262.
Ackerman, John, permission to erect a flour scale, 320.
Ackland, James, on petition in 1738, 262.
Adryasen, Frederick, Sr., runaway servant, 97.
Albany Basin and "Old Albany Basin," 371.
Albany Post from Thurman's Dock in 1754, 263 ; Rider from Oswego Market in 1774, 331.
Albany Turnpike, not opened, 63.
Alcock, Ensign, wounded by rioters, 88.
Aldrich, Vice-Director, notices the prices of provisions in 1657, 31.
Allaire, James P., added an ice-house to Grand Street Market, 456.
Allen, Stephen, Mayor, a singular resignation to, 501; the death of, 577.
Alner, Captain James, Inspector of Vessels, 119.
Ambuscade and Boston, engagement between, and colors presented to the Tammany Society, 299.
"Amelia," privateer, in 1814, Capt. Adams, 440.
Amos, John, petition for place in the markets, 186.
Amos, Rich'd, petition for place in the markets, 186.
Ammerman, Peter, Clerk of three markets, 402.
Amsterdam, Fort, 15, 27, 29, 38, 44.
Anderson, Dr. Alexander, incidents in the life of, 208-9, 296, 317, 377.
Andross, Sir Edmund, Governor of New York, 56-7, 70-1, 75.
Animal carcasses sold in the public markets in 1816-18, 235, 351.
Annett, James, fisherman of Washing. Market, 424.
Anthony, Allard, dispenser of the Burger Rights, 50.
Anthony, John P., on first N. R. steamboat, 195.
Arcularius, Alderman Philip J., report on butchers' stands, 342-3.
Arbuthnot, Admiral Mariot, answer to the Chamber of Commerce, 122.
Armstrong, Colonel William, engaged in the Miranda Expedition, 215.
Ashbey, Joseph, Fly Market fisherman, 224.
Assize, General Court of, in 1664, 42; in 1675, 70.
Assize Law for all kinds of provisions, 140-5; unfavorably received—changed on meats, &c., 148-50.
Asia, British man-of-war, removal of, 119; cannonading the city, 288.
Asten, Isaac, sweeper of Fulton Market, 496.
Astor, John Jacob, laying a foundation for wealth, 185.
Atkinson, John, known as "Speaking Trumpet Jack," 440.
Avery, Thomas, fisherman of Washing. Market, 424.

Baker, Daniel, fisherman of Fulton Market, 500.
Baker, Elisha, fisherman of Fulton Market, 500, 513.
Baker, Elisha A., fisherman of Fulton Market, 513.
Baker, Mr. and Mrs. Gardiner, keepers of the Tammany Museum, 300-2.
Baker, Jared, fisherman of Fulton Market, 513.
Ball and supper at the Centre Market, 472-4; second one by the butchers at the Apollo, 475.
Banta, Mrs. Frances, of the Oswego Market, 331-2, 461.
Banta, Paulus, has property for sale in "Dirick Dye's Street," 332.
Barcker, John, complaint against and fined, 39, 40.
Barker's, Jacob, "Exchange" and "Washington and Warren" Banks, 578-9.

Barr, "Aunt Katy," of the Collect, Centre, and Union Markets, 584-5. (See 207.)
Bartow, John, connected with the Free Bridge, 64.
Battin, John, the centenarian, recollections of the Bear Market, 313.
Battle of Queenstown, Lieut. John L. Fink in the, 415-17.
Battoes to be built in all the market-houses except one, 91; description of, and uses, 252-3.
Baum, Leon., Dep. Clerk of Washington Market, 427.
Bauman, Col., in the Doctors' Mob, 334.
Bauman, G., on the character of a butcher, 199.
Bauman, J., Committee on first N. R. steamboat, 195.
Baxter, William, Fly Market fisherman, 225.
Bayard, Nicholas, suit at law before, 47.
Bayard, N., Mayor, orders certain lots to be surveyed, 61.
Bayard, Nicholas, wishes a market-house in the Fields, (Park,) 275; lessee of the public slaughterhouse, 366-7.
Bayard, Samuel, servant woman's time to be sold by, 101.
Bayard, Stephen, sells goods, &c., 92.
Bayard, William, ferry from Hoboken started from the place of, 314.
Bayard's Vault, sketch of, and the last occupant, 358-9.
Bayard's Mount, or Bunker Hill, incidents of, 317, 357-9, 389, 460.
Bear, curious suit and verdict about a half-eaten, 40-1; found in and near the City of New York, 311-12.
Bear Market established, 307-8; size of, 308; known as Oswego Market, 308-11; foundation-stones laid, 308; butchers' and farmers' petition to remove from, 309-10; hay scales placed in, 311; bear killed near which originated the name, 311-12; the name known in 1773, 312-13; called "Bare Market" by several authors, 312; known as "Hay Market" in 1776, 313; used as a store-house and barracks, 313; condition after the Revolution, 314; known in the Records as "Upper" and "Lower Hudson Market," 314, 322, 324, 326-7; lots sold near in 1784, 314; ferry at, sold at public auction, 314-15; hay scale removed, 320-1; raising the buildings and leasing the cellars, 321; additional market-houses, 321, 324; called Buttermilk Market, 322-4; an original "true state of," 322-3; bell added, 324; the grounds to be sold, 326; butchers petition to be removed, 326; temporary sheds erected for them, 407; transferred into the new Washington Market, 407; the old buildings torn down and the business removed, 327.
Beaver skins, value of, about 1660, (see Currency,) 31.
Beckwith, Russell, Fly Market fisherman, 225.
Beekman, Alderman Theophilus, one of the "Bridewell Court," 190.
Bennett, William, Bobolink Bob, a dancing negro, belonging to, 344.
Benson, Dirck, lessee of the ferry, 1703, terms proposed to, 88.
Benson, Samson, wishes to desert the Bear Market, 309-10.
Berg, Christian, assisted with Goveneur Market, 404.
Berwick, Robert, Deputy Sheriff, murdered, 342.
Betts, Judge Samuel R., "Butcher Causes" tried before, 239.

Bicker, Walter, on the character of a butcher, 199.
Biddle, Col. Geo. H., "Drill-Room Committee," 476.
Bill of Fare of the States by "Eboracus," and easy living, 181.
Binninger, Mr., near the Oswego Market, 340.
Birch, Brig.-Gen. Samuel, proclamations, &c., 123–4, 292–3.
Birds, wild. found in New Netherlands, 19, 21.
Bisley, Cyrus, fisherman of Catharine Market, 366.
Black cattle, a convenient place to land, 80.
Blagge, Alderman Benjamin, erects a hay scale in the Bear Market, 311; removed, 320–1.
Blanchard, James, lessee of the public slaughter-house, 298, 367–8.
Bleeker, G. N., evidence of a market in Broad Street, 255.
Bleecker, James, auctioneer for the sale of stands in Fulton Market, 492.
"Blind Man of Jefferson Market," 572–3.
Bluke, J., Secretary, signs an order to clear Peck Slip Market, 303.
Blunt, E. & G. W., No. 147 Fly Market, advertises, &c., 241.
Blunt, N. B., Corporation Attorney, 530.
Bogardus, Colonel Robert, in the war of 1812, 525.
Bogert, Gilbert Outen, repairs meal market, 251.
Bogert, Alderman John, report on butchers' stands, 342–3.
Bogert, Nicholas C., sold lottery tickets to pay a market debt, 330. (See 272.)
Bolting Act repealed, 87.
Boogert, Johannis, on petition in 1733, 262.
Bosch, Albertus, in the slave-trayd, 246.
Boston, first newspaper printed in, 97.
Bowne. Samuel, at Burling Slip, 278.
"Bowery Boys" and "Broadway Boys"—Fight Streets, 358.
Braiden, James, on first North River steamboat, 195.
Brannon Street, change to Spring Street, 376.
Brasher, Alderman Philip, on market regulations, &c., 216–7, 324.
Bread famine in 1696, 86–7; police regulations of, 174–5.
Brevoort, Henry, petition for place in the markets, 186.
Bremner, John, appointed Clerk of Catharine Market, 350.
Brennan, O. W., lessee of grounds at the Washington Market, 450-1-2.
Bridewell Court, proceedings before in 1795, 189, 190–2.
Bridge, first built connecting New York Island with the main-land, 62; Dyckman's free, how built, 63; "Kissing," location of, 137.
Bridge, (Custom-House or Great,) and weigh-house, market-place near the, 71, 73, 75, 77, 78.
Bridges over the Heere-Graft or Canal in Broad Street, 77–8, 84; Little, 77, 84; afterwards called Long Bridge, 84–5, 114, 265, 279, 286, 370–1.
Briggs, Walter, treasurer for a free bridge, 64.
Bright, Daniel, opposite the Meal Market, 247.
Brinley, George, Commissary of Forage in 1778, 313.
British flag taken down in New York City, 1783, 295–6.
British troops, intention to evacuate the city, 177. (See 292, 296.)
Broad Street surveyed and laid out, 32–3.
Broad Street Market established, 77; repaired and cost, 83–4; used as an Exchange by the merchants, 84–5; called the "Exchange" and "Exchange Market-house," 85; on David Grim's Map "Broad Street Market." 85· ceased to exist. 85.
Broadway in 1770 and 1794, 274–5; lengthened by adding St. George, or Great George Street to it, 275.
Broadway Market, petition to establish, 263–4; as a meal market, 268; meat allowed to be cut and sold in, 247, 268; enlargement of,. 268; called "Oswego Market" and Crown Market, 271–6; the cost of sweeping in 1770, 274; Jersey bills lost in, 105; indicted as a nuisance, 274; removal of, 276.
Broadway Shambles established, 44; rebuilt "and covered with tiles," 44–5; the only meat market, 59; "flesh meat to be kept," 61, 85; demolished, 70.

Brookins, Susanna, permission to sell coffee, &c., in Duane Street Market, 391.
Brooklyn, (Breucklen, Brookland,) a fair or market to be held at, 56; Corporation land at, and ferry, 93; water lot for fishermen cars, 223.
Brouwer, Evardus, on petitions in 1733, 262.
Brouwer, Jacob, on petition in 1733, 262.
Brouwer, Johannes, on petition in 1733, 262.
Brown, Burnel, ship-chandlery, dancing-ground near, 344.
Brown, Charles, built the first steamboat for Albany, 195, 198.
Brown, Seymour, a fisherman of Cath. Market, 366.
Brown, William, fisherman of Fulton Market, 513.
Brownell, Judge J. Sherman, personal qualities, 232.
Brownell, Mrs., a remarkable incident in her life, 229–32.
Bruce, Brig.-Gen., permits for Staten Island, 292.
Buckman, A., lessee of a part of Duane Street Market, 392.
Buel, Dr. W., letter on yellow fever, 373.
Buffalo or Bison kept at the Corlaers Hook Market, 389.
Bull, Joseph, examines fishermen's claims, 119.
Bull-Baiting on Bunker Hill, or Bayard's Mount, 358, 389; Brooklyn, 286.
Bull-Dogs, use of in "Olden Times," 83.
Bull's Head or Cattle Market first established, 37–8. in the Bowery Lane, 158; cattle illegally taken from, and legally put back, 157–9; sale of stolen cattle, &c., at, 174; the yards of, 337; Richard Varian, keeper of, 366.
Burger's (or Burgher's) Right, advantages of, 49, 50–1; path lots to be sold near the, 86; or slip battery. 86; ferry at. 88; market-house at, 92–3; called Smith Street, 101–2; and Old Slip, 86.
Burgher, (Burger, Buger,) Harmannus, petitions for payment of an executed slave, 245–6.
Burgomasters appoint certain hours of the day for work, 37.
Burgomasters' and Schepens' decision in a bear case, 41; appoint "sworn butchers," 37, 45.
Burling, Edward, in favor of a market-house in the Fields, (Park,) 275; name given to a slip and market-place, 278.
Burling, James, corner Smith's Fly and Golden Hill, 278.
Burling's Slip, formerly known as Rodman's and Lyons' Slip, 278.
Burling's Market, established, 278; marked on Maerschalck's map of 1755, as "Burlin's Market," 278; petition against, and removed, 278.
Burnet, Governor William, erected a trading-house at Oswego, 271.
Burnt Mill Point, or Branda Munah Point, 394.
Burr, Aaron, letter to concerning a free bridge, 63–5; petition of, 375; counsel for Levi Weeks. 378.
Burtsell, Alderman William, report on butchers' claims, 239–40-1.
Bussing, Abraham, petition for a market-place, 327.
Bussing, Peter, wishes to desert the Bear Market, 309–10.
Butchers, sworn and confirmed in 1656, 36–7; additional, and the fees allowed—Jew refuses the oath in 1660, 37, 45; additional, and increased fees in 1665, 51–4; not allowed to be tanners, curriers, or shoemakers, 54; obliged to keep meat in two market-places, 61; complaint· against, 83; prosecuted, fines distributed, 90; slaves engaged in the "Great Negro Plot." 1741, 93–6; report on, 130; refuse to agree with the Corporation, 131; the "Press" severe on them, and country people, 145–6; their position in London, 146; contemptuous on account of the Assize Law, 145–8–9; advertise runaway negro slaves, 157; Tories subject to insult. 179; anecdote of, 184–5; ordered personally to attend their stands, complaint against. S. N., 202; desert the markets on account of yellow fever, 210; died of yellow fever in 1798, 206–7–9–10; complaint of Henry Astor for forestalling cattle, 210–11; in the Miranda Expedition, 214–6; appointed Inspectors by the Board of Health, 221; in politics—favoritism

defeated, 221-2; shirks, or sharks, 222-8-9, 503; license, cost of, 232; welcoming silver currency back in 1817, 233-4; (see 418;) meeting against taking uncurrent paper money, 234; (see 418-9;) "Coat of Arms" in 1788, 316; furnish a roasted ox for the Federal procession, 317; plan of doing business, 345-7 notice served on, 351-2; in the Federal procession, 357; Columbian Volunteers composed of, 366; ordered into the markets, 373; character and apprenticeship before eligible for license, 401-2; petition against the sale of stands at public auction, 411-12-21-22; patriotism in the war of the Revolution, 159-60-62, 298, 318-19-36, 413-14; of 1812, 415-18, 431-3, 439-40-1; election of Committee, 438; meeting in relation to sale of stands in Fulton Market by auction, under certain "terms and conditions," (see 489.) 490-4; confined in jail, 498-9; in the Canal Celebration, 506-8; petition in relation to market laws, 532-4; petition for a return of premiums, 547; called "Permit Butchers," 576.

"Butchers' Arms" in the Bowery, 213.

Butchers' Benevolent Society in the Canal Celebration, 507.

Butchers' Executive Committee appointed, and their assistance requested, 438; duties of, 485. (See 581-2.)

Butchers' shambles—but one in 1691, 59.

Butchers' stalls of olden time, 324-5.

Butcher stands, a register ordered to be made of, 228; called "premium stands," 360-1, 436-7; gift or drawn, 509-10, 540-1-7, 551-53, 581-2.

Butler, John, sweeper of the Exchange Market, 374.

Butler, Rose. colored girl, executed for arson, 480-1.

Butler, William. extract from a letter of, on New York City, 289-92.

Butter received as rent, xiv: bad seized, 148; arrival of from Ireland, 148, 234; reputation of the for exportation in 1753, 148; price sold at in 1762, and the assize price, 143; changed, 150; high prices, and meeting of grocers in relation to, 408; premiums given for the best found in two markets, 409; the guinea roll of, 409.

Buttermilk Channel in 1678, (see 15,) 71.

Buyce, Mathew, wishes to desert the Bear Market, 309-10.

Cain, Benjamin, on petition in 1733, 262.

Campbell, George, on petition for place in the markets, 186.

Campbell, Lieut.-Gen., on Long Island in 1783, 292.

Canal (or Here-Graft) in Broad Street, first prepared for use, 31-2. (See 35, 40, 71, 77, 254.)

Canal celebration, butchers engaged in the, 506-8.

Cannon, Abraham, one of the originators of Corlears Hook Market, 388.

Cannon bursted, killed and wounding several persons, 84.

Capoens, Christyne, stolen from the house of. 52.

Carmer, Alderman Nicholas, Market Committee in 1796. 200.

Carroll, Colonel Nicholas, Centre Market Drill-Room Committee, 476.

Carter, Aaron, fisherman of Washington Market, 424.

Carter, William, fisherman of Fulton Market, 500.

Catharine Market established. 341, (see 306;) first fisherman and shed at, 341; great excitement by the people near, 341-2; additions to, 342, 347-9, 350, 353; negro dancing at, 344-5; a great fish market, 348; the shark catcher, 348-9; removed to Chatham Square, 348; a bell hung on the, 349; fees collected, 350-1; a public scale added to, 352; grocers near petition to open trade on Sunday mornings, 352; butchers complain of speculators in Bowery, 353; when a good country produce market, 353-4; petition for better accommodations, 354-5; unsatisfactory arrangement for farmers, 355; country people and hucksters removed, 360; attempted removal, 360; new market-houses erected, 360-4; paying a large interest, 364; iron market-houses built, 369; visit on a Sunday morning in 1859, 369-70; number of premium stands. 547.

Cattle. introduction in New Netherlands, loaned on halves, xii., xiv.; increase and hogs, 17; English and Dutch cattle—crossed, 17; English not permitted to be sold, 26-7; killed by Indians, 34-5; first market or bull's head for the sale of, 37; ordered to be branded, 43-4; not allowed to be slaughtered below Wall Street, 54-5; fees for those killed, 60; the prices of, and horses in 1692, 67-8; place for landing black, 78, 80-2; numbers killed in 1684 and 1698, 87; fat sent to the war in 1755, 272; straying from camp, 161; order to seize, 163; disposition of stolen. 174; exported, also horses and mules from Connecticut in 1790, 186; stolen, 168; complaint of a farmer about the price, &c., 186-7; crossing the ferry, the risk and loss, 187-9; landing-place near Col. Rutgers', 189; butchers petition against forestalling. 211; high prices of, 234, 410; display of, and fat beef, 237, 322, 340, 397, 403, 419-21, 467-8, 477-8, 507; the first drove direct from Ohio to New York City, 411.

Centre Market, established. 460-1; first meat sold in, 461; bell placed on, 461-2; additions to, 462-4-8, 471-2-6-8; butchers' memorial and petition, and stands sold in, 465-6; "against the world" in fat beef, 467-8; butchers send fat beef and letter to President Jackson—his answer, 467-8; paying large interest, 470-1; butchers obtain an injunction against the city, and stop sale of stands, 471; brick market-house erected. 471-2; grand balls and suppers, 472-5; rooms appropriated to military, &c., 475-6-8; fish-stands drawn for 476; railroad laid alongside, 476; heaviest fat ox known sold in, 477-8; cost of. 484; premium stands in, 547; "Centre Market Place," the name given to the street on the east side of. 477.

"Censora" complains of rudeness in the markets, 39, 40.

Chamber of Commerce, their valuation of gold, silver, and paper money, 104-5; Committee from, to designate premiums on the fishery, 117-19; on regulating the markets, 120; on fishery, 122; meet in the Exchange, 283.

Chappell, Samuel, fisherman of Wash Market, 424.

"Cheap meat for boarders," 227.

Cherry, George, victualer for British vessels, 163.

Childs, Heman W., Superintendent of Lamps and Streets, report on markets, 548-9, 569

Cholera of 1832, an incident of the. 429-30.

Christiansen. Hendrick, introduces the first small animals in New Netherlands, xiii.

Christie, Jas., Commissary for Cattle and Sheep, 163.

Chrystie. Lieut.-Col. in the war of 1812, 415-18.

Church-Wardens ordered to loan money to a poor butcher, 91; to mark the clothes of city poor, 128.

Churches in New York in 1748. 270; Quaker meeting-house in Crown Street, 272.

Cistern, proposition to build one near Widow Rutgers' brew-house, 133.

Civill, William, keeper of a public hay-scale, 392.

Clark and Lewis. speculators in the Bowery near, 353.

Clark, Palmer, fisherman of Fulton Market, 500.

Clark, Wm., a fisherman of Catharine Market, 366.

Clarke. John, letter on criminals and the fate of a drunkard, 53.

Clay, Henry. steamboat, destroyed by fire. 577.

Clerk of Markets, duties of in 1691. 60; 1781, 124; rewarded for doing their duty, 183; pay per day, 352; one performing duty for five markets. 392.402.

"Clermont," the first steamboat to Albany, 194-5.

Cliff Street, origin of the name, 126.

Clinton, Gov. Sir Geo., a large water-melon at. 261.

Clinton, Governor George. on yellow fever. 373.

Clinton, Sir Henry, proclamation of in 1778. 166-7.

Clinton Market, established, 527; grounds valued by a jury, 528; name derived from, 528, butchers' stands sold at public auction. 528; country market erected, 530; leased to H. R. R. R. Co., 548; butchers' stands drawn for, 531; number of premium stands, 547; shed additions, 548-9; country market-house torn down, 549; oyster and clam trade, 549.

Clopper, Cornelius, blacksmith, the origin of Smith's Fly, 127.

Cochran, William G., fisherman of Washington Market, 424.
Cockfer. John, the death of old, 152.
Coddrington, Captain Thomas, property at Harlaem for sale. 85.
Codwise,Geo., Hooks and Ladders removed from,306.
Coenties Slip Market established, 109-10; a fire near in 1741, 94; known as the "Great Fish Market," 110, 114-15; origin of the name, and differently spelled. 114; enlarged, 116-7; narrow escape from fire, 117; used as a store-house, &c., 122; proclaimed again a public market-place, 123-4; starting-place for Newark. N. J., 125; not used after the Revolution, but the slip as market for live stock and country produce. 125.
Coffee-House, Old, afterwards Tontine was added, 242.
Cait. Samuel, fisherman of Fulton Market, 500.
Cold winters of 1717, 91; 1720. 91-2; 1739-40, 249; 1746-7. 250; 1773-80-82, 168-9; 1817-18, 379; 1821-29-36, 456-7.
Cole. Jacob, shot Cornelius Fonck for a bear, 312.
Collect, known as Kolch, Kalch Hook, Kolck, Colleck, market near, 397; origin of the name, 398; view of. 357; well at the, 266-68.
Collect Market established, 395-6; origin of the name, 398; known as the "Arsenal" and Mosquito Market, 397; fat beef on sale, 397; report on change of location, 398; butchers and others opposed, 398; removed, 398-9; butchers and other stand-holders removed into Centre Market, 461
Colve, Capt. Anthony, Governor of New Orange, (formerly New York,) 56.
Comptroller's report against the original contributors of Bear Market, 326-7; Flagg on Washington Market, 447; action with the lessees of stands in the Fulton Market, 498; report against the claims of the licensed butchers, 541; answered, 541-7; books of imperfectly kept, 548.
Comstock. John, fisherman of Fulton Market, 513.
"Conditions" made to encourage settlers in New Netherlands, xiii., xiv.
Congress bill sold at auction, 106.
Conlin, Chas., detected in cheating—permit revoked, 226-7.
Continental butcher ordered to catch fish, 291.
Continental troops supplied with provisions, 157-8.
Cooley, Simeon, performs an "amende honorable," 284.
"Cooper Union " — the princely donation of Mr. Peter Cooper, 554-6.
Cooper, Widow Helena, timber used for gun-carriages, 89.
Coote, Governor Richard, Earl of Bellamont, 127.
Coppie Gillie, last of the Negro Plot of 1741, 335.
Copper coin at a discount, also Jersey money, 182.
Corlaers Hook Market, established, 387-8; known as Grand Street Market, 387-8; origin of the name, 388; bell added, 388; a fish market added, 388; butchers removed into the Grand Street Market, 390; market-house sold and removed, 390.
Corlies, John B., on rebuilding the Washington Market, 453.
Cornbury, Lord, appealed to, to prepare defence for the city, 89; no confidence in him, 90; thrown into prison, 90; address to the Board of Trade, 110-11; imprisons ministers of religion, 128; proclamation on slaves, 243.
Cornelissen, Mayke, a bought servant, 96.
Cornell, William, petition to enlarge the Meal Market, and abatement of rent on ferry, 247-8.
Corporation bills or tickets issued, 233-4, 371-2, 418.
Cortland. Aug. V., name on freemanship, 336.
Cortlandt, (Courtlandt,) Augustus, C'k, invites contracts, 155.
Cortlandt's, Col., ferry landing near, 88.
Cortlandt, Alderman Philip, committee to locate the public slaughter-house, 81.
Cortlandt, Philip, in favor of a market-place near White Hall Slip, 276; Catharine, daughter of Philip, killed on a holiday, 84.
Cortlandt, Mayor Jacobus V., Clerk of Markets, 90.
Cosby, Governor William, accident while keeping a holiday under, 84.

Countess Key, (or Slip,) the foot of Maiden Lane, so called in 1698, 127-8; changed to Smith's Fly Slip, 132.
Coutant, Gilbert, petition for place in the markets, 186.
Cox, John, loses chain near the Hay (Bear) Market, 313.
Cozine, Cornelius, Sr., wishes to desert the Bear Market, 309-10.
Crandall. Roger, Fly Market fisherman, 224.
Crane, J., on first North River steamboat, 195.
Creple, bush or swamp, 127.
Criminals, punishment of, 52-3, 102-3, 156, 246, 255.
Croburn, Robert, repairs meal market, 251.
Crocker, Jonathan, Fly Market fisherman, 224-5.
Crofts and Houston, fishermen of Cath. Market, 366.
Crosby, Henry, leases the "Broadway Shambles" for seven years, 68.
"Crossing the ferry " "in olden time," 193-4.
Croton Water introduced into public markets, 485.
Crowell. Joseph, bought State Prison property, 387.
Crown Market established, 327-8; accepted as a public market, 311; known as Mesier's and Thurman's Market, 328; origin of the name, 328-9; burnt in the great fire of 1776, 329.
Cruger. Alderman John, on a committee of public slaughter-house, 81; Mayor, account of victims of yellow fever, 250; on freemanship, 336.
Crystal Palace destroyed by fire, 424.
Culbertson, James, Clerk of Market, rewarded, 183. (See 189.)
Currency, Indian, Dutch, and English, 16, 29, 30-1, 41-2, 67, 99, 104-6, 116, 182, 253, 290.
Curtenius, Peter T., certifies to the character of a butcher, 199; opposite the Oswego (Broadway) Market, 272.
Curtius, Dominie Rector, Alexander Carolus, defendant in a hog case, 47.
Curtis, Cyrus C., fisherman of Fulton Market, 500.
Custom-House in 1700, 78.
Custom-House Bridge Market established, 70; repaired and used as a warehouse, 74; shed taken down and sold, 76; resolution to restore back to a public market-place again, 76; posts put up to keep the cows out, 77-8; declared a nuisance, and removed, 77. (See pages 84, 113.)
Cutler, Ebenezer, fisherman of Fulton Market, 513.

Darow, Nicholas, Fly Market fisherman, 205.
Darrow, Ira, fisherman of Washington Market, 424.
Dartmore Prison, witness of the massacre, 439-41.
Dash, John Balthus, tinman, removed from Oswego (Broadway) Market, 272.
Davies, Judge Henry E., appoints receivers for market property, 451.
Davis, Alderman A. B., communication read by, 541.
Davis, Wm J., anecdote of Sam'l Fraunces, 305.
Dawson, Roper, at the Long Room over the Exchange, 280.
Day, Johnny, of Fly Market, 229-32.
Dayton, S., fisherman of Fulton Market, 513.
Deane. Richard, offers to remove the public slaughter-house, 315.
De Backer, Henry, a great shot, 20.
Deberville, Monsieur, expected attack by, 89.
Decay, (Dekay,) Elizabeth, on petition in 1733, 262.
De Four, David, sues Roelof Jansen for an ox, 49.
De Haas, Andries, the keeper of the market key, 45.
De Kay, Teunis, on a committee in 1691, 77.
De Klyn's Ferry, location of, 383.
Delafons, John, Agent, victualer for the British ships, 171.
De Lancey, Hon. James, Lieut.-Gov., near Oswego (Broadway) Market, 272.
De Lancey, Oliver, leases the Exchange, 279; Adj.-General, 171, 292; property confiscated, 162.
De Lancey, Stephen, merchant, imports the first fire-engines, 258.
De Lancey's Square, location of, 455.
De Langloiserie, Lewis Hector Piot, a porpoise fisherman, 111-12.
Delamater, Samuel, wishes to desert the Bear Market, 309-10.

De Longchamps, Mon. Chevalier, killed in a duel, 357.
Demilt, Anthony, appointed Keeper of the Ware (Market) House, 74–5.
Denton's notice of New York, &c., in 1670, 42–3.
Depeyster, Isaac, in favor of a market-place near White Hall Slip, 276.
Depeyster, Captain John, Fly Market near the house of, 128.
Depeyster, John, Jr , weigher of hay, 273.
Dervall, William, Mayor of New York in 1674, 56.
De Voe, James, and others, petition for repairs to Free Bridge, 66.
Devoo, Frederick—*Jack*, a dancing negro, belonging to, 344, 355.
De Vries, account of Indian agriculture, &c., 24–5.
De Witt, Simeon, laid out a grand market-place, 393.
Doctors' Mob in 1788, incidents in the, 333–4.
Dogs, dangerous running loose, 83.
Domestic animals first introduced into New Netherlands, xiii ; prices of, 30.
Donaldson, James, recommends M. Vogel, 208.
Dongan, Governor Thomas, removes market-house, to be employed as a warehouse, 74.
Dopzen. Joris. complaint against, 40.
Doughty, Major-General, rooms in Centre Market for the use of, 476.
Duane, Hon. James, Mayor, letter to in 1785, 254; liberality of. 296. (*See* 274.)
Duane Street Market, established, 390; called Washington Market, 391; a bell placed in, 392; removed, and ground claimed by Trinity Church, 393, 558
Ducking stool, built in 1691, 110.
Duer, Hon. Wm. A., recollections, &c., 297, 300, 333.
Duke Street, formerly called Bayard Street, now Stone Street, 92.
Dundas, Captain, the last tenant of Bayard's Vault, 358–9.
Dunscomb, Colonel Samuel S., commanded a New York Regiment, 525.
Durie, John, fisherman of Fulton Market, 513.
Durie, Thomas, in the Federal procession, 316.
Durning, Daniel R., interested in the Miranda Expedition, 215.
Duryee, (*Duryea*,) George, appointed Deputy Clerk of Fulton Market, 501; also Franklin Market, 518.
Dutch Boors racing horses and fighting, 58, 72.
Dutch language in the markets, 335, 408.
Dutch laws repealed, 53.
Dutch mile, length of a, 22; names for fish, 21; pound weight. 56.
Duykinck, Gerardus, sells goods near Old Slip Market, 92.
Dyckman, Isaac, Ex-Alderman, 63.
Dyckman, Jacob, erects a free bridge on his land at Kingsbridge, 63–4.
Dyckman, Jacobus, petitions to repair said bridge, 66.

Earle, Job. on petition in 1733, 262.
Earthquake of 1727, driving hoops out of fashion, 256.
East Hampton, proclamation of a cattle market, sent to, 38.
Eckford, Henry, friendship for, 359; property near Manhattan Market, 524.
Edgar, William, certifies a butcher, 199.
Edwards, Johnny, the eccentric scale-beam maker, 480.
Eizenhart, Nathan. Clerk of Catharine Market, 350.
Eldridge, Daniel, fisherman of Wash'n Market, 424.
Eldredge, Thomas, fisherman of Fulton Market, 500
Elliott, Andrew, Superinten't-General of Police, 163.
Ellis, or Oyster Island, to be sold, near the Bear Market, 315.
Ellison. John, lease of a part of the market-house to, 75; petitions to catch porpoises, 76.
Ellsworth, William, in favor of a market-house in the Fields, (Park,) 275.
Ely, Richard, exalted upon a wooden horse, 103.
Embargo laid, and business suspended, in 1706,89,90.
Emmet, Thomas Addis, Counsel in the "Butcher Causes," 239.
English cattle introduced into New Netherlands, 38.
English weights and measures to be used, 56.

Engs, P. W., vouches for Frederick Johnson, 470.
Essex Market, established, 479; name derived from, 479–80; high grounds around, 480; removed, and new building erected, 481, 552; rearrangement of the stands, 483; premium butchers' stands sold, 481–4; number in, 547; drawn stands, 485; ordered taken down and replaced, 485–6; rooms above occupied for public purposes, 486–7; fortunate in having an honest Clerk above twenty years. 487–8.
Etherige's, Sir George, way of making love, 255.
Evacuation of the city in 1783, early intention of by the British troops, 177.
Everzen, Wessels, complaint against, 40; engaged in building a house. 46.
Ewen, Colonel John, Centre Market Drill-Room Committee, 476.
Exchange, (in Broad Street,) when erected—location, 279; two buildings of the same name, 279; room used for various purposes, 280, 298; known as the "New and Royal Exchange," 280. 291; a large clock put up, 280; New York Society Library holds election in. 280; a market for home-manufactured goods, 281; Chamber of Commerce meet in, 283; cupola repaired. 286; Saint George's Ferry near, 286; houses near cannonaded, 288; "London Coffee-House" opened in the, 292; Marine Artillery meet in. 292; ordered to be used as a public market-place, 297; Tammany Society Museum held in, 299, 300–2; murder and suicide near, 301–2; removed, 302; butchers removed, 371.
Exchange and Washington and Warren Banks of Jacob Barker, 578–'.
Exchange Market, established, 370–1; stage-office in, 374; sawed into three pieces and removed, 374; removal, 375.
Exchange Place, its names in olden time, 254.

Fairs at New Amsterdam in 1641, 17; after the Feast of St. Bartholomew, 29.
Fair or market ordered by the Court of Assize, 56.
Fairfield, proclamation of a cattle market sent to, 38.
Fanton, John, fined and imprisoned for selling "blown geese," 410.
Farmer's, Anthony, market-house near, 77.
Farmers suffering from a deep snow, 91–2 ; stand against the Assize Law and an invitation to visit them for products. 146–7.
Fauconier's, Peter, slave executed for conspiracy in 1712, 245.
Feat, a remarkable, and battle, 339–40.
Feat of a countryman in Fly Market, 180.
Featherstone-Hough, Lieut. Wharton, murdered in a riot in 1705, 88–9.
Federal procession in 1788, butchers in the great, 316–17–18; ended on Bayard's Mount, 357.
Feeks, Samuel L., served with Col. Robert Bogardus in 1812, 525.
Ferguson. John, a humane freak of, 209.
Ferries, established across the Harlaem River, 39; to Long Island. 78; old location, 79; from Countess Key. or Fly Market, 88, 286; how conducted, 139; incidents and accidents, 187–98; from Peck Slip, 286; Coenties Slip Market. 286; Saint George's, foot of Broad Street, 286; De Klyn's, 383.
Ferry-boats from Long Island to land on certain days at different places, 88; description of, 187; first steam to Hoboken, 194; to Jersey City, 195; to Brooklyn, 198; do. horse. 197–8; do. to Williamsburgh, 198; Fulton Market. 488.
Ferry-house built on Nassau (Long) Island in 1698, 79; in Broad Street, 254.
Ferry rates and regulations across Harlaem River, 39; East River in 1698, 79, 80; 1732, 249; 1814, 198.
Field, Francis, wounded by a king's soldier. 154.
Fink, Philip. on fat cattle, 419–20–21.
Fire, Trinity Church on, 259; great in 1776 329; in 1778, 107–8; excitement in 1796, 204–5, at the State Prison. 387; in Brooklyn. arrested by the New York firemen, 196–7; on the present site of Fulton Market. 488; great in 1835, 520; officers of the Army and Navy publicly thanked for services in, 521.
Fire-buckets, how used, 258, 371–2.

Fire-engines first introduced and used in New York, 258–9; floating, in 1812, 196.

Firemen in olden time, 371; publicly thanked for services at Brooklyn, 196–7; turn their fire-caps in a body, 582–3.

Fire-wood, scarcity and high price in 1759, 136.

Fish, found in New Netherlands, 21–2; Coenties Slip Market the great market for, 110–12, 223; great catch of, 112, 135; permission to catch, and scarcity, 120; timely and remarkable supply of, 226; without a supply, 224–5; to "get a bunch of," 348.

Fishermen, complaint against the Dutch, 40; encouragement given to, 117–9, 121–3; impressed in 1764, 115–6.

Fisk, Ebenezer, fisherman of Wash'n Market, 424.

Flag of the British troops taken down in N. Y. City, 1783, 296; the first United States at N. Y. City, 295.

Fletcher, William, a bought servant, run away from service, 100.

Flattenbarrack Hill, known also as Verlettenburgh, "Old Boys" on, 254, 329.

Flatten Barrack Market-Place, established, 252; why so named, 253; David Grim's account of, 255; whipping-post, pillory, and stocks near, 255; first engine-house near, 258; permission to erect a market-house, 260.

Fly Market, established, 125–8; the origin and meaning of the name, 125–6; in 1720, called "The Market-House at Countess Key, 129; first called by its proper name, 129; used to build battoes in, 128–9; in 1735 the rival of the Old Slip, 93; enlarged in 1736, 131; in 1754, 134; in 1771, 155–6; in 1784, 180; in 1788, 182; in 1796, 200; (see 205;) fire near in 1737, 132; in 1741, 94; fish market-house burnt, 1796, 204; slaves sold at, 132; sewer built under, 132–3; proposition to build a cistern near, 133; battle between Sons of Liberty and king's soldiers near, 152–5; tables prepared in, 155; Fly Market Street ran alongside of, 170–1; bell cut down and carried away, houses threatened to be prostrated, 178–9; an egg feat, or feast, in, 180; fish market repaired, 182; arrangement of the stands in 1787, 182–3; suits at law ordered against subscribers, 183; butchers' stands sold in 1796, 201; (see 343;) hucksters' petition in relation to the sale of fruit, 203–4; all the stands occupied, 211; petition, and disappointment of twelve Republican butchers, 221–2; a Philadelphian's visit to, 223; fishermen petition for slip-room, 223–4; fish-cars removed to Brooklyn, 224–5; fishing-smack successful in capturing a British vessel of war, 225; a butcher punished for making a false return, 226–7; a return of all the butchers in 1819, 232–3; animals killed and sold in 1816–18, 234–5; large show of premium beef in, 237; on the removal, 235–8; a sewer one of the causes, 527; last sale of meat in, 238; butchers' suit for claims, and settled, 238–39–40–41; (see 343;) deserted, 238; torn down, 238; damages awarded to the butchers, 241; materials to be removed, 353; part to Spring Street Market, 380; part to Centre Market, 462; and part to the Old Slip Market, 517–8.

Fonck, Cornelius, mistook for a bear, and shot dead, 312.

For-fathers and Foremothers, and their generations, 185–6.

Forestalling by Indians and others, 40; report on, 216–7; (see 425–6;) trial, 227.

Fort George, buildings burnt in, 94; meeting at, 248.

Fowler, Daniel, poultry dealer at Fulton Market, 513.

Fowls, domestic, found among the early Dutch, 18.

Francis, Dr. John W., communication on the Collect Market, 396–7.

Franklin Market, established, 517–8; bell presented for the, 518; stands sold for a premium, 518; above the cost of the building, 519; business removed in consequence of yellow fever, 519; old residents near, 520; destroyed by fire in 1835, 520–1; shed erected on ruins, 521; rebuilt, 521–3; the rooms employed for religious purposes, 523.

Franklin, Thomas, on Corporation bills, 233.

Fraunces, Samuel, house struck by cannon-balls, 288; Washington's household steward, 304–5.

Frecke, John C., house near Fly Market, 205.

"Freedoms and exemptions" offered to settlers, xiii.

Freedom of the city, value of, and how obtained, 149.

Frost, Ezra, appointed Deputy Clerk of Fulton Market, 496; resignation of, 501.

Fruit found in New Netherlands, 25–6.

Fulton Market, established, 488; sale of stands advertised, with terms and conditions, 490–1; meetings of butchers in relation thereto, 490–4; sale of stands and cellars, 492–7; unselfish action of the butchers, 497; stands vacated and surrendered, 497, 500; many widow hucksters in, 499; transfer of stands, 500; petition from "small meat" butchers in, 503–4; an Englishman visits, 505; additions to, 508–14–15; fishermen, change of stands, 499, 500–8–12–13–14; petition for slip accommodations, 511–2; fish-trade at, 514–6; butchers' stands drawn by lot, 509; number of premium stands, 547; paying over 9½ per cent. interest, 581; present condition, 517.

Fulton, Robert, produces the first best steam ferry-boat, 195–6.

Furman, Alderman Gabriel, trouble with ferrymen, 189–90; signs a "vote of thanks," 208.

Furman, Alderman Richard, report on butchers' stands, 342–3.

Furs and skins, prices of, (see Currency.) 57.

Gabrie, Timothy, Collector of Excise on Cattle, complaint against, 53–4.

Gaine, Hugh, sells tickets for an exhibition in the Exchange; 280; editorial, 284; solicits permission to erect a market-house, 375.

Garden Street, called Garden Alley, Garden Lane, Church Street, and Exchange Place, 254.

Gardie, Madame, murder of an actress named, 301–2.

Gardner, Noah, the reformed State prisoner, 384–5.

Gazette, N. Y., first paper published in N. York, 99.

Geoffrey, Thomas, Fly Market fisherman, 205.

George, Thomas, recovers fines and penalties against butchers, 90.

General Assembly passed an act to hold fairs and markets annually, 61; small-pox in the House of, 258.

Geneva Club, party of slaves called, 265.

Gerbrants, Marcellus, on a petition for a market-place, 327.

Gerrits, Otte, complaint against Joris Dopzen, 40.

Ghost, George Ship's, 337–9.

Gilbert, Garrit, offer to establish a market at Greenwich, 399.

Gilbert, James, Clerk of three markets, 402.

Gilbert, William, one of the Tammany Society, 299.

Giles, Aquilla, in the Federal procession, 316.

Golden Hill, battle of, 153–4–5.

Gordon, Geo. A., fisherman of Cath'e Market, 365–6.

Goveneur Market, established, 404; name from, 404; new market-house, 405; stands sold at auction, 405; another new market-house—the old sold, 406.

Government value of stock and provisions, &c., in 1665, 42.

Grafht, (see Canal.)

Graham, William, on petition for place in the markets, 186.

Grain, found in New Netherlands, xii., 24–5; price of, 16, 30, 42, 58, 72, 91; export of prohibited, 34, 56; ferry-boats to carry, 79; scarcity of, 86–7.

Grand market-place laid out, and boundaries, 393–4; reduced in size, 395; grounds released to the former owners, 395. (See Poppleton's Map, 1817.)

Grand Street, origin of the name, 455.

Grand Street Market, established, 455; enlarged, 457; arrangement of the stands, 457; butchers petition for stands in Manhattan Market, 458; neighborhood petition for and against a larger market-house near, 458–9; new market-house erected, 459; butchers and the Common Council on the disposal of stands, 459; an obstruction to the street, 586; replaced by the Monroe Market, 460; butchers and others transferred, 587.

Grant, Percer W. fisherman of Wash'n Market, 424.

Grant, William, fisherman of Wash'n Market, 424.

Great or Delancey's Square, 479.

Greenwich, origin of the name, 399, 400; (see 376, 382–3; Upper and Lower Village of, 378, 399, 401–3; yellow fever assisted to their formation, 400–1.

Greenwich Hotel, near the State Prison Market, 383.

Greenwich Market, established, 399; enlarged, 401–2; fat beef sold in, 403; torn down, and grounds appropriated for standing-place for country wagons, &c., 403; butchers transferred into the Weehawken Market, 578.

Griffen, P. S. fisherman of Fulton Market, 513.

Griffing, James, Jr., Fly Market fisherman, 225.

Grim, David, map notices Broad Street Market, 85; fire in 1778, 108; Flatten Barrack Market-Place, 255; map of, 260; in favor of a market-house in the Fields, 275; the city gates and wall, 372.

Grinnell, Captain Richard, escapes from the prison-ship Scorpion, 169.

Gulick, James, Chief Engineer, removed—conduct of the firemen, 583.

Guicks, Captain, crew in a riot and murder, 88.

Gysbert, Mr., mixed up in a law-suit, 47.

Haerlem, N., (Village,) keeps hogs on Baren Island, 48.

Haley, Jeremiah, fisherman of Washington Market, 424.

Half-Moone Battery, location of, 55.

Hall, Charles Henry, sale of Tompkins Market property, 550.

Hall, Ald. William, (General,) on Franklin Market, 522–3.

Hall, Willis, fisherman of Centre Market, 476.

Hallet, James, coachmaker in Broadway, 315.

Hallett, Samuel, on petition for place in the markets, 186.

"Hamadryad," (English war-vessel,) Captain Chatham, 440.

Hamilton, Alexander, engaged as counsel for Levi Weeks, 378.

Hampton, John, Presbyterian minister, imprisoned, 128.

Harbor of New York, defenceless condition of in 1705, 88.

Harding, James, delinquent ferrymaster, 82–3; lands ferry-boats certain days at Burger's Path, 88.

Harlem Market established—location, 588–9; cost of, 590; leased to the Brothers Hardenbrook, 591; last public market, 591.

Harris, Henry, Fly Market fisherman, 205.

Harris, Nathaniel, Fly Market fisherman, 225.

Harris, Richard, account for a public dinner in 1704, 68–9.

Harrison, Francis, Sheriff, paid for executing slaves, 245.

Harrison, John, house burnt in the fire of 1776, 329.

Havemeyer, Mayor W. F., report on Washington Market, 446.

Hay, law to establish the sale of, and where sold in 1762, 273; scale at Bear Market removed, 321.

Haynes, Godfrey, drowned in Burling Slip in 1766, 279.

Hazard, Ald'n Thomas, orders repairs to Peck Slip Market, 304.

Hell-Gate in 1678, 71.

Hendricks, Gerrit, leases the Excise, and the first Inspector of salted meats, 37.

Henigar, Maria M., waiting-maid of Mrs. Washington, 162.

Herring, Elbert, on the Duane Street Market, 393.

Hertell, Thomas, on the Duane Street Market, 393.

Hewlet, John, ordered to seize the Rebels' cattle and sheep, 163.

Hicks, A., fisherman of Washington Market, 424.

Hicks, Dr. John B., card about the body of John Young, 342.

Hicks, Smith, fisherman of Washington Market, 424.

Hicks, Mayor Whitehead, lays the foundation-stone of Bear Market, 308.

Hicks, William S., Committee on first North River steamboat, 195.

Hiscox, Samuel, fisherman of Wash'n Market, 424.

Hoax—"sawing the Island off," 462–4.

Hoebuck Ferry from the Bear Market, when established, 314–5.

Hoffman, James Ogden, one of the Tammany Society, 299.

"Hog-cart," sketches of the, 482–3.

Hogs in New Netherlands in 1641, 17–8, 27; price of in 1650, 30; in 1665, 42; 1693, 68; fairs for the sale of, 38; slaughtering, 35–7, 45, 130; trading one for a petticoat, 41; suit about, 47; lost, 48; ferriage on, 80, 249.

Hoghlandt, Adrian, the slave of executed for murder, 245.

Holland, Edward, in favor of a market-place near White Hall Slip, 276.

Holmes, Eldad, opposed to the removal of Catharine Market, 361.

Holmes, Joel, taylor—the Albany post-rider puts up at, 331.

Holt, John, the Patriot editor and printer—editorial, 280; suffering of, 290.

Hooks, Thomas, slaughter-house near, 80.

Hoonik, Jacob, on petition in 1733, 262.

Hoop-fever, when ladies had the, 255–7.

Hopper, John, wishes to desert Bear Market, 309–10.

Horsen, (Harsen,) Cornelius and John, wish to desert Bear Market, 309–10.

Horsefield, (Brothers,) slaves tried, convicted, and executed, 94.

Horsmanden's account of the great Negro Plot of 1741–2, 93.

Hours of amusements in the "olden time," 306.

House in Broad Street, the rent of in 1772, 253–4.

Howe, General, unsuccessful attempt to bribe made by, 161–2.

Howell, Hezekiah, of Orange County, N. Y., fat cattle by, 340.

Hubbard, N. T., grocer, secretary of a butter meeting, 408.

Huddleston, Ann, on petition in 1733, 262.

Hudson, Hendrick, what he said about New Netherlands, xii.

Hughes, James M., one of the Tammany Society, &c., 299.

Hughson, John, keeper of a public house, and leader of the negro conspiracy of 1741, tried, convicted, and, with his wife, (Sarah,) hung, 95–6. (See 265.)

Hulft, Peter Evertsen, introduced first cattle in New Netherlands, xii., xiii.

Humbert, Jonas, benevolence of, 420.

Hunt, John E., lessee of the basement of the Franklin Market, 523.

Hunter, James, made additions to Corlaers Hook Market, 388.

Hunter, Robert, appointed Governor, 90; action in the slave conspiracy of 1712, 243–5; orders all the market-houses (except one) to be used for war purposes, 252; speech on Oswego, 271.

Hutchins, John Nathan, the first almanac-maker, 272.

Huygen, Leonard, near Old Slip Market, 87.

Illumination of the city and butchers' stalls on account of naval victories, 407–8.

Impressment of four fishermen, 115–6.

Inhabitants, distressed situation of in 1643, 27; in 1779, 109; in 1783, 296; character of in 1670, 42, in 1692, 67; preparing for war in 1653, 33; in 1705, 88, 90–1; 1709, 128–9; 1745, 115; amusements in 1704, 69; in 1759, 136; (see 306;) refugee leaving in 1783, 177–8, 292; comfortable situation of the working classes in 1825, 354.

Indians, native, food and address, xii.; manner of grinding corn, 24; attack on settlers, 27, 34; complaints against, 35; conveying products to market, 71.

Ingolsby, Lieutenant-Governor Richard, put in and out of office, 90.

Inspectors of private slaughter-houses appointed, 368.

Invitation to the English farmers to send cattle to market, 38.

Ireland, Joseph, jury on market grounds, 528.

Ireland. Alderman William H., report on butchers' claims, 255–40–1.
Island of Nassau, (L. I.,) a new ferry to the, 78.

Jackson, General Andrew, President of the United States, present to, and answer, 467–8.
Jacobzen. Captain Jan, sale of a hog, 47.
Jaes, Aaght, singular suit against Cornelius Jansen Vanhorn. and decision of the Court, 40–1.
Jansen, Pieter, a witness, 48.
Jarrott. Allen, slave executed for conspiracy in 1712, 245.
Jay, John, letter on grading Broadway, 254; Governor, feeling against in 1795, 357–8; proclamation in relation to State prisoners, 383.
Jay, Peter A., counsel for butchers' claims, 239–41.
Jeffray, James. fisherman of Wash'n Market, 424.
Jeffray, Robert, fisherman of Wash'n Market, 424.
Jeffray, Thomas, fisherman of Wash'n Market, 424.
Jeroleman. Mrs., in the Oswego Market, 335.
Jersey money in 1774, 105; in 1787, 182.
Jews, Professor Kalm's notice of the, 270.
Jewish seals, a butcher punished for affixing false on meat, 202
Jefferson Market, established and named, 558–9; butchers' stands built in, 559–60; public use made of the grounds at, 560–5–70–1; a well and supply-pump at, 560; hydraulic press, additions to, 561–3; butchers'stands drawn for in, 561; number of premium stands, 547; a centre passage ordered. 561–2; not a loss to the city, 570; bell-tower destroyed by fire. new one erected. 570–1; heart-rending scenes at the, 571–2; "the blind man of," 572–3; Lieutenant-General Scott at the, 573–5; necessary influence to erect a new building, 576.
Johnson, Ben. the hangman, escaped being hung. 53
Johnson, Bernard, large number of shad caught by, 135.
Johnson, David, house burnt in the fire of 1776, 329.
Jones, Major-General James I., rooms in the Centre Market for the use of. 476.
Jones, Samuel. advises the removal of the Broadway Market, 276.
Jones, Thomas, Recorder. lays the second stone in the erection of Bear Market, 308.
Jubeart, John, convicted and hung for counterfeiting, 103–4.
Justices and Vestrymen invite contracts, 155.

Kalm, Professor, describes servants, 99; fish, 116; battoes, 252; market boats on the North River, 261; a large water-melon, 261; N. Y. City, 269–70.
Keen & Lightfoot open a coffee-room in the Exchange. 280.
Kelly. John. petitions for privilege to erect public slaughter-houses. 80; report on, 81.
Kemper, Daniel. son executed in the Miranda Expedition, 216.
Kennedy. Archibald. in favor of a market-place near White Hall Slip. 276.
Kenneydy, James, on petition in 1733, 262.
Kerry. Margaret, convicted and executed for conspiracy. 96.
Kettleman. Valentine, store near the State Prison Market. 383.
Kettletas. Garret. officer of Company Beat No. 20, 1776, 106.
Kettletas, Peter, appointed to examine fishermen's claims, 119.
Kettletas. William, defence of two ferrymen, 190–2.
Key, an old name for a slip about 1700, 127.
Kieft, Sir William, Governor, successor to Governor Van Twiller, 16; Indians' address to, xii.; confessions of wrong to the settlers. 26–7; attack on the Indians—their retaliation, 27; recalled, 28.
Kiersted, (Kierstede) Dr. Hans, first market-place appointed near the house of, 36; descendants of, 248–9; recipe of. 249.
Kiersted, General Henry T., descendant of Dr. Hans, 249.
Kiersted, Dr. Roelof, vessels examined by the Health Officer, 248.
King, Adam, on petition in 1733, 262.

King, Peter, City Surveyor and Carpenter, lays out vacant lots in and near the present Broad, Pearl, Moore, and Coenties Slip, 32–3. 61.
King, Hon. Chas., on the Chamber of Commerce, 121.
King's Bridge, when first built, 62; a toll-bridge, 62–5; with house and farm to let, 66.
Kingsland, Aaron, fisherman of Fulton Market, 513.
Kip, Henry, in favor of a market-house in the Fields, (Park,) 275.
Kip, Jacobus, Alderman, on a Committee, 81.
Kipp, Johannes. on a Committee in 1691, 77.
Kissam, Benjamin, offers the estate of Petrus Rutgers for sale, 328.
Kissam, Dr. Richard S., card about the body of John Young, 342.
Kissing Bridge, why called so, and location of, 137.
Kline, Elizabeth, first allowed to sell refreshments in Catharine Market. 347.
Knapp, John Coghill, (Coggil,) gift of, 164; house in Broad Street, 253.
Knight, Madame, in New York in 1704, 62–9, 70.
Kock, Pieter, property stolen from, 52.
Kray, Teunis, petitions for his wife to superintend the market, &c., 44.
Krigier, Martin, Captain of the "Night-Watch," censured, 33.

La Cheen, Solomon, (La Chair,) complaint of the wife of. 30; leases the excise for slaughtered cattle, 36.
Ladies of olden times, industry of the, 282.
Laight, Edward, appointed to examine fishermen's claims, 119.
Lamb, agreement of citizens not to use, 151; an effectual way to stop the killing of, 282; not to be killed in certain months, 288.
Lamb, Anthony, appointed to the care of fire-engines, 259.
Lamb, John, certifies to character of a butcher, 199.
La Montayne. Johanus, suit against. 47.
Lamphier. Truman, fisherman of Fulton Market,513.
Lamps, no oil for the public in, 1772, 113.
Lasher, John, certifies to character of a butcher,199.
Latham, Jasper, Fly Market fisherman, 205, 224.
Latham, Joseph, Fly Market fisherman, 205, 224.
Latham, Lodowick, fisherman of Wash. Market, 424.
Latham, William, fisherman of Fulton Market, 500.
Lawrence, Jonathan, sold lottery tickets to pay market debt, 330.
Lawson, Captain, arrival at Phila. with servants, 99.
Lawyers consulted in relation to high prices of meat, 250.
Leake, Robert. on a petition for market-place. 327.
Lear, Tobias, Secretary of Gen. Washington, 162.
Lefferts. John, in the Federal procession, 316.
Lefferts, Leffert, the daughter of, killed, 293–4.)
Leitch, Major, death of, 161.
Lenox, Alderman Robert, on the Bridewell Court in 1795, 190; one of the Market Committee in 1796, 200.
Le Roy, Daniel, in the Federal procession, 316.
Lewis, Joseph, Fly Market fisherman, 205.
Lewis, Elias, Fly Market fisherman, 205.
Liberty Boys, battle with king's soldiers, &c., 152–5, 160.
Liberty Pole cut down, 152.
Lindsay, William, has large fire-engine for sale, 259.
Lininseer, Sering, on a petition for a market-place, 327.
Linsey, James. fisherman of Centre Market, 476.
Lispenard, Leonard, petition for a market-house opposite. 375.
Litschoe. Daniel. old tavern kept by, 242.
Livingston, Edward, in the Federal procession, 316.
Livingston, John R., in the Federal procession, 316.
Livingston, Philip, ferry landing near, L. I., 286.
Livingston. Robert G., offers for sale the "Fly or Meadow" and upland. &c., 126; between the Fly and Meal Market. 133, 247.
Livingston, Col. William S., in the great Federal procession, 316.
Lloyd. Thomas, collector of the City Revenue, a defaulter, 362–3.

Lloyd, Major-Gen., rooms in Centre Market for the use of, 476.

Lockard, Captain, complaint against a butcher, 60.

Lockwood, A. & Co., fisherman of Cath. Market, 366.

Lodowicke, Charles, on the growth of domestic animals, 67.

"Long Bridge Boys," a party of slaves in 1741 called, 95, 265.

"Long Island Star" on the removal of the Fly Market, 488–9; Fulton Market stand-holders, 498.

Long Island and Jersey negroes at Catharine Market, 344–5, 370.

Long Island Sound closed with ice near Bridgeport, 456–7.

Loosley and Elms Tavern, illumination of, 289.

Loper, David, fisherman of Fulton Market, 500.

Lorton, Lewis, and others, build Spring Street Market, 375.

Lots laid out near the dock in 1688, 32, 61; others ordered to be sold. 86.

Lovelace, Governor Francis, in 1669, orders the merchants to meet, &c., 85; the Dutch retake New York under the rule of, 56.

Lovelace, Lord John, arrival of the Governor in 1708, death of, 90.

Low, Henry, on petition for place in the markets, 186.

Low, Isaac, remarks on the fishery in 1781, 121–2.

Ludlow, Gabriel H., appointed to examine fishermen's claims, 119.

Lupold, Ullrick. complained of for extortion, 16–7.

Lyell, Sarah, on petition in 1733, 262.

Lyman, Elisha, fisherman of Fly and Fulton Markets, 225, 500.

Lymes, John Hendrick, the Sheriff, killed by accident, 84.

Maettaysan, Nichlas, in the slave-trayd, 246.

Maiden Lane, in 1691 known as "Green Lane." 126; before and after the Revolution a part of known as "Fly Market" and "Fly Market Street," 170–1; in 1824 the whole was, by resolution, named Cortlandt Street, 171.

Maiden Slip, foot of Maiden Lane, called in 1692. 127; in 1698. "Countess Key." after "Countess Slip," 127–9, 131–2, 156; in 1740. as "Smith's Fly Slip," 132–3; after this, as Fly Market Slip.

Main, Rufus W.. fisherman of Wash'n Market. 424.

Malcolm. General W., in the Doctors' Mob. 334.

Mandeville, Yellis, (Jellis.) on petition for place in the markets, 186; wishes to desert Bear Market, 309–10.

Manhattan Island ceded to the Dutch by purchase, xiii.; a small island near "Burnt Mill Point" called, 394–5, 524; town of changed to the City of New Amsterdam. 34; again changed to N. Y.. 53.

Manhattan Market established, 524; bell added. 525; distance from Grand Street Market, 459: a failure, 525; butchers petition, and represent promises which induced them to purchase stands for a premium, 526; stand-holders removed into the Union Market. 526, 581.

Manhattan Water, butchers' petitions for, 210; from the Kolch Well, 372.

Manhattan Well. how originated. (see 338.) 376; a horrible murder connected with the. 377–8.

Mann. John. on vote of thanks for Mathew Vogel. 208.

Manning's. Captain, two servants convicted of crime and punished, 53.

Mansfield. Thomas, fisherman of Fulton Market, 513.

Manwaring. Silas, fisherman of Fulton Market. 513.

Marselus. Rev. N. I.. what he saw in 1822, 400.

Marcus, Rev. Moses, of the Church of St. George the Martyr, 393.

Marine Society meets at the Exchange in 1771. 285.

Marschalk, Alderman Andrew, on a Committee, 81.

Marschalk, John, erects flour scales in the Meal Market, 250.

Martenzen. Mesanck. a thief. examined by torture 52.

Martin. Morris, sale of Centre Market property, 460.

Market-boats usual place to land. 31; accident to, 137–8; laws to protect. 139; regulation of in 1779. 120–1; boatmen not to be impressed. 115; not allowed to visit vessels with a black flag, 373.

Market Committee, ordained with power. yearly invites the services of the Executive Committee of Butchers, 582.

Market-day, Monday of every week, appointed the first, 28–9, 31; change of, 36; the second and additional days appointed. 58–9, 73, 77.

Market fees. how collected in 1691. 60; in 1735 Clerk not allowed to collect, 129–30; appropriated to the use of the poor in 1777, 170; small amount in 1783, 179; in 1786–7–93, 319; laws made and rescinded in 1790, 183; demanded of the butchers in 1798, and changed to renting, 351–2; receipt of in 1833, 484.

Market-Field, origin of, 29, 31; location of, 35.

Market-Girl, the, a poem, 138.

Market-Houses, all used for war purposes, except one, in 1711. 91, 128, 252; ruinous condition of in 1783, 179, 314.

Marketing, how carried home in the olden time, 345–6.

Market Laws in 1656, 36; 1683, 73–4; 1691, 60; 1735, 129–31; 1749, 251; 1758, 135; 1763, 140–5, 149–50; 1774, 156–7; under martial law, 123–4; petition, &c., in 1837, 532–3; resolutions to change parts, 534; report on in 1840, 535–9; petition, &c . 540–1; communication on, 541–7 ; present inefficient, suggestions for improvement, 565–9.

Market people, fees demanded of. before sales, 129; delinquents fined, 184; in jail for assisting the Hessians, 294.

Market-place. the first in New Netherlands, 15, (see 28;) established by Washington. 291; the Harlem Railroad Company. 551; and Charles Oakley, 562.

Market-places, public—Bear, 307; Broadway, 283; Broadway Shambles. 44; Broad Street. 77; Burling's, 278; Catharine, 341; Centre. 460; Clinton. 527; Coenties Slip. 109; Collect, 395; Corlaers Hook. 387; Crown. 327; Custom-House Fridge, 70; Duane Street. 390; Essex. 479; Exchange, (in Broad Street.) 279; Exchange, 370; Flatten Barrack, 252; Fly. 125; Franklin. 517; Fulton. 488; Goveneur. 404; Grand Market. 393; Grand Street, 455; Greenwich, 399; Harlem, 588; Jefferson, 558; Market-Place at the Strand. 35; Manhattan. 524; Meal or Wall Street, 242; Monroe. 586; Old Slip, 85; Oswego, 236; Peck Slip, 102; Spring Street. 375; State Prison. 382; Thurman's Slip. 260; Tompkins. 550; Union. 580; Washington, 400; Weehawken, 576; Whitehall Slip. 276; Common Council takes charge of in 1735. 130; stands in leased, 498; the cost of thirteen, and interest received. 484; (see 581;) expensive system of conducting, 362. 402. 426–7: a more efficient plan proposed in conducting the, 565–9.

Market-Place at the Strand established, and location. 35–6; cattle market, or the first "Bull's Head." near, 37–8; fish sold on the Strand, 40; removal of, 44, 70–1.

Market Street. called Store Street, Winkle Street, near White Hall Street. 15.

Marvin, George, on the character of a butcher, 199.

Masten, J. W., fisherman of Catharine Market, 365.

Mathews. David. Mayor, and an American officer.295.

Mathiessen, Nicholas, brewer, servant-man ran away, 100.

Maverick, Peter, in the Federal procession, 317.

Maybie, A. P., jury on market ground, 528.

Mayor. Aldermen, and Sheriff introduced. 53.

Maynard. Daniel, fisherman of Fulton Market, 500.

McColleck. Jane S.. sketch of, 424.

McCrea, Stephen, on the character of a butcher, 199.

McDougal. Captain Alexander. imprisoned, 284; resolution against killing lamb, 288.

McKemie, Francis, Presbyterian minister, imprisoned, 128.

McNeal. William. on Corporation Bills. 233, 418.

Mead, Isaac. bill of repairs to Bear Market, 321.

Meal or Wall Street Market established. 242; merchants' meeting-place around the, and slaves hired at. 242; privilege to remove or repair as it stands, 246; cost — ordained as a meal market — called "Meat Market" on Lyne's Map. 247; butchers introduced in, 249; flour scales ordered in, 250;

sales at auction near, 251; repairs, and petition for removal, 251; removed, and affixed to Broadway Market, 252.

Meat, unwholesome, how destroyed, 151–2; to be sold by the joint or otherwise, 129; to be sold by the pound weight, 142–49, 251.

Meat-shops established by law, 382.

Meeker, J. M., fat cattle in Greenwich Market, 403.

Meigs, Hon. Henry, forestaller before the, 227; extract of letters from, 381, 431; recollections, 376.

Menus, Captain John, Artillery Company, 160.

Merchants to meet on the ringing of the bell in 1669, 85; in 1711, 242; called rich in 1678, 57; obtain privilege to erect a building in 1700, 76; moving up town, 375.

Merritt, Ald'n Isaac, on Franklin Market, 522–3.

Merritt, Captain William, ferry leased to on conditions in 1683, 79; on a Committee in 1691, 77.

Mesier, Alderman Abraham, wishes a new market-place 327–8.

Mesier, Peter, petition for a market-place, 327.

Michælius, Dominie *Jonas*, on the wants of New Netherlands in 1628, xiii.

Miller's, Rev'd John, plan of New York, 1695, slaughter-houses on, 80.

Miller, Sylvanus, in favor of removing Catharine Market, 361.

Mills, Jacob, attacked by soldiers near the Exchange, 285–6.

Milner, William keeper of a tavern near the Exchange, 285–6.

Milnor, Rev. Dr. James, kindness to "Old Mary Washington," 220.

Ministers a meeting of 3 Dominies or, in 1679, 72–3.

Mingay, Mrs., the "smart and pretty woman" of Jefferson Market 574–5.

Minthorne, Mangle, son of Philip, 331; report on butchers' stands, 342–3.

Minthorne, Philip, the children of, and division of his lands, 331–32.

Minuit, Director, treaty with the Indians, xiii.

Minuse John, Clerk of Market in 1810, complaint, 226; in favor of a market-house in the Fields, (Park,) 275.

Mitchell, Erastus, fisherman of Wash. Market, 424.

Mitchell, Dr Samuel L, the projector of Collect Market, 395–6; with his marketing, 346.

Mitchell, Col. William Centre Market Drill-Room Committee, 476.

Miranda, General Francisco de, expedition of, 213–6.

Monroe Market established, 586–7; unsuitable building, first called "Lafayette Market," "Grand Street Market," butchers transferred in, and stands drawn for, 587; alteration made—committee reported on the sale of part of the building yet standing, 588.

Montgomerie's, Gov., servant's time disposed of, 101.

Montanye, Jacobus, on petition in 1733, 262.

Montayne, John J., on the character of a butcher, 199.

Moon, L., fisherman of Fulton Market, 513.

Moore, Dennis, Committee on first North River steamboat, 195.

Moore, John, merchant, imports first fire-engines, 258.

Moore, William, M.D., bill for medicine and attendance, 334

"Morning Star," ordnance sloop, struck by lightning, 108.

Morris, Elenor, on petition in 1733, 262.

Morris, Col. Geo. P., and 3d Regiment on guard duty, 521; sketches from the "Mirror" and "Journal" of, 335.

Morris, Gouverneur, resolution against killing lamb, 288; laid out a "grand market-place," 393.

Morris, John Clayton, punished for sheep stealing, 103.

Morris, L. P., fisherman of Washington Market, 424.

Morris, Col. Robert C., Centre Market Drill-Room Committee, 476.

Morris's, Roger, house struck by cannon-balls, 288.

Morris, Staats, in the Federal procession, 316

"Mount Pitt," Jones' country-seat called, 455.

"Mount Vernon," location of, known as "Smith's Folly," N.Y. Agricultural Show held at, 237, 419.

Mufford, Samuel, testimony on whale fishery in 1716, 111.

Mulford, Jeremiah, attacked by soldiers, 285–6.

Mumford, Col. S. Jones, Centre Market Drill-Room Committee, 476.

Munroe, Peter Jay, demand against butchers, 396.

Munson, Alderman Reuben, report on butchers' claims, 239, 240–1.

Museum held in the Exchange, 299, 300–2.

Negro dancing, origin of public, 322, 344–5, 370.

Negro plots or conspiracies in 1712, 243–6; in 1741, on St. Patrick's night, 93–6.

Negro slaves. (See *Slaves*.)

Negroes, deaths from small-pox in 1731, 257.

Neilson, William, servants and redemptioners for sale by, 101.

Newcomb, Obadiah, an unsuccessful applicant, 525.

New England, settlers driven from, and Virginia, xiv; weaving introduced, 18; the trade from, 39.

New Englanders excluded from trading in cattle, 26.

New Netherlands, early settlers of, and natives, xi., xii.; the wants of in 1628, xiii.; additions to the settlement of, xiv.

Newtown pippins known as early as 1759, 137.

Newspapers first printed in America, 97.

New York named after the Duke of York, 53; changed to New Orange, changed back again to, 56; County Agricultural Show in 1821, 237, 419, 420; Daily Times, communication on the public markets, 570; Island purchased, xiii.; to be *sawed off* and turned around, 462–4; markets, how the products were brought to in "Olden Time," 137–9.

New Yorkers, origin of, citizens sometimes known as, 233; old, conduct towards imprisoned patriots, 175.

Nicolls, Col. Richard, became Governor of N.Y., 53.

Niblo, Mr. and Mrs, excellent arrangements by, for Centre Market Ball, 473–4. (See p. 400.)

Night-watch, neglect of duty of the, 32.

Noble, Sarah, recollections of a very old woman named, 321.

Non-importation associations in 1769, 283–4.

Nut, Nutten, Noten, or Pagganck, (now Governor's) Island, xiii., 15, 71.

Oak plank, the cost of in 1683, 74.

Oakley Market opened and shut, 562.

Oath taken by sworn butchers in 1665, 54.

Ogden, D. B., counsel in a "butcher cause," 239.

Ogden, Samuel G., interested in the Miranda expedition, 215.

Oil, or oyl, made on Long Island in 1708, 110–1; short supply of for the public lamps in 1772, 113.

Old Slip, origin of, 86. (See 517–8–20–3.)

Old Slip Market established "under the trees by the slipp," where *flesh meat* was to be sold, 85, 86; building lots laid out near, 86; market-house ordered to be built, 87; known as the "Great Flesh Market," 87; ferry-boats to land flour at, 88; known in the laws as "Market-house at Burger's Path," 92–3, 102; in a ruinous condition, 101–2; enlarged and repaired, 93, 101–2; leasing of butchers' stands and cellars, 93, 102; a counterfeiter taken at the, 103; punished, 104; lost, New York currency bill near, 106; a horrid murder near, 106–7; Company Beat No. 20 near, 106; large fire between the Coenties and this market, 107–8; terminated, 109.

"Old style" of date changed and called "new style," 133–4.

Oswego Market established, 330; name applied to the Broadway Market, 271, 330; also the Bear Market, 310–11; how the market-house was built, 330; usually called "Old Swago Market," 330, 340; Albany post-rider started from, 331; complaint of the porters who stand near, 331; the old market woman of, 331; enlarged, 334; Grant Thorburn's visits to, 335; petition of the butchers, 334; the live ghost caught, 337–9; part recommended to be removed, 340; fat beef for sale in, 340; resolution passed to be removed, 340; butchers transferred into the Washington Market, 340.

Oswego Street and landing, 271.

Oliver, William. fisherman of Wash'n Market, 424.

Oothout, Alderman John, report on the market regulations, 216–7; increase of butchers' stands, 324.

Ox, roasted at King's Bridge, 65–6; on Bayard's Mount, 357; attempt to, 379; weight of in 1692, 67.

Oxen drowned, 187; large in Centre Market—"President," 467–8; "Union," (largest known,) 477–8; "Washington," 477. (See Cattle.)

Page, Governor John, compares New York with Philadelphia, 320.

Palmer's, Benjamin. letter to Aaron Burr, 63.

Panburnge, Peter. leases part of a market-house, 75.

Panther killed in the City of New York, 311.

Parade-ground. as laid out by the Commissioners, 393–4.

Park, called "Fields," boat burnt in, 116; petition for privilege to erect a market-house in the Fields, 275.

Parks, Peter, certifies Mr. Vogel, 208.

Parker & Gaine's printing-office at the Royal Exchange, 280.

Parker. Joshua. Fly Market fisherman, 225.

Parsons, John. near the new (Burling's) market, 278.

Pattison, Major-General, desires the assistance of the Chamber of Commerce to regulate the public markets, &c., 120–1.

Patriots, the suffering imprisoned of the Revolution. 175–6; poverty of the returned, 179–80. (See 289.)

Patriotism of Queens and Suffolk Counties in 1755, 271–2; of the butchers in 1812, 431–3.

Pass, no grown person to cross the river into New Jersey without a, 119–20; coming to market protected with a. 138.

Paulding. Hon. James K., and the blind man, 572–3.

Pearsall, Walter, fisherman of Fulton Market, 513.

Peck, Benjamin, his name given to a slip and market-place, 303.

Peck. Geo., paid for repairs to Peck Slip Market, 306.

Peck Slip Market established, 302; first one built of brick, and named after Benj. Peck, 303; known as the "Jersey Market," "New Market at Peck Slip," 303; used as a store-house in the Revolution, after cleared for country people, 303; repairs and additions, 303–4–6; President Washington's residence near, 304; Public Hooks and Ladders removed to, 306; petition to remove, 306; ordered to be sold and removed, 307; butchers removed into Catharine Market, 341.

Peeck, Jan. appointed a translator between the English and Dutch, 38.

Peers, John, on petition in 1733, 262.

Penn, or Pinfold, (Butchers' Pen,) cattle-yard called a, 80–1.

Penniman, Benjamin S., fisherman of Washington Market, 424.

Permit, copy of a market of 1818, 585.

Permits, how obtained—Sunday Leader's unpleasant exposures, 447–9. (See 563–9.)

Pessenger, Seffrenes, captive among the Indians, 159.

Petersen, Cornelius, trade with Ann Jackson, 41.

Petitions on various subjects, 54, 66, 78, 80, 82–3, 127, 158, 182, 186, 199, 205, 210–1, 216, 219, 223, 225–9, 255–6, 239, 240–2, 245–6, 251–2, 260–3, 273–5, 278, 391–2. 398–9. 401, 404, 412–4, 421–2. 436–7, 457–8. 461, 465–6, 468–9. 475–6, 479, 484, 488–9. 493, 498–9, 503, 508, 511, 514, 517–9, 522, 525–6, 532–4, 539, 540, 547, 553, 558–9, 562, 577, 581–2, 584.

Phelps, Williard, fisherman of Fulton Market, 513.

Philips. Adolphus, store-house and yard in 1744, and election, 277.

Philips, Edw'd. answer to Comptroller's Report, 541.

Phillippse. Frederick, builds King's Bridge, 62. (See 64–6.)

Phillips, James. built fish market at Ful. Market 508.

Pierson, Ephraim, a constable, wounded by a slave, 245.

Pierson's Tavern. butchers' meeting in 1806 at, 222.

Pieter. the negro. requests payment for executing sentence on two criminals, 52.

Pigeons, wild, found in New Netherlands, 20; cheapness of, 134–5.

Pintard, John, on Corporation bills, 233, 418; on removal of Oswego Market, 340; complains of Exchange Market, 374.

Pieterson. Adolph, surveys lots near the weigh-house, 32–3, 61.

Plebeanus' opinion of the butchers, 145–6.

Polet, Mary, commonly known as "Long Mary," 109–10.

Population in New Netherlands in 1626, xiii.; in 1643, 27; New York City in 1656, 25; in 1664, 53; in 1678, (able to bear arms,) 57; in 1741, 94; 1742, 250; in 1759, 136–7; in 1772, 155–6.

Pos. Lodowyck, appointed Captain of the "Rattle Watch," 34.

Pot Baker's Hill, location of. 152.

Potter, John, Fly Market fisherman, 205.

Potter, Joseph, fisherman of Fulton Market, 500.

Pound, Rev. Jesse, on the Duane Street Market site, 393.

Power, Stephen N., Committee on first North River steamboat, 195.

Powles Hook ferry-boat accidents, 187–8, 192–3.

Presbyterian ministers arrested and imprisoned, 128.

Preserved meats, &c., first invented, 168.

Price, Mary, the horse of, 255.

Prices of articles according to the currency, 41–2; of skins, hides, sugars, and negroes, 58; of slaves, domestic animals, and real estate regulated by the General Assembly in 1693, 68; of white servants in 1748, 99.

Printers, journeymen, ask for increased wages, 165.

Prisoners, escape from the prison ships, 169 ; acknowledge the receipt of fat beef, 237–8; of State Prison. 386–7.

Privateering in the war of 1812, 439–41.

Proclamation establishing a cattle market or first bull's head, 37–8; translated into English on a cattle market, 38; prohibiting the exportation of corn and flour, 56; to establish a market-place, 70; on impressment, 115; the last by the British Government in relation to markets, 171; of peace in 1783, 292; against slaves, 243.

Produce, a legal tender, at established rates, 42; the manner of bringing it to market, 137–8; early from Long Island, &c., 501–2.

Provincial Congress, petition to about stolen cattle, 158; prohibits the exportation of sheep, and to kill no lambs, 287–8.

Provisions, when scarce or plenty, and prices, in 1637, 16; 1640, 30; 1650, 31; 1653, 34; 1657, 31; 1664, 41–2; 1678, 57–8; 1679, 72; 1691, 60; 1696, 87; 1713 to 1717, 91; 1726, 92; 1731, 257; 1743, 250; 1744, 134; 1746, 250; 1749, 251; 1754, 102; 1756, 135; 1759, 136; (Assize Law, in 1763, 140–50;) 1765, 280; 1771, 155; from 1777 to 1783, 109, 164–8, 172, 175, 179, 289–91; 1793, 373; 1807, 223; from 1814 to 1820. 234, 379–80, 410–11; 1826, 502; 1830, 505; bought on ferry-boats against the laws, 135.

Provoost, Abraham, slave executed. 245.

Public markets. (See Market-Places—Public.)

Public officers. advantages of having good, 183–84; acts and influence of unprincipled, 227–8; golden opportunities for the dishonest, 563–65.

Public Press, the benefits of an honest, 591.

Public Whipper, the pay of, 103.

Pumpkin pies at an early period, 23.

Purdy, Ald. Elijah F., apprised of a defalcation, 363.

Putnam's, General, orders in (1776) relation to provisions and vessels, 119.

Quackenbos, Walter, and the king's soldiers, 152–3.

Queens County, patriotism of, 271–2; complaint of a farmer of, 186–7.

Quincy, Josiah, offer for a fishing right, 111.

Rack, Mattys, petition in 1733, 262.

Racket, Daniel H., fisherman of Fulton Market, 513.

Racket, Jeremiah H. fisherman of Fulton Market, 513.

Rand, Dr. Wm., of Boston, servant-man ran away, 101.

"Rangers," foraging party known as, 172.

Rankins, Charles, fisherman of Fulton Market, 513.
Rathbun, Nathan, fisherman of Wash'n Market, 424.
"Rattle-Watch," attempt to establish, 33; succeeded, 34.
Read, John and Joseph, advertise white servants, 99.
Reade, Joseph, repairs Meal Market-House, 247–8.
Records kept in both Dutch and English, 56.
Redemptionists, persons called, 96, 101.
Refrigerators first invented and commonly used, 347; introduced in the markets, 485.
Refugees, leaving for Nova Scotia, &c., 177–8; lottery for the poor, 175; arrival of German in Philadelphia, 99.
Regnier's. Jacob, slave tyed and whipped, 245.
Remsen, Henry, ferry-landing near Long Island, 286.
Remsen, Peter, and the king's soldiers, 153.
Report on Free Bridge at Spiten Devil, 66–7; on Fly Market stands, 239–41; on refreshment peddlers in markets, 325–6; to amend market laws, 504–5, 535 –9; from Comptroller on Butchers' Claims, 541.
Reservoir, New York City, 560.
Revere, Abraham, "tea-water man," commits suicide, 267.
Richards, Paul, in favor of a market-place, 276.
Riker, John, petition to remove Burling's Market-House, 278–9.
Riker, J. R., appointed Chief Engineer—conduct of the firemen, 583.
Rhoda, Lewis, Engineer, killed, 198.
Rivington, James, consents to advance wages, 165; printing materials destroyed, 288–9; return from England, 289; his Royal body left behind in 1783, 179; the name of his paper changed, 179.
Robins, Ezekiel, certificate, 199.
Robinson, John, a bear found in the orchard of, 311.
Rodman, John, purchases the old City Hall, 78.
Rodman's Slip, known as Lyon's Slip, 278.
Rogers, Albert, fisherman of Fulton Market, 513.
Rogers, George. Fly Market fisherman, 224.
Rogers, George F., fisherman of Fulton Market, 513.
Rogers, Maxen, fisherman of Fulton Market, 513.
Rogers, William, fisherman of Wash'n Market, 424.
Romaine, Nicholas, on petition for place in the markets, 186.
Romayne, Nic's, M.D., bill for medical services. 334.
Romme's, John, house, in which negroes cabaled, 95.
Roome, Henry, sold lottery tickets to pay market debt, 330.
Roorbeck, S., on the character of a butcher, 199.
Roos, (Rose,) Gerrit Jansen, keeper of Public Slaughter-House, 55, 242.
Roosevelt, Cornelius, in favor of a market-house in the Fields, (Park,) 275.
Roosevelt, Jacobus, petition for a market at Peck Slip, 302.
Roosevelt, Alderman John, on a Committee 81.
Roosevelt, Nicholas J., Adjutant Third Regiment, in Doctors' Mob, 334.
Rosevelt, Nicholas, the slave of executed for conspiracy in 1712, 245.
Rose, Thomas, on petition for place in the markets, 186.
Royael, Charles, fisherman of Fulton Market, 513.
Ruckel, Philip C., petition for a bell on Centre Market, 461–2.
Rutgers, Adrian, offers the estate of Petrus Rutgers for sale, 328.
Rutgers, Captain Harman, wife's name given to Catharine Market, 341.
Rutgers, Helena, premises for sale, (see 327,) 328.
Rutgers, Henry, prominent in establishing Catharine Market, 341.
Rutgers, Petrus, on petition in 1733, 262.
Rutherford, John, laid out a Grand Market-Place, 393.
Rutledge. William, witness in the Miranda Expedition, 216.
Ryerszen, Gristie, sues Dirk Van Schelluyne, 96.
Ryerson, Martin—Ned, a famous negro dancer, belonging to, 344.
Rymes, Captain Samuel, advertises a runaway servant, 97.
Ryno, Anson, fisherman of Fulton Market, 513.

Samler John, on petition for place in the markets,186
Sandford, Major-General, rooms in Centre Market for the use of. 475.
Sands, Juliana Elmore, the murder of, 377–8.
Sarkett, Richard, sells three lots for slaughterhouses, 80.
"Sawing New York Island off," 462–3–4.
Schemelzel, Alderman John B., on Franklin Market, 522–3.
Schermerhorn, Simon, "Permit Master" for marketboats on the North River, 119.
Schieffelin, Colonel H. M., Centre Market Drill-Room Committee. 476.
School, public, calamity near the Jefferson Market, 571–2.
Schryver, Jans, witness in a hog case, 47.
Schuyler, Capt. Brandt, on a Committee in 1691, 77.
Schuyler. Harmannis, on petition in 1733, 262.
Scott, John Morin, offers the estate of Petrus Rutgers for sale, 328.
Scott, Lieut.-General Winfield. in battle of Queenstown, 415; letter to Lieut. Fink, 417; at market, 573–5.
Seabright, John. of Albany, large ox fatted by, 397.
Sears, Captain Isaac, battle with King's soldiers, 152–3.
Sebring, Cornelius, petition for a ferry. 78; shoots a bear in New York harbor, 311–12.
Servants (white) and redemptionists, 96–7; difference between and negro slaves, 97, 100; time for sale, 101.
Sharp, Richard, offers the estate of Petrus Rutgers for sale, 328.
Sheep first introduced, xii., xiii.; not cared for, 18; price of, 30; fees for slaughtering. 37, 45; assessed value of, 42; toll on, 62, 249; increase, 67, 87, 151; stealing, 103, 172–4; fees on sold in markets, 130, 268; none to be slaughtered in, 157; ram's horn a useful weapon, 152–3; order for collecting, 163; dead — "cheap meat for boarders," 227; perished from cold, 249; for the army, 271–2; not allowed to be exported. 287–8; number slaughtered in 1816, 351; fat. 419.
Sheldon's. Col., dragoons retake stolen animals, 173.
Shepard's, Ruth, slave executed for conspiracy in 1712, 245.
Shirley, William, general order for battoemen, 253.
Simpson, Jane, and others, petition for reduction of fees, 423.
Simpson, (Washington,) Mary, the humane colored woman, 219–20.
Sinclair, Sir John D., Quartermaster-General in 1756, 253.
Sison, Francis, fisherman of Washington Market, 424.
Sitcher, Colonel Andrew, "New York Volunteers" under the command of, 439.
Skaats, Rinier, rewarded for honesty and diligence, 183.
Skating to market, 72.
Slaughter Farmer, (see 35,) excise leased for one year, 36–7; grants extra privileges, 45–6; must inspect the cattle, 53–4; trouble to do so, 55.
Slaughter-houses in the city ordered outside, 54; public to be erected in the Fly above the Wall, 55; used for a powder-house, 55; cattle landed near, 80; removed to the east end of Queen Street, 81; leased to prominent men, 81; location of in 1784, 297; removed to Corlaers Hook, 298, 367; Nicholas Bayard lessee,366; purchased by James Blanchard, who is sued. 367; butchers buy Blanchard's lease, and it terminates, 368.
Slaves, value of, 1678, 57; 1693.68; 1719. 246; in Negro Plot. 1712, 243–5; in 1741, 93–6; sold at Fly and Meal Markets, 132, 242; not allowed to cross ferry, 243; a law against, 264; called "Free Masons," "Geneva Club," "Smith's Fly Boys," and "Long Bridge Boys," 265; troublesome on Long Island and New Jersey, 265–6; dancing, 344; relics of, 370.
Slocum, William, of Rensselaer County, fat cattle in 1824, 421.
Slosson, William, counsel in a "butcher case," 239.

Small-pox, mortality of in 1731, 257; in the House, with the General Assembly, 258 ; preparation against in 1739—cause of scarcity in 1743, 250.

Smith, Bernardus, Fly Market near the house of, 128.

Smith, Ephraim, Clerk of the Markets in the Revolution, 124, 178-9.

Smith, Dr. E. H., letter on yellow fever, 373.

Smith, James, chairman of a *butter* meeting, 408.

Smith, Jonathan, fisherman of Fulton Market, 500.

Smith, Melancthon, of Tammany Society, 299.

Smith, Richard, Deputy Clerk of Markets, 374, 410-14.

Smith, Colonel William, engaged in Miranda Expedition, 215-6.

Smith, William S., Collector of the City Revenue, 468.

Smith's Fly, (*Queen Street, afterwards Pearl Street,*) 125-7.

"Smith's Fly Boys," name of a negro club, 95.

"Sons of Freedom," call on, for a free bridge, 65.

Southampton, proclamation of a cattle market sent to, 38.

Southhold, proclamation of a cattle market sent to, 38.

Spingler, Henry, on petition for place in the markets, 186.

Spingler Institute, named after Henry Spingler, 203.

Spitenduyvel crossed without paying ferry rates, 39, 40.

Spiting Devil, else Kingsbridge, in 1704, 62.

Spring Street Market established, 375; assistance at Trinity Church—named "Market-house in Brannon Street" and Greenwich Market, 376; butchers on the stands—a bell hung—market-house raised, and name changed with the street, 376; number of stalls in, 458; enlarged—butchers fined and imprisoned, 380-1; ordered to be discontinued and taken down, 528; sale and removal of the building, 382.

Stadt House, or City Hall, location and use of, 110; sold. 78.

Stagg, John, receiver of subscriptions for Bear Market. 308.

Stagg, Nicholas, house of, 272.

Stagg, Thomas, petition for compensation, 326.

Stalls and standings to let in 1754, 134; in 1777, 170.

Stamford, proclamation of a cattle market sent to, 38.

Stamp Act, effect of and repealed, 281-2; the cause of raising more sheep, 287-8.

St. Amore, Thomas, butcher in the Bear Market in 1771, 309.

Staten Island, mail taken down on the ice to—persons walked from Long Island to, 456-7.

State Prison, sketch of, 383-7; grounds sold, part reserved for a market-place, 576.

State Prison Market established, 382-3; removal of butchers in—Greenwich Hotel near, 383; occupants transferred into the Greenwich Market and removal of the old shed. 387.

Steamboat, first for Albany, 194, 372.

Stebbins, William Fly Market fisherman, 225.

Steenwyck, Cornelius, Heer Schepen, engages in slaughtering. 45-6 (See 52.)

Stevens, Ebenezer, on fat cattle 419-20.

Stevens, Col. John runs the first passenger steam ferry-boat. 194-5.

Stewart's, Captain the first vessel in New York harbor to hoist the U S. colors, 295.

St. Clair John, Sr., to British **general** commanding in the Revolution. 124, 171-2.

St. John, Alderman Samuel, resolution to change Maiden Lane to Cortlandt Street, 171.

Stilwell, Samuel, recommends M. Vogel, 208.

Stone Bridge in Broadway, 398.

Storer, William B fisherman of Fulton Market, 513.

Storms, Gen Henry, order for funeral honors to Captain J. L Fink, 418.

Stout, Harme, on petition in 1733, 262.

Stoutenburgh, Jacobus, on petition in 1733, 262.

Stoutenburgh, John, on the character of a butcher, 199.

Strand or Beach, location of, 31; trading at, 34. (See market-place at, 35.)

Stratford, proclamation of a cattle market sent to, 38.

Street sweepings sold at auction, 464.

Strong, Selah, on first North River steamboat, 195.

Stryker, Major-Gen., rooms in the Centre Market for the use of, 476.

Stryker, Garrit, wishes to desert the Bear Market, 309-10.

Stryker, James, wishes to desert the Bear Market, 309-10.

Sturman, Edward, recommends M. Vogel, 208.

Stuyvesant, Gov. Peter, last of the Dutch governors —character and success, 28; interview with the Captains of the night-watch, 33; changes the market-day, and appoints a market-place, 36; surrender of the City, when its name was changed, 53.

Stuyvesant, Peter, stage-driver from Powles Hook, 125.

Suffolk County, patriotism of, 272.

Superintendent of Markets first appointed, 361.

Swartwout, Tomas, requests the "small Burgher-right," 51.

Tammany Society meet at the Exchange in 1790, 298, 300.

Tappan, Charles B., Superintendent of Buildings, on Franklin Market, 522-3.

Tavern prices for board and lodgings in 1786, 180-1.

Taylor, George, Jr., recommends M. Vogel, 208.

Taylor, James B., lessee of grounds at the Washington Market, 450-2.

Tea-Water Well. Comfort's, 95, 265-8; pump, (Kolch.) called "Fresh-Water Engine," 266; reported failure of supply, 267; bad, and replaced by Manhattan well water, 268.

Teller's, Jacob, house near Old Slip Market, 87.

Templeton, Oliver, commandant of Company Beat No. 20, 1776, 106.

Ten Eycke, Coentract, near Coenties Slip Market, 114.

Theobald's, Captain, slip near, 78.

"Third Avenue Trotting Course," 551-2.

Thomas, Allan, Clerk of Essex Market, 487-8.

Thompson, William C., keeper of the "Tea-Water Pump," 267.

Thong, Alderman Walter, duties around a market-house, 76-7.

Thorburn, Grant, from his Life, communications to the Press, and letters to me, 217-8, 220, 272, 297, 322, 335, 371-2, 384.

Thurston, William, schoolmaster near "Koenties Market," 114.

Thurman's Dock, the *Albany Post* started in 1754 from, 263.

Thurman, John, petition of, 261; fire at the dwelling-house of, 262.

Thurman, John, Jr., on petition for a market-place, 327-8.

Thurman, Ralph, on petition for a market-place, 327.

Thurman's Slip, great landing-place, 261-2.

Thurman's Slip Market-Place, petition to establish granted, 260, (see 327;) intended location of, 261; petition asking to select another location, 362; report unfavorable—petitioners ask for one at the foot of Cortlandes Street. rejected, 263.

Tiemann, Mayor D. F., communication from, 451-2.

Tinker, Allen, fisherman of Catharine Market, 365.

Tinker, Edward, Fly Market fisherman, 225.

Tinker, Jeremiah, Fly Market fisherman, 225.

Tinker, Juory, Fly Market fisherman. 225.

"Tompkins, Governor," privateer, (Capt. Shaler,) in 1812, 439-40.

Tompkins, Governor D. D., and Lieutenant John L. Fink, 416.

Tompkins, Colonel William W., on Catharine Market, 365-6.

Tompkins Market established, 550-1 ; p emium stands sold in, 551, (see 547;) additions to, 551-3; Bull's Head, Browning's, near, 554; "Cooper Union" opposite, 554-6; resolutions passed to build an iron market-house—wooden sheds erected, 555-6; market-house finished—satisfactory arrangement of the stands, 556-7; a new article introduced in, and the occupants, 557.

Tories, butchers, printers, and other citizens, 177, 179, 294-6.

Totten, Ephraim, a soldier wounded in the Doctors' Mob, 334.

Tourneur, Daniel, brings suit against Frans Janzen Van Hooghten, 47.

Trading, Jan Peeck appointed to assist in, 38; price between pork, beef, and negroes, 41; hog for a petticoat, 41.

Tremaine, Lyman, Attorney-General, orders a surrender of market grounds, 451.

Trinity Church, on fire in 1753, 259; lots near, 254; burnt in the fire of 1776, 329; contributes towards establishing Bear, 308; Spring Street, 376; Duane Street, 390, and Greenwich Markets, 399; claims Duane Street Market grounds—exchanges, 393.

Trumans, Clark, Fly Market fisherman, 225.

Trumbull, Jonathan, Secretary to General Washington in 1781, 291.

Trumpeter, Albert, complaint against Daniel Tourneur, 48; complained of for selling fish, 48.

Tryon, Governor, known as a cattle thief, 172; a public dinner given to at the Exchange, 286-7.

Tucker, Elstein, fisherman of Centre Market, 476.

Tucker, Wm. A., fisherman of Catharine Market, 366.

Tudor, Captain John, a messenger and lessee of a part of the market-house, 74-5.

Tuthill, S. B., fisherman of Fulton Market, 513.

"Twelve Men" chosen and disbanded, 26-7.

Ulshofer, Lawrence petition for place in the markets, 186.

Ulshoeffer, M., counsel in a butcher case, 239.

Union Market established, 580-1; cost of the land, 484; market-house built by "Charles Overton" named — butchers and others transferred from Manhattan Market in—resolution passed to have six butchers' stands drawn by lot, 581; petitions for examined by Executive Committee of Butchers, and drawn for under their direction, 582; destroyed by fire, and rebuilt—deduction of rent, 582-3; a remarkable woman in—death of, 584-5; dangerous condition of, and rebuilding of a larger building, 586; rooms used for public purposes, &c., 586.

Ury, John, a priest, convicted and executed for conspiracy, 96.

Vail, William, made additions to Corlaers Hook Market, 388.

Valentine, Alderman Abraham, and Fly Market butchers, 237.

Valentine, Alderman Abraham M., promises not recognized by the Common Council, 525-6.

Valentine, David T., locates the old ferry, 79; origin of a market-place, 127.

Van Alst, Jacob, anecdote of, 356.

Van Borckeloo, Willem Jansen, a witness, 48; complained of, 51.

Van Boskerk, Loaurens Andr., complains of a bound servant, 97.

Van Buskirk, Abraham, uses a flying machine, 315.

Van Corlaer, Jacobus, Corlaers Hook from, 388.

Van Dalsen, John, petition for a market-place, 327.

Van Dam, Anthony, Secretary of Chamber of Commerce, 104.

Vanderbilt's, John, store at No 3 Catharine Market, 351.

Van der Donk's account of New Netherlands, xii.; domestic and wild animals, 17-9; birds, waterfowl, 19, 20; fishes, 21-2, 110; vegetables, corn, fruit, 22-6.

Van der Mezlen, Joannes, mediation of, 47.

Van der Spygel, Lawurens, and Sarah Webber's marriage, 52.

Van der Wel, Lourens Cornelius, claims Burgher-Right for performing valiant deeds, 50-1.

Van Duzen, Isaac B., in sea-service of the war of 1812, 525.

Van Dyck, Fiscal, keeper of the first pound, 28.

Van Dyck, Richard, in Hanover Square, 247.

Van Elsant, Claas, application denied, 44.

Van Gelder, Abraham, lessee of the public markets, robbed, 156.

Van Hatten, Arent, Captain of the "Night-Watch," censured, 33.

Van Hooghten, Frans Janzen, suits against, 46-7.

Van Hook, Isaac, Weigher of Hay, 273.

Van Hook, Isaac, Jr., loses his hay-scale book, 313.

Van Hoorn, Derick, the slave of executed, 266.

Van Horn, Cornelius, a candidate for the General Assembly, 277.

Van Horn, Cornelius Jansen, the trial of, 40-1.

Van Horn, Captain Garrit, an election in the place of the deceased, 277.

Van Mepplen, Roelof, complaint against, 40.

Van Ness, Abraham, residence, formerly Lady Warren's, 400; petition for a market, 577.

Van Orden, Johannes, on petition in 1733, 262.

Van Orden, Samuel, petition for place in the markets, 186.

Van Schelluyne, Dirk, sued by Gristie Rutzersen, 96.

Van Tilburgh, Peter, slaves fire the house of, 243-4.

Van Tuyl, Alderman Andrew, of the "Bridewell Court," 190. (See 200.)

Van Twiller, Governor, plantations and improvements, &c., 15-6.

Van Tienhoven, Secretary, a trading suit before, 41.

Van Voerheise, Albert, the slave of executed, 266.

Van Waart, (Weert,) Marten, a thief, punishment of, 52.

Van Wagennen, Garrit, on first North River steamboat, 195.

Van Zant, Alderman Tobias, orders repairs to Peck Slip Market, 304.

Van Zandt, Alderman Winant, Jr., on the increase of stands, 324.

Varian, the name, oldest in the profession, &c., 366-7.

Varian, Isaac, on petition for place in the markets, 186.

Varian, Jonathan, fat cattle in Bear Market, 322.

Varick, John, appointed Clerk of five market-places, 392.

Varick, Mayor Richard, on Bridewell Court, 190; granting a market stand, 319.

Vegetables found in New Netherlands, 22-4.

Verdier, Captain, in a duel on Bayard's Mount, 357.

Vermillias, Thomas, free bridge on the land of, 64.

Verveshe, Johannes, establishes a ferry across Harlaem River, 39; complaints against travelers, 40.

Vogelsangh, Marcus, requests a Burgher-Right, 50.

Wages of mechanics and laborers in 1778, 165.

Wagner & Son, fishermen of Catharine Market, 366.

Waldron, David, on a market-house in the Fields, (Park,) 275.

Waldron, Petrus, wishes to desert the Bear Market, 309-10.

Waldron, Resolvert, commissioned to superintend the Graft, 32.

Waldron, Samuel, purchases a whale, 113.

Wallace, Henry, fisherman of Washington Market, 424.

Wallace, Thomas, on first North River steamboat, 195.

Walter, Alderman John, petition to enlarge Old Slip Market, 93.

Walton, Thomas, suit against Roelof Jansen, 40.

Walton, Hon. William, removed from near the Exchange in 1754 into the "Walton House," 127; residence of, 1759, 126; petition for Peck Slip Market in 1763, 302.

War between the Dutch and English in 1653, 33; in 1664, 53; English and French in 1705, 88, 91; in 1709, 128-9; in 1745, 115, 159; of the Revolution, (see 106,) 119, 157, 160-2, 288, 298, 303, 313-4, 336, 413; war of 1812, 196, 225, 336, 410, 415-8, 431-3.

Warren, Sir Peter, proclamation, (Lady of, residence,) 115.

Watch-House in Broad Street, 260; first district in 1815, 410.

Water, a cooling element with fighting Dutch Boors, 72.

Watkins, Joseph, with others, build Spring Street Market, 375.
Watson, Fanny, of Centre Market, 461, 585.
Way, Sam, the shark catcher, 348–9.
Washington, General, incidents of his life, 160–2; burlesque on proclamation, 173–4; appointed a market-place, 291; residence in New York, 304–5; funeral procession in New York, 377.
Washington Garden, first kept by Brannon, then after by Tyler, 376.
Washington Greys, First Troop, Captains of the, 366, 434.
Washington, John, fisherman of Washington Market, 424.
Washington Market—established, 406–7; the building of, 340; butchers of the Bear transferred in—illumination of, 407–8; the last buttermilk woman, 408; premiums for butter in—the guinea roll purchased, 409–10; First District Watch at—a blower imprisoned, 410; animals slaughtered and sold in, 411; sale of a stand recommended—stopped—drawn for, 412; petition and success of an old butcher. 413–14; sketch of a patriot, 415–18; butchers resolve to take no uncurrent money, 419; fat beef in, 419–21; petition against the sale of butchers' stands at auction,421–2; enlarged—removal of to St. John's Park, 422; petition of the hucksters, 423; of fishermen, 424; country woman and forestaller, 425; forestalling, 425–6; additions to—an honest Clerk, 427; Report on the Basin, 428; author's experience at, 429–30; butchers' stands made "premium stands," 436–7; number of in, 547; petitions of country people, and disposition of their stands, 442–4; (see 454;) additional sheds added, 443–9; new-made grounds at, 446–52; stands, how obtained—unpleasant exposures, 447–50; "Sunday Atlas" on the abuses, 450; State of New York leases grounds at, 450–3; fire at, 452; the "World's" opinion of an attempt to rebuild—plan of, 453; condition of the buildings—indicted as a nuisance, 454; business, supplies, trade, and want of system at the, 454–5.
Waterman, Thomas, Washington Market, fire in a shed of, 452.
Wearing & Comstock, fishermen of Catharine Market, 366.
Webbers, John, wishes to desert the Bear Market, 309–10.
Weehawk, an Indian name, 576.
Weehawken Market established—known as Greenwich Market, 576–8; butchers' stands sold, and gift stands placed in, 578; not successful—part leased, 579–80; deserted, 580.
Weeks, Levi, tried for murder, 377–8.
Weigh-House, lots laid out near, 32; market-places near, 58, 61, 71, 74.
Weights and measures, English adopted, 56.
Wells, Benedict, fisherman of Wash. Market, 424.
Wells, James N., jury on market grounds, 528.
Wells, Reuben P., fisherman of Washington Market, 424.
Wells, Thomas, fisherman of Wash'n Market, 424.
Wessels, Mathias, first fisherman in Catharine Market, 341.
Wessells, Warner, refusal of the currency by, 30.
Westervelt, John J., cellar under Duane Street Market leased to, 391.
Weston, Richard, weigher of hay, 273.
West India Company, introduction and trade of, xii.; their inducements for colonization, xiii., xiv.; location of warehouse which supplied the town with provisions, 15, 28–9, 35; dishonest servants, 17.
Wetmore, G. O., committee on first North River steamboat, 195.
Whale Company in 1669, 111.
Whales seen and taken about the harbor of New York, 22, 110–3.

Wheelbarrows used by the butchers of olden time, 345.
Whigs and Tories in 1783, 296.
Whigs and Federalists, excitement between, 299.
Whiley's, Mr. John, near the White Hall Slip Market, 277.
Whipping-Post, pillory, and stocks, (see 102.) 255.
White Hall Slip Market established, 276; location of an old market-place, and known as Market house at the end of Pearl Street, 276; name derived from —an old landing-place near, 277; removed, 278.
Widows of deceased butchers, petition for privileges, 210.
Wiggins, Bradley S., Fly Market fisherman, 225.
Wilcocks, Thomas, Fly Market fisherman, 205.
Wilkins, Erasmus, accused of murdering Lieutenant Featherstone-Hough, 89.
Willet, Edward, near Oswego (Broadway) Market, 272.
Willett, Colonel Marrinus, certifies to the character of a butcher, 199; witness in Miranda Expedition, 216; in favor of a market-place in the Fields, (Park.) 275.
Willet, Thomas, (Tomas.) fined by the Court, 37; furnish provisions, 41.
Williams, John, fisherman of Fulton Market, 500.
Williamson, David, on petition for place in the markets, 186.
Williamson, D. D., Comptroller, Report against the rights of butchers, 541.
Willis, Asa, fisherman of Washington Market, 424.
Willson, Captain Ebenezer, leases the Slaughter-House in 1696, 80.
Wilson, John L., on first North River steamboat, 195.
Wilson, Robert, fisherman of Washington Market, 424.
Wiseburn, Barbary, ("Aunty Wiseburn,") sketch of, 423–4.
Wiseburn, Daniel, sketch of, 423–4.
Women of olden time, 159, 185; an incident, 331–3.
Wood, high price and scarcity of in 1739–40, 1746–7, 249–50; in 1759, 136; 1816, 234; 1836, 457.
Wood, W., mail-carrier from Thurman's Dock to Albany, 263.
Wood, Willbur, petition to Provincial Congress, 158.
Woodward, John, Captain of Company in Doctors' Mob 334.
Wooley, Rev. Mr., Journal of, 57, 71–3.
Working-people, certain hours fixed for labor, 37.
Wright, William S., fisherman of Fulton Market, 500.
Wright, a muff-maker, died of rum, 53.
Wyckoff, Alderman Henry J., Report on butchers' claims, 239–41.

Year, beginning of changed in 1696 and 1752, 133–4.
Yellow fever years, 1742–3, called "distemper or plague," 250; in 1791 several prominent citizens died of, 205; in 1793 proclamation of Gov. Clinton in relation to, 373; in 1795 great many victims—markets deserted, 205–373; in 1798 very fatal—many butchers died, 206–10, (see 322, 373, 400;) in 1799 began early, not so fatal, 373, 400; in 1803 fatal to many whole families, 206, 218, 400; in 1804 not so bad—in 1805 butchers ordered to leave the markets—cats left starving, 219–20, 374, 400; in 1822 markets removed—lower part of the city deserted—vegetation grew in the streets, and the village of Greenwich greatly added to, 380, 400–1, 422–3, 498, 519, 560.
Young, Mrs. Johanna Christian, punished for crime, 102.
Young, John, the remains of, found in Catharine Slip, 342.
Young, William, fisherman of Fulton Market, 500.

Library of
Early American Business And Industry

I.   John Leander Bishop, A HISTORY OF AMERICAN MANUFACTURES FROM 1608 TO 1860, with an introduction by Louis M. Hacker, 3 volumes.

II.   Albert S. Bolles, THE INDUSTRIAL HISTORY OF THE UNITED STATES, Copious Illustrations, with an introduction by Louis M. Hacker.

III.   Freeman Hunt, LIVES OF AMERICAN MERCHANTS, with an introduction by Louis M. Hacker, 2 volumes.

IV.   George S. White, MEMOIR OF SAMUEL SLATER, Illustrated with engraving, woodcuts and folding diagram.

V.   Rolla M. Tryon, HOUSEHOLD MANUFACTURES IN THE UNITED STATES, 1640-1860. A study in Industrial History.

VI.   J. D. B. DeBow, THE INDUSTRIAL RESOURCES, etc. of the Southern and Western States, 3 volumes.

VII.   TENCH COXE, A VIEW OF THE UNITED STATES OF AMERICA, with folding tables.

VIII.   Charles F. Adams, Jr., and Henry Adams, CHAPTERS OF ERIE and other Essays.

IX.   Stuart Daggett, RAILROAD REORGANIZATION.

X.   Stuart Daggett, HISTORY OF THE SOUTHERN PACIFIC.

XI.   Nelson Trottman, HISTORY OF THE UNION PACIFIC, a financial and economic survey.

XII.   Howard D. Dozier, A HISTORY OF THE ATLANTIC COAST LINE RAILROAD.

XIII.   Timothy Pitkin, A STATISTICAL VIEW OF THE COM-
MERCE OF THE UNITED STATES OF AMERICA.

XIV.   Katherine Coman, ECONOMIC BEGINNINGS OF THE
FAR WEST, 2 volumes.

XV.   William R. Bagnall, THE TEXTILE INDUSTRIES OF
THE UNITED STATES.

XVI.   Witt Bowden, THE INDUSTRIAL HISTORY OF THE
UNITED STATES.

XVII.   Melvin T. Copeland, THE COTTON MANUFACTURING
INDUSTRY OF THE UNITED STATES.

XVIII.   Blanche E. Hazard, THE ORGANIZATION OF THE BOOT
AND SHOE INDUSTRY IN MASSACHUSETTS BE-
FORE 1875.

XIX.   Albert Gallatin, REPORT OF THE SECRETARY OF THE
TREASURY ON THE SUBJECT OF ROADS AND
CANALS, 1807.

XX.   Henry S. Tanner, A DESCRIPTION OF THE CANALS
AND RAILROADS OF THE UNITED STATES.

XXI.   J. Warren Stehman, THE FINANCIAL HISTORY OF
THE AMERICAN TELEPHONE AND TELEGRAPH
COMPANY.

XXII.   Kathleen Bruce, VIRGINIA IRON MANUFACTURE IN
THE SLAVE ERA.

XXIII.   Abraham Gesner, A PRACTICAL TREATISE ON COAL,
PETROLEUM AND OTHER DISTILLED OILS, revised
and enlarged by George W. Gesner.

XXIV.   Alexander Hamilton, INDUSTRIAL AND COMMERCIAL
CORRESPONDENCE OF ALEXANDER HAMILTON
ANTICIPATING HIS REPORT ON MANUFACTURES,
edited by Arthur H. Cole. With a Preface by Prof. Edwin
F. Gay.

XXV. Lewis Henry Haney, A CONGRESSIONAL HISTORY OF RAILWAYS IN THE UNITED STATES, 2 volumes in one.

XXVI. Adam Seybert, STATISTICAL ANNALS. Quarto.

XXVII. Samuel Batchelder, INTRODUCTION AND EARLY PROGRESS OF THE COTTON MANUFACTURE IN THE UNITED STATES.

XXVIII. Tench Coxe, A STATEMENT OF THE ARTS AND MANUFACTURES OF THE UNITED STATES OF AMERICA FOR THE YEAR 1810.

XXIX. (Louis McLane), DOCUMENTS RELATIVE TO THE MANUFACTURES IN THE UNITED STATES (Executive Document No. 308, 1st Session, 22nd Congress.

XXX. B. F. French, THE HISTORY OF THE RISE AND PROGRESS OF THE IRON TRADE OF THE UNITED STATES.

XXXI. Frederick L. Hoffman, HISTORY OF THE PRUDENTIAL INSURANCE COMPANY OF AMERICA, 1875-1900.

XXXII. Charles B. Kuhlman, DEVELOPMENT OF THE FLOUR MILLING INDUSTRY IN THE UNITED STATES.

XXXIII. James Montgomery, A PRACTICAL DETAIL OF THE COTTON MANUFACTURE OF THE UNITED STATES OF AMERICA.

XXXIV. Henry Varnum Poor, HISTORY OF THE RAILROADS AND CANALS OF THE UNITED STATES.

XXXV. Henry Kirke White, HISTORY OF THE UNION PACIFIC RAILWAY.

XXXVI. Frank B. Copley, FREDERICK W. TAYLOR, FATHER OF SCIENTIFIC MANAGEMENT, 2 volumes.

XXXVII. Edward Winslow Martin, HISTORY OF THE GRANGE MOVEMENT: or, The Farmer's War Against Monopolies.

XXXVIII. J. T. Henry, THE EARLY AND LATER HISTORY OF PETROLEUM.

XXXIX   Arthur C. Bining, PENNSYLVANIA IRON MANUFAC-
TURE IN THE EIGHTEENTH CENTURY.

XL   Thomas F. De Voe, THE MARKET BOOK, a History of
the Public Markets in the City of New York.

XLI   James M. Swank, HISTORY OF THE MANUFACTURE
OF IRON IN ALL AGES and particularly in the United
States from Colonial Times to 1891. 2nd Edition (1892).

XLII   Charles H. Ambler, A HISTORY OF TRANSPORTATION
IN THE OHIO VALLEY; with Special Reference to its
Waterways, Trade and Commerce from the Earliest Period
to the Present Time (1932).

XLIII   Pery W. Bidwell and John I. Falconer, HISTORY OF
AGRICULTURE IN THE NORTHERN UNITED STATES
1620-1680 (1925).

XLIV   Jules I. Bogen, THE ANTHRACITE RAILROADS. A Study
in American RAILROAD ENTERPRISE.

XLV   Helen Cowan, CHARLES WILLIAMSON; Genesee Promo-
ter, Friend of Anglo-American Rapprochment (1941).

XLVI   J.B.D. DeBow, STATISTICAL VIEW OF THE UNITED
STATES . . . Being a Compendium of the Seventh Census
to which are Added the Results of Every Previous Census
. . . in Comparative Tables (1854).

XLVII   Lewis C. Gray, HISTORY OF AGRICULTURE IN THE
SOUTHERN UNITED STATES TO 1860. 2 vols. (1933).

XLVIII   Robert Henriques, BEARSTED. A Biography of Marcus
Samuel, First Viscount Bearsted and Founder of "Shell"
Transport and Trading Company (1960).

XLIX   Malcolm Maclaren, THE RISE OF THE ELECTRICAL
INDUSTRY DURING THE NINETEENTH CENTURY
(1943).

L   Lorenzo Sabine, REPORT ON THE PRINCIPAL FISH-
ERIES OF THE AMERICAN SEAS (1852).

LI   Lawrence H. Seltzer, THE FINANCIAL HISTORY OF THE AMERICAN AUTOMOBILE INDUSTRY. A Study of the Ways in Which the Leading American Producers of Automobiles Have Met Their Capital Requirements (1928).

LII   George W. Stocking, THE OIL INDUSTRY AND THE COMPETETIVE SYSTEM. A Study in Waste (1925).

LIII   William Strickland, *et al*, eds., REPORTS, SPECIFICATIONS AND ESTIMATES OF THE PUBLIC WORKS IN THE UNITED STATES OF AMERICA (1841).

LIV   C. W. Ackerman, GEORGE EASTMAN. With an Introduction by E. R. A. Seligman (1930).

LV   James Hall, STATISTICS OF THE WEST at the close of the year 1836.

LVI   Samuel Hazard, Ed., HAZARD'S UNITED STATES COMMERCIAL AND STATISTICAL REGISTER. Documents, Facts, and other Useful Information Illustrative of the History and Resources of the American Union, and of Each State, 6 volumes.

LVII   Freeman Hunt, WORTH AND WEALTH, a Collection of Maxims, Morals and Miscellanies for Merchants and Men of Business.

LVIII   Samuel A. Mitchell, MITCHELL'S COMPENDIUM OF THE INTERNAL IMPROVEMENTS OF THE UNITED STATES, Comprising Notices of all the Most Important Canals and Railroads.

LIX   E. D. Kennedy, THE AUTOMOBILE INDUSTRY, 1941.